OF

THE NATIONAL INSTITUTE OF
ECONOMIC AND SOCIAL RESEARCH

Economic and Social Studies

XXXI

BRITISH ECONOMIC POLICY
1960-74

The National Institute of Economic and Social Research is an independent, non-profit-making body, founded in 1938. It has as its aim the promotion of realistic research, particularly in the field of economics. It conducts research by its own research staff and in cooperation with the universities and other academic bodies. The results of the work done under the Institute's auspices are published in several series, and a list of its publications up to the present time will be found at the end of this volume.

BRITISH ECONOMIC POLICY

1960-74

BY

F. T. BLACKABY (*Editor*), M. J. ARTIS, R. ELLIOTT
K. JONES, P. MEADOWS, A. D. MORGAN
P. MOTTERSHEAD, R. W. R. PRICE, J. H. B. TEW

CAMBRIDGE UNIVERSITY PRESS

CAMBRIDGE

LONDON · NEW YORK · MELBOURNE

Published by the Syndics of the Cambridge University Press
The Pitt Building, Trumpington Street, Cambridge CB2 1RP
Bentley House, 200 Euston Road, London NW1 2DB
32 East 57th Street, New York, NY 10022, USA
296 Beaconsfield Parade, Middle Park, Melbourne 3206, Australia

First published 1978

Printed in Great Britain
at the University Press, Cambridge

Library of Congress Cataloguing in Publication Data
Main entry under title:
British economic policy 1960–74.
(Economic and social studies; 31)
Bibliograph: p.
Includes index.
1. Great Britain – Economic policy – 1945– .
I. Blackaby, Frank Thomas. II. Series:
National Institute of Economic and Social Research.
Economic and social studies; 31.
HC256.6.B7623   338.941   77–28282
ISBN 0 521 22042 4

CONTENTS

3   PUBLIC EXPENDITURE   77
by R. W. R. Price

TABLES

CHARTS

PREFACE

This book is the joint product of a group which met regularly at the National Institute over a number of years. Its aim is to cover the whole field of economic policy over the period 1960–74 – except for regional policy, on which the National Institute has already published *The Framework of Regional Economics in the United Kingdom* by A. J. Brown. All the chapters went through a number of drafts, which were discussed by the group and amended in the light of the discussions; however, the final responsibility rests with the author of each chapter. Pamela Meadows, in addition to her chapter on planning, prepared a great deal of material for the chapters on monetary policy and incomes policy.

We are grateful to the large number of commentators from outside the National Institute – too numerous to mention individually – who have given us comments. We are also grateful to the Director, who painstakingly read through the whole book; to Miss Gillian Little, who undertook the immense labour of preparing the work for the printer, and by careful editing brought the book down to manageable length; to Mrs Evelyn McInulty, who was mainly responsible for typing the long succession of drafts and redrafts; and to Mrs Susan Price, who prepared the index.

The study was financed by a grant from the Treasury; this in no way impinged on the independence of those engaged on the work.

F.T.B.

NIESR
October 1977

'A government in modifying its laws... should collect with care documents necessary to prove, at a future date, whether the results obtained have answered their expectation. Laws are made and repealed with such precipitation that it is most frequently impossible to study their influence.'

(*A. Quetelet*, Lettres à S.A.R. le Duc Règnant de Saxe-Cobourg et Gotha sur la Théorie des Probabilités Appliquée aux Sciences Morales et Politiques, *Hayez, Brussels, 1846. Translated by Olinthus Gregory Downes, London, 1849.*)

SYMBOLS USED IN TABLES

.. not available

n.a. not applicable

— nil or negligible

roman numerals for quarters of the calendar year

CHAPTER I

INTRODUCTION

by *F. T. Blackaby*

This book is a study of British economic policy from 1960 to 1974. Its starting-point is a description of what happened and its raw materials are government decisions and actions. The book is not addressed solely to an academic audience; we hope it will also be useful to those concerned with policy-making and we have tried to write it in a way that is relevant to their experience.

The study is not just descriptive, but includes explanation and assessment. The basic questions to which answers are sought in the descriptive material are: What was the government trying to do – what were its objectives – and why did it select the methods it did? Also, how far were its policies successful, and what were the reasons for the success or failure? Throughout the book, we have concentrated particularly on studying major changes in the direction of policy, such as the spasmodic adoption of incomes policies, the floating of the exchange rate in mid-1972, and the decision to join the Common Market if possible.

In attempting to answer the question why the government chose certain policies, we have tried to trace any influence on these choices of the various views and theories current at the time. In answering questions about success or failure we have gone as far as we can, but we would not claim to have found many definitive answers; it is not so much a problem of evaluating effects as of deciding what they were. In many cases – indeed perhaps in most cases – the evidence on the effects of particular policies is thin, so that any conclusion about success or failure has to be highly tentative. In chapter 14 we survey and comment on the general appraisals of British economic policy which have been made during this period – a period in which the performance of the economy fell far short of the policy-makers' hopes.

COVERAGE

In the 1950s the study of economic policy was concerned mainly with demand management – with 'the practical application of...the broad rule – to stimulate demand when it is deficient and to restrain it when excessive...'.[1] A study of economic policy in the 1960s has to cover a wider area. For a number of reasons demand management lost its pre-eminent position – its semi-identity with economic policy.[2] For one thing economic growth became a dominant objective, and this was considered to need a quite different set of policies; to take another example – by 1962 the Prime Minister was reaching the conclusion that demand management was no longer effective in moderating inflation,[3] so he began the process of attempting to devise new institutions. The study clearly has to cover the experiments with incomes policy, with planning, and with the extension of industrial policies.

There are a number of demarcation problems with the term 'economic policy'. There is no clear line between economic and other political decisions; virtually every government decision has some economic content, however small; thus if it is decided to turn the consulate in Peking into an embassy, government expenditure is fractionally increased. The most helpful criterion is probably that of the *main* objective of policy; if the government acts in any field *mainly* with an economic objective in mind, then that action can be counted as part of economic policy. Ideally all such actions should be considered in the study, since one of its purposes is to compare, and study the effectiveness of, the whole range of policies which were addressed to any particular objective. Economic policy is concerned with the selection of instruments to achieve certain objectives; it is not possible to evolve a sensible selection without a full inventory of the instruments available. A bird's eye view of the whole terrain of economic policy is needed for any attempt to answer questions such as: Which (if any) of the many measures adopted to encourage economic growth appears in retrospect to have had any success? Or, how far did policy in one area conflict with policy in another (for example, competition policies and planning)?

The term 'government' also raises a problem of border definition. There is local as well as central government, and there are many 'para-governmental' bodies – the Monopolies Commission, the Industrial Reorganisation Corporation (IRC), the National Board for Prices and Incomes (NBPI), the National Economic Development Office (NEDO), the Pay Board and the Price Commission – as well as the nationalised industries themselves. Some demarcation problems are fairly straightforward: business decisions by nationalised industries are excluded, but

---

[1] R. L. Hall in the Foreword to J. C. R. Dow, *The Management of the British Economy, 1945–60*, Cambridge University Press, 1964.

[2] This change of emphasis is illustrated by the coverage of W. Beckerman (ed.), *The Labour Government's Economic Record, 1964–1970*, London, Duckworth, 1972; of the nine chapters only one is specifically concerned with demand management.

[3] See page 20.

government policies towards them and directives to them are included; local authorities' expenditure is, of course, included in public sector expenditure, local authorities being considered essentially agents of the central government's economic policy. The harder problems are with bodies which the government sets up to execute particular strands of policy, such as the IRC, NBPI, or NEDO. It is particularly awkward when certain strands of policy are sometimes hived-off to separate bodies of this kind and sometimes kept within the administration itself. For example, the preparation of some kind of general economic plan was at one time the responsibility of the National Economic Development Council (NEDC); at another time it was the direct ministerial responsibility of the Secretary of State for Economic Affairs. In the same way, some of the functions of the IRC were later taken over by the Department of Trade and Industry. In these instances the work of bodies such as the NEDC or the IRC is included in the study.

Government decisions and actions have been stressed in the discussion so far because we are particularly interested in the reasons for changes in the government's economic strategy, and changes are normally marked by some decision or action. However, in some areas of economic policy the process of government intervention is, as it were, continuous – in fiscal policy there is a continuous flow of taxation and expenditure – and inaction – the decision, for instance, not to make any changes in income tax in a time of rapid inflation – can be just as much a policy decision as action. It is sensible in these circumstances to talk about the stance of policy and changes in that stance; these changes may be discretionary – resulting, for instance, from government decisions to alter taxes – or they may be automatic – resulting from the application of the same tax rules to an economy which has changed in other ways. There may be particular statistical series which can be used as a measure of the stance of policy; the point is discussed on page 183 for fiscal policy, pages 280–5 for monetary policy.

FRAMEWORK OF THOUGHT

In the last decade, a good deal of academic work on economic policy has used the approach first developed by Professor Tinbergen:[1] that a government has a set of economic policy objectives and a range of instruments which it can use to try to reach those objectives.

Economic policy is intended to further a number of general *aims*; these give rise to a set of more precisely defined economic *objectives*. Governments, in attempting to achieve these objectives, employ a variety of *instruments*, and

[1] J. Tinbergen, *Economic Policy: principles and design*, Amsterdam, North-Holland, 1956.

take certain *measures*... The government's main policy problem is to select, from a wide range of instruments, the ones which will, in its opinion, most nearly achieve its objectives. The use of an instrument does not normally bring about changes in objectives directly; it operates on other economic quantities. For instance, a government may have expansion of production as its objective. It may choose to increase private consumption, investment or exports, and to effect these increases it can select from a large number of possible instruments – such as a guaranteed minimum wage or export subsidies.[1]

This approach, with multiple objectives instead of the single aim of maximising general welfare over time, certainly brought the analysis of economic policy closer to the real world. The objectives most often cited – full employment, economic growth, stable prices and an adequate balance of payments – were ones which policy-makers could recognise as corresponding to their experience. Further, Tinbergen's approach lent itself admirably to the kinds of quantification which econometricians and economic forecasters thought (rightly or wrongly) they could provide. So this framework not only made sense to policy-makers, it was one within which a large amount of the work done on economic relationships could be used.

Tinbergen's approach has been elaborated in a number of ways. First, with multiple objectives there is the problem of accommodating their complementarity or conflict. If two objectives are in conflict, how much of one must be sacrificed to get a given improvement in another? The practical development of this idea has been limited for a number of reasons. First, given the changing nature of the economic system and our imperfect knowledge of it, there is not much agreement among economists about the technical trade-offs; indeed, it is quite difficult to think of any trade-off between the four objectives listed above which could be said to be reasonably well established. Secondly, the trade-offs between any two objectives are not characteristics of the objectives themselves, they vary with the instruments used. To take one example: a possible instrument for achieving price stability is the lowering of tariffs, which would lead to a worsening of the balance of payments; on the other hand, the same objective might be pursued by a freeze on home prices, which would probably improve the balance of payments as manufacturers looked for higher prices abroad.

For a full model of Tinbergen's type, one would need to know not only all the possibilities of particular combinations of objectives (given a certain set of instruments), but also the preferences of the policy-makers – that is what the relative values are they give the various

[1] E. S. Kirschen *et al.*, *Economic Policy in Our Time*. Vol. 1: *General Theory*, Amsterdam, North-Holland, 1964. This book develops some of Tinbergen's ideas.

objectives. Attempts have been made to construct preference functions for policy-makers; questionnaires have been devised in which they indicate, for example, whether they would accept a rise in unemployment from 2 to $2\frac{1}{2}$ per cent if in consequence the rise in prices would be moderated from 4 per cent to 3 per cent.[1] There is, however, a certain artificiality about these exercises, since they try to make policy-makers think in a way which may be foreign to them. Further, it is difficult to conduct surveys about past changes in preferences; a questionnaire completed now cannot establish whether or not the emphasis given to economic growth increased during the 1960s. Changes in the relative importance of objectives have to be inferred from other evidence – for example, the varying levels of unemployment which at different times served as triggers for reflationary action. However, this is not straightforward, since belief in the efficacy of certain instruments may change over time; that is, policy-makers may become less (or more) confident about their ability to achieve the various objectives, even though these are still given the same relative values.

In this book we have used the general concepts of objectives and instruments, but we have not tried to put the whole of our description and analysis of what happened into this framework. The object of the book is not to build an ideal model of economic policy, but to describe, explain and assess what happened. The classification of actions according to the objectives served is of some help in explaining reasons for changes in policy – but of rather limited help (see page 620). Of a great many changes in the general direction of economic policy during this period comparatively few can be explained by changes in policy-makers' objectives; many have to be explained in other ways. The following section sets out some of the limitations of the 'objective' or 'instrument' classification for the purpose of this book.

OBJECTIVES AND INSTRUMENTS

It is not possible in practice to compile a satisfactorily comprehensive list of quantifiable objectives which describe past policy. Clearly in a book discussing actual policy, the objectives have to be what the policy-makers were trying to do, rather than some ideal set. The difficulty is that the policy-makers did not have a full set of quantified, published economic objectives by which their actions were determined.

In the field of demand management there were quantified objectives of a kind. At least it was generally accepted which series should be used as indicators of relative success or failure in respect of unemployment,

[1] E. S. Kirschen (ed.), *Economic Policies Compared: West and East*. Vol. 1: *General Theory*, Amsterdam, North-Holland, 1974, pp. 280 *et seq.*

the price level and economic growth. For the balance of payments – which must also certainly be included in any assessment of the success or failure of demand management in Britain in the 1960s[1] – there was doubt about the appropriate measure; at times the emphasis was on the level of the gold and foreign exchange reserves, at times on the current account balance, at times on the current and long-term capital account balance, and at times on the exchange rate itself.[2]

Sometimes explicit targets were set for the various objectives – as, for example, in the National Plan.[3] However, policy-makers tended on the whole to avoid publishing target figures for unemployment or for retail prices. In practice there was, at any particular time, an upper limit for unemployment, so that if it was exceeded it could be assumed that the government would take some action. For both retail prices and unemployment it can reasonably be inferred that the targets shifted over time; at the end of the period, policy-makers appeared to tolerate a higher level of unemployment and a higher rate of price increase than they would have done at the beginning.

For the four objectives relevant to demand management there was at least a reasonably agreed measure of achievement, but this was not true for other important objectives of economic policy. If these are taken to be something which the government of the day considers desirable for its own sake, and to which it devotes a significant amount of policy action, then we should include regional development, an improvement in the distribution of income, the promotion of competition, the promotion of rationalisation, the protection of particular industries and the extension of the international division of labour, but for none of them was there a quantified target or measure of achievement. Any precise comparison of objectives and achievements is possible, therefore, only over a fairly narrow field of economic policy and, even in unquantified terms, it is not easy to establish a definitive list of economic policy objectives apart from those relevant to demand management.

There is, moreover, a danger that making lists of 'ultimate' objectives, and trying to allocate policy actions to them, may give a wrong impression of the way in which economic policy was in fact conducted. In particular, in addition to the 'ultimate' objectives of the kind we have just been considering, there were 'intermediate' objectives through

---

[1] In some 'normative' lists of objectives the balance of payments is not included on the grounds that it should be considered an intermediate rather than a final objective: an adequate balance of payments is needed only because without it economic growth and full employment become impossible. In a description of economic policy, however, an objective must be accepted as such if in fact a significant amount of policy action was directed towards it. This was certainly true of the balance of payments in the United Kingdom.

[2] See pages 305–9.

[3] Department of Economic Affairs, *The National Plan*, Cmnd 2764, London, HMSO, 1965.

which the ultimate objectives were pursued. On occasions these inter-mediate objectives became ends in themselves – the all-important guides to policy-making – without any reconsideration of ways of reaching the ultimate objectives they had been supposed to serve. Thus, on occasions economic policy seemed to be centred on the preservation of a particular exchange rate, or on a particular figure for the public sector borrowing requirement, or on the need to introduce legislation to deal with unofficial strikes. Further, the historical section of the book suggests that for fairly long periods economic policy followed the pattern of 'one thing at a time, and one idea at a time', rather than the pattern of a careful balancing of ultimate objectives.

Nor would any account of the objectives of economic policy be com-plete without some reference to elections. Certainly it is reasonable to assume that a government which has general success in its economic objectives will thereby improve its electoral chances – to that extent there is no conflict between electoral and economic objectives. How-ever, there are obviously times when the economic situation appears to the electorate better than in fact it is – when, for example, an upswing has increased real earnings and reduced unemployment, but has only just begun to worsen the balance of payments. Obviously electoral con-siderations of this kind have influenced the timing of economic policy measures; hence a certain general coincidence between the economic cycle and the electoral cycle. Indeed it is rather surprising when, as in 1970, they do not coincide.

The clear distinction between 'instruments' and 'objectives' which appears in most models of economic policy is also at variance with what happens in practice. In most models, whereas the valuations put on different objectives are for the politicians to decide, the choice of instruments is assumed to be purely a technical matter. In real life instruments are not neutral in this way, but are value-loaded, and both Chancellors and Parties have shown strong preferences from time to time for particular types of instrument. Sir Alec Cairncross has referred to this complication:

The fact of political conflict means that what at first sight seemed purely technical issues become the subject of party debate. Governments may be inhibited from using particular instruments of policy such as bank rate by ideological considerations or by the force of popular feeling which they have stirred up earlier when in opposition. They may commit themselves publicly to doctrines about how the economy should be run that rest on little more than assertion and then find it impossible to retract when the doctrines are put to the test.[1]

[1] Sir Alec Cairncross (ed.), *The Managed Economy*, Oxford, Blackwell, 1970, p. 21.

Any explanation of changes in policy would be incomplete unless it took account of these strong preferences for one type of instrument over another. Indeed, most of the more strongly expressed disagreements about economic policy have not been about objectives but about instruments: for example, about monetary policy or incomes policy, or investment allowances as against investment grants, or selective employment tax as against value-added tax (VAT). There is a more general difference which underlies many of these differences about the choice of instruments – with one Party showing, from time to time, a strong preference for reducing the amount of government intervention as much as possible and the other Party giving this consideration little weight.

For some acts of policy the metaphor contained in the term 'instrument' is inappropriate. It is suitable enough for a single change in some parameter, like the 10 per cent surcharge on indirect taxes, but for other actions, in particular all those which establish new institutions, or require some kind of negotiated consensus with interest groups, the metaphor is inappropriate. Over the period considered in this book, a growing proportion of economic actions consisted in bringing about institutional change of some kind, and it is especially difficult to establish the need for, or the effects of, this kind of change. The efficacy of the policy may depend upon the workability or acceptability of the new institution, and in such cases there is no satisfactory way at present of judging in advance what outcome is to be expected. So there is here a problem of assessment which is much more difficult than the problem of assessing the consequences of (say) a tax change.

UNCERTAINTY

Economic policy models tend to assume that the working of the economic system is known. If this had been so, actual economic policy in Britain would have been very different. If there were an agreed body of economic knowledge about the full effects of all major economic instruments, so that the technical trade-offs between particular objectives could be precisely calculated, there might be little reason for substantial disagreement about policy. Such a state of knowledge did not, and does not, exist. Admittedly there are some generally accepted calculations of the effects of particular tax changes on aggregate demand, but such cases are exceptional. Most of the wider effects are highly uncertain; that is, there is no general agreement among economists and there are rival views. For example, there is no agreement about the determinants of economic growth nor the kind of government actions which might accelerate it; we do not know which policies (if any) were responsible for such acceleration as there has been in the underlying trend of productivity – indeed there are differing views about whether this acceleration took place, and when; there is uncertainty about the effects of devaluation and about the possibility of preserving any competitive advantage so obtained; there is no agreement about the existence of long-term dynamic effects from joining the Common Market, nor about the sensitivity of rates of increase in wage rates or earnings to demand pressure as measured by unemployment.

A symptom of these uncertainties was that a number of conflicting views (or doctrines or theories) about the working of parts of the economic system were elaborated and presented by economists during this period. Policy-makers were subjected to a constant commentary on their actions – so long as their policies were successful the pressure to change was weak, but when their policies began to appear unsuccessful (as they usually did, since Britain's general economic performance was relatively poor) an alternative set of ideas, based on an alternative view of the working of the economy, was normally at hand. For example, when demand management by fiscal and monetary means appeared to be failing to control price rises, it was natural for policy-makers to turn to incomes policy; the idea had been extensively written about and widely discussed, and there was a theory of inflation to support it. Chancellors, it is true, were not much concerned with the theoretical backing – and in any case normally felt some obligation to explain that the new policy was essentially a continuation of the old policy in another form.[1] Nonetheless, policies were not normally developed far, or for long, without some theoretical backing, however rudimentary, to support them.

Part of the story of economic policy lies in links between changes in the direction of policy and the range of views and theories being discussed at the time. These links can only be explored in a general way; it is rarely, if ever, possible to identify the exact route by which an idea developed outside the government was eventually incorporated into policy. However, the absence of firm knowledge about the working of the economic system, and the presence of rival views and theories provided the background to such marked oscillations of policy as the rise and fall of planning, and the acceptance, rejection, and reacceptance of incomes policy.

[1] Conversely, when governments change, differences rather than similarities are emphasised, so that a policy which may be virtually identical with one pursued by a previous government is presented as being in some way basically different.

CONCLUSION

The description and analysis of actual economic policy therefore requires concepts rather more complex than simply a list of objectives and instruments. Policy-makers were uncertain about their objectives; they often pursued intermediate objectives, tended to concentrate on one thing at a time, and found that differences in political philosophy often revealed themselves in choices of instruments rather than objectives. Partly because knowledge of the working of the economic system was imperfect, policies were liable to considerable instability; as one set of policies appeared unsuccessful, another set, which implied a different view of the working of the economy, was ready and waiting in the wings.

CHAPTER 2

NARRATIVE, 1960–74

by *F. T. Blackaby*

INTRODUCTION

Most of this book is concerned with analysing particular strands of policy – either the use of a particular family of instruments (fiscal policy or monetary policy), or the examination of policies addressed to a particular area (industrial policy, for example). Nonetheless a narrative chapter is needed to provide a general political framework for economic policy decisions – there were two changes of government during this period and six changes in Chancellors of the Exchequer – and, more generally, because there are important questions about economic policy – priorities and the dominance of particular themes at particular times – which the disaggregated analysis does not cover.

Economic policy is, after all, considered as a whole to some extent; the major decisions are either brought to the Cabinet or discussed among a small circle of Ministers. It would be going too far to say that at any point during this period there was a fully articulated and comprehensive economic strategy; certainly a good many policy decisions consisted of reactions to circumstances. However, by no means all economic policy can be explained in this way; Parties came to power with programmes and priorities which had some influence on their behaviour.[1] In addition, at various times particular issues appeared to become dominant and occupied the centre of the stage; this is clear from political biographies. An example is the attention paid by the Conservative government from the middle of 1972 until the election in 1974 to the problems of devising an effective incomes policy. It is the job of a narrative chapter to describe these shifting preoccupations and priorities.

Frequently in this account of the last twelve years a distinction has to be made between the picture as it appeared to policy-makers at the time, on the basis of figures then available, and the picture as it appears now, on the basis of figures available in 1977. This certainly compli-

---

[1] Also, senior Civil Servants are diligent in attempting to establish in their own minds what the general line of policy is; indeed they sometimes appear to impose a more coherent philosophy on the policies than the politicians do themselves.

cates the narrative, but there is no way of avoiding it. The differences are sometimes substantial: for example, in the first half of 1961, 1960 was looked back on as a very disappointing year, during which national output between the fourth quarters of 1959 and 1960 had risen by only $1\frac{1}{2}$ per cent, whereas the best estimate available in 1977 is that the rise was $3\frac{1}{2}$ per cent. Revisions of this order are not uncommon.

It would not be fair, therefore, simply to use today's series in assessing policy; it must also be judged against the background of the figures available at the time. Further, there is no finality here; substantial revisions to the data are still likely, particularly for the later years covered in this book. It is an important point that the statistical foundations on which demand management is based are shaky; it makes a good deal of difference to the general conclusions drawn about economic policy in chapter 14.

THE YEAR 1960

Throughout 1960 – and indeed well into 1961 – although there were some long-term policy initiatives of importance, the decisions on short-term demand management were reactions to successive alarms (interspersed by short periods of reassurance) accompanying the publication of the figures for trade or reserves. Ministers were pre-occupied with the reserves and the size of the trade gap; to a lesser extent, they were concerned with any weakening in the exchange rate. (Publication of the balance of payments accounts themselves seems to have had less influence, since they came out after quite a long delay.) It is clear from Harold Macmillan's account of economic policy in this period that, although other factors (such as the progress of wage demands) were minor background influences, what caught his eye (and were recorded in his diary) were exclusively trade or reserves statistics.[1] There was a change after mid-1961, when the 'battle of the pay pause' began.

The arguments within the government about the nature of the 1960 budget are worth elaborating in some detail, because it is one of the few cases where we have reasonably good documentation of a difference of opinion among Ministers and of the arguments deployed on either side. From early in 1960 the Chancellor of the Exchequer and the Governor of the Bank of England were both in favour of deflationary measures;[2] the Prime Minister was opposed.

---

[1] The references in this section to Macmillan's views are from chapter 8, 'A touch on the brake' in H. Macmillan, *Pointing the Way 1959–1961*, London, Macmillan, 1972.

[2] The Governor joined the Chancellor, it seems as an equal partner, in initial discussions with the Prime Minister on the economic situation in mid-February.

The Chancellor and the Governor were concerned at the risk of an inflationary boom. There was then nothing in the figures to indicate any slackening in the rise in demand: unemployment was continuing to fall, the trade gap had widened in the second half of 1959 and the reserves had fallen in the fourth quarter by substantially more than the annual payments of capital and interest on North American loans. It is true that the latest balance of payments figures available – for the third quarter of 1959 – still showed a current surplus, but they were by then four months out of date. The figures for the past which would have been under consideration are set out in table 2.1; the Chancellor probably had, in addition, a gloomy balance of payments forecast for 1960. These were the arguments for a tough budget.

The Prime Minister was disturbed at what he considered to be a 'loss of nerve'.[1] Only three months earlier he had led his Party to its third successive electoral victory, with an increased majority for the third time, and one of the themes had been the 'preservation of prosperity'. In a letter to the Chancellor, he presented these arguments:

(a) a deflationary budget would be 'either very foolish or very dishonest';

(b) an additional £50–£100 million of taxation would have practically no effect – 'after all, the national income is of the order of £20,000 million';[2]

(c) there would be a danger of companies changing their investment plans – for example, the motor companies might cancel their planned expansion on Merseyside;

(d) the balance of payments forecast on which the Chancellor based his desire to deflate was not to be trusted;[3]

(e) the economy was not yet at full stretch;

(f) if deflationary measures were needed, the best weapon was Special Deposits – 'if you like, add hire purchase, to taste'.

For all these reasons, Macmillan recommended a stand-still budget.

It is clear that the Prime Minister was most nervous of a budget – with all the publicity surrounding it – which appeared to reverse the previous one. To an economist it might seem sensible to use the budget to increase demand in one year and to reduce it the next. A politician, however, knows that he will be accused of cheating – as Butler was after

[1] He also surmised that Treasury officials were 'calmer' about the economic situation than the Chancellor.

[2] There is a certain inconsistency in his arguments. Here he is saying that the increase in taxation would not have much effect; elsewhere in the same letter he says: 'It cannot be sensible to cheer the economy on vigorously one moment and then push it violently back the next.'

[3] 'My confidence in the accuracy of figures of this sort is just about as much as I have in Old Moore.'

Table 2.1. *Some indicators available at various times during 1960*

	Monthly trade gap[a]	Gold and foreign exchange reserves[b]	Current balance of payments[c]	Unemployment[d]
	(£ million)	($ billion)	(£ million)	(%)
Available 25 January 1960				
1958	−36	3·15	+348	2·10
1959 I	−49	3·14	+19	2·51
II	−32	3·17	+96	2·22
III	−43	3·28	+48	2·06
IV	−53	2·74	..	1·92
October	−38	3·02	..	1·98
November	−72	2·97	..	1·92
December	−57	2·74	..	1·87
Available 25 March 1960				
1959 IV	−53	2·74	−18	2·03
1960 January	−48	2·68	..	1·73
February	−70	2·72	..	1·59
Available 25 July 1960				
1960 I	−56	2·78	+46	1·70
April	−65	2·83	..	1·65
May	−80	2·86	..	1·54
June	−71	2·89	..	1·55
July	..	..	..	1·56
Available 23 September 1960				
1960 II	−70	2·89	−9	1·58
July	−104	3·00	..	1·56
August	−74	3·07	..	1·62
September	..	..	..	1·53
Available 23 December 1960				
1960 III	−83	3·11	..	1·57
October	−133	3·14	..	1·59
November	−70	3·17	..	1·61
December	..	..	..	1·65

SOURCE: *National Institute Economic Review* (various issues).

[a] Seasonally adjusted and adjusted for dock strikes.
[b] At end of period.
[c] Not seasonally adjusted.
[d] Seasonally adjusted; for Great Britain only; includes temporarily stopped.

his autumn budget in 1955 – which is one of the political constraints on counter-cyclical action.

The figures which became available between the first discussions about the budget and the final decisions would have appeared, on balance, to support the Chancellor's thesis (table 2.1). Unemployment dropped sharply; in January and February the trade gap was running higher than in the fourth quarter of 1959, for which period a current deficit of £18 million was estimated for the balance of payments –

although negligible by today's standards, this was treated seriously at that time. Nonetheless the Prime Minister got his way about the budget (he was in a relatively strong position because the Chancellor had some time before indicated that he was anxious to return to private life) and the net tax change was negligible (see page 194). The Prime Minister even checked through the budget speech to make sure that there was 'no note of despondency or alarm; reversal of engines, end of expansionist policies, or any of the horrors which the Chancellor and the Treasury were threatening up to a few weeks ago'.[1] He reports 'I have won this battle quite definitely. I feel ... that we shall not *talk* ourselves into a crisis – as we did ... in 1957.' A public reversal of policies had been avoided.

During the rest of 1960 the statistical background to the decisions on demand management – dominated as always by trade and the balance of payments – was confused. The trade gap continued to widen and further measures were taken in response. On the other hand, the gold and foreign exchange reserves stopped falling and began to increase again; 1960 was a year in which the dollar rather than sterling was suspect and there was a substantial inflow of short-term capital (page 309). Curiously, when the first balance of payments figures for the year were published in July, they showed a return to a current surplus (table 2.1); revisions which turned this surplus into a deficit were not made until 1961. Unemployment continued to fall up to September.

By the end of April, reacting to the trade figures, the Prime Minister agreed to a 'touch on the brake' – Special Deposits at 1 per cent and the reimposition of hire purchase restrictions. He commented that he '... did not wish to be pressed to any panic measures; so many things can be done if they are done quietly and without confusion or alarm.' With a further widening of the trade gap, Bank Rate was raised from 5 to 6 per cent and Special Deposits from 1 to 2 per cent towards the end of June,[2] but there were no further restrictive measures that year.

At the end of July, Heathcoat Amory retired as Chancellor and was replaced by Selwyn Lloyd. The reserves survived an official shipping strike during August, and in October the situation was judged to have improved sufficiently for Bank Rate to be reduced from 6 to $5\frac{1}{2}$ per cent. A Cabinet debate on the economic situation at the end of November led apparently to general bafflement, certainly to no new measures; various enquiries were instituted on different aspects of the balance of payments and the Prime Minister decided to preside over a committee

[1] The Prime Minister was even rather bothered at the thought that the speech would be delivered by the Chancellor in a very lugubrious voice.

[2] It is clear from frequent references that Macmillan considered that changes in Bank Rate had significant internal deflationary or reflationary effects.

on increasing exports. At the end of the year the trade gap seemed at least to have stopped increasing, and the Governor of the Bank of England declared that he was not particularly worried about the immediate future.

In the division of opinion between the Chancellor and Prime Minister, in one sense both sides were right and both wrong. The current balance of payments did worsen, as the Chancellor expected. After the first quarter, exports stopped rising. The American expansion came to an early end, the rise in world trade slowed down and, more important, the British share of world trade fell faster than before. The share of imports in national expenditure rose rapidly. On the other hand, the sharp rise in demand and output petered out after the first quarter without substantial deflationary measures. Consumers' expenditure rose little; the hire purchase and credit restrictions produced a slump in the demand for consumer durables, whose sales (in real terms) were 15 per cent lower at the end of 1960 than they had been at the end of 1959. These factors together brought about a virtual levelling off in total output after the first quarter. However, fixed investment was rising through the year, and investment in stocks stayed high up to mid-year.

During 1959 there had been an extraordinary gap in wage bargaining – the wage-rate indices hardly moved. 1960 was much more active, with unions pressing hard for reduced hours as well as for wage increases. The effect was to push up the hourly wage-rate index by $6\frac{1}{2}$ per cent during 1960, as against a rise of only 1 per cent during 1959. This, together with the slow rise in output in the second half of the year, pushed up wage costs, but the effect on final prices was small during 1960: retail prices went up through the year by less than 2 per cent, with import prices contributing nothing to this.

1961 TO MID-1962

In 1961, as in 1960, it was balance of payments considerations which were dominant. In 1960 the trade gap had widened, but an inflow of hot money had prevented any fall in the reserves. In 1961 this process was reversed: the trade gap narrowed but the hot money flowed out again, so that in July there was a balance of payments crisis, leading to a package of deflationary measures. The pattern was familiar; the only difference was that the inflow of hot money had postponed the crisis for a year.

Partly because it was a familiar pattern, it caused a good deal of discontent – among Ministers as well as the electorate. The simple principle which had governed demand management since the war – of reducing demand when it was excessive and increasing it when it was inadequate – began to appear more and more threadbare, so that moves were made to evolve longer-term policies – medium-term planning and new institutions for an incomes policy.

The first balance of payments crisis came in March, when the Deutschemark (and the Dutch guilder) were revalued by 5 per cent. Macmillan defines precisely the consequences of this:

(a) The *fact* of revaluation reminded all speculators and owners of hot money that fixed exchanges can, after all, be changed. If once, why not again?

(b) The fact that the up valuation is far too small to correspond to realities has led everyone to think the first move in this direction may be followed by a second. Since this could only be upwards, it's an absolutely safe bet to sell dollars and sterling in order to buy Deutschemarks. This has been done on an absolutely unprecedented scale. We lost £67 million [in] *one day* (£26 million was the worst post-Suez day). Altogether we have lost about £187 million of *hot* money from the reserves.[1]

The pound was supported under the Basle Arrangements (page 350).

This run on sterling was part of the background to the budget; in addition, revised balance of payments figures published on 1 April roughly doubled the estimate for the balance of payments current deficit in 1960 (table 2.2): in January this had been estimated at £150–£175 million; in April it was revised to £344 million. At home the signals were uncertain: by March the industrial production index had been flat for a year, but unemployment, which (on a seasonally adjusted basis) had risen a little in the fourth quarter of 1960, fell back again slightly in January and February. The budget was virtually neutral in its effect on demand: £5000 rather than £2000 of earned income was now exempt from surtax and two so-called 'regulators' were introduced. Powers were taken to increase the national insurance stamp by up to four shillings a week for each employee, also to vary most indirect taxes by 10 per cent up or down.[2] However, the idea of varying national insurance contributions was subsequently dropped.

Pressure on sterling continued. At the end of April and the beginning of May there was an unofficial London dock strike, so that when the May trade figures came out they showed a substantial widening in the trade gap. Further, in early June there were widespread rumours of a revaluation of the Swiss franc. It became clear that the Bank of England would have difficulty in arranging more help from the other central banks. Ministers were also getting more and more exasperated with difficulties on the labour front: Macmillan comments on '... the

[1] Macmillan, *Pointing the Way*, pp. 371–2.

[2] Macmillan comments: 'We thus introduced into the management of the economy the now popular concept of the stimulant and the tranquillizer' (ibid. p. 373).

Table 2.2. *Some indicators available at various times during 1961*

	Monthly trade gap[a]	Gold and foreign exchange reserves[a]	Current balance of payments[a]	Unemployment[a]
	(£ million)	($ billion)	(£ million)	(%)
Available 22 March 1961				
1960 I	−54	2·78	+44	1·70
II	−69	2·89	−9	1·56
III	−82	3·11	−101	1·55
IV	−83	3·23	..	1·59
1961 January	−68	3·25	..	1·59
February	−65	3·19	..	1·47
Available 25 May 1961				
1960 I	−54	2·78	−37	1·70
II	−69	2·89	−42	1·56
III	−82	3·11	−148	1·55
IV	−83	3·23	−117	1·59
1961 I	−64	3·02	..	1·49
April	−41	2·95	..	1·41
Available 24 November 1961				
1961 I	−69	3·02	−68	1·49
II	−45	2·77[b]	−15	1·36
III	−33	3·55[c]	..	1·48
October	−55	3·53	..	1·74
November	..	..	..	1·74

SOURCE: as table 2.1.

[a] See notes to table 2.1.

[b] This fell to 2·45 at end-July.

[c] Includes drawing on the IMF stand-by, on which repayment began in November.

utter irresponsibility of labour in some of the *new* industries (motor cars, aviation and the like) and the *hopeless conservatism* of labour in some of the *old* industries (shipbuilding, etc.)'.[1]

There was a good deal of argument about the size of the deflationary package. The International Monetary Fund (IMF) was clearly pressing for cuts in government expenditure and on this Macmillan has an illuminating note: 'If we are to get our "drawings" from the International Monetary Fund, we shall have to make – or *pretend to make* – large savings on government expenditure.'[2] There was a division of opinion at home as well. The Governor of the Bank of England was pressing for a tightening of hire purchase terms and the use of the so-called 'payroll' tax. The Chancellor objected that hire purchase would hit the same industries as had been hit by the first regulator and that the payroll tax was so unpopular with both employers and trade unionists that it would militate against the success of his pay pause.

[1] Ibid. p. 375.   [2] Ibid. p. 376 (italics not in the original).

The issue was put to the Cabinet, which endorsed the Chancellor's position.

The July package had four components: fiscal measures, monetary measures, measures designed to affect the balance of payments directly, and the pay pause. The fiscal measures comprised the use of the new 'regulator' – a 10 per cent increase in indirect taxes – and public expenditure cuts. The monetary measures included a rise in Bank Rate, a call for Special Deposits and a discouragement of personal loans. On the balance of payments, new controls were introduced on private investment outside the sterling area, and British firms were to be encouraged to repatriate more of their overseas profits. Finally, a pay pause was imposed on wage increases in the public sector, in the hope that the private sector would follow suit.

These measures were successful in stopping the run on sterling. They also stopped the tentative recovery in output; after the middle of the year industrial production stopped rising and unemployment began to increase quite quickly. From July onwards there was a shift in ministerial preoccupations: the balance of payments was no longer immediately dominant, as the trade gap narrowed and the reserves rose, so that repayment of the IMF drawings began before the end of the year. The new battlefield was at home, with the objective of making the pay pause effective. As Macmillan saw it, 'The short-term measures ... will all be nullified if we put up personal incomes by £1,000 million in the next 12 months, as we have in the last 12 months.'[1]

The pay pause and incomes policy

The metaphor of a battlefield is not inappropriate. After the normal summer break in wage negotiations the government had a succession of skirmishes with various unions in the public sector. It also had a succession of encounters with the standard problems thrown up by a pay pause or freeze: for example, what should be done about any automatic cost-of-living clauses? Should arbitration procedures be suspended, or should there simply be a postponement of their judgements? What specific powers did the government have to control wage awards made by boards of nationalised industries?

The government's first major defeat was in November 1961 by the Electricity Board, which had informally agreed with Ministers the maximum offer it could make and that it should not be paid before 1 April, at the end of the pause. The negotiators then rang up the

---

[1] Ibid. p. 379. It is clear that in Macmillan's picture of the economy rises in wages had a 'real' reflationary effect. It was not until the early 1970s that the alternative view was widely accepted – that, after taking account of the effect on prices and taxes, the real reflationary effect of wage increases was, after a short interval, negligible and might become negative.

Minister of Power late one night to say that they had no alternative to offering more and to making payment as from 28 January, at which the · Minister protested but took no further action. The Prime Minister publicly deplored this and the chairman of the Board was rebuked, but privately Macmillan admitted that it could be regarded as a tactical retreat from a salient which could not be defended.[1] However, in subsequent skirmishes the government was more successful. The Post Office workers' work-to-rule was called off, as was the threat of a go-slow by some of the Civil Service unions, on the promise that unfettered arbitration would be resumed when the pay pause ended.

As the pay pause continued, the Prime Minister became increasingly concerned with the policy which should follow it, for he had come round to the view that a permanent incomes policy of some kind was needed. He considered that the orthodox theory had in the past proved a good working rule: when the system became 'overheated' (the signs were over-employment, an unfavourable balance of payments, pressures on sterling, rises in wages unjustified by productivity increases) it had to be cooled down by deflationary touches of various kinds. But in 1962 for the first time a resistance had begun to appear. The 'conventional and lowering regimen' had been applied, but it seemed to be having no effect on wage demands. The Prime Minister complained that he got little support in developing new ideas from 'the practitioners of most repute', so he himself took on responsibility for evolving a more permanent incomes policy.[2] His plan was essentially for a 'guiding light' (page 363), together with a commission on pay, to be a permanent body; he considered at some length how to make the commission effective, and came down against compulsion (for example, a fiscal penalty, or depriving a recalcitrant trade union of the protection of the 1906 Trade Disputes Act) and in favour of the pressure which would arise from the 'full public disclosure of the facts'.

Meanwhile certain tentative moves had been made by the Chancellor and the Treasury. The Chancellor wrote to the General Council of the Trades Union Congress (TUC) early in January 1962, asking for their cooperation in keeping the increase in earnings during 1962 within the limits set by the probable increase in productivity, put by the Treasury at $2\frac{1}{2}$ per cent; in February the Treasury issued what was, in effect, a discussion paper,[3] mainly concerned with the criteria by which wage demands should be judged – should an increase in the cost of living be a justification, for example (see page 363)? However, the Prime Minister was becoming increasingly exasperated by the dilatori-

[1] H. Macmillan, *At the End of the Day, 1961–1963*, London, Macmillan, 1973, p 47.
[2] Ibid. pp. 84–5.
[3] Treasury, *Incomes Policy: the next step*, Cmnd 1626, London, HMSO, 1962.

ness of the Chancellor and the Treasury in working out concrete institutional proposals. He was concerned at the Party's loss of popularity in the country; also by June he was anxious about the need for some reflation, which he felt was impossible without an effective incomes policy. 'At present we dare not re-inflate, because our system is open at both ends – wages and imports. Increased wages mean (without increased productivity) more imports and less exports.'[1]

The Prime Minister's economic preoccupations of this period were, therefore, largely with trying to devise new incomes policy institutions, and it seems to have been this which led to his decision to replace Selwyn Lloyd as Chancellor; what is not clear, though, is how far 'dilatoriness' in this matter was due to a disbelief in incomes policies.

Establishing the NEDC

The initial proposal to do something about 'planning' had been made in a rather vague way by Selwyn Lloyd as part of the package of measures announced on 25 July 1961. The proposal clearly divided the Cabinet quite sharply and formal approval for an invitation to both sides of industry was not obtained until 21 September. The trade union side was nervous; they suspected that the invitation was part of an incomes policy trap and only eventually consented to join on condition that the Council was not used as an agent for wage restraint.

At this time policies for encouraging faster growth were being widely discussed. The *National Institute Economic Review* for February 1962 argued that 'a necessary, and almost sufficient condition for rapid growth is for businessmen in general to expect that the demand for their products will continue to grow rapidly'.[2] For this to hold true, businessmen must be confident that total demand in the economy as a whole would expand unhampered by balance of payments difficulties or excessive price rises. It was suggested that there were two distinct policy problems – how to achieve competitiveness in the first place and how to maintain it once it was achieved. For the first, devaluation was recommended while there was spare capacity. For the second, three suggestions were put forward:

(a) an incomes policy to ensure that relative costs did not get out of line;

(b) a policy to ensure that the higher investment needed was forthcoming;

(c) a planning mechanism to ensure, among other things, that the improved demand prospects were appreciated at key points in industry and that industry made its plans in the light of higher growth prospects.

[1] Macmillan, *At the End of the Day*, p. 89.
[2] *National Institute Economic Review*, no. 19, February 1962, pp. 55–6.

The NEDC's first meeting was in March 1962. The main contribution of the Council in its early days was (for good or ill) to establish a 4 per cent annual growth rate as the target for the British economy for the period 1961–6; this figure certainly influenced policy over the next two years.

The 1962 budget

The figures available at the time of the 1962 budget are shown in table 2.3. The trade and balance of payments figures were no longer particularly disturbing, but the recovery was fairly muted. The current balance of payments was still just in deficit in the third quarter of 1961, but the reserves had begun to rise again, apart from the IMF drawing; probably the best description of the balance of payments was 'convalescent'. On the other hand, the latest production figures available showed a distinct falling-off at the end of 1961 and seasonally adjusted unemployment had been rising since July to about 1¾ per cent at the end of the year.

Table 2.3. *Some indicators available at end-March 1962*

	Monthly trade gap	Gold and foreign exchange reserves	Current balance of payments	Unemployment	Index of industrial production	Quarterly change in: Retail price index	Quarterly change in: Weekly wage rates
	(£m.)	($b.)	(£m.)	(%)	(1958=100)	(%)	(%)
1961 I	−69	3·02	−49	1·51	113	+0·5	+1·8
II	−45	2·77	−11	1·39	115	+1·3	+0·7
III	−33	3·55	−1	1·50	115	+1·3	+0·6
IV	−45	3·32	..	1·67	112	+1·1	+0·8
1962 Jan.	−68	3·61	..	1·82	111	+1·4	..
Feb.	−44	3·42	..	1·78	..	..	..

SOURCE: *National Institute Economic Review*, no. 20, May 1962.

Note: see notes to table 2.1.

Nonetheless the budget was essentially neutral. In his speech the Chancellor stressed the risk of excess pressure of home demand by the end of the year, for the official forecast was that output would be rising at some 3–4 per cent through the year, but this rested heavily on a very optimistic export forecast and on only a slight dip in private investment. Further, the Treasury at this time was probably more afraid of underestimating than overestimating demand; they certainly did not want unemployment to fall again and would not have been unduly disturbed if it had risen somewhat further.

MID-1962 TO OCTOBER 1964

The Prime Minister clearly considered that the change of Chancellor on 13 July 1962 and the Cabinet's adoption of an incomes policy provided the necessary conditions for a move towards expansion. Reporting on the economic debate held at the end of July 1962, he comments: 'We were now definitely set upon an expansionist course, and the whole purpose of the changes at the Treasury was to ensure that this should take place without further delay ... We regarded the Incomes Policy as essential in order to sustain expansion without incurring the evils which inflated costs following inflated wages had brought ...'[1]

However, there were in fact no immediate expansionary moves; no action was taken until the late autumn and then it was tentative and cautious. The main reason for this was that Treasury officials were reasonably confident, until the autumn, that output was rising satisfactorily. 'Throughout 1962 the big economic argument about expansion was not whether it was desirable, but whether it was happening.'[2] At the time of the budget the official forecast had been that by the end of the year there would be a greater risk of excess than of deficient demand, and the figures which became available up to August or September provided some support for this view – the seasonally adjusted industrial production index recovered from its dip at the end of 1961 and went on rising into the third quarter. But as the year wore on it became increasingly difficult to reconcile this with the general mood of business pessimism. If production was rising rapidly why were businessmen so gloomy? Further, there was some difficulty in reconciling the unemployment figures with relatively rapid expansion; there were precedents for unemployment continuing to rise after production had begun to recover, but it did seem surprising when October and November too showed quite sharp increases in seasonally adjusted unemployment. One suggestion was that a change in the underlying rate of increase in productivity explained the phenomenon; this change could have resulted from new policies on hoarding labour, an increased rate of introducing automation, and so on.

There were other reasons for official caution. A number of economists, both inside and outside the government, favoured trying to establish a rather wider margin of spare capacity than in the past; although by June unemployment had been rising for a year, it was still just under 2 per cent (according to the definitions then used), so that there were certainly those who were quite ready to see it rise a little further. Secondly, on the figures then available the balance of pay-

---

[1] Macmillan, *At the End of the Day*, p. 108.
[2] *National Institute Economic Review*, no. 23, February 1963, p. 4.

ments on current account had only just moved into a small surplus in the first quarter of 1962; also, the Chancellor's attempt at the IMF annual meeting to get an agreed increase in international liquidity had been unsuccessful.

Nonetheless some measures were taken. Special Deposits required from the banks were reduced from 2 to 1 per cent in early October and qualitative restraints on bank lending were abolished. In addition, on 3 October £42 million of postwar credits were released and an increase of £70 million in public investment was announced. Then in early November an attempt was made to stimulate investment, with increased investment allowances for industry, a quicker 'write-off' for heavy capital goods and an inducement to invest in research; to this was added a cut in purchase tax on cars from 45 to 25 per cent. The attempt to stimulate investment appears to have been the Prime Minister's idea; he noted in mid October: '... my fear is that in view of the uncertainty as to (a) Europe, (b) General Election, we have little chance of getting any natural increase in private investment during the next year unless we can stimulate it by some such means as I have proposed.'[1] It is quite possible that among officials in the Treasury there was a good deal of scepticism about the effectiveness of this kind of stimulus.

Developments during the winter of 1962/3 forced the government to more vigorous expansionist policies. First, official confidence that expansion was proceeding satisfactorily was punctured when the initial estimate of the industrial production index for October 1962 showed a fall of 3 per cent. This was a sharp shock and, although revisions later modified the collapse, they still showed a fall in October and November from the third quarter. Secondly, 1962/3 was a very bad winter; unemployment – seasonally adjusted in the normal way – rose to 3·3 per cent in January 1963 and to 3·6 per cent in February; it was very difficult to put the blame for these figures entirely on the cold weather. At the beginning of 1963 there were longer-term pressures too. Nearly a third of the period 1961–6, for which the NEDC had adopted a target annual growth rate of 4 per cent a year, had gone; to reach that objective the growth rate from 1963 to 1966 would have to be nearly 5 per cent. The case for a substantial stimulus was put in the *National Institute Economic Review* for February 1963, which recommended an additional budget stimulus of roughly £400 million.[2]

There were some further mild reflationary measures in early 1963, but the important question was the amount of reflation in the budget. Throughout the early months of the year the Prime Minister was clearly pressing for a high figure. He had his political difficulties: the

[1] Macmillan, *At the End of the Day*, p. 386.
[2] *National Institute Economic Review*, no. 23, February 1963, p. 43–6.

Labour Party was far ahead in the polls, and there was a substantial movement within the Conservative Party to replace him as Prime Minister. At the end of January he noted that the economy was still not responding; he also recorded his 'instinctive and violent' reaction against economists who accepted the higher level of unemployment. His strategy was firmly that of expansion with an incomes policy – that is, 'expansion without inflation', which was the budget theme.

In the event the budget tax reliefs were worth £261 million in the year 1963/4, mainly benefiting lower income groups, with the object of trying to obtain trade union support for an incomes policy. The full-year effect was, however, substantially greater (£406 million allowing for the effects of the additional investment reliefs introduced); further, the Chancellor's speech indicated that he was ready to meet by international borrowing, or by running down the reserves, any deficit caused by the temporary bout of stockbuilding which tends to accompany a recovery.[1] Of course this was much weaker than the statement made by another Conservative Chancellor nine years later, when Anthony Barber indicated that he was prepared to see the exchange rate go rather than forfeit expansion (page 64). Nonetheless Maudling's statement was an important milestone in the long progression by which 'the strength of sterling' was demoted from its position as a dominant objective of economic policy at the beginning of the 1960s.

In retrospect the recovery in output during 1963 seems clear enough; so also is the succession of stimuli which set it going. They began at the end of 1962 with the relaxations on bank credit, the repayment of postwar credits and the reduction in purchase tax on cars. At the beginning of 1963 purchase tax was also reduced on other durables and from the second quarter of 1963 there was some net stimulus from changes in national insurance benefits and contributions. By the third quarter of 1963 some effects were beginning to be felt from the rise in public investment intended for the fiscal year 1963/4. The tax concessions in the budget probably added some $1\frac{1}{2}$ per cent to consumers' expenditure in both the third and the fourth quarters.[2]

---

[1] 'Moreover, in so far as there is a stocking-up movement related to expansion, in effect the building up of working capital, then I think that it is perfectly reasonable and sensible to finance such a movement out of our reserves or out of borrowing facilities in the International Monetary Fund and elsewhere. This is surely what these various facilities exist for. It is wrong to use reserves or borrowing facilities to boost up an internal position which is unsound because costs, prices and incomes have got out of hand. But it is equally unsound to refuse to use reserves and borrowing facilities for the purposes for which they exist, namely, to deal with temporary situations and prevent temporary difficulties obstructing the proper long-term development of the economy' (*Hansard*, 3 April 1963, col. 471).

[2] However, one of the first of the expansionary measures – the improved terms for investment and depreciation allowances announced in November 1962 – seems not to have had much effect, certainly not immediately; private investment was only just beginning to recover at the end of 1963.

However, during 1963 there was much less certainty about the solidarity of the recovery, for two reasons. First, the high figures for the second quarter might simply have been a rebound from the effects of the very bad winter, so it was only as figures came in for the third quarter that confidence improved. Secondly, in 1962 there had been a recovery in the first half of the year which petered out in the second half – might not this pattern be repeated? However, by the late autumn it was clear that the recovery was well established – and by the beginning of 1964 – only a year after the turning-point – a cut-back in the rate of increase in output was already being suggested.

A useful summary of the background to policy decisions in 1964 is provided by the *National Institute Economic Review* for February of that year. Total demand was forecast to rise in real terms by some 5–6 per cent a year from the end of 1963 to the middle of 1965, the main driving forces being the upturn in private investment which had only just begun, the rise in public investment (intended to fill the gap caused by the drop in private investment) coming in late, substantial stock-building and a continuing rapid rise in exports. It was argued that this rate of increase in demand should be brought down because it would produce too low a figure of unemployment – perhaps about 1·3–1·4 per cent in mid-1965 and probably still falling – when incomes would be 'likely to rise considerably faster than productivity, even on fairly optimistic assumptions about the effect of a high pressure of demand on productivity trends'.[1] (The lagged relationship between output and employment, and therefore between output and unemployment, was by then well known.) The *Review* did not argue that the expansion up till then had been too fast, but that now it was 'sensible to look ahead to the point of full employment; and since there is no sign that the rise in demand is slowing down of its own accord, the government must be prepared to make the adjustment needed'.[2]

The argument for restraint at the beginning of 1964 was not based on any actual acceleration in price increases; indeed through 1963 the movements in both wages and prices had been moderate, even by the standards of the time. Between the fourth quarters of 1962 and of 1963 hourly wage rates had risen only 3½ per cent – virtually in line with the 'guiding light' – and over the same period the retail price index had risen only 2·2 per cent.

The balance of payments forecast took second place to unemployment in the argument for restraint. There were those who contended

[1] *National Institute Economic Review*, no. 27, February 1964, p. 10.

[2] Ibid. p. 11. When this was written, the estimate of the rise in national output between the fourth quarters of 1962 and 1963 was 5 per cent; on the latest figures now available, it is 6½ per cent. Had the latest figure been available at that time, the tenor of the passage quoted would probably have been rather different.

that, if at an acceptable level of unemployment Britain ran a balance of payments deficit, the remedy was not restraint but devaluation. The basis for discussion of the balance of payments in 1964 was the 'balance on current and long-term capital account, including a normal balancing item', which had already worsened during 1963: current estimates showed a change from a surplus of £43 million in the first half of 1963 to a deficit of £8 million in the second half, and this deficit was forecast to be £200 million in the first half of 1965. As to how far this emerging deficit might be considered temporary, it was conceded that some of it could be explained by stockbuilding, but probably not all of it.[1] (Throughout 1964, of course, successive balance of payments forecasts got steadily worse.)

The case presented, therefore, was for what Macmillan would have called 'a touch on the brake'. The standard argument was that it was better to take mild deflationary action early rather than severe deflationary action late. 'A policy of moderating the rise in demand, when it appears too high to be sustained, is not a "stop/go" policy: rather the opposite. The avoidance of "stop/go" does not mean that the Government should abandon the short-run regulation of the economy entirely, but rather that it should intervene in good time so that drastic action, leading to long periods of stagnation, is not needed.'[2]

The restraint urged was certainly moderate. Although it was argued that the forecast level of home output should be reduced by 2 per cent by mid-1965, a cut of only about 1 per cent was suggested for the rate of increase in real expenditure (public and private), on the grounds that if this was done soon further adjustments could be made later if needed. By mid-1965 perhaps a reduction in demand of the order of £400 million would be required, but a first instalment of £200 million was recommended. In the event the Chancellor halved this figure: he put up taxes on drink and tobacco to bring in an additional £100 million in 1964/5. He agreed that the growth rate of the economy should be reduced to 4 per cent, but judged that a relatively small amount of deflation was needed to do this.

During the rest of 1964, up to the election on 15 October, policy-makers and commentators were mainly preoccupied with the worsening balance of payments. Imports rose sharply and exports did not; by May 1964, the National Institute's forecast for the current and long-term capital deficit for the year was £300 million; by August this had risen to £500 million. In mid-October the estimate put before the new government was that the deficit was most unlikely to be below £700 million and might well reach £800 million; however, this last

[1] At that time it was assumed that stockbuilding had a particularly high import content.
[2] Ibid.

figure does not apparently take into account the 'balancing item', which was then assumed normally to provide a credit of some £60 million. Again, this was on a definition which is now not used; the figure we have in 1977 for the current deficit in 1964 is the much less formidable figure of £355 million.

The Chancellor's other concern in this period was with incomes policy. As unemployment came down wage rates began to move up rather faster and left the 'guiding light' behind; through 1964 the increase in weekly wage rates was about $4\frac{1}{2}$ per cent, and the rise in prices accelerated to about the same figure. It was too near an election for the TUC to come to any agreement with a Conservative government.

Partly because of the worsening overseas balance, the rise in output through 1964 was below the forecast; the figure now is that it rose about $4\frac{1}{2}$ per cent. Given that output rose less than expected, unemployment came down rather more sharply than forecast – to $1\frac{1}{2}$ per cent by the fourth quarter of 1964. The transition to a Labour government, therefore, came – conveniently for the narration – at the end of a period of re-expansion.

The years 1962–4 tend to be discussed as if they were in some important way different from other periods of re-expansion. However, the difference was more in words than in actions: first, there was an explicit statement that some balance of payments risks would be taken; secondly, there was a medium-term growth target of 4 per cent a year in the background, so that the relapse to a growth rate of under 3 per cent seemed more of a failure; thirdly, it was intended that an incomes policy should prevent the expansion worsening the price trend and thus the balance of payments, but this objective was never attained.

OCTOBER 1964 TO DEVALUATION

Introduction

In the period up to devaluation – and indeed until the middle of 1969 – economic policy was dominated to an even greater extent than usual by balance of payments considerations – more specifically, by the need to stop or to prevent runs on sterling. It is hard to think of any important demand management measures which were not taken with the balance of payments mainly in mind. This preoccupation comes out clearly in the first sentence of the Foreword to Harold Wilson's record of the Labour government, whose life he describes as dominated by an inherited balance of payments problem.[1]

Over this period there was a series of crises, followed by packages

[1] H. Wilson, *The Labour Government 1964–1970: a personal record*, London, Weidenfeld and Michael Joseph, 1971, p. xvii.

of crisis measures, often followed by false dawns, which then gave way to crises again. Nor was this pattern immediately broken by devaluation, which was, after all, to another fixed exchange rate that also had to be defended. For well over a year afterwards devaluation appeared to have been unsuccessful.

Policy decisions during this period give the impression that the government must have been struggling throughout 1965 and 1966 with a very large current balance of payments deficit. In fact, on the figures we now have, this was not so. There had certainly been a large current deficit in 1964. But from the beginning of 1965 to the end of the third quarter of 1967 the current account was virtually in balance on average. Over the whole of these eleven quarters, on the figures we have in 1977 there was in aggregate a balance of payments current surplus of £5 million. The problem was clearly not on current account at all, but on capital account.

There is a sharp divide between the policies which the Labour government found itself forced to pursue and the economic strategy which it had planned while in opposition, when four years of economic policy almost wholly constrained by the balance of payments had certainly not been envisaged.

Labour came to power firmly believing that it could improve on the Conservatives' growth record. Ministers had a clear picture of the 'stop-go' cycle, which they intended to replace by steady expansion: '... every four or five years a deliberately engineered consumption boom is generated which, after a few months, calls forth spectacular increases in national production ... A rapidly expanding home market exerts a dangerous pull on exports; a disproportionate rise in imports is needed to feed our factories and shops. So the green light changes to amber, interest rates rise, social programmes are cut back, and within a year the red light of economic crisis – with 7 per cent bank rates, additional taxation, and cuts in social expenditure – bring the economy grinding to a halt.'[1] In the discussion of ways of breaking out of the 'stop-go' cycle, Wilson put the emphasis on incomes policy and on selective intervention to improve the industrial structure. On industrial intervention he suggested, *inter alia*, a speedier write-off for plant (or special investment allowances) for exporting industries, 'decisive' investment allowances for particular types of automative equipment installed in manufacturing industry, help with research and finance when import-saving industries were being established, new, publicly owned industries based on science and the expansion of certain industries – such as chemical engineering and chemical plant

[1] H. Wilson, 'Labour's economic policy' in *The New Britain: Labour's plan*, Harmondsworth, Penguin, 1964, pp. 23–41.

manufacture; the expansion, also, of industrial training. Two new Ministries were proposed in the same speech: a Ministry of Technology and a Ministry of Economic Planning – which, in the event, became the Department of Economic Affairs. Clearly the intention was to reduce the Treasury's role in economic policy.

Thus the Labour Party came to power intending to give medium-term and long-term structural changes priority in its economic policy; instead, it found itself reacting to the day-to-day movements in the foreign exchange market.

The initial crisis

The new government made its major institutional change in the economic field straight away by establishing the Department of Economic Affairs under George Brown. The concordat which laid down the relative responsibilities of the new department and of the Treasury seems not to have been very clear, although, even if it had been, there would almost certainly still have been some struggle for power.[1] The original conception had been that the Department of Economic Affairs should lay down economic policy and the Treasury should be the administrative arm in financial matters, but since the new Chancellor of the Exchequer ranked third in the Party hierarchy it could hardly have worked out that way whatever the words of the agreement. The Civil Service put up a paper suggesting that the short term should be the Treasury's responsibility and long-term planning that of the Department of Economic Affairs, but the Prime Minister did not accept this; he wished the distinction to be between monetary matters and real resources. Either division would have been very difficult to define in terms of detailed responsibility for particular branches of policy. Most policies have both long-term and short-term effects and, in much the same way, virtually all policies have both real and monetary consequences. In fact, the new department had not been set up because Labour Party politicians saw a distinct division of responsibilities which they felt would be carried out more effectively if separated; rather it was that they distrusted the Treasury as being too preoccupied with demand management and too little concerned with structural economic change, so that they wished for a countervailing power to champion the long-term cause in economic policy decisions. Inevitably, therefore, there was a large overlap in the responsibilities of the two departments, both of which had to be concerned in major

---

[1] 'We did manage to draft something that I called a "Concordat", but it never got itself formally accepted between Jim Callaghan, the Prime Minister and myself' (G. Brown, *In My Way*, London, Gollancz, 1971, p. 92). The use of the term 'concordat' is illuminating; it suggests an agreement between parties with potentially conflicting interests.

economic decisions. Eventually the Treasury dominated and the Department of Economic Affairs expired because the problems determining policy through most of this period concerned the balance of payments and foreign currency reserves, where the Treasury and the Bank of England could speak with authority and the Department of Economic Affairs could not.

Certainly the new division of responsibilities had little relevance to the government's immediate problems. The Treasury had presented to the Cabinet an appraisal and forecast of the economic situation which suggested that, in addition to the balance of payments deficit on current and long-term capital account of £800 million in 1964, there would be a continuing substantial deficit in 1965 a good deal higher than the published unofficial forecasts which had been available before the election. The Treasury indicated that, in addition to demand management measures, something was needed with a more immediate effect on the foreign balance. Three possibilities were put forward: devaluation of sterling, quantitative restrictions on imports, or a surcharge on a wide range of imports. The three economic Ministers chose the surcharge. The background to the decision not to devalue is set out on pages 311–12; it seems stranger now, in a world that has got used to exchange-rate changes, than it did then. Quotas were also rejected, probably mainly on the basis of Wilson's own experience of administering them in the 1940s, when he was President of the Board of Trade. This left the surcharge as the least damaging to the home economy of the three proposals, but the main objection to it was that it contravened international obligations, particularly those of the General Agreement on Tariffs and Trade (GATT) and of the European Free Trade Area (EFTA).

The government announced a 15 per cent surcharge on imports of manufactured goods on 26 October. This was accompanied by a published statement which included the estimate of a current and long-term capital deficit for 1964 of £800 million, but also indicated that the government did not consider the general pressure on resources excessive, so that there was no need to move to a higher level of unemployment.[1] Government expenditure was to be reviewed – Concorde was singled out – an export rebate system was announced and there were one or two other minor measures. The initial reaction abroad was rather sharp, particularly by members of EFTA, who had been given no advance warning. However, there was at this stage no run on sterling.

On 11 November the Chancellor introduced an autumn budget. He announced a big increase in pensions to take effect from March

[1] Prime Minister's Office, *The Economic Situation*, London, HMSO, 1964.

1965, together with an increase in national assistance benefits; prescription charges were abolished.[1] National insurance contributions were to be increased at the same time; in addition, petrol tax was put up and advance notice given that income tax would be raised in the 1965 budget. The Chancellor also gave notice that he would be introducing a capital gains tax and altering the system of company taxation. In crude terms, the increase in budget revenue was well in excess of the Exchequer contribution to the new benefits. However, the National Institute's analysis suggested that, since the rise in income tax would be at the expense of personal and company savings, and since employers' contributions work only partially and belatedly through to consumer prices, the combined net effect of the changes in benefits, the budget and the import surcharge would be to raise the demand for home output at the end of 1965 by around 1 per cent.

The budget started speculation against sterling, which continued into the next week. Bank Rate was, however, not raised on Thursday 19 November, as generally expected; according to Wilson, George Brown objected.[2] This was also the day on which other EFTA countries demanded and got a promise that the import surcharge would be reduced 'in a matter of months'. Bank Rate was eventually put up by 2 per cent on 23 November, but this still failed to check the speculative outflow.[3] Wilson describes a succession of interviews which took place during this period with the Governor of the Bank of England (Lord Cromer), who stressed the need for cuts in government expenditure as a necessary condition for stopping the outflow. The Prime Minister indicated that, rather than cut social expenditure in deference to foreign financial opinion, he would go to the country again and float the exchange rate; he asked Lord Cromer to see what he could raise from other central banks in support for sterling. Within a day the Governor announced that he had successfully raised £3 billion, thus ending the first of the Labour government's speculative crises.

It has been argued that the management of policy in these first two months was maladroit: that it was foolish to announce publicly the size of the expected deficit, to delay the increase in Bank Rate for four days, to announce in advance the introduction of capital gains tax and corporation tax without saying more precisely what their provisions would be, and so on. However, these errors of timing – if they were errors – cannot have mattered very much; in the light of the specula-

[1] The estimated cost of the changes in national insurance benefits and war pensions was £300 million. The other two measures were to cost much less: £23 million for the increase in national assistance benefits and £22 million for the abolition of prescription charges.

[2] Wilson, *The Labour Government 1964–1970*, p. 36.

[3] It is interesting that at that time it was considered necessary to inform the United States government in advance of the Bank Rate change; rather elaborate steps were taken to do this.

tion which took place against sterling during the next three years, it seems most unlikely that it would have been prevented just by the omission of a figure from a White Paper, or by raising Bank Rate four days earlier – there would have been some other trigger on some other occasion. The more serious criticism is that the initial deflation was inadequate, and that it would have been better if the government had begun in 1964 with the policies it eventually followed from 1966 onwards. If it was in any case going to take steps which increased unemployment to $2\frac{1}{2}$ per cent, then it should have started on that policy right from the beginning. This is a much wider question. In 1964, of course, $1\frac{1}{2}$ per cent unemployment was not considered abnormally low; it was only after 1966 that $1\frac{1}{2}$ per cent was gradually replaced by $2\frac{1}{2}$ per cent as a kind of norm.

The criticism of the Labour government's initial autumn budget is only part of a general criticism of the policy up to devaluation. That policy had, as its objectives, a substantial improvement in the balance of payments without the need to devalue the pound, and an acceleration of the growth rate. It failed on both counts, but it does not necessarily follow that more severe initial deflation would have been any better without other policy changes.

The second speculative crisis

International credit reinforcements stemmed the run on sterling, but did not stop it altogether; sales of sterling were still substantial in December. The pressure was eased further, however, when very good trade figures were announced for December. Throughout this period, and indeed right up to the present day, Ministers have repeated again and again that no weight should be attached to one month's trade figures, but this has made no difference to the tendency for confidence to swing according to the latest figure.

In the period between the two budgets, the Department of Economic Affairs made the first moves on an incomes policy; it also began to construct a National Plan. On incomes policy, employers' representatives and trade unionists were persuaded to sign a joint statement of intent on productivity, prices and incomes in the middle of December; by mid-February there was an agreed White Paper on the machinery of policy;[1] in mid-March Aubrey Jones was appointed chairman of the NBPI, and the TUC General Council agreed to a 3–$3\frac{1}{2}$ per cent norm for wage increases, which was endorsed in April by a conference of executive committees of affiliated unions. On planning, the target figure for the growth rate, announced well in advance of the National

[1] Prime Minister's Office, *Machinery of Prices and Incomes Policy*, Cmnd 2577, London, HMSO, 1965.

Plan itself, was a 25 per cent increase in output between 1964 and 1970. Linked to this ambitious target, the Chancellor announced in February that public expenditure was to increase in real terms by an average of 4½ per cent a year between 1964/5 and 1969/70.

However, in preparing for the budget the Chancellor was naturally concerned with the more immediate problems of the balance of payments. The credits from other central banks had been renewed for a further three months in early February and, in response to intense EFTA pressure, it had been announced that the surcharge on imports of manufactures would be reduced to 10 per cent in April. The National Institute continued to insist on the need for more deflation of home demand to allow a transfer of resources into the balance of payments. It argued that: 'The main aim for policy therefore must be to find ways of improving the balance of payments in 1966 by a figure of the order of £300 million, without adding to the total pressure of demand.'[1] A direct attack limiting investment and government expenditure overseas might conceivably produce a net improvement of £100 million, so that an increase in taxation sufficient to reduce final demand by £200 million from the level it would otherwise have reached was recommended.

In fact the budget followed this prescription fairly closely. United Kingdom residents who sold investments held outside the sterling area had to exchange 25 per cent of the proceeds for sterling at the official rate rather than the investment premium rate (see page 328), and there was a declaration of intent to save £50–£100 million in overseas military expenditure. In addition to the increase in income tax which had already been announced, higher taxes were imposed on drink and tobacco and motor vehicle licence fees were raised. The estimated effect on demand in 1966 was not far short of the figure which the National Institute had suggested.[2] Already an incongruity was beginning to appear between the declared growth target and the requirements of the balance of payments. The effect of the budget, according to the National Institute forecast in May 1965, would be to slow down the rise in output by the first quarter of 1966 to a rate of 2½ per cent a year.

After the budget the government felt, not unreasonably, that it had done enough to ward off further speculative attacks. Monetary policy was tightened in April, when there was an additional call for Special Deposits, and in May controls on bank advances were reimposed. Also in May there was a further drawing from the IMF, most of which was used to repay borrowings from the other central banks. Then in June,

---

[1] *National Institute Economic Review*, no. 31, February 1965, p. 12.

[2] About £150 million at factor cost in 1966 from the increases in taxation on drink, tobacco, and motor licences (*National Institute Economic Review*, no. 32, May 1965, p. 20).

when it seemed that there were neither external nor internal reasons for maintaining Bank Rate at 7 per cent, the Bank was persuaded to lower the Rate by a whole point, contrary to the old doctrine of 'up by ones, down by halves'. This also gave the government the option of increasing Bank Rate again if pressure developed on sterling in the autumn. But, presumably because of nervousness about foreign reaction, the Bank Rate reduction was coupled with tightening of hire purchase controls, to which the Department of Economic Affairs objected; the proposed measures were, however, endorsed by the Cabinet.

We know now that the current balance of payments improved very substantially between the second half of 1964 and the first half of 1965; on figures now available the current deficit fell from £251 million to £10 million. However, while the trade figures available at the time had improved very sharply to a deficit of only £13 million a month in the first quarter of 1965, in April this widened to £30 million and in May to £49 million – which was as bad as in the second half of 1964. A speculative run on sterling began again on publication of these figures and the June figure, at £33 million, was not sufficiently improved to stop the outflow.

The package of deflationary measures therefore announced on 27 July 1965 is generally accepted as 'tough', but, as with all packages which contain large cuts in public investment, it is hard to say just how tough in fact it was. Starts of public investment projects – except for industrial building, housing, school-building and hospitals – were postponed for six months; nationalised industries' investment and local authorities' building programmes were cut; local authority mortgages to private house-buyers were limited; building licences were introduced for commercial projects; hire purchase terms were tightened again and importers were required to make pre-payments on goods brought into the country. The whole package was supposed to reduce demand by £200 million in a full year, but it is very hard to say whether or not this figure was exaggerated. There was at the time a heavy load on the building industry, so that the postponement of starts may simply have accelerated completions. No public investment programme for 1965/6 had been published, so that, as the *National Institute Economic Review* remarked: '...cuts of an unknown size are being made in an unknown sum, to take effect at an unknown time'.[1] It is true that in August of that year the National Institute's forecast of output was significantly more pessimistic than in May, when it had

---

[1] Ibid. no. 33, August 1965, p. 8. The 1965/6 investment programme appeared in *The National Plan*, published in September; the impact of the investment cuts is appraised in this context on pages 113–14 below.

envisaged that output would be rising at about $2\frac{1}{2}$ per cent a year from mid-1965 onwards; by August that figure had been brought down to $1\frac{1}{2}$ per cent. However, the July measures were not the only reason for the change.

The third speculative crisis

As usual, it was uncertain for a time whether or not the measures would be successful in stopping the speculation. In the meantime the Prime Minister, the Chancellor and the Governor of the Bank of England discussed whether they could all go on holiday at the same time as planned, but sterling survived their simultaneous absence, helped by very good trade figures for July, with a deficit of only £3 million.

However, a great deal of the foreign lines of credit had been used up in the defence of sterling and there was no substantial reflux of short-term capital. It was clear that there would soon have to be further support for sterling and the American Secretary of the Treasury was a key figure in this operation. In particular, he pressed the British government to tighten up on its incomes policy because he doubted whether the voluntary policy would be able to withstand the pressure for wage increases.[1] The government therefore decided early in September to introduce legislation making the NBPI a statutory body, giving the Secretary of State power to defer any wage or price settlement while enquiries were continuing, and providing for an 'early warning' of price increases and wage settlements. The TUC General Council reluctantly accepted this Bill, but extracted the compromise that a special Order in Council would be required to activate the legislation; in the meantime the TUC had agreed to strengthen the voluntary system by requiring all wage claims to be submitted to their General Council for vetting by new machinery. The Bill was in fact introduced, but it had not passed through all its stages before the general election in March 1966, so that it lapsed and had to be reintroduced in the next Parliament. Enough had been done, however, to meet the American point and, on 10 September, further international support for sterling was announced.

On 13 September *The National Plan* was published;[2] two other longer-term measures of note at this time were the introduction of investment grants in place of investment allowances and the establishment of the IRC.

Throughout the second half of 1965 the trade figures were improving, with exports rising well. Unemployment stayed low, which seemed very surprising at the time, for the current estimates were that national

---

[1] Wilson, *The Labour Government 1964–1970*, pp. 131–2.
[2] Department of Economic Affairs, *The National Plan*.

output had only risen $1\frac{1}{2}$ per cent in the year up to the fourth quarter of 1965. (The figures now available suggest a rise of $2\frac{1}{2}$ per cent, and the failure of unemployment to rise becomes more explicable.) Thus the economic background for an election was not unfavourable: the government could claim significant progress in improving the balance of payments, unemployment was still very low and, in a pre-election statement of his assessment of the economic situation, the Chancellor suggested that there would be no need to increase taxation in the budget.

By the beginning of 1966 it was becoming clear that it would be very difficult to reconcile the two objectives of faster growth and improving the balance of payments. The National Institute throughout this period was putting forward the view insistently, and indeed repetitively, that on current policies there would be slow growth only, and for this to change it was necessary for export competitiveness to improve and the propensity to import to moderate. At the beginning of 1966 it was suggested that it might be better to revise the target figures for the National Plan, since it seemed probable that the annual growth rate in the first two years of the Plan would be at best $2\frac{1}{2}$ per cent, which would leave an impossible requirement for the remaining four years.

From the beginning of 1966 the trade gap began to widen again. The government took monetary measures in February: the ceiling on bank advances was continued and restrictions on hire purchase tightened further. After the election the Chancellor found that the Treasury assessment of the economic situation had changed; unemployment had still not begun to rise – indeed it was lower in the first quarter of 1966 than in the fourth quarter of 1965 – so that a fairly substantial further reduction in demand was recommended. The form this took was the selective employment tax (discussed more fully on pages 150–3). The main disadvantage of its introduction in the 1966 budget was the time-lag before it could be implemented; collection did not start until September. The Chancellor also announced that the import surcharge would be removed in November 1966.

From the budget onwards events moved towards the third speculative crisis, of July 1966. The proximate cause was the seamen's strike, which started on 12 May and did not finish until 1 July. Again the background was not one of major underlying weakness in the balance of payments: when the 1965 crisis took place the balance of payments – as we now know – was running a very small deficit; at the time of the 1966 crisis there was a small current surplus of £84 million for the year as a whole.[1]

---

[1] The quarterly figures are distorted by the strike, so that the whole of the surplus is recorded in the fourth quarter of the year, but there was probably a small 'underlying' surplus by the second quarter.

The strike naturally caused a run on sterling. However, during the strike the pressure was contained at the cost of some loss to the reserves; the announcement of new swap facilities, agreed at the annual meeting of the Bank for International Settlements on 13 June, no doubt helped. When the strike ended on 1 July, it appeared to the policy-makers that they had weathered the storm. However, when the reserve figures were announced on 4 July there was a further rush to sell sterling; speculation had caused the fall in reserves, which in turn caused further speculation. Another possible factor was a French statement at the time of M. Pompidou's visit to Britain, which appeared to suggest that devaluation of sterling would be necessary before the idea of Britain joining the Common Market could be entertained.

The moves made in the attempt to handle the crisis have again been criticised. It is true that initially they failed, but in such a situation it is very difficult to know what moves might be successful. On 11 July stories of forthcoming deflationary measures were emphatically denied; on 12 July the Chancellor announced a continuation of a tight monetary policy – retaining the existing ceiling on bank advances, with no relaxation to help firms finance the interval between payments and refunds of selective employment tax; on 14 July Bank Rate was raised by 1 per cent, increased calls were made for Special Deposits and it was announced that deflationary measures would be introduced in about a fortnight's time. These moves were all unsuccessful; on 20 July a very substantial deflationary package was announced.

This time there was a devaluation party in the Cabinet. George Brown had come round to the view that further deflationary measures without a devaluation would finally dispose of any hope of significant economic expansion. For a while, in early July, it seems that the Chancellor too was willing to entertain the idea, but the Prime Minister persuaded him that there was no alternative to fighting on to the end in defence of the exchange rate. On 19 July the matter was discussed in the Cabinet, where there was some support for devaluing the pound and apparently some Ministers put the case for floating the pound, but the vote went heavily in favour of holding the exchange rate.

The package included a further tightening of hire purchase terms, the use of the regulator to raise indirect tax rates by 10 per cent, increases in Post Office charges, a surcharge on surtax for one year, an extension of the coverage of building licences, cuts in public investment and overseas expenditure, the introduction of a travel allowance and a six-month standstill on incomes and prices, to be followed by a further six months of severe restraint. The National Institute's assessment of the consequences of these measures was that they would put the economy on a 1 per cent growth path; however, at this cost – of virtually stopping any rise in output – the balance of payments should move into surplus in 1967 on current and long-term capital account.

The prelude to devaluation

After July 1966 there was a gradual return of confidence. Sterling received further support from abroad in September and the trade figures improved considerably. The impending abolition of the surcharge at the end of November explained a large part of the improvement: importers postponed purchases until the surcharge was removed. Nonetheless, in the winter of 1966/7 there was an appreciable reflux of short-term capital.

When George Brown, having piloted the Prices and Incomes Bill through the House of Commons, left the Department of Economic Affairs to be Foreign Secretary, it was probably the end of any substantial influence by this department on the main issues of economic policy. The TUC reluctantly acquiesced in the government's incomes policy, which was endorsed by a majority at the annual Congress in September. It remained a voluntary policy until October, when it was successfully challenged in the Courts by the Association of Supervisory Staffs, Executives and Technicians and the government activated the compulsory provisions of the Prices and Incomes Act (see page 372). There were in fact no strikes against the wage freeze.

It was at this time that the decision was taken to explore again the possibility of joining the Common Market; at the beginning of 1967 the Prime Minister and the Foreign Secretary began a tour of the six existing member countries of the European Economic Community (the EEC).

Early in 1967 official assessments of the economic situation and prospects became more confident. The reflux of short-term funds meant that by the end of March nearly all central bank assistance had been repaid. The trade gap in the first quarter of the year stayed small. The National Institute continued to forecast a surplus on current and long-term capital account in 1967; it also published a medium-term assessment which attempted to forecast export possibilities, deduce from them the volume of imports which could be purchased and so see what rate of expansion the balance of payments might allow. The conclusion was that: 'Allowing for a minor change in the competitiveness of British manufactures in home as well as export markets, the import availability...would be adequate, with a little to spare, for a 3 per cent growth-rate from 1967 to 1970.'[1]

The preoccupation with the balance of payments began to diminish a little and there were the first signs of concern about rising unemploy-

[1] *National Institute Economic Review*, no. 39, February 1967, p. 23.

ment. The budget was basically neutral; the Chancellor's message, introducing it on 11 April, was: 'We are back on course. The ship is picking up speed. The economy is moving. Every seaman knows the command at such a moment, "steady as she goes".'

There was a series of minor reflationary measures. As far back as November 1966 the Bank of England had indicated that credit was available to priority borrowers. In December the government had announced that there would be an additional 5 per cent on investment grants for investment undertaken in 1967 and 1968 only; then Bank Rate was reduced and restraints were tacitly eased on public investment programmes. In June the government announced increases in national insurance benefits to take effect from the end of October.

However, in the second quarter things began to go wrong: exports failed to rise and the trade gap worsened. The National Institute's forecast for the 'basic' balance in 1967, which had been £175 million in February, fell to £105 million in May and £35 million in August; from mid-May onwards confidence in sterling began to weaken again. Partly this was, of course, due to the Middle East war and the closure of the Suez Canal, but possibly also the British application to join the Common Market had led many people to conclude that the sterling parity would have to be changed before the application could be successful.[1]

In the third quarter of the year policy became uncertain: the balance of payments outlook was deteriorating but, on the other hand, unemployment was still rising. In July the Chancellor announced that the rise in public expenditure for three years from 1967/8 would be held to 3 per cent in real terms, but as late as the end of August there was further reflation – the restrictions on hire purchase terms were relaxed. The confidence which had been expressed earlier in the year was waning; the National Institute forecasts in August were for only a negligible basic balance in 1967, with no improvement in 1968; the appraisal noted:

If, looking further ahead, it turns out that with a 3 per cent growth-rate the balance of payments outcome is still inadequate, the Government could hardly meet this situation by deflating demand in the private sector once again. Last July, deflation by itself was a practicable alternative to devaluation or import controls, first because unemployment was still low; and secondly because there was the prospect of a very rapid rise in public sector expenditure which would partly counterbalance the check to private sector

[1] In the nature of things, suggested influences on the foreign exchange market have to be surmises. Reactions are not easily predictable; it was suggested, for example, that an increase in electricity charges had a bad effect (see S. Brittan, *Steering the Economy* (rev. edn), London, Penguin, 1971, p. 348).

spending. Now unemployment is high, and the increase in public sector spending is being cut back... If in such circumstances a further change of course is needed, and if the Government moved again to deflate private demand, the check might quickly slide into the first major postwar recession.[1]

However, at the beginning of October the position was still far from critical. Wilson states in his memoirs that the strength of the economy was not then in question. He clearly takes the view that we were forced to devalue, not by an underlying weak position, but by the particular circumstances of 1967.[2] It is doubtful, however, whether the Chancellor and the Treasury were so sanguine about the underlying position. Certainly between August and November the 'pre-devaluation' balance of payments forecasts by the National Institute deteriorated substantially: in November they were for basic deficits of £275 million in 1967 and £250 million in 1968. The official forecasts at the time are reported to have shown even larger deficits. Within the Treasury a number of people had long been in favour of running the economy with unemployment at about 2 per cent. Consequently they had been quite ready to accept the deflationary measures of July 1966, since they considered them desirable in any case and they regarded it as possible that if unemployment rose the balance of payments would improve sufficiently for devaluation to be avoided. In 1967 the position was different with unemployment above 2 per cent throughout the year, so that they were no longer prepared to advocate simple deflationary measures. Thus, the underlying situation cannot really be described as 'strong', but there is no doubt that it was made worse both by the dock strikes and by fairly wide-spread discussion in Europe of a possible British devaluation.

The dock strikes began in Liverpool, Manchester, London and Hull on 18 September, when the process of the de-casualisation began, and continued spasmodically for two months; the Merseyside dockers went back at the end of October, but in London the dockers at the Royal Group did not return until 27 November. In consequence, the trade figures announced in both October and November showed very large deficits. In October also a Common Market Commission reporting on the British application expressed substantial doubts about the sterling area and, by implication, about the sterling exchange rate. This theme was picked up by M. Couve de Murville in a speech where he compared the current British position with France's position in 1958, when the franc was devalued just before the Common Market began.

The actual sequence of meetings which led up to devaluation is best described in Harold Wilson's memoirs.[3] The Chancellor came to see

---

[1] *National Institute Economic Review*, no. 41, August 1967, p. 10.
[2] Wilson, *The Labour Government 1964–1970*, p. 439.   [3] Ibid. p. 447 *et seq.*

him on 4 November; pressure on sterling had increased because of rumours on the continent; the Ministerial Finance Committee of the Six, due to meet on 14 November, apparently had on its agenda an item on what the Six would do if Britain devalued. Wilson records that for the first time both he and the Chancellor expressed doubts about whether they could hold the position; he was concerned to avoid a major lurch into deflation, but also that too many other countries should not follow the pound if devalued. He stated that he favoured floating rather than a lower parity.

A number of moves were then made to consult other countries – asking them essentially whether they were ready to see sterling devalued, and if so whether they would want to follow us down, or whether they would promise help for sterling to avoid a disruption of world finance. The Chancellor had a meeting with the Secretary of the Finance Committee of the Six, and the Governor of the Bank of England consulted the European central bank Governors at their monthly meeting in Basle.

In Britain, further Ministers were informed of the possibility of devaluation on 8 November at a meeting of the Steering Committee on Economic Policy, where the agenda included a paper on import quotas, but the Prime Minister let it be known that alternative action could be discussed. Consequently devaluation *was* discussed and the Treasury began work on the deflationary package which would be needed to accompany it. The Treasury and the Bank also began to consider which countries might follow: they apparently suggested that the Scandinavians were likely to do so, but the Six were uncertain and so was Australia; if Australia devalued, Japan, Malaysia, Singapore and Hong Kong would do the same. If all these countries also devalued, gains from the change of parity would be problematical.

Of the foreign institutions consulted, it appears that the United States Treasury was the most horrified; they proceeded to try to organise an international package. However, it appears that the general opinion at Basle among the central bankers was that there should not simply be another set of stand-by facilities arranged between central banks; it should be routed through the IMF, the Secretary-General of which indicated that this would require intensive IMF supervision of the British economy – for example, strict credit control, a tighter prices and incomes policy, a limitation on growth, and an agreement not to float during the currency of the loan. A loan on these conditions was rejected and, although they were apparently qualified to some extent, under American as well as British pressure, the qualifications were insufficient. The decision to devalue was therefore taken on 13 November; the next day a group of Ministers met to decide on the accompanying deflationary measures; the Cabinet was informed on 16 November. By this time there were stories in the press about a massive $1 billion loan from foreign banks; a question was asked about this in the House of Commons and the Chancellor, while stone-walling in reply, appears to have given the impression that the stories were erroneous. Operators in the foreign exchange markets therefore leapt to the conclusion that the other possibility – devaluation – must be right and throughout the next day there was an enormous run on sterling. To allow time for the IMF Board to meet, the Treasury statement announcing devaluation was not issued until 9.30 on Saturday evening. In the event very few countries followed sterling down.

The demand restrictions which accompanied devaluation are widely reported to have been smaller than the Treasury or the Bank of England wished; the Prime Minister refused to accept a rise in the standard rate of income tax. They consisted of a moderate increase in hire purchase restrictions, a ceiling on bank advances and an increase of $1\frac{1}{2}$ per cent in Bank Rate; there were to be cuts in defence spending and also other public spending totalling £200 million a year; export rebates were to be withdrawn, also selective employment tax refunds to manufacturers except in development areas; corporation tax was increased. At the same time it was announced that an application would be made for stand-by credits of $1·4 billion from the IMF and $1·6 billion from other central banks.

THE AFTERMATH OF DEVALUATION

Introduction

Devaluation did not immediately transform economic policy. For a year and a half there was the same overriding preoccupation with the balance of payments; the same need was felt to defend the exchange rate which had, after all, moved to a new fixed parity. There were, as before, speculative runs on sterling, and again these forced the government to take deflationary measures. Until the middle of 1969 the government was waiting for the effects of devaluation to appear. Successive forecasts postponed the move into balance of payments surplus further and further into the future, until by the beginning of 1969 a number of people were doubting whether devaluation would ever improve the balance of payments.

The Treasury had warned the politicians from the beginning that the effect would not be immediate, that the balance of payments would get worse before it got better and that the improvement would not be apparent until the second half of 1968. In a Letter of Intent to the IMF on 23 November 1967, the Treasury stated the government's balance of payments target as: 'an improvement of at least £500 million a year... which on present prospects for world trade...should mean a surplus in the second half of 1968 at an annual rate of at least £200 million'. It was the failure of the balance of payments to improve in this way which dominated economic policy in this period. It is clear why the forecasts went wrong – they underestimated the buoyancy of imports.

'Making room'

The Letter of Intent of 23 November stated: 'The next review of the position and prospects of the United Kingdom economy...will, in the normal course of business, be carried out in February 1968. At this time, it should be possible to assess more accurately than can be done at present the effects of the decisions announced on 18 November 1967.' However, the government was forced to act earlier than this; undoubtedly one reason was that the reflux of short-term funds lasted for only a few days after devaluation, and at the end of November and the beginning of December there was renewed pressure on sterling. At this time there was a move into gold because the dollar was also suspect, and no doubt the speculators assumed that if the dollar were devalued sterling would go down with it. So in December the Prime Minister announced a very wide-ranging review of public expenditure.

In an *ex post* justification of the timing of the measures taken, published in mid-March 1968, the government claimed in effect that it was all part of a carefully planned strategy:

The Government recognised that further measures to release resources would be needed. But given the high level of unemployment,[1] and the necessary uncertainty about the timing and magnitude of the response of exports and imports to devaluation, it did not wish to engineer this release before the additional demand for exports (and import substitutes) induced by devaluation had started to come through. It proposed therefore to act during the course of the coming months, first on public consumption (since cut backs in that field necessarily take time to become effective) and later on private consumption.[2]

Or, as Roy Jenkins had put it more graphically in the House of Commons on 5 December 1967: 'We do not want to dig a hole and leave it empty. We want it to be there only when the export demand is ready to fill it.' This exposition is, however, not wholly convincing; certainly it is open to question whether the review of expenditure would have been so severe had there been a bigger reflux of short-term capital.

[1] Unemployment at 2·4 per cent (United Kingdom, excluding school-leavers) was then considered high.
[2] Treasury, *Economic Report on 1967*, London, HMSO, 1968, p. 7.

The public expenditure cuts occupied a long series of Cabinet meetings in early January 1968; the results were finally announced on 16 January. Cuts of this kind are always difficult to quantify sensibly, since they are reductions not from previous levels but from future programmes. The total decrease in expenditure plans estimated for 1968/9, including the £200 million cuts announced on 18 November, amounted to £500 million; larger reductions on existing commitments were estimated for subsequent years.

Chart 2.1. *Public expenditure on goods and services,[a] 1964–72*

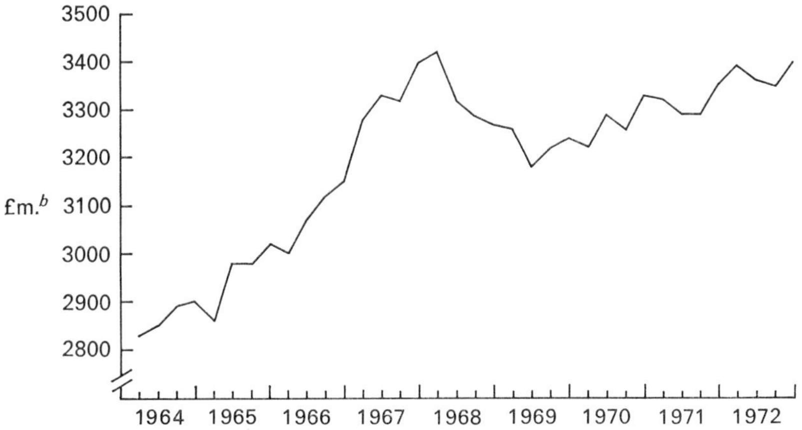

SOURCE: CSO, *Economic Trends, Annual Supplement 1976*, pp. 14, 46 and 47.

[a] Current and capital expenditure; iron and steel investment excluded throughout to avoid a discontinuity from nationalisation in 1967.

[b] At 1970 prices, seasonally adjusted.

The 1968 cuts are significant in two ways: first, they marked the end of British aspirations to be a world power, with accelerated withdrawal from east of Suez; secondly, superimposed as they were on previous reductions, they helped to bring about a sharp check in the rising trend of public authorities' expenditure on goods and services (current and capital) (chart 2.1). The first quarter of 1968 was a peak in the trend of this expenditure; from the beginning of 1964 to the beginning of 1968 it had risen at 4½ per cent a year in real terms. From the beginning of 1968 the trend changed sharply; public expenditure on this definition was falling through the rest of 1968 and again in 1969. Many public expenditure cuts in the postwar period may be open to question, but there is no mistaking the genuine change in trend after the beginning of 1968.

In early March sterling came under pressure again in consequence of the rush into gold. At that time private buyers could purchase gold from the 'gold pool' at $35 an ounce – the price collectively maintained by the gold pool countries.[1] Speculation increased when it became known that the chairman of the Federal Reserve Board was attending the meeting of the central bankers in Basle on 10 March, and statements both from Basle and the Bank of England that the gold price would continue to be held down failed to stop the movement. The drain from official reserves became formidable; it was decided to close the gold pool and create a two-tier market. The foreign exchange markets were closed on 15 March, a step which in Britain required a meeting of the Privy Council. The episode appeared at the time much more important than it does in retrospect; some of the comment even suggested that it was a major world monetary crisis. The whole incident was inflated by the resignation of George Brown from the government on the grounds that he had not been consulted.

The 1968 budget was perhaps the most formidable deflationary budget since the war; the full-year effect of the tax increases was estimated at £923 million. There was an immediate increase in a wide range of indirect taxes; selective employment tax was to be raised in September, by which time the delayed response in exports and import substitution to devaluation should have become more powerful; the standard rate of income tax was unchanged, but there was a levy on investment income. The Chancellor left himself with the possibility of using hire purchase restrictions later in the year. The tax increases, it was estimated, would reduce consumers' expenditure by about 2 per cent; the combined effect of the expenditure reductions and the tax increases was intended to keep the 'borrowing requirement' well below the upper limit of £1000 million mentioned in the Letter of Intent. For the first time the budget was accompanied by a quantified economic forecast.

Two further moves were made about this time. A new phase of incomes policy was announced: it provided for a nil norm;[2] a maximum increase of 3½ per cent was allowed in exceptional circumstances, with additional exceptions for productivity bargaining, and the government's power to postpone settlements was extended to twelve months. By this time incomes policy was meeting with much stronger trade union opposition; in the autumn both the TUC annual Congress and the Labour Party conference rejected incomes policy legislation by overwhelming majorities.

Also in the spring of 1968 consultations were begun to protect

---

[1] At that time: Belgium, Italy, the Netherlands, Switzerland, the United Kingdom, the United States and West Germany. France had left the pool at the end of 1967.

[2] That is, the normal increase in wage rates should be nil.

sterling if sterling area countries, after devaluation, wished to diversify their reserves and reduce their sterling balances. These consultations resulted in September in the Basle Group Arrangement, under which a dozen other central banks offered credits to offset any reductions in sterling holdings by sterling area countries and the British government gave dollar-value guarantees on the bulk of the holdings. This effectively removed one threat to sterling.

Movements in the balance of payments

Improvement in the balance of payments was slow. It soon became clear that the target set in the Letter of Intent – a surplus in the second half of the year – would not be met; in successive forecasts, the estimated point at which the balance of payments would cross into surplus was shifted further and further into the future (table 2.4). The precise quantifications of the official forecast which accompanied the budget make it possible to compare the government's expectations with what actually happened (table 2.5). The volume of exports responded to devaluation as vigorously as expected; imports did not – partly, but only partly, because consumers' expenditure was maintained despite an expected fall.

Throughout 1968 the National Institute was arguing the case for import controls. The government tried tightening monetary policy in May: a ceiling was fixed on bank advances implying they should be held at roughly their existing level and the banks were asked 'especially to intensify restrictions on the granting of credit associated with imports of manufactured goods for home consumption or imports for stock accumulation'. The next moves were not made till November, when the balance of payments prospect looked much worse again and hire purchase restrictions were tightened. Then speculation in favour of the Deutschemark brought about the last of the series of speculative attacks on sterling which dominated economic policy under the Labour government.

A conference was called in Bonn, but the German government was not prepared to revalue. It introduced an export tax and an import subsidy equivalent to a 3 per cent 'back door' revaluation, and took steps to discourage the inflow of hot money. The Chancellor came back to announce a further deflationary package: the full use of the regulator, a further tightening of control on bank lending, with a 2 per cent reduction in non-exempt advances to be brought about by March, and an import deposit scheme which required importers to deposit 50 per cent of the value of goods for six months. There was, however, no immediate effect on confidence; at the beginning of December there were wide-spread rumours that the government was breaking up, with

Table 2.4. *Successive forecasts and estimates of the current balance of payments, 1967–70*

£ million

	1967		1968		1969		1970	
	1st half	2nd half	1st half	2nd half	1st half	2nd half	1st half	2nd half
By National Institute in:								
November 1967	−85	−265	−250	−125	..	..	..	..
February 1968	−108	−392	−75	+75	+200	..	..	..
May 1968	−99	−415	−335	−40	+175	..	..	..
August 1968	−514		−310	−140	+90	+260	..	..
November 1968	−404		−337	−169	−79	+121	..	..
February 1969[a]	n.a.		−430		+39	+89	+85	..
May 1969[a]	n.a.		−429		−96	+49	+125	+205
August 1969[a]	n.a.		−429		−14	+117	+91	+264
November 1969[b]	n.a.		−265		+93	+282	+327	+523
Latest official estimate (October 1976)	−298		−272		+150	+310	+416	+317

SOURCES: *National Institute Economic Review* (various issues); CSO, *Economic Trends, Annual Supplement 1976*, p. 98.

[a] Published forecasts excluded the cost of United States military aircraft and missiles; estimates for these are added to the above figures.

[b] The first figures which were corrected for the under-recording of exports disclosed in June 1969.

Table 2.5. *Some indicators for 1968: Treasury forecasts and actual out-turns*

Indices, 1967 (2nd half) = 100[a]

	1st half, 1968		2nd half, 1968	
	Forecast[b]	Actual[c]	Forecast[b]	Actual[c]
Consumers' expenditure	99·6	101·4	98·1	101·0
Public authorities' current spending	101·7	100·9	103·0	99·5
Gross fixed investment	102·7	103·5	105·7	104·6
Exports[d]	112·7	112·8	113·1	118·2
Imports[d]	102·3	105·6	100·6	106·4
GDP[e]	102·0	103·0	103·6	104·9

SOURCES: Forecasts from Treasury, *Financial Statement, 1968–69*, London, HMSO, 1968, table 13; actuals from CSO, *Economic Trends, Annual Supplement 1976*, p. 12.

[a] Seasonally adjusted.
[b] Based on 1958 prices.
[c] Based on 1970 prices.
[d] Of goods and services.
[e] Average of income, expenditure and output estimates.

resignations from the Prime Minister or the Chancellor. However, the November trade figures, announced on 12 December, chanced to be very good, and before the end of the year the speculative attack had spent itself.

The turning-point

On the figures we have now there is a clear turning-point in the balance of payments at the end of 1968:[1] in the first quarter of 1969 the current balance moved into surplus and in the second quarter this surplus – at an annual rate of nearly £400 million – was substantial. However, at the time things seemed to be getting worse rather than better. The trade figures, which had improved considerably in the three months from November 1968 to January 1969, got worse again after that; the trade figures for the three months February–April 1969, available in May, showed a deficit running a good deal higher than in the second half of 1968. Of all the balance of payments forecasts the National Institute made in the period after devaluation that of May 1969 was the most pessimistic.[2] However, there were no further speculative attacks on sterling in the first quarter; it was supported by some inflow of short-term money earning relatively high interest rates (Bank Rate was raised at the end of February) and a number of sterling area countries added to their reserves.

The budget introduced on 15 April was certainly not a confident statement of success. The Chancellor stated his objective in rather negative terms: 'what I must ensure is that there is certainly room for movement in the right direction, and that even a deviation in the wrong direction would not leave us in an intolerable balance of payments situation'; he acknowledged the possibility that he might have been on the wrong tack: 'It is, of course, the case that after a year of progress, real but disappointingly slow, no one in my position could dismiss without thought the views of those who urge some entirely different strategy.' The additional deflation in the budget was not substantial; rates of corporation tax and selective employment tax and a range of indirect taxes were increased, but this was estimated to have a fairly slow effect, perhaps reducing the growth rate of output by about $\frac{1}{4}$ per cent both in 1969 and again in 1970.[3] Taking public revenue and expenditure together, 1969/70 was a year in which the public sector moved into significant surplus on current and capital account combined (see page 203). Nonetheless, the economic forecast which accom-

---

[1] CSO, *Economic Trends, Annual Supplement 1976*, London, HMSO, 1976.

[2] This was before the announcement (in June 1969) of the discovery of under-recorded exports (see page 51).

[3] The effect was on a forecast which had, of course, already taken the public expenditure cuts into account.

panied the budget indicated the official view that output would be rising by just on 3 per cent between the first halves of 1969 and 1970. The National Institute had a lower forecast, of 2 per cent – which was, in fact, the actual outcome on the latest available figures (May 1977).

During the spring the government was concerned with refinancing the $1 billion remaining of the $1·4 billion IMF drawing made in December 1965, which was due for repayment in 1968–70. The conditions for this refinancing were set out in the Letter of Intent published on 23 June. This specified a target for 1969/70 of a £300 million current and long-term capital surplus on the balance of payments, a 1 per cent maximum increase in public expenditure in real terms over the 1968/9 planned level and a £400 million limit to domestic credit expansion (DCE).

However, the main preoccupation of policy-makers at this time was with the Industrial Relations Bill. The government's prices and incomes policies were clearly beginning to break down and the idea was spreading that, if some way could be found of dealing with unofficial strikes, this would be a major advance towards reducing the pressure behind wage demands. Following the publication of the Donovan Report,[1] Barbara Castle, Secretary of State at the re-christened Department of Employment and Productivity, produced a set of proposals published on 17 January.[2] The main contentious proposals were to give the Secretary of State discretionary powers:

(a) to require a ballot before an official strike which 'would involve a serious threat to the economy or public interest';

(b) in unconstitutional strikes or strikes where adequate joint discussions had not taken place, to order 'a conciliation pause' with a return to work for a period of 28 days.

There would be financial penalties for failure to comply.

There was strong opposition in the trade union movement and also in the Labour movement generally; when the proposals were debated in the House of Commons on 3 March some 57 Labour members voted against the government and an estimated 30 more abstained. Nonetheless the government decided to legislate immediately and announced at the same time that the statutory prices and incomes policy would be phased out. In the Industrial Relations Bill which followed the proposed ballot before an official strike was dropped.

Bargaining between the government and TUC over this Bill continued until early June. The TUC eventually produced alternative

[1] Royal Commission on Trade Unions and Employers' Associations, 1965–1968, *Report* [Donovan Report], Cmnd 3623, London, HMSO, 1968.

[2] Department of Employment and Productivity, *In Place of Strife: a policy for industrial relations*, Cmnd 3888, London, HMSO, 1969.

suggestions: on 12 May the General Council approved a 'programme for action', which gave them increased scope for intervention in unconstitutional strikes and inter-union disputes; this was endorsed by an overwhelming majority at a special Congress held on 5 June. Eventually the government, realising that there was a serious risk that it would be unable to get the Industrial Relations Bill through the House of Commons, negotiated a compromise, by which the TUC agreed to a 'solemn and binding undertaking' about the manner in which the programme for action was to be implemented. This was signed on 18 June.

The fact that a substantial balance of payments recovery was under way at last became apparent in June 1969. The trade deficit in May narrowed very considerably; then it was discovered that exports had been under-recorded for some time – the under-recording having built up to an annual rate of £140–£150 million by 1969; thirdly, there was a revised estimate of the rate at which net invisible earnings were running. The figure which perhaps finally persuaded the doubters that the position had been transformed was a visible trade surplus for August of £40 million; the declared balance of payments target figure, of a £300 million current and long-term surplus for 1969/70, was reached in the first half of that year.

The Labour government's final period

The government had thus at last achieved what it had set out to do and produced a substantial balance of payments surplus; it was in no hurry to change policies. The import deposit scheme was renewed in October, at the slightly reduced rate of 40 instead of 50 per cent; the first significant relaxation came with the abolition of the restricted travel allowance from the beginning of January 1970.

Given the slow rise in output, the slight upward movement in unemployment and the impending general election, the government might have been expected to reflate the economy significantly. One reason for caution, however, was that, with the effective ending of incomes policy, both wage rates and earnings were beginning to rise much faster. Possibly the official forecasts assumed that this would have some real reflationary effect; certainly they predicted a considerable rise in consumers' expenditure. Secondly, there were those who still held the view that if unemployment were allowed to fall significantly the increase in wage rates would accelerate even more. The budget made some income tax and surtax concessions, mainly on allowances, estimated at around £200 million for a full year, with an estimated net effect of increasing output by about $\frac{1}{2}$ per cent. The official post-budget forecast was again over-optimistic – a rise in output of $3\frac{1}{2}$ per cent between the first halves of 1970 and 1971 – in the event the rise was only a little over 1 per cent.

At the change of government, therefore, the economy was running with a considerable balance of payments surplus; however, output was increasing only very slowly and unemployment was gradually rising.

THE CONSERVATIVE PERIOD FROM MID-1970 TO SPRING 1972

Introduction

In 1964 the Labour government had come to power determined to change the course of the British economy and alter the pattern of economic policy by getting away from 'stop–go' towards planning for the medium term; the attempt failed. In 1970 the Conservative government came to power with equally high ambitions; as Edward Heath said in October 1970: 'We were returned to office to change the course of history of this nation – nothing less.'[1] Their policy had a rather different motif – to transform the economy by reducing the extent of government intervention, stimulating self-reliance and improving the efficiency of the government machine. This attempt must also be judged a failure.

During its period in opposition the Conservative Party had set up a number of policy study groups. (Such groups, of course, inevitably look for distinctive policies, sharply different from those of the Party in power.) A number of industrialists took part in these groups; many of these were present at one of the culminating conferences at Sundridge Park in September 1969; the final, better known, conference was at Selsdon Park in January 1970. At these conferences prospective Ministers were told how important it was to have reasonably detailed programmes, so that it would be easier to overcome bureaucratic opposition. This, again, is a common assumption of any opposition Party – that, in bringing about the changes it wants, it will have great difficulty in moving the bureaucratic establishment.

The philosophy put forward at these conferences, and as expounded to the Party conference in 1970, was not mainly concerned with techniques of economic management in the traditional sense. The emphasis was first on government withdrawal and, secondly, on improving the government's cost-effectiveness: 'less government, but of a better quality'.

Government was to withdraw 'from all those activities no longer necessary either because of the passage of time or because they are better done outside government, or because they should rightly be

[1] National Union of Conservative and Unionist Associations, *Verbatim Report: 88th Conservative Conference, Blackpool, 1970*, London, 1970, p. 129.

carried on, if wanted at all, by individual or by voluntary effort'. Individual citizens were to be made more self-reliant and encouraged 'to stand on their own feet, to accept responsibility for themselves and their families'.[1] In industrial relations, if firms gave way to irresponsible wage demands the government would not step in to rescue them from the consequences of their own actions. The functions of government and industry were different; the role of government was to create a framework, within which the free enterprise system should operate. There was not to be a partnership in the sense of mutual absorption or penetration. To make the government more efficient, new techniques would be used to bring about a systematic and continuous process of questioning and analysis of the objectives of the government's activity; new recruits from the business world would bring about a change of direction and attitude throughout Whitehall. The exposition of this new philosophy certainly persuaded commentators at the time that there was going to be a radical new approach to the running of the economy; there were frequent references to the end of consensus politics. The emphasis in this new approach was not so much in praise of the market economy, but in dispraise of government intervention. Further, it was the character-building virtues of government withdrawal which were emphasised, rather than the economic consequences.

The other main commitments of the Conservative Party were to bring the trade unions within the framework of the law and to renew the attempt to join the EEC. The process of negotiation with the EEC is not described in this chapter. The negotiations themselves are for the political rather than the economic history of the time and the actual accession on 1 January 1973 did not have significant economic consequences in the period covered by this book.

The first year

The economy which the new government inherited was in substantial current balance of payments surplus. However, the trade gap had widened between the first and second quarters of the year, so that the National Institute's forecast of the balance on current account in 1970 fell from £675 million in May to £475 million in August,[2] and, given the required debt repayments, current surpluses of this order were no more than adequate. Further, the new government had, on the one hand, an official forecast made at the time of the budget that national output would be rising in line with productive potential and, on the other hand, a slow but steady rise in unemployment from the middle of

---

[1] Ibid. pp. 131–2.

[2] Before these estimates are compared with actual figures they should be adjusted for the further under-recording of exports announced in November 1970.

1969. They were also in the middle of a wages explosion: basic hourly wage rates, which had risen only $5\frac{1}{2}$ per cent between the fourth quarters of 1968 and 1969, were rising at 12–13 per cent during 1970; the price rise was also accelerating, though not so sharply.

Before the election future Conservative Ministers had clearly considered the possibility of breaking into the wage–price spiral by reducing indirect taxes, and possibly also by damping down nationalised industries' price increases, so reflating the economy and reducing prices at one and the same time. Once in office they decided against this; the reasons can be surmised. First, it was not as clear then as it is now that rapid increases in money wages have very little, if any, real reflationary effect. Secondly, and more generally, it seemed perverse to reflate at a time of rapid inflation. Although by 1974 the Treasury had come round to the view that the rise in wage rates was insensitive to the movement of unemployment within a fairly wide band, this was probably not their view in 1970. Further, there were still some anxieties about the balance of payments because the trade balance had worsened so much between the first and second quarters.

There was, in consequence, no significant reflationary action in the second half of 1970; indeed, at the end of July the Bank of England asked the clearing banks to slow down the growth of advances. The budget introduced on 27 October was in no sense primarily concerned with demand management; the Chancellor indicated that it was intended to be 'broadly neutral' in its effect upon demand in 1971/2, and to demonstrate this he quoted the estimated £329 million cut from public spending as against the £315 million cost to the revenue of the cut in income tax. The National Institute suggested that in fact there would be a small reflationary effect, with an increase in 1971/2 of the order of £120 million in gross domestic product (GDP) at market prices.

The main concern of this budget was putting into practical effect some of the principles of 'less government, but of a better quality' and of selective rather than general assistance. A long list of changes can be classified under these headings: the abolition of investment grants and their replacement by tax allowances; the announcement that the regional employment premium would be phased out; the repeal of the Industrial Expansion Act; the move from deficiency payments to British farmers to levies on imported food; the shift of emphasis in financial support for local authority housing from subsidising rents to subsidising individuals; the reduction of taxpayers' support for the Consumer Council and the British Productivity Council; the elimination of subsidies for London commuter trains; the introduction of admission charges for museums; increases in charges for school meals and dental treatment; the ending of cheap welfare milk and free school milk for the over-sevens. At the same time the income limit for free school meals and welfare milk for younger children was raised and a new scheme, the family income supplement, was introduced to benefit the poorest families. The intended net effect on the long-term trend in public expenditure between 1971/2 and 1974/5 was to reduce the annual rate of increase from 3·5 to 2·8 per cent. (This was the first of a long series of changes in public expenditure forward plans which are discussed on pages 117 *et seq.*) In the debate on 4 November 1970 the Secretary of State for Trade and Industry, John Davies, set out the principles according to which the government would be reducing the scale of its intervention in industry: '...the vast majority lives and thrives in a bracing climate and not in a soft, sodden morass of subsidized incompetence...We believe that the essential need of the country is to gear its policies to the great majority of people, who are not lame ducks, or do not need a helping hand...'.

The Chancellor had indicated when introducing the budget that in his view output over the next six months would be growing broadly in line with productive potential. However, the tone of his assessment suggested that he preferred to err on the side of caution: 'If one takes into account the continuation of the rapid rise in costs and prices which we have experienced over the past year or so, it follows that it would be wrong to take any steps likely to increase further the pressure of demand.' The National Institute's assessment at the time was that the trend of growth in real output would be nearer 2 per cent than 3 per cent, so that unemployment would continue its gradual upward movement. The upward movement did indeed continue, but soon ceased to be gradual (page 59).

Conservative policies towards inflation

During the winter of 1970/1 the pattern began to appear of the Conservative government's policies in the fields of inflation, industrial intervention and the trade unions.

In combating inflation the government was concerned to disengage itself from intervention in wage settlements. In November 1970 it announced that the NBPI would be wound up; it was left to employers ro resist excessive wage demands, given the risk that they might bankrupt themselves if they failed to do so. Indeed, as part of the process of disengagement, the conciliation work of the Department of Employment was reduced.

The problem for this policy lay in the public sector. The principle that responsibility for negotiating pay settlements must rest on employers applied in theory to the nationalised industries and the public services just as much as to private industry. In fact the government could hardly remain indifferent to settlements in the public sector and it gradually became more and more involved in them. It acted indirectly on the nationalised industries' finances by refusing to grant in full the price increases they requested (this happened with the Coal Board in the autumn of 1970 and with the Central Electricity Generating Board in the spring of 1971; it would have happened with the Post Office's increase in postal charges if the new stamps had not already been printed). The government also became increasingly identified with a view about the right kind of figure to be granted in specific cases, so that wage claims in the public sector came to be treated more and more as confrontations with the government.

In public sector negotiations in the winter of 1970/1, the government could at least claim it had not given way. The first episode – the 'dustmen's strike' – was a claim on behalf of 770,000 manual workers employed by local authorities. Here, the Department of Employment said that its conciliation services would only be available on the understanding that the settlement did not exceed 14 per cent and strike action began in September. After about four weeks both sides agreed to submit the case to a Committee of Inquiry under Sir Jack Scamp, which conceded most of the claim. At the end of November the miners voted in favour of accepting a 12 per cent increase offered to them by the National Coal Board. An increase of about the same size was offered to the electricity supply workers at the beginning of December, but they rejected it and began a work-to-rule and overtime ban. This caused considerable public irritation and in mid-December the union said they would call off their industrial action if the government would agree to a Court of Inquiry. The government was only prepared to accept this if the terms of reference included consideration of 'the public and national interest'; the unions were reluctant to agree, but eventually did so. However, the Court of Inquiry, under Lord Wilberforce, recommended an increase well above the Electricity Council's final offer; precise quantification is difficult, because the award included a lead-in payment starting at £1 a week to workers who accepted in principle an incentive bonus scheme.[1] Finally, the Post Office workers went on strike at the end of January, rejecting an 8 per cent offer. This strike was not successful; in the end the union agreed to the setting up of a Committee of Inquiry, which, on this occasion, added only

[1] Department of Employment, *Report of a Court of Inquiry into the Electricity Supply Industry*, Cmnd 4594, London, HMSO, 1971. The Department of Employment's *New Earnings Survey* (annual) shows that the average weekly earnings of manual workers in the electricity supply industry rose 14 per cent between April 1970 and April 1971, and 18 per cent between April 1971 and April 1972.

about 1 per cent to the 8 per cent offer. Thus, in this first round of settlements in the public sector, the government could generally be said to be holding its own.

Industrial intervention

The Conservative government's new policy on industrial intervention was also tested in the winter of 1970/1. In November the government refused to grant a bridging loan to the Mersey Docks and Harbours Board, intending it as a first lesson that they would not continue to rescue companies from the consequences of their own mistakes. Debenture holders of the Board's undertakings had always assumed that they had in effect a government guarantee for the security of their capital; when they discovered they had not this first move to industrial disengagement was not popular in the City. The second incident was on a much larger scale. The successive moves in the Rolls-Royce affair are set out on pages 454–6. In February 1971 Rolls-Royce was allowed to go bankrupt, but in spite of this rather extreme measure the government agreed to continue with the production of the RB 211 engine for Lockheed on terms which almost certainly implied a continuing Exchequer subsidy. The third problem for the government in this field came in June 1971, when further cash was refused to Upper Clyde Shipbuilders; this led to a sit-in and to the eventual solution described on page 467.

The Conservative election manifesto had also indicated there would be significant 'hiving-off' of some of the peripheral activities of the nationalised industries. The moves made in the government's first year were not very far-reaching: in August 1970, as part of the process of establishing the second-force private enterprise airline which came to be known as British Caledonian, this airline was given British Overseas Airways' West African routes; then in January 1971 it was announced that Thomas Cook would be sold off, as also would be the state-owned public houses and bars in Carlisle, Gretna and Cromarty.

Industrial relations

The government in its first year was also getting through its Industrial Relations Bill, designed to bring the trade unions 'within the framework of the law' (page 580). The clauses which led to a struggle with the trade union movement over the whole period of this government were mainly those providing for the registration of unions, establishing the new concept of unfair industrial practices, with compensation for those injured by them, creating the National Industrial Relations Court (NIRC) and extending the existing Industrial Tribunals, and giving power to the government to apply to the NIRC for a 'cooling-off' period lasting up to 60 days, or to call for a ballot where industrial action would cause or continue a national emergency.

The TUC denounced the Bill and the General Council decided to embark on a course of outright opposition to it. In March 1971 a special Congress met at Croydon to decide the line the trade union movement should take. The General Council recommended that affiliated unions should be urged not to register – or if they did to inform the TUC of their reasons for doing so – and unions should not sign any legally binding contracts; trade unionists should not serve on the NIRC or the Commission on Industrial Relations (CIR) and should withdraw from the Industrial Tribunals. There were one-day protest strikes on 1 and 18 March, mainly in the engineering industry; it was estimated that $1\frac{1}{2}$ million workers were involved in the first stoppage and 2 million in the second.

The 1971 budget

The section in the Financial Statement for 1971/2 giving the economic background to the budget begins: 'During 1970 there was a rapid rate of cost and price inflation against the background of slowly rising output and a high and increasing level of unemployment.'[1] This summarises the Chancellor's dilemma. The government's anti-inflationary policy, of leaning on the public sector, had had some success, but there were as yet few signs that this success was being imitated in the private sector. Obviously the policy would only succeed if this occurred, for if the rise in earnings in the public sector was kept below that of the private sector for any length of time trouble would clearly build up. There was no certainty, therefore, that the rate of cost and price inflation was being brought down.

Unemployment had risen, but up to the spring of 1971 the rise had been fairly slow – in March 1971 the number wholly unemployed was 90,000 higher than a year earlier. In the National Institute's assessment of the situation before the budget, there seemed no prospect of any substantial reflationary force; it was assumed that the effect of devaluation on the volume of exports had come through and neither public nor private investment seemed likely to rise much. The Institute argued for a stimulus of the order of £500 million as a first step; in a judgement repeated a number of times during this period, it concluded that the effect of a reflation of this order on the trend of costs and prices would be roughly neutral on balance.

The Chancellor did in fact further reduce taxes so as to reduce expected revenue in 1971/2 by rather over £500 million. However, only about £160 million of this – arising from the increase in child

[1] Treasury, *Financial Statement and Budget Report, 1971–72*, London, HMSO, 1971, p. 5.

allowances – was quick-acting; three-fifths came from halving selective employment tax and from a further reduction in corporation tax, neither of which was likely to do much to stimulate effective demand immediately. The Chancellor considered that his measures would bring the economy back to a 3 per cent growth path by early 1972, but this proved, once again, over-optimistic; in any case something more would have been needed to check the rise in unemployment. During 1971 unemployment was reacting to the previous two years of slow growth – from the end of 1968 to the end of 1970 national output had been rising at around 2 per cent a year, which was below the country's productive potential.

The 1971 budget was again not simply an exercise in demand management. The main feature was the announcement of a two-year programme of fundamental reforms in the fiscal system, which included the replacement of purchase tax and what was left of selective employment tax by VAT. In addition, the Chancellor proposed to recast personal taxation, amalgamating income and surtax and replacing the earned income allowance by an investment income surcharge; corporation tax was to be reformed to eliminate disincentives to distribute. There were Green Papers on the proposals[1] and, in the case of corporation tax, a Select Committee of the House of Commons to consider alternative methods.

During the rest of 1971 it was the rise in unemployment which increasingly dominated economic policy. During 1970 unemployment had been increasing at 4000–5000 a month; from the beginning of 1971 this accelerated to around 20,000 a month. An objective of the budget had been to stabilise the level of unemployment; in his speech on 30 March the Chancellor said, 'I cannot make any promise that unemployment will fall until we get a substantial reduction in the level of pay settlements...I could have brought about a reduction in the level of unemployment by giving a still larger boost to consumer demand than I have. But everything I have said supports the view that it would have been irresponsible to do so.' In June he still held the view that the budget measures would slow down and eventually stop the increase in unemployment, but he also referred to the possibility that after the Treasury's regular summer review of the economy there might be a change. The main change in July appears to have been that the Treasury revised past figures rather than the forecast for the future; though they were firmly persuaded that an expansion was under way, they concluded that it was starting from a lower base than they had thought.

[1] Treasury, *Reform of Corporation Tax*, Cmnd 4630, and *Reform of Personal Direct Taxation*, Cmnd 4653, London, HMSO, 1971.

The package of measures introduced in the summer contained a £100 million public works programme for the development areas. In June there had already been a large increase (£46 million for two years) in the allocation for house improvement grants. Otherwise the measures were designed to have a relatively quick effect, and this was clearly right; also, perhaps more important, they formed part of an informal 'social contract' with the Confederation of British Industries (CBI), by which an attempt was made to break into the wage–price spiral from the prices side.

Hire purchase controls were abolished entirely, in line with the recommendations of the Crowther Report;[1] this was certainly a quick-acting measure. The improved capital allowances for industry also had a time-limit – the first-year tax allowance was increased from 60 to 80 per cent for expenditure incurred up to end-July 1973. Purchase tax was cut, clearly in line with the CBI price initiative; for, on the assumption – and indeed the condition – that the government would take action to reflate the economy, the CBI had asked its members to sign an undertaking if possible to avoid raising prices of products or services supplied in the United Kingdom, and to limit any unavoidable increases to a 5 per cent maximum within the twelve-month period ending 31 July 1972. By early September, 176 out of 201 leading companies in the United Kingdom had signed this undertaking. This had radical consequences for government policy towards the nationalised industries, because the CBI said that, if price restraint was to be implemented by the private sector, nationalised industries must be expected to do the same, and the government indicated to the nationalised industries that they should follow suit. This inevitably meant the abandonment of the financial targets which had been introduced in 1961 (page 492), and from the beginning of 1972 subsidies to the nationalised industries, which had been held back between 1968 and 1971, began to rise sharply again (page 511).

In 1971 also the structure of monetary policy was reformed: the Bank of England published 'Competition and credit control';[2] Bank Rate was lowered twice during the year, by 1 per cent in April and a further 1 per cent in September; then on 10 September the new regime for the control of banks and finance houses was announced. From 16 September all 'ceiling' limits on lending were removed and all institutions were required to observe a fixed minimum reserve ratio (page 244); the main consequence was a very sharp rise in bank advances to the private sector in general and to the personal sector in particular.

[1] Department of Trade and Industry, *Consumer Credit. Report of the Committee* [Crowther Report], Cmnd 4596, London, HMSO, 1971.
[2] *Bank of England Quarterly Bulletin*, vol. 11, June 1971.

This was not by any means the end of the sequence of reflationary measures. In November the Chancellor announced an acceleration of government expenditure amounting to £185 million over the next two years; in December he announced the repayment of all outstanding postwar credits (forced wartime savings), amounting to some £130 million. By the end of the year, therefore, the primary objective of government policy had become the checking of the rise in unemployment.

This period of anti-inflationary policy – from mid-1970 to end-1971 – can hardly be counted a success. It is true that the wage awards given in the public sector in the second half of 1971 were substantially lower than those given to the same groups a year earlier. However, there seems to have been no parallel moderation in the private sector which-ever index is used – basic wage rates, average hourly earnings excluding overtime, or wages and salaries per unit of output.[1]

The rise in retail prices did slow down after the middle of 1971; this was helped by reductions in purchase tax and selective employment tax, and by the CBI's price initiative, particularly in its consequences for prices in nationalised industries.

Finally, the policy of 'leaning on the public sector' foundered in a confrontation with the National Union of Mineworkers in the winter of 1971/2.

In September 1971 the National Coal Board offered increases which amounted to an average pay rise of 7 per cent. The president of the National Union of Mineworkers said the offer 'does not even provide us with a negotiating position', and the union imposed an overtime ban from 1 November, which effectively reduced output during December by 15–20 per cent; a ballot was held, which showed that 59 per cent of those who voted were in favour of strike action. The Board raised its offer to an average increase of 8 per cent, but this was refused and the first national coal strike since 1926 began on 9 January. The miners extending picketing from the pits to provide 24-hour cover at coal depots, open coal sites, ports and power stations. On 9 February the Board offered increases of £3 per week for surface workers and £3.50 for underground workers; this too was rejected. The government declared a state of emergency and power cuts were instituted; a Court of Inquiry was set up under Lord Wilberforce. On 14 February fuel rationing was tightened, most of British industry went on a three-day working week and the number of workers laid off amounted to $1\frac{1}{2}$ million. The Court of Inquiry's Report, issued on 18 February, recom-

[1] Basic weekly wage rates rose 13 per cent, and wages and salaries per unit of output 10 per cent, between the fourth quarters of 1969 and 1970. Between the fourth quarters of 1970 and 1971 the comparable figures were 12·3 per cent and 8·8 per cent respectively. Average hourly earnings excluding overtime were 16 per cent higher than a year earlier in October 1970 and 14 per cent higher in October 1971.

mended £5 per week for surface workers and £6 a week for under-ground workers.[1] Then the union, in negotiations with the Prime Minister, won additional concessions in the attendance bonus and an extra five days' holiday a year, all of which cost another £8 million. A ballot showed a 96·5 per cent majority in favour of acceptance and on 25 February the seven-week strike was called off. The settlement raised average earnings in the mining and quarrying sector by some 17–20 per cent.

SPRING 1972 TO SPRING 1974

Introduction

At the beginning of 1972 the government's anti-inflationary strategy was in disarray. First of all, it had been intended simply to hold the level of unemployment at around half a million until the rise in wage rates moderated; it was no part of the strategy that the figure should rise to nearly a million. The government could hardly avoid the conclusion that unemployment had done very little to moderate the rise in basic wage rates. A second strand of anti-inflationary policy – that each suc-cessive settlement in the public sector should be lower than the previous one – had been broken by the miners' strike. Finally, the CBI initiative on price restraint showed few signs of encouraging similar restraint from the unions and, by forcing the nationalised industries to make losses, it had the incidental result of making it additionally obvious that unions in the public sector were negotiating with the government rather than with the boards of the industries.

Looking back now, the sequence of events gives the impression that during the first half of 1972 there was a major decision to change direc-tion. Of course that was not in fact how things happened: the new policies emerged from the old gradually, so that it is hard to say for any particular policy when the transition from the old to the new approach was made. However, there is no doubt that, by the end of its period of office, the Conservative government's stance on economic policy was considerably changed from what it had been in 1970.

The new approach can be summed up as follows. Anti-inflationary policy changed, first, to a process of negotiation with the TUC and the CBI and, after about six months when that attempt was unsuccessful, to statutory intervention. Indeed in the last two years of the Conservative government the dominant economic objective was to make the new anti-inflationary policy effective. Then the high level of unemployment forced the government to take further substantial reflationary measures; this became a decision to aim for a higher rate of economic growth and

---

[1] Department of Employment, *Report of a Court of Inquiry into a Dispute between the National Coal Board and the National Union of Mineworkers*, Cmnd 4903, London, HMSO, 1972.

was accompanied by a declaration that the government would let the exchange rate go if necessary. Thirdly, the government's industrial policy changed – partly because with unemployment so high it was not easy to let large firms go bankrupt in high-unemployment areas, and partly because the government was dissatisfied with industry's investment performance and was therefore less willing than in 1970 to leave the amount of private manufacturing investment to be decided by the firms concerned.

The reflationary budget

Prominent in the background to the budget of 1972 was unemployment, which was, on the latest figures available to the Chancellor (seasonally adjusted) still rising – though a good deal more slowly than during 1971. The last count had been taken on 14 February just before the restrictions on power supplies, so that the figure was probably not much inflated by the effects of the coal strike.[1] The Chancellor would have had some justification for doubting forecasts that, on unchanged policies, it would soon begin to fall, for it had already risen much further than most forecasters had expected. On the other hand, the estimates which he had available suggested that there had already been quite a sharp recovery in national output in the second half of 1971, and there were forecasts on unchanged policies of a continuing rise by about $3\frac{1}{2}$ per cent a year between the second half of 1971 and the first half of 1973.[2] However, the Chancellor had to reckon with the possibility that a rise in output of this order would do no more than keep the level of unemployment roughly where it was at the beginning of the year. The estimate of national productive potential was probably quite high at the time, for productivity had, in an unprecedented way, improved in both 1970 and 1971. In previous periods of recession productivity had stayed low, but in 1971 it had risen by over 3 per cent, so that it seemed quite plausible that the rise during 1972 could be if anything higher.

The government was clearly not prepared to risk leaving unemployment near the million mark, and the explicit aim of the 1972 budget introduced on 21 March was to add 2 per cent to output in the first half of 1973. Quite deliberately, the Chancellor framed this policy in terms of a 5 per cent growth rate: 'The measures I shall put to the House are intended to ensure a growth of output at an annual rate of 5 per cent between the second half of last year and the first half of next...If my

---

[1] It showed unemployment at 3·8 per cent (Great Britain, excluding school-leavers and adult students).

[2] This figure was about the same in the Treasury 'unchanged policies' forecast and in the *National Institute Economic Review* for February 1972.

present expectations are correct, output will have risen by 10 per cent over the two-year period from the first half of 1971 to the first half of 1973.'[1] The Chancellor emphasised 5 per cent because he was concerned to get what stimulus to investment he could from the 'announcement effect' of a rapid rate of growth. For much the same reason, the budget speech contains the famous sentence which indicated that the exchange rate would be sacrificed if necessary: 'Moreover I am sure that all hon. members in this House agree that the lesson of the international balance of payments upsets of the last few years is that it is neither necessary nor desirable to distort domestic economies to an unacceptable extent in order to maintain unrealistic exchange rates, whether they are too high or too low.'

The 1972 budget has become a controversial one; the arguments are essentially about the objectives which the government chose – whether or not it was right to aim at accelerating the growth rate of national output to 5 per cent and bringing unemployment back to around half a million by the end of 1973. Given those objectives, a large stimulus in the budget was inevitable and, for achieving those objectives, the size of the stimulus was roughly right. The target of 5 per cent for the annual rate of growth of output for the eighteen-month period up to the middle of 1973 was in fact roughly achieved and by the end of 1973 unemployment had fallen to around half a million.[2]

The government was already committed to holding back the rise in public expenditure, and it is in any case difficult to get any quick effects in stimulating this element of demand, so that inevitably most of the reflation came from tax reductions aimed at raising personal consumption. The main measure was an increase in the income tax allowances for married and single people; also purchase tax was reduced. In addition the budget contained what the Chancellor termed 'the most powerful combination of national and regional investment incentives... since the war', but these, of course, were not expected to have any quick reflationary effect and certainly did not do so. However, the 1972 budget was notable for reasons other than the aggregate size of the tax reductions. Further major measures of tax reform were promised, with one Green Paper on the possible amalgamation of personal tax allowances with certain social security benefits, introducing in effect a negative income tax, and another on the transformation of death duties into an inheritance tax.[3] In addition there were some minor tax changes designed to benefit particularly those with middle-range incomes: loan

[1] On present figures (CSO, *Economic Trends, Annual Supplement 1976*) this is exactly what happened.

[2] Great Britain, seasonally adjusted, excluding school-leavers and adult students.

[3] Treasury, *Proposals for a Tax-Credit System*, Cmnd 5116, and *Taxation of Capital on Death*, Cmnd 4930, London HMSO, 1972.

interest of over £35 a year was to be tax deductible and, as from April 1971, the first £2000 a year of investment income was to be treated as earned income for tax purposes.

Industrial policy

The budget also took further a change in the Conservative government's industrial policy which had already begun. An original principle had been that enterprises should not be rescued unless there was a firm prospect of a viable independent future. Already, under pressure of unemployment, the government had broken with this principle in February 1972 in its rescue of all four Upper Clyde shipyards (page 467). Then in the budget there was a further retreat from general principles: to stimulate investment, free depreciation, which previously had been available in development areas only, was extended to the whole country. Since this meant that there were no longer any special incentives to invest in the development areas, a new system of 'regional development grants' was introduced, which seemed at least a partial reversal of the previous decision to replace investment grants with tax allowances. In addition, an Industrial Development Executive was set up in the Department of Trade and Industry, with wide powers to assist firms throughout the country.

The substantial change in the direction of industrial policy indicated by these moves is also strongly suggested by various ministerial changes at the Department of Trade and Industry about this time. Two junior Ministers who had been clearly identified with the previous industrial policy were moved and not long afterwards the Secretary of State himself, John Davies, left the department, his place being taken by Peter Walker. This shift in policy is discussed more fully on pages 448–9.

Floating the exchange rate

The undertaking given in the budget speech – that a fixed exchange rate would not be allowed to stand in the way of economic expansion – was a promise which soon had to be taken up. However, before the rate was floated in June, there was in fact a move in the opposite direction. Towards the end of April the six members of the EEC took the first step towards a European Monetary Union by agreeing to narrow the range of fluctuations in their exchange rates.[1] On 1 May Britain, as a candi-

[1] Under the Smithsonian agreement of December 1971 rates for most currencies were allowed to fluctuate between margins of $2\frac{1}{4}$ per cent on either side of their parities against the dollar, so that the rate between any two could vary by $4\frac{1}{2}$ per cent from their cross-parity. Under the agreement of 24 April 1972 EEC countries were committed to ensuring that the rates between any two of their currencies would not diverge from their cross-parities by more than $2\frac{1}{4}$ per cent.

date for the EEC, joined what came to be known as the 'snake in the tunnel'.

The United Kingdom balance of payments still appeared reasonably strong; the estimates available in the second quarter of 1972 suggested that there was still a substantial current surplus, although much reduced from the very high figures of 1971.[1] It is perhaps therefore a little surprising that substantial speculation against sterling developed during June. The reasons suggested for this are that the government appeared to be without any effective anti-inflationary policy and that the trade figures in April and May were judged to be bad.[2] The Labour shadow Chancellor, Denis Healey, forecast an early devaluation in a speech in the House of Commons in mid-June. When speculation threatened to force down the rate, under the new arrangements in the European Monetary Union the pound was supported by the central banks of the EEC countries, but Britain was under an obligation to repay these banks on the next settlement day.

Bank Rate was raised by 1 per cent on 22 June, which led a number of commentators to conclude that no action was going to be taken on the exchange rate. However, the next day the exchange rate was floated 'as a temporary measure'. The official line in presenting this change was that it was made necessary by illogical speculation, that there was 'nothing in the objective facts' to suggest that sterling was over-valued and that the United Kingdom still believed that a world system of fixed parities was desirable; by implication, therefore, once sterling had settled the government would be prepared to fix the parity again. Probably at that time the government did not envisage a virtually permanent floating; it may have had in mind previous German examples, in which the exchange rate for the Deutschemark was allowed to float for a few months and was then fixed again.

The move to a floating rate also marked the effective end of the sterling area. Up to June 1972 the only limit on capital flows to the overseas sterling area was the programme of voluntary restraint begun in 1966, and indeed this had been removed in the 1972 budget. After 23 June 1972 portfolio investors in the overseas sterling area had to pay the same premium as in other areas;[3] further, Bank of England approval was needed for official foreign exchange for direct investment in the overseas sterling area. These new rules were also presented at the time as temporary, but have in fact proved permanent.

The immediate effect of floating was a devaluation of the pound by

---

[1] Estimates now available suggest that in the first half of 1972 the current surplus in the balance of payments was running at an annual rate of rather over £500 million.

[2] In fact the current balance of payments surplus, seasonally adjusted, is now shown to have been larger in the second quarter than in the first.

[3] However, they did not have to surrender 25 per cent on liquidation.

roughly 7 per cent (on a weighted basis against other major currencies). This figure held through the summer, but the pound depreciated further in the autumn.

Negotiations with the unions

In the second half of the Conservative government's period of office the most important change was in anti-inflationary policy. From early 1972 onwards this became the central preoccupation of economic policy-makers: they were concerned, first, with devising a voluntary incomes policy and, when that attempt failed, with instituting and administering a statutory one. Just as at other times the balance of payments was wholly preoccupying, so in 1972 and 1973 the attention of the government was heavily concentrated on holding back the rise in money incomes. This section discusses the events leading up to the introduction of a statutory freeze on wages and prices on 6 November 1972.

The collapse of the government's previous anti-inflationary policy has already been described; from the spring of 1972 there was growing pressure by employers for some action to be taken on wages, because the CBI's price restraint code was due to expire in mid-July and the CBI was reluctant to extend it unless there was some move on the wages side. The first meetings after the miners' strike between the government, the CBI and the TUC took place on 9 and 10 March, but further moves were hampered by the operation of the Industrial Relations Act, which had been brought into full force at the end of February. The government twice invoked the Act during negotiations on railwaymen's pay. In April it applied to the NIRC for a cooling-off period, but in the fourteen days granted the negotiations made no progress. Then in May the government applied for and got an NIRC order for a ballot of railwaymen to see whether they supported the industrial action; the result was a six to one majority in favour, and the final settlement essentially conceded the claim. Thus, in this dispute the use of the Industrial Relations Act was a failure, and throughout the summer there were difficulties when private firms used the Act to bring unions to account for the behaviour of their shop stewards. (See pages 586–8 for a full description of these events.) These situations did not improve the atmosphere for discussions between the TUC and the government; indeed, during this period the TUC was probably rather closer to the CBI. On 21 June the TUC and CBI reached an agreement on a new conciliation and arbitration service which was to be independent of the government.

Nevertheless, preliminary soundings were taken during the early summer and in early July more formal approaches began. The TUC General Council met the Prime Minister on 4 July – their main concern being to press him to repeal or suspend the Industrial Relations Act. The Prime Minister indicated he wished to discuss a wider range of subjects; he suggested the TUC and the government should meet to consider, as a matter of urgency, the problems of conciliation, low pay, and a link between collective agreements and the cost of living. Some members of the TUC Economic Committee, which considered the proposals, thought that there should be no talks with the government until the Industrial Relations Act had been suspended. As a compromise, however, they replied that the NEDC was a suitable forum, and pointed out, incidentally, that the idea of threshold agreements had been suggested by them back in 1971, but at that time the government had not been keen.

Three meetings of the NEDC held before the summer recess to discuss the Prime Minister's agenda appear to have been in the nature of preliminary skirmishes, discussing low pay and prices rather than wages. During August and early September evidence accumulated that the price rise was likely, if anything, to accelerate again. In the *National Institute Economic Review* for August a rise in retail prices of 7–8 per cent through 1972 (and perhaps another 9 per cent through 1973) was forecast. A number of formidable wage demands were being tabled at this time.

Negotiations began again in mid-September. At the first meeting the subjects were again price increases and low pay, but the idea of flat-rate pay increases was introduced and it was agreed that this should be on the agenda for the next meeting. On 26 September the government tabled its proposals:

(a) an extension of its commitment to a 5 per cent growth rate to cover the next two years;

(b) a limit of 5 per cent for the growth of retail prices resulting from increases in costs over the next twelve months (this would require a limit of 4 per cent for price increases of manufactured products, and matching performance from the nationalised industries);

(c) a £2 a week pay rise for everyone, together with 20p a week for each 1 per cent increase in retail prices above a threshold of 6 per cent. The government also undertook to do something about pensions, and tabled some arithmetic to show that the suggested £2 per week, which was assumed to lead in fact to a rise in average earnings of £2.60 per week, was compatible with a 5 per cent price rise and a 5 per cent growth in real gross national product (GNP), with a 61 per cent share of this product going to wages and salaries.

On 10 October the TUC presented counter-proposals. Their arithmetic suggested an increase of £3.40 per week in average earnings; about two thirds of the difference from the government figure of £2.60

was accounted for by different assumptions about the share of national income going to wages and salaries, and about one third by different assumptions about national productivity. Otherwise, as an initial bargaining move, they included virtually every demand they could think of: apart from an assurance on the non-operation of the Industrial Relations Act, they asked for price control, for VAT at $7\frac{1}{2}$ per cent rather than 10 per cent, for the increases in rents due to take place in 1973 under the Housing Finance Act to be abandoned, for a wealth tax, a surcharge on capital gains, and a restriction on dividend payments, and for the Consumer Council to be re-established as soon as possible. They pointed to some of the difficulties in any agreement on flat-rate payments – long-term agreements, the complexity of wage structures, existing incremental scales and the move towards equal pay. On land values, they suggested that betterment profits should accrue to the state and that there should be capital gains tax on speculative transactions; also that some action should be taken on estate duty, that family allowances should be increased, and that weekly pensions should rise by £2 for single people and £3.20 for a married couple, without being recouped to any substantial extent by increased national insurance contributions.

A brisk succession of meetings followed during the rest of October and early November. One working party made considerable progress on the problems of lump sum pay increases; they postponed consideration of what the figure should be by referring to it as £x. The main difficulty was on prices, where the TUC felt that a voluntary system was not strong enough. The Prime Minister put the view that any arrangement would have to be either statutory on both prices and wages, or voluntary on both of them. In a further negotiating move, the TUC tacitly withdrew its demand that there should be statutory price control, and asked instead for a guarantee from the government that the retail price index would not rise by more than 5 per cent in the next twelve months. They were concerned that the government's proposals referred only to price rises resulting from increased costs, which did not include rents, the introduction of food import levies, or any effects of changes in the exchange rate. They stressed the need for action on rents and food prices in particular; indeed they asked for an undertaking that the rise in food prices alone should be kept to 5 per cent.

The negotiations broke down on 2 November. The Prime Minister made a statement at that meeting in which he began by distinguishing between issues affecting prices and incomes, and other matters which were essentially matters of government responsibility. The Housing Finance Act and the Industrial Relations Act, for example, fell into the second category, and therefore could not explicitly be included in the negotiations. The proposals he outlined were basically the same as those which he had set out on 26 September, but he added some possibilities: an increase of 50p in the needs allowance to limit the effect of rent increases in 1973; an extension of the period for which family income supplement, free school meals and free welfare milk were awarded; a lump sum payment to be included in revised pensions; consultation with local authorities to moderate the increase in local rates. The TUC felt that the government had hardly moved from its original position – it had not, for example, taken any notice of the discussion on what the flat-rate pay rise should be – indeed they considered that the Prime Minister had retreated from his early position of offering the TUC a partnership in managing the economy.

The problems of reaching an effective voluntary agreement were indeed very formidable at that time; some concessions would have raised points of constitutional principle – for example, the Industrial Relations Act had passed through Parliament and it is an open question whether it would have been proper for the government to come to an agreement with the TUC that its operation should be suspended. There is no way of knowing how many concessions would have been needed to win TUC acceptance; if the government had given the prices guarantee for which the TUC asked, would this have been enough? Finally, it is not clear, if the negotiations had been successful, how the restrictions on wage and salary increases would have worked on a voluntary basis; what sanctions could the TUC have used against unions which successfully negotiated increases higher than had been agreed?

Statutory incomes policy: Stages I and II

On 6 November the government introduced a wages and prices freeze – the first step in the statutory incomes policy which was to preoccupy them for the rest of their period in office. (The details of the freeze are described on pages 378–9.) There was a gap after both the ending of the CBI period of price restraint (on 31 October) and the breakdown of negotiations with the TUC (on 2 November) in which a number of firms managed to put up their prices; also a number of important wage settlements were made, including the power workers, who settled for around 16 per cent, and about a million local government employees, who settled for around 13 per cent. Caught by the rule that awards had to be completed and operational on or before 6 November were settlements for agricultural workers and bank employees, which were both postponed.

There were protests about the freeze, but no significant industrial action against it. The figures show quite clearly the check to the rise in wage rates, but the check to the rise in retail prices is not so clear, mainly because import prices had by this time begun to increase rapidly. Sharply rising import prices were in fact to bedevil this whole period of incomes policy. Some of this rise is accounted for by sterling's downward float, but the import price index still shows a very big upswing after correction for this.

At the turn of the year the government took action to slow down the rise in the money supply. Between 13 October and 22 December the minimum lending rate (which had replaced Bank Rate on 9 October – see page 252) was raised from $7\frac{1}{2}$ to 9 per cent, and in both November and December the Bank of England made calls for Special Deposits, which reached 3 per cent by January 1973. The government did not intend these measures to slow down the rise in real output. The argument was, first, that under the new incomes policy there would be no need for the money supply to rise as fast as before; secondly, that the very rapid monetary expansion earlier in the year, helped by the restoration of tax relief on interest in the budget, had led to a speculative rise in the price of property. The Bank of England consequently requested the banks to restrict lending for property and share speculation.

In beginning with a 90-day freeze the government had followed the pattern of policy in the United States, and it continued to follow the main outline of the American pattern in the general structure of the second stage of its prices and incomes policy announced on 16 January 1973.[1] The policy was to last from March through to the autumn; the main characteristics (described more fully on page 381) were that for each employee pay increases in a year were to be limited to £1 a week plus 4 per cent of the total wage bill for the employer, with a limit for any employee of £250 a year. A Pay Board and a Price Commission were to be set up; the basic principle of the price code was that only allowable cost increases could be passed on in the form of higher prices.

At the end of February a Green Paper was issued,[2] and some modifications were made, particularly to the proposals for price control, before legislation was enacted. The rules sought to control major settlements and the price policy of large firms in the belief that they set the pattern for the rest of the economy. The proposals also looked ahead to the need to sort out anomalies at some point; the deputy chairman of the Pay Board was required to produce reports on the treatment of anomalies by mid-September and on pay relativities by the end of 1973.

[1] In August 1971 wages, prices and rents in the United States had been frozen for three months. At the end of that period a Pay Board and a Price Commission were set up. One of the characteristics of the system of control – copied in the United Kingdom in 1972 – was that the price movements of large firms and large wage settlements were subjected to particularly close scrutiny; the requirements for small firms and small wage settlements were much less stringent.

[2] Treasury, *Price and Pay Code. Consultative Document*, Cmnd 5247, London, HMSO, 1973.

The trade union movement was, of course, officially opposed to Stage II. A number of unions tried industrial action – including the gas workers, hospital ancillary workers and teachers – but with little success. The provisions were stretched in a few instances – for example, the gas workers were allowed a reduction in pension contributions of 45p a week – but the bulk of settlements were within the rules. Perhaps the most important acceptance was by the miners who, when the National Coal Board's offer was put to a ballot in mid-March, voted against a strike. There were a certain number of protest strikes on 1 May, but these fell far short of a total national one-day stoppage.

Demand management during 1973

By the time of the 1973 budget, presented on 6 March, it was clear that activity was expanding rapidly. However, although unemployment had fallen and was still falling, the level in March (635,000, seasonally adjusted) was still high by historical standards and the Chancellor committed himself to continuing the 5 per cent annual growth rate for at least a further year. Indeed, it seemed that the government was still hoping that the underlying growth rate in the economy might have been shifted above its previous long-term path of 3 per cent a year. Because of the momentum of growth so far achieved as well as the further increases in public investment which were expected, the Chancellor judged that, with private manufacturing investment beginning to accelerate, no further stimulus to demand was required to achieve continued growth at 5 per cent during 1973.

The budget was, therefore, broadly neutral: VAT was brought in at 10 per cent, purchase tax and selective employment tax were abolished and, as promised in 1971, a unified income tax was introduced. However, this gave rise to criticism from some outside observers, who tended to point to the very large borrowing requirement of £4.4 billion which was officially forecast for 1973/4, despite the explanation by the Chancellor that £800 million of this could be accounted for by the once-and-for-all effect on the timing of indirect tax payments of the changeover to VAT. Then, as the output figures for the first half of 1973 were published, it became clear that the economy was growing very fast indeed. A good deal of this could be explained by large rises in consumers' expenditure in anticipation of the introduction of VAT and, rather fortuitously, by the simultaneous switch to positive stockbuilding after nearly two years of run-down. Not surprisingly, the rapid rise in output coming after a very long period of slow growth led to shortages of materials and components.

Policy therefore began gradually to move towards mild restriction of demand. On 21 May the Chancellor announced cuts in public expenditure of £100 million in 1973/4 and £500 million in 1974/5 (at 1972 survey prices[1]); this was partly because the counter-cyclical public spending which should have been maintaining demand some six to twelve months earlier was coming through long after the economy had picked up, when the demands of house-building and other private investment were also becoming very strong, and it was therefore sensible to cut back some of this expenditure. The government also took restrictive monetary measures in the middle of the year; when, in mid-July, the pound began to float down again, the Bank of England called for a further 1 per cent of Special Deposits and, by the end of July, raised the minimum lending rate to $11\frac{1}{2}$ per cent – a record postwar level.

There was a good deal of argument about the extent to which the deterioration of the balance of payments in 1973 should be attributed to excess pressure of home demand, or to the quite exceptional rise in import prices. Non-oil commodity prices, as measured by the *Economist*'s dollar index, rose by 62 per cent in 1973, the largest year-on-year rise ever recorded (the updated index is published from 1860). Quantifying the effects of the commodity boom is complicated by the downward float of sterling during the year. Effectively, the devaluation between the fourth quarters of 1972 and 1973 was about 9 per cent. This must be set against a total rise (in sterling terms) of over 39 per cent in the import unit value index for goods, and of 32 per cent in the more comprehensive deflator for imports of goods and services.[2] Between the second halves of 1972 and 1973 the volume of exports and of imports of goods and services grew by almost equal amounts. The change in the terms of trade, therefore, accounted for virtually all the adverse change in the balance of payments, which hardly suggests an excessive strain on domestic resources.

Statutory incomes policy: Stage III

The TUC agreed to discuss the rules for Stage III with the government once they had been assured that no subject would be barred from discussion at the meetings. Fairly early in the discussions the Prime Minister announced that the government would propose linking wage rises with rises in the cost of living, both the CBI and the TUC having stressed the need for some such linking in principle. The government published its proposals as a consultative document on 8 October;[3] the TUC, while stating their disapproval of the proposals, did not suggest any particular alterations; some small concessions were made in

[1] See page 83, footnote 1 for an explanation of this term.

[2] These figures, which measure the prices of landed imports, are not significantly affected by the rise in the price of oil.

[3] Treasury, *Pay and Price Code for Stage 3. A Consultative Document*, Cmnd 5444, London, HMSO, 1973.

response to the CBI's comments. The new code became operative for prices, profits and dividends on 1 November and for pay on 7 November.

The basic provision for pay (discussed more fully on page 383) was a 'norm' of pay increases of up to 7 per cent for a group, or if preferred increases of up to £2.25 per head per week, with an individual maximum of £350 a year. There were various 'flexibility margins': a further 1 per cent was available in settlements which reduced anomalies and obstacles to the better use of manpower; extra payments were available under new efficiency schemes when genuine savings or a contribution to stable prices had been shown; there were also increased premium payments for those working 'unsocial' hours. The threshold provision was for flat-rate increases of 40p per week payable if, during Stage III, the retail price index rose 7 per cent, and similar increases for every 1 per cent above that level. The provisions on pay were to some extent specifically designed to enable the Coal Board to make a reasonably substantial offer to the National Union of Mineworkers; for prices they were essentially a continuation of Stage II (see page 384).

The last five months

In its last five months in office the Conservative government had to struggle with the problems created by the restriction on oil supplies, the trebling of the price of oil and, finally, industrial action against Stage III, first by the electricity workers and then by the miners.

The oil crisis was first to develop. War broke out in the Middle East on 6 October; on 16 October there was a 66 per cent rise in the posted price of oil and on 17 October the Arab oil Ministers announced a 5 per cent per month cumulative cut-back in oil production. This was further intensified in early November, when the Arab oil-producing nations indicated a minimum 25 per cent cut in supplies to the West; then, just before Christmas, the posted price of oil was doubled from 1 January, but this was coupled with an announcement that the cut-backs in production would be eased from 25 to 15 per cent of September output.

On the industrial front, the series of events which led up to the miners' strike began on 11 October, when the National Union of Mineworkers confirmed their negotiators' rejection of 7 per cent basic pay rises. On 1 November the 18,000 power engineers of the Electrical Power Engineers' Association began industrial action in support of a claim for increases in stand-by payments outside Stage III. The miners decided to start an overtime ban from 12 November and, on 28 November, a meeting between the National Union of Mineworkers and the Prime Minister failed to find a solution.

In reaction to these events the government declared a state of emergency on 13 November; electric advertising signs and floodlighting were prohibited, space heating was controlled in industrial and commercial premises. A week later oil company deliveries of all petroleum products were cut by 10 per cent. A 50 m.p.h. speed limit was imposed on 5 December, with further restrictions on street and office lighting; on 13 December the Prime Minister announced a three-day week from 1 January.

The government also took further steps to cut demand, though they were not, in fact, as formidable as they appeared. The minimum lending rate was raised from $11\frac{1}{4}$ to 13 per cent on 13 November and there was a further call for 2 per cent of Special Deposits. However, in a budget on 17 December the call for Special Deposits was reduced to 1 per cent; instead, new restrictions were placed on the growth of the banks' interest-bearing liabilities (see page 251). In this budget hire purchase controls were reintroduced; also a surcharge on surtax and taxation on property development were announced. However, the main measure was a cut in public expenditure amounting to some £1200 million for 1974/5 – by far the largest cut ever announced for a succeeding year. It was, of course, a cut in a programme announced previously; in the event it did not prevent a substantial rise during 1974/5 in public sector expenditure in real terms.

During January 1974 various attempts were made to solve the miners' dispute. The TUC suggested that other unions should agree that exceptional and distinctive circumstances existed in the mining industry, so that if the government made a settlement possible 'other unions would not use this as a lever in their negotiations'. On 16 January a special conference of trade union presidents and general secretaries overwhelmingly endorsed this initiative, but the government clearly held the undertaking in some doubt.

Meantime, on 10 January the National Union of Mineworkers had decided not to strike, but to keep their overtime ban. By the middle of January the prospect for fuel supplies was easing a little; the Secretary of State for Energy announced the immediate resumption of full electricity supplies for steel production and the likelihood of a four-day week for industry in the near future.

On 24 January the Pay Board's report on relativities was published;[1] the Prime Minister then invited the CBI and the TUC to immediate talks on setting up an independent pay relativities body to consider major claims including the miners'. However, on the same day the National Union of Mineworkers decided to call a strike ballot, and the result, declared on 4 February, showed an 81 per cent vote in favour of a strike to start from 10 February. On 7 February the Prime Minister

[1] Pay Board, *Advisory Report no. 2: Problems of Pay Relativities*, Cmnd 5535, London, HMSO, 1974.

announced a general election on 28 February. The National Union of Mineworkers rejected the Prime Minister's appeal to postpone their strike until after the general election; on 12 February they also rejected a pay offer made by certain industrialists whose identity was not revealed. During the strike, and during the election campaign, the Pay Board sat from 18 to 25 February as a special relativities board considering evidence on the relative pay of miners. Their Report was published on 6 March, after the result of the general election had been announced.[1]

This particular period of policy, therefore, came to a somewhat chaotic end. The attempt had been to combine a move to more rapid economic growth with a statutory incomes policy to prevent inflation at home and a floating exchange rate to protect the balance of payments. Unfortunately the second stage of this particular incomes policy coincided with a very sharp rise in world commodity prices and, in particular, with a trebling of oil prices. The oil price rise (and the accompanying cut-backs in production) did a great deal to strengthen the position of the National Union of Mineworkers in its confrontation with the government and the provision for indexation in the third stage of incomes policy ensured that the rise in commodity prices set off a price–wage spiral in the United Kingdom. (While the Labour government dismantled the Conservative government's incomes policy in general, they allowed the threshold agreements to run on until October 1974. This was one of the driving forces behind the wage and price explosion which followed the fall of the Conservative government, with average earnings rising 28 per cent and retail prices 25 per cent between the second quarters of 1974 and 1975.) The argument remains between those who conclude that the incomes policy experiment of 1972–4 should not have been tried and those who contend that it should not have been abandoned.

[1] Pay Board, *Special Report: Relativity Pay of Mineworkers*, Cmnd 5567, London, HMSO, 1974.

CHAPTER 3

PUBLIC EXPENDITURE

by *R. W. R. Price*

INTRODUCTION

This chapter is concerned with what the Musgraves call the 'stabilisation function' of managing public expenditure – its role in the management of demand.[1] The 'allocation' and 'distribution' functions, which relate to its role in the provision of social goods and the transfer of spending power between individuals, are not considered specifically,[2] although they are generally relevant because the coordination of all three is important in assessing the achievements of each. Combining social objectives with stabilisation policy can be successful, but conflict between the two has, perhaps, been more usual than harmony.

Public expenditure enjoyed an unchallenged pre-eminence in the original blue-prints for postwar stabilisation policy, but in practice it surrendered this position to taxation and the manipulation of consumer demand. If the postwar scene had been dominated by chronic under-investment or prolonged cyclical depression this might not have happened, but stabilisation turned out to require 'fine-tuning', to which variations in public expenditure seemed ill-adapted. By the end of the 1950s the avowed strategy had become to ensure that public spending was neutral *vis-à-vis* internal stability, with the public sector expanding at a rate consistent with the long-run growth of the economy, so that at least one sector would be free from cyclical disturbance. However, adjustments to programmes of a scale and frequency considerably beyond the limits of short-term flexibility originally allowed

---

[1] R. A. and P. B. Musgrave, *Public Finance: in theory and practice*, London, McGraw Hill, 1975, chap. 1.

[2] Concepts of welfare optimisation do not figure in the determination of expenditure and will not be pursued here. With respect to neither priorities for individual programmes nor the overall size of the public sector have governments 'tried to achieve the aims that welfare theories postulate for them, and . . . they are unlikely to do so in future. Consequently these prescriptive theories are simply not operational' (A. T. Peacock and J. Wiseman, *The Growth of Public Expenditure in the United Kingdom*, Princeton University Press, 1961, p. 14). Despite the creation (in the 1970s) of programme evaluation methods explicitly concerned with priorities and cost–benefit analysis (Programme Analysis and Review and the Central Policy Review Staff), fiscal politics and departmental log-rolling still decide most issues in determining expenditure.

for have still been a hallmark of the period covered here. Public expenditure has never wholly shed its short-term role.

It is not, of course, the principal object of public spending that it should act as a counterweight in balancing demand; rather, decisions about its volume and composition should reflect the economic and social considerations specifically attached to it. Concern that using it in a fully active short-term role may entail the sacrifice of these objectives has accompanied doubts about the physical costs of using it as an instrument. Adjustments to programmes (particularly increases) can be made to serve the needs of deficit finance and allocative policies, but only transiently, tending to be followed at short remove by conflict, as economic exigencies force *ad hoc* cuts across-the-board.

How can a framework for decisions on the volume and mix of public expenditure in the medium term be constructed to allow for a contribution to demand management without physical disruption and the sacrifice of other objectives? The principle of planning medium-term expenditure 'in relation to prospective resources', which was endorsed in the *Plowden Report*,[1] and established by the Public Expenditure Survey Committee (PESC), which began operation in 1961, was a first approach to a solution of the problem. This has, however, remained unsolved, so that continuing attempts to construct a more water-tight system are a dominant theme of the period.

The difficulties of applying any system effectively would be great in the best of circumstances; they are exacerbated by the multiplicity of agencies – central government departments, local authorities, nationalised industries and other public corporations – on which the Treasury has to rely both to supply the material on which decisions are based and to implement those decisions. The relationships between the Treasury and the departments, and between central government and the actual spending authorities, have been extensively debated during the period. It is hardly surprising that, despite the continued search for improvement and a number of significant innovations in techniques, the problem of dovetailing the allocative and stabilisation functions of government remains.

The first section of this chapter deals directly with the evolution over the period of public expenditure 'management' – to use a rather inadequate but handy term to describe the process and principles which govern the determination and control of public expenditure. Subsequent sections attempt to provide a quantitative and qualitative assessment of the impact of public expenditure as an instrument in the management of the economy.

[1] Treasury, *The Control of Public Expenditure*, Cmnd 1432, London, HMSO, 1961, p. 6.

THE MANAGEMENT OF PUBLIC EXPENDITURE

The search for improved methods of public expenditure control gives a certain continuity to its historical development, but this can conveniently be considered in three stages. The division between the first two is the *Plowden Report*, which set out the principles of medium-term planning and restricted short-term intervention.[1] Devaluation in 1967 provided a second watershed, because it led to a reappraisal of both medium-term and short-term ground rules; it was the most fundamental influence on policy until the oil crisis.

Public expenditure 1944–61

In 1944 a White Paper had recognised two means of achieving economic stability through regulating public investment. First, it was thought possible to 'maintain the stability of public investment when private investment is beginning to fall off', thus preventing sympathetic movements which tended to accentuate the trade cycle.[2] Secondly, public investment might be deliberately varied in a counter-cyclical way to compensate directly for disturbances in the private sector.[3]

The experience of the 1950s was a mixture of both strategies; so much so that there are two views about which was dominant. The *Radcliffe Report*, certain spokesmen for local authorities and nationalised industries, and the *Plowden Report* saw consistent medium-term planning being compromised by disruptive and destabilising short-term interventions.[4] The other view, expressed by Dow, Dennison and various official publications,[5] clearly allocates a subordinate role in counter-cyclical policy to public expenditure. Actually, during the

---

[1] Ibid.

[2] Ministry of Reconstruction, *Employment Policy*, Cmd 6527, London, HMSO, 1944, p. 21.

[3] The concept of deliberately destabilising public investment was criticised by Beveridge as introducing 'meaningless unprogressive fluctuation'; he advocated instead an expansion of the public sector 'so as to enlarge the area within which investment can be stabilised directly' (W. H. Beveridge, *Full Employment in a Free Society*, London, Allen & Unwin, 1944, pp. 183 and 269). This strategy was designed to maximise the longer-term contribution of expenditure policy to stability, and was reminiscent of Keynes, who foresaw 'the State, which is in a position to calculate the marginal efficiency of capital-goods on long views and on the basis of the general social advantage, taking an ever greater responsibility for directly organising investment' (J. M. Keynes, *The General Theory of Employment, Interest and Money*, London, Macmillan, 1936, p. 164).

[4] Treasury, *Committee on the Working of the Monetary System. Report* [Radcliffe Report], Cmnd 827, London, HMSO, 1959, pp. 167–8, and *Principal Memoranda of Evidence*, vol. 2, London, HMSO, 1960, pp. 183 and 186–7; Treasury, *The Control of Public Expenditure*, p. 10; Institute of Municipal Treasurers and Accountants, *Local Government Finance*, July 1961, p. 157.

[5] Dow, *The Management of the British Economy, 1945–60*; S. R. Dennison, 'Investment in the nationalised industries' (paper given to the Manchester Statistical Society, 11 February 1959) p. 4; Council on Prices, Productivity and Incomes, *1st Report*, London, HMSO, 1958; Treasury, *Public Investment in Great Britain*, Cmnd 1203, London, HMSO, 1960, pp. 6–7.

1950s spasmodic short-term interventions in public expenditure programmes never seriously impeded the development of medium-term
planning, which had explicitly become the axis of stabilisation policy by
the early 1960s. Although short-term adjustments were made to programmes of the nationalised industries, these were generally small, and
became smaller still with experience. Some deflationary interventions –
notably in 1956/7 – may have entailed a cost in terms of disruption, but
in general they only affected programmes where ancillary schemes
allowed some leeway, or where shortfalls from targets (often themselves
due to changed levels of business activity) provided scope for notional
cuts. Both the deflationary intervention of 1958/9 and the reflationary
one of 1959/60 changed investment in nationalised industries by only
3 per cent; the most obvious characteristic of the period as a whole was
the secular expansion of public industry, particularly fuel and power, as
a proportion of the economy. Similarly, although there were five
deflationary interventions by central government in local authority
investment between July 1955 and October 1957, which evoked some
local criticism, these had an extremely small overall impact on planned
spending, partly due to reluctance to interfere with health and education programmes. To ease demand pressures, the government could
accelerate the existing run-down in the public housing programme,
while relying on local environmental projects to provide the remaining
short-term restraint; thus, the natural conflict between central and
local priorities probably accounts for most of the local authority
complaints.

Throughout the 1950s public expenditure was tending, in practice,
towards a stabilisation role that was neutral rather than actively
compensatory. Since it was regarded as being unadjustable at short
notice by more than 2–3 per cent either way without counter-productive
consequences,[1] the characteristic two-year period from high to low was
too short for variations in public investment to be effective. Hence
Plowden's call for the 'greatest practical stability of decisions in public
expenditure',[2] which was hailed by some as revolutionising the conduct
of compensatory finance,[3] but, more properly, regularised what had
already evolved as the *de facto* basis of policy.

[1] This was the official estimate of short-term flexibility in public investment programmes
by the end of the 1950s (ibid; also D. H. Amory quoted in *Local Government Finance*, July
1960, pp. 161–2).

[2] Treasury, *The Control of Public Expenditure*, p. 7.

[3] See House of Commons, *Hansard*, 24 January 1962, col. 221; U. K. Hicks, 'Plowden
planning and management in the public services', *Public Administration*, vol. 39, Winter
1961, p. 304.

Plowden and the planning era

Implementing Plowden's prescription for the medium-term planning of public expenditure with only the most marginal short-term variations depended on a number of factors which made the strategy difficult to put into effective practice. First, once the proper expenditure–resource relationship had been specified, the 'prospective development of income and economic resources' had to be defined and accurately estimated. The *Plowden Report* recognised that economic resources could be predicted five years ahead 'only within broad limits', and that regular surveys would not provide automatic criteria which could be substituted for judgement. Secondly, because targets were set in terms of fifth-year expenditure levels and growth paths in terms of an average rate of growth over the five years, early expenditure plans did not specify by what annual growth rates the average should be achieved. The problem of varying the rate of expansion around the average in order to suit the needs of economic policy was foreseen, but the difficulty was to prevent the timing profile from getting out of touch with short-term needs and the limits of flexibility.

Although the PESC began operation in a climate of restriction, its first tasks being to reduce expenditure to meet the 1961 external crisis, this was meant to be a prelude to a new secular course along a 3 per cent growth path,[1] which had become 4 per cent by mid-1962/3, whilst the 1963 PESC survey eventually projected a real annual average increase of 4·1 per cent between 1963/4 and 1967/8.[2] *The National Plan*, published in September 1965, went further, combining a 4¼ per cent annual average increase in public expenditure (except for investment in nationalised industry) with a 4 per cent annual average growth of GDP from 1964/5 to 1969/70.

In each case the rise in expenditure was to be kept roughly in line with resources, so that the public share of GDP was only scheduled to increase by about ½ per cent in volume terms. In the event, as table 3.1 shows, the demand on resources increased much more than this: between 1963 and 1967 the public sector share of GDP grew by nearly 4 per cent in volume and nearly 5 per cent in value. Of this 0·33 per cent was a planned volume increase and 0·8 per cent a relative price increase;[3] of the balance of 3·65 per cent, over half can be attributed to defective control or policy changes, since by 1967 public expenditure had grown far ahead of schedule, and the rest to over-optimism about the growth of GDP. In the formative years of the PESC, then, the

---

[1] Selwyn Lloyd in the House of Commons, 17 April 1961.
[2] Treasury, *Public Expenditure in 1963–64 and 1967–68*, Cmnd 2235, London, HMSO, 1963.
[3] See page 85 below.

Table 3.1. *The share in GDP[a] of public expenditure:[b]
planned and unplanned changes, 1963–7*

Percentages

	Change 1963–7	Share
1963 share at current market prices		33·26
Planned increase in volume	+0·33	
Unplanned increase in volume:		
Due to GDP shortfall	+1·31	
Due to public expenditure excess	+2·34	
Total increase in volume	+3·98	
Relative price effect	+0·80	
Total increase in value	+4·78	
1967 share at current market prices		38·04

SOURCES: Treasury, *Public Expenditure in 1963–64 and 1967–68*; Department of Economic Affairs, *The National Plan*; CSO, *National Income and Expenditure 1963–73*, London, HMSO, 1974; NIESR estimates.

[a] At market prices.
[b] Excluding imputed rents, net purchases of existing assets (real and financial) and debt interest.

attempt to relate expenditure to resources was not successful and the lessons learnt were negative ones. The subsequent development of expenditure control since devaluation may, indeed, be seen as a reaction to two factors which had become apparent immediately after the *Plowden Report* – the tendencies both to overestimate the resources available and to underestimate public sector demands on them. The PESC procedures relating to these two issues merit further comment.

Since the purpose of the PESC is to provide a framework for taking decisions regarding public expenditure over the medium term, the critical elements have been seen as establishing what prospective resources are available and the 'cost' of pre-empting them for public sector use. Crucial to the former is the concept of the growth of productive potential, or the path of 'constant employment' output from which variations in capacity utilisation have been abstracted.[1] It is this concept rather than the growth of GDP itself which in practice constrains expenditure strategy and determines the growth of expenditure in the medium term.[2] However, since at any base date expenditure may be 'off-trend' in either direction (implying a short-term share of resources greater or smaller than that considered normal or desirable in the

[1] Productive potential increases with both productivity and the labour supply, and 'constant employment' implies absorbing the growth of the latter.
[2] For a discussion of this point see House of Commons, *Seventh Report from the Expenditure Committee, Session 1971–72. Public Expenditure and Economic Management*, London, HMSO, 1972, especially pp. vi–viii and 113–16.

Table 3.2. *Official projections for growth rates of GDP and public expenditure*

Percentages[a]

Forecasts[b]		GDP growth assumed	Public expenditure[c] growth		
Published	Period		Volume[d]	Total cost[e]	Net resource cost[ef']
Dec. 1963	1963/4–1967/8	4·0	4·10	4·85	4·85
Sept. 1965	1964/5–1969/70	4·0	4·25[g]	5·00[g]	5·00[g]
Dec. 1969	1968/9–1971/2	3·0–4·0	2·80	3·00	3·20
Jan. 1971	1970/1–1974/5	..	2·20	2·60	3·10
Nov. 1971	1971/2–1975/6	..	2·20	2·70	3·20
Dec. 1972	1972/3–1976/7	3·5–5·0	2·20	2·50	3·00
Dec. 1973	1973/4–1977/8	3·5–4·5	1·50	2·00	2·50

SOURCES: Treasury, *Public Expenditure in 1963–64 and 1967–68*; Department of Economic Affairs, *The National Plan*; Treasury, *Public Expenditure 1968–69 to 1973–74*, *Public Expenditure 1969–70 to 1974–75*, *Public Expenditure 1969–70 to 1975–76*, *Public Expenditure to 1976–77* and *Public Expenditure to 1977–78*.

[a] Annual average growth rates.
[b] From sources in order given.
[c] Including contingency reserve and shortfall allowance from December 1969 forecast, and excluding investment grants from January 1971 forecast.
[d] At constant survey prices.
[e] At constant out-turn prices, including the relative price effect.
[f] Demand on output in cost terms, as defined, for example, in Treasury, *Public Expenditure to 1977–78*, table 3.1.
[g] Excluding investment in nationalised industries.

longer run), it is legitimate to specify medium-term growth rates for the public sector which diverge somewhat from growth rates in productive potential proper.

Table 3.2 lists these projected official growth rates, as published since 1963, together with the various medium-term output assumptions which accompanied them. From the third and fourth columns it can be seen that there is a fairly consistent decline in the projected volume growth rates of expenditure, both absolutely and relative to the growth of GDP.[1] At first sight this would seem to imply a comparable decline

[1] These volume growth rates are expressed in terms of constant 'survey prices'. The PESC system is integrated with the annual estimates cycle, which forms the basis for financial control: departmental estimates for spending in the next financial year are submitted to the Treasury on 1 December, and the Parliamentary 'Vote on Account' to meet these estimates takes place in mid-February. Including local authority grants, this covers about 55 per cent of government spending, and the components provide the basis for the first year of the PESC survey which follows from March to November. For this expenditure, therefore, 1973 survey prices, for example, mean the pay and prices used to cost the 1973/4 budget estimates, and would refer very roughly to October–November 1972. For other categories of expenditure the precise base point varies, but would normally relate to February–March 1973 (See Treasury, *Public Expenditure White Papers: handbook on methodology*, London, HMSO, 1972,

in the share of the public sector in GDP, but in fact short-term programme increases and GDP shortfalls meant that public expenditure
was being forced into an 'above-trend' position in the short run
and an important reason for the lower projected growth rates for
later periods is the attempt of medium-term policy to correct for
this.

However, the contrast between projections made before and after
devaluation is unambiguous; indeed, the growth of productive potential
had a rather different meaning as a constraint in the two periods. Both
the NEDC experiment and the National Plan were based on the
premise that public expenditure demands would help create their own
supply, thus making the resource 'constraint' endogenous to the growth
path for public expenditure. Following devaluation there was a reaction
from this optimism; projections made in February and December 1969
envisaged an increase in total output of between just under 3 per cent
and about 4 per cent a year over the medium term, with the expenditure plans based on the lower figure.[1] This 'wedge' approach is still
used in expenditure plans, even though the growth objective has
periodically reasserted itself. In 1972/3 and 1973/4 the prospect of
above-average growth was not allowed to influence the longer-run
public expenditure allocation; instead, provision for other demand
items, particularly private investment, was increased.[2]

Generally speaking, the strategy of expenditure management between
1968 and 1973 revolved around a medium-term growth path of
approximately 3 per cent, which the Treasury has described as 'proceeding in a majestic and unvarying way',[3] and which was deduced from
the historical growth record from 1958 to 1970. This has been criticised
by the more optimistic as leading to a self-perpetuating restraint on
growth, but the Treasury has viewed it as 'imprudent to assume a faster
growth rate of available resources without a very clear idea of where the
growth was to come from.'[4]

We have seen in table 3.2 that the National Plan implied a small
increase in the volume of public expenditure relative to GDP, but the
growth of expenditure volume and of GDP were not far from propor-

pp. 23 *et seq.*, and W. A. H. Godley, 'The measurement and control of public expenditure',
Economic Policy Review, no. 2, March 1976, pp. 58–63).

[1] Department of Economic Affairs, *The Task Ahead (Economic Assessment to 1972)*, London,
HMSO, 1969; Treasury, *Public Expenditure 1968–69 to 1973–74*, Cmnd 4234, London,
HMSO, 1969.

[2] See Treasury, *Public Expenditure to 1976–77*, Cmnd 5178, p. 10, and *Public Expenditure
to 1977–78*, Cmnd 5519, p. 10, London, HMSO, 1972 and 1973.

[3] House of Commons, *Seventh Report from the Expenditure Committee, Session 1971–72*, p. 52.
In exact terms, the growth of productive potential was derived as 3·2 per cent per annum,
comprising a 3 per cent increase in productivity and a 0·2 per cent increase in the labour
force (ibid. pp. 113–19).   [4] Ibid. pp. ix and 75.

tional as originally conceived by both administrations. There appears, however, to have been something of a doctrinal divergence between the two Parties on this matter, with Labour coming to regard proportional growth as too low and the Conservatives as too high. Although this latter view was not apparent during Maudling's 'growth experiment', it asserted itself in 1970,[1] when the new approach was 'to consider the need of public expenditure and for what it will be required...first, rather than trying to predict the rate of growth of total output and then seeking to justify the rate of growth of public expenditure in reference to it.'[2] At the root of the difference lies a value judgement about private and public spending and about taxation.

To maintain a given share of national output, the government sector demand for finance (and therefore taxation) has to advance more than proportionately. This is because the productivity increase in the government sector is deemed to be zero,[3] so that the cost of output increases faster than in the 'enterprise' sector, where it is not – the so-called 'relative price effect'. This ensured that public expenditure plans laid down in the early 1960s entailed a continuous rise in their share of GDP at current prices between 1963 and 1967 (0·8 per cent, see table 3.1). This disproportionate demand for finance was recognised from the start;[4] it was at the heart of Chancellors' warnings in the House of Commons about increased longer-term taxation in 1964/5.[5] It was also the basis of the post-devaluation reversal of strategy; the cost of services rather than the level provided having become central to public expenditure planning since 1968. In December 1969 the 3 per cent growth rate for public expenditure was fixed in terms of its cost not its volume (fifth column in table 3.2).[6]

Public expenditure has therefore come to be explicitly identified with the resource transfer (and hence taxation) necessary to finance public spending. But what is the correct measure of this transfer? Public expenditure as it stands is net of charges (for medical prescriptions, for example), but gross of income and expenditure taxes. Direct taxes are generated by some types of current grant and by interest paid on public debt; there is also a significant indirect tax element in government

[1] Treasury, *New Policies for Public Spending*, Cmnd 4515, London, HMSO, 1970.

[2] House of Commons, *Hansard*, 22 February 1971, col. 127.

[3] The failure to measure productivity increases in public services means that (identifiable) output increases come from increased public employment; also, the long-run cost of public services goes up relative to the GDP deflator at a rate equal to average productivity growth in the economy (provided public and private sector earnings increase at the same long-run rate). A constant level of public service output then gives a lower volume share in GDP, but a fixed value share, as the relative price of public services increases at the same rate as GDP.

[4] Treasury, *Public Expenditure in 1963–64 and 1967–68*, p. 10.

[5] Reginald Maudling, 14 April 1964, and James Callaghan, 22 February 1965.

[6] Treasury, *Public Expenditure 1968–69 to 1973–74*.

purchases.[1] Further, where the same function can be fulfilled by either expenditure or tax allowances, changes in spending may involve off-setting changes in revenue (as when switching from investment grants to allowances), so that estimates of the rate of increase in resource demands should take both sides into account. Again, certain items are transactions in existing assets and, while these are significant in them-selves, they do not constitute claims on current production. Finally, since part of transfer expenditure is saved by the recipients, this also can be discounted as a claim on output. By adjusting for all these factors,[2] we can obtain estimates of public expenditure which may be described as 'demand on output at factor cost', changes in which measure the net resource transfer necessary to finance both the growth in public services provided and the redistribution of private spending power (including that to public authority employees through the relative price effect).

This 'weighted' measure of public expenditure – its net resource cost rather than its gross cost – first attained planning significance in 1971/2; as may be seen from the last column of table 3.2, the growth path of public spending was constrained by linking the growth of its net cost to the (past) growth rate of productive potential. In the process, the gross cost projections fell below this by about 0·5 per cent per annum (although the exact difference between the two depends on the com-position of expenditure). Granted that planned public expenditure should be evaluated in this way, the magnitude of public spending is, of course, still a matter for political and economic decision. A proportional (3 per cent) constraint on growth in resource cost can be regarded as a proxy for longer-run (non-inflationary) revenue poten-tial, but as a rule of thumb it cannot have the same force as an explicit long-run income–expenditure budget. It has been advocated that expenditure should be matched directly to tax revenue projections so as to provide a better and more comprehensive method of coordinat-ing public spending with available resources, but here too there have been differences over what rules or datum lines should be specified, and the proposals have not been systematically implemented.[3]

---

[1] In the national accounts charges are netted out of public spending and treated as personal consumption, and the PESC follows this practice. Most of the indirect taxes are included in purchases of goods and services, but selective employment tax introduced a large tax element into the public wage and salary bill, which meant, at the time, an artificial increase in the gross cost of services.

[2] For a fuller description of the adjustments see pages 95–6 below.

[3] The integration of the public expenditure descision-making process with longer-term policy towards taxation was advocated by Sir Richard Clarke, one of the chief architects of the *Plowden Report* (see *The Management of the Public Sector of the National Economy*, London, Athlone Press, 1964, p. 24). It was endorsed in a Green Paper – Treasury, *Public Expenditure: a new presentation*, Cmnd 4017, London, HMSO, 1969 – but the revenue projections in this document were discontinued after the White Paper of the same year (until restored in the

Policy since 1968: medium-term demands and short-term needs

The failure to delineate the growth path of public expenditure between base and target years was recognised with hindsight as a defect of planning in the period 1963–7.[1] It contributed to a tendency to excess spending and made the fifth-year target unachievable without drastic intervention;[2] public expenditure was uniformly ahead of the specified average growth path in 1967/8 (see charts 3.3 and 3.4 on pages 108–10 below) and, though an initial 'hump' in expenditure had been foreseen,[3] its magnitude was an expression of the general fault – that plans were precise five years ahead, but vague as one came nearer to actuality. Since devaluation, therefore, the annual growth path by which the fifth-year target is supposed to be reached has been delineated. This was intended to ease the difficulties of phasing public expenditure to suit the needs of demand management. Inability to manipulate public expenditure in the short term to any marked degree was blamed for the stabilisation problems of the National Plan;[4] a consistent medium-term growth path would therefore help to prevent destabilising variations in the public sector itself and to keep expenditure policy within the bounds of short-term flexibility.

Two further innovations were also supposed to increase the contribution of public expenditure planning to stability. The first was the concentration on the third year, rather than the more nebulous fifth, as the focal point for decision-making. This was portrayed as the most convenient stage at which to confirm or modify provisional expenditure decisions, because it was the year when there was real scope for substantial changes up or down without too great a cost through disruption.[5]

White Paper of January 1978). The innovation was dropped chiefly on the grounds that public expenditure decisions should not be taken on the basis of arbitrarily defined revenue projections (see House of Commons, *Third Report from the Expenditure Committee, Session 1970–71. Command Papers on Public Expenditure*, London, HMSO, 1971, pp. 6–10). Partly this reflected the belief of the incoming Conservative administration that taxation was already too high and ought to be reduced. But there are obvious problems regarding inflationary and real fiscal drag – should tax rates be specified in indexed form or not, and if not what rate of inflation should be assumed? – which may tend to make revenue projections arbitrary unless based on a consistent long-term taxation strategy and/or rules regarding the full-employment budget balance (Cf. R. R. Neild and T. Ward, *The Budgetary Situation: an appraisal*, Department of Applied Economics, University of Cambridge, 1976, and Godley, 'The measurement and control of public expenditure', p. 62).

[1] House of Commons, *Hansard*, 22 January 1970, col. 743.

[2] See H. Heclo and A. Wildavsky, *The Private Government of Public Money*, London, Macmillan, 1974, p. 211.

[3] Treasury, *Public Expenditure: planning and control*, Cmnd 2915, London, HMSO, 1966, pp. 13–14; House of Commons, *Hansard*, 22 January 1970, col. 743.   [4] Ibid.

[5] Treasury, *Public Expenditure: a new presentation*, p. 8; House of Commons, *First Report from the Select Committee on Procedure, Session 1968–69. Scrutiny of Public Expenditure and Administration*, London, HMSO, 1969, pp. 150 *et seq.*

The Treasury have not wished by this approach to create the impression that options are closed before the focal point and open after it, but have emphasised that the inflexibility of programmes diminishes the further one looks ahead to the end of the planning period.[1] However, the PESC system of annual reviews tends to emphasise that the third year is the point at which medium-term and short-term needs converge.[2]

It was hoped that the second innovation would also help with short-term stabilisation; plans were to be made on the basis that it was 'less disruptive later to bring forward plans if there proves to be room for them than it is to stop what has been started if this proves to have been too much'.[3] But the relative merits of reflation over deflation are not so clear-cut; they rest, particularly, on the lower relative *cost* of increasing programmes at short notice than of cutting them – cost being here interpreted as the financial, political and psychological diseconomies of altering existing commitments. In terms of the actual physical and contractual difficulties of changing programmes at short notice, it is doubtful so far as capital expenditure is concerned whether either reflation or deflation has a distinct advantage. Cuts have to be restricted to programmes not yet 'committed' (the last formal stage before the scheme moves to tender); they do not extend to projects already contracted, and only exceptionally to those out to tender.[4] Short-term deflationary potential thus excludes any effect on work-in-progress, which is accepted as zero; it is confined to cuts in orders, which means that a given change in capital expenditure necessitates a much larger alteration in project starts.[5] Against this, reflation has to rely on the extent to which longer-term projects are ready to be put into effect,[6] or on the existence of frustrated demand in, for example, local environmental schemes.

[1] House of Commons, *Third Report from the Expenditure Committee, Session 1970–71*, p.67; Treasury, *Public Expenditure 1969–70 to 1974–75*, Cmnd 4578, London, HMSO, 1971, p. 6.

[2] It is beyond the short-term horizon of $1\frac{1}{2}$–2 years, but allows for positive cyclical phasing within the context of the medium-term economic assessment, as well as minimising the possibility of public expenditure plans becoming cyclically perverse and thus straining the capacity for short-term stabilisation proper.

[3] Roy Jenkins in the House of Commons, 21 January 1970.

[4] Even so, land may be held unproductively and designs shelved or scrapped. The effects on morale and efficiency have frequently been cited by local authorities as one of the costs of programme reductions (see *Local Government Finance*, September 1970).

[5] Occasionally the government may intervene in the 4–6 month period between commitment and commencement, but in the case of local authority projects it has, in fact, no legal right to do so. It took a 50–60 per cent cut in starts to achieve the 20 per cent cut across-the-board planned investment cut in December 1973 (see NEDO, Building and Civil Engineering Economic Development Committees, *The Public Client and the Construction Industry*, London, HMSO, 1975, p. 22; House of Commons, *Fourth Report from the Expenditure Committee, Session 1974. Expenditure Cuts in Health and Personal Social Services*, London, HMSO, 1975, p. ix).

[6] The possibility of a 'shelf' of partially prepared projects has been mooted at various times, in particular in OECD, *Fiscal Policy for a Balanced Economy* by W. Heller et al., Paris, 1968, p. 110. The Treasury objections to such a scheme are set out in House of Commons, *Seventh Report from the Expenditure Committee, Session 1971–72*, pp. 8–9.

With suitable incentives for spending within a particular time (as in 1971–3), reflationary policies can be effective, but persuasion is not equivalent to the direct controls available for implementing cuts – the system acts better as a bridle than a spur. This being so, it has remained the opinion of the Treasury that it is physically 'easier to postpone than to bring forward'.[1]

The real advantage of reflation lies, in fact, in current expenditure. Transfer payments tend to be rigid downwards and elastic upwards, and for technical reasons instruments such as increasing national insurance benefits or government consumption have a more immediate impact on demand than either taxation or investment, which makes them almost irresistible.[2] The trouble is that these instruments tend to be self-defeating in the sense that much of their short-term effect compromises the medium-term strategy from which their usefulness devolves. Except for the peculiar case of postwar credits, repayments of which can be confined within a given period, transfer payments cannot be phased, but necessitate an upward shift in the medium-term expenditure schedule;[3] the same thing applies to current expenditure on goods and services. Short-term cuts may also imply medium-term shifts, but these can be contained more easily than upward changes.

This difficulty of phasing reflations so that they do not spill over inopportunely into the medium term is one reason why there tend to be successive reversals of stance in stabilisation policy. The tendency for reflation to result in increased medium-term commitments,which then have to be cut back, may be partly the result of laxer control during reflations, so that there is an unintentional spill-over, but the documentary evidence on 1972/3 shows that, in fact, discretionary policy decisions are more important in this respect than a looser Treasury hold on the reins.

Reflation began in 1971/2, with the Treasury looking for things which could be started quickly but completed within two years; it was not the intention to 'prejudice the whole of public expenditure for five years ahead'.[4] During the course of 1972, however, conjunctural policy took on a new dimension and as a result there were large programme increases for 1973/4 and beyond.[5] It seems that the authorities had decided

---

[1] Ibid. p. 9.

[2] The impact multipliers for the first year of intervention are relatively large because the lags are shorter and the savings and import offsets smaller. In the case of an uprating the impact effect is also much greater than the eventual leverage because the negative effect of increased contributions (especially those by employers) takes longer to work through than the positive effect of increased transfers.

[3] It is true, however, that, to the extent that they are fixed in nominal terms, the higher the rate of inflation the faster the rate at which increments in transfer payments will be eroded in real terms.   [4] Ibid. pp. xi, 3, 4 and 11.

[5] Treasury, *Public Expenditure to 1976–77*.

that 'there were two ways to go about relieving [unemployment] by means of public expenditure policy. One was the straight counter-cyclical deviation from the plan which would otherwise have been in being. The other was an addition to the programme which would be acceptable in the medium-term.'[1]

The situation is illustrated in chart 3.1. The specifically counter-cyclical action initially scheduled to taper off during 1973/4 constituted an increase of about 1·7 per cent on total 1972/3 expenditure; the

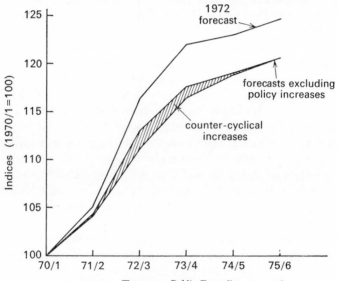

Chart 3.1. *Counter-cyclical and other policy increases in public expenditure^a between the 1971 and 1972 surveys*

SOURCE: Treasury, *Public Expenditure to 1976–77.*

^a Expenditure volume of total programmes excluding investment grants.

medium-term or secular increases more than doubled this, adding 2·8 per cent to that year;[2] they also shifted the expenditure schedule upwards by about 3½ per cent in the following years. In such a process there is a danger that medium-term strategy may be undermined even though the planning constraint fixed in terms of the average annual rate of growth from the base year is not exceeded. In this case the projected rate of growth (the slope of the schedule) was actually reduced from 2·7 to 2·5 per cent in cost terms, the latter, of course, being from a larger base. The facility with which shifts in the expenditure schedule can be compensated for by more shadowy adjustments to the longer-term profile of expansion must be counted a defect of the control system.[1] Even if the intention is to restore the balance later by downward shifts, this might be at a cost, and there is the danger of imbalances in the programmes because the elements which are flexible upwards, and useful in reflations, are not necessarily those available for deflation. Counter-cyclical action proper has concentrated on investment, while (in 1972/3 at least) medium-term action has been through increases in current expenditure (transfers, goods and services). Since the latter are least operable in a deflation, capital reductions are often called upon to compensate.

Whilst the refinement of the PESC system has undoubtedly brought some notable gains in the costing of public expenditure – the focus on the third year and the provision of appropriately cautious datum lines – these cannot be said to have solved the basic problem of making room for contra-cyclical variation of plans within a viable medium-term programme. Since, moreover, the system has been called upon to provide a degree of flexibility substantially and increasingly beyond that envisaged at the beginning of the period, it must remain a cause for serious concern that failure to solve this problem may result in programme imbalances and successive reversals of policy.

Control of the spending authorities

The multifarious agencies actually responsible for the programmes which make up public expenditure exacerbate the problems. Since it is principally upon investment that contra-cyclical adjustments fall, it is the nationalised industries and the local authorities rather than central government which carry the onus of adjustment. Some observers have accordingly criticised the government machine for lack of coordination, with local authority spending a 'rogue elephant'[2] responsible for periodic over-loading of the economy;[3] the belief is also prevalent that short-term adjustments can never be adequately enforced on either the local authorities or the nationalised industries.

Certainly as regards current spending, it is officially admitted that the mechanism of rate support grants constitutes 'strong influence' rather than control.[4] Local authorities have the right to levy their own rates, so

---

[1] For a discussion of the 'fine art' of bartering long-term cuts for short-term increases, see Heclo and Wildavsky, *The Private Government of Public Money*, pp. 236–7.

[2] A. R. Prest, 'Sense and nonsense in budgetary policy', *Economic Journal*, vol. 78, March 1968, p. 5.

[3] Sir John Hicks, *After the Boom*, London, Institute of Economic Affairs, 1966, p. 16.

[4] Treasury, *Public Expenditure White Papers: handbook on methodology*, p. 19.

that their expenditure must be autonomous at the margin, the main constraint being the inflexibility and unpopularity of the rates themselves. But local authority expenditure is in many ways similar to that of the central government, except insofar as priorities determined centrally may call for relative expansion of programmes in the local authority domain (particularly housing and education); some of these (housing, again, in particular) may pose special planning and control difficulties.[1] In respect of capital expenditure local authorities are, in fact, almost satellites of the central government, chiefly as a result of their inability to raise loans without government sanction.[2] Up to 1970/1 loans had to be approved for financing each project, despite the fact that 80 per cent or so of local capital spending was also subject to direct departmental control of some form or another and despite local authority complaints that meticulous control over the other 20 per cent was unwarranted in spheres of essentially local interest. The reforms of November 1970 rationalised the system, so that for 'key sector' programmes – housing, the bulk of education and roads – direct departmental sanction carried automatic borrowing approval; in the 'locally determined' sector local authorities may now set priorities within the framework of a block capital allocation which is fixed annually. It is here – in the environmental sector and the smaller road and education projects[3] – that counter-cyclical policy has traditionally been concentrated, since such projects have low priority and are thought, in the main, to have shorter planning horizons.

[1] See NIESR evidence, 'Local authority finance and the management of the economy', Appendix 6 to Department of the Environment, *Local Government Finance. Report of the Committee of Enquiry* [Layfield Report], Cmnd 6453, London, HMSO, 1976, pp. 48–80. The housing programme, for which local authorities are mainly responsible, largely accounts for the unpredictability which sometimes characterises local authority investment. Otherwise, neither this nor current expenditure has differed in regard to shortfalls, overruns or relative price effects from central government spending. Moreover, the *National Institute Economic Review*, no. 75, February 1976, pp. 86–9, shows that, for the period between 1970/1 and 1974/5, central and local spending did not display separate features *vis-à-vis* the expansion which occurred. The local authority contribution to the excess of 1974/5 spending levels over those planned in November 1971 appears to have been about 17 per cent – cf. Q. Outram, 'The significance of public expenditure plans' (unpublished working paper, Centre for Studies in Social Policy), London, 1975, pp. 16 and 34. There is strong evidence that difficulties in controlling programmes are linked more to the level of capital expenditure and to open-ended subsidies and transfers than to institutional factors, though time and cost overruns also vary significantly (see NEDO, Building and Civil Engineering Economic Development Committees, *The Public Client and the Construction Industry*, pp. 79 *et seq.*)
From the point of view of demand management, of course, it should be noted that rate-financed expenditure has only a second-order effect on fiscal leverage, since the financial balance of the authorities is not affected.

[2] This system was established in 1933 to prevent local authorities from burdening themselves with debt; it provided a readymade instrument for carrying out postwar employment policies (see Ministry of Reconstruction, *Employment Policy*, p. 21).

[3] 'Other environmental services' make up 50–60 per cent of the locally determined sector, education, libraries and the arts about 20 per cent, and roads 25 per cent.

Investment in nationalised industries presents special problems of control; its usefulness as a short-term instrument is limited by its strong market-orientation. The 1944 White Paper mentioned only that ways were being considered by which 'the programming of capital expenditure by public utility companies' could be used for counter-cyclical purposes;[1] local authority investment was supposed to be the principal instrument. In the event governments have been unable to ignore possible contributions to demand management from the nationalised industries, because of the impact of their capital spending on heavy engineering and transport. Public service investment, on the other hand, is predominantly in new building and works, so that the two sectors have complementary roles in stabilisation. The effectiveness of interventions in nationalised industries is, however, particularly questionable, not so much because the system of control is inadequate, nor because the industries do not try to respond to the wishes of the central government, but because their capital programmes are subject to forces – from the market and from suppliers – which tend to make marginal short-term adjustments futile. This is reflected in shortfalls of spending from planned levels, which disguise the effects of cuts and may nullify increases.

It is no doubt true that the control of public expenditure suffers from the divorce of responsible agencies from the centre, but the cause cannot be traced to inadequate institutional procedures. In the control of the purse strings and the legislative determination of priorities, the central government is more-or-less dominant in relation to both nationalised industries and local authorities, with the proviso regarding rates (see page 91 above). The problems lie rather in the efficient use of funds which are spent locally but raised mainly nationally. Agencies outside the central government are responsible for the detailed evaluation of projects and their execution is subject to market pressures. This gives scope for forecasting errors and for putting local and technocratic considerations before national economic ones. When things are favourable this may lead to over-compliance, while in adverse circumstances there may be a tendency to protect plans from short-term restrictions. It is doubtful, however, whether this resistance is any greater than the Treasury experiences within the central government from the spending Ministers and their departments.

[1] Ministry of Reconstruction, *Employment Policy*, p. 21.

PUBLIC EXPENDITURE AND RESOURCES
1959/60 TO 1973/4[1]

Introduction

There is nothing absolute about the share of resources to be pre-empted by the public sector, nor about its measurement. Measuring the public sector by reference to its own output or employment may be valid for some purposes, though there is no direct link between these magnitudes and the expenditure and revenue requirements of the budget. As an employer, the public sector has, during the period under review, used between 24 and 26 per cent of resources at a cost of 29–31 per cent of all employment income, but in spending terms 35 to 41 per cent of resources have passed through government hands.

Table 3.3. *The public sector's employment and wage bill, 1959–73*

Percentages

	Employment/working population				Wages and salaries/total employment income			
	1959	1964	1970	1973	1959	1964	1970	1973
Central government	7·71[a]	7·01	7·55	7·71	9·64	9·09	9·58	9·70
Local authorities	7·04	8·24	10·11	11·28	7·85	8·52	9·73	11·15
Public authorities	*14·75*	*15·25*	*17·66*	*18·99*	*17·49*	*17·61*	*19·31*	*20·85*
Public corporations	9·46[a]	8·22	7·95	7·27	11·56	10·26	10·14	10·00
PUBLIC SECTOR	24·21	23·47	25·61	26·26	29·05	27·87	29·45	30·85

SOURCE: CSO, *National Income and Expenditure 1964–74.*

[a] The Post Office is classified throughout as a public corporation, although it was part of central government until 1961.

Table 3.3 shows public sector employment as a proportion of the total working population (employed and unemployed) and the public sector's wage and salary bill as a proportion of total income from employment. The observations refer to years which were political dividing lines, since there have been quite explicit differences between the Parties on public expenditure and nationalisation. Nevertheless,

---

[1] For an analysis of trends in public spending in a historical context see Peacock and Wiseman, *The Growth of Public Expenditure in the United Kingdom* (for the period 1890–1955); J. Veverka, 'The growth of government expenditure in the United Kingdom since 1790' in A. T. Peacock and D. J. Robertson (eds.), *Public Expenditure: appraisal and control,* Edinburgh, Oliver & Boyd, 1963, pp. 111–27. Inter-country comparisons of expenditure growth between the years 1957 and 1965 are given in OECD, *Public Expenditure Trends in OECD Countries* by M. Garin-Painter, Paris, 1970. A discussion of the definition and measurement problems is to be found in T. E. Chester, 'The public sector – its dimensions and dynamics', *National Westminster Bank Review,* February 1976, pp. 31–44.

such trends as there are appear to hold for all three periods. The public corporations' share of the total workforce declined steadily from 9·46 per cent in 1959 to 7·27 per cent in 1973, despite the nationalisation of steel and as a result of the run-down in the coal industry and rail transport. Central government employment stayed fairly steady throughout, chiefly because the armed forces were reduced; without this it would have expanded fairly continuously, as did local authority employment, which went up over the period from about 7 per cent to over 11 per cent, with its wage bill matching this quite closely. However, the central government workforce is more expensive, so that for public authorities as a whole in 1973 the proportion of income was 21 per cent compared with a proportion of manpower of 19 per cent.

The public sector's demands on resources

Public employment is not an adequate measure of the public sector's impact as a supplier of social goods, as a distributor of resources among sections of the community, or as a vehicle of stabilisation policy. Current expenditure by public authorities includes purchases of goods and services from the private and overseas sectors which amount to about half as much again as is paid in direct wages and salaries. Only a very small fraction of their wage bill (about 1¼ per cent) is charged to capital accounts, since private contractors are used for most public investment projects. Conversely, some public sector employment goes towards satisfying private wants; certain elements of public service are charged for, and may be treated as private goods. Also, the operating accounts of the public corporations do not involve the use of public resources – only their surpluses (as revenue) and deficits (as subsidies to be met by public expenditure) appear in the published accounts, together with their capital spending and debt interest paid to non-government sources. Consolidated with public authorities' spending, these items provide a definition of public sector expenditure which is the basis of the analysis below.[1]

Translated into demands on resources at factor cost (which includes the relative price effect), direct public spending accounted for about 28 per cent of national resources in 1973/4 (slightly less than the 31 per cent public share of employment income), but to this must be added

[1] To comply with international practice, since 1977 a sharper distinction has been drawn – for both PESC and national accounts purposes – between 'general government' spending and that of the public enterprises. The former corresponds to central and local government expenditure; it includes government grants and loans to the public corporations, but not that part of their capital spending which is met by loans from other sources, nor their corresponding payments of debt interest. The use of the 'public sector' definition, which includes both of these, is justified here by the practice of both demand management and public expenditure control over the period under review, as well as by the fact that *all* public investment contributes to the borrowing requirement and to fiscal leverage.

Chart 3.2. *Public sector demands on resources relative to full-employment GDP,*
1959–1973/4

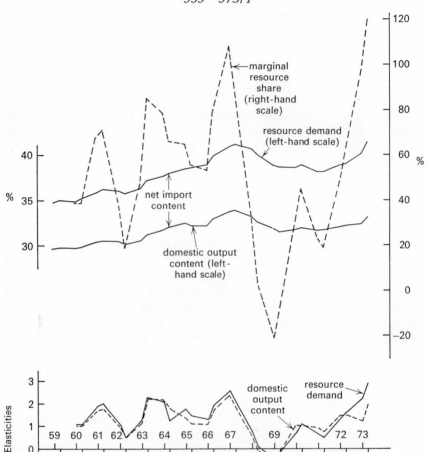

SOURCE: NIESR estimates.

Notes: (i) Public expenditure excludes investment grants and steel industry investment.
  (ii) Full-employment GDP defined as maintaining a level of 325,000 unemployed,
       with underlying productivity growth of 3·2 per cent per annum. Imputed rents
       of private and public sectors are excluded.
  (iii) Resource demand = total public expenditure net of net lending, imputed rents,
        indirect taxes on public expenditure, direct taxes on current grants, net
        purchases of land and existing buildings, estimated private sector savings out
        of current grants and stock appreciation.
  (iv) Marginal resource share is the year-to-year change in resource demand (at
       constant 1970 factor cost) as a ratio of the year-to-year change in real full-
       employment GDP.
  (v) Elasticities in the lower section are the ratios of year-to-year percentage changes
      in public expenditure (at 1970 factor cost) to the annual growth rate of full-
      employment GDP (3·2 per cent).

transfers and subsidies – publicly financed private expenditure – which raised the public share of resources to about 41 per cent. The necessity of raising revenue constrains both direct and indirect public expenditure, so that, in the context of the budget and fiscal policy, it makes sense to combine them into a single measure of aggregate public sector demand on resources. For estimates of this aggregate demand (shown in chart 3.2), the raw expenditure figures have been refined in various ways. First, variations in expenditure associated automatically with changes in the level of activity have been neutralised by recalculating the relevant expenditure at a full-employment level of activity; the items concerned are unemployment benefits and debt interest.[1] Secondly, some items of public expenditure are automatically associated with tax receipts and in such cases (for example, taxable current grants or government purchases subject to indirect taxes) expenditure is taken net of tax. Thirdly, the expenditure figures have been converted into terms of actual demand by allowing for savings offset against current transfers and netting out expenditure on the purchase of existing assets (for example, land). Finally, the short-run consequences for domestic output clearly depend on the import content of the demand for resources and a further adjustment is made for this.

Chart 3.2 therefore shows public expenditure redefined in 'weighted' terms, which enables it to be evaluated directly in relation to full-employment GDP at factor cost. Two measures are important: the estimates of *total* claims, including expenditure abroad, and of the direct demands on domestic production. While 'resource demand' is a measure of total resources pre-empted by public expenditure as a ratio of full-employment GDP, the 'marginal resource share' shows the resources allocated to the public sector out of GDP *growth* – that is, the year-to-year increment in public spending as a ratio of the corresponding increment in full-employment GDP (both at constant prices). The domestic output content is derived, also as a ratio of GDP, by deducting the net import content of expenditure.[2] Again we are talking in terms of

---

[1] Full-employment GDP is defined on the basis of 325,000 unemployed with an underlying growth rate of 3·2 per cent per annum. Expressing public expenditure in terms of constant employment abstracts from it items which involve no opportunity cost (since unemployment-related expenditure does not, by definition, pre-empt resources from alternative employment), while also netting out spending which is 'non-discretionary' through being related to the level of economic activity. The concept of the full-employment budget and its measurement are discussed further in chapter 4. Expenditure is not as sensitive to the level of unemployment as revenue, though unemployment benefits are significant. The adjustment for debt interest is small, being an estimate of the extra interest paid on the difference (in a particular year) between the full-employment deficit and the actual one (see *National Institute Economic Review*, no. 77, August 1976, pp. 21–4).

[2] This includes direct expenditure abroad, indirect imports in the form of inputs into domestic purchases and an allowance for the import content of purchases made by the recipients of current grants. So defined, the import content of public expenditure has crept

public demands on output, but overseas expenditure is excluded, because this does not (in the short run) contribute to domestic activity – that is, we have an estimate of the content of public spending which exercises demand 'leverage' on the domestic economy.[1] Changes in leverage occur both directly (by changes in public sector demand) and indirectly (through the multiplier) when the output content of expenditure changes. The *direct* changes involved in this process are shown in the lower part of chart 3.2 in the form of elasticities, which express the percentage change in the domestic output content of public expenditure as a ratio of the percentage change in productive potential. For comparison, changes in the resource measure of expenditure – gross of import content – are also shown in similar proportionate terms, and the two series can be seen to track each other quite closely.

The chart shows very clearly the profile of expansion up to 1967 (with the elasticity measure almost always in excess of unity), the turn-round after devaluation and the subsequent resurgence. Between 1959 and 1973/4, the total resource cost of public expenditure rose from some 35 to 41¼ per cent of potential GDP – a rate of increase about 1 per cent per annum above the underlying economic growth rate of 3·2 per cent. Indirect claims were the fastest growing element, their share of potential GDP expanding from 10·3 to 14·1 per cent, but direct claims also raised their share from 24·7 to 27·2 per cent. At the peaks of public sector expansion, in 1961/2, 1963/4, 1967 and 1973/4, demands on resources emanating from the public sector increased by between 72 and 130 per cent of the real absolute change in full-employment GDP, or 2–3 times the percentage change. All of these expansions involved a discretionary contra-cyclical element, although in the middle years the expansion was also a function of a conscious longer-run shift in policy.

---

up from 15 to 20 per cent as shown in the chart. In the resource definition of expenditure (as used for planning purposes), the import content is counted as an element of demand, on the basis that in the long run the balance of payments must be zero; consequently, any increase in net public sector demands for imports must be met by a corresponding decrease in the private sector's net imports. In terms of the leverage exerted by public expenditure on domestic output, the import content is given a zero weight, there being no presumption that the net imports of the private sector adjust so as to keep the external balance the same.

[1] Leverage refers to the *net* effect of the budget in raising or lowering aggregate demand. Like expenditure, some elements of taxation have a larger effect on production than others, so these have to be weighted too, the balance of expenditure and revenue then being the 'weighted' budget balance (see chapter 4, pages 183–9). It would be possible to define leverage as the difference between *actual* weighted expenditure and *actual* weighted receipts, but the measure implied here is one which nets out the non-discretionary element associated with the cycle (see R. A. Musgrave, 'On measuring fiscal performance', *Review of Economics and Statistics*, vol. 46, May 1964, and R. A. and P. B. Musgrave, 'Fiscal policy' in R. E. Caves and Associates, *Britain's Economic Prospects*, London, Allen & Unwin, 1968, pp. 40–2). The choice of an 'elasticity' measure to depict direct changes in leverage in the following analysis is presentational, since it perhaps best expresses the degree of expansion and contraction in public spending relative to the underlying expansion of the economy.

Public sector output and the volume of expenditure

The demands of public expenditure on resources include the cost of maintaining the relative incomes of public employees in the face of lower (recorded) productivity growth for the public authorities, which leads to the deflators for public expenditure increasing faster than those for GDP as a whole – the relative price effect. Part of the expansion in public demand relative to GDP has thus been due to (adverse) price trends, not to increases in public output, as may be seen from table 3.4, which shows the annual average growth rates of expenditure for a number of categories over the period 1959–73. Increases in the total volume of expenditure (first column),[1] which represent the growth in the supply of public services, were achieved at an average annual rate of 3·55 per cent per annum (an elasticity of 1·17 with respect to the underlying GDP growth rate), while the total cost of programmes increased at an average rate of 4·3 per cent.[2] The difference of 0·75 per cent can be ascribed to the relative price effect, which is shown in the second column. The *net* resource cost of expenditure, as we have seen above, grows at a slightly different rate from the gross cost, and this is also shown as being 4·15 per cent over this period.

The chief source of adverse relative price effects can be traced to public authority wages and salaries (table 3.3). Current expenditure on goods and services, to which most of this applies, increased by an average of 2·45 per cent in volume from 1959 to 1973, compared with 3·85 per cent in terms of cost (table 3.4); military defence was the main programme held back, whereas the provision of education and other services increased relative to GDP (note *e*). But the slower growth of the health services shows that the relative price effect is an important constraint on expansion. Overall, public authority current expenditure on goods and services has pre-empted an increasing proportion of resources, while forming a diminishing part of output; *ex-post*, it

[1] The derivation of expenditure *volumes* depends on the existence of price indices relating to the various services provided. As far as the national accounts are concerned, deflators are available for current expenditure on goods and services in four sectors – defence, health, education and 'other'. Capital expenditure deflators may be derived for the various assets on which money is spent (new buildings and works, plant and machinery, etc.). Transfers are evaluated notionally, according to the purchasing power of income in the hands of the general public (that is, by reference to the consumer price index, or to the GDP factor cost deflator in the case of items like debt interest). From these deflators it is then possible to derive deflators applicable to the various programmes and spending authorities by referring to the economic analysis of public sector programmes (CSO, *National Income and Expenditure 1964–74*, London, HMSO, 1975, table 58) and to the asset composition of capital spending programmes. For a discussion of the difficulties involved in creating estimates of public sector output, see Godley, 'The measurement and control of public expenditure'.

[2] The price index relevant to the *real* cost of public expenditure is the GDP factor cost deflator.

Table 3.4. *Public expenditure by category in volume and cost terms: changes, 1959–73*

	Volume[a]	Relative price effect	Total cost[b]	Net resource cost[bc]	Volume growth/ GDP growth[d]
	(annual average percentage changes)				(ratios)
Current expenditure					
On goods and services					
Central government	1·10	1·40	2·50	2·65	*0·34*
Local authorities	4·70	1·40	6·10	5·90	*1·46*
Public authorities[e]	2·45	1·40	3·85	3·80	*0·77*
Transfers					
Current grants to persons	5·80[f]	−0·25	5·55	5·70	*1·80*
Subsidies	5·15	—	5·15	4·80	*1·72*
Total transfers[g]	4·75	−0·15	4·60	4·90	*1·48*
TOTAL CURRENT EXPENDITURE	3·40	0·80	4·20	4·20	*1·07*
Capital expenditure[h]					
Central government[i]	6·00	1·05	7·05	6·55	*1·88*
Local authorities[j]	5·90	0·90	6·80	6·55	*1·84*
Public corporations[k]	1·20	−0·15	1·05	1·30	*0·38*
Public sector GDFCF	3·95	0·45	4·40	4·25	*1·23*
TOTAL INVESTMENT	4·30	0·40	4·70	4·55	*1·34*
TOTAL PUBLIC EXPENDITURE[hl]	3·55	0.75	4.30	4.15	*1·17*

SOURCES: CSO, *National Income and Expenditure 1964–74* and *National Income and Expenditure 1970* London, HMSO, 1970.

[a] Expenditure deflated by own-price indices (base 1970), but see notes *f* and *g*.
[b] Expenditure deflated by the GDP factor cost deflator.
[c] As total cost, but 'weighted' to allow for the true demand effect.
[d] GDP growth taken as 3·2 per cent.
[e] Public authorities' current expenditure on goods and services can be disaggregated as follows:

	Volume	Relative price effect	Total cost	Net resource cost	Volume growth/ GDP growth
	(annual average percentages changes)				(ratios)
Military defence	−0·80	1·55	0·75	0·75	*−0·25*
Health	2·80	1·50	4·30	4·30	*0·88*
Education	4·80	1·40	6·20	6·20	*1·50*
Other	4·10	1·15	5·25	5·20	*1·28*

[f] Expenditure deflated by the consumer price index.
[g] Including debt interest and grants abroad which (with subsidies) are deflated by the GDP factor cost deflator.
[h] Excluding net lending and investment grants.
[i] Including grants to universities.
[j] Including housing improvement grants.
[k] Excluding British Steel Corporation.

Table 3.4 cont.

l Total public expenditure can be disaggregated as follows:

	Volume	Relative price effect	Total cost	Volume growth/ GDP growth
	(annual average percentage changes)			(ratios)
Military defence	−0·95	1·70	0·75	−0·30
Health	3·25	1·65	4·90	1·56
Education	5·50	1·15	6·65	1·72
Roads	4·70	1·80	6·50	1·47
Housing*	6·25	0·75	7·00	1·95
Environmental	6·40	1·20	7·60	2·00

* For 1959/60–1973/4, see 'Treasury analysis of public expenditure' in CSO, *National Income and Expenditure 1964–74*, p. 132.

seems that about half of the relative price effect has been met by allowing the cost of such spending to grow at 0.7 per cent per annum above underlying GDP, while the volume growth has been kept below GDP to an equal extent.

Current transfers have been relatively expansionary, the more so in volume terms because of a favourable relative price effect. The increase in current grants and subsidies can be traced to reasons of social and economic policy. Social security benefits have been a method of redistributing income and of reflation, while subsidies combine both these uses with the further one of combating inflation. Neither grants nor subsidies grew very smoothly, both being subject to recurrent bouts of expansion and inflationary erosion.

Despite the popularity of capital expenditure as a short-term deflationary instrument, it has been relatively fast-growing in volume terms (an average annual increase of 3·95 per cent). Fixed investment by central government and by local authorities provided the chief momentum, both expanding at a rate of about 6 per cent per annum. Investment in nationalised industries, on the other hand, was a declining proportion of GDP for the period as a whole (despite a favourable relative price effect of −0·15 per cent); up to devaluation its expansion was very rapid, being based on the unrealised economic growth target of 4 per cent, but this was followed, from 1968 onwards, by a substantial decline. Public authority investment is relatively concentrated on land and construction, where prices rose very fast in the period 1971–3, so that the relative price effect was positive. In general, this effect is less important in capital spending than on the current side, though it is subject to more cyclical fluctuation, making it less predictable. However, there also tend to be 'unforeseen' relative price effects on current spending when public sector incomes are successively held back and given free rein – as happened in the period 1971–4.[1]

The programme which expanded most consistently was education, both this and the National Health Service being subject to medium-term plans, but it has been in housing and the environment that the greatest increases have taken place, both sectors being subject to cyclical fluctuation (note *l*). The housing programme particularly was successively restricted (up to 1962/3 and between 1969 and 1971) and allowed to expand (from 1963 to 1967 and from 1972 through to 1976). Investment in water and sewerage has been the most consistent impetus to the environmental programme, while sub-sectors with lower priority have been restrained or exhorted to expand according to the short-term economic climate; for such elements, average rates of growth would be quite different if a different period was taken.

Growth of public expenditure: its determinants

Ideas vary about the causes of the relative expansion observed in the public sector, with a tendency to seek explanations that are universally valid in the long run for what is considered a general process, rather than to view it against the background of the time. The particular circumstances of the period seem to provide at least an adequate explanation of experience in the United Kingdom, especially the mis-specification of planning constraints, the inadequate appreciation of relative price effects and the displacement effects of counter-cyclical policy.[2] But perhaps these are also expressions of a more general tendency for the sector to expand and there are other more fundamental factors at work as well. Other commentators have stressed in turn:

(a) structural factors linked to the process of growth, industrialisation and demographic trends;

(b) institutional and financial control factors;

(c) behavioural imperfections by consumers of public goods;

(d) 'social disturbance' and factors which force the government to assume temporarily greater responsibilities, but which have displacement effects leaving some of the increase as permanent.

This last hypothesis has been put forward by Peacock and Wiseman as a possible explanation of longer-run historical developments.

In the much shorter historical perspective of the postwar years the applicability of the last theory would seem to be limited, though there are undoubtedly displacement effects resulting from economic contingencies, particularly reflationary reactions to unemployment. Displacement effects linked to changes in administration (the electoral

---

[1] See *National Institute Economic Review*, no. 75, February 1976, pp. 87–9.
[2] Peacock and Wiseman, *The Growth of Public Expenditure in the United Kingdom*, pp. 24 *et seq.*

cycle) also offer a possible explanation, though it is doubtful whether this goes deep enough. Of the structural biases tending to increase public expenditure, the most obvious is the tendency towards a lower real level of public service for a given outlay. This may be partly due to the adverse relative price effect on public output, but may also derive from demographic trends;[1] if these produce (as in the United Kingdom) an increasing proportion of the population above retiring age, an increase in the public sector proportional to GDP would mean a lower growth of services per recipient, so that maintaining a given quality entails a relative expansion in health and social services. On the other hand, a fall in the school population (as experienced in the 1970s) has the opposite effect. Similar arguments stress the effects of economic growth – industrialisation and urbanisation – on the expansion of government activity; others have suggested that the growth of income has a similar effect on public services to that on all services, which tend to have a relatively high income elasticity of demand.[2] But while it is easy to see how all these factors may influence individual programmes, their effect on aggregate public spending is impossible to quantify.

So far as institutional and financial factors are concerned, the analysis above has emphasised the deficiencies of strategic control, which seems to be effective so long as it is negative and restrictive, but less so when it is a matter of positive planning for systematic expansion.[3] The role of the local authorities as *causal* factors in the growth process has been discounted, though the system of local authority finance cannot be said to make for an efficient allocation of resources. The authorities' expenditure functions bear no relation to their income, which comes substantially from the central government, so that the system facilitates overexpansion even when the cause is central legislation. This suggests the wider question of whether (as is frequently argued) the separation between the expenditure and revenue-raising functions of government generally leads to over-expansion of the public sector due to the lack of any short-term budget constraint. As we have seen above, public spending shifts are associated with budget deficits, but this is connected with the stabilisation role of the budget and governments cannot escape from a longer-term budget constraint. The fact that they can do so in the short-term, however, may mean that the inevitable correction in the longer term will be made partly by higher tax rates, leaving a net expansion. If this argument is correct it leads us to discard an alternative

[1] For a list of demographic factors affecting the size of the public sector see OECD, *Public Expenditure Trends in OECD Countries*, p. 54.

[2] Peacock and Wiseman, *The Growth of Public Expenditure in the United Kingdom*, p. 22; C. T. Sandford, *Economics of Public Finance*, Oxford, Pergamon, 1969, pp. 228–31.

[3] Cf. C. T. Sandford and P. N. Dean, 'Public expenditure: the paradox of control', *The Banker*, vol. 120, April 1970, pp. 377 *et seq.*

theory about the expansion of public spending – that it is linked to a process of 'natural budget reaction', by which expenditure responds to the buoyancy of tax receipts.[1] This does not seem to fit the case of the United Kingdom, though fiscal drag is useful *ex post* in financing the net growth of expenditure once deficit-financing has become cyclically inopportune.

The detachment of costs from the benefits of public expenditure may affect individuals as well as governments. If public services benefit particular sub-groups, while tax costs are more widely shared, then over-supply can result because part of the cost can be shifted to non-beneficiaries.[2] Alternatively, there is a more politically influential hypothesis of under-expansion put forward by Professor Galbraith.[3] Whether or not one accepts his idea that individual choices may be distorted from a true preference system by advertising, the possibility that legislators have been influenced to correct for this is very real.[4] Behavioural arguments about a built-in bias in either direction cannot readily be verified, but it is interesting that either may lead to the growth of the public sector – the first automatically, the second by discretionary correction. Like the structural arguments, their net impact is impossible to translate into figures, so that how far the more observable and quantifiable effects of shortcomings in planning and control are proxies for more deep-rooted expansionary impulses remains undetermined.

IMPLEMENTING POLICY: INTENTIONS AND OUT-TURNS

Earlier we set out changes in total public expenditure after adjustment for the automatically stabilising elements within it. As so defined these figures include shortfalls and overruns in comparison with plan; further, changes in the level of spending may be due as much to autonomous factors (such as demographic trends) as to discretionary policy decisions about the 'quality' of service provided. All these elements are important in determining the reliability and flexibility of public expenditure as an instrument of demand management; by the same token, they complicate the task of diagnosing policy success by obscuring both the true nature of 'policy' changes themselves and the extent to which they are implemented. (It was understandable, for example, that the House of

[1] OECD, *Fiscal Policy in Seven Countries, 1955–1965* by B. Hansen, Paris, 1969; however the United Kingdom is not cited as one of the countries subject to this phenomenon. The case that public spending is induced by inflationary tax buoyancy has been used in the argument for indexation (see D. R. Morgan, *Over-taxation by Inflation*, London, Institute for Economic Affairs, 1977, p. 16).

[2] See Musgrave and Musgrave, *Public Finance*, pp. 98–100, for a fuller discussion.

[3] J. K. Galbraith, *The Affluent Society*, London, Hamish Hamilton, 1958.

[4] See M. J. Artis, 'Fiscal policy for stabilization' in Beckerman (ed.), *The Labour Government's Economic Record 1964–1970*, p. 265, and Sandford and Dean, 'Public expenditure', p. 376.

Table 3.5. *Demand management and short-term interventions in public expenditure, 1960–73*

Date of announcement	Effect in financial year	Current expenditure, announced effect		Public investment — Announced effect		Discretionary factor[a]	Realisation factor[b]
		Current prices	1970 prices	Current prices	1970 prices		
		(£ million)				(%)	(%)
23 June 1960	1961/2	—	—	..	−75	—	10
25 July 1961	1962/3	−175	−265	..	−25	—	—
9 Oct. 1962	{ 1962/3	—	—	+15	+21 }	35	100
	1963/4	—	—	+83	+115		
27 July 1965	{ 1965/6	−7	−9	{ −65^c / −50^d	−80^c / −70^d }	50	100
	1966/7	−6	−8	−70^d	−100^d	100	85
20 July 1966	1967/8	−100	−130	−150	−175	70	60
18 Nov. 1967 }	{ 1968/9	−129	−138	−163^e	−184^e	67	94
16 Jan. 1968 }	1969/70	−275	−294	−213	−239	74	100
July 1971 }	{ 1971/2	+3	+2	+33	+30 }		{ 100
to }	1972/3	+147	+124	+270	+241 }	100	70
May 1972 }	1973/4	+62	+53	+197	+180 }		—
21 May 1973	{ 1973/4	−14	−11	−92	−68	10	100
	1974/5	−198	−152	−341	−254	—	100
8 Oct. 1973	1973/4	−19	−15	−97	−72	10	100
17 Dec. 1973	1974/5	−329	−250	−851	−655	60	55

SOURCES: House of Commons, *Hansard* and Expenditure Committee Reports; Annual Reports of Department of Education, Ministry of Housing and Local Government, British Transport Commission, Electricity Council, Gas Council and National Coal Board; Department of Economic Affairs, *The National Plan* (Cmnd 2764); Treasury, *Public Investment in Great Britain* (Cmnd 1203), *Public Investment in Great Britain, October 1961* (Cmnd 1522, London HMSO, 1961), *Public Investment in Great Britain, October 1962* (Cmnd 1849), *Public Investment in Great Britain, October 1963* (Cmnd 2177), *Public Expenditure: planning and control* (Cmnd 2915), *Public Expenditure in 1968–69 and 1969–70* (Cmnd 3515), *Public Expenditure 1968–69 to 1973–74* (Cmnd 4234), *Public Expenditure 1969–70 to 1974–75* (Cmnd 4578), *Public Expenditure 1969–70 to 1975–76*, (Cmnd 4829), *Public Expenditure to 1976–77* (Cmnd 5178), *Public Expenditure to 1977–78* (Cmnd 5519) and *Public Expenditure to 1978–79*, Cmnd 5879, London, HMSO, 1975).

^{a} The proportion of the announced effect which cannot be attributed to estimating changes – identified from discrepancies between programme forecasts and out-turns and from Annual Reports of departments and nationalised industries.

^{b} The proportion of the announced effect actually achieved – aggregated from an analysis of individual programmes. Offsetting changes in exempted programmes (e.g. housing in 1967/8 and 1974/5) not included.

^{c} For public corporations.

^{d} For public authorities.

^{e} Excluding a cut of £80 million in investment grants.

Commons Expenditure Committee should mistrust the 1973 cuts,[1] which were announced at a time when public expenditure was falling short of planned totals.) In what follows an attempt has been made to estimate the authenticity and effectiveness of announced variations in public expenditure after taking account of such elements. The results, summarised in table 3.5, are inevitably subjective to some extent.

Ministerial speeches and White Papers provide a series of announcements of cuts or increases, for each of which, as it affected capital expenditure, two factors have been calculated. The 'discretionary factor' estimates the proportion of the announced intervention which can properly be termed 'discretionary'; it discounts the announced figure for changes due simply to revised estimates for a given programme, or to changes in a programme which would have occurred anyway (for example, a change in school building due to revised demographic forecasts). The 'realisation factor' estimates the proportion of an announced intervention (whether properly discretionary or not) which was carried through. The basis for evaluating each of these components for the various interventions is discussed below in a historical context.

However, it would be a mistake to view the contribution of public expenditure to short-term demand management solely in the light of *announced* interventions. Short-term changes are frequently accompanied by shifts in longer-term programmes, which are relevant to the stabilisation function of the budget because they involve changes in the budget balance. Taking account of these, public expenditure makes a contribution to demand management which is sometimes larger than the announced change, or sometimes in the opposite direction. Table 3.6 therefore shows the announced public expenditure changes in the context of realised changes in both the budget deficit and overall public spending, all expressed as proportions of full-employment GDP.[2]

The effectiveness of policy – both long-term and short-term – depends substantially on the reliability of long-term plans and how far they are implemented. Charts 3.3 and 3.4 therefore show both planned expenditure and short-term deviations from plan against the realised growth paths of the major categories of expenditure, in order to appraise the effectiveness of expenditure management.[3] The hatched areas indicate

---

[1] House of Commons, *Eleventh Report from the Expenditure Committee, Session 1972–73. The May 21st Expenditure Cuts*, London, HMSO, 1973, pp. viii and 14.

[2] A further discussion of this weighted budget impact is to be found in chapter 4; the expenditure figures correspond to those given in chart 4.7.

[3] Public Expenditure White Papers have been published annually since 1969, so that there is a series of plans from that date. Previously, there was a plan from the NEDC, *Growth of the United Kingdom Economy to 1966*, London, HMSO, 1963, and from the Department of Economic Affairs, *The National Plan*; early in the 1960s there were also regular Public Investment White Papers looking two to three years ahead. Budget forecasts have contained one-year forecasts of the major economic spending categories since 1966/7. The plans are

Table 3.6. *Short-term interventions in public expenditure and changes in the budget deficit,[a] 1959/60–1974/5*

Percentages of full-employment GDP

	Public expenditure[b]		Change in budget deficit
	Change in total	Announced intervention(s)	
1960/1	+0·03	—	+0·28
1961/2	−0·75	+0·18	+0·55
1962/3	+0·49	+0·53	+0·64
1963/4	−1·17	−0·24	−1·76
1964/5	−0·76	—	−0·13
1965/6	−0·18	+0·30	+1·47
1966/7	−0·72	+0·34	−0·14
1967/8	−0·89	+0·32	−0·35
1968/9	+1·13	+0·53	+2·75
1969/70	+1·10	+0·84	+2·69
1970/1	−0·38	—	−0·95
1971/2	+0·26	−0·05	−1·09
1972/3	−0·50	−0·55	−1·86
1973/4	−0·85	−0·20	−0·88
1974/5	−2·05	+1·85	−1·93

SOURCES: as table 3·5; NIESR estimates.

[a] Public expenditure and the budget deficit both output-weighted.

[b] The contribution of changes in public expenditure to budgetary leverage, as shown here, is of the opposite sign to the actual spending changes.

announced short-term deviations from plan, while the difference between the plans and the out-turn are shortfalls or overruns. In the light of these it is also possible to make an impressionistic judgement of the true nature of the adjustments as a background to table 3.5.

The first Conservative administration, 1959/60–October 1964

The first two interventions of the period covered by this study seem to have had little effect. The first, in June 1960, was an announcement that public investment programmes for 1961/2 would be kept to the same real level as in 1960/1. Allowing for a possible 3 per cent growth rate, this probably represented a potential saving of £75 million (at 1970 prices),[1] but no short-term adjustment was needed – the savings were to come from an autonomous decline in nationalised industries' programmes, with public authority investment still scheduled to increase

all expressed in terms of constant survey prices, while the out-turns are in terms of 1970 prices. The charts therefore refer to the volume of expenditure and do not contain the relative price effect.

[1] All the intervention figures given below are in volume terms at 1970 prices, though table 3.5 also gives them in current prices.

Chart 3.3. *Public authorities' current expenditure, planned and out-turn,
1959–1974/5*

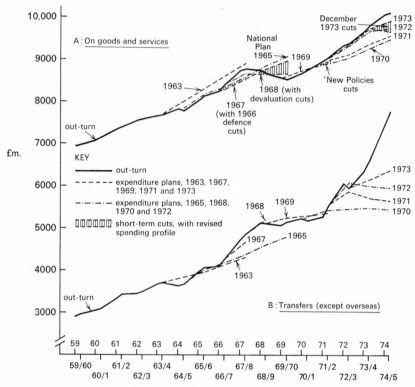

SOURCES: CSO, *National Income and Expenditure 1964–74* and *Economic Trends, Annual Supplement 1975*, London, HMSO, 1975; Department of Economic Affairs, *The National Plan*; Treasury White Papers as table 3.5.

Notes: (i) Expenditure is in volume terms at 1970 prices.
(ii) Expenditure planned in 1971 shown after short-term increases.
(iii) Expenditure on goods and services planned in 1972 shown after cuts in May and October 1973.

substantially. In addition, the pressure of demand in 1960, to which the intervention was a response, began causing shortfalls, so that the real discretionary element in the intervention must have been very small. The extent of the shortfall could not have been accurately known at the time, but, in conjunction with the ceiling, it implied an eventual increase of 5 per cent in public investment for 1961/2. In fact, investment increased by about 8 per cent – some £75 million over the imposed limit – so that even the nominal saving was negligible.

In the summer of 1961 further intervention was needed to salvage the

Chart 3.4. *Public sector capital expenditure, planned and out-turn, 1959–1974/5*

A: *Central government*

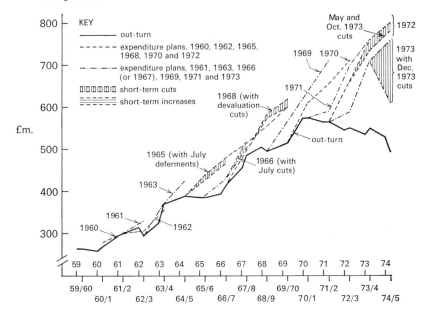

£m.

KEY
— out-turn
--- expenditure plans, 1960, 1962, 1965, 1968, 1970 and 1972
–·–· expenditure plans, 1961, 1963, 1966 (or 1967), 1969, 1971 and 1973
▯▯▯▯▯ short-term cuts
▭▭▭ short-term increases

May and Oct. 1973 cuts · 1972 · 1973 with Dec. 1973 cuts

1969 1970 1971

1968 (with devaluation cuts)

out-turn

1965 (with July deferments)

1966 (with July cuts)

1963

1961 1962

1960

B: *Local authorities*

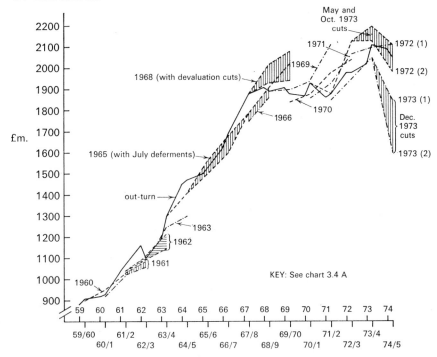

£m.

May and Oct. 1973 cuts

1971 1969 1972 (1)

1968 (with devaluation cuts) 1972 (2)

1970 1973 (1)

1966

Dec. 1973 cuts

1965 (with July deferments) 1973 (2)

out-turn

1963

1962

1961

1960

KEY: See chart 3.4 A

Chart 3.4 *cont.*

C: *Nationalised industries*

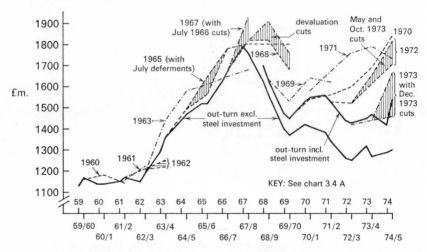

SOURCES: CSO, *Economic Trends, Annual Supplement 1975, Financial Statistics*, October 1975, and *Annual Abstract of Statistics, 1974*, London, HMSO, 1974; Department of Economic Affairs, *The National Plan*; Treasury White Papers as table 3.5.

Notes: (i)   Capital expenditure is gross domestic fixed capital formation in volume terms at 1970 prices.

(ii) Expenditure planned in 1971 shown after short-term increases.

(iii) Planned expenditures by the central government and local authorities do not include the provision for shortfalls made since December 1969 because no separate figures available.

(iv) Local authority investment includes capital grants to the private sector, also health and water investment throughout (although the functions were removed in 1973/4).

(v)   December 1973 cuts by local authorities take no account of increases in housing investment.

(vi) Planned investment by nationalised industries excludes steel up to 1966/7 and includes investment by the British Steel Corporation thereafter.

'critical external situation', but the effect realised was, like that of the previous adjustment, indistinguishable from zero. It was announced that total capital expenditure by local authorities in 1962/3 'should not significantly exceed the (real) level of the current year'. The nationalised industries were excluded because they were now seen as obliged to make a commercial return on capital, so that it was proposed to allow them the investment needed to reach their financial targets.[1] At the same time, however, current expenditure was to be controlled in the medium term in the way that Plowden had suggested by being restricted to a 2½ per cent real increase, which, in fact, reduced it by £265 million. This

[1] House of Commons, *Hansard*, 26 July 1961, col. 435.

saving was part of a general move to bring expenditure into a 'proper relationship with resources likely to be available in the long term'.[1]

Whether the adjustments to investment were intended to be cosmetic or not, they were certainly ineffective; before the year was out strategy was reversed towards reflation, but even before that local authority programmes were expanding faster than was compatible with the restriction. However, the intention to restrict current expenditure was undoubtedly real; although Selwyn Lloyd was to express concern as to whether the objective was being met in the House of Commons on 27 February,[2] the historical record confirms that its volume growth was constrained to $2\frac{1}{2}$ per cent.

The intervention of 1961 was made otiose by the falling off in economic activity which became apparent after the 1962 budget. During the summer and autumn of that year additional investment was authorised for local authorities and nationalised industries, to be phased over the remainder of 1962/3 and 1963/4, with most of the impact in the latter year, when the increases were to be 6 per cent for local authorities and 2 per cent for the nationalised industries. The additions scheduled for 1962/3 were forestalled by the severe winter, but would otherwise have been achieved. As can be seen from charts 3.4B and C, the conjunction of reflationary and growth objectives provided an impetus to the programmes of both local authorities and nationalised industries which carried public expenditure forward (with the help of the National Plan) to 1967. The intervention in nationalised industries looks small in comparison with the subsequent secular additions, while part of the short-term increase in public authority programmes was really a secular adjustment; in housing, for example, there was a prior commitment to an increase to solve the housing and slum-clearance problem of the big cities.[3] A significant characteristic of this reflation was the large secular upswing in expenditure which went with it and dwarfed the actual counter-cyclical (phased) element. The projected public investment increase for 1963/4 was raised from 8 to 22 per cent between October 1962 and October 1963,[4] which must be attributed to the conjunction of short-term needs with the revised medium-term goals implied by the higher growth objectives.

Of these three interventions, therefore, the first two were subject to shortfalls and the third to a large additional upswing, which made the

---

[1] Ibid. 25 July 1961, col. 224.

[2] The estimates for 1962/3 exceeded the target set by £111 million (current) or about 60 per cent of the real intended saving.

[3] Ministry of Housing and Local Government, *Housing in England and Wales*, Cmnd 1290, London, HMSO, 1961.

[4] Treasury, *Public Investment in Great Britain. October 1962*, Cmnd 1849, and *Public Investment in Great Britain. October 1963*, Cmnd 2177, London, HMSO, 1962 and 1963.

realised profile of public investment different from what was intended. Chart 3.5 shows the actual and intended annual growth rates of public investment as ratios of the long-run growth rate of GDP, to give an elasticity measure of the pressure being exerted on the economy by this sector.[1] Defining neutrality as an elasticity of 1, the intention in 1960/1 can be seen to have been neutral, although the actual out-turn was deflationary because supply constraints led to programme shortfalls. The out-turn in 1961/2 was expansionary (an elasticity of nearly 3), although supposed to be moderately restrictive. In 1962/3 the bad winter aborted contradictory attempts at stabilisation; on the other hand, the reflationary strategy of 1963/4 was compounded by secular programme increases, which gave an elasticity of nearly 6 when the real counter-cyclical impact was supposed to have been a third of this.

The medium-term forecasts of public expenditure as a whole which were published in December 1963 envisaged a 4·1 per cent average growth rate after 1963/4 up to 1967/8, with a 5½ per cent average growth rate for public investment;[2] together with the large increase which had already occurred in 1963/4, this represented an expansion of 8·6 per cent per annum over the period from 1962/3. Thus, by 1963 public investment had well and truly taken off.

Labour administrations, October 1964–June 1970

On assuming office in October 1964, the Labour government found in its predecessor's plans 'a lack of balance and absence of proper social and economic priorities'.[3] But the purpose of most expenditure was 'sound enough', so that outside the spheres of defence and social security little was to be altered. In public investment, the strong momentum in nationalised industries' and housing programmes was to be maintained under the National Plan. Both were considered crucial to faster growth,[4] and both were to play a critical part in the expansion of the public sector up to devaluation and subsequently.

The reappraisal of defence expenditure aimed at a saving of £550 million up to 1969/70, with a reduction of £50 million in 1965/6 from cancellation of the TSR-2.[5] Expenditure on defence was to be kept at the same real level as 1964/5 and up to 1967/8 this was almost achieved – the real annual average growth being 0·7 per cent (although this was

---

[1] See below page 117 and cf. the lower part of chart 3.2.

[2] Treasury, *Public Expenditure in 1963–64 and 1967–68.*

[3] Prime Minister's Office, *The Economic Situation,* p. 2.

[4] The evidence suggested 'that the most successful housebuilding countries lead the United Kingdom at least partly because they have chosen to devote a greater proportion of their national resources to housing' (Ministry of Housing and Local Government, *The Housing Programme 1965–1970,* Cmnd 2838, London, HMSO, 1965, p. 3).

[5] House of Commons, *Hansard,* 6 April 1965, col. 280. At 1965 prices the figures were £400 million and £35 million respectively.

only what it had been over the preceding three years). Nevertheless, partly because of this, the National Plan was able to show a reduction in the annual average growth rate of current expenditure on goods and services to 3 per cent (from $3\frac{3}{4}$ per cent in the Conservative plan). However, despite this downward shift (chart 3.3), the out-turn up to 1967/8 was 4 per cent not 3 per cent. Moreover, the shift in the schedule probably had as much to do with the shortfall in expenditure in 1964/5 (for which defence expenditure was largely responsible) as with discretionary action.

Compensating for this reduction, the new administration calculated on increasing current transfers to the personal sector (particularly social security benefits) at a rate of 6 per cent per annum between 1964/5 and 1968/9 (chart 3.3B). A feature of the period up to devaluation was the constant upward revision of this target; in the event this component of current expenditure grew at a real average rate of $9\frac{3}{4}$ per cent per annum up to 1967/8.

There was no substantial attempt at short-term intervention in the current sector until January 1968. Meanwhile, however, there were two deflationary packages aimed at public investment. The first, on 27 July 1965, followed large increases in taxation in the 1965 budget and, while there were no further revenue increases, included tighter hire purchase terms and a six-month moratorium on project starts by public authorities – housing, schools and hospitals being excepted, so that road and local authority environmental expenditure bore the brunt of the adjustment. The cuts were to save £70 million in 1965/6 and £100 million in the following year.[1] This seems to have fallen short of the Treasury's original target,[2] but appears to have been almost fully implemented (see table 3.5). By 8 February 1966 the Chancellor was able to announce that the cuts 'had achieved their purpose'; in particular, the rate of expenditure on capital projects had been appreciably reduced. Though the moratorium did not apply to the nationalised industries, these were urged 'to follow a similar course of action', in deferring the purchase of goods to the 'maximum possible extent' without compromising projects essential for economic growth and the National Plan.[3] Expenditure of £80 million was ostensibly deferred in 1965/6, but a substantial element of this might have come from short-falls in the electricity programme.

Observers at the time and subsequently have tried to identify this intervention as the moment when the government abandoned its

[1] Small savings of £9 and £8 million were announced in current expenditure.
[2] '... by the time we had made exemptions for the things which were either contracted for, or had been committed... its effect was not nearly as big as it was designed to achieve' (House of Commons, *Seventh Report from the Expenditure Committee, Session 1971–72*, p. 9).
[3] Treasury, *Public Expenditure: planning and control*, p. 14.

growth objective.[1] In terms of its public expenditure plans, however, this is not true. First, the deferments did not affect the major programmes at the heart of the National Plan and excess housing investment was to compensate for 40 per cent of the cuts. Secondly, there was the short-fall in central government investment and the nationalised industries' programmes, where the responsiveness of the electricity programme to market factors and to the secular increase in investment in natural gas was to provide a reservoir of readymade 'cuts'. Thirdly, deferment was really what it said – a rephasing – which meant that road and education schemes would be reallocated over the remaining period of the Plan. This was done at the beginning of 1966 and restraint continued only in local authority environmental programmes.

Public investment in 1966/7 still came to a 'formidable total', and the objective of demand management in 1966 remained the moderation of consumption to finance the expansion of the public sector. Though the Chancellor believed that 'government expenditure would not make excessive new claims on the economy', some observers did not agree.[2] The intervention of July 1966, however, was as much a response to the sterling crisis of June – a result of the seamen's strike and the world liquidity shortage – as to inflated demand *per se*. The cuts were in 1967/8 programmes. Reductions of £130 million in defence and over-seas spending were to help the balance of payments directly. Public authority investment was to be cut by £65 million, with the same exceptions and priorities as in 1965. Though there is little doubt that environmental investment was restrained, the cuts in the road pro-gramme were intended to 'reduce the extent to which we shall be mak-ing up ground lost as a result of the 1965 deferment measures'.[3] Part of these cuts might therefore be considered notional, since the same items were being deferred as in the previous year. More important, housing and social services, the main engines of expansion, were not affected, and the intervention looked small in comparison with the eventual excess of £125 million on the housing programme. The nationalised industries were to contribute £110 million, but though these cuts were supposed to exclude slippage, the electricity industry could clearly meet the government's demands, and more, out of autonomous revisions to its programmes;[4] as with public authorities, adjustment to parts was only as effective as the control over the whole body of investment, which in

[1] See Brittan, *Steering the Economy* (rev. edn), p. 309.

[2] Public investment was to increase by 7½ per cent and public corporation investment by 14 per cent (House of Commons, *Hansard*, 1 March 1966, cols. 1115–16, and Bank of England, *Report for the year ended 28 February 1967*, p. 6).

[3] Harold Wilson in the House of Commons, 3 August 1966.

[4] Ministry of Technology, *Electricity Council. Annual Report and Accounts 1967–68*, London, HMSO, 1968, p. 11.

1966 and 1967/8 was influenced especially by the development of natural gas.

Nationalised industries' investment, though reduced, remained at a level above that projected in the National Plan. Public authority total investment was to be only $2\frac{1}{2}$ per cent below the National Plan level in 1967/8, so that, overall, the public sector was still expected to show substantial leverage. As it turned out, public authority investment exceeded the Plan's target by 1 per cent; this was due to the excess housing investment and despite a continuing rigid control over environmental investment, where restrictions on loans effectively curbed expansion. The total impact of the 1966 'cuts' was, therefore, not all that great, though certain component cuts were achieved.[1] Moreover, it was not long before a projected decline in private investment seemed to call for reflation,[2] so that the incentive to implement the cuts disappeared. It is thus difficult to attribute a positive overall impact to the intervention of 1966.

At the same time large increases were being planned in public sector transfers, while current expenditure on goods and services was to turn out almost 3 per cent higher than planned (chart 3.3). The reductions that were achieved have thus to be taken in the context of aggregate increases which were to prove particularly large in 1967. The impetus to public expenditure was still very much intact, despite the attempt at cuts. This problem was highlighted in the negotiations for the first biennial rate support grant in December 1966. The forecasts for local authority current expenditure in 1967/8 and 1968/9 showed increases over the previous year of about 9 and $6\frac{1}{4}$ per cent respectively (at constant prices). These were considered too high, and the grant was fixed to allow local current expenditure on goods and services to increase by $1\frac{1}{2}$ per cent in 1967/8 (compared with a forecast increase twice as big in the same category of central spending). The eventual excess in this area was wholly attributable to the local authorities, whose spending actually grew by $5\frac{3}{4}$ per cent, but it is noteworthy that the overspending was financed wholly by the central government, not from local revenue.

Much of the heat generated in the Cabinet by the 1966 intervention was due to a dispute over the relative merits of devaluation and of public expenditure cuts. With hindsight, it is evident that the structural imbalance created by framing public expenditure programmes against over-optimistic growth rates, which reached its culmination in 1967/8 (see chart 3.2), could be corrected only by a drastic shift in the public

[1] It is only these component cuts which are evaluated in the column for realisation factors in table 3.5, the offsetting changes in exempt programmes being omitted from the calculation.
[2] House of Commons, *Hansard*, 20 March 1967, col. 1313.

expenditure schedule. This was accomplished at the beginning of 1968 in conjunction with devaluation. Immediate cuts of £84 million were made in the nationalised industries' programmes for 1968/9, and this was followed by reductions in other programmes of £238 million, 60 per cent being current expenditure on goods and services.[1] Total public expenditure was planned to increase by 4·8 per cent in 1968/9, compared with the rate of 6·9 per cent scheduled previously, while over the two years to 1969/70 the average rate of growth was to be 2·85 per cent compared with 4·25 per cent. In practice the fall was more severe – demands on real resources (chart 3.2) increased negligibly in 1968/9 and declined by 1 per cent over the two years.

The secular switch of resources away from public expenditure is seen most clearly in the case of current expenditure on goods and services (chart 3.3); in the event the scheduled cuts were exceeded, though current transfers were slower to make a contribution. Once it was acknowledged that the National Plan growth targets were unattainable, there was bound to be a reaction in public investment plans which had been based on those targets. Nationalised industries' investment fell by twice as much again as the announced cuts; housing investment too reacted to devaluation and the high level of activity in previous years, leading to a large shortfall in 1968/9 and four years of continuous decline.[2]

Because most of the overt interventions in the period 1964 to 1967 entailed expenditure cuts and tax increases, the whole tenor of demand management has been interpreted as deflationary. A closer study of the leverage exerted by public spending contradicts this quite emphatically.[3] Chart 3.5 shows that the intended rate of growth of public investment in the years 1965/6 to 1967/8, even taking account of short-term interventions, was still about 2 to 3½ times that of productive potential. The 1965 intervention emerges clearly as a pause (emphasised *ex post* by an underestimate of the expansion in 1964/5), while, for the 1966 intervention to be interpreted as effective, it must be seen as reducing the intended growth of public investment from 5 times to 3½ times that of productive potential. After devaluation, policy was supposed to be neutral in 1968/9 and deflationary the following year. A substantial proportion of the deflationary leverage which emerged in both years is thus attributable to the involuntary reaction of investment in nationalised industries and housing.

[1] Treasury, *Public Expenditure in 1968–69 and 1969–70*, Cmnd 3515, London, HMSO, 1968. These figures exclude a scheduled cut of £80 million (1967 prices) in investment grants in 1968/9.

[2] For a discussion of this and the education programme, where the cuts were not achieved in 1968/9, see NIESR evidence to the Layfield Committee.

[3] Cf. Artis, 'Fiscal policy for stabilization', p. 267.

The second Conservative administration, June 1970–February 1974

The new Conservative administration was at pains to emphasise the differences between its attitude to public spending and that of its predecessors. An immediate review had as its object 'to reduce substantially previous plans for public spending and to permit taxation to be reduced',[1] and resulted in a White Paper in October 1970.[2]

Chart 3.5. *The growth of public sector capital expenditure relative to the growth of full-employment GDP, planned and out-turn, 1960/1–1974/5*

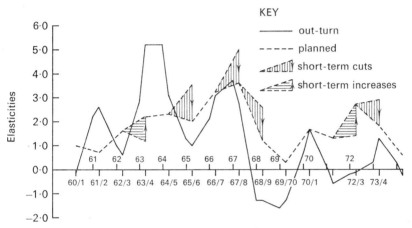

SOURCES: as chart 3.4.

Notes: (i) Capital expenditure is gross domestic fixed capital formation in volume terms (at 1970 prices) excluding steel investment and housing grants.
(ii) Full-employment GDP taken as growing at 3·2 per cent per annum.
(iii) 'Planned' growth observations based on estimates made immediately (0–6 months) before the financial year. 1974/5 level taken before December 1973 cuts.

The objective, as announced by the Chancellor in the House of Commons on 27 October, was the long-term restructuring of public expenditure, with an imputed saving of £394 million in 1971/2 supposed to be 'broadly neutral' in its effect upon the economy when taken with the £315 million reduction in income tax liability.[3] Though by the end of 1969/70 the 'great shift of resources' away from public spending had been completed, and the previous Chancellor had announced on 21 January 1970 the beginning of a period 'when public expenditure can grow as fast as national resources – but not, in the near future, faster',

[1] Treasury, *Public Expenditure 1969–70 to 1974–75*, p. 5.
[2] Treasury, *New Policies for Public Spending*.
[3] After setting off estimation revisions, the net announced impact was £330 million (Treasury, *Public Expenditure 1969–70 to 1974–75*, pp. 4–5).

this was regarded with suspicion. The estimates having been revised upwards, it was stated by Maurice Macmillan in the House of Commons on 22 February 1971 that the calculations of the previous government had been undermined by the 'falling off of industrial investment and the wages explosion'; also, Conservative philosophy on the control of expenditure was different – proportionality with the growth of GDP was considered too high.[1] Although the cuts were not explicitly linked to conjunctural circumstances but rather to secular objectives, it is difficult not to conclude that some deflation to help in combating rising money incomes and prices would have been welcome as a side-effect.

However, the downfall of 'New Policies' was certainly a reversal of conjunctural stance. By 30 March 1971 the Chancellor could announce that increased unemployment had removed the danger that 'demand inflation would be added to the inflation stemming from rapidly rising costs', and the budget aimed to stabilise the situation – that is, to prevent the pressure of demand from falling further. By the summer the government was prepared 'to use the level of public spending and the programmes to which it is applied to meet urgent and immediate needs as an instrument of policy',[2] which involved a series of interventions to increase public investment. Despite attempts to reconcile this expansion with 'New Policies', in practice the principles of that document were being abandoned.

Although some of the reflationary measures which spanned the period from June 1971 to May 1972 were supposed to have a general effect (the repayment of postwar credits, for instance), most of the interventions were aimed at particular sectors (naval shipbuilding, purchases of machine tools and the replacement of rolling stock). The intermediate and development areas featured prominently, as did the construction industry, including housing investment. The impact was to be concentrated over the period up to mid-1973/4, with just over half (£365 million) in 1972/3 and 35 per cent (£233 million) in 1973/4. The effect of this phased leverage seems to have exceeded the Treasury's expectations; there was found to be 'much greater flexibility in public expenditure than people had supposed in the past, or we have ever been able to achieve in the past'.[3] Local authorities' and nationalised industries' capital programmes were increased by 5 per cent, thus substantially exceeding the limit of 2–3 per cent previously entertained in the conventional wisdom on the subject (see page 80 above). The increase in central government investment was slightly less, at 4 per cent.

[1] See above, page 85.

[2] Maurice Macmillan in the House of Commons, 8 December 1971.

[3] House of Commons, *Third Report from the Expenditure Committee* (*Public Expenditure* (*General*) *Sub-Committee*), *Session 1971–72. Changes in Public Expenditure*, London, HMSO, 1972, p. 9.

Including housing, the counter-cyclical increase in local authority investment alone was intended to be 7 per cent in 1972/3. Improvement grants were thought to be 'quicker-acting than new building, and more labour intensive',[1] so that, in June 1971, such grants (for local authority and private improvements in assisted regions) were increased for work which could be completed within two years.[2] This policy was misconceived; improvements are intensive of *skilled* labour, which is not an important element in the pool of unemployed. The counter-cyclical increases, with the simultaneous switch from new dwellings to improvements, resulted in an overload and a sharp increase in tender prices, so that by the spring of 1972 the two-year limit was extended to three.[3] An important element in the upturn of 1972–4 was the way in which a modest counter-cyclical impulse to the housing market grew; in 1972/3 alone the impact, initially estimated at approximately £40 million, was raised to nearer £140 million, with the impetus carried forward into the medium term. Because of this, the housing intervention is not incorporated in the figures in table 3.5.[4] The reflationary impact could not be contained and the concentration on improvements ensured that housing investment reached capacity at a level of output and employment below that which had obtained in 1964 or 1967.[5]

Were the other reflationary measures more effective, or did they too founder on supply constraints that they themselves created, thus leading to the cut-backs of 1973? Prima facie evidence against the reflation constituting a net *ex post* addition to demand is given by the fact that in all three investment programmes there were shortfalls in 1972/3 and 1973/4 greater than the extent of the intended intervention.

In the nationalised industries the shortfall was fairly large, but the Treasury was alert to the problem of ensuring that the measures had their forecast effect at the forecast time. The accelerations were monitored and, by the beginning of 1972, 95 per cent of the work had been authorised, let and started within the time envisaged.[6] Pressure on supplies does not seem to have been as important a factor in the subsequent overall decline in investment as the more endemic problem of

[1] House of Commons, *Seventh Report of the Expenditure Committee, Session 1971–72*, p. 6.

[2] House of Commons, *Hansard*, 22 June 1971, cols. 271–2.

[3] Ibid. 21 April 1972, col. 164; House of Commons, *Tenth Report from the Expenditure Committee, Session 1972–73. House Improvement Grants*, vol. 1: *Report*, London, HMSO, 1973, p. xxix. The switch of emphasis to improvements dated from the Housing Act of 1969.

[4] The White Paper of December 1972 (Treasury, *Public Expenditure to 1976–77*) also dropped the housing intervention from its 'counter-cyclical' definition, in contrast to Treasury, *Public Expenditure 1969–70 to 1975–76*, Cmnd 4829, London, HMSO, 1971.

[5] In 1972 the building labour force was still only 80 per cent of its 1967 level.

[6] House of Commons, *Seventh Report from the Expenditure Committee, Session 1971–72*, pp. 10–11.

the 'planning and execution of major projects'.[1] Attributing a net effect of zero to these measures on the grounds that they pre-empted other projects is probably less realistic than applying to them the usual element of structural shortfall, giving a realisation factor in 1972/3 of about 80 per cent. Supply constraints were more evident in the construction and civil engineering industry, where a large part of the environmental and 'infrastructure' increases was concentrated.[2] Certainly, some of the shortfall in the road and environmental programmes must have been due to excess demand, which makes it doubtful if all the counter-cyclical increases were a *net* addition to demand. About 60 per cent of the authorised short-term increases in public authority investment would seem to have been attained in 1972/3, making a 70 per cent realisation factor for the public sector as a whole.

A substantial proportion of the 1972/3 and 1973/4 shortfalls was due not to supply constraints but to price increases. The price of land, particularly, caused delays in land-intensive programmes (environment and roads),[3] while in other sectors there is evidence of a reaction to increased tender prices.[4] But, to the extent that price increases were a symptom of excess demand, it may be wrong to label shortfalls as the result of one *or* the other. (Equally it would be wrong to equate the two, since increases in the relative cost of investment cannot be categorically attributed to public expenditure policy.)

The first intervention of 1973, in May, seems mainly to have been a reaction to criticism of the December 1972 White Paper.[5] The medium-term increases were attacked for being potentially destabilising – particularly in late 1973/4 and 1974/5[6] – so that £79 million was taken from the 1973/4 programme and £406 million from the following year, in order to make way for the 'strong expansion of industrial investment and exports which we can now expect'.[7] This again evoked criticism on two counts: the first, that the successive shifts of policy for 1974/5 was

[1] House of Commons, *Expenditure Committee (General Sub-Committee), Session 1973–74. Minutes of Evidence, Monday, Jan. 28, Public Expenditure to 1977–78 (Cmnd 5519). Public Expenditure and the Balance of Resources*, London, HMSO, 1974, p. 25; House of Commons, *Fifth Report from the Expenditure Committee, Session 1972–73*, pp. 29–32.

[2] House of Commons, *Eleventh Report from the Expenditure Committee, Session 1972–73*, p. vii, and Anthony Barber in the House of Commons, 21 May 1973.

[3] House of Commons, *Expenditure Committee (General Sub-Committee), Session 1973–74. Minutes of Evidence, Nov. 12, 1973. Control of Road Programme Expenditure*, p. 15, and *Minutes of Evidence, Dec. 3, 1973. Public Expenditure in 1972–73 and 1973–74: forecasts, revisions and out-turn*, pp. 14–16, London, HMSO, 1973.

[4] Ibid. *Minutes of Evidence, Dec. 3, 1973*, pp. 15 and 18; NEDO, Building and Civil Engineering Economic Development Committees, *The Public Client and the Construction Industry*, p. 19. In the environmental sector, the reorganisation of local government and the transfer of functions to the regional water authorities (from 1974/5) may also have contributed to the shortfall.   [5] Treasury, *Public Expenditure to 1976–77*.

[6] House of Commons, *Fifth Report from the Expenditure Committee, Session 1972–73*, p. vii.

[7] Anthony Barber in the House of Commons, 21 May 1973.

contrary to the principle of medium-term stability; the second, that the cuts had come after the belated identification of the large 1972/3 shortfall, so that there was no assurance that they would not merely reduce the shortfall rather than actual expenditure.[1]

The rephasing of building contracts which followed in October 1973 was explicitly a reaction to excess demand – an overload in the construction industry had led to increased tender prices – and was intended to avoid the 'partial frustration' of some programmes.[2] The saving of £87 million imputed for 1973/4 was quite outside the possible timescale for an adjustment to real demand. The proposition that the 1973 measures relied on a 'built-in shortfall that comes to the rescue whenever there is pressure to reduce public expenditure'[3] is thus difficult to refute, though equally it is not clearly demonstrable in the terms expressed by the Expenditure Committee. Because expenditure is unrealised in one year does not mean it will be unrealised the next, and the Treasury's view of how far programmes would be realised in 1973/4 proved more accurate than that of its critics, who expected an even larger shortfall.[4] But, if the cuts were illusory, could they also be disruptive? Paradoxically, the case that the 1973/4 cuts depended on shortfalls is strongest when based on the maintenance rather than the disruption of a given medium-term stance. As can be seen from table 3.7, before the emergence of the 1972/3 shortfall public investment was due to increase by 7·3 per cent in 1973/4 and 2·5 per cent in 1974/5; with the emergence of shortfall these percentages were increased to 10·6 and 5·1 per cent respectively, and the effect of the May and October cuts was only to revert to the *status quo*, with implied increases of 7·0 per cent for 1973/4 and 2·6 per cent for 1974/5. (The discretionary factor for the 1973 policy adjustments has therefore been shown as minimal in table 3.5.)

Current expenditure cuts, which made up 37 per cent of the total in 1974/5, seem to have been more disruptive of medium-term policy, because it was in this area that secular changes were most evident in the reflation of 1972 (chart 3.3). Although there was a shortfall on transfers in 1972/3, current expenditure in 1973/4 exceeded the forecast level even after the cuts, so that it would be difficult to argue that they had been constructed out of a shortfall.

[1] House of Commons, *Eleventh Report from the Expenditure Committee, Session 1972–73*, pp. viii, x and 14.

[2] Treasury, *The Counter Inflation Policy: Stage 3*, Cmnd 5446, London, HMSO, 1973, pp. 9–10.

[3] House of Commons, *Eleventh Report from the Expenditure Committee, Session 1972–73*, p. 14.

[4] See House of Commons, *Expenditure Committee (General Sub-Committee), Session 1973–74. Minutes of Evidence, Dec 3, 1973*, and *Minutes of Evidence, Monday, Jan. 28*; also Treasury, *Public Expenditure to 1977–78*, pp. 147–8.

Table 3.7. *Volume of public sector capital expenditure: projections of gross domestic fixed capital formation and the 1973 programme cuts*

	Forecast Dec. 1972[a]	Forecast December 1973[b]			Out-turn[c]
		Excluding cuts	After May and Oct. cuts	After Dec. cuts	
Change from previous year:					
1973/4	+7·3	+10·6	+7·0[d]	+7·0	+3·0
1974/5	+2·5	+5·1	+2·6[d]	−12·2	−1·0
Change from 1972/3:					
1974/5	+10·0	+16·2	+9·8	−5·9	+2·0

SOURCES: Treasury, *Public Expenditure to 1976–77* and *Public Expenditure to 1977–78;* CSO *Economic Trends, Annual Supplement 1975.*

[a] At 1972 survey prices.   [b] At 1973 survey prices.   [c] At 1970 prices.
[d] Allowing for £100 million shortfall by nationalised industries.

By the beginning of December 1973 public expenditure was planned to increase by 1·4 per cent overall in the year 1974/5, with an intended elasticity of 0·44 in relation to the secular growth of GDP, a strategy designed to make way for a projected increase in industrial investment and exports.[1] This was, however, to prove unattainable. On 17 December 1973, as a reaction to the oil embargo, 20 per cent cuts across-the-board were made in capital programmes (except housing, fuel and power) and there were large accompanying decreases in current expenditure. These cuts reduced the 1974/5 programme by £905 million in total. The reductions were based on a new output forecast, which had been significantly revised downwards, and on the inevitability of increased unemployment.[2] They were, therefore, a real reaction to changed external circumstances and a radical shift in policy beyond anything that had gone before. For capital expenditure, for example, the ostensible result of the intervention was to translate a 2·6 per cent increase into a 12·2 per cent decrease (table 3.7), but two factors make this an overestimate of discretionary change. First, the original forecast was based on quite large increases in investment by central government and nationalised industries, which looked suspiciously optimistic in view of the shortfalls of the previous years (and that of 1974/5 as it turned out). Secondly, reductions in local authorities' investment were accompanied by a switch to housing investment, so

[1] Ibid. p. 10.   [2] House of Commons, *Hansard*, 17 December 1973, cols. 954 and 963.

Table 3.8. *Public expenditure on goods and services: annual growth rates relative to full-employment GDP, 1971/2–1974/5*

Ratios[a]

	Volume			Net resource cost		
	Current	Capital[b]	Total	Current	Capital[b]	Total
1971/2	1·05	−0·70	0·50	1·50	−0·50	0·85
1972/3	1·20	−0·50	0·65	1·25	0·05	0·90
1973/4	1·35	1·30	1·30	1·80	4·20	2·50
1974/5	0·70	−0·45	0·35	3·35	0·70	2·50

SOURCES: CSO, *Economic Trends, Annual Supplement 1975*.

[a] Percentage annual change in expenditure at 1970 prices divided by 3·2 per cent.
[b] Gross domestic fixed capital formation, plus capital grants for housing and universities.

that the volume of public investment was, in the event, hardly to decline in 1974/5, even though it was a deflationary influence on the economy.

Characteristic of the period 1970/1 to 1974/5 was the substantial negative leverage exerted by the volume of public investment, which in no year (as charts 3.4 and 3.5 show) matched the planned profile of reflation and deflation. However, in terms of demands on resources, as described in table 3.8, the picture was substantially different, with adverse relative price effects causing the net resource cost of public investment to increase at 4·2 times the growth of full-employment GDP in 1973/4. The explanation of the persistent gap in this period between planned volumes and out-turns must be found substantially in this relative price shift.

Although current spending on goods and services was expansionary in both cost and volume terms up to 1973/4 (with the severely adverse relative price effect coming through in this sector in 1974/5), taking capital and current spending together, table 3.8 shows a profile of expenditure growth quite different from that intended at the start.[1] Though most of the growth was supposed to come through in late 1971/2 and 1972/3, growth of public expenditure was still lower than that of potential GDP in those years; the impetus was greatest in 1973/4, by which year it was actually meant to level off. The incongruity is particularly marked in terms of total direct leverage derived from net demands on resources; in 1973/4 and 1974/5 these were a substantial expansionary influence – they grew by 2·5 times the growth of potential GDP in both years.

[1] For a discussion of the unforeseen relative price effects operating at this time see page 130; public sector earnings moved ahead of private in an unprecedented fashion in 1974 and 1975 (A. J. H. Dean, 'Earnings in the public and private sectors 1950–1975', *National Institute Economic Review*, no. 74, November 1975, pp. 60–70).

THE PHASING OF PUBLIC EXPENDITURE AND
THE OBJECTIVE OF STABILISATION

There are two reasons why the above analysis cannot be interpreted directly in terms of the effect of public expenditure on economic stability. First, it is arguable that to test a government's stabilisation policy it is necessary to take into account not only the expenditure but also the revenue side of the budget – also, indeed, monetary policy. In other words, one should look at the net impact of all the instruments of economic policy and not confine the analysis to the operation of a single one. Secondly, to appraise the effectiveness of varying public sector demand as an instrument of stabilisation, it has to be considered in the context of private sector demand.

For the first reason economic analysis is properly reticent about attempting to quantify the stabilising properties of public expenditure in aggregate.[1] Nevertheless, it can be argued that stabilisation need not extend to the entire economy, but could also apply to parts of it; in particular, the stabilisation of investment is a subsidiary objective which should not be overlooked. It then becomes legitimate to analyse the impact of counter-cyclical investment policy in its own right, since it has, from time to time, been the express intention to balance demand and supply in investment goods. The direct correlation of movements in public investment with private sector fluctuations can then be defended as valid insofar as the latter may be taken as autonomously determined – or at least unaffected by public investment plans.

Chart 3.6A therefore measures the deviations of public and private investment from their respective linear trends (at constant 1970 prices).[2] Strictly speaking, for stability the requirement would be that the value of the deviations should be equal and opposite in sign. Since, however, the two sectors have been approximately equal in size,[3] the deviations are expressed as percentages of trend, which makes it easier to identify the amplitude of the fluctuations. We shall therefore assume that an optimal result would be for the percentage deviations of the public sector to offset those of the private sector, so that the two summed to zero; a necessary (but not sufficient) condition for a completely stabilis-

[1] Such an exercise was, however, undertaken by A. R. Prest for the period 1955–66, cf. 'Sense and nonsense in budgetary policy', p. 5. For a criticism of the procedure used see G. D. N. Worswick, 'Fiscal policy and stabilization in Britain' in Sir Alec Cairncross (ed.), *Britain's Economic Prospects Reconsidered*, London, Allen & Unwin, 1970, pp. 36–60.

[2] Here the private and public sectors display different characteristics: the former approximates most closely to a fixed percentage rate of change (4·7 per cent per annum), while the latter is best described in terms of a constant elasticity because of the 'hump' in the mid-1960s.

[3] In 1970 investment the private sector (as here defined – see notes (iii) and (iv) to chart 3.6) formed approximately 55 per cent of the total and the public sector 45 per cent.

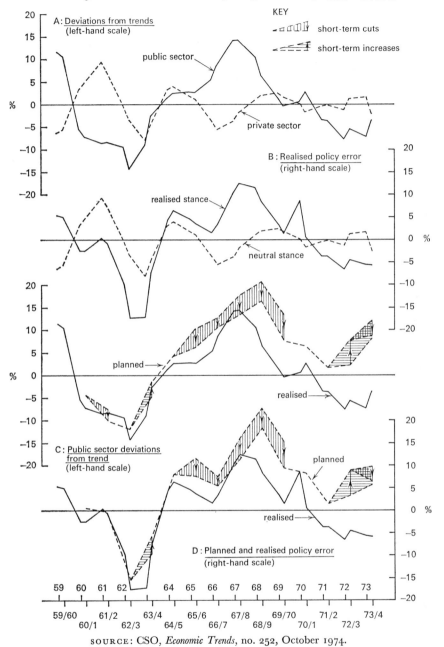

Chart 3.6. *Stabilisation in the capital goods sector, 1959–1973/4*

KEY

short-term cuts

short-term increases

A: Deviations from trends
(left-hand scale)

public sector

%

private sector

B: Realised policy error
(right-hand scale)

realised stance

neutral stance

planned

realised

C: Public sector deviations
from trend
(left-hand scale)

planned

realised

D: Planned and realised policy error
(right-hand scale)

59 60 61 62   64 65 66 67 68 69 70 71 72 73

59/60   61/2   63/4   65/6   67/8   69/70   71/2   73/4
    60/1   62/3   64/5   66/7   68/9   70/1   72/3

SOURCE: CSO, *Economic Trends*, no. 252, October 1974.

Notes: (i) For definitions of trends, see text.
(ii) Policy errors in parts B and D equal to sum of public sector and private sector deviations from trend as a proportion of public sector trend.
(iii) Steel is treated as part of the private sector throughout.
(iv) Capital grants to universities and grants for housing improvement included in the public sector.

ing investment stance would then be that the elasticity of public sector deviations with respect to private should equal -1.

For the data shown in chart 3.6A the coefficient works out at -0.677, which is statistically significant, although the negative correlation with private sector movements is only about 10 per cent.[1] While policy thus seems to have responded correctly to the private sector's cycle, only a small amount of the fluctuations in public investment are explained (or offset) by private sector fluctuations. Thus, the greater source of cyclical deviations in the investment market has been public sector demand, as may be deduced directly from the fact that the trend accounts for 96 per cent of all movements in private investment but only for 87 per cent of public sector movements.

The implications of this generalisation may be best appreciated from chart 3.6B, which expresses the total investment cycle as the sum of private and public sector deviations, which may be interpreted as an index of the realised policy stance. For a perfectly stabilising policy the deviations would always be zero, but where stabilisation is incomplete the index shows how far the actual public sector deviation from trend departed from the optimum and, as may be seen immediately, it has almost always done so. On the other hand, has it increased instability? Had public sector investment followed the 'neutral' policy of trend growth without fluctuations, the cycle in total investment would reduce to the deviations in private investment alone. The 'neutral stance' line in chart 3.6B thus repeats the private sector line of chart 3.6A; it can be seen to run, for the most part, closer to the zero line of optimal stabilisation than the actual total of private and public sector deviations from trend, the exceptions being chiefly at the beginning of the period, but including 1966/7. The early years exhibit a clear counter-cyclical effect, as do the periods 1966–8/9 and 1970–3. Marked pro-cyclical behaviour is limited to 1962–5, but destabilisation is character-istic of all three later periods – in the first the existing cycle was amplified (1962/3) and reinforced (1964/5); in the second and third (especially the former) the public sector created its own amplified counter-cycle.

It appears, therefore, that the degree of public investment has been destabilising, though not uniformly or unequivocally so; a tendency towards over-correction is revealed. This is not necessarily a conse-quence of short-term demand management; the public investment profile is a mixture of short-term interventions and medium-term influences, which may even contain elements of 'planned' instability

[1] $y = x^{-0.677}$ ($t = 1.96$; DW = 1.02; $R^2 = 0.12$) where $y =$ public sector deviations and $x =$ private sector deviations. There are 30 observations for the 15 years (calendar and financial) between 1959 and 1973/4.

(as for instance during the growth experiments).[1] Nor is it necessarily discretionary; the deviations are those that were *realised* and need not represent intended phasing. In particular, failures in the specification of policy may distort the original stance; for example, supply constraints may impose a counter-cyclical pattern in practice.[2]

Charts 3.6C and D attempt to separate short-term from medium-term policy, and discretionary from realised stance. In these charts any immediate (non-cumulative) forecasting errors have been added back to the realised deviations to give an *ex ante* estimate of the effectiveness of stabilisation,[3] including the impact of any short-term changes made. Chart 3.6C is related to 3.6A in that it too shows the amplitude of public sector deviations from trend, not only as they occurred, but as they would have occurred had spending plans been fully realised.[4] Chart 3.6D repeats the test in chart 3.6B for the intended stance of policy before and after short-term changes; that is, it shows the deviations of private (realised) investment added to those of public sector investment, as realised and as intended.

Three general conclusions emerge. First, due to the opportune effects of shortfalls and overruns, policy out-turns proved less destabilising than the original expenditure plans in nine of the fourteen years covered by the chart. Secondly, short-term interventions have been a mixed benefit: where the arrows point towards the zero line they may be taken as stabilising, while a movement away is destabilising. Perverse counter-cyclical reactions can then be identified in 1961/2 and the period 1972/3–1974/5. In later years the intended expenditure plans erred towards reflation, though the realised stance does not show this. The cuts in May and October 1973, however, partly cancelled out the original short-term increases for that year (the cross-hatched area) and can be seen to have been opportune. This also applies to the whole series of interventions from 1963/4 until devaluation; policy was correctly reversed towards reflation in the first of these years, while the deflationary interventions which followed from 1965 can be justified as tending to restore to a proper balance an economy which had embarked upon an extended period of above-trend investment. This brings us to

[1] M. C. Kennedy, 'Employment policy: what went wrong?' in Joan Robinson (ed.) *After Keynes*, Oxford, Blackwell, 1973, pp. 83–4.

[2] Such constraints may also affect private investment, though there seems to be a tendency in some supplying industries to give priority to private sector demand, so that the strain is taken by the public sector.

[3] Adding back the forecasting error naturally affects the trend itself, so that the graph slightly misconstructs the forecast deviations. *Ex ante* policy is thus not the intended deviation, but short-term public investment intentions, expressed as functions of the trend realised between 1959 and 1973/4.

[4] Thus the 'realised' line in chart 3.6C corresponds to the public sector line in chart 3.6A, whilst the 'realised' stances in charts 3.6D and B are also identical.

the third conclusion: that medium-term changes accounted for the major part of policy error, particularly the tendency to over-reflation juxtaposed with the National Plan targets which occurred in the mid-1960s. It is interesting to note that the large devaluation cuts, though opportune, were not initially sufficient to restore balance in investment, given the degree to which the public sector was above-trend and the fact that the private sector had also entered an expansionary phase.

CONCLUSIONS

Expenditure growth and control

The period under review is one in which the public sector has expanded a good deal more rapidly than the economy as a whole. Its share of total full-employment resources rose from 35 per cent in 1959 to $41\frac{1}{4}$ per cent in 1973, implying that exactly half of the extra resources created during the period were allocated to public spending of one kind or another.

It is, on the face of it, paradoxical that a period which began with concern over the need to contain public expenditure, which has seen important reforms in the management of public spending and which has stressed the need to relate public demands to the availability of total resources should have encountered such expansion. It is, of course, essential to note that the *amount* of services provided by the public sector (at least as measured in the national accounts) has increased much more slowly than its cost – an annual average growth rate of 3·55 per cent compared to 4·15 per cent (table 3.4). The relative price effect has been one of the most important influences on the longer-run expansion of the public sector, particularly in the mid-1960s. However, following devaluation not only were resources more realistically defined, but also the relationship of public expenditure to them; the assumptions about the rate of economic growth were more pessimistic, while the cost, not the volume, of public spending was constrained to grow at the same rate as prospective resources. This switch of emphasis involved recognising the fact that an adverse relative price effect must entail a volume growth of public services slower than that of GDP if the current-price resource share of public expenditure is not to rise indefinitely.

Even so, still to be explained are the continuing rise in public spending in the 1970s (after the pause at the end of the 1960s), the failure of the 'New Policies' approach and, although it is really a postscript to the period, the remarkable further expansion of the public sector in the mid-1970s, which raised the ratio of public spending to full-employment

GDP to about 46 per cent in 1974/5.[1] Some commentators have emphasised general underlying factors as the cause of public expansion – for example, the income elasticities of various public services – and political factors are obviously important, but because public spending is subject to fits and starts, one looks for an explanation in the system of control. A whole series of circumstances has made the PESC and the concept of forward planning vulnerable to events. In the first place, the balance of medium-term growth in expenditure tends to be upset when the instrument is used to reflate or maintain demand. Short-term changes tend to imply medium-term shifts in expenditure schedules and to have displacement effects. Once expenditure is raised it is not easy to reverse the process because of the tendency for current expenditure to be flexible upwards but rigid downwards; imbalances then result from the different instruments used to cut back, capital spending being particularly vulnerable. Phasing errors can also help to raise public expenditure in the long term if, as in the period 1972/3–1973/4, reflation is followed by a period of falling activity which, far from allowing a relaxation of public demand, actually calls for a further stimulus.

In any case, the PESC is only as effective as the determination (political and economic) to use it as a control rather than as a signpost to the medium-term horizon – to decide what the direction *should be*, as well as what it *is*. The vulnerability to vertical shifts of the spending schedule is paralleled (and compounded) by doubts over what the longer-run path of public spending should be – in particular, what its relationship should be to the secular growth rate of GDP. This has been respecified several times – in 1963–8 it was more than proportional, in 1969–70 proportional and from 1970 less than proportional – with the Treasury view tending towards the middle strategy. The difficulty is that any such rule can only be defended on pragmatic grounds, since there is no reason why the rate of growth of public expenditure, or its size, should be immutably related to GDP. Yet without some rule there is no clear idea of how far public expenditure should expand and, in the absence of other criteria (such as those provided by output and objective budgeting and the welfare analysis of public expenditure, for which medium-term rules are a somewhat inadequate proxy), it may expand by default. However, the system is not without its built-in constraints; medium-term economic assessment provides a perspective for assessing the claims on GDP of the various categories of expenditure, and it is useful for appraising how far public demands are compatible with the longer-term availability of resources. This check could perhaps

---

[1] See *National Institute Economic Review*, no. 75, February 1976, p. 88, and no. 77, August 1976, pp. 21–4. In January 1977 the aim was to bring this down to about 43 per cent by the end of the decade (Treasury, *The Government's Expenditure Plans*, Cmnd 6721, London, HMSO, 1977).

be made more effective if revenue forecasts were calculated and published, so that the medium-term budget constraint became more apparent – a development invited by the 1969 Green Paper,[1] but not consistently pursued thereafter.

Further, the planning of public expenditure is framed in terms of constant prices with an allowance for the relative price effect. This is, in conception, a relative productivity effect, and otherwise there is no presumption that the cost of public sector expenditure will increase faster or slower than the general rate of inflation. Since public expenditure has been presumed to play no causal role in inflation, it has been a precept of the PESC, as of the rate support grant, that any increase in the general price level will be financed automatically.[2] This system was upset in 1973/4 and 1974/5, when there was a substantial 'unforeseen' relative price effect, which raised the total cost of programmes by an unplanned £1700 million (current) by 1974/5. Not only had the general rate of inflation been underestimated by an amount not included in the £1700 million, but there had also been relatively greater inflation in the price of public goods. Much of this was due to increases in the cost of land and construction, but £500 million was the effect of relatively larger increases in public authority wages. In these circumstances it became necessary to alter the rules, so that changes in the relative price of public goods brought a compensating change in the volume of expenditure (as was evident in the public investment shortfalls of 1973/4) and so that public spending was not seen to be fuelling the fires of inflation. As a bolster to the control of expenditure volume by the PESC, cash limits were introduced in 1975, together with closer monitoring of cash flows on a month-to-month basis.[3] Provided the general rate of increase in earnings can be accurately foreseen and the rate of cash settlement is linked to it, this would cover the normal relative price effect, but not any further adverse changes in the relationship between earnings in the public and private sectors. At the same time, growth in the volume of public spending is constrained, since the application of cash limits implies that the *cost* of public spending increases propor-

[1] Treasury, *Public Expenditure: a new presentation*.

[2] Cf. Godley, 'The measurement and control of public expenditure', p. 58; the use of constant prices is an essential component of any system of medium-term expenditure management, since 'it insulates public expenditure from variations in the *general* rate of cost inflation'.

[3] See House of Commons, *Twelfth Report from the Expenditure Committee, Session 1974–75. Cash Limit Control of Public Expenditure*, London, HMSO, 1975; the intention to use cash limits on expenditure to back up the pay policy was announced on 11 July 1975 and incorporated in the rate support grants for 1976/7 announced on 21 November 1975. Up to 1975/6 the Treasury received quarterly information on cash flows from the spending departments; from 1976/7 this was changed to monthly. From April 1977 it has been supplemented by information on spending volumes and price changes supplied five times a year.

tionately to GDP. In these circumstances, the precise identification and control of the benefits (in terms of output) received from public spending becomes increasingly important if the standard of public services is not to fall; a regime of cash limits on a long-term basis means that 'positive planning' is necessary so that the results of programmes can be appraised other than by measuring public sector output with its conventional assumption of fixed productivity.

Again, the stresses caused by expanding public expenditure tend to be felt most acutely at the local level because of the inelasticity of local revenue and because of the historical tendency for local expenditure to grow faster than that of central government. The PESC has, of course, only incomplete control over local authority current expenditure through the rate support grant, but this accounts for only a small part of the overall deficiency in control, which tends to be general and strategic in origin rather than institutional.

Finally, it is still possible to point to particular deficiencies in control which lead to mis-estimations – either excesses or shortfalls – and serve to underline a basic weakness of the PESC – that the whole is only as strong as the sum of its parts. Certain areas of expenditure are not amenable to control by ceilings; they depend on forecasts. This applies to public transfers in particular, where once the rates of benefit and subsidy have been set, total spending is determined by the rate of take-up, so that expansion of this sector (as from 1972) does not help the cause of aggregate control. Some capital programmes – by nationalised industries and in housing especially – are also not subject to control in any basic sense, but to market and supply conditions. Errors in extrapolating such expenditure add an arbitrary element to attempts at effective demand management – public and national.

The PESC, as a system of control, has not been conspicuously effective as judged by results; on the other hand, it has developed defences against some of its weaknesses. Paradoxically, periodic breakdowns in control only serve to emphasise (as immediately after devaluation) the overwhelming necessity for the concept of the PESC and for a commitment to its effective working.

Short-term demand management

A feature of the period under review is the contrast between the scale of public expenditure interventions at the beginning and the end. Part of this was due to force of circumstances – devaluation and the oil crisis, for instance. But there has also been a calculated reaction against the limited scope for short-term action which was accepted as a fact in the early 1960s. While the Treasury still says that 'short-term management of the economy by fiscal means should primarily be carried out by changes in taxation', it has also discovered greater scope for using public expenditure to this end.[1] On the other hand, there has been continuing doubt about its effectiveness in such a role and concern over disruption and destabilisation.[2]

In the early 1960s the instrument almost atrophied entirely; the interventions of these years were a mixture of rather ineffective medicines and placebos. The need for something stronger arose primarily from the failure of the medium-term strategy advocated by Plowden. Up to devaluation the successive interventions (starting with reflation in 1963 and turning to deflation from 1965) were concerned as much with offsetting the instabilities inherent in public expenditure itself as with counter-cyclical action, but the experience of those years only seemed to confirm the rigidity of the system – particularly the limited scope for cuts. The reversal of strategy after devaluation was based on the belief that it would be easier to reflate, if necessary, than to deflate; the safe margin for the upward adjustment of public expenditure would be greater than for cuts. The extent to which this was confirmed in 1971/2 led to a new found optimism in the Treasury over the potential of public expenditure as an instrument of demand management (and a selective one). Although it would be difficult to argue that this optimism was wholly justified by events, especially given the problems of shortfalls in public spending, it seems safe to say that public expenditure had, by the early 1970s, acquired a somewhat greater potential as a short-run instrument than would have been admitted in the early 1960s.

Certainly experience may have delineated more clearly those areas where little can be expected from attempts at short-term adjustment. The problem of controlling nationalised industries' investment, with its perpetual shortfalls, would seem to prevent action here from having much effect. Housing investment has also proved difficult to predict, and this programme, together with that of the nationalised industries, comprises the major unpredictable element in public spending; forecasting errors in these areas (as may be seen, for example, from chart 3.4) often exceed the scale of short-term interventions. On the other hand, it does not seem that short-term policy is frustrated at the local government level. On environmental projects, where all loans must be sanctioned by the Treasury, control is very effective, while intervention to stabilise demand for new buildings and works appears to have been fairly effective.

Adjustments to current expenditure, insofar as they entail longer-run

[1] House of Commons, *Fifth Special Report from the Expenditure Committee, Session 1974–75. Public Expenditure, Inflation and the Balance of Payments*, London, HMSO, 1975, p. 5.
[2] House of Commons, *Ninth Report from the Expenditure Committee, Session 1974. Public Expenditure, Inflation and the Balance of Payments*, London, HMSO, 1975.

changes in expenditure plans, obviously have a meretricious quality, but in certain respects they may have dependable and desirable short-term effects; this applies particularly to current transfers and even subsidies. On the other hand, much of current spending on goods and services is in the hands of the local authorities, which have much more discretion here than over capital expenditure. Most local spending appears to be in response to central legislation, but in the short run the system of rate support grants gives only limited central control, the government having to rely on the unpopularity of the rates to force local authorities to spend less.

Historically, as table 3.5 shows, it is possible to identify a rather mixed performance in achieving announced changes in spending. Overall, there is not a great deal of evidence that such packages have been merely window-dressing for the sake of opinion abroad, though they do offer potential in this respect and one finds some references to 'pretended cuts'. But instances of under-implementation are probably less common than the opposite tendency, for interventions to lead – frequently with a lag – to an over-reaction. At all events, the picture given is one of effectiveness in some sectors, but this is more than offset by ineffectiveness in others.

As with implementation, the stabilisation record has been mixed. The devaluation cuts could not be said to be destabilising, for instance, and nor could those in 1965, but there is evidence that some attempts at fine-tuning have actually accentuated the cycle in the short-term, while others, though rightly timed in terms of immediate trends in private demand, have had adverse repercussions on stability in the medium term. The problem of timing reflations was brought into particularly sharp perspective in the period 1971–3, and forecasts of private investment – particularly in dwellings – have not proved accurate triggers for intervention. Had it been possible to ensure that public investment exactly followed a consistent medium-term trend, this would have been by some margin superior to the policy actually followed in contributing to economic stability. But it has to be remembered that medium-term planning is itself difficult; it is by no means easy to ensure that such plans do not eventually cause short-term trouble as a result of the difficulties of control listed above.

Since short-term expenditure changes invariably involve cost in terms of disruption, the doubts attached to their potential benefits seem to call for public spending to be relegated to the position of a 'tool of last resort'. It may be more profitable to devote resources to improving the consistency and reliability of medium-term planning than to making the instrument more effective in the fine-tuning of the economy. But this could be to learn the wrong lesson, for if the amplitude of the cycle is to be greater than it was to 1973/4, counter-recessionary contributions from public spending cannot be ruled out. Nor should selective intervention – in particular sectors, with particular skills and inputs of resources – be ignored.

Depending on the scale of the stabilisation problem with which the government is confronted, there would seem to be two possible courses open to it. In the kind of circumstances which faced demand management up to 1973/4 there is little doubt that public expenditure policy would have gained by ignoring the short-term and adjusting programmes only on a planned long-term basis. This would have entailed following a fairly rigid and consistent growth path, in order to minimise the chance of the stance of policy becoming perverse and necessitating short-term action. The second possible course is perhaps more apposite to the period since the oil crisis. If short-term expenditure changes are to make an important counter-cyclical contribution the problems are twofold: first, to establish medium-term rules which prevent unforeseen financing difficulties from emerging as plans get nearer to actuality; second, to adjust any short-term role for the instrument to longer-term needs and resources – the deficit-financing which initially accompanies the use of public expenditure as a short-term instrument must be brought down to more normal levels by phasing expenditure to fit in with medium-term revenue and borrowing potential. This would seem to call for a system of medium-term budgeting, where prospective public sector claims on resources are constrained in the longer run by the limits of non-inflationary taxation potential, and by the need for domestic savings to finance investment and an external surplus. This is already partially accomplished through the medium-term assessment, but would be improved by a more comprehensive regime of full-employment budgeting, which, in the medium term, implies planning against the prospect of economic resources being, at some stage, 'fully' employed.[1] In the past it has never been exactly clear how much of a deficit-financed increase in public spending was supposed to be temporary and how much permanent; grafting a full-employment budgeting system on to the existing short-term one would undoubtedly make this clearer, so helping to prevent an inflationary conflict between stored-up resistance to expenditure cuts and equal resistance to tax increases. In this respect, a full-employment budgeting system may be seen as an important *desideratum* if not the *sine qua non* of an effective counter-cyclical expenditure policy.

[1] For a discussion of the full-employment budget, and the distinction between its medium-term and short-term use, see pages 183–5 below.

CHAPTER 4

BUDGETARY POLICY

by *R. W. R. Price*

OBJECTIVES AND INSTRUMENTS

Economic policy and demand management: a historical perspective

Fiscal policy and public finance are not interchangeable terms. The former refers to government action as a 'balancing factor' in the economy at large;[1] the latter is wider-reaching, embracing, for example, the distribution of costs and benefits. These allocative issues are an important sub-theme to the basic concern of this chapter, which is with macroeconomic management; the precise method by which budgetary policy seeks to balance demand has often been based on the desired shape of the fiscal system in terms of its contribution to income redistribution, enterprise and efficiency. Indeed, the allocative content of budget-making has tended to grow in importance, though with some controversy over the degree of 'neutrality' or 'interventionism' involved – the one philosophy being based on classical beliefs in the efficiency of the market and the need to minimise distortions by the tax system, the other on the belief that the tax system can act in a positive way to improve economic performance.

On the other hand, the tax structure has also tended to develop in an *ad hoc* and even inconsistent way because of the requirements of demand management and because of the absence of longer-term policies concerning either the internal harmony of the tax system or the overall size of the tax take. The character of fiscal policy has been derived primarily and initially from the needs of short-term demand management, the clearest objective of which has always been the maintenance of full employment. But in practice this has borne little resemblance to the diagnosis of Keynes's *General Theory*.[2] Postwar variations in demand were less violent than expected, and by 1960 it had come to be believed that the 'pre-war problem of mass unemployment had gone'.[3] What remained was the problem of responding to cycles of much smaller amplitude and duration, to which the answer appeared to be greater flexibility and rapidity of action – that is, 'fine-tuning'.

---

[1] Keynes, *General Theory of Employment, Interest and Money*, p. 220.
[2] Ibid.   [3] Treasury, *Public Investment in Great Britain*, Cmnd 1203, pp. 6–7.

Accompanying this, there was the problem of reconciling 'expansion and price stability'.[1] The possibility of a link between demand pressure and inflation encouraged the use of demand management to maintain price stability by the creation of unemployment – a prescription which, though never an overriding basis of policy, occasionally emerged as a reinforcing rationale for deflating demand, most notably in 1961/2 and 1970/1. By the end of the period the belief that wages responded gradually to unemployment was explicitly rejected by the Treasury,[2] but even at the beginning disillusionment with 'stop–go' led to a search for alternative prices and incomes policies. Partly this was in response to a growing belief that inflation was cost-induced and thus outside the scope of demand management, but more explicitly the problem had become one of 'limiting the rise in incomes associated with a given level of unemployment to a rate lower than that which would occur on the basis of past experience'.[3]

Similar considerations applied to reconciling expansion with balance of payments equilibrium, which re-emerged, with price stability, as the central problem of economic management in 1960 and 1961. The solution of the two was linked; of the instruments available to affect the balance of payments in the short term, only reducing the rate of cost and price increases appeared not to have any serious international disadvantages. Otherwise, the external consequences of expansion could be tempered by *ad hoc* measures like export rebates, cuts in government expenditure overseas, quantitative restrictions and surcharges on imports, but basically the short-run balance of payments problem was regarded as insoluble because of the temporary flows of imports needed for stockbuilding and re-equipment.[4] However, if the imbalance was temporary only, demand management might achieve longer-run growth provided that the 'virtuous circle' of growth, productivity increases and export competitiveness could be entered from expansion rather than from a shift in the demand schedule for exports.[5] This was the strategy on which the expansion of 1963/4 was based. In this respect, though, policy was also turning towards a more directly structural approach to growth, linked with planning, which was to dominate demand management from the end of 1964 to 1967. On the other hand, the allocative

[1] Ibid. p. 7.

[2] Wages and prices, it came to be believed, do not react to the level of unemployment over a wide range until very high levels are reached (House of Commons, *Ninth Report from the Expenditure Committee, Session 1974*, p. 136).

[3] NEDC, *Conditions Favourable to Faster Growth*, London, HMSO, 1963, p. 45.

[4] Ibid. pp. 32–4 and 47.

[5] The direction of causation between export growth and GDP growth was ambivalent, but 'to some extent, the rapid increase in exports was due to the same factors that led to growth in the economy as a whole' (ibid. p. 34).

effects of public expenditure and the tax system came in for increasing scrutiny.[1]

The development of incomes policy and planning as economic instruments was a reaction to the waning belief that fiscal policy could achieve all economic objectives simultaneously – a belief that tended to flourish in the upswing and wither with the reserves. But up to 1967 no instrument proved sufficient to solve the conflict between full employment and the balance of payments. Devaluation was a landmark in this respect and from that time the proper balance between fiscal policy and exchange-rate policy which was needed for external and internal stability with (demand-led) growth has been an important consideration. In general terms, fiscal policy is usually assigned the role of maintaining internal stability and the exchange rate that of achieving external balance; the two are not taken as independent, but policy tends to be regarded in this way because exchange-rate effects are treated as partial equilibrium relative price effects, with income changes the province of fiscal policy.[2] But the impact of devaluation on the balance of payments depends on the income effects of the extra demand generated by the change – the absorption[3] and savings out of increased income earned abroad – as well as on export and import price elasticities. To gain the maximum effect from devaluation, additional savings should equal the increase in demand resulting directly from the change in relative prices. At levels of employment below the optimum the increase in demand will itself generate some additional private savings, but at full employment fiscal policy must create all the necessary savings to prevent devaluation from producing pure inflation.[4] Thus, at full employment, one cannot have a flexible exchange rate without an active fiscal policy to reconcile full-employment domestic savings with the target balance of payments;[5] in this sense, fiscal policy determines absorption and hence the balance of payments. But below full employment the respective importance given to one or other instrument is dependent on the multiplier; if this (and the marginal propensity to save) is unity, it is the exchange rate that fully secures the balance of payments objective.

[1] The first time the tax system was considered in relation to growth was in Inland Revenue, *Report of the Committee on Turnover Taxation* [Richardson Report], Cmnd 2300, London, HMSO, 1964.

[2] See C. P. Kindleberger, *International Economics* (3rd edn), Homewood (Ill.), Irwin, 1963, pp. 211–12.

[3] Where b is the balance of payments, y output and a expenditure, $\Delta b = \Delta y - \Delta a$ and Δa is termed absorption.

[4] Devaluation can increase real savings at full employment if there is money illusion, or if income is redistributed to relatively high-saving areas, among which export industries may be important.

[5] See N. Kaldor (ed.), *Conflicts in Policy Objectives*, Oxford, Blackwell, 1971, p. 12.

The greatest area of dispute over the combined role of fiscal and exchange-rate policy has concerned the amount of domestic savings forthcoming – the income effects of devaluation. The strategy of 1968/9 involved a large turn-round in budgetary savings, from financial deficit to surplus, and the main question is whether the initial correction was sufficient, or whether the delayed effects of devaluation were symptomatic of excessive domestic absorption. Since there was a rise in unemployment, the usual verdict is that the correction was sufficient and a lagged response by demand to prices can explain the delay, but other features point to the possibility of excessive absorption in 1968 (page 202 below). In any case, the 1972/3 reflation was built upon the lagged effects of devaluation for, domestic demand having been increased, sterling was floated in mid-1972 with the objective of a viable and sustained expansion. This combination of deficit budgeting and a flexible exchange rate gave rise to the so-called 'New Cambridge' controversy, which centred initially on the possibility that the potential gains from floating were being dissipated by domestic absorption – specifically, by budgetary dis-savings which private sector savings (interpreted here as the surplus of current savings over investment) could not be reliably expected to offset and which, as the economy reached capacity, would spill over into the balance of payments.[1]

Pessimism about the private surplus to be expected at the peak of the cycle in 1973/4 then led to a more universal proposition – that the private sector spends all (or almost all) its income in the longer run and cannot *at any time* be relied upon to supply more than a small amount of savings.[2] As a result, even below full employment fiscal policy becomes both necessary and sufficient to determine the balance of payments; the exchange rate (or a similar device) can affect output but not the external balance (that is, absorption offsets completely the price effects of exchange-rate changes). It is this extension of the complete absorption theory from a full-employment context that constitutes the 'new' in New Cambridge. It differs from orthodox Keynesian theory in its different view of the behaviour of private savings,[3] so that within the same framework it arrives at a series of 'elegant paradoxes'; the first is the direct link between the budget deficit and the balance of payments, the second that short-term interventions in demand management are unnecessary, because the private sector is not a source of instability and does not call for compensatory action. But the theory

---

[1] N. Kaldor, *The Times*, 30 March and 21 August 1973; see also page 190 below.

[2] R. R. Neild, *The Times*, 19/20 July 1973, 30 January 1974; W. A. H. Godley and F. Cripps, *The Times*, 22 January 1974; House of Commons, *Ninth Report from the Expenditure Committee, Session 1974*.

[3] Insofar as the original thesis postulated a negligible amount of private sector savings, it has also been seen as a reversion to Say's Law.

stands or falls on empirical proof and in this respect it has not been substantiated.[1] The recession after the oil crisis showed that instability in the economy can stem from changes in overseas or private sector surpluses, and that when such changes are incompatible with domestic full employment fiscal policy reverts to its traditional role of stabilising employment rather than determining the full-employment external balance. However, the danger of absorption from the conjunction of large-scale deficit budgeting and cyclical upturns in domestic and world demand – when the full-employment surpluses of the private and overseas sectors tend to be eroded – suggests that as the economy actually nears full employment the budget balance should be framed more explicitly than in the past to secure the balance of payments objective.

Taxation and compensatory finance

The principle of compensatory finance is that fiscal policy should match public and private savings (or dis-savings) to ensure that aggregate savings are compatible with full employment, but only rough guidance is provided as to the balance of policies; capital expenditure should be used to offset fluctuations in private investment, for instance, but when demand generally is unbalanced the particular mix of policies is indeterminate.

There was, however, a fairly distinct – and asymmetric – pattern of policy response in the period up to the early 1960s, according to which it was by a more restrictive monetary policy, increases in voluntary savings, and short-term and longer-term cuts in public expenditure, as well as through the automatic buoyancy of the revenue, that relief could be found from excess demand; deficient demand, on the other hand, could be countered by tax concessions, chiefly in the personal income tax – where discretionary changes were synonymous with reductions – and purchase tax.[2] Up to 1963/4 the dominant view was that taxation was too high and should be used to balance demand only where that was consistent with reductions. From 1963/4 the situation changed: the background to taxation policy became the rising revenue requirements of the expanding public sector. The Conservatives' return to office in 1970 then brought a restoration of something like their earlier strategy (which was, in turn, reversed by the Labour administration which followed), so that taxation policy shows a marked oscillation, which is described in fuller detail below.

[1] See Lord Kahn and Michael Posner, *The Times*, 17/18 April 1974; G. D. N. Worswick, *The Times*, 5 March 1973 and 28 January 1974; *National Institute Economic Review*, no. 64, May 1973, pp. 20–4; House of Commons, *Ninth Report from the Expenditure Committee, Session 1974*.
[2] The asymmetry of expanding by fiscal policy and retarding by monetary policy was criticised by Paish and others (see J. M. Buchanan, 'Easy budgets and tight money', *Lloyds Bank Review*, no. 64, April 1962, pp. 17–30).

Personal income tax

There have been two influences on the development of the personal income tax system[1] – the level of taxation and the graduation of the tax structure – and in both contradictory forces can be identified. First, the tendency for the public sector to demand resources for its expansion and increase the tax burden accordingly has conflicted with the intuitive but not empirically established view that a progressive tax system acts as a disincentive to work, initiative and growth. Secondly, the administrative convenience of a smaller number of rates and larger steps from one marginal rate to the next (particularly at the threshold) has conflicted with, and largely overridden, the arguments for a more highly differentiated structure; these have been seen as enhancing the progressiveness of the system and mitigating its harmful side-effects on the labour supply and possibly on wage bargaining.

There has, in fact, been an element of all-Party consensus over the possibly stultifying effects of direct tax increases.[2] Nevertheless, there have been noticeable differences between the Parties in the weight given to the argument. The problem is that, whilst the effects of an increase in the marginal rate may well be to substitute leisure for work, any change in average rates which accompanies it will have an 'income effect', so that people may work more to maintain a given post-tax income.[3] This may account partially for the marked difference between income tax policy in the period 1964–70 and the years before and after. The Conservatives' policy was characterised by reductions in income tax rates and rises in income tax and surtax thresholds. Under Labour the expansion of public spending and the switch into exports after devaluation called for an increased standard rate (from

[1] Until they were merged in 1973/4 this incorporated two taxes – income tax and surtax; 94 per cent of the yield in 1972/3 was from income tax and 6 per cent from surtax. National insurance contributions have becoming increasingly akin to an income tax with their transformation from a flat rate to a graduated income-related levy; their position in aggregate personal taxation is described on pages 161–3. Capital gains tax is another element of personal taxation which should be taken into account, but its development has coincided with reform of the company tax structure; it is discussed in the context of taxing retained and distributed profits in the next section.

[2] Cf. Roy Jenkins (in the House of Commons, 19 March 1968), who rejected the case for increasing income tax in the budget after devaluation on the grounds that, even if the disincentive effect of high tax rates was 'more allegation than reality', it was inadvisable to ignore the possibility.

[3] See Royal Commission on Taxation of Profits and Income, *Second Report*, Cmd 9105, London, HMSO, 1954, pp. 42–5. Subsequent studies have confirmed the possibility that this 'income effect' is likely to be stronger than the 'substitution effect' caused by lowering the opportunity cost of leisure (see C. V. Brown and E. Levin, 'The effects of income taxation on overtime: the results of a national survey', *Economic Journal*, vol. 84, December 1974, pp. 833–48, where it was found that the overall effect of tax was very small but led to a slight increase in the hours of overtime worked).

Table 4.1. *Statutory rates of tax, 1955/6–1973/4*

	Personal income taxes[a]				Company taxes[b]		Indirect taxes	
	Threshold	Lowest rate	Basic rate	Highest rate	On retentions	On distributions	Purchase tax	SET per head
	(£)	(%)	(%)	(%)	(%)	(%)	(%)	(£)
1955/6	566	8·75	33·06	92·50	45·00	70·00[cd]	5–90[c]	—
1956/7	566	8·75	33·06	92·50	45·50	72·50[d]	5–90	—
1957/8	630	8·75	33·06	92·50	45·50	72·50[d]	5–90	—
1958/9	630	8·75	33·06	92·50	48·75		5–60	—
1959/60	630	6·80	30·14	88·75	48·75		5–50	—
1960/1	630	6·80	30·14	88·75	51·25		5–50	—
1961/2	630	6·80	30·14	88·75[e]	53·75		5½–55[c]	—
1962/3	630	6·80	30·14	88·75	53·75		{10–45 / 10–25[c]}	—
1963/4	771	15·60[f]	30·14	88·75	53·75		10–25	—
1964/5	771	15·60	30·14	88·75	56·25[c]		10–25	—
1965/6	797	15·60	32·08	91·25	40·00	64·75	10–25	—
1966/7	797	15·60	32·08	96·25[cg]	40·00	64·75	11–27½[c]	1·25
1967/8	797	15·60	32·08	91·25	42·50	66·22	11–27½	1·25
1968/9	797	15·60	32·08	91·25[c]	45·00	67·69	{12½–50 / 13¾–55[c]}	1·88
1969/70	842	23·33[h]	32·08	91·25	42·50[c]	66·22	13¾–55	2·40
1970/1	958	32·08[i]	32·08	91·25	40·00	64·75	13¾–55	2·40
1971/2	1061	30·14	30·14	75·44	40·00	63·25	11¼–45[c]	1·20
1972/3	1234	30·14	30·14	75·44	40·00	63·25	11¼–25	1·20
1973/4	1245	30·00	30·00	75·00[e]	52·00		(VAT, 10%)	

SOURCES: Treasury, *Financial Statement and Budget Report* (annual); Inland Revenue, *Report of the Commissioners* (annual); Customs and Excise, *Report of the Commissioners* (annual).

[a] On earned income. The threshold is that applicable to a married man with two children aged 11–16.

[b] Maximum rates applicable to company accounting periods (or portions thereof) ending in the financial year.   [c] Changes announced other than in the annual budget.

[d] Only applicable if companies paid their taxes out of reserves. Since the maximum distribution ratio was only about 65 per cent if taxes were paid out of current income, the maximum rates of tax in practice were 61·7 per cent (1955/6) and 62·9 per cent (1956/7 and 1957/8) (see A. R. Prest, *Public Finance* (1st edn), London, Weidenfeld & Nicolson, 1960, p. 165).

[e] Changes in surtax, including its threshold (see also note g).

[f] Number of reduced rates cut from three to two.   [g] 10 per cent surcharge on surtax.

[h] Number of reduced rates cut to one.   [i] Reduced rates abolished.

1965/6), surtax and investment income surcharges and a resistance to maintaining the real value of allowances, but also, a general reluctance to increase tax rates, even if not to reduce them like the Conservatives.

As a result, as table 4.1 shows, the basic rate on earned income (defined up to 1972/3 as the 'standard rate' reduced by the full earned income relief of two ninths) was the same (30 per cent) in 1973/4 as in 1959/60, but on higher and lower incomes there were fundamental changes. Until 1970/1 the highest rate of tax on earned income was the standard rate plus surtax because of the cut-off point for earned income relief, but this maximum was reduced in the 1971 budget to 75·44 per cent by extending a 15 per cent earned income relief to all higher incomes. The rate structure was rationalised further in April 1973, when income tax and surtax were unified, the 30 per cent standard rate on earned income being redefined as the 'basic' rate, with 75 per cent as a maximum. At the same time, investment income (above a specified minimum) was surcharged at 15 per cent, the concept of earned income relief being abolished.

Formerly, earned income relief, together with the system of reduced rates, had made income tax appear more graduated, but the elimination of reduced rates in the budgets of 1963, 1969 and 1970 (there is, again, some bipartisanship here) and the absorption of earned income relief into the basic rate imply that administrative simplicity – a relatively low tax threshold, a high initial rate and simple proportionality over a large range of income – has taken precedence over a more graduated income tax.[1] Because increases in personal allowances roughly kept pace with inflation in the end, the real value of the tax threshold was maintained, but the real value of the threshold at which the basic rate became payable was reduced by about half by the elimination of the reduced rate bands.[2]

---

[1] The width of the basic band had been justified by the need to avoid adjustments at the end of the year and the abolition of the reduced rate bands, which removed small income earners from the tax net, by the uneconomical cost of collecting small amounts of tax. By 1963 it had come to be believed that the starting point for liability was 'too low for modern conditions' (Reginald Maudling in the House of Commons, 3 April 1963). However, by 1970/1 the proportion of the working population liable for income tax had regained its 1962/3 level despite the intervening abolition of reduced rates; despite also the increased allowances in the 1971 and 1972 budgets, the proportion grew over the period as a whole.

The negative income tax scheme suggested in the 1972 Treasury Green Paper, *Proposals for a Tax-Credit System*, would have extended simple proportionality below the tax threshold.

[2] The 1973/4 tax thresholds as proportions of their 1959/60 equivalents were (with 1959/60 allowances, including earned income relief, multiplied by an index of consumer prices to convert them to 1973/4 terms):

	Value in 1973/4	Proportion of 1959/60 threshold for:	
		Initial rate	Standard rate
	(£p.a.)	(%)	(%)
Single person	595	163	45·6
Married couple	775	124	49·5
Married couple with 2 children	1245	97	56·2

In terms of the threshold and the initial rate of tax (raised to 35 per cent in 1975/6) the United Kingdom tax structure compares disadvantageously with that of other industrial countries, where the average starting rate is about 14 per cent and the threshold level two thirds higher (House of Commons, *Hansard*, 25 March 1976, col. *247*).

The increased tax rates that these changes implied at lower income levels and the reduction in the higher rates can be clearly seen from chart 4.1, which compares the tax structure in 1959/60 and 1973/4. The marginal and average (also called 'effective') rates of tax are shown for a 'representative' taxpayer – one with income all earned and claiming the marriage allowance. Progressiveness, as measured by an average rate of tax which increases continuously with income, has remained a characteristic of the system, though the reforms of the period

Chart 4.1. *Marginal and average rates of tax on earned income for the 'representative' taxpayer,[a] 1959/60 and 1973/4*

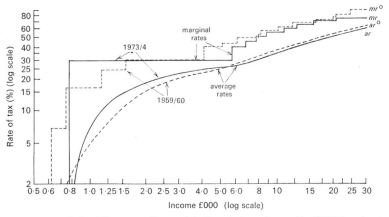

SOURCES: Inland Revenue, *Report of the Commissioners* (annual); NIESR estimates.

Notes: (i) 'Representative' taxpayer defined as a couple with all income earned, claiming only the married person's allowance.
(ii) 1959/60 translated into 1973/4 income terms by multiplying allowances and rate bands by an index of consumer prices.

have mitigated this. However, a significant aspect of progressiveness, especially in an inflationary economy, is the consistency of the rate of change of the average rate. If everyone's tax liabilities increased in the same proportion as incomes increased, the average rate schedule would be a straight line (since it is drawn to a log scale), but its slope is steeper at the lower end, in both 1959/60 and 1973/4, implying that effective rates of tax increase faster for lower income earners. In this respect the system tends to become less progressive as incomes increase (a factor explored more fully below), and this was enhanced by the reforms of the period, since the average rate schedule can be seen to rise more rapidly in its early stages in 1973/4 than in 1959/60.

The taxation of company income and capital gains

Changes in company taxation showed a great deal o f purely conjunctura variation, while there were also major structural reforms on grounds of growth, efficiency and equity. Rates of company tax are a flexible instrument for short-term demand management, particularly popular at times of economic stringency, while investment incentives, operating through allowances or grants, have been prominent in reflations. The relative merits of grants and allowances has been a source of some dispute, as has the issue of differential tax rates on retained and distributed profits.

Up to 1957/8 retained profits were favoured by differential rates of profits tax. Income tax, to which companies were also liable at the standard rate, was levied on the same base as profits tax, but insofar as profits were distributed to the personal sector the income tax already paid was regarded as deducted at source and set off against the liability of the recipient.[1] There were, therefore, three salient features of the system before 1958: first, the company and personal income tax systems were not entirely separate; secondly, payments of income tax by companies counted as payments by the recipient of dividends; thirdly, there was (in 1957/8) a 27 per cent differential in favour of retentions through discriminatory profits tax rates (of 3 and 30 per cent), which, with income tax at 42·5 per cent, meant overall rates of 45·5 per cent on retentions and 72·5 per cent on distributions (table 4.1).[2]

The 1958 budget removed this discrimination through a single 10 per cent rate of profits tax, but left the income tax system unchanged. Capital gains also remained exempt from tax. This reform stemmed from the majority recommendation of a Royal Commission.[3] The minority agreed that in the long run a private enterprise economy was likely to function better without discrimination against dividends, but recommended that the existing differentiation should be abolished only if a capital gains tax was introduced;[4] on equity grounds, however, (which were not accepted by the majority) they were prepared to introduce double taxation of dividends by separating the company and personal tax systems and subjecting distributed profits to both. They

[1] The standard rate is not necessarily the actual rate payable by a recipient on his dividends, since the tax is refundable if his liabilities are less, or surtax may be added. The marginal rate of tax on dividends was about 52 per cent (a quarter more than the standard rate) in 1969/70 (see page 168 below, and cf. A. J. H. Orhnial and L. P. Foldes, 'Estimates of marginal tax rates for dividends and bond interest in the United Kingdom, 1919–1970', *Economica*, vol. 42, February 1975, pp. 79–91).

[2] If all profits were distributed this would have involved a penal rate of tax in the sense that it would have had to be paid out of reserves (see table 4.1 footnote *d*).

[3] Royal Commission on Taxation of Profits and Income, *Final Report*, Cmd 9474, London, HMSO, 1955.   [4] Ibid. pp. 354–70 and p. 388.

recommended that, after the introduction of a capital gains tax, a 'corporation profits tax' should be introduced at uniform rate and, while income tax should not be levied on companies as such, they should act as agents and deduct income tax at the ruling standard rate from dividends.[1]

The reforms introduced by the new Labour administration in the 1965 budget followed exactly this prescription. The company tax system was separated from the personal by the creation of corporation tax, while a 'classical' system of double taxation on distributions was introduced, with companies being made responsible for deducting the standard rate of income tax at source.[2] While the 1962 budget had already made short-term capital gains subject to income tax and surtax, the 1965 budget made realised long-term gains (on assets held for more than a year) subject to a capital gains tax of 30 per cent.[3]

With corporation tax at 40 per cent the new system implied a differential of 24·75 per cent in favour of retentions because of the double taxation of distributions. But the issue remained in dispute and, when returned to office in 1970, the Conservative government announced they would abolish double taxation, and with it discrimination. After some discussion an imputation system was introduced with effect from 1973/4,[4] under which distributions carried a liability to advance corporation tax. This is a payment in advance equivalent to the standard rate of income tax; it counts against the company's eventual corporation tax liability and is 'imputed' to the shareholder by means of a 'tax credit' against his income tax liability.[5] By this reform the separation of the two tax bases was confirmed and it has now become an established principle of British taxation that company profits are

[1] Ibid. pp. 384 and 389.

[2] Treasury, *Corporation Tax*, Cmnd 2646, London, HMSO, 1965.

[3] Treasury, *Taxation of Capital Gains*, Cmnd 2645, London, HMSO, 1965. Company capital gains are chargeable to corporation tax; the distinction between short-term and long-term gains was removed by the 1971 budget.

[4] The absence of debate on the 1965 reforms was seen by many observers as an indictment of the governmental process (see A. R. Prest, *The Capital Gains Tax and the Corporation Tax*, London, Woolwich Polytechnic, 1967), so that the 1973 reforms were preceded by a Green Paper (Treasury, *Reform of Corporation Tax*), the proposals of which were considered by a Select Committee of the House of Commons, which reported in October 1971 (House of Commons, *Report from the Select Committee on Corporation Tax*, London, HMSO, 1971). The White Paper followed in April 1972 (Treasury, *Reform of Corporation Tax*, Cmnd 4955, London, HMSO, 1972).

[5] An alternative method – treating the tax on distributions as income tax and charging corporation tax on distributions at a correspondingly lower rate – was the one favoured initially, but it was considered disadvantageous in respect of distributions overseas and this tipped the balance in favour of an imputation system (see House of Commons, *Report from the Select Committee on Corporation Tax*, pp. ix–x; A. R. Prest, 'The Select Committee on corporation tax', *British Tax Review*, no. 1, 1972, pp. 19–20; J. F. Chown, *The Reform of the Corporation Tax*, London, Institute for Fiscal Studies, 1971, and 'The reform of the corporation tax: some international factors', *British Tax Review*, no. 4, 1971, pp. 215–29).

sui generis, calling for a separate tax regime which is 'something more than a mere attempt to collect personal income tax in advance';[1] hence there is the distinction between 'mainstream' corporation tax, which cannot be set off against income tax, and the imputed element, which can.[2] The reintroduction of a system which is 'neutral' as between the taxation of retained and distributed profits has remained, however, a divisive issue. Advocates of fiscal neutrality have held, on equity grounds, that the personal and company tax systems should be considered in their combined effect and the burden of taxation for a shareholder equalised between his benefits from received and from retained income.[3] There is, however, no determinate answer to the problem of fairness and neutrality. It depends, first, on the true incidence of company taxes, where the evidence is inconclusive but tends to indicate that such taxes are not passed on to the consumer;[4] secondly, on the extent of capital gains and the taxation of these – for a shareholder to be indifferent between distribution and retention of profits, he should be liable to pay company and personal income tax on the one equal to his potential liabilities by way of company tax and capital gains on the other.[5] For a taxpayer at the standard rate, realised capital gains would have borne tax at half the standard rate from 1965, while it appears that for shareholders as a whole both the marginal rate of income tax on dividends and the rate of capital gains tax would have been higher – 50 and 28·5 per cent on average in 1973/4.[6] For the standard rate taxpayer, therefore, distributions would have been taxed at an aggregate rate of 52 per cent (table 4.1), while realised capital gains would have borne a total effective rate of 59 per cent – a bias in favour of distributions. However, the 1973 system appears to have

[1] House of Commons, *Hansard*, 6 April 1965, col. 255; Royal Commission on Taxation of Profits and Income, *Final Report*, p. 164.

[2] With corporation tax at 52 per cent and all profits distributed, the 'mainstream' rate would be 31·4 per cent and the imputed rate 20·6 per cent (three sevenths of the distribution).

[3] The opposite case is that, if company income is *sui generis*, principles of equity require that profits tax should be set off against the individual's tax no more than other payments such as rates (ibid. p. 383). See also the viewpoints of Prest and Kaldor in House of Commons, *Report from the Select Committee on Corporation Tax*, p. vii.

[4] See M. T. Sumner, *The Effect of Taxation on Corporate Saving and Investment*, London, Institute for Fiscal Studies, 1976.

[5] Accounting for the fact that the imputation system allowed income tax at the standard rate to be offset against the grossed-up value of the dividend (that is, the dividend multiplied by 10/7), this condition is $\text{CT} + (1 - \text{CT})(10/7)(\text{IT} - 0·3) = \text{CT} + (1 - \text{CT})\text{CGT}$, or $(10/7)(\text{IT} - 0·3) = \text{CGT}$, where CT is the rate of company tax and 0·3 is the standard rate of income tax, IT is the marginal tax rate on dividends and CGT the rate of capital gains tax. Of course, retained profits are not systematically related to capital gains, which accrue and are realised in an erratic manner. The analysis here is thus fairly simplistic.

[6] See table 4.6 below and *Inland Revenue Statistics 1974*, table 107. For a standard rate taxpayer capital gains tax liability (on the first £5000 of gains) is restricted to the amount that would be due if half of this gain was added to his income as assessed for income tax.

been more neutral than either of the two previous regimes insofar as it removed the discrimination between retained and distributed profits for the *average* shareholder, who would have been taxed at (approximately) 66 per cent on both retentions and distributions. Both of the previous regimes involved a bias against distributions, despite the one operative from 1958 to 1964 being neutral towards the standard rate taxpayer.[1]

The issues of economic management which have entered into the differential tax debate have concerned the effects on aggregate savings and on inflationary pressure. The problem is not so much whether retentions – and hence company savings – are increased, it is rather to quantify the extent of the increase.[2] The *net* savings effect is, however, a different matter. The majority of the Royal Commission was much more hopeful than the minority that increasing distributions would not add much to demand,[3] and the proponents of discrimination have continued to argue that the propensity to save out of distributions is considerably lower than out of (realised or unrealised) capital gains,[4] but the differential may be as low as 10–15 per cent according to one calculation.[5] This might be taken as implying that the economic gains from discrimination are tentative, but part of the argument has

---

[1] For the period as a whole, the company tax system displayed the following properties *vis-à-vis* retentions and distributions:

	Standard rate taxpayer	Average shareholder
1958–64	neutral	bias against distributions
1965–72	bias against distributions	greater bias against distributions
1973	bias against retentions	neutral

When there is no capital gains tax, as in 1958, neutrality would actually demand a higher rate of tax on retentions than on distributions, both to force profits into the surtax net and to act as a proxy for an accrued capital gains tax (see Royal Commission on Taxation of Profits and Income, *Final Report*, p. 163; A. R. Prest, *Public Finance: in theory and practice* (5th edn), London, Weidenfeld & Nicolson, 1975, pp. 362–3).

[2] For a résumé of the evidence see Sumner, *The Effect of Taxation on Corporate Saving and Investment*.

[3] Both majority and minority were of the opinion that restoring neutrality would increase distributions and hence, *in the short term*, share values. The pessimism of the minority over the inflationary pressures that this would cause seems to have been shared by the Treasury, since the discrimination against distributions remained for three years afterwards, and was even increased in 1956.

[4] Kaldor in House of Commons, *Report from the Select Committee on Corporation Tax*, p. 251. See also, T. Balogh, 'Differential profits tax', *Economic Journal*, vol. 68, September 1958, pp. 529–30.

[5] M. S. Feldstein and G. Fane, 'Taxes, corporate dividend policy and personal savings: the British postwar experience', *Review of Economics and Statistics*, vol. 55, November 1973, pp. 399–410.

rested on the 'undoubted psychological link between dividend payments and wage claims'.[1]

However, the weight of the arguments for and against discrimination have come to centre on its effects *vis-à-vis* the size and character of investment. The Royal Commission's finding that retentions did not necessarily encourage ploughing back, but did interfere with the raising of new capital on the market by firms which needed it, implied a net discouragement to investment. The neutralist case, however, has rested on allocative efficiency – the correction of a system which discriminates in favour of monopoly and inefficiency by benefiting existing (large) corporations and encourages investment in relatively unprofitable channels. The reasons put forward for the 1958 reform (which were to be echoed by Anthony Barber in 1971) were that it would 'improve the supply of capital to firms who needed it most, and help remove the distortions in company finance';[2] that the previous system short-circuited the market seems to have been generally agreed on at one time. Among the arguments for reintroducing discrimination in 1965, the most powerful was thought to be that it would shift the tax burden away from 'the faster growing companies, which are generally low distributors, and thus enable them to expand faster'.[3] Empirical evidence is short on this subject, though a good deal of the neutralist case has been based on the finding that companies which retain a relatively high proportion of profits select relatively unprofitable investments.[4]

Theoretically, too, the issue is not clear-cut.[5] In particular, if the marginal rate of tax relevant to investment decisions is the rate on retentions, then the 1965 reform gave an added incentive to invest, as was claimed by the Chancellor at the time, by reducing the operative marginal rate from over 50 to 40 per cent.[6] But this obviously has to be considered in the context of the change from investment allowances to grants, a move prompted by disillusionment in the new administration over the effectiveness of investment incentives given through the tax system.[7] In January 1966 grants replaced investment allowances,[8]

---

[1] Royal Commission on Taxation of Profits and Income, *Final Report*, p. 387; A. Rubner, 'The irrelevancy of the British differential profits tax', *Economic Journal*, vol. 74, June 1964, pp. 350–1.   [2] D. H. Amory in the House of Commons, 15 April 1958.

[3] James Callaghan in the House of Commons, 6 April 1965.

[4] I. M. D. Little, 'Higgledy piggledy growth', *Bulletin of the Oxford University Institute of Statistics*, vol. 24, November 1962, pp. 387–412.

[5] See Sumner, *The Effect of Taxation on Corporate Saving and Investment*, for a summary of the theoretical issues.

[6] House of Commons, *Report from the Select Committee on Corporation Tax*, p. 249; *Hansard*, 6 April 1965, col. 255.   [7] Ibid. cols. 256–7.

[8] Department of Economic Affairs, *Investment Incentives*, Cmnd 2874, London, HMSO, 1966.

and here there is a second source of dispute. The arguments against grants were of the same genre as those against discriminatory tax rates; they were believed to distort the relationship between investment and returns by benefiting firms irrespective of profitability. The reintroduction of allowances in October 1970 was thus based primarily on the danger of 'uneconomic investment leading to waste of resources', though the discrimination against the service industries built into the grants system and the larger element of central administration and direction (not to mention public expenditure) were also considerations.[1] The 1970 reform introduced accelerated depreciation through increased initial and annual allowances (making 60 per cent the 'first-year' allowance on plant and machinery); there was no return to the system of investment allowances which had periodically reinforced initial allowances in the 1950s and early 1960s. It was followed in 1972 by the system of 100 per cent initial allowances (or 'free depreciation').

Indirect taxation

The late 1950s and early 1960s saw a substantial fall in expenditure tax rates on income-elastic goods, prompted by a belief in the economic efficiency of a more uniform tax incidence and greater 'fiscal balance'. By 1959/60 the number of purchase tax rates had been reduced to four, with a range of 5–50 per cent (table 4.1), and this tendency continued up to 1963/4, when there were three rates with a range of 10–25 per cent. Though purchase tax increases were occasionally used in contractions, its absolute and relative impact on a restricted range of goods was a drawback recognised by all Chancellors;[2] in Conservative periods this acted as an incentive to reduce and standardise rates and in Labour periods as a disincentive against increases, though expediency sometimes prevailed (as in 1968).

Debates on the expansion of the tax base which accompanied expenditure tax increases usually brought suggestions of substituting a turnover tax for purchase tax. This, having been rejected in 1958, was raised again in March 1963, but received no encouragement from the Richardson Report, which saw no benefits sufficient to offset the added burden of administration.[3] If a further expansion of the tax base was desirable, this could best be achieved by extending and modifying purchase tax; the committee found that VAT did not, any more than purchase tax, promote exports or growth. However, because of the small amount of purchase tax on industrial inputs such as cars and

[1] Treasury, *Investment Incentives*, Cmnd 4516, London, HMSO, 1970.
[2] See particularly the budget speeches on 6 April 1965 and 3 May 1966.
[3] Inland Revenue, *Report of the Committee on Turnover Taxation*, chap. 5.

stationery which enter into export costs, and because of the discrimination in favour of services (which a sales tax cannot easily cover) such
a reform continued to be favoured in some circles;[1] it became official
Conservative policy in preference to selective employment tax and as
a step towards harmonisation with the EEC. The introduction of VAT
in 1973/4 at a standard rate of 10 per cent was represented as reducing
the 'distortion of consumer choice' which led to allocative inefficiencies,
and as benefiting the balance of payments because the hidden element
of purchase tax and selective employment tax on exported services
could now be refunded in full.[2] Because VAT provided a broader and
more uniform tax base, it was also supported as making stabilisation
policy more effective (the selectivity allowed by purchase tax having
come to be considered as of dubious value).[3] From the late 1950s the
need for more flexible and broader based demand interventions had
become apparent, which led to the introduction of an expenditure tax
regulator in the 1961 budget, so that adjustments to expenditure taxes
as a whole could be made between budgets to a limit of 10 per cent of
existing duties.[4] In 1964 this was altered to allow variations in any one
or more of five groups of duties – purchase tax, tobacco, alcoholic
drink, hydro-carbon oils, and betting and other minor duties – the
object being to exclude items which were thought to be near their
taxable capacity.

While the degree to which the excise tax base as a whole responds to
changes in real income is not as low as sometimes supposed, all the
excise duties decline in real value through inflation and this is probably
the biggest single reason for the prominence of excise duties in discretionary tax increases. There is, though, an important drawback in that they
achieve their effect only by raising consumer prices, with the danger
that they will accelerate the price–wage spiral. Partly for this reason
there was a growing reluctance to correct the declining real value of
excise duties between 1968/9 and 1973/4.

The introduction of selective employment tax in the budget of 1966
was the product of both expediency and refined economic logic, in
that it reflected the need for more revenue and faster long-term growth.
It was a poll tax, levied as a flat-rate surcharge on employers' national
insurance contributions, with broad distinctions as to age and sex.
It was to be refunded to all industries except services and construction;
manufacturers and institutions engaged in scientific research related to
manufacture received premiums.

---

[1] For example, NEDO, *Value Added Tax*, London, HMSO, 1969.
[2] Treasury, *Value Added Tax* [Green Paper], Cmnd 4621, London, HMSO, 1971.
[3] NEDO, *Value Added Tax*.
[4] Excluding protective duties, television licence fees and excise licence duties.

Apart from its structural aspects, selective employment tax was intended to raise revenue for the expansion of the public sector. While its potential as such was welcomed in some quarters,[1] it was not the descendent of the 1944 payroll regulator, which had been revived as a proposal in 1961, but had foundered because it had none of the necessary qualities for flexible action. As the delayed starting date for selective employment tax showed (it was to be effective from 5 September 1966) the instrument could only be slow-acting, while the economic efficiency of a tax on *employers'* contributions could not be great, since its effects on prices and consumer spending were ambivalent and delayed.[2] As a means of eliminating the bias of the tax system in favour of services the new tax could be supported by economic liberals; but it also had strong directional aspects in its discrimination in favour of visible exports, manufacturing and (with the subsequent introduction of regional employment premiums) the regions.

An implicit subsidy for exports was contained in the general rebate to manufacturing industry; the rationale being the relatively high export content of manufacturing in comparison with construction and (allegedly) services. It can be traced to a memorandum submitted to the Committee on Turnover Taxation by Kaldor in 1963;[3] here the suggestion was a value-added tax, the proceeds of which would be used to pay a general subsidy to enterprises on their wages bill. From the point of view of exports and the balance of payments this was claimed to be 'just as effective as a devaluation'. The effect of the premium ($37\frac{1}{2}$p per male worker) in stimulating exports was, however, small. The National Institute estimated the net effect on exports as virtually nil and other commentators did not differ substantially.[4]

The further positive ingredients in the system, which aimed to affect export growth and achieve lasting expansion, were the employment base and the restriction of the base to services and construction. The idea of a permanent payroll tax (of which the poll tax is a variant) had arrived in official circles by way of Sir Robert Hall's diagnosis of the structural weakness in the British economy during the boom of 1960/1.[5] At that time a great degree of spare capacity existed side-by-side with over-employment, preventing output and productivity gains.[6] There was also evidence of labour hoarding, one remedy for which was seen as a tax disincentive, and selective employment tax was a logical solution.

---

[1] See *National Institute Economic Review*, no. 36, May 1966, p. 10.

[2] See Brittan, *Steering the Economy*, pp. 249–50.

[3] N. Kaldor, *Essays on Economic Policy*, vol. 1, London, Duckworth, 1964, pp. 291–4.

[4] *National Institute Economic Review*, no. 36, May 1966, pp. 18–19; S. Brittan, 'The selective employment tax', *The Banker*, vol. 116, June 1966, p. 367.

[5] See Brittan, *Steering the Economy*, p. 248.

[6] Sir Robert Hall, 'Britain's economic problem', *Economist*, 23 September 1961, p. 1133.

Perhaps the more sophisticated argument, which related to the choice of services and construction to bear the burden of selective employment tax, had been set out by Kaldor in 1966.[1] Here a high growth rate for manufacturing output was laid down as the *sine qua non* of high productivity increases, fast-growing exports and high levels of economic growth. The crucial element in Britain's growth performance was distilled from the premise that 'over a run of years it was the rate of growth of production which determined the rate of growth of our exports and not the other way round'.[2] Neither high rates of export demand, nor large amounts of industrial investment were regarded as sufficient in themselves to procure expansion (though necessary) and the conclusion was that 'once it is recognised that manpower shortage is the main handicap from which we are suffering...we shall...tend to concentrate our efforts on a more rational use of manpower in all fields'.[3] Thus selective employment tax aimed to transfer manpower to manufacturing as a potentially more productive sector, emulating the effect that large reserves of agricultural labour had had upon growth in other countries.

This thesis did not gain universal acceptance. A Brookings report found the link between growth and the labour supply unconvincing;[4] moreover, it was disputed that a tax on an employment base was a better means of increasing productivity than one based on total cost or output. Selectivity was considered questionable in its effect on export competitiveness because of the adverse effects on invisible trade and service inputs into merchandise trade,[5] while devaluation reduced the need for such expedients in any case; it also discriminated against investment insofar as construction was not exempt. For these reasons the Conservative government abolished selective employment tax (in two steps, in 1971/2 and 1973/4) as part of a wider programme involving the introduction of VAT.[6]

Reports on the effects of the tax find some savings in manpower in the service industries (particularly distribution),[7] but these results are ambiguous in that the introduction of the tax coincided with the

[1] N. Kaldor, *Causes of the Slow Rate of Economic Growth of the United Kingdom*, Cambridge University Press, 1966.   [2] Ibid. p. 25.   [3] Ibid. p. 31.

[4] Musgrave and Musgrave, 'Fiscal policy' in Caves *et al.*, *Britain's Economic Prospects*, p. 64. See also J. N. Wolfe, 'Productivity and growth in manufacturing industry', *Economica*, vol. 35 (new series), May 1968, pp. 117–26; N. Kaldor, 'Productivity and growth in manufacturing industry: a reply', *Economica*, vol. 35 (new series), November 1968, pp. 385–91.

[5] '... this was bound to be true if the field of tax was defined in terms of establishments, rather than by reference to activities' (W. B. Reddaway, *Effects of the Selective Employment Tax: final report*, Cambridge University Press, 1973, p. 172).

[6] House of Commons, *Hansard*, 30 March 1971, cols. 1392–4.

[7] Reddaway, *Effects of the Selective Employment Tax*; Treasury, *Effects of the Selective Employment Tax. First Report: the distributive trades*, London, HMSO, 1970.

abolition of resale price maintenance and the withdrawal of investment allowances to service industries; also, productivity gains in service industries were accompanied by similar 'abnormal gains' in manufacturing, which may imply that some common factor, such as a shake-out of labour, was at work during the period.[1] The case for selective employment tax – apart from redressing the erstwhile tax imbalance between service and goods industries, now accomplished by VAT – thus remains unproven.

BUDGETARY STRATEGY:
DISCRETIONARY AND BUILT-IN CHANGES IN REVENUE

Introduction

Budgetary policy in the United Kingdom has been based on short-term discretionary action through changes in tax rates. This derives from the historical procedure of annual budget-making, and from the constitutional and political realities of Cabinet government, which have normally ensured the prompt enactment of Finance Bills by Parliament. This is in marked contrast to the American system, for Congress has a more influential role, so that statutory tax changes there are introduced only infrequently and have a Congressional delay of twelve to eighteen months.[2] To compensate, the United States places greater emphasis on automatic stabilisation and has committed resources to improving its effectiveness. In Britain, on the other hand, more attention has been concentrated on enhancing legislative and administrative flexibility in the interests of 'fine-tuning'.

Although British practice has never had explicit rules for operating automatic stabilisers, these have great analytical relevance to fiscal policy. They not only provide the 'built-in flexibility' which damps cyclical movements in the economy, they also define the automatic properties of the system *vis-à-vis* growth and inflation; that is, they specify budgetary rules to identify and even neutralise the biases arising from 'fiscal drag', through either indexation or the direct specification of the level of the full-employment budget balance. Some prescriptions for setting this balance attempt explicitly to eliminate the

---

[1] The attribution of productivity gains to selective employment tax has been questioned by J. D. Whitley and G. D. N. Worswick from a study of the corresponding trends in manufacturing (see 'The productivity effects of selective employment tax', *National Institute Economic Review*, no. 56, May 1971, pp. 36–40; W. B. Reddaway, 'The productivity effects of selective employment tax – a reply', *National Institute Economic Review*, no. 57, August 1971, pp. 62–8, and Whitley and Worswick, 'The productivity effects of selective employment tax – a rejoinder', *National Institute Economic Review*, no. 58, November 1971, pp. 72–5).

[2] On the implications of this lag for stabilisation see P. R. Portney, 'Congressional delays in U.S. fiscal policymaking: simulating the effects', *Journal of Public Economics*, vol. 5, April–May 1976, pp. 237–47.

need for discretionary fiscal intervention,[1] but the concepts of fiscal drag and the 'full-employment surplus' may be better interpreted as delineating discretionary action by providing benchmarks for a 'neutral' policy. In British budgetary practice, for instance, a neutral budget may be defined as one leaving statutory tax rates and allowances unaltered, but because of fiscal drag the effective tax burden may still rise automatically and it has been at the discretion of Chancellors to offset this or not.[2] Discretionary policy should therefore be defined to include both active changes in statutory rates and passive changes due to fiscal drag. In this respect, also, the use of the full-employment surplus can be shown to identify more closely the criteria by which the overall neutrality of the budget is judged, in that it measures the combined effect of fiscal drag and other discretionary policy influences, undisguised by the automatic damping effects on budget revenue which less than full employment has on the actual budget balance.

Accordingly, the following analysis attempts to measure discretionary and built-in policies as they conform to various definitions of neutrality. The definitions used in British budgetary practice are followed in measuring the demand effect of budgetary changes; these statutory changes are then traced through the resultant changes in effective rates and analysed in the context of the accompanying automatic changes in tax rates. Not all such automatic changes are built-in – some are haphazard or non-recurring–so finally we attempt to specify the structural element they contain through their relationship with income. The approach here is to derive first the marginal tax rates applicable to built-in flexibility, then, secondly, the non-proportional effects (elasticities) which are the basis of fiscal drag. Later in the chapter the total stance of budgetary policy is measured with reference to the neutrality rules applicable to the full-employment budget balance.

Discretionary interventions in British budgetary practice

Changes in tax rates and allowances are generally accompanied by an estimate of their revenue effects on both a current-year and a full-year basis.[3] In addition, the Financial Statement issued at budget time shows the total revenue from the various classes of taxes expected to be received during the financial year; it thus provides the basis for break-

---

[1] Cf. M. Friedman, 'A monetary and fiscal framework for economic stability', *American Economic Review*, vol. 38, June 1948, pp. 245–64.

[2] This was recognised in the 1977 Finance Act, which laid down that personal income tax reliefs be changed in following years 'by not less than the same percentage as the increase in the retail price index for the previous calendar year'; to prescribe lesser reliefs the Treasury needs Parliamentary approval.

[3] The difference between the two reflects the lag of accruals on payments and, where the intervention occurs part-way through the financial year (as with the regulator), the fact that the tax change is not operative for the whole of the current year.

ing down the change in total tax between discretionary and automatic effects. The procedure may be clarified by considering a proportional tax system, with tax base B, statutory rate of tax μ and a total yield T; thus:

$$T_t^t = \mu_t B_t \tag{1}$$

$$T_{t-1}^{t-1} = \mu_{t-1} B_{t-1} \tag{2}$$

and
$$T_t^{t-1} = \mu_{t-1} B_t \tag{3}$$

T_t^t being the accrued yield of tax in year t (subscript) derived from the tax function actually operative in that year (denoted by superscript t). Similarly, T_{t-1}^{t-1} is the accrued yield in the previous year, derived from the tax rates which operated in that year, and T_t^{t-1} the yield which would have accrued had the previous year's tax rates operated in the current year. All three estimates appear in the Financial Statement.[1] The first is the actual forecast for the year, and the difference between this and the provisional out-turn for the past year (2) is the total expected change in yield ($T_t^t - T_{t-1}^{t-1}$). The third estimate is the pre-budget forecast, and the difference between this and the actual forecast is a measure of the discretionary change introduced in the budget: $T_t^t - T_t^{t-1}$. The automatic change in yield which would have occurred without budgetary intervention then emerges as the difference between the pre-budget forecast and the past year's out-turn: $T_t^{t-1} - T_{t-1}^{t-1}$. The total change can then be expressed as:

$$
\begin{aligned}
T_t^t - T_{t-1}^{t-1} &= (\mu_t B_t - \mu_{t-1} B_t) &&+ (\mu_{t-1} B_t - \mu_{t-1} B_{t-1}) \\
\text{or} \qquad &= \underbrace{(\mu_t - \mu_{t-1}) B_t}_{} &&\underbrace{+ \mu_{t-1}(B_t - B_{t-1})}_{}
\end{aligned}
\tag{4}
$$

$$\underbrace{\phantom{T_t^t - T_{t-1}^{t-1}}}_{\substack{\text{total} \\ \text{change}}} \quad \underbrace{\phantom{(\mu_t - \mu_{t-1}) B_t}}_{\substack{\text{discretionary} \\ \text{change}}} \quad \underbrace{\phantom{+ \mu_{t-1}(B_t - B_{t-1})}}_{\substack{\text{automatic} \\ \text{change}}}$$

However, the tax base B can change both independently and as a result of discretionary changes in tax rates. It is conventional to ignore induced effects on the tax base so far as income tax is concerned, although if the repercussions of a change on labour supply or any other relevant behaviour were known with some certainty and were not negligible it would be proper to incorporate them. The case of expenditure taxes is quite different, and Treasury estimates of revenue changes allow for the effects of budget-induced relative price changes on the composition of consumers' expenditure, since the post-budget forecast is evaluated at levels of the tax base which take account of substitution effects. Under the previous tax regime the base in year t would have

---

[1] These figures are in terms of tax payments rather than accruals, so that some adjustment is necessary to the published figures to obtain estimates of accruals (*National Institute Economic Review*, no. 65, August 1973, pp. 53–4).

Table 4.2. *Discretionary tax changes,* [a]*1959/60–1973/4*

£ million

	1959/60	1960/1	1961/2		1962/3		1963/4	1964/5		1965/6	1966/7	
	Budget	Budget	Budget	Regulator	Budget	Other[b]	Budget	Budget	Other[c]	Budget	Budget	Regulator
Personal income taxes[a]												
Rates of tax	-61	—	-83	—	—	—	-77[e]	—	+90	+2	—	+25[f]
Allowances, etc.	-105	-20	-15	—	-4	—	-218	—	—	-10	—	—
Total												
Current year	-135	-7	-12	—	-9	—	-221	—	—	-8	+3	—
Full year	-166	-20	-98	—	-4	—	-295	—	+90	-8	+3	+25
Expenditure taxes												
On alcoholic drink	-34	-4	—	+31	-6	—	—	+49	—	+52	—	+38
On tobacco	—	+40	—	+71	-4	—	—	+55	+93	+75	—	+72
On hydro-carbon oils	—	—	—	+43	+42	—	—	-2	—	—	—	+40
Purchase tax	-82	—	+50	+45	-18	-77	—	—	—	—	—	—
SET[h]	—	—	—	—	—	—	—	—	—	—	+240	—
Others	-12	-7	+33	+6	—	—	-53	-6	—	+54	+17	—
Total												
Current year	-103	+29	+79	+130	+14	-31	-36	+91	—	+172	+323	+94
Full year	-128	+29	+83	+196	+7	-77	-53	+96	+93	+181	+257[k]	+150
(Full-year out-turn)	-153	+20	+83	+191	—	—	-53	+78	+104	+206	+350[k]	+180
Company taxes[l]												
Income tax[d]	-63	+65	+70	—	—	-53[o]	—	+5	—	—	—	—
Profits tax	-3	—	+3	—	—	—	—	—	—	—	—	—
Corporation tax	—	—	—	—	—	—	-57[g]	—	+32	+48	+75[m]	—
Investment allowances	-9	—	—	—	—	—	—	—	—	—	-35[f]	—
Total												
Current year	-57	+1	+1	—	—	—	-3	+3	+32	—	+40	—
Full year	-75	+65	+73	—	—	-53	-57	+5	+32	+48	+40	—
Capital taxes												
Capital gains tax	—	—	—	—	—	—	—	—	—	+125	—	—
Estate duty	—	-2	—	—	—	—	-1	—	—	—	+1	—
Total												
Current year	—	-1	—	—	—	—	-1	—	—	—	+1	—
Full year	—	-2	—	—	—	—	-1	—	—	+125	+1	—
TOTAL TAXATION												
Current year	-295	+22	+68	+130	-10	-31	-261	+94	+32	+164	+326	+94
Full year	-369	+72	+58	+196	+10	-130	-406	+101	+215	+346	+298	+175
(Full year at 1970 prices)	-541	+103	+80	+268	+13	-172	-639	+130	+266	+422	+352	+206

£ million

	1967/8 Budget	1968/9 Budget	1968/9 Regulator	1969/70 Budget	1970/1 Budget	1970/1 Other[c]	1971/2 Budget	1971/2 Other[b]	1972/3 Budget	1973/4 Budget
Personal income taxes[a]										
Rates of tax	—	+100[f]	—	—	—5	—350	—38	—	—14	—316[g]
Allowances, etc.	—4	+123	—	—	—186	—	—241	—	—1227	—
Total										
Current year	—3	+164	—	—6	—150	—350	—184	—	—982	..
Full year	—4	+223	—	—	—191	—350	—279	—	—1241	—316
Expenditure taxes										
On alcoholic drink	—	+15	+33	+10	—	—	—	—	—	—
On tobacco	—	+30	+44	+45	—	—	—	—	—	—
On hydro-carbon oils	+2	+76	+97	+52	—	—	—	—	—	—
Purchase tax	—	+163	+76	+130	—	—	—	—	—	—
SET[h]	—10	+152	—	+12	—13[j]	—	—245	—235	—175	—64[i]
Others	—	+156	—	—	—	—	—3	—	—	—
Total										
Current year	—2	+548	+65	+212	—13	—	—292	—110	—141	—
Full year	—8	+592	+250	+249	—13	—	—248	—235	—175	—64
(Full-year out-turn)	—8	+581	+296	+236	—	—	—299	—236	—175	..
Company taxes[l]										
Income tax[d]	—	—	—	—	—	—	—	—	—	—
Profits tax	—	—	—	—	—	—	—	—	—	—
Corporation tax	—	+98	—	+105	—	—90[p]	—105	—	—60	—77[n]
Investment allowances	—	—	—	—	—	—	—	[p]	—205[p]	—
Total										
Current year	—	+57	—	+75	—	—60	—55	—	—17	..
Full year	—	+98	—	+105	—	—90	—105	—	—205	—77
Capital taxes										
Capital gains tax	—	—1	—	—10	+2	—	—16	—	—15	—
Estate duty	—	+11	—	+2	+6	—	—53	—	—123	—5
Total										
Current ye	—	+5	—	—9	+6	—60	—15	—	—71	—2
Full year	—	+10	—	—8	+2	—90	—69	—	—138	—5
TOTAL TAXATION										
Current year	—5	+774	+65	+272	—144	—60	—546	—110	—1211	..
Full year	—12	+923	+250	+346	—202	—440	—701	—235	—1819	—462
(Full year at 1970 prices)	—14	+1027	+270	+368	—285	—430	—618	—202	—1464	—340

SOURCES: Treasury, *Financial Statement and Budget Report* (annual); NIESR estimates.

[a] Full-year budget forecasts on tax accruals unless otherwise defined. Current-year figures are for effects on tax payments in the year of intervention. For extra-year, budgetary interventions and changes (such as SET) operating part-way through the year, differences between current-year and full-year effects arise from both partial operation in the year and an adjustment for accruals.

[b] Changes made by Treasury Order (other than the regulator) in October 1962 and July 1971.

[c] Supplementary budgets in November 1964 and October 1970.

[d] Income tax on distributions is allocated to the personal sector.

[e] Includes abolition of schedule A tax on imputed rent of owner-occupation equivalent to —£48 million.

[f] Surcharges on surtax (1966/7) and investment income (1968/9).

[g] Effect of unifying income tax and surtax.

[h] Excludes SET allocated to public authorities' expenditure.

[i] Effect of replacing purchase tax and SET by VAT.

[j] Excludes the effects of the import surcharge (1964/5) and import deposits (1970/1).

[k] Difference from budget estimate due to discrepancies between payments and accruals of tax refunds.

[l] For income tax and corporation tax, rates are on income assessed in the financial year – usually earned in the previous-but-one calendar year. Profits tax rates were, however, set in advance on income to be earned in the financial year.

[m] Estimated effect of change to corporation tax, with double taxation of distributions.

[n] Nil included for effect of reverting to single taxation of distributions, because with the increase to 52 per cent corporation tax it did not affect overall liabilities (Treasury, *Financial Statement and Budget Report 1972–73*, p. 28).

[o] Effects expected in 1954/5.

[p] Effects of substituting investment grants for allowances (1966/7) and allowances for grants (1970/1–1972/3).

been B_t^{t-1}; post-budget it becomes B_t^t, where superscripts again refer to the tax function and subscripts to the year's income considered. Equation (4) then needs to be modified slightly and, as applied to an individual instrument whose base is sensitive to changes in budget parameters, it becomes:

$$T_t^t - T_{t-1}^{t-1} = \underbrace{(\mu_t B_t^t - \mu_{t-1} B_t^{t-1})}_{} + \underbrace{(\mu_{t-1} B_t^{t-1} - \mu_{t-1} B_{t-1}^{t-1})}_{} \qquad (5)$$

$$\begin{array}{ccc} \text{total} & \text{net discretionary} & \text{automatic} \\ \text{change} & \text{change} & \text{change} \end{array}$$

Treasury estimates of discretionary change prepared on this basis are presented for the principal expenditure taxes in table 4.2, also the income tax changes as derived from equation (4). They are defined as 'full-year budget estimates' of change and are accompanied, for the major categories of taxation, by estimates of the change occurring in the current year. For expenditure taxes the 'out-turn' effects of tax changes on a full-year basis are also given; these may be used to check the accuracy and consistency of the budget estimates themselves, as well as to provide a breakdown according to the sector affected.[1] A change in personal income tax can be attributed wholly to the personal sector, but the proportion of a change in an expenditure tax which affects consumers directly varies substantially. Duty on hydrocarbon oils and selective employment tax particularly impinge to a large extent on industrial inputs, which makes their effect on price levels and spending more diffuse than that of beer or tobacco excise duties, which fall almost wholly on consumers.

The substitution effects on the tax base which cause B_t^t to differ from B_t^{t-1} as a result of discretionary budget changes – equation (5) – may be quite complex and on them depends the efficiency of a particular tax instrument in raising extra revenue. The net discretionary change in equation (5) can actually be divided into a tax rate change and a tax base change, the second usually offsetting to some degree the ex ante effect on revenue of the first:

$$\underbrace{\mu_t B_t^t - \mu_{t-1} B_t^{t-1}}_{} = \underbrace{(\mu_t - \mu_{t-1}) B_t^{t-1}}_{} + \underbrace{\mu_t (B_t^t - B_t^{t-1})}_{} \qquad (6)$$

$$\begin{array}{ccc} \text{net discretionary} & \textit{ex ante} \text{ effect} & \text{substitution and} \\ \text{change} & & \text{income effects} \end{array}$$

[1] The disaggregated tax model used for simulating the effects of tax changes over a period is based on a regression analysis of the various tax bases between 1955 and 1972. The allocation to consumption is given in table 4.8 on page 174 below. The out-turn figures also incorporate the income effects on consumption, which are usually smaller than the substitution effects. The complexities do not allow an ex post check of the Inland Revenue estimates of discretionary changes in allowances, but the effects of standard rate changes can be deduced from published figures of taxable income. For example, the effect of the 1970 change was put at −£350 million; the out-turn shown in table 4.8 for 1971/2 was −£380 million.

The *ex ante* effect is the rate change evaluated at unchanged forecast levels of the tax base. The substitution effect depends on how much tax changes are shifted into final prices, the 'tax content' of prices and the relevant substitution elasticities. A further effect derives from the reaction of consumers to the real income changes caused by the tax change and this may be quite substantial on occasions. The more tax changes are shifted and the higher the tax content of final prices, the greater will be the absolute and relative price change for a good arising from a given tax change, and this, together with the price elasticity, determines the substitution effect.

Table 4.3. *Effects on the tax yield from consumers' expenditure of a 'regulator' change in indirect taxes*

	Relative price elasticity[a]	Substitution effect	Income effect	Net discretionary tax change
		(percentage of *ex ante* tax change)		
Excise duties	-0.35	-20.5	-16.5	$+63.0$
Beer	-0.25^b			
Spirits	-2.10^b	-41.5	-17.0	$+41.5$
Wine	-0.70			
Tobacco	-0.30^c	-14.0	-7.5	$+78.5$
Petrol	—	—	-38.5	$+61.5$
Purchase tax	-1.00	-1.0	-12.5	$+86.5$
Total regulator	-0.80	-15.5	-15.5	$+69.0$

SOURCE: NIESR estimates.

[a] Estimated from a regression analysis for the period 1956–72, using annual Customs and Excise data; see also note *c* to table 4.7.

[b] There is also a strong substitution effect between beer and spirits. The elasticity for drink as a whole is -0.95.

[c] The budget estimates in table 4.2 imply an elasticity of -0.5 in the mid-1960s and of -0.3 in later years. A value of -0.15 is quite plausible (see A. B. Atkinson and T. C. Skegg, 'Anti-smoking publicity and the demand for tobacco in the UK', *Manchester School of Economic and Social Studies*, vol. 41, September 1973).

The extent of the substitution effects will also depend on whether the instrument is used singly or in a package. Even an across-the-board tax change, such as accompanies the use of the regulator, will, however, have quite large substitution effects because of the differing tax content of the various goods affected.[1] As an illustration, table 4.3 presents the substitution effects accompanying the 1968 regulator surcharge of 10 per cent. These, the corresponding income effects on the tax base and the net discretionary effects are all expressed as percentages of the

[1] Cf. W. A. B. Hopkin and W. A. H. Godley, 'An analysis of tax changes', *National Institute Economic Review*, no. 32, May 1965, pp. 33–42.

initial *ex ante* change (as defined in equation (6)). This being 10 per cent, it can be seen that the net effect on tax receipts was 6·9 per cent,[1] with the substitution and income offsets accounting equally for the difference between this and 10 per cent. Overall, excise duties seem to have been less effective than purchase tax in raising revenue, and this is associated, in particular, with the extremely price-elastic duty base for spirits. The sensitivity of the tobacco base to the effect of duty changes seems to have led to some pessimism on the part of the author-ities in the mid-1960s about the usefulness of this instrument in raising revenue and to its exclusion from the 1966 regulator. But since the relevant elasticity is −0·3, and might well be as small as −0·15, this pessimism seems to have been overdone.

Overall, as may be seen from the budget estimates and out-turns in table 4.2, indirect taxes are a fairly reliable instrument of policy, with an average range of prediction error of ± 10 per cent only in the inter-ventions of the period. The unpredictability can, however, be as high as 20 per cent of the announced discretionary change, and this factor, together with the caveats attached to individual instruments, qualifies the verdict somewhat.

Effective rates of tax

Discretionary budget changes may be partly determined by the need to offset unwanted automatic changes in tax incidence. Or, if they are opportune, automatic changes may make discretionary interventions unnecessary. In this respect, effective rates of tax derive from a com-bination of automatic changes (the parameters of the tax system being taken as fixed) and statutory changes in tax rates or allowances. The relative contribution of each is summarised in chart 4·2.[2] Parts B and C

---

[1] This applies to the 80 per cent or so of the regulator surcharge falling directly on con-sumption; the element falling on industrial inputs and other final expenditures would not be subject to substitution and income effects.

[2] Direct and indirect taxes are here evaluated in relation to a base of aggregate personal income (Y), or consumers' expenditure, which are national income concepts and have no statutory existence. The effective rate of tax therefore changes as the ratio of the statutory to the national accounts base changes, even with an unchanged tax rate. In year t, the average rate $\overline{ar}_t^t$ will actually be $\mu_t(B_t/Y_t)$; if the statutory rates operating in year t had applied to the previous year's income, the effective rate would have been $\overline{ar}_{t-1}^t = \mu_t(B_{t-1}/Y_{t-1})$, so that the average rate would have changed automatically if the base had grown at a different rate from income. The actual average rate in the previous year being $\overline{ar}_{t-1}^{t-1} = \mu_{t-1}(B_{t-1}/Y_{t-1})$, the total change in the average rate emerges as:

$$\underbrace{\overline{ar}_t^t - \overline{ar}_{t-1}^{t-1}}_{\text{total change}} = \underbrace{(\overline{ar}_t^t - \overline{ar}_{t-1}^t)}_{\substack{\text{automatic} \\ \text{change}}} + \underbrace{(\overline{ar}_{t-1}^t - \overline{ar}_{t-1}^{t-1})}_{\substack{\text{discretionary} \\ \text{change}}}$$

In general terms, the automatic change derives from the fact that the average rate differs from the marginal rate, a measure of which is given by $\overline{MR}_t = \mu_t(\Delta B_t/\Delta Y_t)$, where

Chart 4.2. *Effective rates of personal sector taxes, 1955/6–1973/4,
with automatic and discretionary changes*

A. *Direct and indirect taxes
combined as percentage
of personal income*

C. *Central government indirect
taxes as percentage of
consumers' expenditure
(excluding housing)*

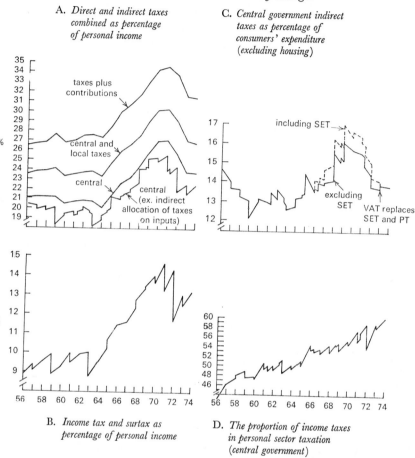

B. *Income tax and surtax as
percentage of personal income*

D. *The proportion of income taxes
in personal sector taxation
(central government)*

SOURCES: Inland Revenue, *Reports of the Commissioners* (annual); Customs and Excise, *Reports of the Commissioners* (annual); NIESR estimates.

Notes: (i) Automatic and discretionary changes are as defined on page 158; the former are shown by lateral shifts and the latter by vertical shifts. Discretionary changes are measured at the income level at the time of intervention. Automatic changes in indirect taxes include all influences on consumption not stemming directly from budgetary changes. Where changes did not take effect from the beginning of the financial year, the actual-year effect is given at the point of intervention and the residual is added to the subsequent year's change.

(ii) 'Personal income' includes national insurance contributions in measuring rates of tax plus contributions and excludes them in measuring tax rates alone.

(iii) Indirect taxes exclude the indirect allocation to consumption of taxes on industrial inputs and local authority rates.

(iv) Horizontal scales refer to financial years ending 31 March (e.g. '74' indicates the end of 1973/4).

show the aggregate average or effective rates of tax on personal income and consumers' expenditure respectively; they are summed and referred to personal income in Part A and table 4.4; the relative movements in each are reflected in the changing mix of direct and indirect taxes illustrated in part D.

Table 4.4. *Changes in the average rate of tax (direct and indirect) on total personal income,*[a] *1955/6–1973/4*

Percentages

	Discretionary change	Automatic change	Total change
Budget 1955/6 to October 1964	−2·98	+2·51	−0·47
Budget Nov. 1964 to end-1970/1	+4·45	+1·50	+5·95
Budget 1971/2 to end-1973/4[b]	−5·34	+2·23	−3·11
Budget 1955/6 to end-1973/4	−3·87	+6·24	+2·37

SOURCES: Inland Revenue, *Report of the Commissioners* (annual); Customs and Excise, *Report of the Commissioners* (annual).

[a] Excludes rates and indirect allocation to consumption from taxes on industrial inputs.
[b] Includes changes announced in October 1970 effective from 1971/2.

The average rate of personal income tax has been influenced by the persistent upward bias imparted by rising incomes under a progressive rate structure (as shown in chart 4.1). This was counteracted up to 1963/4 by discretionary reductions, so that the effective rate remained fairly steady at around 9·5 per cent,[1] but thereafter there was a strong and consistent rise until the end of 1970/1, when the rate reached 14·7 per cent. Of this increase of 5·2 per cent, a small amount (0·6 per cent) was attributable to budget changes, while the bulk was due to automatic changes in yield. In the second Conservative period attempts were made to bring the rate down, but three quarters of the substantial discretionary reductions of 4·5 per cent merely offset the increasing automatic buoyancy of income tax revenue, so that the effective rate of 12·2 per cent in 1973/4 still represented a significant increase over the beginning of the period.

The ratio of central government indirect taxes to consumers' expenditure (chart 4.2C) has the opposite pattern: increases have been effected

---

$\Delta B_t = B_t - B_{t-1}$ and $\Delta Y_t = Y_t - Y_{t-1}$. The marginal rate can differ from the average because of a progressive rate structure, or because the tax base changes at a different rate from income. The automatic changes in the average rate discussed in the text can thus be understood as:

$$\overline{ar}_t^i - \overline{ar}_{t-1}^i = (\overline{MR}_t - \overline{ar}_{t-1}^i)(\Delta Y_t / Y_t)$$

[1] See chart 4.2B. The effective rate is here calculated with respect to personal income as defined in the national accounts (see note (ii) to chart 4.2).

by discretionary action and decreases (apart from purchase tax) have largely resulted from the fact that the quantum base of excise duties fails to keep pace with inflation. The period 1956/7–1964/5 saw the overall rate fall slightly from 14 to about 13 per cent of consumer spending.[1] Between 1964/5 and 1970/1, however, the effective rate increased emphatically, reaching 15·5 per cent, with oil duty, purchase tax and selective employment tax the principal instruments (see table 4.2).

The effects of automatic factors on the combined (direct and indirect) effective rate of tax (chart 4.2A) have been less consistent, chiefly because the buoyancy characteristics of the two types of taxation were partially offsetting, but the effects have almost always been fairly consistently positive and were significantly so overall (table 4.4). They explain the net increase in the tax rate between the late 1950s and 1973/4, when central government taxes accounted directly for about $22\frac{1}{2}$ per cent of personal income. With indirect taxes on inputs into consumption and local rates, the tax take was 27 per cent; with national insurance contributions it was almost 32 per cent. At the same time the proportion of personal taxation derived from income taxes rose from 45 to 60 per cent (chart 4.2D), the consistency of this movement being remarkable, in that automatic biases making for greater dependence on income taxes (the lateral upward movements) were accompanied, but only partially offset, by a discretionary bias towards expenditure taxes (the vertical downward shifts). This significant change in the tax-mix seems to have been at odds with prevailing ideas about the relative merits of direct and indirect taxes.

It was shown in the Richardson Report that the burden of company taxation – as expressed in the effective rate of tax on the income of that sector – had fallen between the mid-1950s and early 1960s despite statutory increases in rates of profits tax;[2] the improvement in capital allowances (especially the introduction of investment allowances in 1954), together with the increase in investment, was largely responsible. Chart 4.3 shows, however, that this trend ceased to operate in the 1960s, despite the increase in investment allowances at the end of 1962 and notwithstanding the switch to investment grants in 1966. The average rate of United Kingdom tax on gross company income (including that on distributions)[3] increased from 23·5 per cent to a peak of

---

[1] This excludes local authority rates and the indirect allocation to consumption from taxes on industrial inputs. Housing expenditure, which bears rates, is correspondingly excluded from consumer spending.

[2] Inland Revenue, *Report of the Committee on Turnover Taxation*, pp. 48–50.

[3] The effective rate is defined in terms of *accruals*, that is taxes levied on income earned during the year irrespective of when they are paid. This broadly corresponds to the national accounts definition, except that that includes additions to reserves made according to anti-

Chart 4.3. *Effective rates of tax on company income, 1959–73*

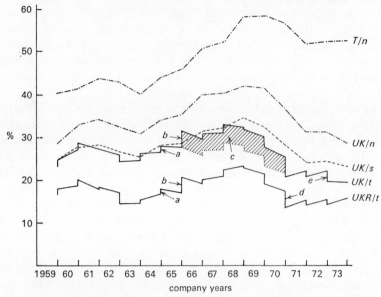

company years

SOURCES: CSO, *National Income and Expenditure 1965–75*; Inland Revenue, *Inland Revenue Statistics* (annual); NIESR calculations.

Notes: Automatic changes shown by lateral shifts and discretionary changes by vertical shifts; the latter are shown at the beginning of the company year in which they started, and any difference between actual and full-year effects at the beginning of the next year.

T = total taxation: United Kingdom accruals (payments plus addition to reserves), with adjustments for retrospective tax changes, and overseas taxes on a payments basis.

UK = United Kingdom taxes as in T, including those on distributions, at standard rate.

UKR = United Kingdom taxes as in T, excluding those on distributions, at standard rate.

t = tax base of total company income net of interest payments.

s = tax base as t less stock appreciation.

n = tax base as s less capital consumption.

a = effect of changing to corporation tax, with double taxation of distributions (see footnote 1, page 165).

b = effect of abolishing investment allowances.

c = estimated accrued value of investment grants, calculated on an 18-month lag in payment, less the effect on depreciation allowances.

d = effect of changing back to investment allowances.

e = change including the effect of reducing the standard rate of tax from 0·3875 to 0·3.

---

cipated tax rates (the rate of corporation tax being fixed retrospectively), whereas here the tax yield refers to actual not expected liabilities. Overseas taxes are given in payment terms. Company income is net of interest payments (debenture and loan interest, cooperative society dividends and interest, building society interest and other interest paid by banks etc. – all as defined in table 5.1 of CSO, *National Income and Expenditure 1965–75*, London, HMSO, 1976). Correspondingly, the income tax on such interest deducted at source is netted out from company tax liabilities.

28 per cent in 1968 (a figure which nets out the tax equivalent of investment grants from the actual effective rate of 32·5 per cent, as shown by the shaded area in the chart). Net of income tax on distributions, the rate on gross profits rose from 16·5 to 23 per cent, while, if taxes paid abroad are taken into account, the aggregate effective tax rate rose from 33 to 38·5 per cent. Discretionary budget changes – increases in the rate of profits tax (in April 1960 and 1961), a rise in the standard rate of income tax (affecting 1964 company income), the net effect of switching to corporation tax with double taxation of distributions (effective from 1966/7)[1] and the increases in the rate of corporation tax which followed devaluation – wholly accounted for this extra burden. The net effect of automatic changes on the company tax rate seems to have been negative, though fluctuating with the rate of investment and tending, with a falling distribution ratio, to become increasingly negative towards the end of the decade.[2]

This and the retrospective reductions in statutory rates introduced in October 1970 and April 1971 caused the effective rate to fall between 1968 and 1970; the downward momentum was kept up by a further series of discretionary measures – the dismantling of the investment grant system, leading to the introduction of free depreciation in 1972/3; the reduction in the standard rate of income tax in 1971/2 and the further reduction in 1973/4 (from 0·3875 to 0·30); finally, the return to equal treatment of distributed and retained profits, also in 1973/4.[3] These later changes seem, however, to have been partly offset by a tendency to greater buoyancy, mainly because investment was failing to keep pace with gross company income, while stock appreciation (part of the base for company taxation) was forming an increasing proportion of gross profits.[4] The result, as table 4.5 shows, was that United Kingdom taxation formed a lower proportion of gross company income in 1973 than in 1959 (19 per cent including tax on distribu-

---

[1] It was announced in the 1965 budget that the intention was not to increase the burden of tax but to redistribute it; for this purpose a 35 per cent corporation tax was thought to suffice (House of Commons, *Hansard*, 6 April 1965, col. 257). Ideas about the correct equivalent rate were subsequently revised upwards, but the actual rate of 40 per cent probably still represented a 1½ per cent increase in overall effective incidence (ibid. 3 May 1966, cols. 1449–50).

[2] A feature of the two-tier tax on distributions operating between 1965 and 1972 is that the buoyancy of the tax is a function of the distribution ratio: a fall in the ratio leads, *ceteris paribus*, to negative buoyancy.

[3] The effect of reducing the standard rate was to reduce tax liabilities on distributions (and with it total liabilities) by £160 million, though part of this was recouped by the 15 per cent surcharge on investment income over £2000. The effect of eliminating double taxation was neutral, since the revenue loss was recovered by the change from 40 to 52 per cent in the rate of corporation tax.

[4] A measure of tax relief on stock appreciation was introduced in the November 1975 supplementary budget.

Table 4.5. *Effective rates of company taxation,*[a] *1959 and 1973*

Percentages

	United Kingdom tax		Total (including overseas)
	Excluding tax on distributions[b]	Including tax on distributions[b]	
On gross income[c]			
1959	16·5	23·5	33·0
1973	15·5	19·0	35·0
On gross income less stock appreciation			
1959	16·5	24·0	33·5
1973	18·5	23·0	42·0
On gross income less stock appreciation and capital consumption			
1959	20·0	28·5	40·5
1973	23·0	28·5	52·5
Change 1959–73			
Discretionary	*+ 1·5*	*− 1·5*	*− 1·5*
Automatic	*+ 1·5*	*+ 1·5*	*+ 13·5*
Total	*+ 3·0*	—	*+ 12·0*

SOURCES: CSO, *National Income and Expenditure 1965–75*; Inland Revenue, *Inland Revenue Statistics* (annual); NIESR estimates.

[a] United Kingdom accruals, overseas payments (see text).
[b] At the standard rate of income tax.   [c] Net of interest payments.

tions, $15\frac{1}{2}$ per cent without). But this reduction can be seen as partly illusory by substituting true economic profit – the maximum level of payments which a company could make while maintaining its ability to produce the same level of goods and services – for the conventional accounting definition;[1] that is, company income should be net of stock appreciation and capital consumption at replacement cost. As can be seen from table 4.5, United Kingdom effective rates in relation to profits net of stock appreciation were only slightly lower in 1973 than in 1959; netting out capital consumption as well, the effective rate of United Kingdom tax was the same in both years. However, the effective tax burden on companies, including tax paid abroad and offset against corporation tax (double taxation relief), increased quite emphatically from 40·5 to 52·5 per cent and this is perhaps the most accurate indicator available.[2] Moreover, since the net effect of discretionary

[1] See M. A. King, 'The United Kingdom profits crisis: myth or reality?', *Economic Journal*, vol. 85, March 1975, pp. 35–7.
[2] It is not strictly possible to derive the effective rate of taxation on United Kingdom *domestic* income because of lack of data on the amount of United Kingdom tax borne by

changes was slightly beneficial, this increase occurred automatically as a result of a slower investment trend and stock appreciation – adverse influences which would have caused the United Kingdom effective rate to rise were it not for the growing element of double taxation relief. The net automatic changes in the United Kingdom effective rates were small, so that fiscal drag as applied to the buoyancy of United Kingdom revenue was negligible; as applied to company tax liabilities the effect was much more marked.

Marginal rates of tax and built-in flexibility

A positive marginal rate of tax damps the multiplier and reduces the amplitude of the economy's response to exogenous demand disturbances. If tax revenue fluctuates positively with income, the system is said to contain 'built-in flexibility', which is usually measured by the marginal rate of tax – that is, the amount of any change in income which adds to or subtracts from government revenue rather than personal disposable income. The extent to which this built-in flexibility also constitutes built-in stability depends upon the damping effect which the marginal rate has through its inclusion in the multiplier.[1] Where an increase in wages and prices is related to increased activity, built-in stability may also imply greater price stability, but here it is necessary to consider how far built-in flexibility applies to movements in money incomes which are offset by price rises ('inflationary' income movements). Estimates of the marginal rates of both direct and indirect taxes on personal incomes are given separately for movements in real income and 'inflationary' income in table 4.6.

The concept already developed of the automatic change in revenue in any particular year provides the first means of estimating marginal rates of tax. The automatic change in tax yield divided by the change in income which accompanies it is the simplest definition of a marginal rate,[2] but it is subject to two deficiencies. First, such a rate has no

income earned abroad. However, on the assumption that no United Kingdom taxes were charged on such income, then the effective tax rate (including taxes on distributions) on domestic income net of stock appreciation and capital consumption would have risen in similar proportion to the third column of table 4.5 – from 38.5 per cent in 1959 to 54.5 per cent in 1973. The effective rates of tax on United Kingdom manufacturing companies may, however, have behaved somewhat differently, the rate at the end of the period probably lying in the range 25–30 per cent (ibid. p. 46).

[1] Built-in stability is measured by the fraction of the change in income which is prevented by the existence of built-in flexibility (see, inter alia, R. A. Musgrave and M. H. Miller, 'Built-in flexibility', American Economic Review, vol. 38, March 1948, and, in a British context, A. T. Peacock and G. K. Shaw, The Economic Theory of Fiscal Policy, London, Allen & Unwin, 1971, pp. 115 et seq.; E. T. Balopoulos, Fiscal Policy Models of the British Economy, Amsterdam, North-Holland, 1967).

[2] Following the methodology described above: $MR_t^i = (\mu_t \Delta B_t / \Delta B_t) (\Delta B_t / \Delta Y_t)$. In this formulation built-in flexibility is the product of two factors – the flexibility of the tax base and

Table 4.6. *Marginal rates of tax,[a] 1959/60–1973/4*

Percentages

	Income tax rates on personal income[b]			Expenditure tax rates on disposable income[c]		Total personal tax rates[d] on personal income[b]		Tax plus NI rates on total personal income[e]	
	'Average' for year	Year-beginning	Year-end	Real income	'Inflationary' income	Real income	'Inflationary' income	Real income	'Inflationary' income
1959/60	17·0	16·5	17·3	12·7	5·2	27·9	21·6	28·1	21·8
1960/1	18·0	17·3	18·4	12·5	4·9	28·6	22·4	28·8	22·6
1961/2	18·0	17·6	18·5	12·5	4·9	28·6	22·3	29·2	23·0
1962/3	13·5	17·7	18·6	12·2	4·8	28·6	22·6	29·5	23·4
1963/4	18·0	17·5	18·0	12·5	4·8	28·2	22·5	29·7	23·4
1964/5	18·5	18·0	18·7	13·6	5·1	29·9	22·8	30·8	23·8
1965/6	20·0	19·4	20·9	14·3	5·1	32·2	24·9	33·1	25·9
1966/7	17·5	19·9	20·3	14·7	5·2	32·1	24·5	33·2	25·5
1967/8	21·5	20·2	21·2	15·6	5·3	33·6	25·4	34·6	26·6
1968/9	22·0	21·3	22·2	16·8	5·7	35·4	26·6	36·3	27·7
1969/70	23·0	22·0	22·9[f]	17·9	6·1	36·8	27·6	37·9	28·8
1970/1	25·0	23·0	25·1	17·7	6·2	38·4	29·5	39·7	31·0
1971/2	23·0	22·9	24·9	16·9	5·8	37·6	29·0	39·1	30·7
1972/3	23·5	21·7	23·4	16·2	5·4	35·8	27·5	37·4	29·6
1973/4	23·0	20·5	22·4	15·7	5·9	34·6	26·9	36·7	29·4

SOURCES: Inland Revenue, *Survey of Personal Incomes 1969–70*, London, HMSO, 1972; CSO, *Economic Trends*, no. 264, October 1975 and *National Income and Expenditure 1964–74*, tables 21–7; NIESR estimates.

[a] Tax accruals not including capital gains tax.

[b] Personal income as defined in the national accounts, including the income of non-profit-making bodies and life and superannuation funds, but excluding contributions to national insurance, etc.

[c] Personal income less accrued income taxes, but including the indirect allocations to consumption from expenditure taxes on industrial inputs.

[d] The combined marginal rate is $\overline{mr} + (1 - \overline{mr})\,\overline{mr}^*$, where $\overline{mr}$ is the marginal rate of income tax and $\overline{mr}^*$ the marginal rate of expenditure tax, the base for which has to be adjusted by $(1 - \overline{mr})$ to make it equivalent to personal income.

[e] As personal income, but including contributions to national insurance, etc.

[f] For 1969/70 for example, this rate is the weighted average of the following marginal rates on different categories of income: employment income, 24·6 per cent; self-employment income, 25·3 per cent; current grants, 5·1 per cent; other personal income (excluding imputed rents), 36·8 per cent. Within this last category, the marginal rate on dividends received by persons was 52·5 per cent, on rental income 41·75 per cent and on occupational pensions 8·05 per cent.

the statutory marginal rate of tax (see L. Cohen, 'An empirical measurement of the built-in flexibility of the individual income tax', *American Economic Association Papers and Proceedings*, vol. 49, May 1959, pp. 532–41; J. A. Pechman, 'Yield of the individual income tax during a recession' in National Bureau of Economic Research, *Policies to Combat Depression*, Princeton University Press, 1956, pp. 123–48).

operational significance: for instance, for an individual taxpayer who crosses the 30 per cent threshold half way through the year, his marginal rate at the beginning would have been zero and at the end 30 per cent, whereas expressing the annual change in his tax liabilities as a ratio of his change in income would give a marginal rate of 15 per cent. The latter could be described as his average marginal rate for the year and, in similar vein, this is how the first column of table 4.6 should be interpreted for the economy as a whole; the rates actually operative at the beginnings and ends of financial years would be rather different. The second deficiency relates particularly to indirect taxes, the yield of which can fluctuate for a number of reasons beside their relationship to income and still be reflected in the automatic change over the year. These fluctuations make the marginal rates erratic; they cannot, in any case, be interpreted strictly in terms of built-in flexibility, which is an income-related concept;[1] average marginal rates are therefore not given for indirect taxes in the table.

The problems of estimating the marginal rates of income and expenditure taxes operating at any particular time are principally those of aggregation (since statutory rates are known for individuals and commodities) and (particularly for indirect taxes) the specification of the relationship between the tax base and the national accounts definition of personal income. For income tax the required aggregate marginal rates can be derived from Inland Revenue statistics as weighted averages of the rates for individuals, which is how the estimates in table 4.6 were generated. The Inland Revenue's annual *Survey of Personal Incomes* collects tax and income data by income range; within each range the average tax paid per person (x_i) is T_i/N_i (where T_i is the total tax paid and N_i the number of tax units in income bracket i). The average effective rate is also immediately apparent as $(T_i/N_i)/(Y_i/N_i) = T_i/Y_i$, but the marginal rate has to be derived by a regression analysis of the average tax paid per person against the average income per person: $x_i = f(y_i)$.[2] Since such a function only operates when the parameters of the tax system are unchanged, a series of functions must be calculated,

[1] Automatic changes in yields of expenditure taxes can be due to factors such as hire purchase restrictions or the impact of anti-smoking campaigns. Such effects introduce an apparent randomness into the marginal relationship between expenditure taxes and personal income, and *seemingly* impair the built-in stability of the system (see OECD, *Fiscal Policy for a Balanced Economy*, p. 67).

[2] This relationship is a proxy for the progressive structure of the income tax system and on estimation yields a marginal rate rising with income: $x_i = \alpha + \beta_1 y_i + \beta_2 y_i^2 + \beta_3 y_i^3 + \beta_4 y_i^4$, where $x_i = T_i/N_i$ and $y_i = Y_i/N_i$. The marginal rate is then

$$\hat{mr}_i = \beta_1 + 2\beta_2 y_i + 3\beta_3 y_i^2 + 4\beta_4 y_i^3$$

and the aggregate marginal rate can be deduced as

$$\overline{mr} = \Sigma_{i=1}^n \hat{mr}_i w_i$$

where $w_i = Y_i/\Sigma_{i=1}^n Y_i$ (see R. W. R. Price, 'Some aspects of the progressive income tax structure in the UK', *National Economic Institute Review*, no. 65, August 1973, pp. 52–63).

yielding a tax schedule and a set of income-class marginal rates, $f_t(y_{it})$, for each budgetary year. The rates given in the third column of table 4.6 are then calculated by weighting these according to the proportion of income accruing to each income class. Each tax function thus generates a marginal rate of tax applicable to the level of personal income during its year of operation; specifically, since income is to be thought of as a flow, a rate applicable to the level of income reached at the *end* of that year. Applying the same function to the level of income at the beginning of the year (the end of the previous year), as in the second column, the difference between the two estimates will be the automatic change in the marginal rate, and the two estimates should approximately bracket the average marginal rate for the year given in the first column (which they do in most cases[1]). The discretionary change in the marginal rate in any year is given by the difference between the figure in the second column and the previous year's figure in the third column.[2]

In the light of the large differences between the marginal rates of tax on different kinds of income (as noted in the table for 1969/70),[3] it might be expected that changes in the distribution of income as between sources would contribute to instability in the aggregate marginal rate. In fact there is a high degree of consistency in the pattern of its development over time; like the average rate of income tax, the marginal rate was kept fairly steady by discretionary tax reductions, at 17–18 per cent during the late 1950s and early 1960s; it was allowed to rise to 25 per cent in 1970/1, and from then until 1973/4 its tendency to increase automatically was more than offset by discretionary tax cuts. At the end of the period the rate was just over 22 per cent, which still represented a significant increase.

Marginal rates of income tax relate to both real and inflationary income because tax rates are set in money terms. This is not so for

---

[1] The major exceptions are 1962/3 and 1966/7. In terms of automatic changes in the tax yield, the differences involved are, respectively, £60 million (2·7 per cent of the tax yield) and £30 million (0·9 per cent of the tax yield).

[2] These relationships can be clarified by denoting end-year estimates as

$$\overline{mr}_t^t = \Sigma_{i=1}^n [f_t'(y_{it})\, w_{it}]$$

and beginning-year estimates as $\overline{mr}_{t-1}^t = \Sigma_{i=1}^n [f_t'(y_{\overline{it-1}})\, w_{it}]$, where the subscript denotes the year's income taken and the superscript the tax function used. The year-to-year changes in the third column can then be broken up into:

$$\underbrace{\overline{mr}_t^t - \overline{mr}_{t-1}^{t-1}}_{\text{total}} = \underbrace{(\overline{rm}_t^t - \overline{mr}_{t-1}^t)}_{\text{automatic}} + \underbrace{(\overline{mr}_{t-1}^t - \overline{mr}_{t-1}^{t-1})}_{\text{discretionary}}$$

Since the two estimates used to calculate the automatic change are based on the same income weights (and therefore imply a fixed distribution of income), it is perhaps interesting that there have not been more occasions on which they have not bracketed the average marginal rate.

[3] The differences are the result partly of different tax rates – on investment income for example – partly of the pattern of exemptions and partly of the size of incomes within each category.

expenditure taxes, where some rates are set in quantum terms and where, at an aggregate level, improved living standards have markedly different effects on spending patterns from income changes which merely offset increases in the cost of living. Aggregate marginal rates of total taxation on consumer spending are therefore presented in both real and 'inflationary' terms in table 4.6;[1] the figures are derived from regression analysis of the individual tax bases;[2] they show a stable and consistent increase in the built-in flexibility of the indirect tax structure. Some elements of tax on consumers' expenditure may be fairly income-inelastic, but the marginal rate with respect to real disposable income rose from 12·7 per cent in 1959/60 to 15·7 in 1973/4, as consumption patterns changed towards income-elastic and highly taxed goods. Combined with the marginal rate of personal income tax, the aggregate marginal rate of tax on real personal income increased steadily from under 28 per cent to about $38\frac{1}{2}$ per cent in 1970/1, three quarters of the increase being due to income tax; budgetary changes subsequently brought the rate down to about 35 per cent in 1973/4. Taking national insurance contributions into account,[3] the marginal rate of all deductions from real personal income also increased substantially, from 28 to nearly 37 per cent. A change of this order, most of which can be traced to underlying automatic increases, represents a significant restructuring of the built-in properties of the system; like the effective rates of income tax and indirect tax, and the tax-mix, the structure of marginal rates has developed automatically rather than by design.

Much the same process occurred in the marginal tax rates applicable to 'inflationary' income changes, though here the increase was almost wholly due to income tax. Despite the introduction of VAT, the marginal rate for indirect taxes rose only from $5-5\frac{1}{2}$ per cent at the beginning of the period to 6 per cent at the end. Including national insurance contributions, the total rate of tax on 'inflationary' income changes was just over 29 per cent in 1973/4 compared with 22 per cent in 1959/60.

Income elasticities and fiscal drag

While built-in flexibility is defined in terms of the marginal rate of tax, the concept of fiscal drag has come to be defined in Britain in terms of the change in the average rate which takes place as incomes rise. This

---

[1] These estimates refer to either central government or public authority taxation, since local authority rates have a zero marginal relationship with respect to both real and money income.

[2] Since the relationships of the individual tax bases have been specified mainly in constant elasticity form, the procedure was to weight these elasticities (see below page 173) in order to create an aggregate expenditure tax elasticity $(\bar{e}_t)$ and to derive the marginal rate as a product of the elasticity and the average rate: $\overline{mr}_t = \bar{e}_t \overline{ar}_t$. Measured at the levels of income obtaining *in* the year, the rates are calculated on the same income basis as the third column of the table. [3] See note 1, page 174.

can be thought of in terms of the difference between the marginal rate of tax and the average rate, since this determines the 'elasticity' of the tax yield – the proportionate change in taxes relative to a proportionate change in income. To the extent that this elasticity exceeds unity, an increase in (real or money) incomes will generate an increase in the average rate of tax and fiscal drag is produced.[1]

In the presence of fiscal drag, calculations of the full-employment budget balance would show that in a growing economy the deficit (surplus) was falling (rising) as a proportion of national income, even if the growth of public expenditure was keeping pace with the underlying growth rate of the economy.[2] If fiscal drag is associated with inflationary increases in money incomes (real incomes being constant) the full-employment budget deficit (surplus) will tend to fall (rise) as a proportion of income, causing real changes in the balance.[3] When fiscal policy is measured by changes in the full-employment budget deficit, therefore, fiscal drag is the agent of automatic fiscal tightening in the context of income growth, while negative drag (which emerges when the tax elasticity is below unity) causes automatic fiscal relaxation. The measurement of fiscal drag is therefore of obvious and direct significance to the analysis of fiscal policy.

Since the presence of fiscal drag is identified by tax yield elasticities in excess of unity, this propensity can be shown, as in table 4.7, by computing the relevant elasticities; these are derived in the same way as the marginal rates in table 4.6 and correspond to them. Estimates of fiscal drag in value terms are given in table 4.8.

It emerges that the income elasticity of the income tax yield has fluctuated between 1·6 and 1·9, with a tendency to decline as incomes rise partly accountable (together with the introduction of lower

---

[1] That is, where the elasticity of the tax yield $(\bar{e})$ at any point in time is $\overline{mr}/\overline{ar}$, the proportionate change in the average rate of tax from a proportionate change in incomes will be $(\overline{dar}/\overline{ar})/(dY/Y) = \overline{mr}/\overline{ar} - 1$.

[2] Where national income grows at a constant longer-run rate, aggregate demand must keep pace if unemployment is not to occur, and net public demand (revenue less expenditure) must keep pace for the stance of stabilisation policy to remain unchanged. For the same reason, a neutral growth path of public receipts may be taken as one which maintains proportionality with potential national income. Ultimately, however, fiscal drag has to be measured with reference to the neutrality rules governing the longer-run planning of public expenditure (which are described in chapter 3), so that, from a balanced budget position, *net* fiscal drag would occur if $\bar{e} > \bar{g}$, where $\bar{g}$ is the ratio of the longer-run growth of public expenditure to the longer-run growth of national income; only if this was unity would fiscal drag be the same in gross and net terms. For a further discussion of fiscal drag in the context of expenditure plans, see below, page 184, and A. S. Blinder and R. M. Solow, 'Analytical foundations of fiscal policy' in *The Economics of Public Finance*, Washington (DC), Brookings Institution, 1974, p. 19.

[3] Tax receipts may rise in proportion to the price level without causing real tax rates to change; the non-proportional element in taxation will, however, have consequences for real incomes (ibid. p. 20 and page 179 below).

Table 4.7. *Income elasticities of personal sector taxes,[a] 1959/60–1973/4*

Ratios

	Income taxes[b]	Expenditure taxes[c]		Total personal taxation[b]		
		Real income	'Inflationary' income	Real income	'Inflationary' income	Average[d]
1959/60	1·87	1·03	0·42	1·36[e]	1·05[e]	1·35
1960/1	1·85	1·04	0·41	1·38	1·08	1·28
1961/2	1·84	1·03	0·40	1·37	1·07	1·09
1962/3	1·86	1·02	0·40	1·37	1·09	1·20
1963/4	1·89	1·06	0·41	1·39	1·09	1·31
1964/5	1·84	1·09	0·40	1·40	1·07	1·19
1965/6	1·81	1·13	0·40	1·42	1·10	1·17
1966/7	1·75	1·12	0·39	1·38	1·05	0·86
1967/8	1·72	1·15	0·39	1·39	1·05	1·22
1968/9	1·66	1·17	0·40	1·37	1·03	1·07
1969/70	1·63	1·19	0·40	1·37	1·02	1·07
1970/1	1·71	1·22	0·42	1·42	1·09	1·18
1971/2	1·74	1·26	0·42	1·45	1·12	1·18
1972/3	1·80	1·29	0·43	1·50	1·15	1·31
1973/4	1·67	1·31	0·48	1·45[e]	1·13[e]	1·18

SOURCE: NIESR estimates.

[a] Accruals of central government taxes, not including capital gains tax.

[b] With respect to personal income as defined in note *b* to table 4.6.

[c] With respect to disposable income as defined in note *c* to table 4.6. Elasticities for individual expenditure taxes are calculated in R. W. R. Price, 'A model of the indirect tax system in the UK, 1956–72' (unpublished NIESR working paper), 1977.

[d] The responsiveness of the tax yield to total (real and 'inflationary') income changes during the year.

[e] Elasticities of total taxes including national insurance contributions with respect to total personal income (see note *e* to table 4.6) were as follows:

	Central government		Total public authority	
	Real income	'Inflationary' income	Real income	'Inflationary' income
1959/60	1·17	0·90	1·05	0·81
1973/4	1·28	1·02	1·16	0·92

statutory rates) for the 1973/4 elasticity being at the lower end of this range. Indirect taxes, on the other hand, have tended to become more buoyant as spending patterns have changed in favour of goods with a high tax incidence and high income elasticity of demand, like petrol, wines and spirits, and durables. The real income elasticity applicable to the excise yield rose from only 0·87 at the beginning to 1·53 at the end of the period and, while statutory reductions in tax rates on income-elastic goods brought down the elasticity of purchase tax quite

Table 4.8. *The effects of fiscal drag and discretionary tax changes on personal sector taxes,[a] 1959/60–1973/4*

£ million

	Income taxes		Expenditure taxes			Total personal taxation		
	Discretionary change	Fiscal drag	Discretionary change[b]	Fiscal drag	Other effects[c]	Discretionary change	Fiscal drag	Total automatic effects[d]
1959/60	−166	+90	−129	−10	+125	−295	+80	+205
1960/1	−20	+140	+20	−35	−85	—	+105	+20
1961/2	−98	+90	+149	−60	−40	+51	+30	−10
1962/3	−4	+110	+59	−60	−45	+55	+50	+5
1963/4	−295	+140	−39	−35	+65	−334	+105	+170
1964/5	—	+175	+121	−90	+60	+121	+85	+145
1965/6	−8	+225	+216	−115	−145	+208	+110	−35
1966/7	+25	+55	+329	−90	+110	+354	−35	+75
1967/8	−4	+210	+58	−80	+40	+54	+130	+170
1968/9	+223	+200	+517	−160	−150	+740	+40	−110
1969/70	—	+225	+335	−175	+5	+335	+50	+55
1970/1	−191	+435	−7	−210	+75	−198	+225	+300
1971/2	−659	+485	−345	−255	+90	−1004	+230	+320
1972/3	−1241	+690	−218	−160	—	−1459	+530	+530
1973/4	−316	+760	−64	−355	—	−380	+405	+405

SOURCES: Treasury, *Financial Statement and Budget Report* (annual); NIESR estimates.

[a] Full-year effects on tax accruals.

[b] Extra-budgetary changes apportioned between the year of intervention and the following year.

[c] Effects stemming from automatic changes in effective rates which are not attributable to income changes.

[d] Other effects on expenditure taxes plus total fiscal drag.

markedly (from 1·32 to 1·17), there was a continuous trend towards a higher overall elasticity of indirect taxes – from just above unity to 1·3. Together with the growing importance of income taxes in the tax-mix, this accounted for an increase in the real income buoyancy of overall personal taxation from an elasticity of 1·36 in 1959/60 to about 1·45 in the early 1970s. On the other hand, local rates and the flat-rate element in national insurance contributions have, in principle, an elasticity of zero with respect to income.[1] The downward bias that this seemingly imparts to overall fiscal drag is, however, somewhat illusory, for both forms of tax are regularly increased in line with prospective

[1] Apart from the responsiveness of flat-rate contributions to employment, the relationship to national income has depended on graduated contributions, introduced in April 1961. These have made up an increasing proportion of the whole, being 13 per cent in 1961/2 and 48 per cent in 1973/4; from April 1975 the whole system became earnings-related. As can be seen, the overall elasticity has risen with the proportion of graduated in total contributions.

expenditure, which can be regarded as having some relationship to income, though not a rigid one.

The 'inflationary' income buoyancy of the revenue system is quite different from its real income buoyancy. Excise yields, which react to inflation only through its effects on consumer spending patterns, maintained a fairly constant elasticity of 0·2,[1] and the overall buoyancy of expenditure taxes fluctuated narrowly around 0·4 until the introduction of VAT raised it nearer to 0·5. Any increase in buoyancy in personal taxes overall (1·13 at the end compared with 1·05 at the beginning of the period) is due to this and the increasing incidence of progressive income tax.

Together, personal income and expenditure taxes displayed an emphatically positive real income drag and an only slightly positive inflationary income drag. The extent of the bias in terms of receipts depends both on the rate of change in money incomes and on the real and inflationary composition of this change. The estimates in table 4.8 measure the aggregate annual effects on the tax yield of both real and inflationary income movements,[2] while the 'average' column in table 4.7 shows the implied overall elasticity of tax receipts with respect to total 'money' income changes – in effect, an average of the real and inflationary income elasticities weighted by the proportions of real and inflationary income changes in the total change for the year. As can be seen from comparing the fiscal drag estimates with the effects of discretionary tax changes, the former have made an important contribution to budgetary stance throughout the period, the revenue gain in the 1960s being between £30 and £130 million, with overall revenue elasticities between 1·07 and 1·35 (last column, table 4.7).[3] The indirect tax base has, however, behaved rather erratically from year to year due to influences not systematically related to income, and these 'other effects' in table 4.8 have to be set against fiscal drag proper. In the early 1970s – due to increasing inflation and the gradual rise in tax elasticities – the contribution of fiscal drag to the Exchequer rose to about £700 million from income taxes and between £400 and £500 million in total (net of the negative drag associated with indirect taxes). Budgetary policy had thus to offset a substantial – and growing – bias

---

[1] Prices of goods subject to specific duties rise more slowly than the general price level and so their relative price falls; their consumption therefore increases (cf. table 4.3) and excise yields expand by about a fifth of the rate of inflation.

[2] The calculations are made on the same basis as the automatic changes in average rates defined in footnote 2, page 160; i.e. fiscal drag (£ million) = $(\overline{ar}_t^i - \overline{ar}_{t-1}^i) Y_t$. Since fiscal drag is defined as a function of income, this leaves the effects of other factors on the average rate of tax, which are particularly important in the case of indirect taxes (table 4.8).

[3] Because the inflationary buoyancy of the revenue was not enough to offset the effects of the fall in real income in 1966/7, the amount of drag accruing in that year was (exceptionally) negative and the average elasticity of the revenue less than unity.

BBE

in the tax system before it could achieve a net reduction in effective tax rates.

Distributional effects of fiscal drag

Fiscal drag has important consequences for the distribution of the tax burden and of post-tax incomes. This section analyses these effects for income tax, which has been the centre of greatest controversy.

A progressive tax system implies that the tax burden is concentrated on higher income earners, so that post-tax incomes are more equally dispersed than pre-tax ones. Chart 4.4 tests the income tax system for these attributes. It shows, first, cumulative percentages of the income tax burden (plotted vertically) ranked against cumulative percentages of pre-tax income; a proportional tax system would give a curve linking the two along the diagonal, while the more progressive the system the more the curve is pushed to the right.[1] The chart shows, for example, that in 1973/4 the lower 50 per cent of incomes yielded 32·5 per cent of taxes, while the top 50 per cent of incomes accounted for 67·5 per cent of taxes. But in 1959/60 the tax burden had a more marked concentration as measured by the gap between the tax distribution curve and the diagonal; here, the lower 50 per cent of incomes bore only 19 per cent of taxes. By this measure the degree of progressiveness has thus declined quite markedly and, although this was partly due to discretionary changes in the tax system, automatic changes accounted for a substantial part also.

The effect of taxation in redistributing income may be deduced from Lorenz curves of pre-tax and post-tax incomes; chart 4.4, however, gives a shorthand account of this by also ranking cumulative percentages of pre-tax and post-tax incomes against each other. Again a proportional tax system would give a curve linking the two along the diagonal, which in this context is to be interpreted as a line of unchanged income distribution; taxation reduces income inequality if these curves are to the left of the diagonal.[2] In both 1959/60 and 1973/4, the first 50 per cent of gross incomes received about 53·5 per cent of post-tax incomes and neither the 1973/4 curve nor the 1959/60 one is unequivocally more progressive, since they intersect in the fifth decile of pre-tax incomes. Below this level the 1973/4 curve distributes incomes more equally, whilst the 1959/60 curve shows greater equality above this level. It

---

[1] In contrast to a conventional Lorenz diagram, which ranks cumulative gross incomes against cumulative income units and where deviations to the right of the diagonal reflect inequality and inequity, an unequal distribution of the tax burden by concentration on higher incomes is progressive and equitable.

[2] As with the tax distribution curves, movements *away* from the diagonal (this time to its left) are progressive so long as the income distribution is not reversed.

appears that the regressive structural reforms of the period have been partly offset by the compensating changes which have taken place automatically as incomes have risen.

Chart 4.4. *The distribution of the tax burden and of post-tax incomes with respect to cumulative gross incomes, 1959/60 and 1973/4*

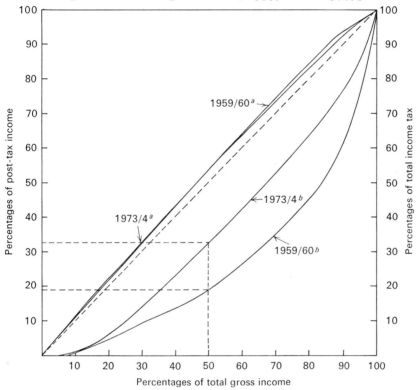

SOURCES: CSO, *National Income and Expenditure 1965–75*, table 4.8, and *National Income and Expenditure 1969*, London, HMSO, 1969, table 23; NIESR estimates.

[a] Post-tax/pre-tax income distribution curves.   [b] Tax distribution curves.

Intuitively it might be expected that fiscal drag would be accompanied by a tendency to greater concentration of the tax burden and a fairer distribution of income as taxpayers were pushed into higher tax brackets; that is, that a progressive system would become more progressive over time as incomes rose. Yet, with the advent of high rates of inflation, this was qualified by concern that rising money incomes were shifting the tax burden relatively on to lower income earners, which became one of the chief arguments for index-linked allowances.[1] At first sight, however, this is difficult to square with the fact that post-tax incomes became more dispersed for the lower 45 per cent of incomes between 1959/60 and 1973/4.

To resolve this paradox it is necessary to review the criteria for a stable tax system – that is, one which maintains the distribution of the tax burden and of post-tax incomes in the face of proportional increases in gross incomes. It can be shown that for the distribution of the tax burden to remain stable and progressive it is necessary and sufficient that the elasticity of the average rate schedule (as defined for chart 4.1 – the proportionate change in average tax rates relative to income) should be positive and constant.[2] This follows intuitively from the fact that, for the proportion of aggregate tax each person pays to remain the same, his tax liability should increase at the same rate as everyone else's. With a given growth in money incomes, a declining elasticity causes the effective rate of tax to increase proportionally faster for lower income earners, so that their contribution to the overall tax burden rises, and this can be shown to apply in large measure to the income tax system. Chart 4.5 plots the elasticity of the average rate of tax for the 'representative' taxpayer (as defined for chart 4.1). Corresponding to the definition of aggregate fiscal drag given above (page 172), we have here a measure of the extent of fiscal drag on individuals' tax liabilities:

$$ar' = \frac{dar}{ar} \Big/ \frac{dY}{Y} = \frac{mr}{ar} - 1 \qquad (7)$$

It can be seen that, whilst initially (up to the threshold) the elasticity is zero, it rises to infinity at the point of the threshold and then declines towards zero, because the average rate increases while the marginal rate is fixed. Then, as higher tax rates are reached, each new marginal rate causes a discrete jump in the curve, giving a 'saw-tooth' effect as the rate declines towards zero within each band. This imparts a certain amount of consistency to the elasticity of the average rate, which does not deviate markedly from 0·5, but this is lower than the responsiveness to income changes of tax on incomes under (about) £2000. For a given proportionate change in money incomes, the increase in the effective tax rate would be greater below this level than above it, the more so the nearer to the threshold the income is.

Furthermore, since the elasticity can be defined as the *non*-proportional change in tax yield that accompanies automatic income changes (the difference between the tax yield elasticity and unity), it can also

---

[1] See Morgan, *Over-taxation by Inflation*; R. I. G. Allen and D. Savage, 'Inflation and personal income tax', *National Institute Economic Review*, no. 70, November 1974, pp. 61–72.

[2] See U. Jakobsson, 'On the measurement of the degree of progression', *Journal of Public Economics*, vol. 5, Jan.–Feb. 1976, pp. 161–8.

be shown to measure the increase in real tax liabilities which arises from inflationary fiscal drag. Tax yields can, of course, increase at the same rate as inflation (covered by offsetting increases in money incomes)

Chart 4.5. *The responsiveness to changes in income of average tax rates and the ratio of pre-tax to post-tax income: 'representative' and 'average' taxpayers, 1973/4*

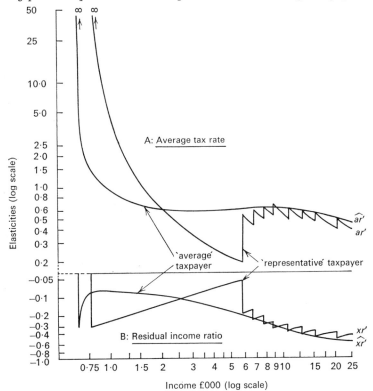

SOURCES: table 4.1; CSO, *National Income and Expenditure 1965–75*, table 4.8; NIESR estimates.

Notes: (i) 'Representative' taxpayer defined as for chart 4.1; 'average' taxpayer defined in terms of average tax liability for all persons with a given gross income (derived from Inland Revenue, *Survey of Personal Incomes*, see text).

(ii) elasticities: above zero, the proportionate change in the average tax rate from a proportionate change in income; below zero, the proportionate change in the ratio between pre-tax and post-tax incomes from a proportionate change in pre-tax income.

without affecting real tax liabilities; so the curve for the representative taxpayer can be interpreted in terms of the consequences of inflation for the tax distribution. The elasticity of the yield applicable to aggregate United Kingdom income tax in 1973/4 was 1·67; that is, for an 'inflationary' change in money incomes of 1 per cent, the real increase in the yield would have been 0·67 per cent, as also would have been the percentage increase in the effective rate of tax. But a 'representative' taxpayer receiving less than £2000 a year would have suffered a larger real increase than this; at an income of £1000, for instance, the increase in the effective rate would have been approximately 3·5 per cent.

It does not necessarily follow that the distribution of post-tax incomes has also become less progressive. A necessary condition for this distribution to remain stable is that the proportionate change in the ratio of post-tax to pre-tax incomes should be negative and constant.[1] By increasing the government's share of income more than proportionally, fiscal drag automatically reduces the proportion retained by recipients, so that this decrease should occur at the same rate for all income earners if their share of post-tax income is to remain unchanged. It is, however, possible for the burden of taxation to be thrown increasingly on lower income earners – through a declining tax elasticity – while the post-tax income distribution remains constant or improves. Whether or not this is the case in the United Kingdom is a matter for some debate. The lower part of chart 4.5 shows the proportionate reduction in the ratio of post-tax to pre-tax income from a proportionate growth in gross incomes for the 'representative' taxpayer; it also measures the proportionate reduction in real post-tax income that occurs with inflation, since

$$xr' = \frac{d(1-ar)}{(1-ar)} \bigg/ \frac{dY}{Y} = \frac{(1-mr)}{(1-ar)} - 1 \qquad (8)$$

where $(1-mr)/(1-ar)$ is the 'residual income elasticity', defined as the proportionate change in post-tax income with respect to a proportionate change in pre-tax income.[2] This would be less than unity under a progressive tax system. But if real post-tax incomes are to maintain their value they *must* keep pace with inflationary income increases, when xr' would be zero; the further below zero this value falls, the more the rate of increase in post-tax incomes is falling behind the rate of inflation.

Up to the threshold, recipients retain all their income and pay no tax to be affected by inflation. At the threshold the ratio of post-tax to pre-tax income begins to fall, the proportionate increase in post-tax income being 70 per cent of the proportionate increase in pre-tax income and, if this was an inflationary increase, the proportionate decline in real income would be 30 per cent of the rate of inflation. But after this the responsiveness of the ratio to income growth begins

[1] Ibid.
[2] R. A. Musgrave and T. Thin, 'Income tax progression, 1929–48', *Journal of Political Economy*, vol. 56, December 1948, pp. 498–514.

to decline, reaching a low point at the end of the basic rate band, where the decline in real post-tax income would be only 5·5 per cent of the rate of inflation. After that responsiveness changes in a saw-tooth manner with increases in marginal rates and the curve reaches a high point at the beginning of the top rate of tax, where a 1 per cent inflationary increase would cause a 0·49 per cent decline in real post-tax income.

Using the aggregate marginal and average rates derived above for 1973/4, it would be expected that 1 per cent inflation would lead to a 0·12 per cent decline in real spending power (as measured by total personal post-tax incomes). Compared with this overall effect, it can be seen from chart 4.5 that those with annual incomes less than £2500 or more than £5775 suffer a greater decline, while those within this range suffer less. The fact that lower income earners appear to suffer more than average has been a fundamental part of the case for indexing tax allowances to prevent inflation from increasing tax liabilities more than proportionally.

However, while the validity of these conclusions is not in doubt for taxpayers with different incomes but identical circumstances, it is not strictly possible to generalise from this to what would happen to the relationship between post-tax and pre-tax incomes as shown in the distribution diagram, where the horizontal axis cumulates the incomes of people with the same gross incomes but different allowances. A part of such allowances is income-related (payments of mortgage interest, life assurance premiums, etc.), so that at any particular level of gross income there is an array of taxpayers facing different average rates and even different marginal ones. Thus, for any given movement up the scale of gross incomes there will be people on both the rising and falling parts of the curves for the representative taxpayer in chart 4.5 – they may be moving either across the threshold or into higher tax brackets. If sufficient people are being drawn into new tax brackets to offset the automatic decline in elasticity experienced by those who are not, the average effect will be to maintain the post-tax income elasticity and with it the existing post-tax income distribution. But to estimate whether or not this is the case, it is necessary to calculate the average elasticities at each level of gross income. For these it is again possible to rely on the Inland Revenue's *Survey of Personal Incomes* and the income-class marginal and average rates used to derive the aggregate tax rates described above. From the relationship between these it is possible to calculate the average of the tax and post-tax income elasticities which apply at various points on the income scale.[1] These

---

[1] From footnote 2 page 169 above we already have the marginal rate $\hat{mr}_i$; the corresponding average rate is $\hat{ar}_i = \alpha y^{-1} + \beta_1 + \beta_2 y + \beta_3 y^2 + \beta_4 y^3$. The elasticities of the system are then derived as $\hat{ar}' = \hat{mr}_i / \hat{ar}_i - 1$ and $\hat{x}\hat{r}'_i = (\hat{ar}_i - \hat{mr}_i)/(1 - \hat{ar}_i)$.

calculations provide the 'average' taxpayer elasticities for 1973/4 shown in chart 4.5, and may be taken as determining the effects of proportional gross income changes on the tax and post-tax distribution lines in chart 4.4. It can be seen that the tendency for the tax burden of the average taxpayer to increase faster at lower levels of income is confirmed, but to a more limited extent than for the 'representative' taxpayer. Nevertheless it is marked and accounts for the flattening of the tax distribution curve towards the line of equal tax distribution in chart 4.4. But the effect on the post-tax income distribution expected from the curve for the average taxpayer is predominantly progressive; the responsiveness of the post-tax income ratio to changes in income increases for an annual income above (about) £1000, though it diminishes for the short range between the threshold and this point. People at or very near the threshold are still relatively badly affected, but for most of the range up to £2500 per annum inflation would have caused a lower proportionate decline in real incomes than for those above £2500. The effect of inflation and real income growth seems, therefore, unequivocally progressive for the upper 90 per cent of incomes, not the converse as would be expected from the 'representative' curve. The distribution curves corroborate this insofar as the 1973/4 post-tax income distribution is more progressive for the lower 45 per cent of incomes than the 1959/60 distribution; the fact that for the upper 55 per cent the curve became less progressive reflects reforms in higher rates which offset the automatic progressive tendencies of the tax system.

The effects of fiscal drag on income tax liabilities seem therefore to be, for the most part, progressive vis-à-vis disposable incomes (income tax being the principal adjustment in calculating personal disposable income as defined in the national accounts). But other factors, including indirect taxes and benefits from subsidies and transfers, obviously need to be considered. Taking account of expenditure taxes on consumption, in 1973/4 a 1 per cent growth in real incomes would have led to a 0·86 per cent growth in real personal disposable incomes, while a 1 per cent growth in inflationary incomes would have led to a 0·04 per cent decline (compared with the 0·12 per cent decline due to income taxes alone).[1] Although the distributional effects are indeterminate without knowing individual indirect tax elasticities, the conclusion that automatic income changes are biased towards a more progressive distribution of disposable income is still likely to hold.[2]

[1] The income tax effect is related to disposable income at market prices, the total effect to disposable income net of indirect taxes.

[2] The assumption behind the aggregate expenditure tax elasticities in table 4.7 is one of constant elasticities for the individual tax bases, leading to an increasing elasticity overall as the consumption of income-elastic goods increases. This is not necessarily the best description of the way elasticities change over a scale of gross incomes, but the implication is that the

THE PUBLIC SECTOR FINANCIAL BALANCE
AND FISCAL LEVERAGE

Introduction

In this section the taxation and public expenditure sides of fiscal policy are brought together to give measures of the full-employment budget.

In one form or another, the balance of total public sector receipts over expenditure as an indicator of public sector (dis)savings probably represents the most concise summary of the stance of fiscal policy. However, two important considerations suggest that the raw data which emerge as the public sector financial balance should be modified: first, tax receipts vary (to an extent already explored in the previous section) with the growth of incomes and fluctuations in economic activity; secondly, a given change in the balance may occur as a result of changes in receipts or expenditures which are offset by private sector savings in varying degrees.

Taking the first consideration, it is clear that changes in the actual budget balance will occur both as a result of fiscal interventions and because of the two types of automatic change described above – fiscal drag and built-in flexibility.[1] The weakness of the public sector financial balance as an indicator of fiscal stance is that it fails to distinguish the influence of the budget on the economy from the influence of the economy on the budget.[2] The concept of the full-employment budget balance seeks to resolve these problems by normalising the level of

---

distribution of tax and of post-tax incomes will become more progressive as incomes rise. So far as the 'inflationary' income elasticities of the indirect tax system are concerned, there is little reason to suppose that these change much in aggregate and, this being so, inflation would not be expected to have a noticeable effect on the distribution of the indirect tax burden.

[1] Using the distinction between discretionary and automatic budget changes developed on page 160 and distinguishing between long-run and short-run changes in income, the change in the balance (P) can be separated into four components:

$$P_t - P_{t-1} = \underbrace{\Delta \overline{ar}_{t-1}^{\Delta t} Y_{t-1}}_{\substack{\text{discretionary} \\ \text{tax change}}} + \underbrace{\overline{MR}_t (Y_t^{fe} - Y_{t-1}^{fe})}_{\substack{\text{long-run} \\ \text{automatic} \\ \text{tax change}}} + \underbrace{(\overline{MR}_t - \overline{G}_t)(U_t - U_{t-1})}_{\substack{\text{automatic} \\ \text{stabilisers}}} - \underbrace{(G_t - G_{t-1})}_{\substack{\text{public} \\ \text{expenditure} \\ \text{change}}}$$

where the leftmost term $P_t - P_{t-1}$ is the *total change*.

where $\Delta \overline{ar}_{t-1}^{\Delta t}$ = the discretionary change in the effective tax rate evaluated at the level of income in year $t-1$ (as defined in footnote 2 page 160), $\overline{MR}_t$ = the average marginal rate of tax in year t, Y^{fe} = full-employment income, $U_t = Y_t - Y_t^{fe}$ (the difference between actual and potential national income: the 'GDP gap'), $\overline{G}$ = the marginal rate of change in public expenditure relative to changes in U, and G = other government expenditure.

[2] It can be demonstrated that as a target of fiscal policy it may lead to perverse fiscal action, in that a shortfall in employment will lead to a shortfall in receipts, thus increasing the deficit and prompting *deflationary* action to correct for this (see *National Institute Economic Review*, no. 79, February 1977, pp. 43–4).

economic activity and real income at which the balance is measured; this nets out the effects of built-in flexibility and leaves an index of fiscal policy containing the effects of discretionary changes and long-run automatic changes in revenue.[1] The 'weighted' full-employment balance attempts to account for the differential incidence of private savings on different forms of revenue and expenditure by scoring the items in question according to their net impact on demand and output; the weights used are discussed below and in chapter 3.

The full-employment budget balance represents the initial (or *ex ante*) stance of the budget in regard to savings at the full-employment level of income; it is initial in the sense that, if there is an imbalance of aggregate savings intentions, the multiplier will generate a different level of national income and employment and a new level of public receipts, in which process neither full employment nor the full-employment balance need be realised. Changes in the full-employment balance thus reflect changes in fiscal stance which, with the multiplier consequences, cause aggregate demand to diverge from or gravitate towards its full-employment level. Since the economy grows at a certain underlying rate over time with productivity increases, a fixed policy stance would normally be one where the proportion of public savings in full-employment income remained the same; a change in policy would then be reflected in a change in this proportion, causing demand to diverge from its long-run growth path and so altering the rate of unemployment. Such a change would be composed of discretionary interventions and net fiscal drag. The weighted full-employment balance represents the initial demand leverage of the budget;[2] it is interpreted in the same way as the unweighted balance, the only difference being that the weighted variant translates the budget balance into a 'first round' demand impact by netting out budgetary transactions which do not represent claims on output. The full leverage of the budget is determined by this and the multiplier.

Because it nets out the secondary demand and revenue effects which

---

[1] Discretionary changes in tax rates are evaluated as the change in yield which would occur at full-employment income; expenditure plans (G) and long-run automatic tax changes are not affected. Thus (where P^{fe} is the full-employment balance):

$$P_t^{fe} - P_{t-1}^{fe} \;=\; \underbrace{\Delta \overline{ar}_{t-1}^{\Delta t} Y_{t-1} + \Delta \overline{MR}(Y_{t-1}^{fe} - Y_{t-1})}_{\substack{\text{discretionary change at} \\ \text{full-employment income}}} \;+\; \underbrace{\overline{MR}_t(Y_t^{fe} - Y_{t-1}^{fe})}_{\substack{\text{long-run automatic} \\ \text{tax change}}} \;-\; \underbrace{(G_t - G_{t-1})}_{\substack{\text{public expenditure} \\ \text{change}}}$$

$\underbrace{\phantom{P_t^{fe} - P_{t-1}^{fe}}}_{\text{total change}}$

The discretionary change is thus the *actual* discretionary change, plus the difference in yield which would accrue by evaluating the GDP gap at the new marginal rate, where $\Delta \overline{MR} = (\mu_t - \mu_{t-1})\,(\Delta B_t / \Delta Y_t)$.

[2] This balance can be interpreted as the multiplicand (M_{fa}) in Musgrave's measure of 'fiscal leverage' (see Musgrave, 'On measuring fiscal performance', pp. 216-17).

disguise the original stance of policy, the full-employment balance has obvious advantages over the actual balance as an indicator of fiscal policy, but it still suffers from two potential drawbacks. First, because errors occur in forecasting public expenditure and receipts, policy will be imperfectly implemented. A distinction should thus be drawn between the intended initial stance of policy and its out-turn. Insofar as it is possible to derive the intended stance – from forecasts of actual GDP and the actual balance made at budget time – these are presented, with the out-turn, in table 4.9 on page 187 below. The second drawback is due to the fact that the overall change in GDP leverage exerted by a change in the weighted full-employment balance is a function not just of that change but also of the multiplier attached to it, which in turn depends on the marginal rate of tax. It is possible for the total effect on GDP leverage to be in a different direction from the initial change in the full-employment balance if changes in the marginal rate of tax cause a change in the multiplier which more than offsets the change in the initial leverage. In this case changes in the full-employment balance would even mislead as to the direction of change in fiscal stance.[1] Although, over our period, the multiplier has been reduced by the steady increase in marginal tax rates, it does not appear that the direction of change implied by changes in the full-employment balance was, in fact, ever contrary to the change in total leverage; however, when allowance is made for this, at the end of the period the leverage implied by a given change in the full-employment balance was about 10–15 per cent below that at the beginning.

[1] For example, assuming zero full-employment balances in other sectors, and thus an equilibrium full-employment budget balance of zero, the change in GDP leverage exerted by the budget is $-(P_t^{fe} k^t - P_{t-1}^{fe} k^{t-1})$, where k^t = the multiplier with post-intervention tax rates and k^{t-1} = the previous multiplier. Alone, a discretionary tax change would give a leverage change of:

$$\Delta GDP^{\Delta t} = -\Delta \overline{ar}_{t-1}^{\Delta t} Y_{t-1} k^t = -[\Delta \overline{ar}_{t-1}^{\Delta t} Y_{t-1} + \overline{\Delta MR}(Y_{t-1}^{fe} - Y_{t-1})] k^t - P_{t-1}^{fe} \Delta k$$

discretionary change in GDP / tax yield effect calculated at full-employment income / multiplier change

Where, from a position of unemployment (full-employment surplus), a cut in the effective rate also involves an increase in the marginal rate, the change in the full-employment multiplicand may (depending on the GDP gap) show a change towards greater surplus. The reflationary stance of policy is not picked up by the change in P^{fe}, but is actually contained in the effect of a lower multiplier on the existing full-employment surplus ($P_{t-1}^{fe} \Delta k$). The further the economy is from full employment, the more this possibility must be taken into consideration (see Blinder and Solow, 'Analytical foundations of fiscal policy', p. 17; W.H. Oakland, 'Budgetary measures of fiscal performance', Southern Economic Journal, vol. 35, April 1969, pp. 347–57; OECD, Fiscal Policy in Seven Countries, 1955–1965, pp. 25–6).

The public sector financial balance, 1959/60–1973/4

The out-turn and forecast levels of the actual and the full-employment public sector financial balance are set out in table 4.9.[1] The actual balance was in surplus only during the two years after devaluation, while the full-employment balance was also in surplus in 1970/1. Initial public savings were at a peak during 1969/70 and 1970/1 (at about £1200 million), though it was the latter year which saw the most restrictive intended stance of policy, as reflected in a forecast full-employment surplus of £1580 million. Differences between the forecasts and out-turns of the actual balance reflect, among other things, the effects on income-related receipts and expenditure of mis-estimating economic activity; differences between the forecasts and out-turns of the full-employment balance, on the other hand, arise principally from short-falls and overruns in public expenditure, from mis-forecasts of inflation and from mis-estimating the pattern of demand in its effect on revenue. The differences illustrate the ambiguity involved in treating changes in the out-turn of the full-employment balance as policy changes; this is especially marked for 1972/3 – the year which (with 1973/4) shows the largest realised deterioration in the full-employment balance (−£1545 million) and an intended change in fiscal stance of −£2105 million. In 1973/4, on the other hand, the full-employment balance was almost exactly as intended, despite the difference of −£800 million between the intended *actual* balance and its out-turn, which was almost wholly attributable to the GDP shortfall in that year.

The estimates of the weighted full-employment balance follow the principles set out in calculating the domestic output content of public expenditure in chapter 3. The changes in private savings set off against tax changes are the obverse of those allowed against transfers and subsidies, though substantially more important. Government direct expenditures are not affected by such offsets, while the recipients of grants and transfers tend to have a lower propensity to save than tax-payers as a whole, and a good deal lower than surtax payers or recipients of unearned income. The 'economic efficiency' (to use Kaldor's term for the output-content of public sector transactions) of surtax seems to be about 64 per cent, of taxes on 'other personal income' about 74 per cent, of taxes on wages and salaries 90 per cent, and of taxes on

---

[1] For the definition of full-employment national income see above, page 84. Since the full-employment balance is derived by measuring what the budget would be at full-employment *income* under existing tax rates and expenditure plans – including existing expenditures by other sectors of the economy, where only consumption is taken as income-related – compositional errors in its calculation are confined to errors in the allocation of full-employment income between companies and persons (which are subject to different marginal rates of tax). The composition of full-employment expenditure is not an issue here.

Table 4.9. *The public sector financial balance with full-employment corrections,[a] 1959/60–1973/4*

	Actual balance		Full-employment balance		Weighted full-employment balance[b]	
	Forecast[c]	Out-turn	Forecast	Out-turn	Out-turn	Proportion of full-employment GDP
	(£ million)					(%)
1959/60	..	−620	..	−560	−1619	−7·61
1960/1	..	−720	..	−460	−1644	−7·33
1961/2	..	−619	..	−680	−1612	−6·75
1962/3	..	−602	..	−460	−1549	−6·11
1963/4	..	−1098	..	−1020	−2102	−7·87
1964/5	..	−857	..	−670	−2273	−8·00
1965/6	..	−697	..	−450	−1989	−6·53
1966/7	−473[d]	−1169	..	−810	−2174	−6·67
1967/8	−1317	−1828	..	−1120	−2425	−7·02
1968/9	−857[d]	−548	−530[d]	−270	−1570	−4·27
1969/70	+538	+662	+900	+1290	−625	−1·58
1970/1	+1138	+114	+1580[d]	+1165	−1117	−2·52
1971/2	−378[d]	−508	+1285[d]	+780	−1827	−3·61
1972/3	−2441	−1994	−1325	−765	−2992	−5·23
1973/4	−2853	−3646	−2415	−2375	−4056	−6·30

SOURCES: CSO, *Economic Trends, Annual Supplement 1975, National Income and Expenditure 1970 and 1975* and *Annual Abstract of Statistics 1975*; NIESR estimates.

[a] Full employment is defined as the 1960 level of 325,000 unemployed and the full-employment growth rate is taken as 3·2 per cent per annum (see text). The full-employment correction is calculated on the basis that inflation, the exchange rate, exports and investment are exogenous and fixed, the adjustment being to derive discretionary, or *ex ante*, public sector savings. The responsiveness of public sector receipts to a 1 per cent change in GDP has risen from 0·94 to 1·02 per cent over the period.

[b] Net of steel industry investment. The savings offsets are derived from regression analysis and the import weights from CSO, *Input–Output Tables for the United Kingdom* (various issues). The expenditure figures are as defined in chapter 3, pages 97–8 above. The results should be taken as representing orders of magnitude rather than absolute expressions of the economic impact of the budget, with year-to-year changes more relevant than actual levels. The accruals adjustments have been given a weight of zero.

[c] Forecasts of the actual balance have been given officially in the Financial Statement only since 1966/7 and official forecasts of GDP (needed to convert the actual figures to a full-employment basis) only since 1968/9.

[d] Excluding subsequent extra-budgetary interventions.

transfers 99 per cent, compared with an overall 85 per cent efficiency for across-the-board tax changes such as general adjustments to expenditure taxes.[1] Allowing for these and other offsets on the receipts side, the net impact of the budget on demand will always tend to be

[1] See M. J. C. Surrey, 'Personal incomes and consumers' expenditure' in K. Hilton and D. F. Heathfield (eds.), *The Econometric Study of the United Kingdom*, London, Macmillan, 1970, p. 108; J. C. Dorrington and G. A. Renton, 'A study of the effects of direct taxation on consumers' expenditure' in G. A. Renton (ed.), *Modelling the Economy*, London, Heinemann, 1975, pp. 557–609.

greater than is apparent, the weighted balance being on the negative side of the actual balance, with greater implied leverage.

More attention should be paid to changes in the weighted full-employment balance than to its actual level, but its impact in 1959/60–1960/1 is estimated at about $7\frac{1}{2}$ per cent of full-employment GDP, declining to about 6 per cent in 1962/3;[1] the upturn of 1963/4–1964/5 then brought it to a peak of 8 per cent, which declined to between $6\frac{1}{2}$ and 7 per cent in the next three years. The extreme reaction which followed devaluation and lasted until 1972/3 is quite apparent: the weighted full-employment balance fell to a low of about $1\frac{1}{2}$ per cent of full-employment GDP in 1969/70, rising gradually to 3·6 per cent over the next two years. The reflation of 1972/3 relaxed the budgetary stance by 1·6 per cent (the intended increase was nearer to 2·5 per cent) and the supposedly 'neutral' budget of 1973/4 further increased the weighted full-employment deficit to 6·3 per cent of full-employment GDP.

These year-to-year changes in the weighted full-employment balance are shown in chart 4.6 in terms of the separate contributions of changes in expenditure and in revenue. Since decreases in receipts have the same expansionary effects as increases in expenditure, all changes plotted to the right of the diagonal 'neutrality' line, where expenditure changes exactly offset revenue changes, add to budgetary leverage, while leverage is diminished to the left.[2] During the 1959/60 and 1963/4 reflations, and in the upturn of the 1970s, both sides of the accounts acted in the same direction (tax decreases being relatively more important in stimulating the economy in 1959/60 and 1972/3, and expenditure dominating in 1963/4). Similarly, the deflationary leverage exerted in 1968/9 and 1969/70 was the product of both sides. On the other hand, the combination of expansionary expenditure policies and restraining taxation changes was a dominant feature of the period 1964/5–1967/8, with only 1965/6 showing net deflationary leverage. In 1971/2 there was an example of the opposite – expansionary revenue policies (tax cuts) offset, in leverage terms, by restraint on the expenditure side (to which shortfalls on capital spending made an unintentional contribution).

[1] The budgetary impact in first-round terms is, of course, positive where the budget balance is negative.
[2] This exposition follows in some respects that of Artis, 'Fiscal policy for stabilization' pp. 292–4, as described in M. J. Artis and R. H. Wallace, 'Assessing the fiscal impact' in, N. Runcie (ed.), *Australian Monetary and Fiscal Policy: selected readings*, London University Press, 1971, pp. 378 *et seq.*

Chart 4.6. *Changes in budgetary stance (with full-employment corrections),[a]*
1959/60–1973/4

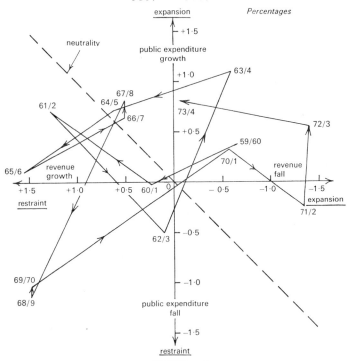

SOURCE: NIESR estimates.

[a] Changes in the ratios of weighted full-employment receipts and expenditure to full-employment GDP.

Sector balances and 'fiscal adequacy'

Estimates of the full-employment budget balance, as developed here, do not in themselves contain any built-in judgement about the adequacy of appropriateness of the fiscal stimulus which they measure. To develop such a judgement at least two further ingredients are required: comparable full-employment estimates of the private sector and overseas balances, and a view on the appropriate rate of adjustment from the current position to full employment.

The full-employment budget balance is a comparative static concept. It says nothing about lags in the response of the economy to changes in fiscal policy. The time-path of response to alternative fiscal stimuli can only be illustrated by appropriate simulations on an econometric model. However, when measuring the full-employment adequacy of the budget, short-run dynamic responses can reasonably be set aside;

then, comparably calculated full-employment balances for the private and overseas sectors can, in principle, be set against the full-employment budget balance to test the adequacy of a given fiscal policy for realising full employment, or the likelihood that it will generate excess demand (relative to the full-employment target). The test to be applied is whether the intended full-employment budget balance is equal and opposite in sign to the sum of the intended overseas and private sector balances, also evaluated at full-employment income levels. If the net result is a deficiency of aggregate intended savings, there is a presumption of excess demand; if it is a surplus, deficient demand is presumed. In either case, the implication is that fiscal policy is inadequate in the short term to achieve either full employment or the full-employment budget balance as measured, though in the medium term such a balance may become appropriate and sustainable as the private and overseas sectors vary cyclically.[1]

In this context the particular contribution of the 'New Cambridge' school was to suggest that the private sector surplus could be taken as being a small and stable fraction of GDP.[2] Granted an exchange rate or 'degree of competitiveness' sufficient to ensure an acceptable balance of payments (the inverse of the overseas sector's balance) at full employment, the approach determines an appropriate full-employment public sector balance for a balance of payments target of zero as the obverse of the long-run private sector surplus. The private savings behaviour implied in this approach has, however, remained contentious, no less than the assumption that the overseas sector could be relied upon to provide no marked destabilising influence.[3]

For purposes of evaluating short-run policy, however, if some assumptions can be made about the full-employment values of the potential overseas and private sector balances, the comparative static

[1] Where, for instance, a calculation of the full-employment balances reveals both a surplus in the public sector and a greater savings surplus in the economy at large, there will be a shortfall in demand and GDP which can be corrected by fiscal action only at the expense of the full-employment surplus itself; that is, the public sector balance must be altered so that its deficit offsets the surplus of potential savings in other sectors. In the context of medium-term budgeting and resource planning, however, the full-employment public sector balance has a somewhat different significance, since the assumption is that full employment can be sustained at the peak of the cycle, when 'full-employment budgeting' actually implies a planned public sector balance compatible with fully employed resources.

[2] See pages 138–9 above. Subsequently this was adjusted to a 'small and predictable' rather than a 'small and stable' fraction (see House of Commons, *Ninth Report from the Expenditure Committee, Session 1974*, p. 15).

[3] The claim that fluctuations in output have been '*entirely* the consequence of stabilisation measures' (ibid. p. 5) clearly rests as much upon assuming stability in the overseas sector balance as in the private sector surplus. It was the claim of the 'New Cambridge' school in this regard that 'during the past twenty years or so, purely by chance, the fluctuations of UK exports, to the extent that these were induced by changes in world trade, have been roughly offset by changes in import prices attributable to the same cause' (ibid. p. 5).

adequacy of fiscal policy can be appraised, but the extent to which it is useful to do this hinges on the difficulty of estimating such values, or proxies for them, and on the confining framework of the comparative static analysis itself. The approach does not produce hard and fast quantification, but it does suggest that it might be fruitful to view fiscal policy in the light of the state of world demand and the implied changes in the (full-employment) overseas sector balance. Such considerations feature in the next section, which is devoted to a narrative account and running assessment of fiscal policy; they are subsequently brought to bear in a test of the cyclical appropriateness of fiscal policy.

IMPLEMENTING BUDGETARY POLICY

An account of fiscal policy in terms of full-employment budget balances is inevitably abstracted from the sequence of short-term pressures under which fiscal policy decisions are actually made. The purpose of this section is to correct the perspective by giving a narrative account of the background to fiscal changes.

The formulation of fiscal policy in the short run hinges on the forecasting of real demand variables to the relevant horizon (usually eighteen months to two years), and an account of policy must clearly aim to distinguish failures due to forecasting errors from those which have their roots in other causes. Official forecasts were not published explicitly until the 1968/9 budget; before that we have to rely on the indications (frequently only qualitative) given in budget statements by Chancellors of the Exchequer. An alternative is the published National Institute forecasts, which have been used in place of official ones up to 1967/8; they were available to the Chancellor and, though they are not likely always to have been identical with those on which policy was based, it has been assumed that by and large the differences were not marked.

The rate of growth of GDP is the most critical element in any demand forecast, since this must be the same as the growth in productive potential for the unemployment rate to remain constant. Growth rates are generally expressed as percentage changes from the same period in the previous year,[1] though the average year-on-year change is also emphasised on occasions. Chart 4.7 presents both, together with the errors in forecasting GDP, which are the sum total of errors in forecasting its components. Consumers' expenditure is, of course, the principal component, so that forecasts and forecast errors are also given for this. Since errors in forecasting imports have also been important

---

[1] In the Financial Statement the Treasury publishes forecasts based on half-year to half-year percentage changes, while the *National Institute Economic Review* analyses quarterly changes, with particular emphasis on fourth quarter to fourth quarter (year-end to year-end).

Chart 4.7. *Total final demand: quarterly and annual percentage changes, forecast and out-turn, 1959–73*

A: *Total final expenditure*

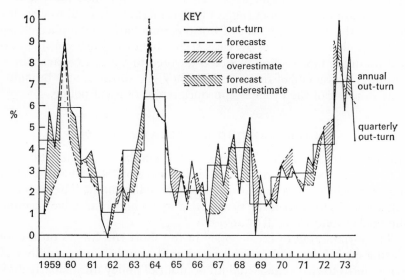

B: *Gross domestic product at factor cost*

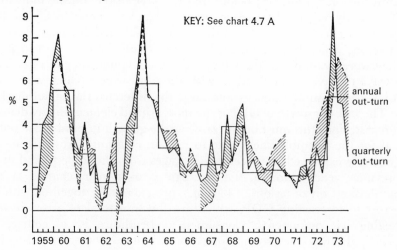

Chart 4.7 (*cont.*)

C: *Consumers' expenditure*

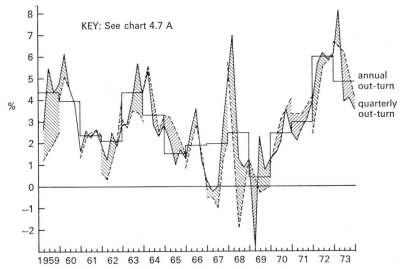

SOURCES: CSO, *Economic Trends, Annual Supplement 1975*; Treasury, *Financial Statement and Budget Report* (since 1968); *National Institute Economic Review* (May issues) to 1967; Neild and Shirley, '*Economic Review*: an assessment of forecasts, 1959–1960'; M. C. Kennedy, 'How well does the National Institute forecast?', *National Institute Economic Review*, no. 50, November 1969, pp. 40–52.

Notes: (i) Quarterly changes are changes from the same quarter of the previous year; annual changes are changes over four quarters up to the end of the calendar year in question.

(ii) Forecasts at budget-time (including the budgetary intervention) are corrected for subsequent interventions, including variations in hire purchase controls. Up to 1968, data from *National Institute Economic Review*, except where there is evidence (as in 1962) that this conflicted with the Treasury's unpublished forecasts; since 1968, forecasts are half-yearly ones published in the *Financial Statement*.

(iii) The compromise (average) estimate of GDP is used.

to managing the economy, forecasts of aggregate demand (total final expenditure) are given in part A of the chart, the difference between these and the GDP forecasts consisting of the import (and net indirect tax) content of expenditure.

The first Conservative period, 1959/60–October 1964

By the beginning of 1960 the economy had been expanding rapidly for some time and, following the reflationary boost given in April 1959, people were beginning to look for signals indicating the need for budgetary moderation.[1] Such signals began to appear when figures for

---

[1] *Economist*, 2 January 1960.

GDP showed that the pace of the expansion had been far greater than anticipated – in the final quarter of 1959 GDP was over 6 per cent higher than in the same quarter of 1958, as against an increase of about $2\frac{1}{2}$ per cent forecast previously.[1] The unwelcome result of this was a weakening in the balance of payments, which dominated budget-making up to July 1961.

The 1960 budget, resting on the prognosis of a diminishing rate of growth towards the end of the year, was, however, absolutely neutral. Profits tax was raised by $2\frac{1}{2}$ per cent, but this was not intended to cut back private investment, for which capital allowances remained unchanged. Because of the balance of payments weakness, this budget involved a 'balancing of risks', but as far as total demand was concerned the forecasts appear to have been correct. However, they were wrong in regard to the balance of payments: the propensity to import was underestimated, while the falling off in export demand (due to a decline in world activity) was not foreseen. These two circumstances led to demand management packages in the spring and early summer which relied on credit controls and public expenditure cuts. But the alterations in hire purchase terms, which had proved 'prompt and substantial' in their effects, bore too heavily on a certain range of goods, particularly consumer durables. In the 1961 budget the Chancellor deduced the need for the more extensive and uniform use of the existing expenditure tax base through an 'economic regulator' – a device enabling the Treasury at any time to institute across-the-board changes in duties up to a maximum of 10 per cent.[2]

The 'wait and see' possibilities offered by this innovation helped to make the budget fairly neutral once more. Apart from raising an extra £68 million of revenue in the current year (principally from the oil duty), the opportunity was taken to mitigate the effects of higher rates of tax on earned incomes, where the surtax threshold was raised from £2000 to £5000;[3] this was scheduled to cost £83 million in 1961/2 and was to be paid for by an increase in profits tax from $12\frac{1}{2}$ to 15 per cent.

With final demand expected – correctly – to increase by about $2\frac{3}{4}$ per cent in 1961, and with imports levelling off as predicted, the forecasts

[1] On the failure to foresee the upswing in demand see R. R. Neild and E. A. Shirley, 'Economic Review: an assessment of forecasts, 1959–1960', National Institute Economic Review, no. 15, May 1961, pp. 12–29.

[2] Treasury powers to surcharge or rebate revenue duties 'with a view to regulating the balance between demand and resources' (Finance Act 1961, s. 9) have to be renewed in each Finance Act. The 1961 Act also contained a provision for the Treasury to introduce surcharges on employers' national insurance contributions, up to a maximum of 4s. per week per employee, but this power was not subsequently renewed (see page 17 above).

[3] Earned income relief was extended from income tax to surtax and a further earnings allowance of £2000 was introduced.

for both an improved external balance and output growth matching productive potential would have been fulfilled for the year as a whole. But this did not prevent the introduction on 25 July of a 10 per cent regulator surcharge which, together with measures affecting public expenditure and credit, increased taxation by £130 million in 1961/2. This coincided with the end of the boom, for from the last quarter of 1961 GDP fell below the rate necessary to maintain full employment.

How far this denouement was deliberate and how far an unintentional coincidence of deflation with a declining trend in activity is open to question.[1] In favour of the latter interpretation are the statements about increased demand forecasts which accompanied the intervention,[2] but, on the other hand, the Chancellor spoke of the need for a 'pause' in activity. However, the episode gives rise to a more fundamental question of the soundness of the decisions to reflate in 1959 and to stay neutral in 1960, since these implied coincidence of the budgetary cycle with the world demand cycle (chart 4.8) and a deterioration in the current account; this might have been avoided or diminished by more cautious policies, but in the event led to speculative losses from the reserves and the eventual deflationary 'stop'.

The crisis of 1961 encouraged a re-evaluation of the adequacy of demand management for achieving growth with stability. The future need for new instruments – incomes policy and planning – was officially accepted in the July intervention and the budget of 1962. In the meantime, though, it was the deflationary school arguing for a higher margin of unused resources whose ideas appeared to be in the ascendant.[3] The output pause became endowed with strategic significance, since a period of lower demand pressure was seen in some quarters as a means of keeping money wage increases below the world level, thus restoring competitiveness.[4] The deflationary strategy was not, in the event, long-lasting, but the episode illustrates how demand management interventions tend to be seen as turning-points when new strategic approaches to the achievement of *all* the major objectives of policy are adopted. This was to be even more true of the subsequent reflation, which was not merely an exercise in balancing aggregate demand and supply, but an attempt to break through into the 'virtuous circle' of growth and stability on all fronts.

---

[1] See Brittan, *Steering the Economy*, pp. 251 *et seq.*

[2] Selwyn Lloyd in the House of Commons, 25 July 1961. Though correct as to the year-on-year growth of output, the budget forecast itself had tended to overestimate output growth in the second half of 1961 (chart 4.7).

[3] This school might, in general, be termed 'Paishite', but Brittan (*Steering the Economy*, p. 254) refers to the spare capacity argument as a 'recurrent intellectual fashion' to which *some* Treasury officials were drawn.

[4] On this argument see *National Institute Economic Review*, no. 19, February 1962, p. 56.

Chart 4.8. *Changes in initial fiscal leverage, and the export and investment demand cycles, 1958/9–1973/4*

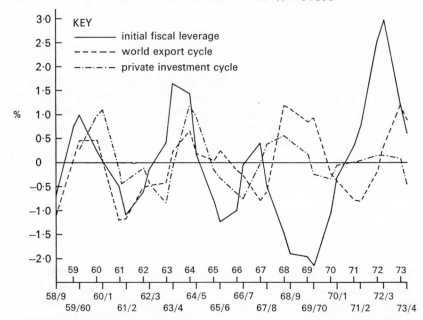

SOURCES: table 4.9; chart 3.6; United Nations, *Monthly Bulletin of Statistics* (various issues); NIESR estimates.

Note: Annual changes (financial and calendar years) in the ratios to full-employment GDP of:

    (*a*) the (intended) weighted full-employment budget balance – initial fiscal leverage;

    (*b*) export demand, deduced from fluctuations around their trend of world exports of manufactured goods;

    (*c*) private investment demand, represented by fluctuations around the trend described in chapter 3.

The Treasury forecast for 1962 anticipated a growth in output through the year of some 4 per cent and on the strength of this the budget itself was neutral in its overall impact, though, in consolidating the regulator surcharge of the previous July, it was decided to continue reshaping purchase tax by extending the tax base and rearranging the existing rates to keep the same yield. A new rate of 15 per cent was introduced on confectionery, soft drinks and ice-cream and the range of existing rates was changed from 5½–55 per cent to 10–45 per cent (table 4.1). At the same time, the anachronistic 'breakfast table duties' were abolished[1] and speculative capital gains were brought within the

---

[1] These were duties on tea, cocoa, coffee and sugar, yielding a revenue of about £15 million.

charge to income tax. By September it had become clear that the budget demand forecasts were optimistic. Public investment increases announced in early October were accompanied by increased investment allowances for the private sector, while the two highest rates of purchase tax were reduced to 25 per cent at a cost of £77 million in a full year.[1]

The process of reflation was continued in the 1963 budget in order to make up the ground lost on the (by then) official growth target of 4 per cent per annum. £218 million of taxation was remitted by way of increased personal and child allowances, though this rise in the tax threshold was accompanied by the elimination of the lowest reduced rate of tax, which increased the initial rate from 6·8 to 15·6 per cent (table 4.1). A further £77 million was remitted through the abolition of income tax on personal owner-occupation (schedule A), which had actually been announced in the previous budget. Overall, the budget concessions amounted to tax cuts of £349 million in a full year (£257 million in 1963/4), to which should be added the effects of improved investment allowances (table 4.2).

In terms of aggregate demand the developments of 1963 were almost identical with those of 1959, though this time the expansion was, for the most part, intentional, being based on the explicit acceptance of the balance of payments deficit likely to occur in the early stages of growth.[2] The circumstances of budget-making in 1964 were therefore remarkably similar to those in 1960, except for the crucial commitment to continue the expansion through 1964. There were certain differences, however, in that the forecasts were showing a faster year-end rate of growth for 1964 than had been predicted for 1960 (5½ per cent growth of GDP compared with 3 per cent), with investment (particularly public investment) mainly responsible for the difference. In these circumstances, the budget strategy for 1964 was based on the need to effect 'the transition to 4 per cent, and to avoid the danger of "overheating"'.[3] However, the extra £100 million raised by the budget seems to have been more influenced by the danger of 'checking expansion rather than moderating it'.[4]

[1] The duty on cars was reduced with effect from 6 October; other goods formerly taxed at 45 per cent were affected from 1 January 1963. It is interesting that the regulator was *not* used.

[2] Given the actual annual growth of GDP of nearly 4 per cent in 1963 as a whole and of 6¼ per cent as the year-end rate, against a post-budget forecast of 5½ per cent, the extent of the upswing was still underestimated. This was true of consumption, where the year-end rate was 4¼ per cent against an anticipated 3, of exports, where the out-turn was 4¾ per cent to the forecast 3, and of total investment, where the final quarter increase of 20 per cent over the final quarter of 1962 was extremely similar to the situation in 1959/60.

[3] Reginald Maudling in the House of Commons, 14 April 1964.

[4] Ibid. There seems to have been an emphasis here on the importance of not giving 'confidence' an untoward jolt; the National Institute in its February forecast and policy

The overall out-turn for 1964 – with the rather critical exception of the balance of payments, where the current deficit was about twice what had been expected – lay well within the limits of forecasting accuracy, so that, whilst the errors of the 1959 reflation could largely be attributed to forecasting mistakes, the errors of the period 1963–4 are essentially the result of the medium-term strategy which was adopted. That strategy consciously provided for maintaining expansion by running down the reserves and using additional policy instruments to modify the trade-off between external stability and internal expansion;[1] the rapid deterioration of the basic balance[2] and the change of administration ushered in a policy package in November which contained just such an instrument in the form of an import surcharge and export rebate. In contrast to the 1961 'stop', policy throughout 1964 sought, quite directly, to avoid a deliberate output pause, whilst intending to deal with the balance of payments problem by alternative means. The difficulty with this policy – as it was with the overall growth strategy which had been adopted – was that, though providing a short-term solution to the problem of 'stop–go', it still gave no permanent answer to the reconciliation of faster growth with a stable currency and the transfer of resources into the balance of payments.

The November 1964 budget effectively marks the end of the second of the two cycles which characterised the period 1959–64. Both of the upturns on which these were based derived from experiments in domestic demand-led growth, which sooner or later created a need to free resources for investment and the balance of payments, and this was likely to prejudice the momentum of growth itself. While the ensuing balance of payments difficulties may have been a matter of fundamental competitive inadequacies, it is possible that they were also, to some extent, expressions of excess demand resulting from the type of strategies actually followed. Both budgetary cycles shadowed those in world demand, so that policy (partly by commission, partly by omission, since export demand was frequently misread) failed to

---

appraisal for 1964 was quite explicit about this. Having calculated that the transition to 4 per cent growth required the extraction of some £400 million from demand, it went on to recommend a smaller adjustment (of £200 million as compared with the Chancellor's £100 million) on the grounds that considerations of confidence argued against so large a change (*National Institute Economic Review*, no. 27, February 1964, p. 11).

[1] In his budget speech on 14 April 1964 Maudling entertained the use of import controls 'if we should be facing severe balance of payments difficulties which could not be dealt with in better ways'. Work had been put in hand on alternative schemes of import quotas or a surcharge, which the ex-Chancellor claimed he would have used rather than deflation (see Brittan, *Steering the Economy*, pp. 284–5).

[2] The deficit on current account was similar, in real terms, to that in 1961 – at 1970 factor cost the current deficit in 1964 was £450 million as compared with about £400 million in 1961.

exploit the balance of payments and growth possibilities from this direction.

Demand management deficiencies also played a part in the pattern of pro-cyclical budgeting which seems to have emerged. Forecasting performance was mixed; although policy-makers seem to have been given the right signals for much of the time, the exceptions were rather critical – the 1959/60 upturn was not foreseen and the extent of the recession in 1962/3 was underestimated, both of which led to reflationary over-reaction. The upturn having once started, it is probable that strategic (growth) considerations did most to determine the budgetary inaction which tended to follow.

Labour administrations, October 1964–June 1970

The new administration in October 1964 sought a wide-ranging contribution from fiscal policy towards the realisation of its economic and social objectives,[1] while endorsing the trend towards 'new' instruments of policy. The character of fiscal policy itself became more interventionist, with a greater emphasis on income redistribution. Corporation tax and capital gains tax, which became effective in 1966/7, introduced, for reasons of equity and economic policy, extra tiers of taxation on income accruing to shareholders; investment grants, which replaced allowances against tax in January 1966, were designed to give more discretionary power over the direction of investment and, like selective employment tax, were strongly *dirigiste* in conception.

The prognosis accompanying the November 1964 budget was that 'there was no undue pressure on resources calling for action', though there were specific areas of imbalance.[2] The overall demand impact of the fiscal changes – with increases in social security benefits countering the effect of an increase in the standard rate of income tax (due to take effect in 1965/6) and a further rise in duties on hydro-carbon oils – was in fact broadly neutral;[3] it was consistent with the latest output forecasts, which foresaw GDP growth slowing down from 5 per cent in 1964 to about 3 per cent in 1965.[4]

By the time of the 1965 budget, however, the estimates of consumers' expenditure had risen and the tax increases of £164 million (on a

---

[1] 'In all these ways', the Chancellor stated in November 1964, 'budgetary policy must contribute to our objectives: a healthy foreign balance, stable prices and full employment, social justice for the needy, fair play for all taxpayers, sound planning of public expenditure, rewards for the energetic and sustained economic growth' (House of Commons, *Hansard*, 11 November 1964, col. 1025).

[2] Prime Minister's Office, *The Economic Situation*, para. 7.

[3] See *National Institute Economic Review*, no. 30, November 1964, p. 8.

[4] Ibid.

current year basis) which were introduced,[1] brought its forecast growth (of 2 per cent through 1965) back down to the levels forecast in November. GDP was expected to rise by $3\frac{1}{2}$ per cent up to the end of 1964 ($2\frac{1}{2}$ per cent through the financial year), so no effect was anticipated on unemployment,[2] and since the balance of payments was forecast to improve, there were favourable indications for the compatibility of external and internal stability, which the record shows were justified (charts 4.7 and 4.8). Nevertheless, speculation against sterling and supply pressures in the construction industry resulted, in July, in measures using credit restrictions (but not taxation) to hold consumption to a forecast 1 per cent growth rate through 1965. With the accompanying public investment cuts, these were intended to hold GDP to $2\frac{1}{2}$ per cent growth through 1965/6, with an $8\frac{1}{2}$ per cent growth in exports partially offsetting the less expansionary stance of the budget (table 4.9 and chart 4.6).

The strategy of transferring resources into the balance of payments without cost to employment seems to have been successful initially and the prospects for 1966 seemed reasonably favourable. The momentum behind public expenditure was maintaining the leverage exerted by the budget, though relying on the public sector to sustain demand while private expenditure bore the brunt of the adjustment necessary to safeguard the balance of payments was to create special difficulties. Excise duties on alcohol and tobacco were thought to be near their taxable ceiling, whilst income tax increases were ruled out as prejudicial to savings and investment. Hence the hasty introduction, in the 1966 budget, of selective employment tax (to become operative only in September), which supplied most of the extra £326 million revenue to be raised in 1966/7. In the meantime however, disappointing balance of payments figures and the seamen's strike provoked more precipitate action; the deflationary package of July aimed at raising an extra £94 million in 1966/7 through the regulator (tobacco duties were exempted on this occasion), with a surcharge on surtax liabilities expected to bring in a further £25 million in 1967/8. In the context of the continuing growth of public expenditure, however, direct fiscal leverage remained very much the same as in the previous year, of the order of $6\frac{3}{4}$ per cent of full-employment GDP (table 4.9). The balance of taxation and spending increases by which this was achieved implied the strict

---

[1] The reliance on excise duties derived from the worry that purchase tax increases would prove damaging to industrial investment (House of Commons, *Hansard*, 6 April 1965, cols. 288–90).

[2] With the trend in productive capacity at $3\frac{1}{4}$ per cent a year the National Institute diagnosed some shortfall, but did not expect to see this translated into unemployment because employment was at the time 'a good deal out of adjustment' (*National Institute Economic Review*, no. 32, May 1965, p. 4).

restraint of private consumption; originally forecast to rise by some $1\frac{1}{2}$ per cent through 1966/7, after the July measures a fall of a similar magnitude was forecast (reduced, in the event, to an actual decline of about $\frac{1}{4}$ per cent).

With the private sector depressed, the Chancellor chose not to intervene in the budget of 1967, relying on the recession for further improvement in the balance of payments, while restricting the decline in activity by means of public expenditure and automatic stabilisers. The actual budget deficit was intended to increase by £450 million in the calendar year 1967, with an improvement in the current balance of £200 million.[1] In the event, the current balance deteriorated by some £400 million, an outcome accounted for partly by disappointing export results, partly by an underestimate of the buoyancy of internal demand, in which an overrun by public expenditure played a role. The 2·1 per cent GDP growth in the year as a whole was double the 1 per cent originally forecast, aided in part by a relaxation of credit in June and August. The expansionary leverage of the public sector is particularly notable in retrospect, rising to 7 per cent on a weighted full-employment basis (table 4.9).

Devaluation in November was followed by fiscal adjustments designed to release resources in appropriate amounts at the appropriate time, thus combining the transformation of the balance of payments into surplus with continued high utilisation of resources. Initially cuts were announced in public expenditure plans; then taxes were increased in the 1968 budget, which was brought forward to March for that purpose – revenue being increased by £923 million. Apart from the commitment to recover the full amount of the recent increase in family allowances from income tax, the Chancellor was keen to avoid using this instrument, concern over possible adverse effects on savings being by this time fairly pronounced. However, since profits and equity prices were expected to increase, corporation tax was raised by $2\frac{1}{2}$ per cent, but an increase in the rate of capital gains tax was ruled out because it was thought that its use as a short-term instrument might cause an immediate reluctance to realise profits and thus possibly a fall in yield. Instead, a special surcharge on investment income was added to surtax for 1967/8, yielding a once-and-for-all £100 million. The economic impact of these measures seems to have been less important to the Chancellor than the effects on equity and the financing requirement. Spending power was constrained by raising indirect taxes (beer duty being excepted because it was considered regressive); in all £923 million was added to tax accruals in 1968/9, the effective rate of personal sector taxation (chart 4.2A) being raised by $1\frac{1}{2}$ per cent.

[1] See *National Institute Economic Review*, no. 40, May 1967, p. 8.

The financial deficit in 1968/9 was expected to be about £1000 million less than in 1967/8. In terms of demand aggregates, the effects of this were to be reflected in consumption growing at 0·25 per cent in 1968, with private investment recovering by $4\frac{1}{2}$ per cent; exports were forecast to increase by $7\frac{3}{4}$ per cent in volume and imports by $1\frac{3}{4}$ per cent, giving a GDP increase of 3 per cent over 1967. All these figures turned out to be underestimates, which necessitated reinforcing measures, in the shape of a regulator surcharge, in November. This was to have a full-year impact of £250 million, so that consumption growth through 1968 was eventually held to 1·2 per cent.

The balance of payments turned round slower than expected (the improvement in the year was only £26 million compared with earlier forecasts of improvements as large as £500 million[1]) which, together with the underestimates of consumption and the necessity for supplementary intervention in November, raised questions about the effectiveness of the original fiscal strategy. This had been planned with the tax measures delayed until 1968 on the calculation that the 'elasticity effects' of devaluation would not begin to make themselves felt until the second half of that year.[2] In fact it was not until late in 1968 that the public sector financial balance began to show substantially less expansionary leverage than it had in 1967[3] and, although this was consistent with the strategy, it seems less appropriate in the light of the underestimate of the upturn in domestic and world demand (charts 4.6 and 4.7), and the capacity constraints that emerged in early 1968.[4]

The 1969 budget aimed at raising an extra £272 million in 1969/70, again through indirect taxation because income tax was ruled out.[5] The Chancellor considered whether 'even in a year as difficult as this, it would be justifiable for incentive reasons and for the encouragement of savings,

[1] *National Institute Economic Review*, no. 43, February 1968. By May this forecast had been trimmed back to an expected improvement of £140 million.

[2] Ibid, no. 42, November 1967, pp. 10–11.

[3] At an annual rate (for the four quarters up to and including the quarter in question) the public sector balance was as follows:

£ million

1967 II	1967 III	1967 IV	1968 I	1968 II	1968 III	1968 IV	1969 I
−1227	−1447	−1648	−1828	−1795	−1608	−1136	−548

[4] The situation at the time was confused. Unemployment still seemed high, but the relationship between unemployment and vacancies had changed and the latter, like the statistics of capacity utilisation and overtime rates, suggested that demand pressures in 1968 were quite as high as they had been in the boom years of 1961 and 1964 (see *London and Cambridge Economic Bulletin*, November 1968 and January 1969).

[5] There were also a number of constraints on indirect taxation. Duties on tobacco and spirits could not be raised because it was feared that this would diminish revenue. It was also preferred to expand the base of purchase tax rather than to increase rates, which might have been seen as encouraging those who had tried to anticipate this by pre-budget spending.

to mitigate slightly the rates of tax on high earned incomes';[1] an increase in the earned income allowance was regarded as a high priority for a later budget.[2] Meantime, the tax threshold was raised by a combination of higher personal allowances and the abolition of the lowest reduced rate (which raised the initial rate to $23\frac{1}{3}$ per cent) without any net effect on demand. The public sector financial balance as a whole, which had improved by £1280 million in 1968/9, was meant to improve by about a further £1100 million, bringing a surplus of over £500 million despite an unexpectedly large increase in unemployment (table 4.9).

In the two years following devaluation, the discretionary budgetary leverage provided by the public sector was greatly reduced, from 7 per cent of full-employment GDP to about $1\frac{1}{2}$ per cent, the contribution of changes in taxation and in public expenditure being about equal (chart 4.6). Further, a current account surplus of £727 million was achieved and GDP grew at an annual average rate of about 3 per cent, so that in this respect fiscal policy and devaluation may be said to have worked. It is possible that the immediate budgetary action accompanying devaluation was inadequate viewed from the cyclical situation at the time, but, this apart, the most salient point about the devaluation strategy was that even the somewhat tardy turn-round in the full-employment public sector balance was uniquely stabilising, in that *for the first time* (as chart 4.8 shows) the domestic budgetary cycle was inversely phased with the world demand cycle – a characteristic which has otherwise been conspicuously absent in the United Kingdom.[3] This implied, however, that at some time after the 1969 budget fiscal policy should have been relaxed to compensate for the relative falling-off of world trade and investment which then ensued. Because the consolidation of an external surplus appeared paramount this was not done, and the fact that no reflationary action was taken (despite the advice of outside commentators such as the National Institute) until the other sectors of demand were picking up again (chart 4.8) is crucial to the understanding of stabilisation policy in the early 1970s.

The second Conservative period, June 1970–February 1974

The legacy of the planning era was thus potentially beneficial as well as detrimental to the economy. On the detrimental side there was the excessive growth of the public sector, so that from 1969/70, when both the public sector balance and the overseas balance moved into surplus, fiscal policy could turn to reducing the accumulated burden on the private sector. A good deal of this had been built up through hidden

---

[1] House of Commons, *Hansard*, 15 April 1969, col. 999. [2] Ibid. cols. 1031–2.
[3] This is not to say that exploiting the world cycle is an answer, in itself, to competitive inadequacy, but it is potentially a factor to compensate for the inadequacy.

increases in the average rate of income tax, with company taxes and indirect taxes being increased by discretionary means. (The first relaxation had come in Roy Jenkins' 1970 budget, which reduced the personal income tax by £191 million; this reform followed the 1969 pattern by raising the tax threshold and abolishing the one remaining reduced rate, so raising the initial rate of tax to 32 per cent (table 4.1).)[1] The move towards reducing income tax – and taxation in general – was taken much further by the incoming Conservative administration, which undid several of the structural tax reforms introduced during Labour's period of office. A series of structural measures was announced in the 1971 budget: the unification of the personal income and surtax systems, with lower marginal rates on earned income; the substitution of VAT for purchase tax and selective employment tax; the abolition of the second-tier tax on company distributions; the proposed unification of the social security and income tax systems through the mechanism of tax credits; the immediate substitution of investment allowances for grants (in October 1970).

Demand management continued for a time in the same cautious vein, aimed at keeping demand roughly in line with productive potential. The stimulus to export demand had continued throughout 1969/70 (the volume increase being 11 per cent), but was expected to fall to 4 per cent through 1970/1. The budget, though introducing a measure of relaxation, implied the same weighted *ex ante* leverage as in the previous year: at 1½ per cent of potential GDP (table 4.9), this was extremely deflationary in view of the lack of stimulus from other sources. The projected 3¼ per cent growth rate was, in the event, optimistic, and the realised budget surplus, not least because of the downturn in activity, was £1000 million less than forecast.

The emergence of the two evils which were to plague economic policy in the 1970s – cost inflation and unemployment – was rather ambivalently contributing to the cautious stance of budgetary policy at this time. On the one hand there was a belief that the two were causally connected,[2] so that reduced public spending plans tended to be rationalised partly on grounds of the slower growth of the economy and the increased cost of programmes.[3] On the other hand, it was the

---

[1] Such had been the alteration in the balance of direct and indirect taxation (chart 4.2) that the Chancellor even considered substantially raising indirect taxes in order to finance even larger reductions in income tax, but he was dissuaded by the belief that price rises occurring as a result would be a stimulus to inflation (House of Commons, *Hansard*, 14 April 1970, cols. 1242–3).

[2] The rise in unemployment in 1970/1 was due to the relatively slow growth of output, but it also reflected 'rapidly rising wage costs', which had forced employers to cut down on labour (House of Commons, *Hansard*, 30 March 1971, col. 1362).

[3] Treasury, *New Policies for Public Spending*.

Chancellor's belief that the fight against inflation would not be aided by a further reduction in the pressure of demand, even though fiscal policy should avoid creating the additional danger of demand inflation.[1] Budgetary policy, as expressed in the interventions of October 1970 and March 1971, was cautious, preferring to err towards a lower pressure of demand, though trying to maintain a rate of growth equal to productive potential.

The first package was avowedly neutral in its effects on demand, the projected cut in the standard rate of income tax in 1971/2 nominally offsetting the expenditure cuts. The decrease in the rate of corporation tax was, however, intended to have a longer-term effect on investment;[2] on a weighted basis the whole package was slightly reflationary. The out-turn leverage of the budget was still, however, only 2·5 per cent of full-employment GDP – much less than even in 1962/3.

Maintaining such a stance through 1971/2 would have meant a shortfall from potential, so the 1971 budget introduced some correcting measures to increase the growth rate from a projected 2 to 3 per cent. Through a combination of income tax changes (amounting with the cut in the standard rate in October 1970 to £500 million in 1971/2), a further reduction in the rate of company tax and the partial abolition of selective employment tax, the total discretionary revenue decrease in 1971/2 was over £850 million. Even so, the change in the weighted *ex ante* leverage was slight, partly because of the effects of fiscal drag. It required a further reduction in purchase tax rates on 19 July 1971 and a series of public expenditure measures to increase budgetary leverage from 2·5 to 3·6 per cent of potential GDP in 1971/2 (table 4.9). This was sufficient, with a recovery in export demand in the second half of the year, to keep GDP growth up to the original target of 3 per cent in 1971, with an increased current account surplus. (The real extent of the employment gap implied by four years of growth below potential, had, however, caused a revision of the growth target in mid-1971, to 4–4½ per cent through 1971/2, so that the out-turn represented a shortfall from this.)

In the 1972 budget the Chancellor chose to continue the momentum he saw in the economy by raising the growth target to 5 per cent between the second half of 1971 and the first half of 1973. To achieve this, £1200 million was to be remitted in taxation and the budget deficit was expected to increase substantially to £2441 million. To safeguard the balance of payments the exchange rate was to be allowed to float if necessary – a significant factor in view of the sharply rising tide of

---

[1] House of Commons, *Hansard*, 30 March 1971, col. 1369.
[2] The cut in the rate applied to taxes on 1969 profits and involved refunds where payments had already been made.

imports, which had begun to swell towards the end of 1971/2 and was accounting for much of the shortfall in domestic output through that year.

The Chancellor relied mainly on income tax for reflationary effect, £982 million being remitted through an increase in personal allowances (against which should be set fiscal drag of about £700 million). A boost to consumption greater than its nominal value (£7 million in a full year) was given by allowing loan interest over £35 against tax – a concession that did not apply to hire purchase debt. The rest of the package was made up of cuts in purchase and company tax (table 4.2). Overall, the budget introduced the largest discretionary change in leverage of the whole period by a considerable margin. The intended stance, in weighted full-employment terms, was approximately 6·15 per cent of full-employment GDP and, though this represented a return only to the 1965–7 level of intervention, the implied change in direct budgetary leverage from the previous year was – at about 3 per cent of GDP – without precedent. Neither this nor the growth objective were, in the event, achieved; GDP increased only at a 3¼ per cent annual rate over the eighteen months to mid-1973, and the full-employment budget balance turned out at 5·23 per cent in 1972/3 because of substantial shortfalls in public expenditure. The current account balance deteriorated by £1215 million to −£237 million.

At the time of the 1973 budget the erosion of the external position was already apparent, although the output target still seemed achievable.[1] The budget therefore followed a strategy of 'no change', maintaining the objective of 5 per cent growth through 1973/4, while being 'broadly neutral' on the tax front.[2] April 1973 was, however, the date for the inception of several tax reforms announced previously, and these were to cost about £460 million in a full year. The unified income tax system entailed a tax reduction of £300 million, though the savings content of this must have been fairly high because much of the benefit was to unearned incomes and higher levels of earned income; on the other hand, both the changeover to an imputation system of company taxation and the introduction of VAT at a standard rate of 10 per cent were fairly neutral in effect. The extra leverage exerted by the full-employment balance in 1973/4 was in fact to come from the expenditure side, with the nominal deficit increasing to an intended £2853 million and the weighted full-employment balance to 6·3 per cent of full-employment GDP (an increase of about 1 per cent over the 1972/3 out-turn). Expecting an upturn in manufacturing investment, the

[1] The 1973/4 Financial Statement gave a GDP growth rate of 6·8 per cent between the second half of 1971 and the first half of 1973.

[2] House of Commons, *Hansard*, 6 March 1973, col. 249.

Chancellor avoided demand cuts which would prejudice this; in addition, export demand was expected to recover strongly. In 1973, which turned out to be the peak of the world demand cycle (chart 4.8), there was thus a reversion to the pre-devaluation pattern, by which burgeoning export and investment demand coincided with expansion in other sectors of the economy led by a fiscal deficit. This time the output targets were achieved for 1973, though the oil crisis and the three-day week gave a different result for the financial year, but it was at the expense of, or in conjunction with, a further deterioration of £1263 million in the current balance, which reached −£1500 million.

Whether this conjunction of expansionary budgeting and a deteriorating payments position was causal or coincidental is a matter of some dispute among economists, the 'New Cambridge' school being only the most prominent of the critics of the official position. The basic judgement of policy-makers and those who supported their position throughout this episode was that the economy began by carrying very substantial excess capacity (estimated by the National Institute at 6 per cent of GDP in 1971[1]) and the continued 5 per cent growth target (granted that underlying productive potential was growing at over 3 per cent per annum) was no more than consistent with the steady removal of this unused capacity. The floating of the exchange rate was seen primarily as a protection against the contingency that the recovery would be prematurely halted by speculation against the pound. The initial diagnosis of excess capacity is, however, disputable, because the behaviour of unemployment was inconsistent with that of other indicators; by other measures (vacancies, capacity utilisation, etc.), the margin of excess capacity was not great in 1973 – it was indeed comparable to that existing in the boom year of 1964. Moreover, there is no doubt that, whatever the 'aggregate' margin of spare resources, there were numerous specific bottlenecks encountered at this time.

A second problem is that, even if there were a clear agreement on the margin of spare resources, this does not readily translate into an agreement over policy, which involves a calculation not only of the added amount of demand required, but also of the rate at which demand should be augmented. It is not implausible to argue that the rate of change of demand is as significant as the level for its inflationary potential;[2]

---

[1] Assuming 'full employment' at a registered unemployment rate of 1½ per cent (cf. *National Institute Economic Review*, no. 63, February 1973, pp. 44–5).

[2] There is not much empirical evidence on this issue. However, the argument is eminently plausible that if demand is added to an economy at a high rate this will exceed the rate at which production schedules can easily be raised and the gap will be filled by imports, rationing and price rises. On the importance of the *speed* of the upswing in creating pressures and bottlenecks, see F. P. R. Brechling and J. N. Wolfe, 'The end of stop-go', *Lloyd's Bank Review*, no 75, January 1965, pp. 23–30; for a sceptical viewpoint, see P. M. Oppenheimer,

here, it is important to note not only that the turn-round in fiscal policy attempted in those two years was very large,[1] but also that it was accompanied by an expansive convulsion in monetary policy of an unparalleled kind.

These considerations suggest that fiscal policy in this period may very well have attempted too much too quickly. The 'New Cambridge' school were more definite in their criticism, which was based upon the proposition that the projected public sector deficit (£2853 million in 1973/4) could not be matched by private sector savings at the foreseen output levels and therefore could only be realised if there was a direct spill-over into the balance of payments (excess demand was here put in the region of £500-£600 million).[2] The uniqueness of this view – and the source of greatest dispute – rests on the precision with which private sector savings are held to be predictable and hence the precision with which the spill-over can be identified.

Another element of 'New Cambridge' criticism was of earlier origin and more general validity. It was that domestic demand-led growth is a chimera, for in the long run the growth of the economy must be determined by the growth of exports.[3] Relying on domestic demand for reflation disposes towards budgetary immobility at the top of the cycle, since 'governments have been plagued with the dilemma whether to restrain consumption so as to provide more resources for investment or exports, or to allow relatively free rein to consumer demand to ensure the growth of capacity'.[4] By relying on export growth, the confidence effects on investment (such as they are) caused by reining back domestic demand may be avoided and the greater scope for productivity gains thought to attach to the export sector exploited. The 1972/3 episode was the last and perhaps the most dramatic of the attempts to use domestic demand to break through to the 'virtuous circle' of demand-induced growth and investment. As history stands it failed.

BUDGETARY POLICY AND STABILISATION, 1959/60–1973/4

It would be a mistake to see the conduct of demand management as related immutably to one particular objective of policy. At times, it has been used (with and without the added help of other instruments)

'Is Britain's worsening trade gap due to bad management of the business cycle?', *Bulletin of the Oxford University Institute of Economics & Statistics*, vol. 27, August 1965, pp. 177–83.

[1] Out-turns were less expansive than intended (especially in 1972/3) largely because of shortfalls in expenditure, some of which may have been due to market difficulties.

[2] R. R. Neild, *London and Cambridge Economic Bulletin*, July 1973; W. A. H. Godley and F. Cripps, *The Times*, 6 September 1973. See also pages 137–8 above.

[3] W. A. H. Godley and F. Cripps, *The Times*, 9 January 1973; Kaldor (ed.), *Conflicts in Policy Objectives.*   [4] Ibid. p. 15.

as a means of achieving all the major economic objectives; at other times there has been a conscious trade-off between them – particularly unemployment and the balance of payments. Nevertheless, there remains a dimension to demand management which is summed up in its effectiveness as a stabiliser, in which it is dependent on the reliability of short-term forecasts. It is true that such forecasts can be overridden by political expediency, but the process of budget-making in the United Kingdom is based on the belief that aggregate demand can be forecast, and then balanced by appropriate intervention.

Fiscal neutrality

In assessing fiscal policy the first requirement is to establish some concept of neutrality.[1] One such rule specifies neutrality as unchanged tax rates; that is, statutory tax rate changes provide indices of deviations from neutrality. This is attractive because the budget is the ultimate balancing exercise. Tax changes are, however, frequently made in order to pay for public expenditure changes, so that they cannot be thought of simply as means of offsetting changes in other components of demand; more to the point, we have seen how powerful automatic tax movements can be, so that effective rather than statutory tax rate changes might be more logical indicators of changes in fiscal stance. Fiscal drag would then be implicitly defined as discretionary, which conforms with policy-makers' frequent use of the buoyancy of the revenue as a substitute for (or supplement to) discretionary action proper.

Even so, changes in revenue can only be partial indicators of policy action, so that the public sector financial balance can be regarded as the best measure of fiscal policy stance, provided that it is translated into full-employment terms and, according to the form of analysis to which it is subjected, weighted or not for the differential impact on demand of different types of revenue and expenditure.

The record of stabilisation

Discussion of the success of budgetary policy in stabilising the economy usually starts from Dow's pessimistic conclusion for the 1950s that 'budgetary and monetary policy must be regarded as having been positively destabilising'.[2] Tests of stabilising adequacy, however, conventionally require an estimate of the domestic output cycle in the absence of intervention. Policy is then presumed to have damped fluctuations in the economy if this cycle (net-of-policy) shows greater variation than the actual cycle. Representing fiscal policy by discretion-

[1] Worswick, 'Fiscal policy and stabilization in Britain', p. 50, and page 154 above.
[2] Dow, *The Management of the British Economy, 1945–60*, p. 384.

ary tax changes,[1] the results of such tests have been ambiguous. Whereas, for the period 1955–65 Bristow's verdict was that policy had been marginally stabilising, Artis's results for the periods 1958–70 and 1965–70 showed it to have been slightly destabilising.[2] However, perhaps most noticeable was the smallness of the effects either way (as well, indeed, as the smallness of the fluctuations to be offset). The effects of total budgetary leverage were also found to be slightly destabilising by the OECD country study of the period 1955–65, which concluded that the United Kingdom was unique in this respect.[3] The 'pure cycle' (net-of-policy) appeared to have been amplified by 11 per cent for the public sector or 13 per cent for the central government. Following a different approach, the Brookings Institution also criticised budgetary policy for being destabilising: from a reaction function analysis of policy changes over the period 1951–65, it appeared that interventions had been triggered by changes in unemployment – an indicator which lags GDP changes by about a year and which, if used as a basis of policy formulation, must of necessity lead to instability.[4] Despite the methodological and other misgivings attached to all tests of demand management, there remains a consensus against a positive contribution to stability from budgetary policy.

Simulation procedures used for testing the impact of interventions

[1] Testing for the stabilising effectiveness of policy by comparing fluctuations in the economy with and without discretionary tax interventions is not strictly a test of counter-cyclical policy, since the changes in tax may, in fact, be compensating for variations in the public sector itself (cf. chapter 3, page 124). It is, however, a test of short-term budgetary adequacy as practised in the United Kingdom, where tax changes are ultimately called on to balance *all* sources of excess or deficient demand.

[2] J. A. Bristow, 'Taxation and income stabilisation', *Economic Journal*, vol. 78, June 1968, pp. 299–311; Artis, 'Fiscal policy for stabilization'. Bristow's analysis was based on Hopkin and Godley, 'An analysis of tax changes', while Artis analysed the model described in J. R. Shepherd and M. J. C. Surrey, 'The short-term effects of tax changes', *National Institute Economic Review*, no. 46, November 1968, pp. 36–41, which included an allowance for accelerator effects on investment, whereas the previous model did not. Bristow found that for the cycle net-of-policy the ratio of GDP to its logarithmic trend was 0·90, compared with a ratio of 0·91 for the actual cycle; that is, that 0·01 of instability had been offset by policy. Artis's results showed that for both periods policy had increased instability by 0·01 (1958–70: 0·99 net-of-policy, 0·98 with-policy, and 1956–70 : 0·97 net-of-policy, 0·96 with-policy).

[3] OECD, *Fiscal Policy in Seven Countries*, pp. 69–71. Of the countries studied, the United States appeared to be the only one which offset over half of the exogenous fluctuations in the economy, the others having been mainly 30–40 per cent successful.

[4] Caves *et al.*, *Britain's Economic Prospects*, p. 489. Changes in total public sector leverage and in tax rates appear to have been expansionary when unemployment was increasing and deflationary when unemployment was falling (the statistical significance of the relationship between total leverage and unemployment being quite small). The general methodology of the Musgraves has been criticised by Worswick, 'Fiscal policy and stabilization in Britain', pp. 42–7, but it is true that up to the 1960s the lagged relationship between employment and output was not well known. There was a formal reappraisal of reactions between these two indicators in the early 1960s, so that after this it cannot be said that policy was premised on ignorance of the lags involved (cf. W. A. H. Godley and J. R. Shepherd, 'Long-term growth and short-term policy', *National Institute Economic Review*, no. 29, August 1964).

call for a full-scale model of the economy and a knowledge of the lags involved. On pages 190–1 above an alternative method of testing budgetary adequacy was set out which overcomes the problem of lags.[1] If the (intended) full-employment public sector balance is accepted as the indicator of fiscal policy, fiscal adequacy can be assessed by comparing changes in the value of that indicator with changes in the overseas and private sector balances, also evaluated at full employment. A regression using the intended change in the weighted full-employment balance (P'^{fe}) and, as proxies for the *ex ante* changes in overseas and private sector financial balances, world exports of manufactures (X) and investment in the private sector (I) (all expressed as ratios of full-employment GDP) gave the following result:[2]

$$\Delta P'^{fe} = 0\cdot52\Delta(I+X) \quad (\text{SE} = 0\cdot20, \quad t = 2\cdot49, \quad R^2 = 0\cdot21) \qquad (9)$$

The negative sign expected if fiscal policy was stabilising does not appear;[3] indeed, discounting the two years after devaluation, the budgetary cycle appears to have been positively phased with the private investment and export cycles, as is borne out by chart 4.8. As far as the relationship of the budgetary cycle with the investment cycle is concerned, reflationary budgeting has tended to lead (in 1959/60, 1963/4 and late 1971), but with a tendency for an overlap as the upturn in activity takes hold. At this point budgetary leverage usually ceases to exert any *extra* demand leverage, though the budgetary stance (for reasons considered below) tends to be maintained at peak level by so-called 'neutral' budgeting (1960/1, 1964/5 and 1973/4). This conjunction of peak budgetary leverage and investment demand has then tended to be followed by reinforcing downturns (1961/2–1962/3 and 1965/6). The pattern seems to have been broken in 1966/7 and 1967/8, when the budgetary turn-round was checked, and by devaluation in 1968/9, though this favourable conjunction gave way in 1970/1 to an unfavourable one, when reflationary action was delayed – a reversion

---

[1] Musgrave 'On measuring fiscal performance', p. 261. However, the caveats attached to the use of a 'reaction function' analysis of this comparative static type should be kept in mind (page 189 above).

[2] Changes in the intended *ex ante* balances should be used to avoid problems caused by forecasting errors, but in practice the precise data required are not available. The proxies used here are the *ex post* figures of the (change in) deviation from trend of gross domestic capital formation in the private sector (as described in chart 3.6) and world demand for exports (given by the United Nations volume index for manufactures). Both cycles being translated into GDP terms (chart 4.8), perfect stabilisation would give a coefficient of -1.

[3] Regressions were also run against each of the two proxies separately:

$$\Delta P'^{fe} = 0\cdot69\Delta I \quad (\text{SE} = 0\cdot39, \quad t = 1\cdot79, \quad R^2 = 0\cdot12)$$
$$\Delta P'^{fe} = 0\cdot72\Delta X \quad (\text{SE} = 0\cdot34, \quad t = 2\cdot16, \quad R^2 = 0\cdot17)$$

All the equations discount the extremely stabilising budget changes of the two post-devaluation years and are based on the calendar and financial year data in chart 4.8.

to the usual pattern of reinforcing recessionary pressures. There has been a similar tendency for the budgetary cycle to reinforce the world demand cycle, except immediately after devaluation, and in this case the conjunction in trends has tended to appear almost immediately (1959/60, 1963/4 and 1972/3), with a degree of symmetry also appearing at the top of the two cycles as domestic and external leverage is maintained (1960/1, 1964/5 and 1973/4).

Pro-cyclical budgeting

However, the less than beneficial effect of fiscal policy on domestic stability needs two qualifications: first, it is not implied that stability has been markedly worsened, only not improved, since public demand can fluctuate at least as much as non-government demand before the impact becomes worse than if the cycle applied to the economy as a whole. Secondly, variations around the trend of output in the United Kingdom have not, including demand management effects, been as great as in other (faster-growing) countries.[1] Nevertheless, it still has to be explained why demand management has been pro-cyclical, and one can advance three hypotheses: first, the techniques and instruments of demand management may have been insufficient, and forecasting inaccuracies may have misled policy; secondly, demand and output instability might be explained by the electoral cycle; thirdly, since the tactics of demand management have not been applied in an unchanging strategic framework, output stability may have been sacrificed from time to time to the balance of payments, or risked by 'growth experiments'. The performance of stabilisation policy seems explicable in terms of each of these factors, though it is a matter for subjective judgement which was most important.

As instances of forecasts misleading policy, there were the wrong diagnosis in 1962 and the underestimate of the downturn in 1970, while the 1959/60 and 1972/3 reflations seem to have been guided by pessimistic views of the actual demand forces in the economy. However, once the economy gets off course it becomes increasingly difficult to withstand political pressures for action, so that there has also been a tendency for output forecasts to be overruled for short-term gains. Excessive reflation, for instance, has been explained by reference to the electoral cycle[2] – the expansions of 1953/4, 1958/9 and 1963/4 closely preceded elections, though that of 1972/3 did not. Moreover, 'neutral' budgeting at the height of the boom might be partly attributable to

---

[1] See A. Whiting, 'An international comparison of the instability of economic growth', *Three Banks Review*, no. 109, March 1976, pp. 26–46.

[2] See memoranda by G. D. N. Worswick in House of Commons, *Ninth Report from the Expenditure Committee, Session 1974*, pp. 28–33.

reluctance to be seen altering course once an election has taken place, particularly if it might appear in breach of a pre-election declaration; the 1960 dispute between Macmillan and his deflationist Chancellor comes into this category, as does the budget of 1966. But interventions for immediate economic and political ends can come to be represented as strategic changes. Deflations may be seen as transferring priorities towards the balance of payments, or as lowering the pressure of demand to mitigate inflation and even improve export performance.[1] Correspondingly, reflations tend to become opportunities not just for filling a particular demand gap, but for solving all the problems of economic policy by expansion, which may be part of the explanation of reflationary over-reaction. Although it may also depend on the under-forecasting of upturns, consumption-led growth (possibly mixed with public expenditure-led growth, as in 1963/4) has been the dominant philosophy behind expansionism in the United Kingdom and it is a characteristic of such a strategy that it becomes difficult to rein consumption back once the upturn is under way, because it is believed that to do so would adversely affect investment.

The idea that the British economy has been subject to recurrent bouts of 'planned instability' arising from deliberate deflationary policies[2] may be extended to the successive switches between expansion and contraction, during which stabilisation policy proper has been compromised. In this sense, it may have been that too much has been expected of demand management and that, if the successive policies have failed, it is because productive potential has not been pushed up as hoped, secondary export expansion (through increased competitiveness) has not been achieved and the balance of payments constraint has never been overcome. Because faster growth has been impossible to achieve, stability has also been impossible.

To summarise, it seems that the pro-cyclical tendency of budgetary policy may be ascribed to a combination of all three factors. Forecasting errors have certainly played their part, but are by no means more important than the other elements, for the political pressures accompanying adverse employment and balance of payments indicators have always been powerful enough to override, in the last analysis, any mechanistic forecast-linked demand management policy; at the same time, it has been a notable feature of fiscal policy that it has been used not simply for 'fine-tuning' of demand but to try to break through supply constraints. Domestic stability appears to have been compromised by failure to raise the growth of productive potential in this way.

---

[1] On the 'toothpaste tube' approach to exports – that when demand is squeezed exports are extruded – see Worswick, 'Fiscal policy and stabilization in Britain', p. 53.

[2] Kennedy, 'Employment policy: what went wrong?'.

CONCLUSIONS

The operation of budgetary policy

Budgetary policy in the United Kingdom has been characterised both by an active short-term policy towards tax rates and by the pursuit of longer-run structural reform. Discretionary interventions have been largely identified with income tax decreases and expenditure tax increases, but this asymmetry has to be seen in the context of the automatic biases in the system associated with inflationary fiscal drag. These have resulted in increases in the effective rate of personal income tax and decreases in indirect tax rates, with the net result that the overall reliance of the system on personal income tax has increased, though not as a conscious act of policy.

With respect to both real and inflationary income movements, the aggregate yield of taxes on personal income (direct and indirect) has exhibited an elasticity greater than unity, which tends to increase without discretionary correction. The net fiscal drag which has resulted has been behind the increase over the period in the aggregate effective rate of tax; the rapid inflation of the early 1970s accelerated this, so that budget-making became increasingly involved with offsetting, rather than exploiting, the bias. This factor, together with the unwanted changes in the tax-mix, the augmented 'patronage powers' of Chancellors who can remit large increases in taxes, and the fact that automatic movements disguise the true discretionary stance of the budget, formed the basis of the case for 'indexing' the tax system – that is, fixing tax rates in real terms to eliminate inflationary fiscal drag. The case for this has also been argued from other points of view, most notably because of the regressive effects which fiscal drag may have on the distribution of the tax burden and of post-tax incomes. But, though inflation tends to have especially adverse effects on lower income earners at and near the tax threshold, fiscal drag has actually been associated, by and large, with a movement towards a more progressive distribution of post-tax incomes.

Whilst discretionary budgetary policy has become increasingly pre-occupied with the offsetting of automatic biases, the built-in properties of the system have themselves grown in relative strength. British budgetary practice has never explicitly employed automatic stabilisers, preferring to adjust tax yields in order to balance demand, but the built-in damping potential of the tax structure tends to be augmented unless corrected by discretionary action, as marginal rates and elasticities automatically increase with the growth of incomes. This has been particularly marked in the case of marginal rates (built-in flexibility), which determine the strength of automatic stabilisers; it has also, to a lesser extent, been a feature of the aggregate elasticities of the tax system, which determine fiscal drag.

The period has seen a substantial overhaul of the tax structure. The personal income tax system has been simplified administratively by the abolition of reduced rates of tax and the unification of income tax and surtax. The relatively high maximum rates of tax on earned income have been abated and the graduation of the system at its lower end has been reduced; among advanced industrial countries the British tax threshold has become one of the lowest and the 30 per cent initial rate of tax (raised to 35 per cent in 1975/6) one of the highest. The indirect tax system has also been simplified (the revised rate structure being associated with increased costs of collection). Doubts on economic grounds about discriminating against income-elastic goods led to a reduction and standardisation of purchase tax and eventually to the introduction of VAT at a single standard rate. But this trend was not consistent: selective employment tax, while removing one element of discrimination by taxing services, was still based on a preference for manufacturing industry. The clash between 'interventionist' and 'neutralist' attitudes towards the role of the tax structure in resource allocation, which was evident here, had a parallel in the shaping and reshaping of company taxes to be neutral towards or discriminate against distributions. Here, and in the tax system at large, the net outcome over the period was in favour of a more 'neutral' and uniform structure, a process in which efficiency (either administrative or economic) has been advanced over the redistributive functions of the system, which might be better served by a more highly differentiated and progressive structure.

The reforms and counter-reforms of the period have been criticised as introducing a degree of uncertainty and instability. A number of fundamental changes sprang 'fully armed from the Chancellor's head',[1] with no prior public discussion and little chance of consensus. In this respect, the practice of issuing consultative documents in the form of Green Papers in the latter part of the period extended the boundaries of debate and increased the possibilities of reform with stability. Parallel improvements can be identified in the operation of budgetary policy, where the reform of the Exchequer accounts was followed, in 1968/9, by publication of forecasts for the financial balance and borrowing requirement of the public sector, enabling the overall leverage of budgetary policy to be interpreted more easily. There still exists, however, no coordinated longer-term strategy with respect to either the internal balance and structure of the tax system, or the balance of public spending and taxation, such as would emerge from a medium-term (or full-employment) budgeting system (see page 130 above).

[1] Prest, *The Capital Gains Tax and the Corporation Tax*, p. 19.

The effectiveness of budgetary policy

The effectiveness of short-term fiscal action has been questioned to a considerable degree. Besides criticisms which depend on alternative models of economic behaviour, there are judgements on the performance of fiscal policy within its own terms of reference *vis-à-vis* the objectives of demand management. Full employment (in some degree) has been achieved, but only associated with balance of payments deficits and inflation which have made it unsustainable for more than a short period. However, it has long been recognised that price stability needs a separate instrument, while it is difficult to reconcile full employment with balance of payments equilibrium when the economy is competitively inadequate. Fiscal policy should not, therefore, be judged by objectives which it could not be expected to achieve.

Nevertheless, budgetary policy has exerted a pro-cyclical influence; indeed, fluctuations in the economy would have been reduced if budgetary leverage had not fluctuated. However, whilst forecasting errors (including those relating to public expenditure trends) have at times been misleading and encouraged policy-makers to leave correction too late, fiscal (and other) policy has not always aimed at stabilising demand in a mechanistic way. Political pressures and external crises have sometimes evoked responses which sacrificed domestic stability, while deliberate attempts to induce faster growth (as opposed to cyclical recovery) have fundamentally compromised stability; because domestic demand was the instrument chosen to influence growth, there was a tendency for excess demand to emerge at the peak of the cycle, with some spill-over into the balance of payments. In this respect policy is particularly open to the criticism that it did not (part knowingly at least) exploit the periodic upswings in world demand as opportunities to improve the balance of payments and growth simultaneously. Only at the time of devaluation was there a conjunction of deflationary budgeting and output growth based on the world and domestic output cycles, but this advantage was lost by delaying the subsequent reflation.

The short-term element in demand management, as practised in the United Kingdom and epitomised in the term 'fine-tuning', was the product of the circumstances in which it has operated. The cycles in activity up to 1973/4 were not in fact very deep, so that conclusions about the period 1959/60–1973/4 may be peculiar to the circumstances of the time; even if the verdict were unfavourable, it would not rule out using budgetary policy when the troughs of activity were deeper (as after the oil crisis), or where there was a secular unemployment problem. It may be, however, that the short-term horizon of eighteen months to two years is too short, which is an argument for extending medium-term budgeting techniques.

In budgetary circumstances similar to those which obtained up to 1973/4 it might be that there should be a greater emphasis on medium-term policy, with correspondingly less on balancing demand in the short term. This at any rate is a possible verdict of experience, but such a conclusion cannot be drawn unambiguously from the record of stabilisation. Short-term policy *has* actually been subordinated, from time to time, to strategies for economic growth which may to some extent be called medium-term, and stabilisation has been compromised. Requiring that budgetary policy be framed around medium-term consistency therefore somewhat begs the questions of what the rule should be, how it should be maintained against immediate political and other pressures, and how it can be prevented from eventually becoming destabilising in the short run.

If a solution is to be found to the relative roles of short-term and medium-term policy, it is probably neither in continuing what has gone before nor in adopting some unbending rule of medium-term neutrality. Past expansions have been pro-cyclical because the strength of exogenous demand forces – world demand and investment – have been underestimated and because relying on domestic demand-led growth involved a conscious policy choice. In other words, policy has never been intentionally counter-cyclical in any very meaningful sense, so that there remains the option of clearly adhering to this aim in future. This, in turn, would mean greater reliance on the medium-term (cyclical and trend) prognosis, so as to ensure (as was not the case in the past when expansions started from balance of payments surplus) that any upturn can be sustained in the longer run and does not entail competition for resources between deficit-financed expenditure, investment and exports.

CHAPTER 5

MONETARY POLICY

PART I

by *J. H. B. Tew*

INSTRUMENTS AND OBJECTIVES

The 'new approach' to monetary policy, inaugurated by the Bank of England's consultative document 'Competition and credit control' of May 1971,[1] did not represent a break in the continuing objectives of that policy. But there were changes in the instruments by which the authorities sought to achieve their objectives and in the views of officials about the mechanism by which their actions are transmitted through the economy so as to achieve the desired objectives.

In the postwar period the objectives of British monetary policy have indeed changed very little. The two main external objectives, both treated in chapter 7, were (until June 1972) to peg the spot exchange rate for the dollar by official transactions in the foreign exchange market and to discourage excessive capital outflows. The predominant internal objective has always been demand management. In the 1950s there was also the potentially conflicting objective of keeping down the interest burden of the national debt, but by the mid-1960s this had been subordinated to demand management,[2] which has meant in practice avoiding a level of demand either so low as to lead to a politically unacceptable amount of unemployment or so high as to drain away our international reserves.

The instruments of British monetary policy are official regulations and official transactions. In both cases there were changes under the 'new approach', so initially we shall consider the evolution of such instruments prior to 1971.

There were then (apart from exchange controls, to be considered in chapter 7) three main groups of *regulations*, of which the first were the balance sheet ratios observed by the clearing banks. From 1946 the London clearing banks had observed an 8 per cent minimum cash ratio,[3]

---

[1] Reprinted in *Bank of England Quarterly Bulletin*, vol. 11, June 1971.

[2] 'Official transactions in the gilt-edged market', *Bank of England Quarterly Bulletin*, vol. 6, June 1966; see especially p. 146.

[3] 'Cash' included notes, coin and demand deposits at the Bank of England. 'Liquid assets' included cash, call money and Treasury and commercial bills. 'Call money' here means

and from 1951 they also undertook to observe a liquid asset ratio somewhat vaguely defined as 28–32 per cent of their deposit liabilities.[1] In 1957 this was made more precise, as a minimum of 30 per cent, reduced in 1963 to 28 per cent. From 1960 the authorities attempted to improve the efficiency of the minimum liquid asset ratio by activating a scheme for Special Deposits, under which part of the liquid assets of the London clearing banks could be rendered non-liquid by being blocked in Special Deposit accounts at the Bank of England. A variant of the scheme applied to the Scottish clearing banks, which also undertook to maintain whatever liquid asset ratio each had observed hitherto. The second group of regulations took the form of lending requests. From the early 1950s onwards the banks had been accustomed to receive from time to time official advice on the composition, and subsequently also on the total amount, of their sterling lending to the private sector. In the 1950s requests were addressed only to the London and Scottish clearing banks, but as from 1961 they were extended to other banks and to the larger finance houses. The third group of regulations – controls on hire purchase terms for consumers' durable goods – were exercised with only short intermissions from 1952 to 1971. In addition to these official regulations, the London clearing banks, with the support of the authorities, operated an interest-rate cartel, which related their deposit and lending interest rates to Bank Rate.

Official *transactions* are conducted in three markets – the foreign exchange market, the money market and the gilt-edged market. There are also transactions in national savings media, but these appear not to have been used to any significant degree as an instrument of monetary policy.

From the reopening of the London foreign exchange market in the early 1950s up to the floating of the pound in 1972, the spot pound–dollar rate was pegged by official transactions in the market and, though the peg was changed from $2.80 to $2.40 in 1967, the technique of intervention remained much the same throughout the period. In the forward market, however, there was an important change in official tactics as from November 1964 (see chapter 7).

In the money market, official policy from 1951 onwards has been for the Bank to control money market rates, especially the Treasury bill rate, by acting as the residual supplier of finance to the discount houses, whether by purchases (and occasionally by sales) of bills

short-term lending to discount houses, bill brokers, Stock Exchange jobbers and money brokers, and the banks' own holdings of tax reserve certificates.

[1] European Communities Monetary Committee, *Monetary Policy in the Countries of the EEC. Supplement 1974 (The United Kingdom)*, Brussels, EEC, 1974, p. 22.

through its bill broker, or by transactions through the discount office. In this way the Treasury bill rate has been held on a target by broadly the same means as the pre-1972 exchange rate, though in this case the target has been readily varied since 1951, if needs be from day to day, instead of being changed only rarely and reluctantly as with the exchange rate.

In the gilt-edged market, however, official transactions, conducted by the Government Broker, have not aimed at holding the bond rate on a target – at all events not since Hugh Dalton's 'cheap money' target of $2\frac{1}{2}$ per cent was abandoned. What the Government Broker has sought to do instead was affected by policy shifts at about the beginning of the 1960s and again towards the end of the decade (culminating in the 'new approach' of 1971). In the period between these two shifts, official policy in the gilt-edged market was to 'lean against the wind': that is, to buy as well as to sell in the market, and to do so in such a way as to moderate and slow down the fluctuations in interest rates which market forces tended to bring about, while still always permitting any persistent pressure of market forces to move rates upwards or downwards.

The way in which the various instruments of British monetary policy are matched with the objectives is in many cases straightforward, as is also the transmission mechanism[1] by which the former serve to achieve the latter. Thus, prior to the floating of the pound in 1972, the objective of exchange transactions in the spot market was to peg the exchange rate; the objective both of exchange control and of exchange transactions in the forward market was to mitigate excessive external capital movements; the objective of hire purchase restrictions and of lending requests was demand management. Credit extended by the clearing banks was also controlled for purposes of demand management by the imposition of the minimum liquid asset ratio and by calling for Special Deposits.

However, the 8 per cent cash ratio imposed on the London clearing banks was not a demand management device like the liquid asset ratio. As we have already seen, the main aim of the Bank of England's transactions in the money market was to achieve control of interest rates, especially the Treasury bill rate.

Treasury bills can therefore always be turned into cash without much disturbance of the market rates of discount on them. It follows that the Bank cannot restrain the lending operations of the clearing banks by limiting the creation of cash without losing its assurance of stability of the rate on Treasury bills. It is because of this circumstance that the effective base of bank

---

[1] The term is not here used in the technical banking sense of the cheque clearing system.

credit has become the liquid assets (based on the availability of Treasury bills) instead of the supply of cash.[1]

What, then, was the purpose of the cash ratio? It seems to have served no purpose other than to stabilise the London clearing banks' demand for cash and thus to enable the Bank of England to forecast more accurately the amount of finance which the discount houses could expect from these banks, and hence how much would have to be provided by the Bank of England to achieve its desired level of interest rates in the money market. Thus, the cash ratio, together with the fixing of Bank Rate and the transactions undertaken by the discount office and the Bank's bill broker, were all instruments for controlling the level of rates prevailing in the money market.

A further instrument for controlling short-term rates – more specifically the London clearing banks' rate on 'regular' call money lent to the discount houses,[2] their overdraft rates and the rates they paid on deposit accounts – was the cartel interest-rate agreement, by which the London clearing banks, at the instigation of the authorities, used Bank Rate as the basis for determining the rates at which they themselves borrowed and lent. By making use of these various devices, the Bank had a very effective control over what may be called 'traditional' short-term rates, in particular the rates in the traditional money market – broadly those on the discount houses' assets (other than certificates of deposit) and on their liabilities.[3] On the other hand, this control did not extend to the rates prevailing in 'London's new markets for money',[4] which expanded rapidly in the 1960s, nor to deposit rates paid by the non-clearing banks, whose business was expanding no less rapidly (table 5.1).[5]

In their control of short-term rates the authorities had a mixture of objectives: to keep down the cost of the short-term national debt; to regulate demand insofar as capital expenditure was sensitive to variations in short-term rates;[6] to avoid undermining confidence in the

---

[1] Treasury, *Radcliffe Report*, para. 376.

[2] 'The rate of interest on "regular" money lent to the market by the clearing banks does not normally vary with the week-to-week fluctuations in the Treasury bill rate: it is only changed when Bank Rate is changed' (Treasury, *Radcliffe Report*, para. 360).

[3] See the evidence of the Chief Cashier as quoted in para. 360 of the *Radcliffe Report*.

[4] *Midland Bank Review*, August 1966, p. 3. See table 5.6 on page 243 below.

[5] 'Banks' in this chapter means banks in respect of which the Bank of England publishes statistics (listed in *Bank of England Quarterly Bulletin*, vol. 12, December 1972, pp. 573–5). They subdivide into 'deposit banks', 95 per cent of whose sterling deposits were at the London and Scottish clearing banks, and the following categories of other banks which will be collectively labelled the 'non-clearing banks': accepting houses; British overseas and Commonwealth banks; American banks; foreign banks and affiliates; other overseas banks; other banks in the United Kingdom.

[6] The Radcliffe Committee clearly thought that capital expenditure was fairly insensitive to variations in short-term rates.

Table 5.1. *An analysis of bank deposits,*[a] *1963-9*

£ million

	Held by UK residents		Held by overseas residents	
	At deposit[b] banks	At non-clearing[b] banks	At deposit[b] banks	At non-clearing[b] banks
1963	8,734	738	408	2,374
65	9,669	1,137	429	3,397
67	10,702	1,610	426	5,395
69	11,330	2,500[c]	459	12,883[d]

SOURCE: Bank of England, *Statistical Abstract*, no. 1, London, 1970, p. 28.

[a] At end-years; includes both sterling and other currencies, but excludes inter-bank deposits and certificates of deposit.

[b] See footnote 5 page 221.   [c] Of which approximately £2000 million in sterling.

[d] Of which a little over £1000 million in sterling.

bond market by undue irregularities in bill rates; to influence short-term external capital movements by variations in London short-term rates relative to those in foreign centres.[1] Nevertheless, although motives were mixed, it is apparent from the timing of the actions taken by the authorities that by 1960 the last objective had come to pre-dominate.

There remains to note the purpose of official transactions in the gilt-edged market and in sales of savings certificates and other national savings media. Both are potentially relevant to demand management; the former was actively used to this end, though with disappointing results, in preference to pursuing other possible objectives; the latter was, however, very little used – the terms and yields on the various national savings media being adjusted, often belatedly and inadequately, to those prevailing in the private sector.

OFFICIAL REGULATIONS IN THE 1960s

Balance sheet ratios

Prior to the new approach of 1971 the only innovation in officially imposed balance sheet ratios was the introduction of the Special Deposits scheme to improve the effectiveness of the liquid asset ratio. Throughout the history of this scheme the Bank of England was

[1] There was a fifth objective in the second half of the 1950s, namely to create a demand for Treasury bills among the non-bank public by increasing the Treasury bill rate relative to the clearing banks' deposit rate, thereby depriving the clearers of liquid assets. However, with the availability of higher yielding local authority temporary debt and later of other 'new' money market assets, industrial companies and other large non-bank investors mostly lost interest in Treasury bills.

constantly expressing the hope that Special Deposits could be used as a substitute for control of advances; the hope was constantly frustrated. When the scheme was first activated in 1960, the Chancellor hoped that the banks would moderate advances rather than sell gilt-edged stock, but there was nothing in the scheme to prevent them doing this and the Government Broker's strategy of leaning against the wind[1] enabled them to unload their gilt-edged stocks without serious capital losses. So the initial intention to use the new instrument on its own was abandoned. In July 1961 the call for Special Deposits, effective as from 16 August, was part of a package which included restrictions on advances; thus Special Deposits were used as a reinforcing rather than a substitute measure. The banks were specifically told that the impact should fall primarily on advances.

During the remainder of the decade this pattern continued; nevertheless, the authorities still from time to time expressed the hope that they would be able to use Special Deposits without recourse to lending ceilings and in April 1967 actually applied such a regime to the clearing banks, the Chancellor explaining that Special Deposits would be used in future in a new and more flexible manner so as to maintain a continuous control over bank lending. He did not, however, remove the ceilings from non-clearing banks, because there was no alternative system of control for them in existence at that time.[2] The experiment lasted only until November, when a lending ceiling was again applied to all banks.

The use of Special Deposits as a means of reinforcing the Bank of England's directives on lending was given a new twist in May 1969. For some time lending by the clearing banks had been above the ceiling imposed in November 1968; they had been given until the middle of March to attain it, but in April and May were still exceeding it. The Bank therefore halved the rate of interest paid on Special Deposits. This provoked a strong reaction from the clearing banks, who protested that they were already carrying out official instructions to the best of their ability. The full rate of interest was restored in April 1970, when the ceiling was raised somewhat; the banks were then within the new ceiling.

One of the problems of the Special Deposits scheme was that part of the banking sector was exempt from imposed balance sheet ratios; the growth of this part (the non-clearing banks) had exceeded all expectations during the 1960s (table 5.1). The Bank of England was therefore concerned to find a means of controlling over 150 diverse non-clearing banks, with differing liquidity needs and practices. The Cash Deposits scheme announced in February 1968 was designed to

[1] See page 231 below. [2] *Midland Bank Review*, May 1967, p. 26.

fill this role,[1] although it never actually came into operation. As with Special Deposits, Cash Deposits had to be made in frozen accounts at the Bank of England at the request of the Bank; they were to be levied as a percentage of all sterling deposits and all foreign currency deposits switched into sterling. Interest would normally be paid at the Treasury bill rate, but the Bank reserved the right to pay a lower rate if the response to official guidance on the development of bank credit was deemed insufficient.[2] This penal aspect of the scheme was important, since, unlike Special Deposits, Cash Deposits could not act in any way other than as a penalty on profits; the non-clearing banks did not observe a conventional liquid asset ratio and so in their case there was no fulcrum against which the authorities could press.

Lending requests

Formally at least the institutions receiving requests have cooperated on a voluntary basis; indeed in one instance they voluntarily acquiesced in penalties for infringement (page 223, above). Implicit statutory backing is, however, provided by the Bank of England Act, 1946, which gives the Bank qualified powers to 'direct' the commercial banks.

The *Radcliffe Report* regarded lending restrictions as an instrument only suitable for use in emergencies, although in such circumstances it foresaw the possible need to widen the coverage of requests to include institutions such as hire purchase finance companies. However, it was confident that in normal circumstances official market transactions could be made to exercise sufficient influence over the lending of financial institutions; moreover, though necessary in a serious crisis, in the longer term credit rationing would be subject to substantial slippage and would lead to a loss of efficiency in the capital market. The Bank's testimony to the Radcliffe Committee also made clear its distaste for restrictions on advances as a permanent or semi-permanent instrument of control.

In the event, far from withering away, lending restrictions were operative in the 1960s whenever official policy was to restrict demand. The first request was in July 1961; in its published form it was not quantified, and only a behind-the-scenes suggestion by the Bank of England led the clearing banks to interpret it as a ceiling on advances at the mid-June level.[3] Commercial bills were to be restricted as well as advances, though not by an explicit ceiling. From May 1965 onwards quantified ceilings were made explicit for both advances and commercial bills; the latter had become very necessary, since firms denied

---

[1] 'Control of bank lending – the Cash Deposits scheme', *Bank of England Quarterly Bulletin*, vol. 8, June 1968.   [2] Ibid, p. 170.
[3] *Midland Bank Review*, May 1962, p. 17.

access to overdraft finance were turning increasingly to bill finance, as is apparent from table 5.2.

The lending requests in the 1950s were addressed only to the London and Scottish clearing banks, but that of July 1961 also went to the non-clearing banks; moreover, the Finance Houses Association was advised that their members should not seek to attract deposits to finance business other than that to which they were already committed and that restrictions of credit should fall primarily on consumers' expenditure.[1] Subsequent requests went to the clearing banks, 'the other lending banking associations' and the larger finance houses.

Throughout the period non-sterling lending and lending to the public sector were excluded from the ceilings. In the six months preceding May 1968 medium-term shipbuilding credits and all lending which could be identified as going to finance exports were also excluded. This wide concession was then discontinued; from May to November 1968 the ceiling covered all sterling lending to the private sector. This was relaxed in November 1968 to exclude advances made under special schemes for exports and shipbuilding.

With each request priorities were laid down. Exports were given high

Table 5.2. *Holdings of commercial and other bills (excluding Treasury bills),[a] 1958–69*

£ million

	London clearing banks		Discount market
	UK commercial bills[b]	Other[c]	Sterling bills
1958	135	..	70
59	141	23	118
1960	133	22	117
61	195	57	183
62	197	71	189
63	231	74	249
64	343	83	302
65	356	100	339
66	354	120	404
67	347	142	437
68	302	223	560
69	258	350	629

SOURCE: Bank of England, *Statistical Abstract*, no. 1, pp. 22, 37 and 39.

[a] At December each year.

[b] Includes medium-term export credits refinanceable at the Bank of England and likewise refinanceable shipbuilding credits. See below, chapter 7, pages 357–9.

[c] Includes Treasury bills of Commonwealth and foreign governments.

[1] *Midland Bank Review*, November 1965, p. 7.

priority on every occasion; in November 1967 this was extended to cover import-saving. Regional policy also had priority, but after May 1968 it was dropped because of the overriding importance of the balance of payments. The same thing happened to productivity-increasing investment in industry and agriculture, and to bridging finance for house purchase. Low priority categories included, in all but one of the requests, lending to personal borrowers; building and property development was similarly classified up to 1967. The financing of imports was added to the low priority list as from July 1965, as was the financing of import deposits in 1968 (chapter 7 below).

Hire purchase restrictions

Although hire purchase regulations are usually regarded as a monetary instrument, they are not administered by the Bank of England and the Treasury, but by the Ministries which have at various times been responsible for trade and consumer affairs. The controls have never been applied to industrial plant and machinery, and their provisions have always regulated the minimum down-payment and the maximum period over which the purchaser has to repay the balance. The problem with the use of this instrument has always been that it has strong directional effects on particular industries. In evidence submitted to the Radcliffe Committee, the Board of Trade argued that as a general principle when restrictions have to be applied, 'measures of wide and general application are preferable to selective measures of narrow application'.[1] They added that the two main reasons for restrictions were to cut down consumer demand and release more capacity for exports, but restricting credit might well redirect consumers' expenditure into other channels and 'the result may well be that the pattern of the economy, e.g. in investment, is distorted in favour of industries which, while being of no greater importance to the national economy, are fortunate enough to escape from the hire-purchase restrictions'.[2] In oral evidence the representatives of the Board of Trade took it that a change in controls would have a once-and-for-all effect on consumer spending on durables, but they thought that a new equilibrium level would be reached after a delay of approximately twelve months.[3]

Controls on hire purchase terms were removed in 1958 and reimposed in April 1960. The demand for cars was increasing and there were regional labour bottlenecks along with a worsening in the balance of payments. The controls were aimed at cutting back demand specifically

---

[1] Treasury *Committee on the Working of the Monetary System. Principal Memoranda of Evidence,* vol. 1, London, HMSO, 1960, p. 232, para. 8.   [2] Ibid. p. 236, para. 71.

[3] Treasury, *Committee on the Working of the Monetary System. Minutes of Evidence, July 11, 1957 to April 30, 1959,* London, HMSO, 1960, question 3159.

in the industries affected, which was a return to the sort of use prevalent in the early 1950s, when they were intended to reduce the excess demand for durable goods. By January 1961 it was clear that the demand for consumer durables had been depressed more than could be justified by the need to restrict domestic expenditure as a whole; the terms were therefore relaxed.[1] In his budget speech the Chancellor admitted that the discriminatory consequences of hire purchase controls were undesirable, but did not propose any alternative. In the summer of 1965, when the controls, having been slightly relaxed in January 1961 and June 1962, were again tightened, the intention was not to depress differentially the demand for consumer durables; rather the measure was part of a general deflationary package and this was true of all hire purchase restrictions in subsequent years.

In 1968 the Crowther Committee was set up to investigate all aspects of consumer credit and its Report was published in 1971. It accepted that there were several reasons why governments liked hire purchase controls: for one thing, unlike taxes, they did not affect the retail price index; they also had an immediate psychological effect and became effective without appreciable delay. Nevertheless, the Committee condemned the use of the instrument:

> It remains true that changes in terms controls have to be very sharp to produce any effect that is significant in relationship to total economic policy, and the industries affected... have the right to enquire whether the net benefit to the community is commensurate with the undoubted damage done to them, particularly since they have not been selected (latterly, at least) for their suitability to play this role, but solely by the accident of being affected by a particular control which is easy to apply.[2]

In addition they pointed out that people of means could avoid the restrictions by paying cash, by taking out personal loans or by second mortgages. They concluded that hire purchase controls should find no place among the weapons of economic policy.

In July 1971 all hire purchase controls were lifted, but there was no commitment to abolish them permanently; in fact restrictions were reimposed in December 1973 (page 251 below).

[1] *Bank of England Quarterly Bulletin*, vol. 1, March 1961, p. 9.
[2] Department of Trade and Industry, *Crowther Report*, p. 352, para. 8.2.4.

OFFICIAL TRANSACTIONS IN THE 1960s[1]

Transactions in the money market

Treasury bills, issued to cover the government's residual need for sterling finance, are offered for tender every Friday. The members of the London Discount Houses Association tender a syndicated bid to cover the whole of each week's issue; in practice they never secure the whole issue. The other tenderers are mostly non-clearing banks and the Bank of England (mainly acting on behalf of other central banks). The London clearing banks do not tender on their own account, but buy their Treasury bills from the discount houses. By agreeing to cover the whole tender the discount houses ensure that each week's issue is taken up, but the size of the tender is usually large enough to cause the discount houses to be short of finance on at least some days every week unless the Bank either buys bills or lends to the market. The Bank can be relied upon to relieve a shortage in one way or the other, though on terms of its own choosing, and by choosing the appropriate terms it determines interest rates in the traditional money market.

In the early 1960s the Bank's practice was to relieve a shortage either on penal terms (traditionally at Bank Rate) at the discount office, or on more favourable ('market') terms by purchasing Treasury bills through its bill broker. But in the course of the 1960s the Bank began to lend at the discount office also at non-penal interest rates. The first step was taken in 1966, when the Bank lent overnight at the market rates charged by the clearing banks.[2] In August 1967 for the first time loans at market rates were given for seven days and in September for five days.[3]

Though the arrangements just described normally kept the discount houses dependent on help from the Bank, it could happen on particular days that the market had an excess of funds, and on such occasions the Bank might well mop them up. In the early 1960s this was done by the Bank's bill broker coming into the market as a seller, but as from 1964 the Bank adopted the additional technique of regulating the maturities of its lending to the discount houses so as to mitigate foreseen fluctuations in the daily balance of their books. In December 1964 the Bank advanced the discount houses £24½ million, half for six and half for eight days,[4] instead of the traditional seven days, and a further development was when in June 1966 the Bank advanced money at Bank Rate overnight, to 'balance out a shortage of money on one day

---

[1] Official transactions in the foreign exchange market are treated in chapter 7.
[2] *Bank of England Quarterly Bulletin*, vol. 6, September 1966, p. 216.
[3] *Bank of England Quarterly Bulletin*, vol. 7, December 1967, p. 342.
[4] *Bank of England Quarterly Bulletin*, vol. 5, March 1965, p. 7.

with an expected surplus on the next'. Such operations 'serve to keep money short, the discount houses' repayments transferring the initial shortage from day to day'.[1]

Transactions in the gilt-edged market

In the 1950s and up to the late 1960s, save on a few brief occasions of seriously inadequate effective demand, the overwhelming preoccupation of the authorities responsible for official transactions in stocks was with what may be termed the 'flooding problem'. To Peter Thorneycroft the monetary system appeared 'like an antiquated pumping machine, creaking and groaning, leaking wildly at all the main valves, but still desperately attempting to keep down the level of the water in the mine',[2] and this preoccupation with flooding is no less apparent in the speeches of the Governor of the Bank, in the official evidence to the Radcliffe Committee and in subsequent articles in the *Bank of England Quarterly Bulletin*.

Table 5.3. *Domestic borrowing, and stock repayments and conversions, by the central government, 1955–73*

£ million

	Domestic borrowing	Stock repayments and conversions
1955–9[a]	252	909
1960–4[a]	152	854
1965–9[a]	69	1274
1970	663	1771
71	3438	1949
72	34	1414
73	2562	1735

SOURCES: Bank of England, *Statistical Abstract*, no. 1, table 1; Bank of England, *Report* (various years); *Bank of England Quarterly Bulletin*, vol. 15, March 1975, table 2, and vol. 17, September 1977, p. 321.

[a] Annual averages.

The water which is seen as flooding into the mine corresponds to the sum of two financial flows (table 5.3). The first is the government's domestic borrowing requirement, which, to the extent that it is not offset by government debt taken up by the public, has to be met by borrowing from the banks. The second flow comprises gilt-edged maturities which have to be refinanced; in the United Kingdom these are unusually large due to our unusually large national debt (table 5.4).

[1] *Bank of England Quarterly Bulletin*, vol. 6, September 1966, pp. 215–16.
[2] P. Thorneycroft, 'Policy in practice' in *Not Unanimous*, London, Institute of Economic Affairs, 1960, p. 1.

If the refinancing cannot be wholly covered by placing new stock with the public, the banks are again called upon to finance the balance.

Table 5.4. *Comparative sizes of national debts,[a] 1968/9*

	Percentages of GNP
Canada	29
France	13
Germany	13
Italy	15
Japan	6
Netherlands	20
United Kingdom	59
United States	29

SOURCE: *Bank of England Quarterly Bulletin*, vol. 14, December 1974, p. 433.
[a] Excluding official holdings and IMF notes.

The Radcliffe Committee, in line with most academic opinion, took the view that the flooding problem could always be resolved by making gilt-edged stock cheap enough to attract the investing public. But witnesses from the Bank of England and the Treasury had taken the contrary view, insisting that 'the market in long-term securities is dominated by expectations of future prices and is therefore seriously liable to react perversely to a movement of prices'.[1] In their oral evidence to the Radcliffe Committee, the Chief Cashier and the Government Broker made it quite clear that they would never hope to sell more stock by reducing its price; not only would it be ineffective, it would also be a breach of faith with people who had bought stock when it was originally issued.[2] Thus, official witnesses to the Radcliffe Committee clearly believed that the Government Broker's role as a salesman, though not wholly passive, gives him little scope for initiative. If the market is rising his skill as a dealer enables him to exploit his opportunity, but if it is not rising he has no opportunity to exploit.

On this issue, despite the criticisms expressed by the Radcliffe Committee, there seems to have been, at any rate up to 1975, no subsequent change in official opinion, which was re-stated with emphasis in an article, 'Official transactions in the gilt-edged market',[3] and was in no way disowned in 'Competition and credit control'.[4]

The shifts in the Government Broker's strategy, which occurred both

[1] Treasury, *Radcliffe Report*, para. 563.
[2] Radcliffe Committee, *Minutes of Evidence*, questions 11967 and 12009.
[3] *Bank of England Quarterly Bulletin*, vol. 6, June 1966.
[4] *Bank of England Quarterly Bulletin*, vol. 11, June 1971.

at the beginning of the 1960s and at the time of the new approach, were not in his selling but in his buying. In the early 1960s the strategy was to lean against the wind in *both* directions: the Government Broker would not only seize the opportunity to sell when demand increased, but would also come in as a buyer when the market was weak. The main reason advanced for supporting a weak market was that otherwise investors 'would be seriously discouraged from investing their funds...the capacity of the market would be permanently reduced and with it the ability of the Government to borrow at long term.'[1]

It is clear that intervention of this kind, in support of a weak market, was not practised to any extent in the decade before 1958; the evidence of the Bank to the Radcliffe Committee in November 1958 suggested that there had been only one occasion since the late 1940s when support of this kind had been given.[2] Yet by 1960 a new strategy of supporting the market was being practised, much to the Prime Minister's displeasure. Referring to the first call for Special Deposits on 28 April 1960, Harold Macmillan noted in a letter to Selwyn Lloyd that the banks, which had promised to adhere to the Special Deposits scheme, had been selling gilt-edged securities to do so and the Government Broker had been frightened into buying.[3] The implication of market support which alarmed Macmillan (the weakening of official control over the behaviour of the banks) does not seem to have troubled the authorities very much before the 'brakes-on' phase of demand management in the second half of the 1960s; indeed in the preceding period of slack demand they reduced the minimum liquid asset ratio from 30 to 28 per cent lest it should unduly constrain bank lending. Macmillan's point was, however, publicly taken by the Bank in 1969, when it admitted that the policy of leaning against the wind had enabled the banks to change their holdings from one form of government debt to another in the short term without much loss.[4] Hence, it was variations in the banks' total holdings of government debt relative to their deposit liabilities, rather than the details of the division between cash, Treasury bills and gilts, which largely determined whether their balance sheets were becoming more or less liquid.[5] The significance of this admission will be apparent from table 5.5, which shows that the London clearing banks' ratio for liquid assets and investments combined, though on a declining trend until 1969, was always in excess of 40 per cent and hence well in excess of the minimum liquid asset ratio, which was consequently ineffective as an instrument of control.

[1] *Bank of England Quarterly Bulletin*, vol. 6, June 1966, p. 147.
[2] Radcliffe Committee, *Minutes of Evidence*, questions 12029–33.
[3] Macmillan, *Pointing the Way, 1959–1961*, p. 361.
[4] *Bank of England Quarterly Bulletin*, vol. 9, June 1969, p. 177.   [5] Ibid. p. 178.

The twin precepts, that the Government Broker should never attempt to sell more gilts by dropping their price and that he should lean against the wind when the market was weak, clearly had far-reaching implications for monetary policy. First, though this strategy was regarded as the best one for maximising official sales of bonds in the longer run, it accepted that in the short run the Government Broker's transactions were largely in response to market conditions and not to the immediate requirements of monetary policy. Hence, unless the market was sufficiently buoyant to enable the Government Broker to sell enough stock to the public to match maturities plus the government's domestic borrowing requirement, the balance sheets of the banks would inflate, with deposits rising on the liabilities side (hence a corresponding increase in the quantity of money) and with public sector debt (in the form of cash, Treasury bills, call money advanced against Treasury bills, and government stock) rising in balance on the assets side. Secondly, the natural reaction of the banks to the increases in their liquidity implicit in this change in their balance sheets would certainly not be to cut their lending to the private sector; rather they would want to lend more to the private sector, which would thereby bring about a secondary increase both in their deposit liabilities and in their assets (this time in the form of advances). Thirdly, since the Govern-

Table 5.5. *London clearing banks' liquid assets and investments as a proportion of gross deposits,*[a] *1958–71*

Percentages

	Liquid assets	Investments[b]	Total
1958	33·9	32·9	66·8
59	31·0	29·1	60·1
1960	31·5	21·3	52·8
61	30·4	16·5	46·9
62	32·6	14·8	47·4
63	30·5	16·0	46·5
64	29·7	14·6	44·3
65	29·5	12·0	41·5
66	30·1	12·0	42·1
67	29·5	13·7	43·2
68	28·7	13·2	41·9
69	29·4	11·7	41·1
1970	29·7	11·8	41·5
71	32·4	10·2	42·6

SOURCES: Bank of England, *Statistical Abstract*, no. 1, pp. 36–9; *Bank of England Quarterly Bulletin*, vol. 11, March 1971, p. 98, and June 1971, p. 246.

  [a] At mid-March, which is near the seasonal minimum for liquid asset holdings.
  [b] Mainly gilt-edged stock. In March 1969 £1064 million out of a total of £1232 million were British government stocks.

ment Broker has so much difficulty in selling enough gilts, his problems should not be exacerbated by an expansionist budgetary policy. Finally, leaning against the wind in order to maximise official sales in the long run must preclude, save in fortuitously favourable circumstances, a demand management policy based on using official national debt transactions to manipulate the pattern of interest rates, as favoured in the *Radcliffe Report*. The Bank of England's article 'Official transactions in the gilt-edged market' is quite explicit on this: one of a number of possible subsidiary aims of national debt management was 'to assist economic policy by promoting or sustaining the most appropriate pattern of interest rates', but these subsidiary aims must not be pursued at the risk of causing damage in the long run to the health and capacity of the market – a limitation that may sometimes preclude all but a fairly narrow choice of policies in the short term.[1]

There was a transitional period of a number of months up to 24 February 1960 when the Government Broker set a floor to bond prices – this being done to stimulate the then depressed economy by making it easy for the banks to unload their bonds in order to increase their advances. But, as from February 1960, leaning against the wind did not imply, save in rare circumstances, that the Government Broker would hold rates to a target.[2] When the market was buoyant his sales would mitigate the rise in prices but not stop it altogether; in this way he reassured investors in gilts that it was possible to make capital gains. When the market was weak his purchases usually served to slow down the fall in prices, rather than to support them with a firm floor.[3] Exceptionally, and then only for short periods (December 1964, May and June 1967, and November 1968[4]) he set a floor to steady a demoralised market; otherwise leaning against the wind meant mitigating short-term fluctuations but not resisting market pressure. The operations of the Government Broker were indeed compatible with a long-term upward trend in yields and appreciable fluctuations from month to month and year to year.

[1] *Bank of England Quarterly Bulletin*, vol. 6, June 1966, p. 146. The Governor had made the same point in 1958; he said, 'It would still not be true to say that the Bank were aiming at any particular range of rates' (Radcliffe Committee, *Minutes of Evidence*, question 11919).

[2] Bank of England, *Report for the year ended 29 February 1960*, p. 12.

[3] See *Bank of England Quarterly Bulletin*, vol. 1, September 1961, p. 12: 'On the 2nd August rumours began to circulate to the effect that the authorities intended to withdraw their support. The Bank therefore reminded the market that it was not the practice of the authorities to support the gilt-edged market in the sense of pegging it at any particular price level: that the authorities would continue to be concerned to ensure orderly market conditions so that dealings at a price could continue; and that prices would continue to depend upon general market conditions.'

[4] *Bank of England Quarterly Bulletin*, vol. 5, March 1965, p. 9; vol. 7, September 1967 pp. 227–8; vol. 9, March 1969, p. 15.

TRANSMISSION MECHANISMS

Changes in the choice of instruments of monetary policy, and in the way they are used to pursue various objectives, may derive from revisions to official views about transmission mechanisms; in the period treated in this book there were such revisions. As from 1972 there was official rethinking about how external balance might better be achieved by greater reliance on variations in the exchange rate.[1] Previous to this, however, rethinking about transmission had been confined to the means for achieving just one of the official policy objectives – demand management. Nor is it surprising that official views on this particular aspect of the transmission mechanism should be specially subject to revision. For the channels by which official action in the monetary sphere may influence the level of demand for goods and services are complex and tortuous; they are, moreover, very imperfectly understood by economists and have, throughout the postwar period, been the subject of inconclusive controversy, in the United Kingdom and elsewhere, in both academic and official circles. Official rethinking about this issue was especially active in two periods – at the time of the *Radcliffe Report* and again towards the end of the 1960s. In both periods the stimulus came from academic economists: in the earlier period from the two academic members of the Radcliffe Committee, Richard Sayers and Alec Cairncross; in the later period (partly via the IMF officials who were engaged in negotiations with the British authorities) from the American monetarist school, which, under the leadership of Milton Friedman, had in the course of the 1960s become increasingly influential in the United States. However, the outcome in the two periods was dissimilar: the new views advanced by the Radcliffe Committee had only a small impact on official action – the Bank's new strategy in the gilt-edged market in the early 1960s did not follow from the *Radcliffe Report's* recommendations. On the other hand, the rethinking which began in the late 1960s was an important element leading up to the new approach of 1971.

In the period up to the late 1960s, when the British authorities were so obsessed with the flooding problem, they seem not to have committed themselves to any particular version of the transmission mechanism by which official transactions in the gilt-edged market might be supposed to influence the demand for goods and services. Though the Radcliffe Committee tried to give a decisive lead on several facets of this issue, it was in response not to their lead but to the influence of the American monetary school that the authorities eventually began rather gingerly to commit themselves.

[1] Chapter 7, below.

Let us look briefly at some of the crucial features of the transmission mechanism on which the *Radcliffe Report* took a definite stand but on which the authorities seem to have maintained an eclectic position. It is common ground that, for the monetary authorities of any country, 'it is not possible to choose the direction of movement of interest rates and of the quantity of money independently',[1] but some economists believe that the authorities should conduct their transactions with their eyes on interest rates as their main target variable, while others (including the quantity theorists and more recently Friedman) believe that their target variable should be the quantity of money. The *Radcliffe Report* strongly backed the former point of view. It argued that a change in interest rates had considerable effect on the readiness of lenders to lend and a slower, more partial, influence on the readiness of borrowers to borrow.[2] The Bank's written evidence to the Radcliffe Committee clearly gave rather greater weight to the latter effect, but also attached some importance to the effect of interest-rate changes on the readiness of lenders to lend.[3] Subsequently the authorities seem to have paid little attention to the issue, if for no other reason than because they did not believe that (given the need to sell as many bonds as possible in the long run) they were free to exercise much influence over gilt-edged rates, apart from ironing out short-term fluctuations.

On the other hand the Radcliffe Committee strongly questioned the value of the quantity of money as a target variable:

...spending is not limited by the amount of money in existence; but it is related to the amount of money people think they can get hold of, whether by receipts of income (for instance from sales), by disposal of capital assets or by borrowing.[4]

and later:

In a highly developed financial system the theoretical difficulties of identifying 'the supply of money' cannot lightly be swept aside. Even when they are disregarded, all the haziness of the connection between the supply of money and the level of total demand remains.[5]

The official evidence to the Radcliffe Committee had attached much more importance than this to the quantity of money. The Bank maintained that 'the basic need remains the ability to regulate the total quantity of currency and bank deposits',[6] and quoted from a communiqué issued after a meeting of the Governor and Chancellor on

---

[1] Radcliffe Committee, *Principal Memoranda of Evidence*, vol. 1, Bank of England's submission, p. 36, para. 14.　　　　　　[2] Treasury, *Radcliffe Report*, para. 983.
[3] See Radcliffe Committee, *Principal Memoranda of Evidence*, vol. 1, p. 37, paras, 22, 24, 25 and 29.　　　　　　[4] Treasury, *Radcliffe Report*, para. 390.
[5] Ibid. para. 523.
[6] Radcliffe Committee, *Principal Memoranda of Evidence*, vol. 1, p. 36, para. 11.

24 July 1956, which indicated that the government would press on with measures influencing the supply of money.[1] All the same, the Bank was certainly not committed to any view as specific as the quantity theory: 'a change in the supply of money is not rigidly associated with a similar change in the amount of spending'.[2] Or again: '...but addition to the money supply is by no means the only factor which increases demand and so puts up costs and prices. There is bound at any time...to be a large volume of spendable money, in the form of bank deposits, cash or easily-realisable assets'.[3] Here the inclusion of the last item, 'easily-realisable assets', indicates that the Bank was concerned with the quantity of money only as one component of the public's total holding of liquid assets, along with, for instance, national savings and building societies' shares and deposits.[4] Significantly, the growing short-term debt of local authorities was a cause of official anxiety.[5] Thus the pre-Radcliffe official view attached importance to the quantity of money because one of the many factors determining the level of demand was the public's holding of liquid assets, of which the stock of money is one component; there is, however, no suggestion that the authorities at this time thought that 'the behaviour of the money supply is an important indicator of the thrust of monetary policy', as the Chief Cashier put it in November 1971 in his explanation of the 'new approach'.[6]

The Radcliffe Committee's view that the quantity of money was unimportant led them to conclude that 'regulation of the banks is required not because they are "creators of money" but because they are the biggest lenders at the shortest (most liquid) end of the range of credit markets'.[7] The official evidence to Radcliffe included a memorandum, 'The control of bank credit in the United Kingdom', which also stressed the role of bank advances;[8] moreover, this official view continued into the 1960s, as witnessed by the fact that, when bank lending to the private sector could not be adequately controlled by official sales of gilt-edged, the authorities did not hesitate to impose lending ceilings.

To summarise: apart from interest rates in the traditional money market, the only target variable which we know for certain the authorities adopted up to the late 1960s was one for bank and finance house lending to the private sector. We know this for certain because, in the credit squeezes which occurred from May 1965, such a target was

---

[1] Ibid. p. 31, para. 114.   [2] Ibid. p. 36, para. 9.
[3] The Governor's Mansion House Speech, 8 October 1957, quoted ibid. p. 50, para. 65.
[4] Ibid. p. 17, paras. 6 and 7.
[5] See the Bank's oral evidence to the Radcliffe Committee on 27 November 1958 (*Minutes of Evidence*, questions 12061–2).
[6] Sykes Memorial Lecture, 10 November 1971.   [7] Treasury, *Radcliffe Report*, para. 504.
[8] Radcliffe Committee, *Principal Memoranda of Evidence*, vol. 1, pp. 9–10.

explicitly incorporated in official requests to the institutions concerned. This does not mean that officials thought the quantity of money or the level of bond rates to be of no consequence, but whatever they thought had little impact on their actions.

THE CHOICE OF INSTRUMENTS OF
POLICY IN THE 1960s

Though in the 1960s the authorities came to rely more and more on lending ceilings, this instrument was always very much a second-best one, which the authorities resorted to only because their preferred instrument, the limitation of liquid assets available to the banks, could not be relied upon to ensure an adequate degree of restraint. Early in the decade the Bank optimistically hoped that lending ceilings could be reserved for emergency use, or even dispensed with altogether. The proportion of public sector debt in the clearing banks' assets was following a downward trend, and the availability of liquid assets to the banks (see table 5.5) contracted so greatly that, in 1963, a year in which the stance of official policy was to stimulate demand, the authorities reduced the minimum liquid asset ratio from 30 to 28 per cent.[1] Yet, whatever optimism the authorities may have felt gave way to disillusionment, and lending ceilings, withdrawn in the recession of 1962, had to be reapplied from December 1964 onwards, with only one brief respite (for the clearing banks only) in 1967. The clearing banks' liquid assets, supplemented by their cushion of gilts, which (thanks to the Government Broker's readiness to support the market) could be 'liquefied' without serious loss, never fell low enough to press against the 28 per cent minimum. Special Deposits were invented precisely to deal with this situation, by converting liquid assets into illiquid ones, but such Deposits were never called on a scale sufficient to make the minimum liquid asset ratio really bite.

Why were the authorities thus forced back on their second-best technique for limiting bank lending? One explanation is the rapid rise in the popularity with British industry of bill finance, which (since such commercial bills usually qualified as liquid assets) added to the liquid assets available to the banking system (table 5.2).[2] However, this problem could presumably have been overcome if the authorities had redefined the liquid assets which counted towards the 28 per cent

---

[1] In March 1963 the banks were permitted to go for the time being 'somewhat below' 30 per cent (*Bank of England Quarterly Bulletin*, vol. 3, June 1963, p. 88). Later in the year this became 28 per cent (*Bank of England Quarterly Bulletin*, vol. 3, December 1963, p. 295).

[2] Commercial bills held by the discount market contributed to the increase in the clearing banks' liquid assets because they increased the market's need for call money, which counted as a liquid asset.

minimum to exclude commercial bills altogether, or at any rate to exclude any in excess of a prescribed amount – as indeed they eventually did in 1971 as part of the new approach (see footnote to page 244 below). A more intractable problem was that the 28 per cent minimum applied only to the London clearing banks, and the authorities saw great difficulty in extending it to cover other banks, which in the course of the 1960s were expanding much faster than the clearing banks, even in their domestic business (table 5.1). Eventually, however, under the new approach, the nettle was grasped and a common 'reserve asset' ratio applied to all banks. Last, but most important, was the fact that the Government Broker's strategy in the 1960s (page 232 above) meant that the amounts of his sales or purchases were, at any rate in the short run, determined by prevailing market conditions and not by the need to regulate the liquid assets available to the banks in the interests of demand management. It was in recognition of this problem that, under the new approach of 1971, official support to the gilt-edged market was to be limited, as in the 1950s, to exceptional circumstances.

THE NEW APPROACH

The new approach to monetary policy, inaugurated in May 1971 with the publication of the Bank of England's consultative document 'Competition and credit control', and put into operation later in the year, can best be described as a change of instruments, and a change in the use of existing instruments, for the purpose of demand management. Lending ceilings on banks and finance houses, which had been in almost continuous operation since 1964, were discontinued, although the possibility of qualitative guidance was retained, and in July hire purchase restrictions were also discontinued for the time being. From September the balance sheet ratios previously imposed on the clearing banks were changed, and their application was extended to the non-clearing banks and to the finance houses. The London clearing banks' interest-rate cartel was discontinued from October 1971; henceforth their borrowing and lending rates were no longer automatically related to Bank Rate. The London Discount Houses Association continued to make a joint bid each week to cover the Treasury bill tender, but no longer at one agreed rate of discount for all members of the Association. The Government Broker's technique for dealing in the bond market was changed; he was no longer in normal circumstances to support the gilt-edged market, although he would continue to buy maturities of under one year.

All these changes, introduced more or less simultaneously, reflected a rethinking by the authorities over a number of years, as we can judge from earlier official actions (sometimes rather trivial in themselves) and also from official pronouncements over the period from 1967 to May 1971. The actual timing of the new approach was influenced by several factors. The change of government in June 1970 returned to power a Conservative administration which wanted to encourage competition and free enterprise. There had been a change in the attitudes of officials towards monetary policy instruments. There had been a rapid falling off of effective demand, so that the time was right to institute a change which would be expansionary in its initial impact.[1] Finally, the external deficit had at last turned into a surplus, so that monetary policy was no longer constrained by the external situation and could for the time being be directed exclusively towards the expansion of the economy.

There are three interrelated strands in the evolution of official thought in the late 1960s. There was a determination to infuse a new spirit of competition into the British banking system. There was a growing optimism that the flooding problem might be less intractable than it had earlier seemed and a willingness to tackle it with a new strategy for conducting official transactions in the gilt-edged market. There was, finally, a 'reinstatement of the money supply as more than just one in a whole range of liquid assets'.[2]

Competition

'Competition and credit control' quoted with approval the Chancellor of the Exchequer's statement in his March 1971 budget that 'it should be possible to achieve more flexible but still effective arrangements basically by operating on the banks' resources rather than by directly guiding their lending'. The idea that the imposition of lending ceilings could be harmful to competition and to the structure of the monetary system had long been recognised by the authorities, in particular in the Bank of England's evidence to the Radcliffe Committee,[3] but also on many subsequent occasions.[4] The authorities had indeed been seeking an alternative solution for some years before 1971. However, the experiment in 1967 with the use of Special Deposits without a lending ceiling for the clearing banks[5] came to an untimely end with the devaluation crisis in November, when severe lending ceilings were reimposed

[1] The removal of lending ceilings could be expected to lead to an increase in bank advances to the private sector. Also, the minimum reserve asset ratio imposed on clearing and non-clearing banks alike had to be fixed at a level which was tolerable to the latter and hence might be unrestrictive to the former.

[2] Chief Cashier, Sykes Memorial Lecture, 10 November 1971.

[3] Radcliffe Committee, *Principal Memoranda of Evidence*, vol. 1, p. 39, para. 7. See also the Governor's reply to question 1818 in the *Minutes of Evidence*.

[4] For example, *Bank of England Quarterly Bulletin*, vol. 9, June 1969, p. 179.

[5] Page 223, above.

and not discontinued until the new approach of 1971. There was even then a proviso in 'Competition and credit control' about qualitative, as distinct from quantitative, guidance on bank lending:

Notwithstanding the abandonment of quantitative ceilings...the authorities would continue to provide the banks with such qualitative guidance as may be appropriate. For example, so long as hire purchase terms control remains in force, banks will be asked that personal loans related to the purchase of goods subject to terms control should be made on terms no easier than those permitted...for hire purchase contracts.[1]

In the event this particular need for qualitative guidelines soon disappeared for the time being with the discontinuance in July 1971 of all restrictions on hire purchase, credit sale and rental agreements.

The authorities took longer to come round to the view that the London clearing banks' interest-rate cartel was also seriously harmful to competition in banking services. As early as April 1963 the Governor of the Bank of England had made a speech in praise of increased competition, which was at the time widely interpreted as inviting the clearing banks to abandon their cartel on interest rates. However, he did not explicitly make this point; his words could be taken to mean simply that the cartel rates should be more competitive with those of the non-clearing banks and other financial intermediaries.

In October 1963 the clearing banks, possibly in response to the Governor's speech, put forward a proposal for an increase of $\frac{1}{2}$ per cent in their overdraft rates, combined with the simultaneous introduction of special savings deposit accounts (maximum holding £500) paying a higher interest rate than the then deposit rate ($3\frac{1}{2}$ as against 2 per cent). This proposal was, however, not welcomed by the authorities, presumably because its aim was competition for deposits mainly with national savings media and building societies; moreover, a rise in overdraft rates was politically unattractive. The banks were therefore told not to proceed with the scheme.

The clearing banks themselves drew a distinction between competition for deposits with other private sector institutions and with public sector institutions. Competition with the latter, for example the Post Office and Trustee Savings Banks, brought them obvious advantages. As the NBPI subsequently put it: 'These public sector institutions lend largely to the Government...cheques [of depositors] will be drawn on the clearing banks with a resultant fall in the latter's reserves with the central bank...',[2] and with a consequent reduction in the clearing banks' liquid assets. Thus competition to retain depositors who might

---

[1] 'Competition and credit control', para. 14.
[2] NBPI, *Report no. 34: Bank Charges*, Cmnd 3292, London, HMSO, 1967, para. 59.

be tempted to redeposit at public sector institutions was to the clearing banks' collective advantage; the obstacle here was that the government did not welcome such competition.

Competition with private sector institutions mainly involved kinds of business (especially 'wholesale' banking in large transactions) which are not transacted through a clearing bank's provincial branch net-work. In such cases the clearing banks preferred to acquire or establish subsidiary or associated banks,[1] which could compete with independent non-clearing banks on equal terms without having to observe imposed balance sheet ratios. In addition, there was at this time a wide-spread view, which the NBPI did not accept, but which it nonetheless thought it necessary to elucidate, that competition for deposits with other private sector institutions brought no advantage to the clearing banks as a whole, in that they could not as a group 'lose' deposits to other financial institutions in the private sector. For when someone transfers a deposit to such an institution from a clearing bank, then a deposit in that person's name at a clearing bank will be transferred to the other institution's account at a clearing bank and, when the other institution lends on the deposit, the borrower will also bank at a clearer, so 'what is involved is merely a transfer in the ownership of the bank deposits [at the clearing banks]...The logical corollary of this line of argument would be that the payment of any deposit rate is a needless cost for the banks.'[2] The clearing banks seem at one time to have attached importance to this argument, though progressively less so in the course of the 1960s.

There matters rested until the publication in July 1968 by the Monopolies Commission of a Report on the proposed merger between Barclays Bank, Lloyds Bank and Martins Bank, which came out strongly against the practice of regulating the banks by lending ceil-ings.[3] This, taken together with the NBPI Report, made out a strong indictment against the cartel and also a case, again with the aim of encouraging competition, for banks to reveal their inner reserves and true profits in their published accounts. The indictments of the cartel in

[1] The subsidiary or associated banks of the clearing banks did their English banking business from London, not from provincial offices.

[2] NBPI, *Report no. 34*, para. 58. The Board's own (critical) appraisal of this argument is in para. 59, which, after dealing with competition with public sector institutions, reads as follows: 'Secondly, there are the private sector financial institutions – e.g. hire purchase companies. Deposits transferred to them from a clearing bank will enable them to increase their lending, thus driving down interest rates and tending to raise the level of spending and income, with possible adverse effects on the balance of payments. In such a case the monetary authorities would need to take offsetting action, e.g. the sale of bonds, so as to reduce the lending power of the clearing banks themselves ... the reserves and deposits of the clearing banks suffer in the last analysis a decline.'

[3] Monopolies Commission, *Barclays Bank Ltd, Lloyds Bank Ltd and Martins Bank Ltd. Report on the Proposed Merger*, London, HMSO, 1968.

the two Reports may be briefly amalgamated into the following line of argument. The cartel had a soporific effect; it also led to excessive non-price competition, especially in the opening of too many branches. Moreover, its abolition would enable the clearing banks to regain ground lost to the non-clearing banks; this would, of course, require them to take over a higher share of total bank lending, as well as a higher share of total deposits. Finally, the NBPI maintained that some of the business then conducted by the clearing banks through subsidiaries was conducted in this way, and not directly in their own names, solely because of the cartel agreement and because of official restrictions imposed on the clearers alone; some such business could, however, be more efficiently conducted by the clearers in their own right. Hence there was a case not merely for abolishing the cartel, but also for assimilating the regulatory balance sheet ratios imposed on different kinds of banks and finance houses.

The case for reform did not go unheeded. Pressed by the authorities, the London and Scottish clearing banks agreed in 1968 to observe the full disclosure provisions of the Companies Act, even though banks are, under the Act, specifically exempted; the first annual accounts on the new basis were in respect of 1969. Action on the other impediments to competition was delayed until 1971, but it is clear from a speech by the Governor of the Bank on 17 October 1968 that the issue was under official review.[1]

There were difficulties in the way of reform, both as regards the abolition of the interest-rate cartel and as regards the imposition of more or less uniform balance sheet ratios on all banks and finance houses. In the case of the cartel, the original official fear that freer competition for deposits would reduce the flow of savings into national savings media and the building societies remained to the end. Even in 'Competition and credit control' the Bank envisaged the possibility of imposing official controls (having an equivalent effect to that of the cartel) on the terms offered for savings deposits.

Another problem was that the Treasury continued to fear that the abolition of the cartel would mean unacceptably high interest rates on advances to industrial firms.[2] A further problem was that the abolition of the cartel would break the automatic link between Bank Rate and the London clearing banks' deposit and lending rates, and thus cut off one route (traditionally regarded as of considerable importance) by which the authorities could influence the economy. However the importance of this bit of transmission mechanism was being eroded by the development in the course of the 1960s of London's new markets for

---

[1] *Bank of England Quarterly Bulletin*, vol. 8, December 1968, p. 411.
[2] Monopolies Commission, *Report*, para. 206.

money (table 5.6), in which interest rates were settled by unfettered competition.[1] The rapid growth in the 1960s of the non-clearing banks, who took in 'wholesale' deposits at interest rates uncontrolled by the London clearing banks' cartel and lent on to the private sector within the limits of their lending ceilings, or otherwise to local authorities, was further developed by their issuing, as from October 1968, sterling certificates of deposit (table 5.6).[2] One result of these developments was that the new 'free' rates became the important ones for a significant part of the British economy. Hence, when in 1971 the authorities decided to press for the abolition of the London clearing banks' cartel, this was to weaken a policy instrument which had already become much weaker than it had been in the 1950s.

Table 5.6. *New money markets: sterling funds outstanding, 1961–73*[a]

£ million

	Local authorities' temporary money[b]	Inter-bank deposits	Certificates of deposit	Finance houses' deposits
1961	1079	..	—	337
62	1142	260	—	337
63	1349	350	—	390
64	1712	462	—	494
65	1740	588	—	654
66	1728	712	—	648
67	1854	924	—	591
68	1870	1333	165	612
69	1896	1728	442	636
1970	1879	1978	1089	688
71	1974	2200	2372	823
72	2408	4760	4930	437[c]
73	3368	7694	5983	477[c]

SOURCES: European Communities Monetary Committee, *Monetary Policy in the Countries of the European Economic Community. Supplement 1974 (The United Kingdom)*, table 11; CSO, *Financial Statistics*, February 1975, tables 31, 41 and 66.

[a] At end-year.

[b] Deposits and revenue bills of up to one year. In the years 1965–71 inclusive, deposits taken net of bank deposits by local authorities.

[c] Excluding figures from institutions recognised or confirmed as banks in January 1972 and previously classified as finance houses.

[1] Of the markets distinguished in table 5.6, the local authority short-term market dates from the 1950s. The inter-bank market developed somewhat later; its main dealers were the merchant banks, foreign banks in London and British banks operating abroad, together with some subsidiaries of clearing banks. The clearing banks themselves did not take part, though it was deposits at the clearing banks which the non-clearing banks, operating as principals, transferred from one to another in their inter-bank market operations (*Midland Bank Review*, August 1966, p. 6). Subsequently, under the regime of 'Competition and credit control', the clearing banks also began to operate in this market as principals, and on a large scale.

[2] The advantage of a certificate of deposit as against a time deposit of the same maturity is that the former is a negotiable instrument which can be traded in a secondary market conducted by the discount houses.

A final problem posed by the abolition of the cartel was that the London clearing banks could represent its existence as a reasonable *quid pro quo* for the favourable terms they extended for medium-term export credits and for their observance of two onerous balance sheet ratios (the 8 per cent cash ratio and the 28 per cent liquid asset ratio) from which non-clearing banks were exempt. Of these objections, the first was eventually met by an upward adjustment of the relevant interest rate,[1] while the second was met in 1971 by imposing uniform reserve and Special Deposit ratios on all banks.

The need for uniform ratios had not been readily admitted. The Bank of England had initially shied away from it; in the 1968 proposal for a Cash Deposits scheme (which remained a dead letter)[2] it was represented as impractical to have the same balance sheet ratios imposed on such a diverse collection of institutions as banks. There was also the problem that controlling banks through imposed balance sheet ratios requires that the prescribed reserve assets should be in inelastic supply. This condition could not be fulfilled if reserve assets were to include 'new money market' assets (such as local authority deposits), and in the 1960s the non-clearing banks normally relied for their liquidity on such assets and on the inter-bank market, rather than on traditional money market assets such as Treasury bills. Yet in the end the Bank overcame its scruples; the new approach replaced the 28 per cent liquid asset ratio hitherto imposed on the London clearing banks by a $12\frac{1}{2}$ per cent ratio for all banks of 'reserve assets' (not including 'new money market' assets) to liabilities.[3] A common Special Deposit ratio, fixed from time to time at the discretion of the Bank, was also to be imposed on all banks. Finance houses with liabilities over £5 million also had to observe a minimum reserve asset ratio of 10 per cent and became liable to calls for Special Deposits, which in practice have been at the same percentage rate as in the case of banks.

The uniformity of these regulations was mildly infringed by the fact that the London clearing banks, but not other banks, were required

---

[1] The rate was raised from $5\frac{1}{2}$ per cent to 7 per cent in October 1970.

[2] See above, pages 223–4.

[3] Reserve assets comprise balances with the Bank of England (other than Special Deposits); Treasury bills; money at call with the discount houses, bill brokers, Stock Exchange jobbers and money brokers; British government stocks with one year or less to final maturity; local authority bills and (up to a maximum of 2 per cent of eligible liabilities) commercial bills eligible for rediscount at the Bank of England.

Liabilities are taken to comprise the sterling deposit liabilities of the banking system as a whole, excluding deposits having an original maturity of over two years, plus any sterling resources obtained by switching foreign currencies into sterling. Inter-bank transactions and sterling certificates of deposit (both held and issued) are taken into the calculation of individual banks' liabilities on a net basis, irrespective of term.

to hold $1\frac{1}{2}$ per cent of their $12\frac{1}{2}$ per cent reserve asset ratio in the form of (zero-interest) demand deposits at the Bank of England. In addition, the fact that notes and coin were not to be counted towards the reserve asset ratio, as they had been towards the old 28 per cent liquid asset ratio, involved what might be regarded as discrimination against the clearing banks, the nature of whose business requires them to hold a higher proportion of their assets in these forms than the non-clearing banks.

The flooding problem

Towards the end of the 1960s the authorities came to have doubts as to whether supporting the gilt-edged market in the face of selling pressure was a necessary, or even a desirable, element in the Government Broker's dealing technique. The Bank's paper of October 1969 on 'The operation of monetary policy since the Radcliffe Report'[1] noted that a more flexible policy on interest rates had given more scope for flexible tactics in debt management. In particular, as from May 1969 the official buying price for stocks within three months of maturity was no longer tied to the Treasury bill rate, and from July the authorities no longer announced the price at which they were prepared to sell tap stocks but instead considered bids made by the market.[2]

The change of dealing technique proposed in 'Competition and credit control' was explained as follows:

(i) the Bank will no longer be prepared to respond to requests to buy stock outright, except in the case of stocks with one year or less to run to maturity;
(ii) they reserve the right to make outright purchases of stock with more than a year to run solely at their discretion and initiative;
(iii) they will be prepared to undertake, at prices of their own choosing, exchanges of stock with the market except those which unduly shorten the life of the debt;
(iv) and will be prepared to respond to bids for the sale by them of 'tap' stocks and of such other stocks held by them as they may wish to sell.[3]

This modification by the Bank of their mode of operation in the gilt-edged market represented a return towards the position which they had occupied in the 1950s. Looking back in 1971 on the market support which the Bank had provided in the 1960s, the Chief Cashier suggested that it

...probably contributed to the attrition of the market's resources. So long as the Bank were prepared in effect to put substantial resources into ensuring the marketability of gilt-edged there was no particular reason why others should do so...Also, it is the essence of a market that there should be a

[1] *Bank of England Quarterly Bulletin*, vol. 9, December 1969.   [2] Ibid. p. 456.
[3] 'Competition and credit control', para. 13.

variety of views among operators of similar size. The Bank's close presence in the market often meant that in practice there were only two views – those of the Bank and those of everybody else.[1]

All the same, the Bank's close presence in the market was not something that could be spirited away by the new tactics of official intervention. Year in and year out the Government Broker still had to sell stock on an enormous scale, and he continued to do this, as in the 1960s, by waiting for a rising market, not by dropping his price ahead of the market in an attempt (futile, as the authorities continued to believe[2]) to tempt more buyers for his wares. The only time when his presence was less in evidence than in the 1960s was in a weak market, for under the new approach he became less ready to afford support and then only at the Bank's discretion. Thus, his transactions still continued to be determined very largely by the state of the market, even if not quite so closely as in the 1960s.

The quantity of money

The first sign accepted by outside commentators that the British authorities might have come to regard the money supply as more than just one in a whole range of liquid assets was the official Letter of Intent sent to the IMF in connection with the stand-by drawing right nego-tiated just after the devaluation of sterling in November 1967. This stated that the growth in the money supply in 1968 should be limited to its estimated growth in 1967, both absolutely and as a proportion of GNP. Then in 1968 and 1969 the British authorities became unusually receptive to the idea of relying more heavily on monetary policy, since in both Britain and the United States deflationary fiscal policies seemed disappointing in their results. In Britain the post-devaluation deflationary measures were unaccountably slow in taking effect, while in the United States the 10 per cent surcharge on income taxes, imposed in 1968, was no less disappointing. The views of Milton Friedman and his American followers had begun to be reflected in United Kingdom publications as from 1968. Thus in December 1968 *The Banker* invited leading proponents of differing points of view, among them Milton Friedman, to put their cases,[3] and Samuel Brittan wrote a number of articles in the *Financial Times* in 1968 and 1969 on the control of the money supply.[4] A. A. Walters, in a pamphlet published in January 1969, argued that monetarist theory explained

---

[1] Sykes Memorial Lecture, 10 November 1971.   [2] At any rate up to 1975.
[3] M. Friedman, H. Wincott and F. W. Tooby, 'The money supply debate', *The Banker*, vol. 118, December 1968.
[4] For example, 'Money supply: the great debate' in the *Financial Times*, 25 October 1968; 'Four propositions about the money supply' in the *Financial Times*, 23 January 1969, and other articles in the *Financial Times* of 8 and 10 July, and 13 November 1969.

the behaviour of the British economy very well up to 1945, although less well in the postwar period.[1] The Governor of the Bank of England in his Mansion House speech in October 1968 showed that he was aware of the monetarist school of thought, though he was not prepared to accept its teaching without due reservations,[2] and the same may be inferred of the Chancellor of the Exchequer, in the light of his budget speech in April 1969.

One of the chief catalysts of official thought was a seminar held in London in October 1968 for Bank of England and Treasury officials and representatives from the IMF.[3] Its main subject was DCE, a concept which had been invented by a senior IMF official,[4] who was himself one of the IMF representatives at the seminar. The new concept became important with the second Letter of Intent to the IMF of May 1969, which set a quantitative target for DCE in the year ending 31 March 1970 of not more than £400 million.[5]

How did those responsible for British monetary policy make use of the new concept? It would seem that they regarded it as just one of a number of diagnostic devices at their disposal, but in no sense a prescription for treatment. If a DCE target were exceeded, this was prima facie evidence that something might be amiss with the United Kingdom economy; in such circumstances all other available evidence should be analysed in the hope of achieving a correct diagnosis and then (but only then) a suitable course of treatment should be prescribed.[6]

In his April 1970 budget statement Roy Jenkins was able to report that DCE had been negative in 1969/70, so that his expectation that the expansion would be less than £400 million had thus been more than fulfilled. Looking forward to 1970/1, his expectation was for an expansion of domestic credit of under £900 million, and he expected the money supply to rise by less than DCE.[7] In his 1971

---

[1] A. A. Walters, *Money in Boom and Slump*, London, Institute of Economic Affairs, 1969. Other contributions to the public debate in 1969 were Anna Jacobson Schwartz ('Why money matters', *Lloyds Bank Review*, no. 94, October 1969), Judith A. Waters ('Money supply and credit – theory and practice', *National Westminster Bank Review*, November 1969), and Laurence Harris, 'The Chicago school of thought', and P. R. Herrington, 'Walters on money – a review article', (both in *The Bankers' Magazine*, vol. 208, July 1969).

[2] *Bank of England Quarterly Bulletin*, vol. 8, December 1968, p. 410.

[3] *The Banker*, vol. 118, December 1968, p. 1094.

[4] J. J. Polak, 'Monetary analysis of income formation and payments problems', *IMF Staff Papers*, vol. 6, November 1957; see also page 50 above.

[5] DCE corresponds to the change in the money stock on its M_3 definition (see footnote to table 5.7 below) plus the balance of payments deficit (defined for this purpose, broadly speaking, as the deficit on current account less net private sector borrowing overseas).

[6] See Treasury, 'Money supply and domestic credit', *Economic Trends*, no. 187, May 1969, p. xxi; also the Governor of the Bank of England's Jane Hodge Memorial Lecture in December 1970 (*Bank of England Quarterly Bulletin*, vol. 11, March 1971, pp. 43–4).

[7] In the event, DCE in 1970/1 was £1400 million and the increase in the money supply (M_3) £2031 million.

budget the new Chancellor did not lay down a specific money supply target, but he thought it would be inconsistent with his budget judgement to restrict the growth of money supply much below 3 per cent per quarter.

The DCE concept is so defined as to include not only the current deficit in the balance of payments (which is appropriate in an indicator to be used as a guide to demand management), but also a wide variety of external capital movements (for example, much of the short-term capital inflow which occurred in 1971). If therefore such capital movements are erratic and unpredictable, DCE becomes to that extent an unreliable indicator for demand management purposes, and the case for having a DCE target would have to rest on the control of the external balance being no less important as a policy objective than the control of effective demand – a presumption which was unquestionably invalid in 1971, when our external position was unusually strong. Hence it is not surprising that in his 1971 budget speech the Chancellor adduced the strength of sterling as a reason for not setting a DCE target. However, when in 1972 and 1973 our external balance deteriorated, official interest in DCE as an alternative monetary indicator to the stock of money was not resumed (though it came into use again in 1976).

Though officials lost interest in DCE, they did not in the money stock. A greater emphasis on the money supply was an ingredient in at least some of the official rethinking which characterised the new approach of 1971. Thus the Chief Cashier, in his Sykes Memorial Lecture of November 1971, spoke of a theoretical reappraisal,[1] which had led to the conclusion that the Bank's operations in the gilt-edged market should have more regard to quantitative effects on monetary aggregates; hence there was a need for a better official dealing technique in the gilt-edged market to give the authorities a better control over the monetisation of the national debt. The greater emphasis which some officials now gave to the money supply also supported a presumption against forms of control which affected only certain kinds of credit, for example bank advances and hire purchase contracts. It equally supported a presumption in favour of imposing a uniform control over all private sector institutions whose liabilities are conventionally regarded as 'money'; hence the imposition of uniform reserve asset and Special Deposit ratios on all banks.

[1] Some at least of the results of the Bank's 'theoretical reappraisal' have appeared in its Quarterly Bulletin. See in particular 'The importance of money', *Bank of England Quarterly Bulletin*, vol. 10, June 1970, 'Timing relationships between movements of monetary and national income variables', vol. 10, December 1970 and 'The demand for money in the United Kingdom: a further investigation', vol. 12, March 1972.

THE NEW APPROACH IN OPERATION

The period from the adoption of the new approach in 1971 until the general election in February 1974 saw an intensification of competition in banking, as had of course been intended by the authorities. Among the developments within the banking system was the entry of the London clearing banks in their own right into the market for certificates of deposit, both as issuers and as holders. Moreover, besides offering their traditional seven-day deposit account facilities through their branches to their regular customers, they now negotiated competitive terms for large 'wholesale' deposits and participated in the inter-bank market, both as deposit takers and as lenders.

The period also saw many changes in the use of the various instruments of monetary policy. Finally, it saw a complete change in the stance of official policy, since the pressure of effective demand moved from inadequate to adequate, or even excessive, and the balance of payments deteriorated from favourable to unfavourable, or even alarming. The main preoccupation of the authorities throughout the period was with demand management – initially to stimulate demand and later to restrain it. During most of the stimulation phase the balance of payments was not a constraint; though it deteriorated rapidly after 1971, the floating of the pound in June 1972 gave a further year's respite, so it was not until July 1973 that there arose any conflict between internal and external objectives.

The first touch on the monetary brakes, a slightly belated touch in retrospect according to views of the Governor of the Bank in October 1972,[1] occurred in mid-1972 with an abrupt upward movement in interest rates in the two months between the end of May and the end of July. Then about a year later, with the first indication that concern for the balance of payments was beginning to operate as a constraint on official action, the Bank of England took steps in July 1973 to bring about 'a sharp upward shift in short term rates in London', which, in the words of the Governor, 'achieved our primary objective of stabilising the sterling exchange rate...Apart from the external need I should have preferred a less sudden change.'[2]

[1] Address prepared by the Governor and delivered by the Deputy Governor at the Lord Mayor's dinner on 19 October 1972; *Bank of England Quarterly Bulletin*, vol. 12, December 1972, p. 516.

[2] Speech at Lord Mayor's dinner on 18 October 1973; *Bank of England Quarterly Bulletin*, vol. 13, December 1973, p. 476.

Official regulations

The period we are now considering was one of rapid increase in bank deposits and bank advances, likewise (see table 5.7) in the money stock, whether defined narrowly (M_1) or broadly (M_3). Up to the middle of 1972 all the evidence points to monetary policy being unrestrictive. Even after mid-1972 the figures of actual reserve ratios suggest that banks were being allowed to continue on a fairly loose rein. However, the behaviour of short-term interest rates after mid-1972 seems to suggest that the banks were beginning to compete more actively for reserve assets. Under the new approach every bank, including the London clearing banks, was now free to bid for wholesale deposits or to issue certificates of deposit at competitive interest rates as a means of preserving, or improving, its share of the total available reserve assets. Hence a rise in certificate of deposit and inter-bank interest rates in relation to rates on reserve assets, such as occurred very markedly from mid-1972 until February 1973, can probably be interpreted as implying that the discipline of the $12\frac{1}{2}$ per cent minimum reserve asset ratio was making itself felt, even though the figures of actual reserve asset ratios remained appreciably above $12\frac{1}{2}$ per cent.

Table 5.7. *Growth rate of the money supply, 1968–73*

Percentages

	$M_1{}^a$	$M_3{}^b$
1968	5·0	7·3
69	—	3·2
1970	9·3	9·4
71	15·4	13·5
72	14·4	28·1
73:*c*		
March	10·1	26·8
June	12·3	23·8
September	8·0	28·2
December	5·8	27·9

SOURCE: *Midland Bank Review*, May 1974, p. 4.

a Defined to include notes and coin in circulation with the public plus sterling current accounts owned by the private sector.

b Includes notes and coin in circulation with the public plus all United Kingdom private and public sector deposits, both sterling and other currencies, with banks and discount houses.

c Percentage change on 12 months earlier.

In the second half of 1973 official restrictions were progressively tightened. In August the Special Deposit ratio was increased by 1 per cent to 4 per cent, which immediately touched off a rise in certificate of deposit and inter-bank interest rates,[1] both absolutely and in relation to the rates on reserve assets. Further increases in Special Deposits followed in November.

In August 1972 the Bank had reverted to lending priorities, with a request that property and Stock Exchange speculation were to be accorded low priority. This request was later made more forcibly and supplemented by other measures: in December 1973 hire purchase controls were reintroduced and at the same time a new device, Supplementary Deposits – which could even less be reconciled with the competitive philosophy of the new approach – was introduced. This new device provided for non-interest bearing deposits to be made with the Bank whenever the interest-bearing sterling deposit liabilities of each bank (or finance house) grew at more than a certain rate, which was fixed at 8 per cent for the next six months.[2] Thus, the Supplementary Deposit scheme (like the old ceilings on advances) imposed a limitation on each individual bank, not just on banks as a whole, so that competition between banks (for depositing customers in this case, for borrowing customers under the old lending ceilings) was inhibited or at any rate discouraged.

Finally, though the banks' freedom to indulge in competition for deposits was encouraged by the abolition of the interest-rate cartel in 1971, an official ceiling of $9\frac{1}{2}$ per cent was imposed in September 1973 on interest payable on bank deposits of under £10,000. The official justification was:

In the consultative document of May 1971, the Bank recognised (paragraph 15) that the greater freedom of the banks to compete for personal savings could have implications for the savings banks and the building societies. The increases in short-term interest rates which took place in the first half of the year under review curtailed the flow of funds into the building societies, which were constrained in raising their own rates because of the effect on the cost of mortgages.[3]

The imposition of so many restrictive controls in the second half of 1973 provoked a comment in the following year from Lord O'Brien, who had then just retired as Governor of the Bank of England, to the effect that the recent changes in the credit control mechanism had brought the money supply under control, but they carried some of the same dangers to competition in the banking system as did the old techniques.[4]

[1] *Midland Bank Review*, May 1974, p 8.
[2] For details, see 'Credit control: a supplementary scheme', *Bank of England Quarterly Bulletin*, vol. 14, March 1974, p. 37.
[3] Bank of England, *Report and Accounts for the year ended 28 February 1974*, p. 7.
[4] *Financial Times*, 13 September 1974.

Official transactions in gilt-edged

Though under the new approach there was not the systematic support for the gilt-edged market that occurred in the 1960s,[1] support was afforded in June and July 1972, following the floating of sterling on 23 June, and again from time to time in 1973. In 1972 the Bank made facilities available to the banking system for the temporary sale and repurchase of short-dated gilt-edged stocks, under which it bought £358 million of stocks on 30 June which were resold to the banks on 14 July.[2] In 1973 there were some sharp fluctuations in the market, which, on occasion, involved moderate net purchases by the Bank, particularly during the period early June to mid-September.[3] However, despite the Bank's occasional support for gilt-edged, prices in the market in 1972 and 1973 fluctuated much more than in the 1960s. This seems to have been at least partly responsible for three firms of jobbers withdrawing from the gilt-edged market in July 1972; however the Bank was not unduly concerned.[4]

Official money market transactions

Since 1971 there have been three changes in official tactics in the money market. First, in October 1972 the Bank's traditional rediscount rate, Bank Rate, was superseded by an automatically determined 'minimum lending rate', which had the advantage of avoiding the dramatic announcement effect of changes in Bank Rate. The new arrangement was practicable because the significance of Bank Rate as a conventional reference point for other money market rates had been reduced, notably because the clearing banks had ceased to tie their deposit and lending rates to it and instead had each announced its own 'base' rate from time to time. The Bank's new minimum lending rate was to be determined every Friday at $\frac{1}{2}$ per cent above the average rate of discount for Treasury bills at the tender, rounded to the nearest $\frac{1}{4}$ per cent above, but a change in the rate independent of these arrangements was not excluded if this was required to signify a shift in monetary policy.[5] In fact such a change was made in 1973, when in November the Bank raised the rate (from $11\frac{1}{4}$ to 13 per cent) by specific announcement rather than in accordance with the new formula.

Secondly, the balance sheet constraint, initially imposed on the discount houses in 1971 with the aim of limiting the undue expansion of call money (a reserve asset) for the finance of non-public sector debt,

---

[1] Except in the case of bonds maturing within one year.
[2] Bank of England, *Report and Accounts for the year ended 28 February 1973*, p. 15.
[3] Bank of England, *Report and Accounts for the year ended 28 February 1974*, p. 14.
[4] *Bank of England Quarterly Bulletin*, vol. 12, September 1972, pp. 318–19.
[5] Bank of England, *Report and Accounts for the year ended 28 February 1973*, p. 6.

was amended in July 1973. Under the original arrangements the discount houses had undertaken to hold at least half their assets in specified forms of public sector debt, thereby artificially stimulating the demand for such assets (page 254 below). Under the revised arrangements, holdings of non-public sector debt were limited to a maximum of twenty times each house's capital and reserves.

Thirdly, the tradition under which the Bank did not undertake transactions in the new money markets was broken in late 1973 and early 1974.[1] It is perhaps too soon to judge whether these will be seen to have created an important precedent; so far they seem not to have done so.

There can be no doubt that under the new regime the Bank's transactions in the traditional money market, whether at the discount office or through its bill broker, continued to afford the Bank as effective a control over rates on reserve assets as it had enjoyed in the 1960s.[2] The transition from Bank Rate to the new minimum lending rate in October 1972 was not intended to abdicate the Bank's control over rates on reserve assets. As regards interest rates in the new money markets, it has become very apparent that, with the new reserve asset ratio, the differential between the rates prevailing in the traditional and new money markets (as measured, for example, by the excess of the certificate of deposit rate over the Treasury bill rate) is very sensitive to whether or not the banks are experiencing, or expect to experience, a shortage of reserve assets. When there is no shortage, as for instance in the first half of 1972, the differential can be very small, but when the banks fear that they are going to be squeezed the differential increases, since the way that the banks compete for scarce reserve assets is to offer higher rates on the 'wholesale' deposits which they borrow and on certificates of deposit which they issue.[3] This is what happened in the second half of 1972 and early 1973, and then again in the course of roughly the same months one year later.[4]

---

[1] Bank of England, *Report and Accounts for the year ended 28 February 1974*, pp. 12 and 13.

[2] Bank of England, *Report and Accounts for the year ended 28 February 1973*, p. 12.

[3] The clearing banks' rates on 'retail', i.e. seven-day branch deposits, are conventionally related to their base rates, as pre-1971 they were to Bank Rate.

[4] The following table permits a comparison of the differential:

Percentages

	Treasury bill rate	3-months CD rate
25 February 1972	4·36	5·19
23 February 1973	8·06	10·81
22 February 1974	11·82	14·31

SOURCE: *Bank of England Quarterly Bulletin*, vol. 14, September 1974, table 30.

The Bank's amendment in July 1973 of its restriction on the discount houses' portfolios was probably intended to mitigate the tendency for the differential between the certificate of deposit and Treasury bill rates to widen at times of a squeeze on reserve assets. In the preceding squeeze it had been found that the differential had been increased not only because the banks competed for reserve assets by bidding up the certificate of deposit rate, but because the discount houses, in attempting to supply the banks with more reserve assets (in the form of call money they borrowed from the banks), bid more fiercely for Treasury bills, since they could take £2 more call money for every additional £1 of Treasury bills in their portfolios.[1] Thus, up to the reform of July 1973 both the banks and the discount houses had an incentive to widen the differential between the certificate of deposit and Treasury bill rates. However the reform did not improve matters much; during the next period of squeeze, which began in mid-1973 and reached a climax at about the turn of the year, the differential between the certificate of deposit and Treasury bill rates was as wide as ever.

The quantity of money

The practice of announcing monetary targets lapsed in 1971 (page 248 above), and was not resumed until 1976. By the time of the first budget after 'Competition and credit control', in March 1972, the authorities had adopted a policy of reflating demand and the Chancellor was prepared to accept a growth of money supply high by standards of past years to ensure that adequate finance was available for the extra output; he rejected the constraint of a numerical target. In fact, an accelerating rise in the money stock was tolerated, even though (according to Patrick Jenkin, Chief Secretary at the Treasury) it was accepted that an excessive expansion of money supply could store up trouble in the future, since the full effects of monetary policy are likely to be felt only after a lag of perhaps a year or even more.[2] A rapid increase in the money supply was at the same time tolerated on econometric grounds, in that the Bank of England's research on demand functions for money (on various definitions of the money stock) strongly suggested that when real income is increasing a much more rapid rise is needed in the money stock than in money national income if unacceptably high rates of interest are to be avoided.[3] This conclusion

---

[1] Since one half of their portfolios had to be in public sector debt, for example Treasury bills, their acquisition of £1 of such debt enabled them to acquire a further £1 of private sector debt, for example certificates of deposit, so that they could then make use of £2 additional call money. [2] Reported in the *Financial Times*, 17 July 1972.

[3] L. D. D. Price, 'The demand for money in the United Kingdom: a further investigation', *Bank of England Quarterly Bulletin*, vol. 12, March 1972. An earlier version of this paper had been presented at a conference in September 1971.

reconciled the Bank for the time being to a remarkable fall in the velocity of circulation (GNP divided by M_3), which brought its value down from a plateau of about 3·0 in 1970 and 1971 to about 2·7 in the third quarter of 1972.

The first sign of a change from acquiescence by the authorities in an increase in the money supply came in mid-1972 with a sharp rise in short-term rates (page 249); then in mid-September 1972 came a warning that the highest priority must now be given to the reduction of the rate of inflation, since the real growth of the economy had speeded up to the government's target rate of 5 per cent and concern had shifted to the rapid rise in prices. Moreover, in the course of 1973 confidence in the Bank's demand functions for money was undermined; the econometric case for tolerating a rapid rise in the money stock was weakened by the recognition that recent structural changes in the financial system had decreased the reliability of the M_3 statistical series as a useful measure of the money stock.[1] In particular:

(1) Six years of lending ceilings had driven some business out of banking channels, for example into inter-company loans. This had now come back into the banks and helped to swell the figure for bank deposits and hence for the money stock.

(2) The new competitive environment allowed the banks, especially the clearing banks, to extend their range of deposit facilities, including sterling certificates of deposit, and thus provide new homes for funds awaiting investment. Bank deposits, unlike some of the alternative homes for such funds – such as deposits with local authorities – are included in the figures of the money stock.

(3) Towards the end of 1973 some bank customers came to believe that the Bank and the government – faced with this rapid expansion in money and credit – would be forced to reintroduce credit ceilings. This led to some precautionary borrowing, with customers making use of their facilities for advances while the going was good, and thereby causing an equivalent increase in bank deposits.

(4) At times a perverse relationship developed between clearing bank borrowing and lending rates, so that borrowing became relatively cheap, and bank customers were able to draw upon their facilities for advances and use them to build up their deposits – sometimes drawing money solely in order to reinvest it in sterling certificates of deposit or in large wholesale deposits which earned relatively high market rates.

[1] The alternative series for measuring the money stock, M_1, was no less unsatisfactory. As the Deputy Governor explained in an address on 11 April 1973, the Bank's estimates of M_1 were inherently of poorer quality than those for M_3 and had been available on a consistent definition for little more than a year. Hence the Bank had during 1973 become increasingly sceptical of the value of either M_1 or M_3 as intermediate variables in the formulation of monetary policy (*Bank of England Quarterly Bulletin*, vol. 13, June 1973, p. 198).

This was the process which came to be known as the 'merry-go-round' or 'round-tripping'.[1] The reasons why this occurred included: first, the existence of the overdraft system, which gave customers sizable unused facilities which they could draw upon at will; secondly, the fact that the cost of those facilities was related to base rates which the banks were reluctant to raise – partly because they were already embarrassed by the high profits they were known to be making as a result of the generally high level of interest rates. In this situation the banks preferred to respond to pressure on the reserve ratio by bidding aggressively for large amounts of wholesale deposits rather than by raising rates on advances. And the more deposit rates rose in relation to lending rates, the greater the demand for credit and the greater the pressure on reserve ratios. Hence there was a vicious circle of rising market rates, associated with an expansion of bank advances and deposits, and also of the quantity of money.

The rise in the money stock had eventually to be slowed down – even though some of the rise may have been only a statistical distortion – and clearly Special Deposits were an inappropriate instrument for this purpose since they would merely aggravate the pressure on reserve ratios. So, in December 1973, the Supplementary Deposit scheme was introduced, which imposed a direct limit on the rate of growth of the banks' interest-bearing liabilities, which are a substantial component of the money stock. This scheme allowed a reasonable rate of growth in the banks' balance sheets, while discouraging them from bidding for funds and creating the distorted interest-rate pattern described above. It was also intended to encourage the banks to be more cautious in extending facilities for advances, for there is no doubt that in the first flush of freedom following the introduction of 'Competition and credit control' in 1971 many banks took on lending commitments far beyond what they could have reasonably expected to have the resources to finance.

As compared with the lending ceilings of the 1960s, which applied to a particular area of bank lending (namely the private sector), the new arrangements had the advantages of allowing banks more freedom to arrange their assets as they wished and to run their own business within the given overall rate of growth, and of providing more control over the money stock. It was also hoped that the scheme would be more easily applied for a temporary period than the lending ceilings had proved to be. (It was, in the event, suspended for the time being in February 1975.)

---

[1] The merry-go-round effect was the subject of an initiative by the Bank later in 1973, which led to decisions by the clearing banks to adjust their base rates to respond more rapidly to movements in market rates and to link their lending rates to certain customers (in particular local authorities, finance houses and other banks) to money market rates rather than to base rates.

The Supplementary Deposit scheme did its job well, in the sense that the growth in the money supply was quickly checked. After a few months the scheme was made less necessary by the falling demand for credit from the private sector; in the event very few banks came up against the prescribed limits. Yet in the first half-year of its operation it was thought by the Bank to be contributing to the banks' greater restraint in extending credit.

CHAPTER 6

MONETARY POLICY

PART II

by *M. J. Artis*

INTRODUCTION

This chapter is addressed principally to the problem of evaluating the effects of monetary policy. As such, it would ideally incorporate, if not summary statistics measuring these effects, then at least orders of magnitude illustrating the importance of monetary measures. In fact, it is only for a few types of measure and a limited range of monetary variables that this ideal can even be approached, and then not often with great confidence. However, the consequent rather uncertain and patchy verdict on monetary policy is consistent with the findings of other investigators;[1] it accords with the relative absence from the major United Kingdom macroeconometric models of convincingly detailed and powerful monetary influences.

There is ample room for speculation on why this state of affairs prevails and it is worth dwelling for a moment on some of the conditions required for the effects of monetary policy, whether at an aggregated or disaggregated level, to be isolated and measured. In the first instance it is obviously necessary for monetary policy (or more modestly monetary variables), somehow measured, to have varied sufficiently to exert a measurable influence on real factors – a condition which is met by only a few monetary variables (hire purchase terms, for example) in our period; indeed, a popular broad-brush view of British monetary policy in the 1960s is that it was essentially passive. It is also necessary to establish that any variation in monetary policy was independent of other factors; but here there is the awkward fact of a very intimate relationship between fiscal and monetary policy in British conditions –

[1] See, for example, the Bank of England's paper 'The operation of monetary policy since Radcliffe' in D. R. Groome and H. G. Johnson (eds.), *Money in Britain 1959–1969*, London, Oxford University Press, 1970. However, there are some monetarists who have attached unequivocal importance to the price and real output consequences of variations in the money supply; two recent examples are D. E. W. Laidler's 'Brief note on fiscal policy, inflation and the balance of payments' presented to the House of Commons Expenditure Committee (see House of Commons, *Ninth Report from the Expenditure Committee, Session 1974*) and J. M. Parkin's ' Where is Britain's inflation going?', *Lloyds Bank Review*, no. 117, July 1975.

a relationship which is liable to frustrate attempts to demonstrate the effects of monetary policy alone even by the most convinced *aficionados* of its potency.[1] Then, as a third requirement, it has to be possible to quantify monetary policy, but in those views of its transmission mechanism that stress the significance of volatile expectations – 'threshold effects' and the imperfection of capital markets – quantification is by no means straightforward. Finally, the task is made more difficult by evidence that the monetary reforms of 1971 introduced under the title 'Competition and credit control'[2] constituted a structural break with the 1960s; thus, later observations, relating to a period in which several important monetary variables conveniently (at first sight) varied much more than they had in previous years, fail to confirm the significance of relationships established for the earlier period.

These considerations suggest that it will be best to consider separately the problems raised by the conceptual isolation and measurement of monetary policy, the nature of the transmission mechanism and the events following the publication of 'Competition and credit control'.

INSTRUMENTS, INDICATORS AND OBJECTIVES

The theory of macroeconomic policy provides a framework in which instrumental variables[3] – those over which the authorities have direct control – are sharply distinguished from goal variables – those whose magnitudes 'really matter' to policy-makers. Between these two sets stand 'intermediate' variables, whose values are capable of being closely determined by the authorities through their instrument setting and which can be thought of, in turn, as either influencing, or being an early indicator of, the goal variables of the system.[4] According to this approach monetary policy could be defined as changes in those instruments which have, on some principle, been classified as monetary instruments; the effects of monetary policy can then be identified, in two stages, with the effects of monetary actions on the intermediate variables and the effects of changes in these upon the goal variables of the system. Alternatively the sequence can be viewed in reverse, and attention focused upon the response of monetary instruments to

[1] Walters, for example, whilst clearly stating his belief in the 'power' of money, rightly draws attention to this problem in *Money in Boom and Slump*.

[2] *Bank of England Quarterly Bulletin*, vol. 11, June 1971.

[3] This term, used here in a policy context, appears also in the literature on econometric estimation, where it has a different meaning.

[4] This account is oversimplified to some degree: the authorities may have grounds for thinking that intermediate variables 'really matter' too, apart from their significance for the goal variables of the system; an example would be the rate of interest on government debt. Most studies of the monetary authorities' reaction functions also seem to assume that the authorities attach 'disutility' to *changing* their instrument variables.

deviations in the goal variables from their preferred values; this is the object of the authors of various investigations into the 'reaction functions' of the authorities (see pages 279–80 below).

This scheme invites us to look at monetary policy actions and effects in a relatively disaggregated fashion, at least to the extent of the multiple goals and instruments which can be identified. As such, it stands in some contrast to the emphasis of a large bulk of literature, both theoretical and empirical, where the effect of monetary policy is identified with the impact of changes in the money supply or the monetary base. There are some considerations (commented upon further below) which can help to resolve the apparent contrast between the two approaches, but our view of the transmission mechanism of monetary policy and of the monetary authorities' goals implies that it cannot be completely removed. Accordingly, some analysis of the effects of changes in individual instrumental variables is in order.

Regulatory instruments

Monetary instruments are classified in the preceding chapter into instruments of a regulatory character and those involving the authorities in direct market transactions. Among the former are bank lending 'requests', Special Deposits and variations in the terms of hire purchase borrowing. Each of these has been the subject of academic enquiry and the use of these instruments, more especially of the last two, was perhaps the most obvious outward sign of monetary action in the period up to 1971 with which we are concerned at this point.

The occasions on which *bank lending requests* were used and their general character have already been described in the preceding chapter; a summary is given here in table 6.1. It is perhaps surprising in view of the importance of this instrument in the 1960s that relatively little attention should have been paid to quantifying its effects. Published investigations appear to be restricted to three papers, of which only that by Norton is of much help.[1] His procedure was to classify the requests into two groups, 'severe' (calling for zero or negative growth) and 'mild' (allowing for restricted but positive growth), and then to use this scoring as a dummy variable in a multiple regression analysis to explain the level of bank advances.

---

[1] F. P. R. Brechling and G. Clayton, 'Commercial banks' portfolio behaviour', *Economic Journal*, vol. 75, June 1965, pp. 290–316; W. E. Norton, 'Debt management and monetary policy in the United Kingdom', *Economic Journal*, vol. 79, September 1969, pp. 475–94; W. R. White, 'Some econometric models of deposit bank portfolio behaviour in the United Kingdom, 1963–1970' in Renton (ed.), *Modelling the Economy*. Brechling and Clayton are mainly concerned with the 1950s, whilst White (who was at the Bank of England at the time) gives an econometric expression to requests and the series affected by them which cannot be replicated from published sources; it is therefore difficult to derive from them any illustrative order of magnitude for the effect.

Table 6.1. *Ceilings on lending to the private sector,[a] 1961–71*

	London and Scottish clearing banks	Other banks	Larger finance houses
July 1961	Unquantified request for restraint[b]		
Oct. 1962	Restraint removed		
May 1965[c]	105% of mid-March 1965	105% of March 1965	
April 1967	Ceiling removed	Unchanged	
Nov. 1967	100% of mid-Nov. 1967		100% of end-Oct. 1967
May 1968	104% of mid-Nov. 1967		Unchanged
Nov. 1968	98% of mid-Nov. 1967[d]	102% of mid-Nov. 1967	98% of end-Oct. 1967
April 1970	105% of mid-March 1970[e]	107% of mid-March 1970	105% of end-March 1970
March–June 1971	107½% of mid-March 1970[e]	109½% of mid-March 1970	107½% of end-March 1970

SOURCE: 'Monetary surveys' in *Midland Bank Review* (May issues).

[a] Requests covered commercial bills as well as advances from May 1965 onwards, and leasing facilities from November 1967 onwards.

[b] Interpreted by London and Scottish clearing banks as 100 per cent of mid-June 1961.

[c] Followed a request to all institutions in December 1964 to slow down the rate of growth of lending. Institutions were told in February 1966 that the ceiling for the ensuing year would remain at 105 per cent of the March 1965 figure.

[d] This level was to be attained by March 1969; in October 1969 it was unofficially relaxed to 104 per cent of the official ceiling.

[e] Ceilings applied to London and Scottish clearing banks in aggregate, not to individual institutions.

A similar procedure was followed in estimating the equations reported in table 6.2; the incidence of requests, scored in the same manner, is shown against a time-series graph of London clearing bank net advances in chart 6.1. The results in table 6.2 are an excerpt from a long series of trials, using alternative formulations of the dependent variable and a wide array of independent variables. Requests were regularly highly significant with the appropriate sign, and virtually all the equations indicated a very slow rate of adjustment, often not significantly different from zero. Two basic models were employed: in the first, advances were treated (following Norton) as demand-determined, subject to requests acting as constraints upon the adjustment process;[1] in the second, a reduced form of supply and demand was estimated, with structural equations based on the assumption that market-clearing occurred in

[1] That is, the long-run demand for advances, A^*, was thought of as subject to the partial adjustment process, $A - A_{-1} = \alpha(A^* - A_{-1}) + \beta D$, where the subscript indicates a one-period lag, α the coefficient of adjustment and D the request dummy, acting as a constraint upon the adjustment process.

Table 6.2. *The effect of lending requests on bank advances,[a] 1956 III–1971 III*

	Equation numbers				
	1	2	3[b]	4	5
Constant term	128·25 (2·05)	218·18 (2·80)	−66·59 (3·25)	−1077·24 (1·91)	−739·30 (1·31)
Regression coefficients for:					
Permanent income[c]	0·17 (3·76)	0·18 (3·31)	n.a.	0·15 (3·78)	n.a.
Disposable income[d]	−0·17 (3·6c)	−0·17 (3·17)	−0·04[e] (3·98)	−0·16 (4·15)	−0·07 (2·89)
Bank Rate[f]	−4·81 (0·39)	−42·04 (3·73)	n.a.	n.a.	−2·17 (0·19)
Short bond rate	n.a.	n.a.	−1·81 (2·39)	n.a.	n.a.
Special Deposits	n.a.	n.a.	1·36 (2·73)	n.a.	n.a.
Banks' free resources[g]	n.a.	n.a.	n.a.	0·07 (2·35)	0·01 (0·84)
Total private investment	n.a.	0·07 (0·87)	n.a.	n.a.	n.a.
Stockbuilding[h]	0·01 (0·80)	n.a.	n.a.	n.a.	n.a.
Capacity utilisation[i]	n.a.	n.a.	124·45 (5·94)	1193·18 (2·01)	1305·41 (1·89)
Lagged dependent variable	0·98 (41·29)	0·97 (32·17)	n.a.	0·93 (35·24)	0·82 (15·59)
Time trend	n.a.	n.a.	0·83 (7·08)	n.a.	16·84 (3·05)
Lending request dummies:[j]					
Mild	−74 80 (2·89)	−0·29[k] (1·93)	−2·37 (2·11)	−83·59 (4·06)	−65·96 (2·74)
Severe	−139·20 (5·29)		−3·79 (3·50)	−157·58 (8·98)	−137·17 (5·64)
$\bar{R}^2$	0·999	0·999	0·900	0·998	0·998
DW	2·04	1·55	1·11	2·14	2·11

SOURCE: M. J. Artis and P. Meadows, 'Lending requests' and 'Lending requests: addendum' (unpublished NIESR working papers), 1974.

[a] Net advances by the London clearing banks, excluding those to nationalised industries. Seasonal dummies not listed. t-statistics shown in brackets.

[b] Dependent variable scaled by deposits.

[c] As defined in Norton, 'Debt management and monetary policy in the United Kingdom': $(1-k) \Sigma_{i=0}^{10} k^i Y_{t-i} / (1-k^{11})$, where Y is GDP at factor cost and $k = 0.95$.

[d] Also as defined by Norton: $Y - T$, where T is total direct tax payments.

[e] Coefficient multiplied by 10. [f] Quarterly average.

[g] Deposits minus required liquid assets and Special Deposits.

[h] Value of physical increase in stocks. [i] Deviation from trend.

[j] Taken as zero: 1958 III–1961 II, 1962 IV–1964 IV, 1971 III; mild: 1962 III, 1965 I–1966 I, 1967 II–1968 II, 1970 II–1971 II; severe: 1956 III–1958 II, 1961 III–1962 II, 1966 II–1967 I, 1968 III–1970 I. [k] A 0, 1, 2 dummy scaled by the consumer price index.

non-observable 'quality' variables.[1] The dependent variable of the estimated equation is defined for equations (1), (2), (4) and (5) as London clearing bank net advances and for equation (3) as advances scaled by deposits; in equation (2) the dummy variable was also scaled by the consumer price index.

Chart 6.1. *Bank advances and their ratio to personal disposable income,*
1957–72

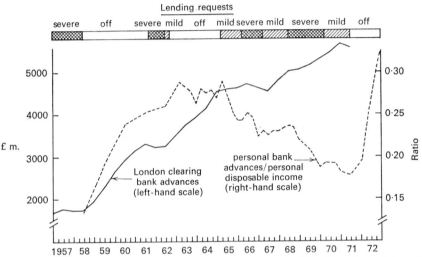

SOURCES: Bank of England, *Statistical Abstract,* no. 1, table 9(1); CSO, *Financial Statistics* and *National Income and Expenditure* (annual).

Notes: (i) London clearing bank advances (excluding those to nationalised industries), seasonally adjusted.

(ii) Personal bank advances and personal disposable income (at current prices) not seasonally adjusted.

These equations reflect the generality of results obtained in the investigation of bank advances. Interest rates were of variable significance in determining bank advances, and Special Deposits hardly ever significant (although they do influence the value of the variable 'banks' free resources', which was occasionally significant – as in equation (4)).[2] But bank lending requests proved significant on almost any specification of the equations, the 'mild' request having an impact effect of the order

[1] That is, assuming that $A_s = a + bQ + cS$ and $A_d = a' - b'Q - c'Z$, where Q is the unobservable market-clearing factor and S and Z are exogenous influences on supply and demand, the weighted sum of A_s and A_d is formed as $w_1 A_s + w_2 A_d = A$, with $w_1 = b'/(b'+b)$ and $w_2 = b/(b'+b)$, so as to yield an estimating equation, $A = w_1 a + w_2 a' + w_1 cS - w'_2 cZ$. A similar procedure was employed by M. H. Miller in 'An empirical analysis of monetary policy in the UK, 1954–1965' (unpublished Ph.D. thesis, Yale), 1971.

[2] In equation (3) Special Deposits, though significant, have the 'wrong' sign.

of £70 million and the 'severe' dummy an effect approximately twice as large. The results suggest that the cumulative effect of requests on the *level* of bank advances was considerable, building up slowly over a long period. For example, they imply that the requests imposed at the beginning of 1965 and maintained until 1971 were responsible by the end of this period for reducing the demand for bank advances by some £1500 million. It seems, indeed, reasonably clear that the requests affected the level of bank advances significantly and that their prolonged use resulted in a substantial frustration of the demand for bank credit.[1] This was probably especially true of advances to the personal sector, as was the evident intent of the qualitative advice accompanying the requests and as is strongly suggested by chart 6.1. It is, of course, a matter for separate consideration how far the effect of requests on advances was reflected in a parallel modification of spending behaviour.

It is difficult to find any reason (or evidence) for believing that *Special Deposits* played a significant part in monetary policy in the 1960s. The authorities appear to have regarded them, alternately, as possible substitutes for, or as complements of, bank lending requests. But in the latter role they were essentially redundant and in the former largely ineffective. The suggestion that they were largely ineffective is reinforced by the relatively small scale on which they were employed: as table 6.3 shows, up to September 1971 cumulative calls never exceeded $3\frac{1}{2}$ per cent for the London clearing banks and $1\frac{3}{4}$ per cent for the Scottish banks. After 'Competition and credit control', however, calls for Special Deposits cumulated to 6 per cent of eligible liabilities.

That Special Deposits were largely redundant as a complement to bank lending requests follows from the apparently high degree of compliance with those requests by the institutions concerned. Only once, in 1969, did the Bank of England publicly display concern at non-compliance (and temporarily penalised the banks for it by restricting the interest paid on Special Deposits), although it is true that the series to which requests were applicable are not available in detail in the

---

[1] This is not to claim that the determination of bank advances and the role of requests is well understood, however. For example, although the equations in table 6.2 point to the existence of a large pent up demand for advances by 1971, their technical characteristics actually suggest that the response of advances to the removal of requests (as to their imposition) should have been very gradual; as is evident from the value of the coefficients obtained on the lagged dependent variable, the results could have been generated from an instantaneous flow model rather than the partial stock adjustment model outlined in footnote 1, page 261 – that is, the value of α could have been taken as zero. Yet the evidence is that the response of advances to the removal of the requests was in fact very rapid, an observation which can be squared with the results reported only by appealing to the argument that conditions changed so fundamentally in 1971 that observations before and after 'Competition and credit control' must be regarded as belonging to structurally distinct regimes (see pages 298–9 below).

Table 6.3. *Special Deposits required from the clearing banks, 1960–73*

Percentages

	Called		Released		Cumulative total	
	London	Scottish	London	Scottish	London	Scottish
April 1960	1	½	—	—	1	½
June 1960	1	½	—	—	2	1
July 1961	1	½	—	—	3	1½
May 1962	—	—	1	½	2	1
Sept. 1962	—	—	1	½	1	½
Nov. 1962	—	—	1	½	—	—
April 1965	1	½	—	—	1	½
July 1966	1	½	—	—	2	1
April 1970	½	¼	—	—	2½	1¼
Oct. 1970	1	½	—	—	3½	1¾
Sept. 1971	—	—	3½	1¾	—	—
Nov. 1972	1		—		1	
Dec. 1972	2		—		3	
July 1973	1		—		4	
Nov. 1973	2		—		6	

SOURCES: *Bank of England Quarterly Bulletin* (various issues); CSO, *Financial Statistics.*

published statistics, so that it is not possible to be sure how far non-compliance was a significant (if unpublicised) problem in other periods. However, the data that are available do not suggest there could have been major difficulties of this kind.

The ineffectiveness of Special Deposits as a substitute follows from different considerations, of which two are important. First, there is reason to believe that throughout the period the banks were adjusting their portfolios to increase the ratio of advances to deposits far above the level prevailing in 1960; thus, the prewar ratio was in the region of 60 per cent, by which criterion the steady upward trend shown in chart 6.2, depressed as it was by the incidence of requests, strongly suggests that, when Special Deposits were imposed on bank portfolios, the assets for which they were substituted were bonds and not advances. Seen in this light, the analysis appropriate to a situation in which a call for Special Deposits fell upon banks initially in a position of equilibrium can be dispensed with.[1] Secondly, the policy followed by the authorities in the bond market, was as described above (chapter 5) one of 'leaning against the wind' – implying a willingness to absorb the greater part, if

[1] In this situation, there are two counter-posed factors to consider: to the extent that Special Deposits reduce liquidity, banks may wish to hold more bonds to compensate; but, to the extent that profitability per unit of assets is reduced, there is an 'income effect' operating to increase advances. A useful review of these and associated issues appears in A. D. Bain, *The Control of the Money Supply*, London, Penguin, 1970.

not all, of the bond sales induced by a call for Special Deposits. Taken together, these two factors suggest that calls for Special Deposits were largely absorbed by a reduction in bond holdings in bank portfolios, with little or no repercussion upon the total volume of deposits or advances. Researchers into the effects of Special Deposits have usually concluded in this vein,[1] although most have placed greater emphasis

Chart 6.2. *Ratios of advances to deposits and of Special Deposits to gross deposits, 1960–71*

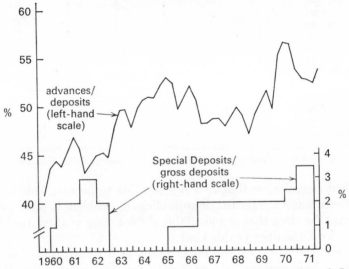

SOURCES: Bank of England, *Statistical Abstract*, no. 1; *Bank of England Quarterly Bulletin*.

Notes: (i) Ratio advances/deposits, quarterly averages, not seasonally adjusted.
       (ii) Ratio Special Deposits/gross deposits, end-quarter figures.

upon the effects (or lack of them) on deposits – an emphasis that was misplaced, since the authorities firmly singled out advances as the goal of Special Deposits. One investigation, however, revealed some effect of Special Deposits upon advances,[2] although no such impact was

[1] For example, N. J. Gibson, 'Special deposits as an instrument of monetary policy', *Manchester School of Economic and Social Studies*, vol. 32, September 1964, and 'Monetary, credit and fiscal policies' in A. R. Prest (ed.) *The UK Economy: a manual of applied economics* (2nd edn), London, Weidenfeld & Nicolson, 1968; R. L. Crouch, 'Special Deposits and the British monetary mechanism', *Economic Studies*, vol. 5, no. 1, 1970. J. M. Parkin, M. R. Gray and R. J. Barrett, 'The portfolio behaviour of commercial banks' in Hilton and Heathfield (eds.) *The Econometric Study of the United Kingdom*, found it appropriate to assume that both deposits and advances were exogenously determined; they concluded that a call for Special Deposits would induce a more than equivalent shift out of bonds with an accompanying increase in holdings of Treasury bills and call money.

[2] R. T. Coghlan, 'Special Deposits and bank advances', *The Bankers Magazine*, vol. 216, August 1973.

discernible in any persistent manner in the investigations described earlier in this chapter.

Hardly less than bank lending requests, changes in the terms of *hire purchase credit* typified monetary action in the 1960s. The terms controlled were the minimum down-payment and maximum repayment period applicable to credit for particular goods; table 6.4 summarises the changes imposed.

Table 6.4. *Hire purchase controls, 1960–71*

	Minimum deposit				Maximum repayment period			
	Cars	Motor cycles	Radio, TV, etc.	Furniture[a]	Cars	Motor cycles	Radio, TV, etc.	Furniture[a]
	(percentages)				(months)			
April 1960	20	20	20	10	24	24	24	24
Jan. 1961	20	20	20	10	36	36	36	36
June 1962	20	20	10	10	36	36	36	36
June 1965	25	25	15	10	36	36	36	36
July 1965	25	25	15	10	30	30	30	36
Feb. 1966	25	25	25	15	27	27	24	30
July 1966	40	40	$33\frac{1}{3}$	20	24	24	24	24
April 1967	40	25	$33\frac{1}{3}$	20	24	27	24	24
June 1967	30	25	$33\frac{1}{3}$	20	30	27	24	24
Aug. 1967	25	25	25	15	36	36	30	30
Nov. 1967	$33\frac{1}{3}$	25	25	15	27	36	30	30
Nov. 1968	40	$33\frac{1}{3}$	$33\frac{1}{3}$	20	24	24	24	24
July 1971	—	—	—	—	—	—	—	—

SOURCE: *Board of Trade Journal/Trade and Industry*.

[a] Excluding cookers, on which the minimum deposit was 10 per cent and the maximum repayment period 48 months throughout.

Investigations of the effect of these controls have usually proceeded in two stages – by first identifying the change in outstanding debt due to specified changes in the controls and then the associated change in consumers' expenditure.[1] The change in outstanding debt can be identified with the difference between new credits and repayments. In Garganas's recent study, the latter are considered to arise as a distri-

[1] These investigations leave no doubt that outstanding debt responded significantly to the controls (see R. J. Ball and P. D. Drake, 'The impact of credit control on consumer durable spending in the United Kingdom, 1957–1961', *Review of Economic Studies*, vol. 30, October 1963, pp. 181–94). This was confirmed more recently by Garganas, using an approach based on the earlier study, but modified to take account of additional factors (see N. Garganas, 'An analysis of consumer credit and its effects on purchases of consumer durables' in Renton (ed.) *Modelling the Economy*). Additional confirmation is provided by A. M. El-Mokadem in *Econometric Models of Personal Saving. The United Kingdom, 1948–1966*, London, Butterworths, 1973.

buted lag of the former, in which the profile of the lag distribution depends on the repayment requirements in force and the deviation of disposable income from its trend. New credits are explained in a stock adjustment framework, with significant determinants including disposable income, an index of hire purchase terms, an interest-rate variable and unfilled vacancies (the latter being interpreted as an attitudinal index). Since the two dimensions of hire purchase control are multi-

Chart 6.3. *Ratio of hire purchase debt to disposable income with and without controls, 1960–73*

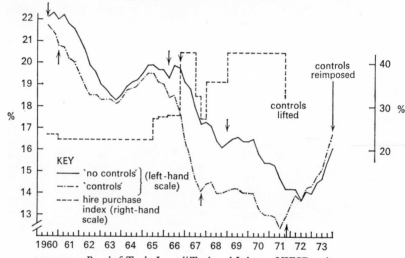

SOURCES: *Board of Trade Journal/Trade and Industry*; NIESR estimates.

Notes: (i) Hire purchase index calculated as $d + (100 - d)/m$, where d is percentage minimum deposit and m maximum repayment period in months. End-quarter figures for cars only are used.

(ii) Arrows indicate major interventions.

collinear, either one of them may be dropped, or they may be combined into a composite variable; the latter is the course followed by Garganas and the value of this composite index for one major group of durable goods (cars) is superimposed on chart 6.3.[1] It is fairly clear that a restriction on hire purchase terms has a largely short-term effect; the initial reduction in new credits is subsequently offset by the lower rate of repayments on outstanding debt, which is smaller than it otherwise would be.

Garganas's system can be used to simulate the effect of the controls on outstanding debt. First, outstanding debt is estimated in the presence

[1] The composite variable is defined as $dp_d + (100 - d)p_d/m$, where d is the minimum average deposit, m the maximum average repayment period and p_d the relative price of consumer durables. For purposes of chart 6.3 variations in the term p_d were suppressed.

of the controls; this is shown, as a proportion of disposable income, by the 'controls' line in chart 6.3; next the level of debt is recomputed on the assumption that the controls remained at their (minimal) 1959 level – this is shown in chart 6.3 as the 'no controls' line, again expressed as a ratio of disposable income. Within the limits of what can be expected from such a simulation, the results indicate that the controls may have frustrated hire purchase credit to a maximum of some $2\frac{1}{2}$ per cent of disposable income (the level of disposable income being regarded as exogenous). The controls were suspended in 1971 and not renewed until 1973; thus, in the intervening period, as might be expected, the two simulation runs come close together, the 'controls' run lying slightly above the 'no controls' because of the lagged effects of lower inherited debt levels (implying, for comparable demands for new credit, reduced repayments and a faster rate of rise in outstandings). The major interventions are shown by arrows in the chart, and it is worth noting that, although the 'controls' simulation shows quite a marked response to the severe restrictions of 1965 and 1966, there would still have been a fairly steady decline in the debt–income ratio in a 'no controls' situation. Indeed, the extent of this decline might lead one to suspect the 'no controls' simulation was biased downwards were it not for the fact that the value of the ratio in the 1973 period of 'freedom' showed no signs of approaching the 1959 levels, despite a probable incentive to anticipate the reimposition of controls. It seems likely that by this time bank credit had become an increasingly effective substitute for hire purchase debt; as we have seen, the debt–income ratio for personal sector bank advances displayed a very marked rise in this period (chart 6.1). As in the case of bank advances, econometric investigation of a period dominated by controls can always be suspected of failing to deliver an accurate verdict, but there appears little reason to doubt that variations in hire purchase terms had a significant short-run impact on levels of debt; but once again, the question of how this impact was transmitted to the demand for consumer durables remains to be investigated (see page 295).

Market instruments

Bank lending requests, calls for Special Deposits and variations in hire purchase terms have all been considered as instruments falling in the general category of monetary regulations. The authorities also had at their disposal the instruments of 'classical' monetary policy – the ability to buy and sell government debt – through which they are traditionally thought of as being able to influence the supply of money and the maturity composition and sectoral holdings of the national debt, or to control decisively the general level and structure of interest rates. It is axiomatic that they are unable to follow independent policies in these respects – to determine *both*, say, a certain growth rate for the money supply *and* any level of interest rates they choose.

As indicated in chapter 5, in the 1960s the monetary authorities pursued distinct policies in the short and longer ends of the market in government debt. In the former they appear to have been overwhelmingly concerned with steering interest rates so as to stabilise the spot exchange rate with the assistance of other devices such as intervention in the forward market. At the long end they followed a policy designed, as they saw it, to maximise sales of debt in the long run and so achieve their objective of funding. However, their view of the bond market led them to pursue a policy of smoothing out the fluctuations around the trend of bond prices ('leaning against the wind') which in effect removed their ability to control the money supply in the short run except through bank lending requests. It was in modifying this policy in the bond market (or rather, in accelerating the previous gradual shift in policy) that 'Competition and credit control' was particularly significant, for the authorities continued, as before, to display a desire to control interest rates at the short end of the market quite firmly, although in a context which had changed markedly.

The significance of movements in Bank Rate (and operations to make it effective) is a well-worn theme in British monetary history. Throughout the period covered by this book, changes in Bank Rate (after October 1972, minimum lending rate) were almost invariably rationalised by reference to the external situation,[1] the desire to exploit the confidence effects of adjustments meaning that increases typically occurred in steps of one or two percentage points (sometimes accompanied by a 'package deal' of other measures) and decreases were usually by half a point (table 6.5). Estimates of reaction functions (pages 279–80 below) confirm that Bank Rate is sensitive to external considerations and suggest that it will eventually rise by something approaching half a point in response to a loss of £100 million in the published reserves.[2]

---

[1] On the basis of the various statements made in the *Bank of England Quarterly Bulletin* and other official sources, the only possible exceptions seem to be the increases from 4 to 5 per cent on 27 February 1964 and from 7 to 8 per cent on 27 February 1969, when domestic objectives were given pride of place. Decreases in Bank Rate were regarded as almost always desirable domestically whenever external considerations permitted.

[2] See D. Fisher, 'The instruments of monetary policy and the generalised trade-off function for Britain, 1955–1969', *Manchester School of Economic and Social Studies*, vol. 38, September 1970; C. A. Pissarides, 'A model of British macroeconomic policy, 1955–1969', *Manchester School of Economic and Social Studies*, vol. 40, September 1972. R. T. Coghlan, 'Bank competition and bank size', *Manchester School of Economic and Social Studies*, vol. 43, June 1975, relates Bank Rate to changes in net reserves, defined as published reserves minus official short-term and medium-term borrowing, and finds that it would require a loss of something like £500 million in reserves so defined to provoke a half point adjustment in Bank Rate. The 'window-dressing' of published reserves was quite substantial in this period (see table 6.7 on page 280 below).

Table 6.5. *Changes in Bank Rate,ᵃ 1960–72*

No. of changes

	Total	In 'package deals'
Increased by:		
½%	2	—
1%	6	3
1½%	1	1
2%	2	1
Decreased by:		
½%	15	—
1%	3	—
1½%	—	—
2%	—	—
All changes	29	5

SOURCE: *Bank of England Quarterly Bulletin* (various issues).

ᵃ Minimum lending rate from October 1972.

As well as improving confidence, increases in Bank Rate were intended to provide or restore an incentive to capital inflows. However, studies of the general effect of interest-rate changes on capital flows provide only indirect evidence on this aspect, because these studies use local authority rates as the representative short rate in the United Kingdom. Chart 6.4, however, shows a broad sympathy of movement between Bank Rate and local authority rates, although it is difficult to be specific about the direction of causation. But, up to the time of 'Competition and credit control', a change in Bank Rate did have immediate effects upon a number of important administered rates (especially those of the London clearing banks) and these, together with reinforcing operations in the money markets, could be expected to lead through arbitrage to sympathetic movements in yields on local authority paper. Even so, this control was indirect and palpably less precise than that of the Treasury bill market, which became in this period a largely captive market of overseas monetary authorities and domestic institutions required to hold such paper.

Subject to these caveats, the estimates provided by Hodjera and, more recently, Hutton can be thought of as indicating an order of magnitude for the short-term capital inflow consequent upon a change in the relevant interest differential.[1] A key result of

[1] See Z. Hodjera, 'Short-term capital movements of the United Kingdom, 1963–1967', *Journal of Political Economy*, vol. 79, July–Aug. 1971, pp. 739–75; J. P. Hutton, 'A model of short-term capital movements, the foreign exchange market and official intervention in the

Chart 6.4. *Bank Rate and the local authority three-month rate,[a] 1963–73*

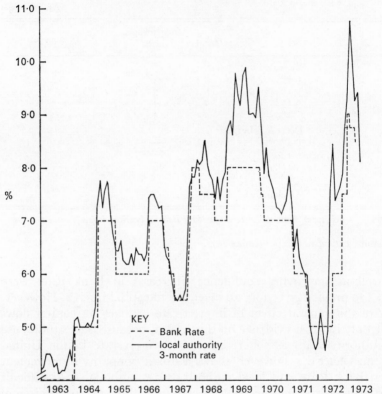

SOURCES: Bank of England, *Statistical Abstract*, no. 1; *Bank of England Quarterly Bulletin*.

[a] Taken at the last Friday in each month.

Hodjera's study is provided in the equation (estimated quarterly for 1963–7):

$$SC_t = 109 \cdot 6\Delta UD_{t-1} - 0 \cdot 80\Delta BT_t + 1 \cdot 6\Delta \overline{BT}_{t-4/3} - 140 \cdot 2D$$

where SC is short-term capital inflow defined to include the balancing item, UD the uncovered differential between the 90-day local authority rate and the Eurodollar rate, BT the visible balance

UK 1963–1971' (mimeo.), 1974. A revised version of this paper giving estimates for 1963–70 was subsequently published in *Review of Economic Studies*, vol. 44, February 1977. A further study (OECD, *Capital Movements in the OECD Area: an econometric analysis* by W. H. Branson and R. D. Hill, Paris, 1971) of the combined capital account in the United Kingdom failed to produce plausible interest-rate effects and has been ignored in what follows. The determinants of direct investment have been studied in B. D. Boatwright and G. A. Renton, 'An analysis of United Kingdom inflows and outflows of direct foreign investment', *Review of Economics and Statistics*, vol. 57, November 1975.

of trade, $BT_{t-4/3}$ the lagged two-quarter moving average of the balance $= \frac{1}{3}(2BT_{t-1}+BT_{t-2})$, and D a dummy variable for speculation based on the relationship of the forward rate to the lower limit of the permitted swing in the value of the spot rate. The lagged visible balance is interpreted as a speculative variable, with a (therefore) appropriate positive sign, the negative sign on the current value of the visible balance being taken to indicate trade financing. Further analysis by Hodjera showed that, when capital inflows are related to the covered differential, a 1 per cent rise in the latter encourages an inflow of some £475 million (with a one-quarter lag); this is, however, clearly not an alternative estimate of the effect of a rise in the United Kingdom rate of interest, since the cost of cover can be expected to increase as a result of any induced inflow. This mechanism is made explicit in Hutton's treatment, where again a key result is that a rise of 1 per cent in the uncovered differential will lead to an inflow of just over £90 million – the same order of magnitude as the £110 million suggested by Hodjera.[1] The confidence effect of a Bank Rate increase is omitted from these estimates, and it is impossible to impute anything to such an effect *per se*, particularly when reactions can be perverse.[2]

Whilst the close interest of the authorities in controlling short rates primarily for external reasons remained an unvarying theme, policy in the longer end of the market underwent significant changes. The emphasis on damping fluctuations in the price of bonds (whilst not resisting their 'trend') gave way after the mid-1960s to a series of modifications culminating in 'Competition and credit control' (see pages 239–45 above). This change in priorities is reflected in chart 6.5, which shows that an index of the variability of bond prices effectively doubled in value between the mid-1960s and the early 1970s.

[1] Hutton models the determination of short-term capital flows (1963–71) by considering separately the behaviour of arbitrageurs (who obtain forward cover) and of spot speculators (who do not). An amalgamated equation provides:

$$SC_t = 5{\cdot}515\Delta UD_t - 2{\cdot}673\Delta C_t + 1{\cdot}867G + 1{\cdot}075BT_{t-1}$$

where, of the new variables, C_t is the cost of forward cover and G a dummy variable covering specific speculative crises. A second equation determines the forward rate as:

$$F_t = 0{\cdot}682\,(S-UD) + 0{\cdot}313\,(S-100) + 0{\cdot}055BT_{t-1} + 0{\cdot}120BT_{t-2} - 0{\cdot}846D_1 + 0{\cdot}273D_2$$

where F is the forward rate, S the spot rate, and D_1 and D_2 are speculative dummies. When the effect on the forward rate of an increase in UD is allowed for in the second equation and the resultant effect on the cost of cover accounted for in the first, the net result for an increase in the uncovered differential of 1 per cent is an inflow of capital in the same quarter of $\frac{1}{4}(5{\cdot}515 - 2{\cdot}673 \times 0{\cdot}682) = $ £92·3 million. (In the revised 1977 version Hutton obtains a slightly higher estimate of £126·8 million.)

[2] Perhaps the most notorious example of such a perverse effect occurred after the rise in Bank Rate from 5 to 7 per cent on 23 November 1964, which took place, unusually on a Monday. Sales of sterling on the succeeding days were reported to be even higher than those that had taken place before the increase.

Chart 6.5. *Bond prices and sales of government debt*

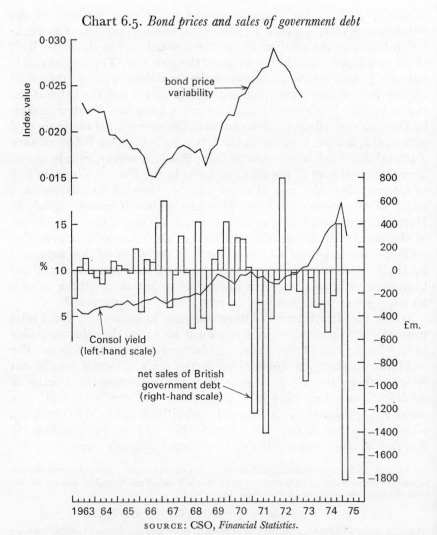

SOURCE: CSO, *Financial Statistics.*

Note: Bond price variability measured by the standard error of a 36-month moving average of logarithmic first differences in the Consol rate, end-quarter values.

Both the policy of 'leaning against the wind' and the withdrawal from it were based upon the authorities' (changing) beliefs about the stability of the bond market. It is difficult to confirm or refute these beliefs. The inference that open-market operations feeding speculative demand for gilt-edged stocks would lead to a positive correlation between sales of debt and increases in bond prices seemed to be borne out for earlier periods by graphical evidence produced in the *Radcliffe Report* and confirmed by a regression result quoted by Goodhart.[1] This correlation is less obvious for the period with which we are concerned (see chart 6.5) and an attempt to replicate Goodhart's equation with data for this period failed. Most probably this should be attributed to the fact that the available data are quarterly, so that the relevant day-to-day movements may be obscured; similarly, the movement of Consol prices may be a poor indicator of changes in the complex of gilt-edged prices. Norton has suggested that the speculative behaviour observed by the authorities was the mirror-image of their own counter-speculative operations, which, being known to the market, caused a fall in bond prices to be taken as the herald of a continuing decline as the authorities sought to ease the rate of fall, and consequently as the signal for immediate speculative sales.[2] Although this suggestion was not in fact rigorously confirmed by Norton's results, it seems to have been seriously entertained by the authorities as good cause for modifying their strategy.[3]

By attempting to steady the price of government securities, the authorities removed the possibility of using their operations to effect quantity adjustments designed, say, to influence the growth rate of the money supply. The cash ratio became otiose as a fulcrum of open-market operations, since the authorities had to be prepared to defend the level of short rates at any time. This point was clearly taken by the Radcliffe Committee, which was, however, associated with the view that the liquid asset ratio could be substituted for the cash ratio as such a fulcrum: '...the effective base of bank credit has become the liquid assets (based on the availability of Treasury Bills) instead of the supply of cash'.[4] This would have been true if the authorities could have controlled the supply of assets which might be substituted for Treasury bills to satisfy the liquid asset ratio, and if they had been prepared to accept the implications for the prices of longer bonds of any move designed to squeeze the banks' reserve of liquid assets,[5] but in the event neither of these conditions was met. A number of studies have shown

---

[1] Treasury, *Radcliffe Report*, p. 204; C. A. E. Goodhart, 'Monetary policy in the United Kingdom' in K. Holbik (ed.), *Monetary Policy in Twelve Industrial Countries*, Boston (Mass.), Federal Reserve Bank of Boston, 1973, where the regression is of bond sales on the change in Consol yield, the latter having a significant negative sign.

[2] Norton, 'Debt management and monetary policy in the United Kingdom'.

[3] At least, this is a possible interpretation of the Chief Cashier's remarks published in 'Competition and credit control'. Norton's results suggest that the public's demand for government bonds contains a speculative element; they also indicate that the authorities responded to increased demand for stock by gradually letting the price rise. The idea that the former behaviour depends on the latter is, however, an embellishment of the results not necessary to their interpretation.   [4] Treasury, *Radcliffe Report*, para. 376.

[5] The Radcliffe Committee accepted the latter point (ibid. para. 378), although the significance of controlling the Treasury bill issue seems to have been overstressed at the expense of ignoring the problem posed by the existence of substitutable liquid assets.

that the decline in the supply of Treasury bills relative to the banks' needs could be, and was, countered by substituting alternative liquid assets eligible for inclusion – commercial bills, call money placed outside the discount market, and so on – and also by increasing the proportion of discount market call money secured on assets other than Treasury bills.[1] In any case, even had the assets eligible as liquid reserves been such that their supply was clearly in the hands of the authorities, a policy of varying this stock with a view to influencing the supply of money would not have been consistent with the defence of bond prices in the short run at something close to their existing levels. Pressure on the banks' technical liquidity, granted their excess holding of government bonds, would have evoked sales of bonds, decreases in bond prices and intervention by the authorities to temper the fall by purchasing bonds, thus undoing the effect of the liquidity squeeze. This explains why Special Deposits could not be expected to function as a variable reserve requirement, and perhaps also why the authorities did not bother (before 'Competition and credit control', that is) to redefine eligible liquid assets so as to preclude the substitution of alternative assets for Treasury bills. The stock of money in this period was not the immediate object of the monetary authorities' operations; when and to the extent that it became so, it is not surprising to find that policies in the bond market changed.[2]

Thus, a textbook caricature of the 1960s system would be that the authorities assured a horizontal 'LM' schedule (at a shifting interest rate 'peg')[3] – a policy which can be rationalised as consistent with the belief that the demand for money was unstable.[4] It is tempting, at this level of abstraction, to bring together the rising tide of research findings

---

[1] See, for example, R. L. Crouch, 'A re-examination of open-market equations', *Oxford Economic Papers*, vol. 15 (new series), July 1963, and 'The inadequacy of "new orthodox" methods of monetary control', *Economic Journal*, vol. 74, December 1964; also, D. J. Coppock and N. J. Gibson, 'The volume of deposits and the cash and liquid assets ratios', *Manchester School of Economic and Social Studies*, vol. 31, September 1963; W. T. Newlyn, 'The supply of money and its control', *Economic Journal*, vol. 74, June 1964. At the beginning of the 1960s Treasury bills were the largest single component of bank liquid assets – as compared with notes, coins and Bank of England balances, money at call, commercial bills and 'other' bills – but by 1970 they were the smallest of these components.

[2] See chapter 5 above, pages 246–8.

[3] Following the analysis originally due to J. R. Hicks ('Mr. Keynes and the "classics": a suggested interpretation', *Econometrica*, vol. 5, April 1937) and subsequently embodied in most macroeconomic texts, the LM schedule is taken as tracing out combinations of the interest rate and income at which money demand and supply are equal. A horizontal LM schedule is immediately implied by an infinitely interest-elastic *demand* for money, or (as here) by an infinitely elastic *supply* schedule. Cf. B. Griffiths, 'Resource efficiency, monetary policy and the reform of the UK banking system', *Journal of Money, Credit and Banking*, vol. 5, February 1973 (pt 1).

[4] Cf. W. Poole, 'Optimal choice of monetary policy instruments in a simple stochastic macro model', *Quarterly Journal of Economics*, vol. 84, May 1970.

that the demand for money was stable, and the theoretical proposition that in the face of such a stable demand policies should 'aim at' the money supply rather than at interest rates – that is, that the horizontal 'LM' schedule should be abandoned. Such a conjunction provides an appealing analytical rationale for 'Competition and credit control' – and one with an awkward twist in its tail in the light of the re-emergent doubts about the stability of the demand for money in the last few years. But, whilst these caricatures serve to highlight the role of changing beliefs about the demand for money and the consequent irony of experience since 'Competition and credit control', it should be emphasised that the positions described are no more than caricatures. In particular, before 1971 the authorities did not, even in their most rigid phase, aim to peg bond prices and interest rates, only to reduce their fluctuations; nor, since 1971, did they abandon their predilection for selling on a rising market and, more certainly still, did not come to regard fluctuations in bond prices with complete indifference.[1]

Fiscal and monetary policy

Inhibitions about using interest rates as an aid to funding the national debt implied also that additions to the debt arising from a positive public sector borrowing requirement were in general closely associated with an expansion of the money supply; because the non-bank public's demand for such debt rose only to the extent dictated by long-term factors – essentially increasing wealth (including some wealth effects associated with the deficit itself) – the residual supply, to the extent it was not sold overseas, had to find its way into the portfolios of the banks. Thus, to this extent, fiscal policy, as measured by the public sector deficit, and monetary policy, as measured by the change in the stock of money, tended to be highly correlated. At the same time, a monetary policy of this character tended to imply a (short-run) 'high multiplier' fiscal policy, and helped to validate calculations of the effect of tax changes which ostensibly take no account of the means of financing the deficit.[2] Also at the same time, this strong connection between monetary and fiscal policy inevitably frustrated the attempt to measure separately the contributions of fiscal and monetary policy to changes in the level of income.

However, whilst these propositions seem to hold true in a rough and ready way of the 1960s, they do not hold true of experience in more recent years. Table 6.6 shows that the public sector borrowing require-

---

[1] For an account of the authorities' move in the direction of controlling the 'monetary aggregates' and their actions in the bond market, see pages 245-6.

[2] Such calculations have frequently appeared in, for example, the *National Institute Economic Review*. In the language of the 'IS–LM' macro-model, the horizontal 'LM' curve validates the assumption of an unconstrained multiplier process.

Table 6.6. *The fiscal deficit and monetary expansion, 1963–74*

£ million

	Public sector financial deficit[a]	Public sector borrowing requirement	External financing	Domestic borrowing requirement[b]	Increase in money supply (M₃)
1963	833	832	40	729	766
64	1004	989	571	418	653
65	851	1205	22	1183	938
66	854	961	413	548	479
67	1472	1863	503	1360	1345
68	1033	1279	1111	168	1152
69	−429	−466	−593	127	503
1970	−740	−17	−1353	1336	1586
71	421	1373	−2670	4043	2366
72	1612	2047	1564	483	5299
73	2585	4168	−121	4289	7232
74	4857	6336	1462	4874	4221

SOURCES: CSO, *National Income and Expenditure* and *Financial Statistics*.
[a] Net acquisition of financial assets with the sign reversed.
[b] Public sector borrowing requirement minus external financing.

ment (which represents the financing problem) has become less closely identified with the public sector deficit, and the domestic borrowing requirement (after allowing for external financing) less closely identified with the total public sector borrowing requirement;[1] finally, the domestic borrowing requirement has become less closely identified with changes in the money supply. In consequence, 'Kaldor's rule' of the association of changes in the money supply and the public sector borrowing requirement has ceased to hold.[2]

Even under conditions in which the monetary authorities have gained substantial freedom to use interest rates actively, fiscal and monetary policy are, of course, quite likely to be closely connected in practice. The principle which might separate one from the other – fiscal policy being identified with alterations in public sector indebtedness, monetary policy with the management of the distribution (by sector and by maturity)[3] of the *stock* of debt (including its increment) –

[1] The difference between the public sector deficit and the borrowing requirement is approximately the net amount of transactions in existing assets in which the public sector is involved.

[2] N. Kaldor, 'The new monetarism', *Lloyds Bank Review*, no. 97, July 1970, maintained, on the basis of simple correlation analysis, that the money supply increased almost pound for pound with the public sector borrowing requirement.

[3] Account needs to be taken here of government debt which may change its effective maturity in the hands of the public (for example, when acquired by banks). Also 'management' needs to be defined to include control of the secondary effects of debt management, for example when controls over bank advances frustrate the expansion to which the banks' acquisition of government debt would otherwise give rise.

does not in itself permit the presumption that the two will be independent in practice. It is fairly clear, for example, that very expansive fiscal policies (as in 1972/3) tend to lead to correspondingly expansive monetary policies, whilst policies for containing the growth of the money supply are usually associated with a tighter rein on the borrowing requirement.

Reaction functions

We have reviewed above evidence on how far certain monetary instruments are effective in influencing intermediate variables. The theoretical framework of the instruments–objectives view of economic policy readily allows the complementary study of the authorities' reaction functions. Such studies seek to reveal how far changes in instruments are prompted by deviations from their preferred values of the variables measuring the authorities' ultimate 'goals'.

Table 6.7 draws upon three published studies; it indicates for the three instruments mentioned, and for Bank Rate, a reasonably systematic relationship with the 'goal' variables distinguished. Increases in the price level and decreases in foreign exchange reserves and unemployment are associated with deflationary changes (increases) in the instrument variables, the greatest doubt about the significance of the relationships concerning that between Special Deposits and reserves, whilst the response of lending requests to changes in the price level appears insignificant when other objectives are considered.

It is tempting to try to wring more out of these estimates and in some of the studies cited an attempt is made to do so, but at this stage of sophistication it is far from clear that much can be gained from such attempts. The estimates allow at best for only a limited range of substitution between policy instruments;[1] they are also poor material from which to draw conclusions about the destabilising effect of policy[2] and do not allow us to deduce the trade-off between policy goals implied by the authorities' actions, unless we have convincing estimates of their 'model' of the effect of instruments on goals. The interpretation of the presence of the lagged dependent variable on the right hand side of the equation is open to question, as are also the underlying assumption that the authorities minimise a quadratic disutility function[3] and the disregard of their use of forecasting apparently implied by the presence of current values

---

[1] See A. R. Nobay, 'A model of the United Kingdom monetary authorities' behaviour 1959–1969' in H. G. Johnson and A. R. Nobay (eds.), *Issues in Monetary Economics*, London, Oxford University Press, 1974, for effective criticism on this point.

[2] For a detailed argument to this effect see Worswick, 'Fiscal policy and stabilization in Britain'.

[3] For an alternative model see P. Mosley, 'Towards a "satisficing" theory of economic policy', *Economic Journal*, vol. 86, March 1976, pp. 59–72.

Table 6.7. *Reaction function estimates^a by Fisher, Pissarides and Coghlan*

	Regression coefficients for:				
	Reserves^b	Unemployment rate	Price level^c	Lagged dependent variable	R^2
Fisher (1955–68)					
Bank Rate	−0·68	−0·76	0·10	0·45	0·734
	(2·72)	(2·85)	(2·00)		
Special Deposits	13·49	−28·59	0·99	0·91	0·954
	(1·13)	(2·96)	(2·30)		
Hire purchase deposit^d	−4·17	−5·05	0·19	0·70	0·803
	(1·31)	(2·02)	(1·97)		
Pissarides (1955–68)					
Bank Rate	−0·20^e	−0·63	0·78	0·57	0·752
	(2·30)	(3·12)	(3·70)		
Tax rate^f	−0·05^e	−0·44	2·62	0·56	0·808
	(1·22)	(3·47)	(3·98)		
Hire purchase deposit^d	−0·02	−6·32	26·04	0·66	0·689
	(1·84)	(2·56)	(2·57)		
Coghlan (1962–70)					
Bank Rate	−0·07^e	−0·77	0·04	0·15	0·863
	(4·40)	(2·91)	(2·80)		
Special Deposits	—	−0·24	0·04	0·62	0·914
		(1·50)	(4·99)		
Bank lending requests^g	−0·03^e	−0·47	0·01	0·59	0·841
	(3·47)	(2·98)	(1·03)		

SOURCES: Fisher, 'The instruments of monetary policy'; Pissarides, 'A model of British macroeconomic policy'; Coghlan, 'Bank competition and bank size'.

^{a} t-statistics shown in brackets, but suppressed for the lagged dependent variable, where not given by Fisher. Constant terms also suppressed as not given by Fisher.

^{b} Official gold and foreign exchange reserves (Fisher and Pissarides); net reserves, i.e. minus official short-term and medium-term borrowing (Coghlan).

^{c} Consumer price index (Pissarides); retail price index (Coghlan); unspecified (Fisher).

^{d} Minimum percentage down-payment on cars. ^{e} Coefficients multiplied by 10^2.

^{f} Discretionary change in tax yield as a percentage of GDP.

^{g} Dummy variable scored 0 = no request, 1 = mild request, 2 = severe request.

only of the goal variables.[1] Whilst these studies open a promising avenue for further research, their present value in illuminating the use of monetary policy seems accordingly rather limited.

Indicators

Within the spirit of the instruments–objectives model, an intermediate variable can be justified as a measure of economic policy. Popular measures of this kind in the fiscal field include the initial fiscal stimulus

[1] However, this *might* be regarded as 'allowed for' (in a naive fashion) by the presence of the lagged dependent variable.

and the full-employment budget deficit. It can be argued that, although such indicators are inferior in principle to comprehensive simulation results, they command attention where such results are not available and it is desired to have a measure of policy, necessarily approximate. The suggestion that an intermediate variable be chosen for this role stems from the problem that the 'actions' of the authorities – in the case of the monetary authorities, sales and purchases of bonds, calls for and releases of Special Deposits, imposition and cancellation of lending requests, and the like – lack in themselves a common scale upon which they can be aggregated. An intermediate variable is expected to provide just such a common scaling; it should also register and reflect the actions of the monetary authorities without being overwhelmingly determined by forces exogenous to those actions. A further requirement is, however, that changes in the variable concerned should, *ceteris paribus*, have an influence over the goal variables of the system, and this requires some presumption that it has a stable relationship with its determinand. In short, the selection of a policy indicator requires some presumption about the transmission mechanism of monetary policy.

How do these considerations work out in the choice of a policy indicator of monetary action?[1] Is there an obvious analogue with the measures used in the analysis of fiscal policy?

Perhaps the least of the difficulties involved in selecting an indicator is the multiplicity of the monetary authorities' goals. The same consideration applies, after all, to fiscal policy indicators and it can be finessed in the same way by explicitly selecting aggregate demand as the policy goal of interest, setting other goals aside. Using this simplification, it becomes clear that a source of contention will be different views of the transmission mechanism. We present our own view of that mechanism in the following section; at this stage the main point to be noted is that we give some emphasis to rationing and expectational effects in the operation of monetary policy, and to that extent suggest that there are discontinuities and threshold effects. This is in contrast with, or at least an important modification of, the customary 'textbook' view, as exemplified in the use of the 'IS–LM' framework of analysis. However, it is worth enquiring what are the requirements of such a framework in the choice of an indicator.

In a stochastic version of such a framework,[2] variations in the money supply are a good indicator of policy and superior to interest rates to the extent that the demand for money is stable, whilst to the extent

---

[1] For further discussion of these issues the reader may consult, *inter alia*, M.J. Artis, 'Monetary policy in the 1970s in the light of recent developments' in Johnson and Nobay (eds.), *Issues in Monetary Economics*; D. Fisher, 'Targets and indicators of British monetary policy', *The Bankers' Magazine*, vol. 216, August 1973, pp. 97–116.

[2] Poole, 'Optimal choice of monetary policy instruments'.

Chart 6.6. *Indicators of monetary policy, 1963–73*

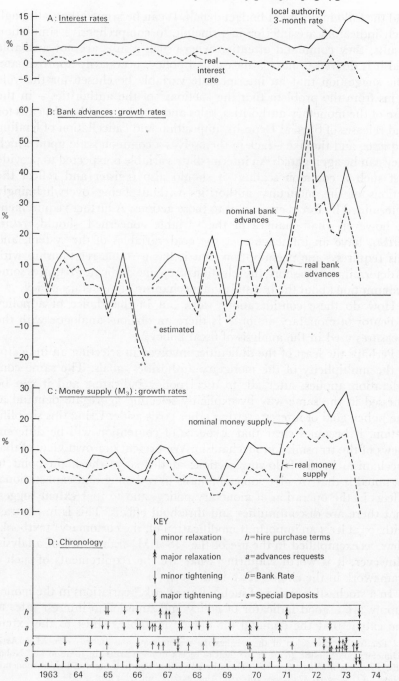

SOURCES: Bank of England, *Statistical Abstract*, no. 1; CSO *Economic Trends* (monthly) and *Financial Statistics*.

that the demand for money is unstable the reverse conclusion holds. This seems plausible; it is, however, arguable by appeal to modern monetarist analysis that, since in an open economy it is domestic credit rather than the supply of money over which the monetary authorities ultimately have control, the former should be the indicator. This proposition is, however, only applicable to the long run; besides assuming a stable demand for money, it also assumes a degree of capital market integration and stability of the real economy that makes it uncertain at best in the short run.

It may, therefore, seem reasonable to say that, to the extent to which the demand for money is stable, the growth rate of the money supply is a reasonable proxy indicator of monetary policy. But this assumes that any actions which do not affect the money supply can be neglected and so cuts across the line of argument that stresses the significance of credit flows (particularly bank advances) in an imperfect capital market. The same point applies, *mutatis mutandis*, to interest rates and in both cases inflation is an additional complication. Both the monetary growth rate and interest rates should allow for inflation (strictly, expected inflation) when used as indicators and there is no simple way of doing this. It is sometimes suggested that inflation improves the claims of the former as opposed to the latter, but this is not as obvious as it sounds. Certainly the same nominal rate of interest differs in significance with different levels of on-going ('expected') inflation, but the same is true of the monetary growth rate. The consequences for *real* demand of a monetary growth of 20 per cent differ according to whether inflation is occurring at zero or at 20 (or any other) per cent.[1]

Enough has perhaps been said to show that there is no very clear presumption in favour of any particular indicator; an eclectic viewpoint therefore seems most appropriate. This conclusion is reflected in the set of graphs shown in chart 6.6, the third panel of which shows the rates of growth of M_3 and the 'real' money supply, the second panel growth in bank advances and the top panel the level of interest rates. At the bottom, the chronology of monetary policy 'actions', given a partial subjective scoring, is also shown. The adjustments made to each series are indicated in the footnotes. Finally, an indicator of financial

---

Chart 6.6 (*cont.*)

Notes: (i) 'Real' rate of interest calculated as $100\ (R_t - \dot{P}_t)/(100 + \dot{P}_t)$ where R_t is local authority three-month rate and $\dot{P}_t$ is the first central difference of the rate of change in prices measured by the deflator of total final expenditure.

(ii) Bank advances to 1966 IV, quarterly totals; no distinction between residents and non-residents, or between currencies available. From 1967 I, quarterly advances to United Kingdom residents.

[1] A different presumption in favour of the money supply arises, of course, from the assumption that the real economy is stable over not too long a run, so that monetary policy, and consequently a monetary indicator, is focused on the control of the price level or its rate of increase. From this viewpoint is seems clear that the monetary growth rate is preferable to nominal interest rates.

stringency was taken from the regular CBI survey, in which firms are asked to indicate the most important factor or factors limiting their output on a check list of seven possibilities (including a residual category). The proportion of respondent firms indicating 'credit or finance' as a constraint is plotted in chart 6.7 against the real money supply to see whether the two series show any sympathy, and there is, it would seem, a loose degree of sympathy, at any rate in the case of the larger movements.[1]

Whilst the quarter-to-quarter concurrence of the various possible measures is not very close, there is some uniformity in the story they tell about the major movements: in particular, it seems that monetary policy was relatively stringent in 1966, and again in 1969 and 1974/5, and

Chart 6.7. *The growth rate of the 'real' money supply and the CBI credit stringency factor, 1963–74*

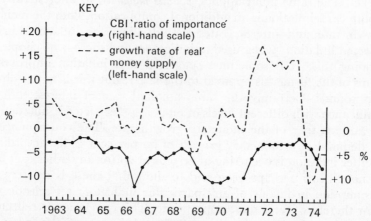

SOURCES: *Bank of England Quarterly Bulletin* (various issues); CSO, *Economic Trends*; CBI, *Industrial Trends Survey* (4-monthly).

Note: CBI Survey 3-monthly from 1972.

particularly 'easy' in 1967, the latter part of 1971, and in 1972 and 1973. Much the same could be inferred from a chronology of monetary policy actions. It does not seem possible to advance much upon this position; the fiscal policy indicators do not have any very precise analogue in monetary policy and, although the strength of this dichotomy may be partly misleading (in as much as it attributes more cer-

---

[1] This must be seen, however, in the context of the source of data. Since firms responding to the questionnaire are asked to tick the *most important factor or factors* limiting output, cyclical behaviour in the computed 'ratio of importance' of 'credit or finance' could be induced by the pressure of a cycle in other factors, even where there has been no cycle in monetary conditions.

tainty to the effect of fiscal actions than is probably warranted), it reflects in large part our relatively sketchy understanding of the effects of monetary actions, or, to put it in a more flattering way, the complexity of the transmission mechanism of monetary policy. Two points are, perhaps, most crucial: first, the question of the stability of the demand for money and, second, the significance of capital market imperfections. The interaction of these and other considerations is considered more extensively below.

THE TRANSMISSION MECHANISM

The transmission mechanism of monetary policy consists in the linkages between changes in the instruments of monetary policy (or, going forward one stage, the intermediate variables affected by these instruments) and the goal variables of the system. An account of this mechanism is thus a description of the process whereby changes in monetary variables affect the economy. Clearly an understanding of this process is important in appreciating the potential for monetary policy of the design of policy in terms of the instruments used and the size of adjustments made; also, as suggested above, in the selection of a monetary indicator or proximate target of policy. Accordingly, differences of opinion about the transmission mechanism and changes in the balance of these opinions over time can be seen as underlying dissension over the effectiveness of policy and contributing towards change in policy design – of which 'Competition and credit control' is an example in our period. In principle, then, some of the differences of opinion about monetary policy should be resolved as firm knowledge of the transmission mechanism is obtained by empirical study. To that extent, the disparity of prevailing views attests to the still very incomplete knowledge of the mechanism that we possess, with considerable room left for speculative views and hunches, in some apparent contrast to fiscal policy, where the effects are thought to be known with a much higher degree of certainty.

In default of detailed accounts of the mechanism, some attention has been paid in recent years to the study of so-called 'reduced form' relationships, in which, with details suppressed, attention is focused upon the strength and nature of the relationship between an indicator variable, usually the money supply, and a goal variable, typically GDP or the price level. Studies of this kind have commonly, if not exclusively, been associated with examining propositions due to the monetarist school and have very often taken the form of replicating with British data hypotheses first tested on American data. Certain caveats are necessary in interpreting this kind of evidence. First, since such studies explicitly bypass the exploration of the transmission mechanism, they are open to the charge that all they provide in place of such an exploration is a 'black box'. This would be less troublesome if the reduced form under study could be shown to be a valid reduced form, rather than a casual single equation; unless this is the case there remains an unresolved technical difficulty in interpreting the coefficients obtained, and an ambiguity about what structural system the reduced form results are supposed to be consistent with. Secondly, many of the studies rely implicitly upon time-lags to free the results from the attribution of 'reverse causality', but precedence in time is a treacherous indicator of causality, however attractive superficially.[1]

It so happens, however, that as far as British studies are concerned these cautions are somewhat otiose. Single equation estimates of the 'money multiplier' for the United Kingdom seem to destroy the theory that 'money is all that matters', if indeed the sign and size of the coefficient obtained carry any unambiguous implication.[2] A test on British data by Artis and Nobay was notable chiefly for the lack of statistical significance achieved,[3] not dissimilar results being obtained subsequently by Goodhart and Crockett.[4] Evidence based more explicitly on timing is similarly weak in suggesting any significant relationship between the money supply and either income or prices.[5] Finally, the assertion that the timing profile of the effects of a change in the money stock involves first and soon a change in real output and then (after a lag of 18–20 months) an effect upon the price level, which has become a standard prediction of the monetarist school,[6] has at best a somewhat ambiguous validity. Chart 6.8 shows a scatter diagram of inflation rates and money supply growth rates, with the latter lagged

[1] The classic demonstration of the pitfalls involved in using timing as evidence of causality is given in J. Tobin, 'Money and income: post hoc ergo propter hoc?', *Quarterly Journal of Economics*, vol. 84, May 1970, pp. 301–17.

[2] The money multiplier in question here may be identified with the value of the coefficient b in an equation of the general form:

$$\Delta Y_t = a + b\Sigma_{i=0}^n (w_i \Delta M_{t-i}) + c\Sigma_{i=0}^n (x_i \Delta Z_{t-i})$$

where $\Sigma w_i = \Sigma x_i = 1$, Δ indicates a first difference and Y, M and Z stand for GDP (nominal), money, and other factors (e.g. fiscal policy), respectively. Quite often Z is omitted from equations of this type.

[3] M. J. Artis and A. R. Nobay, 'Two aspects of the monetary debate', *National Institute Economic Review*, no. 49, August 1969, which was modelled on an American study, L. C. Anderson and J. L. Jordan, 'Monetary and fiscal actions: a test of their relative importance in economic stabilization', *Federal Reserve Bank of St. Louis Review*, vol. 50, November 1968.

[4] C. A. E. Goodhart and A. D. Crockett, 'The importance of money', *Bank of England Quarterly Bulletin*, vol. 10, June 1970, where it was found, however, that money multiplier relationships could be strengthened by substituting industrial production (scaled by the wholesale price index) for GDP.

[5] See A. D. Crockett, 'Timing relationships between movements of monetary and national income variables', *Bank of England Quarterly Bulletin*, vol. 10, December 1970.

[6] For example, the contributions by Laidler and by Parkin (see footnote to page 258).

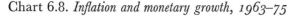

Chart 6.8. *Inflation and monetary growth, 1963–75*

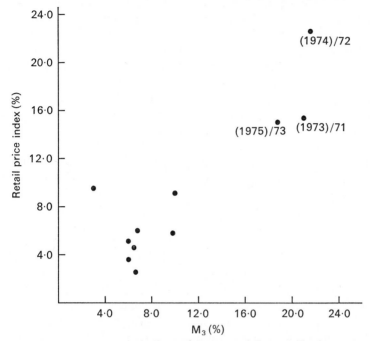

SOURCE: CSO, *Financial Statistics* and *Economic Trends*.

Note: End-year rate scentred on fourth quarter, as $100(Q2 - Q2_{-1})/Q4_{-1}$, where Q denotes the quarterly value and the subscript a lag of one year. The retail price index is plotted two years ahead of M_3, for example, RPI for 1974 with M_3 for 1972.

two years on the former. As is evident, confirmation of this two-year lag by a line of best fit would turn upon treating the more recent and the earlier observations as derived from the same sample; taken by themselves the earlier observations do not support such an association.[1] It therefore remains an open question, on statistical grounds alone, whether such a relationship has a solid foundation. The assertion that a lag of this length can be supported by reference to structural estimates of the demand for money and the relationship between inflation, excess demand and expectations has recently been examined by Miller.[2]

The British evidence does not, therefore, seem to confirm 'reduced form' relationships between 'money' and demand or prices; although

[1] Elsewhere, of course, the *variability* of the lag has been emphasised. For a sympathetic and subtle account see J. S. Flemming, *Inflation*, London, Oxford University Press, 1976.

[2] M. H. Miller, 'Money, output and inflation: a critique of some recent monetarist developments in the UK', *Manchester School of Economic and Social Studies* (forthcoming).

we have already noted that evidence of this kind, even if confirmed, would be far from conclusive, it appears that British evidence is out of line with that derived from American data. This suggests at least two possibilities: that British evidence should be treated as an instance of the non-universality of the monetarist association and to that extent a counter-example to the doctrine, or that there are features of the British economy which make these tests inapplicable and their results correspondingly irrelevant. An argument of the latter kind is that, for most of the period with which we are concerned, the money supply in the United Kingdom has been demand-determined because the monetary authorities have been overwhelmingly interested in defending the level of interest rates at any point of time. A suggestion to similar effect derives from the more recent amendment of monetarist theory to apply to 'small' open economies, according to which, at least in the long run, the stock of money is endogenous to the economy. The latter argument, except to the extent it is mirrored in the first, is the less easy to accept, insofar as the monetary authorities may be assumed to be able to sterilise money flows and inhibit adjustment through the use of exchange controls. However, if the stock of money is demand-determined, then the reduced form regressions are 'incorrect', in as much as the regressor – the stock of money (or a transformation of it) – is not exogenous, so that the results of such estimation will be biased; whilst this clearly does not imply that money has no effect, it does mean that the magnitude of the effect cannot be properly estimated in this way. A test which might help to clarify matters in this respect was carried out by Williams, Goodhart and Gowland,[1] in an attempt to determine whether it could be inferred either that the money supply was demand-determined or that it was exogenous to income. Their results were, however, less than clear-cut and cannot be said to provide very strong support for either view – again in some contrast to the American evidence, which rather strongly favours the view that money is exogenous to income.[2]

However, to the extent that it is accepted that the money supply was demand-determined during the 1960s, it would seem that there should be little ambiguity in the results of single equation estimation of the demand for money – that is, technically there is no identification

[1] D. Williams, C. A. E. Goodhart and D. H. Gowland, 'Money, income and causality: the UK experience', *American Economic Review*, vol. 66, June 1976, pp. 417–23. They applied to British data the Sims–Granger test for 'causality' (see C. A. Sims, 'Money, income and causality', *American Economic Review*, vol. 62, September 1972, pp. 540–52).

[2] Williams, Goodhart and Gowland, 'Money, income and causality', found some evidence of 'causality' running from nominal incomes to money, but *also* some evidence of 'causality' running from money to prices. The Sims–Granger test leans heavily on *post hoc ergo propter hoc* principles and does not exclude simultaneous causality in either direction, as the authors point out (ibid. p. 423).

problem and so no real doubt that such estimates are indeed estimates of the demand for money function and not of the supply function or of some indeterminate mix of the two. Such estimates were made by a number of investigators,[1] and were generally felt to confirm that a stable function for demand for money did exist, that it was characterised by a significant but low interest elasticity and an income elasticity in the region of unity, and that differences between the various measures of money supply caused no technically insuperable problems.

Findings like these, to the extent they can be regarded as robust (and this is commented upon further below in the light of experience since 'Competition and credit control'), have been widely regarded as highly significant for the interpretation and formulation of monetary policy. It is true, of course, that they cut across the line of thinking about monetary policy which stresses the instability and high interest elasticity of the demand for money, views characteristically attributed to the *Radcliffe Report*; by the same token, they reinforce the case for regarding the money stock or its growth rate as a suitable indicator of (and target for) monetary policy. Finally, by suggesting the viability of a policy of controlling the money stock through interest-rate adjustments, these findings very probably accelerated the 1971 reforms and reinforced the case for moving away from the previous controls with their heavy emphasis upon bank lending ceilings.[2]

But whilst the existence of a relatively stable demand for money is of significance in these ways, it does not in itself illuminate the transmission mechanism, nor guarantee the potency of monetary policy.[3] It leaves open the questions how, and by how much, demand is influenced by monetary factors. It is these questions which continue to vex investigators and to which the answers remain somewhat untidy and unsatisfactory.

The modern theory of portfolio analysis suggests that intervention by the monetary authorities causes a rearrangement of portfolios across a wide spectrum of assets. Because the point of intervention of classical monetary policy is the government bond market, the effect will be felt in that market first. But, as Friedman has reiterated on a number of

---

[1] For example, D. E. W. Laidler and J. M. Parkin, 'The demand for money in the United Kingdom, 1956–1967: preliminary estimates', *Manchester School of Economic and Social Studies*, vol. 38, September 1970, pp. 187–208.

[2] Cf. C. A. E. Goodhart, 'Problems of monetary management: the UK experience' in A. S. Courakis (ed.), *Inflation, Depression and Economic Policy in the West: lessons from the 1970s*, Oxford, Blackwell (forthcoming).

[3] Within the framework of textbook IS–LM analysis, it can be shown that the size and stability of the money multiplier depends both upon the characteristics and fit of the money demand and supply functions, and upon the nature of the real expenditure functions (see D. E. W. Laidler, 'The influence of money on economic activity – a survey of some current problems' in G. Clayton, J. C. Gilbert and R. Sedgwick (eds.), *Monetary Theory and Monetary Policy in the 1970s*, London, Oxford University Press, 1971).

occasions, this is only a 'first round' effect,[1] which upsets the overall portfolio equilibrium and leads to further adjustments involving a wider range of assets, including real assets and paper claims to them. Eventually these adjustments may be expected to spill over from the 'capital account' to the 'current account' at the point where the rise in price of existing assets makes it profitable to buy new ones; thus, new investment will be stimulated.[2]

At the customary level of abstraction it is supposed that these adjustments take place in a perfect capital market. It seems clear, however, that in practice much of the flavour of how monetary policy works, and particularly how it worked in Britain in the 1960s, is lost if this assumption is accepted unquestioningly. The inescapable contingency of bankruptcy and the mediation of capital markets by financial institutions with lending rules and administered interest rates make alterations in the availability of internal funds and in the degree of credit rationing significant sources of stimulus or constraint, in addition to the impetus supplied by calculations of the rate of return and the cost of capital, such as dominate the conventional account of the transmission mechanism of monetary policy. In particular, there appear to be significant differences in ease of access to funds for the personal and for the corporate sectors, which are important in the *modus operandi* of monetary policy and indeed were deliberately exploited by such policy in Britain. One of the consequent dilemmas of the monetary authorities was the conflict between the short-run exploitation of capital market imperfections and the desire to improve the efficiency of those markets.

Finally, because the calculation of expected returns involves anticipating the actions of others and prognosticating the effects of current and future monetary (and other) policies, a monetary intervention can affect current demand by influencing expectations of the future. The monetary authorities cannot avoid this effect and may indeed choose to use it deliberately, as seems often to have been the case when monetary intervention has been announced in 'package deals'.

Traditional theory suggests that one should look to fixed investment

---

[1] For example, M. Friedman, 'A theoretical framework for monetary analysis', *Journal of Political Economy*, vol. 78, March–April 1970, pp. 193–238.

[2] This way of putting it is 'Keynesian' in the distinction which is drawn between adjustments to 'capital account' and to 'current account' – a dividing line which is blurred or eschewed in much monetarist analysis. Nevertheless, the accounts of the transmission process detailed by, for example, M. Friedman in several places (see his joint work with A. J. Schwartz, 'Money and business cycles', *Review of Economics and Statistics*, vol. 45, February 1963, and his paper with D. Meiselman, 'The relative stability of monetary velocity and the investment multiplier in the United States 1897–1958' in Commission on Money and Credit, *Stabilization Policies*, Englewood Cliffs (NJ), Prentice-Hall, 1963), appear to differ not in principle, but rather in the range of possible substitutions, and (implicitly) the scale and perhaps the speed of the process.

as the lever to which monetary policy is applied. But for the period and for type of interventions with which we are concerned this seems unhelpful. It is not so much that there is little firm evidence of variations in interest rates having significant effects on such investment, although this still continues to be true,[1] but rather that monetary interventions were not aimed directly at this target. Variations in real long-term interest rates were not large and, insofar as the exploitation of market imperfections was concerned, policy was usually intended to squeeze the personal sector, whilst cosseting manufacturing investment, in which the more significant policy interventions were fiscal ones (see pages 144–9).

Chart 6.9. *Building societies' differentials and the flow of funds, 1960–73*

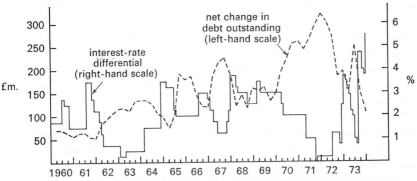

SOURCE: CSO, *Financial Statistics* (and supplement), February 1973, table B.

Notes: (i) Debt outstanding equals building society liabilities, deflated by an index of house prices.
(ii) Interest-rate differential calculated as minimum lending rate (or Bank Rate) minus the building society rate.

The case of dwelling investment was rather different. The conventional wisdom has it that variations in monetary conditions affect the rate of such investment in a number of ways; indeed that these effects have been sufficiently powerful and their associated political repercussions sufficiently important to provide a constraint on monetary action in the form of a politically determined 'ceiling' on interest rates.[2] The routes by which monetary conditions affect the housing market

[1] But cf., for example, the study by A. G. Hines and G. Catephores, 'Investment in UK manufacturing industry, 1956–67' in Hilton and Heathfield (eds.), *The Econometric Study of the United Kingdom*. There has as yet been no convincing examination of the attractive hypothesis that the rate of adjustment of the capital stock is significantly influenced by the availability of funds, so that monetary policy can play an indirect role in determining the current rate of investment in this way (see S. Nickell, 'Tax structure and financial policy' in M. J. Artis and A. R. Nobay (eds.), *Studies in Modern Economic Analysis*, Oxford, Blackwell, 1977).
[2] Goodhart, 'Monetary policy in the United Kingdom'.

comprise the influence of mortgage rates on the demand for mortgages and of bank lending rates on the building trades; also, there is the impact of mortage rationing and the general portfolio adjustment through which an excess supply of money may spill over into an increased demand for housing. However, despite public concern, surprisingly little quantification of these effects has been attempted and it is difficult to be precise about their relative importance. Nevertheless, it is well known that, due to the stickiness of their administered interest rates, the building societies' inflow of funds is very volatile; when market rates rise the inflow tends to decline until the share and deposit rates are brought in line (chart 6.9, which uses the minimum lending rate as an index of market rates, illustrates this point). At the same time, mortgage rates appear to be determined primarily as a mark-up on share and deposit rates, so that in periods when the inflow of funds is restricted the societies adopt non-price rationing to restrain the demand for mortgage finance.[1] A study by Artis, Kiernan and Whitley set out to explore the links between the mortgage market and dwelling investment; in a subsequent (unpublished) extension of this work it was found that both mortgage rationing and the mortgage rate were significant influences (the latter with an implied elasticity of -0.35), and that a speculative term in the increase in (real) house prices was also significant.[2] The implication is that an easing of rationing and a decline in mortgage rates are capable of stimulating the volume of dwelling investment considerably, both directly and also because the induced tendency for (real) house prices to rise will tend

---

[1] C. St J. OHerlihy and J. E. Spencer, 'Building societies' behaviour, 1955–70', *National Institute Economic Review*, no. 61, August 1972, pp. 40–52, showed that deposits and withdrawals were highly sensitive to variations in Bank Rate and the share rate. The following results indicate the long-run effect on deposits and withdrawals of a 1 per cent increase in each of these rates:

Percentages

	Effect on	
	Gross deposits	Withdrawals
1 per cent rise in:		
Bank Rate	-12	$+5$
Share rate	$+50$	-8

[2] See M. J. Artis, E. Kiernan and J. D. Whitley, 'The effects of building society behaviour on housing investment' in A. R. Nobay and J. M. Parkin (eds.), *Contemporary Issues in Economics*, Manchester University Press, 1975. In the original study rationing of mortgage funds was not found to be significant. This seems to have been due to mis-specification of the rationing variable and failure to allow for a lag between changes in mortgage rationing and the impact on investment. In the later study 'rationing' was identified with a variable involving the ratio of the current quarter's inflow of funds into building societies to the average of the previous twelve quarters' inflow, the effect of changes in this variable being registered upon investment with a lag of four quarters.

to be extrapolated, thus stimulating a speculative demand. As the process is subject to considerable lags, this goes some way to making sense of the sequel to the authorities' deliberate policy of stimulating the housing market in 1971/2; this resulted in a significant increase in dwelling investment in 1973 and a strong rise in house prices (which the authorities clearly regretted).[1]

Except for the positive stimulus in late 1971 and 1972, however, dwelling investment does not seem to have been the main object of the monetary authorities' attention, although it was a frequent casualty of their policies and a constraint upon them. Indeed, the history of the period is littered with attempts to insulate the mortgage market, usually the mortgage rate, from the effects of monetary action.[2] In contrast, consumers' expenditure (particularly on durable goods) was the frequent object of monetary interventions in the form of hire purchase controls and bank lending ceilings. There is evidence that these interventions were successful in their limited aim. Moreover, simply by reason of its relative scale, consumption rather than investment may well be the component of expenditure through which monetary policy has its greatest impact on aggregate demand.[3] General considerations suggest three main ways in which monetary factors might bear upon consumers' demand. First, in several popular forms of the consumption function wealth has an important role and short-run fluctuations in the value of measured wealth are usually dominated by changes in stock and bond prices; secondly, changes in the rate of interest may exercise a general influence apart from their wealth effects upon the decision to save or consume; finally, credit rationing by financial institutions and its formal reinforcement by official controls also affect consumer spending.

There is little firm evidence that changes in the rate of interest, apart from their revaluation effects, influence overall savings levels and there

[1] Whereas the 'Commentary' in the *Bank of England Quarterly Bulletin*, vol. 11, December 1971, noted with apparent satisfaction that 'monetary relaxations have helped to stimulate a pronounced increase in personal spending on cars and other durable goods and on housing' (p. 453), in the issue for December 1972 the Governor is quoted as having said 'the state of the property and housing market had become unruly with prices moving wildly ahead, unnecessarily far to provide an incentive for new building' (p. 517).

[2] These measures have included temporary government loans to the building societies and control of competitive bank deposit interest rates (both in 1973); earlier, building societies were asked to defer mortgage rate increases, were referred to the NBPI and were encouraged to merge with a view to reducing the mark-up of mortgage rates over share rates.

[3] Modigliani has indeed reported simulations for the United States which show that monetary policy (interest-rate) effects which work through consumption are larger and faster than those which work through investment, a result due to the greater relative scale of consumption offsetting its smaller elasticity (see F. Modigliani, 'The channels of monetary policy in the Federal Reserve–MIT–University of Pennsylvania econometric model of the US' in Renton (ed.) *Modelling the Economy*).

is a well-known ambiguity about the direction of the effect to be expected.[1] On the other hand, two studies of the United Kingdom consumption function have obtained results consistent with capital gains and losses having an impact on consumption,[2] but the scale does not appear to be large. To quote Deaton: '...in normal circumstances ignoring wealth effects causes little error; [although] in times when stock market values change very rapidly...there is a significant impact.'[3] A similar analysis motivated a suggestion in the *National Institute Economic Review* for November 1968 that the stock market boom of that period might have boosted consumption.[4] Nevertheless, it must be noted that empirical studies of these models have usually measured wealth, implicitly or explicitly, by the integration of current savings, thus leaving revaluation effects out of account;[5] also, most observers have reservations about the influence of revaluation effects, partly because capital gains and losses are likely to be associated in the short run with speculative effects and partly because the ownership of stocks and bonds is highly skewed.[6]

As for credit rationing, it was argued above that the officially approved changes in bank and hire purchase lending terms seem to have affected the outstanding totals of bank and hire purchase debt. For such instruments to influence consumption it is also necessary that consumers should not have ready access to alternative forms of finance, or be able easily to liquidate assets to make good the frustration of their borrowing potential. The widely voiced criticism of the inequity and narrow effectiveness of hire purchase controls (falling with particular severity upon certain industries producing durables) is in itself testimony to the fact that the controls worked in this sense, but the extent to which bank lending ceilings were similarly effective is less

---

[1] Recent work offers some suggestive evidence in favour of a positive effect, but so far it stands alone in this regard and cannot be considered conclusive (see El-Mokadem, *Econometric Models of Personal Saving*).

[2] See K. Hilton and D. H. Crossfield, 'Short-run consumption functions for the UK, 1955–66' in Hilton and Heathfield (eds.) *The Econometric Study of the United Kingdom*; also A. S. Deaton, 'Wealth effects on consumption in a modified life-cycle model', *Review of Economic Studies*, vol. 39, October 1972.

[3] Ibid. p. 451.

[4] *National Institute Economic Review*, no. 46, November 1968, pp. 9–11. Hilton and Crossfield concurred with this suggestion ('Short-run consumption functions for the UK', p. 80).

[5] A prominent example is the study by R. Stone, 'Private saving in Britain past, present and future', *Manchester School of Economic and Social Studies*, vol. 32, May 1964, and most of the studies reviewed in F. Modigliani, 'The life cycle hypothesis of saving twenty years later' in Nobay and Parkin (eds.), *Contemporary Issues in Economics*, share this feature.

[6] See J. J. Arena, 'Postwar stock market changes and consumer spending', *Review of Economics and Statistics*, vol. 47, November 1965, pp. 379–91; Modigliani, 'The life cycle hypothesis of saving twenty years later', however, reported on unpublished work by Ando which showed that there was no significant difference between the response of consumption to capital revaluations and to other changes in wealth.

well documented.[1] However, for the bulk of the period covered by our study, forecasting practice at both the Treasury and the National Institute incorporated a consumption function in which the change in debt outstanding (bank advances and hire purchase debt combined) appeared as an important determining variable.[2] This form of consumption function was investigated in some detail by Surrey;[3] similar estimates are shown in table 6.8. From there it will be seen that the equation containing the amalgamated (unweighted) debt term fits marginally better overall than that containing the two forms of debt separately, and that the long-run coefficient for the change in debt is approximately unity. The justification for estimating such an equation is that the 'change in debt' is primarily due to variations in monetary controls; the results can therefore be taken as implying that these controls were effective in stimulating or restraining consumer spending. This suggestion can be further elaborated for hire purchase terms alone by extending the simulation exercise described earlier, where the object was to determine the effect of variations in hire purchase controls on the level of outstanding hire purchase debt. On the assumption that the system is recursive, these simulation results can be extended to measure an impact upon consumption.[4] When this was done, it was found that the *cumulative* restraint of consumers' expenditure attributable to all variations in the controls over the period from 1959 reached a peak of some $3\frac{1}{2}$–4 per cent in 1969/70, broadly similar results being obtained whether an aggregated or disaggregated consumption function was employed; in either case, the impact of any isolated change in the controls was found to be short-lived, with a strong tendency to reverse itself after about a year.

The effectiveness and *modus operandi* of monetary policy depends on the instruments employed and the transmission mechanism by which changes in monetary factors affect demand and output. The Bank of England in 1969 described its policy as having been 'Radcliffean'. In some important respects this could be said to be misleading for, as demonstrated elsewhere, policy in practice ran clean against some of

[1] It might be presumed that bank customers would have easier access to alternative forms of finance and greater ability to liquidate existing assets in face of a frustrated demand for credit. This would at any rate be consistent with Norton's finding in 'Debt management and monetary policy in the United Kingdom' that dummies representing controls on bank advances were significant in determining the public's demand for national savings, and perhaps also with the puzzling experience of conditions since 'Competition and credit control' (see pages 298–9).

[2] See, for example, the paper by A. D. Roy, 'Short-term forecasting for central economic management of the UK economy', and that by M. J. Artis, 'Short-term economic forecasting at NIESR', in Hilton and Heathfield (eds.), *The Econometric Study of the United Kingdom.*

[3] Surrey, 'Personal income and consumers' expenditure'.

[4] Garganas, 'An analysis of consumer credit'.

Table 6.8. *The effect of income and credit rationing on consumption,[a]*
1958 II–1969 IV

Eqn no.	Constant term	Regression coefficients[b] for:				$\bar{R}^2$	DW
		Personal disposable income	Change in bank advances[c]	Change in hire purchase debt	Lagged dependent variable		
(1)	319·30 (2·46)	0·42 (5·66)	0·22 (0·48)	0·70 (2·31)	0·50 (5·53)	0·989	2·19
(2)	298·80 (2·38)	0·42 (5·65)	0·52[d] (3·25)		0·51 (5·70)	0·990	2·26

SOURCE: NIESR estimates.

[a] All data quarterly, seasonally adjusted, at 1970 prices. Dependent variable is consumers' expenditure.

[b] Short-run; long-run coefficients are as follows:

	Eqn (1)	Eqn (2)
Personal disposable income	0·84	0·85
Change in bank advances	0·43 ⎫	1·04
Change in hire purchase debt	1·38 ⎭	

[c] To persons.

[d] For combined variable of change in bank advances plus hire purchase debt.

the leading Radcliffe prescriptions,[1] but insofar as it was based on influencing credit flows policy could claim to be 'Radcliffean' at root. The *Radcliffe Report* had argued on a geological analogy that the capital market contained certain major faults,[2] of which one, very roughly, divided the corporate and personal sectors, and policy consisted, to a large extent, in exploiting this fault by the devices of hire purchase controls and bank lending ceilings. This was deliberate, and to some degree effective, but monetary policy also clearly affected the housing market, where most of the fluctuations do not seem to have been intended. Otherwise, the main purpose of monetary policy was to influence the balance of payments by a combination of confidence effects and incentives to flows of funds, whilst seeking to protect manufacturing investment from the worst rigours of the direct effects of policy (it could not, of course, be insulated from indirect effects stemming from the induced fluctuations in consumer demand). The most appropriate model of the transmission mechanism of these years seems, therefore, to be 'Radcliffean' in the loose sense that it used credit flows to exploit the limits which exist in some major sectors of the

[1] See pages 230 and 235–6 above.   [2] Treasury, *Radcliffe Report*, para. 319.

economy on the extent to which one form of finance can be substituted for another.

A dilemma underlying such a model is readily apparent; in exploiting imperfections in the capital market the short-run goals conflict with the long-run target of an improved and less imperfect market; it can also be argued that such a policy is inevitably inequitable in requiring disproportionate sacrifice from certain sectors of industry and the community for its success. It may, however, have appeared to policy-makers in a slightly different guise. Over the course of time it is fairly certain that a policy based on rationing will breed 'black markets' or their legal equivalent, and as a result it must become less and less certain what the effects of policy actually are (we have already noted the difficulties of interpreting evidence from a period dominated by controls, which is another aspect of the same problem). In these circumstances it might have seemed that the effects of the policy, as well as increasingly uncertain, became increasingly small. Such a judgement might not be wholly justified, but it is a natural one and would be an argument against continuing active discrimination and in favour of a more anonymous and generalised policy. It is not implausible that this was an element in the radical change associated with the introduction of 'Competition and credit control'.[1]

'COMPETITION AND CREDIT CONTROL'

The purpose of this section is not to provide a detailed account of the period which begins with the inauguration of 'Competition and credit control' (such an account appears in chapter 5 above), but rather to draw attention to the interruption in this period – real or apparent – of two of the more significant 'regularities' which characterised the 1960s. The first of these is the role of credit factors in the consumption function and the second the demand for money. The stability of these relationships is relevant to the analysis and interpretation of monetary policy in the 1960s, as is already evident from the preceding account, and in this light evidence of their possible interruption takes on a special significance.

Table 6.9 shows for various estimation periods the coefficients for personal disposable income, lagged consumption and the change in consumer debt (bank advances and hire purchase debt combined) used as variables explaining the level of consumption. Such a relationship, as we have already seen, characterised forecasting practice in the 1960s, and equation (1) (the same as equation (2) in table 6.8 above) may be taken as broadly representative, being estimated on data for

[1] Goodhart, 'Problems of monetary management'

Table 6.9. *The effect of income and credit rationing on consumption*[a]
in different periods

Eqn no.	Period of estimation	Regression coefficients[b] for:		
		Personal disposable income	Change in consumer debt[c]	Lagged dependent variable
(1)	1958 II–1969 IV	0·42	0·52	0·51
(2)	1958 II–1973 III	0·41	0·37	0·49
(3)	1970 IV–1973 III	0·34	0·88	0·40

SOURCE: NIESR estimates.

[a] All data quarterly, seasonally adjusted, at 1970 prices. Dependent variable is consumers' expenditure.

[b] Short-run; long-run coefficients are as follows:

	Eqn (1)	Eqn (2)	Eqn (3)
Personal disposable income	0·85	0·80	0·57
Change in consumer debt	1·04	0·73	1·48

[c] Bank advances to persons plus hire purchase debt.

the period 1958 II–1969 IV. The other two equations in the table show the changes in coefficient values observed when the data period is extended to include, or is confined to, the 1970s and indicate that such data cannot be assimilated in the relationship measured in equation (1). This was confirmed by a simulation of equation (1) using actual values of lagged consumption, which produced very substantial over-predictions of consumption.

Although not obvious from the table, it is clear from graphical inspection and from the apparent stability of relationships involving hire purchase debt alone, that this difficulty is associated with the very rapid rise in bank advances after 1971 (cf. chart 6.1). This poses an awkward problem. The principal justification for estimating equations like those in tables 6.8 and 6.9 is that the values of the 'change of debt' terms were constrained by monetary controls; otherwise they would be choice variables determined simultaneously with consumption and of dubious value as independent regressors. If the controls were successful in suppressing consumption, as such equations suggest, their removal should stimulate it. It is true that, at some point, when consumers have re-established an equilibrium in the absence of controls, the justification for fitting such equations would not be so obvious, but in the intervening period it would not seem unreasonable to suppose that the release of controls would lead to an increase in consumption which could be predicted by such an equation, whereas in fact consumption is substantially over-predicted. Indeed, it is not easy to see where the effect of the increase in bank advances was felt. There is no sign that it significantly affected Stock Exchange prices (which did not rise strongly after the first half of 1971); it may perhaps have helped to boost the rise in house prices, but the series in question purports to exclude loans for house purchase; neither does it seem that an explanation involving broader expenditure categories is of any help.[1] The most likely explanation seems to be that following the release of controls a large part of the expansion in bank advances accommodated a reshuffling of asset (and debt) portfolios, which involved the substitution of bank credit for less preferred forms of debt. This would indeed have been consistent with one of the purposes of 'Competition and credit control', but by the same token it suggests that rather more of the 'effect' of bank lending controls than first appeared may have been offset by drawing down financial assets and repaying other forms of credit, perhaps including trade credit for which data are very inadequate.[2] It must, of course, be admitted that the case for including bank advances together with hire purchase debt was never very firmly established in the first instance and the success of the composite term may merely have reflected a statistical correlation with little of the economic justification suggested. On the other side of the balance sheet, it is still too early to be sure how far this apparent breakdown in the relationship reflects a transitional shock associated with the new conditions. Whatever the case, it would seem that the experience of the recent period implies the need for some caution when interpreting the use of bank lending ceilings in the 1960s.

However, perhaps a more problematic (but not unrelated) issue concerns the demand for money. As already mentioned, one of the achievements of empirical monetary economics in the 1960s had been to demonstrate the existence of a stable function for the short-run demand for money, sensitive, but not greatly so, to variations in the rate of interest, very simply specified, and applicable with minor and plausible modifications to any of the definitions of the money stock available.[3] Fitting in as it did with comparable evidence for other

[1] Indeed, it is noticeable that in the econometric explanation of private expenditure afforded by Cripps, Godley and Fetherston (in the 'New Cambridge' tradition), bank advances for the period in question were replaced by a transformation of hire purchase debt (see House of Commons, *Ninth Report from the Expenditure Committee, Session 1974*, Minutes of Evidence, pp. 1–12).

[2] There was a debate about the role of trade credit in the *Economic Journal*, commencing with the investigation published there by F. P. R. Brechling and R. G. Lipsey, 'Trade credit and monetary policy', *Economic Journal*, vol. 73, December 1963, pp. 618–41. It seems fair to say that no conclusive evidence has been produced as to whether movements in trade credit amplify, offset, or are simply neutral with respect to variations in monetary conditions.

[3] The stability of the demand for money is of course crucial to monetarist models of the economy – an intellectual fashion of growing importance in the period – but it is also quite

countries, and running clean contrary to the views of the *Radcliffe Report*, this relationship allows one to suggest that, whilst monetary policy was primarily accommodating in that period, it might possess the potential for more active use; it also allows one – as indicated earlier – to conceive of a monetary policy which did not rely upon bank lending ceilings and direct controls in the manner of the 1960s. The significance of an interruption to the previously observed relationship between money, income and interest rates is then obvious, for, if genuine, it undermines all these conclusions.

It should not have been surprising that the simply-specified demand for money should begin to appear an inadequate explanation of the behaviour of the money stock in the 1970s, for the 'own rate' on money was omitted from the calculations, whilst 'Competition and credit control' allowed the banks to compete for funds.[1] Artis and Lewis argued that allowance should also be made for the increased variability of bond prices in the 1970s, since, *ceteris paribus*, this would diminish the attractiveness of bonds and increase that of money.[2] However, even when these variables were included, the demand for money exhibited considerable instability when the 1970s were added to the estimation period: table 6.10 illustrates this for the broad definition of the money stock (M_3), where, admittedly, the problem was the most pronounced.[3] When demand functions estimated from data for the 1960s were used to predict the level of the money stock in the 1970s, given the actual levels of income and interest rates prevailing, a substantial degree of under-prediction was discovered.[4] Three hypotheses might explain this

---

acceptable to other schools of thought, including the Keynesian; indeed there is an argument that many typical monetarist propositions turn on the assumption of an interest-*in*elastic demand for money (see, for example, J. Tobin, 'Friedman's theoretical framework', *Journal of Political Economy*, vol. 80, Sept.–Oct. 1972) – a characteristic definitely rejected by the United Kingdom evidence. (An early finding by Laidler and Parkin of interest inelasticity seems to have been due to an inappropriate choice of the interest-rate variable. See Laidler and Parkin, 'The demand for money in the United Kingdom, 1956–67'.)

[1] This omission might seem a curious one, but it can be related to the absence of an obvious data series for the 'own rate' and perhaps to its presumed relative lack of variation. In any event, the functions for the demand for money estimated without it were widely judged to be satisfactory.

[2] M. J. Artis and M. K. Lewis, 'The demand for money in the United Kingdom 1963–1973', *Manchester School of Economic and Social Studies*, vol. 44, June 1976, pp. 147–81.

[3] The results of equation (1) can be used to estimate long-run elasticities (for income +1·08 and for interest rates −0·25) obtained by dividing the short-run coefficients by the complement of the coefficient on the lagged dependent variable. Such a procedure is implausible for equation (2) because of the value (in excess of unity) obtained there on the lagged dependent variable.

[4] See M. J. Artis and M. K. Lewis, 'The demand for money, stable or unstable?', *The Banker*, vol. 124, March 1974, pp. 239–47; also G. Hacche, 'The demand for money in the United Kingdom: experience since 1971', *Bank of England Quarterly Bulletin*, vol. 14, September 1974.

phenomenon: first, that the demand for money is indeed unstable; secondly, that it was subject to a shock associated with the introduction of 'Competition and credit control'; thirdly, that the under-prediction reflected a disequilibrium position of excess supply which the market had failed to clear within the periods of observation.

Table 6.10. *Estimates of the demand for money function* $M_3{}^a$

| Eqn no. | Period of estimation | Constant term | Regression coefficients for: | | | | R^2 | DW |
			GNP at market prices	Interest rates[b]	Index of bond price variability[c]	Lagged dependent variable		
(1)	1963 II–1970 IV	0·13 (0·95)	0·24 (2·17)	−0·06 (1·91)	0·03 (1·80)	0·78 (7·05)	0·998	1·96
(2)	1963 II–1973 I	−0·21 (1·38)	0·05 (0·41)	−0·07 (1·80)	0·06 (3·36)	1·01 (9·34)	0·998	1·94

SOURCE: Artis and Lewis, 'The demand for money in the United Kingdom', table 2.

[a] Data quarterly, GNP and M_3 seasonally adjusted in nominal terms; dependent variable is M_3 logarithmic.
[b] The differential between the Consol rate and the 'own rate' on money.
[c] Based on the standard deviation of a moving average of logarithmic first differences in Consol prices (see source).

Investigations by the Bank of England using disaggregated functions favour an interpretation along the lines of the first or second of these explanations.[1] They suggest that the behaviour of the corporate sector was particularly important and was strongly influenced by an unusual combination of lending and borrowing rates which made it worthwhile for companies both to lend and to borrow from banks simultaneously; also, that competition for bank deposits was much sharper after 'Competition and credit control'. Nevertheless, these factors, insofar as they could be measured, did not appear to provide a full explanation, so it was concluded that 'it is unwise to be confident in the survival of stable demand-for-money relationships when there are changes in regulations affecting banks'.[2] On the face of it, this statement seems to impugn the independence of demand and supply which is normally assumed, but it would be naive to reject the conclusion solely for this reason. It must, after all, be acknowledged that there are many measurement problems where, although the 'true' demand function is independent of supply conditions, the quantification of the relevant relationships is unable to capture the true function. These measurement problems embrace, in particular, lack of data on the 'own rate' and

[1] Ibid.   [2] Ibid. p. 297.

the poor quality of the disaggregated data on sectoral money holdings. Secondly, even assuming no difficulties of measurement, the extent of the change in the supply regime was arguably such as to imply that at least the associated lag structure – if not strictly the form of the demand function – might be altered.[1]

Artis and Lewis attempted to pursue this line of argument. They adopted as an initial hypothesis the position that the demand for money had remained stable,[2] but that variations in supply conditions were responsible (in the absence of a full market-clearing in the short run) for the appearance in later years of a marked disequilibrium and excess supply, which gave the (misleading) appearance of a 'breakdown' in the demand for money. This they associated particularly with the release of bank lending controls in 1971 and the size of the budget deficit in 1972 and 1973. The data available were insufficient to avoid some compromise with the theoretical standpoint they had adopted initially and the final results were somewhat inconclusive.[3]

At the time of writing, therefore, the question still remains unsettled. Confidence in the stability of the demand for money has been impaired but not destroyed, which implies that confidence in the further implications of a stable demand for money has also been impaired, if not destroyed.

CONCLUSIONS

At the beginning of this chapter we remarked that it was not feasible to represent the effects of monetary policy by a set of figures and that in only a few instances can we have much confidence in relationships bearing upon these effects. They seem clear enough in the case of hire purchase controls, the housing market and capital flows; otherwise, it cannot be claimed that much is known. Bank lending controls were unquestionably effective in controlling advances and, probably there-

---

[1] Brechling offered a perceptive comment on this problem in his contribution to the proceedings of a conference held in 1968. He argued in part that: 'It seems especially plausible to suppose that the demand for money adjusts to its equilibrium position quite rapidly when the supply of money is infinitely elastic and that interest rates, prices and permanent income react sluggishly to exogenous changes in the money stock, thus causing considerable disequilibrium in money holdings. In such a case, the existence of a stable demand function in the sample period may not tell us much about this function in the period of active money supply policy.' (See F. P. R. Brechling's discussion paper on the paper by Laidler in Clayton, Gilbert and Sedgwick (eds.), *Monetary Theory and Monetary Policy in the 1970s*, p. 138.)

[2] Artis and Lewis, 'The demand for money, stable or unstable?'. However, they allowed for the influence of the 'own rate' on money and variability in bond prices – variables suppressed in earlier estimates of the demand function.

[3] Some support was revealed for the proposition that the 'narrow' money supply series M_1 had not been so severely disturbed as M_3, which was compatible up to a point with the findings of Hacche, 'The demand for money in the United Kingdom', and explicable on the argument that M_1 remained primarily demand-determined even in periods when M_3 was in excess supply.

fore, the money supply; that they had much direct effect on spending is more questionable. Variations in the money supply were not particularly marked until the 1970s and the model of a largely accommodating monetary policy seems the most appropriate, for, whilst interest rates were not pegged, the authorities pursued a policy of 'leaning against the wind' in an endeavour to increase the stability of bond prices and the attractiveness of bonds as an asset to hold. This policy in the bond market had to be accompanied by a comparative and complementary stability of rates at the short end of the market, subject, however, to the need to offset incipient balance of payments crises by interest-rate adjustments designed to attract capital inflow, or to stem the outflow. The premise that policy could have had larger positive effects depends on a view of the demand for money which has come under a cloud recently, also upon evidence of the sensitivity of expenditure to interest-rate changes which most investigators have found it difficult to obtain. Clearly the period in which monetary policy was most open to criticism was that of the strong expansion in 1971–3, although this has to be considered in conjunction with fiscal policy in that period, which is discussed elsewhere in this book (chapter 4) as an important episode in its own right. Apart from this, it seems unlikely that monetary policy did very much for good or bad in this period; it did not do very much at all, and was not supposed to.

CHAPTER 7

POLICIES AIMED AT IMPROVING THE BALANCE OF PAYMENTS

by *J. H. B. Tew*[1]

INTRODUCTION

In every year from 1961 to 1968, except for a temporary respite in 1962 and 1963, balance of payments difficulties were serious enough to threaten the exhaustion of the reserves of gold and foreign currencies held by the Exchange Equalisation Account. The government was at intervals faced with crisis situations, which were resolved partly by improvised measures designed to make the external balance less unfavourable, partly by hastily negotiated rescue operations to supplement the reserves. The task was not made easier by the fact that confidence in sterling was at best precarious, each crisis being characterised by large outward short-term capital movements, motivated by the fear that the United Kingdom would be forced to devalue – a fear that was eventually justified in November 1967, when the pound was devalued from \$2.80 to \$2.40.

In the course of 1969, and at any rate in part as a delayed reaction to the devaluation, there began an improvement in the United Kingdom's external position so dramatic as to exorcise, albeit only temporarily, the anxiety about the balance of payments. From 1972, however, there was a growing suspicion that the old spectre had not after all been finally laid, as the balance started to deteriorate again. In June 1972 sterling was allowed to float and exchange control was extended to transactions with the sterling area, but by 1973 there was once again a large deficit on the current balance.

Intermingled with emergency measures intended to tide over the periodic crises were longer-term reforms intended permanently to reduce the net flow overseas of government payments and private investment. It was hoped prior to November 1967 that these reforms, together with others described elsewhere in this book aimed at countering inflation and improving the efficiency of British industry, would so strengthen our balance of payments in the longer term that, without

[1] The sections on the import surcharge and the temporary import deposit scheme (pages 344–9) are by M. J. Artis; appendix 1 is by A. D. Morgan.

recourse to devaluation, emergency measures could be dispensed with eventually. Some of the measures adopted at times of crisis come under the headings of demand management, priorities in bank lending, or interest-rate policy and, as such, have already been treated in chapters 5 and 6; others, such as more drastic exchange control or the imposition of the import surcharge, will be considered in the present chapter.

EVIDENCE OF BALANCE OF PAYMENTS DIFFICULTIES

At the start we need to be clear about what is meant by 'balance of payments difficulties'. Broadly there are four kinds of evidence that such difficulties may exist.

Table 7.1. *United Kingdom current and basic balance of payments, 1958–73: private and government transactions distinguished*

£ million

	Current balance			Basic balance		
	Government a/c[a]	Private a/c	Total	Government a/c[a]	Private a/c	Total
1958	−360	+704	+344	..	..	+148
59	−355	+510	+155	..	..	−100
1960	−430	+185	−245	..	..	−437
61	−496	+518	+22	−490	+574	+84
62	−506	+634	+128	−589	+611	+22
63	−514	+645	+131	−578	+554	−24
64	−550	+195	−355	−651	−61	−712
65	−578	+552	−26	−675	+422	−253
66	−626	+727	+101	−672	+688	+16
67	−630	+332	−298	−635	+236	−399
68	−696	+424	−272	−663	+264	−399
69	−791	+1251	+460	−946	+1245	+299
1970	−743	+1476	+733	−957	+1525	+568
71	−720	+1804	+1084	−886	+2020	+1134
72	−707	+861	+154	−849	+230	−619
73	−1005	+269	−736	−1089	+9	−1080

SOURCES: CSO, *United Kingdom Balance of Payments 1972*, table 3, and *1965–75*, tables 2, 3 and 13; CSO, *Economic Trends*, no. 200, June 1970, p. xxxi.

[a] Includes public sector interest, profits and dividends.

In the first place there are statistical series of the external balance defined in various ways. On a monthly basis there has always been the balance of visible trade, preliminary figures for which have been available with little delay. On a quarterly basis there have been a number of other statistical series, of which the current balance (of

visible and invisible trade) and the basic balance (the current balance
together with the balance of long-term capital transactions) were the
most widely used in the 1960s (see table 7.1); a difficulty with these
quarterly series is that they become available only after a time-lag
and are subject to considerable retrospective revision. Originally
officials preferred the current balance, but in 1957 preference shifted
to the basic balance. In 1970 it was back to the current balance, when
the Treasury concluded that the basic balance had become less useful,

Chart 7.1. *Short-term sterling liabilities (net of claims), 1959–69*

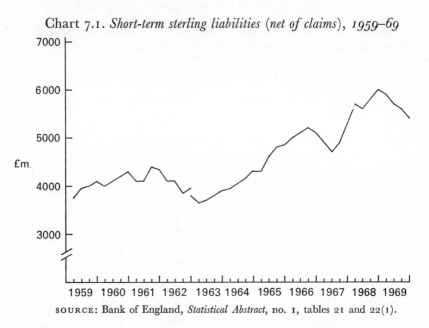

SOURCE: Bank of England, *Statistical Abstract*, no. 1, tables 21 and 22(1).

mainly because of the increasing difficulty of distinguishing long-term
from short-term capital investment.[1] From then on the balances
judged to be most significant were the current balance, as showing
success or failure in paying our way, and the total currency flow, for
the facts about our ability (or inability) to build up reserves and repay
official borrowing.

A second type of evidence is changes in the stock of British external
assets and liabilities. In the 1960s total assets always comfortably
exceeded total liabilities, so that the only cause for concern was the
balance of short-term assets and liabilities, which was much less satisfactory. The so-called 'sterling balances' held overseas were widely
accepted as a measure of short-term sterling liabilities; these were
usually taken net of certain short-term sterling claims, as shown in

[1] Treasury, *Economic Progress Report*, no. 7, September 1970.

chart 7.1. The short-term assets were official reserves in various forms: holdings of gold, foreign currencies, IMF Special Drawing Rights (as from 1970) and the reserve position in the IMF general account, and these are shown in the first column of table 7.2. To be offset against these resources were official liabilities contracted specifically to replenish reserves, so that the latter can best be judged when taken net of such liabilities, which are also shown in table 7.2. These statistics were known to officials accurately and without delay, and may well on that account have weighed heavily with them in deciding on urgent official action. Unfortunately no published information is available about official *forward* commitments, which at times were very large and which would be as important as outstanding official borrowing.

A third type of evidence consists of the spot and forward exchange rates. Since the spot pound–dollar rate was pegged throughout the 1960s, initially at $2.80 and later at $2.40, pressures against the pound revealed themselves as a fall in official reserves, or as a rise in official indebtedness, rather than in the spot exchange rate. The latter was therefore an important indicator of our external position only from the time that the pound was floated in June 1972. The forward pound–dollar rate is also a possible indicator, but its value as such was much reduced when (mainly in the years 1964–7) it too was being officially supported. At such times pressures against the pound in the forward market would be revealed better by the outstanding official position in forward dollars, which, though never published, would be known to officials. At other times, thanks to arbitrage, the discount or premium on forward sterling would normally tend to reflect the differential between sterling and dollar market interest rates; hence those occasions when the discount appreciably exceeded the interest-rate differential can fairly confidently be regarded as occasions of considerable pressure against sterling in the forward market. As may be seen from chart 7.2 there were a number of such occasions, in particular in 1968 and 1969.

The fourth kind is qualitative evidence about confidence in sterling coming into the official machine through the Bank of England, which enjoys privileged access to such information by virtue of its close relations with other City institutions and overseas central banks. We know from Harold Wilson's memoirs that such information was of vital importance in government decision-making, particularly on the timing of official action.[1]

The years in the 1960s in which the British authorities judged the United Kingdom to be in balance of payments difficulties were those in which outstanding official short-term and medium-term borrowing

[1] Wilson, *The Labour Government 1964–1970*.

Table 7.2. *United Kingdom reserves and outstanding official short-term and medium-term borrowing from abroad, 1959–73*

$ million

		Reserves^a and related items^b	Official financing and liabilities^c			
			Net drawings from IMF^d	Borrowing from other monetary authorities^e	Public sector borrowing^f	Total
1959	Dec.	2736	325	—	—	325
1960	June	2892	232	—	—	232
	Dec.	3231	—	—	—	—
1961	June	2772	—	904	—	904
	Dec.	3318	1040	—	—	1040
1962	June	3433	535	—	—	535
	Dec.	2806	—	—	—	—
1963	June	2713	—	—	—	—
	Dec.	2657	—	—	—	—
1964	June	2704	—	15	—	15
	Dec.	2316	1000	605	—	1605
1965	June	2792	2383	629	—	3012
	Dec.	3004	2370	913	—	3283
1966	June	3276	2430	683	—	3113
	Dec.	3100	2410	1738	—	4148
1967	June	2834	1862	628	—	2490
	Dec.	2695	1508	3453	—	4961
1968	June	2683	2908	4538	—	7446
	Dec.	2422	2723	5348	—	8071
1969	June	2443	2700	4543	50	7293
	Dec.	2528	2650	3744	120	6514
1970	June	2791	2381	1125	120	3626
	Dec.	2827	2328	958	120	3406
1971	June	5319	1620	—	316	1936
	Dec.	8832	1081	—	366	1447
1972	June	8115	—	2608	366	2974
	Dec.	5646	—	—	366	366
1973	June	7012	—	—	1337	1337
	Dec.	6476	—	—	2982	2982

SOURCES: Bank of England, *Statistical Abstract*, no. 1, table 27; *Bank of England Quarterly Bulletin*, vol. 16, March 1976, table 23 and pp. 79–80.

^a Sterling reserves converted at $2.80 to the pound up to mid-1967 and then at $2.40 until 1969; thereafter reserves are valued as in *Bank of England Quarterly Bulletin*, vol. 16, March 1976, table 23.

^b Foreign currency taken out of reserves by official swaps with overseas monetary authorities included as follows: June 1971 $1700 million, December 1971 $2251 million, June 1972 $1150 million.

^c Non-dollar borrowing valued as in *Bank of England Quarterly Bulletin*, vol. 16, March 1976, pp. 79–80.

^d Drawings net of repayments by the United Kingdom and of drawings of sterling by other countries; interest and charges in sterling excluded.

^e Foreign exchange obtained by the Bank of England as deposits or by swaps.

^f Foreign currency borrowing (net of repayments) by the British government and by other public sector institutions under the 1969 and subsequent exchange cover schemes.

increased, namely 1961 and 1964–8 inclusive (see table 7.2). The only year in which other evidence appears to conflict with this table is 1960, when the current balance and the basic balance both suggest a 'difficult' year (table 7.1). However short-term capital inflows in that year (reversed in 1961) delayed the strain on our reserves until 1961, and it was only then that decisive official action, appropriate to balance of

Chart 7.2. *Covered interest-rate differential between local authority temporary loans and Eurodollar deposits in London, 1966–73*

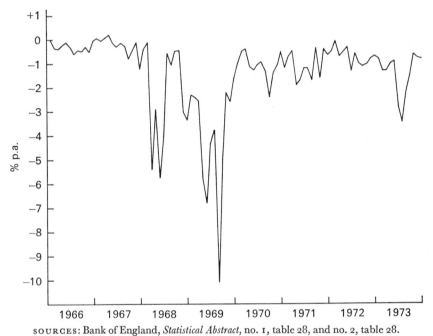

SOURCES: Bank of England, *Statistical Abstract*, no. 1, table 28, and no. 2, table 28.

Note: The differential represents the excess of the sterling rate over the dollar rate, minus the forward premium (per cent per annum) on the dollar.

payments difficulties, was taken. (The only action taken in 1960 was to raise Bank Rate and impose controls on hire purchase.) In the 1970s there was a temporary anxiety about the middle of 1972, associated with the floating of sterling in June, and this accounts for the $2.6 billion of official borrowing shown in table 7.2. Then balance of payments troubles resumed in earnest in 1973 and led to strong official encouragement to public sector institutions to borrow in foreign currencies to improve our reserves.

EXCHANGE-RATE POLICY

An issue which claims our attention at the outset of any discussion of policies to improve the balance of payments is why the authorities were so reluctant to devalue the pound. The spot value of sterling had been pegged within the limits $2.78–$2.82, giving a small margin on either side of the $2.80 parity, ever since the devaluation of 1949. The government's attitude to this rate had, however, been subject to vicissitudes during the 1950s. The Conservative administration which came to power in November 1951 had initially toyed with a scheme 'Operation Robot' for introducing non-resident convertibility with a floating rate for the pound, or at any rate widening the swing on either side of $2.80, and discussions were held within the OEEC about the technical implications of such a move.[1] But as the news of the discussions leaked out there followed a run on sterling, which was only stopped by the Chancellor of the Exchequer's firm denial, in his speech at the annual IMF meeting in September 1955, that any change in the pegging arrangements for sterling was contemplated.[2]

Thereafter the government's commitment to $2.80 hardened. Peter Thorneycroft, in his budget statement of 1957, spoke of the austere policies he had adopted to improve our balance of payments at the existing dollar value of sterling and in the following year his successor, Heathcoat Amory, said that the strength of sterling remained the primary objective of economic policy. Harold Macmillan was no less determined to avoid devaluation, though his grounds were political rather than economic. He stated that devaluation mattered politically because sterling had become a symbol, but he seemed doubtful whether, otherwise, maintaining the parity 'matters as much as we all think'.[3]

Outside comment did not give such unqualified approval to the $2.80 peg. For example, in 1955 James Meade was writing in favour of a floating rate,[4] while the deterioration of the balance of payments in the first half of the 1960s provoked considerable public controversy on the merits of abandoning $2.80 in favour of either a lower peg or a floating rate. However outside opinion, and particularly academic opinion, was deeply divided.[5] At that time none of the protagonists seemed to think it necessary, or indeed possible, to quantify with any

[1] The Earl of Birkenhead, *The Prof in Two Worlds*, London, Collins, 1961. pp. 284–92.

[2] A. Shonfield, *British Economic Policy since the War*, Harmondsworth, Penguin, 1958, p. 201.

[3] Macmillan, *Pointing the Way*, *1959–1961*, p. 376.

[4] J. E. Meade, 'The case for variable exchange rates', *Three Banks Review*, no. 27, September 1955.

[5] T. W. Hutchison, *Economics and Economic Policy in Britain 1946–1966*, London, Allen & Unwin, 1968, pp. 219–33.

accuracy the fall in the exchange rate appropriate to improving our external balance by the required amount, or even to specify what the required amount was. Yet without quantification the debate was almost bound to be inconclusive, since the possible adverse side effects of a departure from the $2.80 peg (retaliation by other countries; speculation against the pound; deterioration in our terms of trade; a rise in the cost of living, leading possibly to a wage–price spiral; breaking faith with overseas holders of sterling; damage to the City's prestige) all depended very much on the percentage by which the pound's external value would have to fall. (As was pointed out in a more sophisticated public controversy which took place in 1967, the disadvantages of a large devaluation were disproportionally greater than those of a moderate one.[1])

In any case, the inconclusive public controversy in the first half of the 1960s seems to have had no impact on the policy of the Conservative government. The various measures adopted in 1961 enabled us to weather the storm without altering the exchange rate and, when our external balance began to deteriorate again in the course of 1963, Reginald Maudling rejected the proposition that a vigorous economy and a strong position for sterling were incompatible, and planned to deal with what he diagnosed as only a temporary external deficit by drawing down reserves and by recourse to external credit.[2]

Despite Maudling's optimism, the Labour Chancellor James Callaghan, who succeeded him in October 1964, was faced with a formidable balance of payments problem: the basic balance for the year was £717 million in deficit and was believed at the time to be even worse. The incoming Labour government was therefore faced immediately with the major issue of whether to maintain the $2.80 peg or to abandon it. Some of the academics who moved into Whitehall in 1964 had participated on both sides of the public controversy several years earlier and this suggests that there must have been a debate of some kind.[3] Indeed Samuel Brittan says the issue was discussed very thoroughly.[4] But if we are to believe Brandon's account of what happened behind the scenes,[5] whatever debate there may have been was cut short by a decision to hold fast to the $2.80 peg, taken by Harold Wilson and a small group of colleagues at a meeting on 17

---

[1] M. FG. Scott, 'Should the pound be devalued?', *The Bankers' Magazine*, vol. 203, April 1967, p. 227.

[2] Budget statement, 1963.

[3] For example, T. Balogh was in favour of holding to the $2.80 peg, R. R. Neild and N. Kaldor were in favour of abandoning it (Hutchison, *Economics and Economic Policy*, pp. 219–22).

[4] Brittan, *Steering the Economy* (rev. edn), p. 393.

[5] H. Brandon, *In the Red: the struggle for sterling 64/66*, London, Deutsch, 1966, p. 43.

October 1964 immediately after taking office. Callaghan, according to Brandon, had already for some time been committed to \$2.80, and he and Wilson remained steadfast to their commitment right up to 1967, when there was no feasible alternative to abandoning it. Indeed, once the decision had been taken, Brittan tells us that all reference to the subject was forbidden and it became known as 'the great unmentionable'.[1]

Wilson's own account of the decision gives more prominence to the political implications of devaluation than the economic ones.[2] He says that he and his colleagues were obviously tempted by the idea, since the responsibility could have been put on the previous government. His first argument against devaluation is that international opinion, remembering that the decision to devalue in 1949 had been made by a Labour government, would conclude that Labour would always take the easy way out by devaluing. Secondly, he argues that – whereas by 1967 there was general international acceptance of devaluation – this would not have been the case in 1964. On the economic side, he argues that devaluation would have required a 'severe and rapid' shift of resources from the home to the overseas sector. In addition, he was strongly influenced by the view that the physical and structural improvement of the British economy, to which he was deeply committed, would make Britain so much more competitive with other countries that our balance of payments would in due course improve adequately without devaluation.[3] Of course, the physical and structural reform of the British economy would take time, but meanwhile the deficit could be reduced by various expedients and whatever balance remained could probably be financed with official help from other major powers, especially the United States. The United States was indeed anxious to help with any policies which offered a credible alternative to a British devaluation, which was seen as menace to confidence in the dollar and hence to the whole international monetary system.

The view that the devaluation of sterling would have such catastrophic consequences is clearly one which was put to Wilson in 1964 by the Governor of the Bank of England, who advocated draconian alternatives, including all-round cuts in public expenditure, to relinquishing the \$2.80 peg.[4] Another consideration which may have weighed in 1964 was that devaluation or a free float could jeopardise

[1] Brittan, *Steering the Economy* (rev. edn), p. 292.

[2] Wilson, *The Labour Government 1964–1970*, p. 6.

[3] Balogh had argued in a similar vein in his written evidence to the Radcliffe Committee (Treasury, *Committee on the Working of the Monetary System. Principal Memoranda of Evidence*, vol. 3, London, HMSO, 1960, p. 40).

[4] Wilson, *The Labour Government 1964–1970*, p. 37.

the success of a prices and incomes policy, which was itself an alternative way of making British goods more competitive. This point of view was being advanced at that time by the National Institute.[1]

Alongside the various arguments against devaluation, there developed in the 1960s a quite different approach, pioneered by Paish,[2] which cannot be so readily reconciled with the views of the Labour leaders at the time of the crucial decision of October 1964. The central idea was that the problems which beset the British economy, including the balance of payments problem, were mainly attributable to excess demand. For, unlike other critics of 'stop–go' policies of demand management, who favoured stabilising demand at the level achieved in the 'boom' phase of the cycle, Paish wished to stabilise it at the level of the 'recession' phase, corresponding to an unemployment rate of 2 per cent or slightly more. Such a margin of excess capacity would serve to maximise the rate of real growth in the long term and at the same time contain the annual rise in wages and prices within acceptable bounds; a highly desirable side effect of the policy would be the avoidance of the balance of payments troubles associated with the high-demand phase of previous cycles.

To those economists, inside as well as outside the government, whose views on the British economy came to be broadly in line with Paish's, the $2.80 peg, at any rate up to mid-1966, was never an undesirable constraint on demand management, since from the end of the war up to that time demand had almost never been inadequate – and had intermittently been excessive. In the high-demand phase the constraint had been beneficial, in that it served to reinforce the government's resolve to deflate demand to a level which this school of thought regarded as more appropriate to the domestic objectives of demand management.

'The great unmentionable' remained unmentionable in government circles until 1966, when George Brown insisted on raising the devaluation issue with his colleagues.[3] But only a minority, though a substantial one, was in favour, so instead of devaluation there was in July a further package of deflationary measures.

Mid-1966 was thus an important milestone on the road to eventual devaluation, in that from then onwards the Cabinet was alive to the issue, and indeed as seriously divided on it as outside opinion.[4] More-

[1] *National Institute Economic Review*, no. 33, August 1965, p. 18.

[2] See F. W. Paish, *Studies in an Inflationary Economy: the United Kingdom 1948–1961*, London, Macmillan, 1962, in particular his chapter on 'Output, inflation and growth'.

[3] Brown, *In My Way*, p. 114.

[4] D. J. Robertson in his introduction to a symposium on the British balance of payments in the *Scottish Journal of Political Economy*, vol. 13, February 1966, said that few of the contributors believed that devaluation alone would help the British balance of payments in any

over, arguments in favour of holding to the $2.80 peg were advanced with noticeably less conviction. In particular, those who (on Paish's line of argument) had previously regarded it as more or less compatible with the domestic aims of demand management began to lose faith in this harmony of objectives. It still had its defenders, but they were mainly people burdened with especially heavy responsibilities in the field of international monetary affairs – Wilson and Callaghan in the Cabinet,[1] officials on the international side of the Treasury and the Bank of England, City bankers concerned with international business – plus a number of outside commentators. Many of the statesmen and officials concerned had so solemnly pledged themselves to maintain the $2.80 peg that they would have found it embarrassing to escape from their commitment, but there is no reason to doubt the sincerity of their professed dread of the consequences. The last major change in exchange rates that they remembered – the revaluation of the German and Dutch currencies in 1961 – had provoked speculative movements of short-term funds on a scale which they hoped never to experience again.[2] They feared defections from the sterling area; they feared for the continued prosperity of the City if sterling should go out of favour as a commercial currency throughout the world; they were impressed (unduly so, as we now know from subsequent experience) by the inconveniences which varying exchange rates occasion for firms engaged in international trade. Moreover, those who were critical of the government's administrative competence also noted that our balance of payments was in deficit almost entirely because of the large deficit on official transactions (table 7.1) and believed that if only the government were less spendthrift the problem would disappear without any need to tamper with the $2.80 peg.[3]

The decision taken in mid-1966 to hold to the $2.80 peg remained the basis of official policy until late in 1967, when it had to be abandoned. The decision to devalue to $2.40 was taken in the crisis atmosphere of November 1967 and is described by Wilson in his memoirs. He characterises the IMF's conditions for supporting sterling as

---

permanent way, though some might feel that a price advantage would be immediately beneficial. However, the pro-devaluationists were at this time cautious about presenting their case in public lest they should rock the boat. One of the rare published arguments in favour of devaluation was presented by M. FG. Scott ('Should the pound be devalued?') in *The Bankers' Magazine* of April 1967, p. 225, together with a criticism by R. J. Ball ('The case against devaluation of the pound').

[1] Wilson suggests (*The Labour Government 1964–1970*, p. 452) that Brown's move to the Foreign Office caused him to become very mindful of the international consequences of devaluation, which he came to view less favourably than he had in July 1966.

[2] Macmillan, *Pointing the Way, 1959–1961*, pp. 371–2.

[3] Richard Fry explains this view, which however he did not himself share, in 'Government spending overseas: how it has risen', *The Banker*, vol. 118, June 1968, p. 493.

unacceptable: they included stricter credit control, a tighter prices and incomes policy, and a pledge that sterling would not be floated.[1]

The die-hard defenders of the $2.80 peg, including Wilson and Callaghan, came to be criticised in post-mortems on devaluation conducted in 1970 and subsequently. But in the period up to the second half of 1969 few commentators dared to interpret what was then still recent history in this way. For initially it was the unwanted consequences of devaluation which were most in evidence, while the desired consequences – export-led growth and a marked improvement in the balance of payments – were delayed longer than anyone, including the Treasury and the National Institute, had expected. The National Institute had by May 1968 revised downwards from £500 million to between £300 and £400 million the surplus on current account for 1969 forecast immediately after devaluation.[2]

In the course of 1969 the belated improvement in the balance of payments became apparent and in 1970 there followed a massive swing into unprecedented surplus, which most people were well content to attribute to the 1967 devaluation without much allowance for other factors operating in the same direction, notably further deflationary measures in 1968 and 1969 and an upsurge of world demand for exported manufactures. More careful assessment of the probable effects of the 1967 devaluation, as they would have been had other things remained equal, suggests a more qualified enthusiasm for its efficacy. This is apparent from appendix 1, which sets out various estimates, made at the time and subsequently, of the consequences of devaluation.

The new $2.40 parity seems not to have come up for reconsideration before President Nixon's speech of 15 August 1971, which suspended the gold convertibility of the dollar and ushered in a regime of floating rates until the Smithsonian conference in December 1971, at which sterling and many other currencies were re-pegged with different dollar parities. The lesson drawn by the major powers from this episode was, however, that parities would probably need to be more adjustable in the 1970s than in the 1960s; with the possible exception of Canada none of them (and certainly not Britain) then favoured floating rates. Indeed, as late as his 1972 budget speech (only about three months before he unpegged sterling) Anthony Barber's pronouncements on exchange rates contain no explicit reference to the case for floating.

The float of June 1972 was always described as temporary, but the government was in no hurry to re-peg. Our national interest was

[1] Wilson, *The Labour Government 1964–1970*, p. 453. Right up to the last minute Wilson seems to have favoured floating the pound to devaluing to a lower peg, so the freedom to float was presumably important to him (ibid. pp. 38 and 448).

[2] *National Institute Economic Review*, no. 44, May 1968, p. 11. The Institute's analysis includes the first published reference to the now famous J-curve (see appendix 1, page 356).

probably thought to be best served by encouraging other countries to peg while ourselves retaining the freedom to float. All the same, our readiness to float, even on this basis, reflects an appreciable shift of government opinion in the first half of 1972. Outside commentators who favoured floating rates had certainly been pressing their case in the preceding year.[1] Moreover, recent experience had shown that floating was practicable and could be efficacious, at any rate as a means of discouraging excessive short-term capital movements. The Canadian dollar had been floating since 1 June 1970; the mark had floated between 29 September 1969 and the following 24 October, while both the mark and the florin floated from May 1971 until the Smithsonian settlement of December 1971; almost all currencies had floated between 15 August and 21 December 1971. Thus Barber's action in June 1972 was not without precedent.

His resolve to continue the float was soon backed by other countries' actions. The Swiss franc was floated as from January 1973; the crisis of February 1973 left the lira and the yen floating; that of March 1973 left all the major currencies floating, though eight countries of continental Europe operated a joint float. The United Kingdom was invited to join the joint float, but the Chancellor laid down conditions which were so far-reaching that his EEC partners were unable to accept them and the pound continued to float individually. The conditions were that:

(1) The initial exchange rates must be acceptable to each member state and each member state must have the 'unimpaired right', after consultation with the Council of Ministers, to alter the value of its currency in relation to currencies of other members.

(2) There must be financial support of the most far-reaching kind – all EEC countries being prepared to grant unlimited support without conditions and without obligation to repay.[2]

At the beginning of the floating regime the pound was allowed to find its own level, but in 1973 the Bank of England intervened in the market. In mid-May intensifying speculative pressures against the dollar propelled the pound to $2.58 and the Bank of England entered the market to moderate the pace of advance. Thereafter, however, the Bank's intervention was in support of the pound, the first occasion being in July.[3]

[1] For example Brittan in the *Financial Times*, 31 March 1971.
[2] The Chancellor said that the system could only be made proof against speculative capital flows if there was clear knowledge that support was unlimited (*Financial Times*, 5 March 1973).
[3] *Bank of England Quarterly Bulletin*, vol. 13, September 1973, pp. 275–6.

'BRITAIN ALONE' POLICIES

M. FG. Scott, writing at the end of the 1950s, identified a strand of economic thought, as exemplified in the then recent writings of Alan Day and Andrew Shonfield, as favouring what he called a 'Britain alone' solution to our external problems.[1] This solution envisaged that the United Kingdom should shed her international commitments in various ways; it had two facets – remedies for the weakness of the balance of payments and remedies for the illiquidity of the country's balance sheet of external assets and liabilities. The former, according to Shonfield writing in 1959, required both a drastic cut-back in long-term investment overseas and a thorough-going reappraisal of government expenditure abroad, although (on Shonfield's priorities) expenditure on aid to the developing countries was to be reviewed more sympathetically than expenditure for military and political objectives.[2]

The case for discouraging investment was partly fiscal: the investor in his private interest preferred an overseas investment to one in the United Kingdom whenever the yield after tax on the former exceeded the yield after tax on the latter, whereas in the national interest the comparison ought to be made net only of overseas taxation paid on overseas investments, since the tax revenue collected by the British government was enjoyed by the British economy no less than the interest or dividends received by United Kingdom residents. In addition, however, Day questioned the wisdom, from a national point of view, of permitting British companies to maintain their foothold in overseas markets by setting up local production facilities whenever this became more profitable than exporting from the United Kingdom.[3]

The remedy for excessive investment abroad was mainly to be sought in a stricter exchange control on outward capital transactions, and especially in putting an end to the exemption of sterling area transactions from the provisions of United Kingdom control.[4] There were admittedly other devices available for discouraging investment in the sterling area, but these had hitherto been only very mildly restrictive.

The second facet of the 'Britain alone' solution was, according to Day, 'that of reducing the risks arising from our illiquid capital position'.[5] The relation between Britain's short-term assets and liabilities made her (in a banking sense) illiquid and, since a substantial and allegedly volatile part of her short-term liabilities was the liquid

---

[1] M. FG. Scott, 'What should be done about the Sterling Area?', *Bulletin of the Oxford University Institute of Statistics*, vol. 21, November 1959, p. 228.
[2] Shonfield, *British Economic Policy since the War*, p. 265.
[3] Radcliffe Committee, *Principal Memoranda of Evidence*, vol. 3, p. 74.
[4] Shonfield, *British Economic Policy since the War*, pp. 252 and 273.
[5] Radcliffe Committee, *Principal Memoranda of Evidence*, vol. 3, para. 34 on p. 74.

sterling debts, such as Treasury bills, held overseas, both Day and Shonfield were concerned to find remedies for the 'problem of the sterling balances'.

Various kinds of relatively minor alleviations were proposed, several of which were later adopted by the British authorities. Thus both Day and Shonfield recommended an exchange-rate guarantee on sterling balances, and this was given on the bulk of such balances under the Basle Group Arrangement of 1968 (see page 352 below). Another suggestion was to sell British-owned long-term investments, as Callaghan subsequently did in 1966 and 1967 in the case of the official portfolio of dollar securities. Yet another was to tighten up the exchange control on short-term credits extended by London banks to overseas customers, as was actually done by a series of modifications to the exchange control regulations in September 1957 and on various subsequent occasions.

Apart from such minor alterations Day recommended a much more fundamental change which is strongly reminiscent of the stillborn Barber Plan put forward at the IMF Annual Meeting in 1971.[1] He wrote:

> The direction to explore, therefore, is that of finding some international organ to act as financial intermediary and, in effect, to take over London's work as an international central banker...If we could judiciously hand over to an international organisation sterling's functions as a reserve currency, it should be possible to retain most of our commercial banking business, making London into a sort of super-Amsterdam.[2]

This point of view gained more and more adherents, especially as in the course of the 1960s the City had demonstrated its ability to do business in non-sterling currencies, particularly dollars.[3] The overseas sterling area had been diversifying its reserves and was liable to switch out of sterling at times of balance of payments difficulties; from 1968 dollar-value guarantees had to be given to holders of sterling in the overseas sterling area. Moreover, overseas holdings of sterling represented a constraint on our interest-rate policy. Finally, our future EEC partners were unhappy about the role of sterling as a reserve currency and we had to give assurances, as a condition for joining, that we were prepared to contemplate the possibility that this role should be ended.

---

[1] Barber suggested that IMF Special Drawing Rights should become the *numéraire* in terms of which parities should be denominated, should eventually replace national currencies held as reserve assets (apart from working balances of intervention currencies) and should be issued in future in amounts adequate to meet the total need for additional reserve assets.

[2] Radcliffe Committee, *Principal Memoranda of Evidence*, vol. 3, pp. 75 and 76.

[3] Speech on 8 December 1971 by the Governor of the Bank of England (*Bank of England Quarterly Bulletin*, vol. 12, March 1972, pp. 84–5).

The more important of the 'Britain alone' policies actually adopted – the measures to reduce government expenditure overseas, changes in taxation of overseas profits and the tightening up of exchange controls – are considered in the next three sections.

GOVERNMENT EXPENDITURE OVERSEAS

In the 1960s both political Parties professed to be aware of the need to economise on government expenditure overseas in the interests of a healthier balance of payments. Harold Macmillan's memoirs relating to mid-1961 record the need to cut down defence expenditure and overseas aid in the light of the serious fall in invisible earnings.[1] Selwyn Lloyd, in his budget statement of 1962, said that the country still had a considerable way to go to achieve a satisfactory balance of payments surplus having regard to heavy and continuing obligations for defence, aid and investment overseas. The first Chancellor in the 1964 Labour government, James Callaghan, held substantially similar views; in particular, in his budget statement on 3 May 1966 he referred to the fact that the scale of government investment overseas, which over the last decade had been allowed to grow out of proportion to resources, imposed a heavy burden on the balance of payments. But the resolve to effect economies in such expenditure is not so apparent (at any rate as measured in current values) in the *ex post* statistics as set out above in table 7.1.

The first item of overseas expenditure to consider is aid to developing countries, which would have been exempt from Shonfield's proposed economy campaign but which the British government made determined efforts to contain within a ceiling.[2] Aid did rise slowly in the first half of the 1960s, but it remained static in the second half (chart 7.3).

The limitation of the aid programme was a policy which both political Parties adopted only with reluctance. In the case of the Labour Party, Harold Wilson had constantly argued in favour of the need for large capital flows to the developing countries as part of an international plan;[3] while in the 1964 election manifesto there was a promise to 'increase the share of national income devoted to essential aid pro-grammes, not only by loans and grants but by mobilizing unused industrial capacity to meet overseas needs'. In the case of the Conser-

[1] Macmillan, *Pointing the Way, 1959–1961*, p. 374.
[2] In the fiscal year 1965/6 official aid was subject to a ceiling of £205 million (*House of Commons, Seventh Report from the Estimates Committee, Session 1967–68. Overseas Aid*, London, HMSO, 1968, p. vii, para. 11); in 1966/7 it was £225 million and in 1967/8 £205 million (Bank of England, *Report for the year ended 28 February 1967*, p. 5). The ceiling remained at £205 million up to and including 1970/1; in 1971/2 it was raised to £251 million.
[3] D. Seers and P. Streeten, 'Overseas development policies' in Beckerman (ed.), *The Labour Government's Economic Record, 1964–1970*, pp. 118–19.

vative Party, Edward Heath, then Secretary of State for Industry, reaffirmed at the United Nations' Conference on Trade and Development (UNCTAD) in Geneva on 16 June 1964 the United Kingdom's support for the multilateral aid programme of the United Nations and gave a list of additional British multilateral aid to be given.[1]

Chart 7.3. *United Kingdom expenditure on overseas aid, 1961–73*

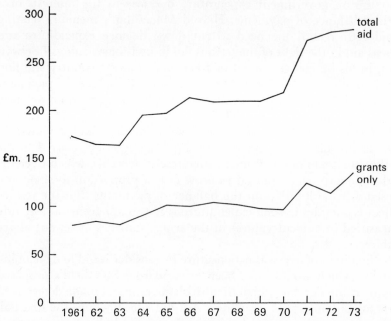

SOURCES: CSO, *United Kingdom Balance of Payments 1972*, table 42 and *1964–74*, table 36; column 4 of table 7.3.

But aid was recognised as a burden on our balance of payments. Heathcoat Amory's budget statement in April 1960 quoted from a speech by the Prime Minister in March arguing that overseas aid required the limiting of the growth of consumption at home and an increase in exports so as to provide a margin of foreign exchange.[2] The National Plan of 1965 argued that it would be necessary to scrutinise the aid programme with particular care so long as the balance of payments was under strain,[3] and the Labour government remained cautious in

---

[1] *Board of Trade Journal*, 19 June 1964, p. 1326.

[2] Speech delivered on 15 March 1960 to the Commonwealth and Empire Industries Association.

[3] Department of Economic Affairs, *The National Plan*, p. 71.

its attitude to aid throughout its period of office – some Labour supporters indeed thought that the Party had betrayed its ideals.[1]

Apart from aid to the developing countries, the main items of government expenditure overseas (table 7.3) are 'administrative and diplomatic' and 'military', the latter being much the more important. Callaghan, in his budget statement of April 1965, drew attention to the serious consequences of the growth of overseas military expenditure, which since 1959 had 'gone up year by year and from about £175 million to over £300 million'. *The National Plan*, published in the same year, quoted the Prime Minister as saying that the government 'are determined to achieve a saving of £50 to £100 million in overseas military expenditure' and noted the government's intention 'to restrict the Defence Budget at constant prices to the level of the 1964/5 Estimates, and to bring about an absolute reduction in that part which is incurred overseas'.[2]

From 1965 the balance of payments implications of defence were a constant theme in the annual *Statements on the Defence Estimates*. That of February 1965 drew attention to the heavy burden on our

Table 7.3. *Balance of payments on government services and transfers, 1960–73*

£ million

	Credits		Debits		
	Military	Other	Military	Aid grants[a]	Other
1960	41	4	213	..	..
61	41	5	239	80	59
62	33	6	257	84	58
63	35	5	272	81	69
64	38	7	306	91	80
65	25	21	293	101	99
66	25	17	307	100	105
67	25	11	292	104	103
68	28	16	294	102	114
69	27	21	298	98	119
1970	29	22	314	97	125
71	28	31	334	125	127
72	41	31	369	114	153
73	40	103	444	139	358

SOURCES: CSO, *United Kingdom Balance of Payments 1971*, table 12, *1972*, table 42, and *1964–74*, tables 8 and 36.

[a] The items in CSO, *United Kingdom Balance of Payments 1964–74*, table 36, with a cross-reference to table 8.

[1] Seers and Streeten, 'Overseas development policies', p. 150.
[2] Department of Economic Affairs, *The National Plan*, p. 71.

balance of payments of our forces in Germany.[1] In February 1966 it was argued that the maintenance of military tasks and capabilities outside Europe would impose an unacceptable strain on the economy and on our reserves of foreign exchange; consequently it had been decided that Britain would not undertake major operations of war except in cooperation with allies, nor would she provide another country with military assistance unless it was prepared to provide us with the facilities we needed to make such assistance effective in time; finally, there was to be no attempt to maintain defence facilities in an independent country against its wishes.[2]

Various policy measures were adopted in the course of the 1960s to mitigate the burden of military expenditure. In the first place, sterling expenditure in the United Kingdom was seen to have implications for our balance of payments and procurement policies were modified accordingly. Thus, in 1965, when the TSR-2 was cancelled, Callaghan (in his budget statement) emphasised that this would release resources to assist the balance of payments. However, more concern was apparent in the case of expenditure in foreign currencies. The policy was spelt out in February 1966: the British contribution in Europe was to be kept at roughly the same level, but only if some means were found of meeting the foreign exchange costs; substantial savings were to be made in the Mediterranean and the Middle East; in the Far East there was to be some limitation to the scale and nature of our military effort.[3] Little could be done to reduce expenditure in Europe (which in practice meant mainly in Germany) and in the event little was done, as table 7.4 shows. Instead the main effort was directed to finding some means of meeting the foreign exchange costs, in practice through the so-called 'offset agreements'. Table 7.4 also shows that the reductions in forces in the Mediterranean (Gibraltar, Malta and Cyprus) did not succeed in reducing costs measured in current values; the really important run-down in overseas military expenditure occurred east of Suez. This run-down eventually proceeded further than envisaged in February 1966, or even February 1967, when, though it was noted that on the independence of South Arabia in 1968 'we shall withdraw all our forces', nonetheless our continuing intention to maintain a military presence east of Suez was emphasised.[4] By July 1967, however, we had 'declared our intention to withdraw from South Arabia and

[1] Ministry of Defence, *Statement on the Defence Estimates 1965*, Cmnd 2592, London, HMSO, 1965, p. 8.
[2] Ministry of Defence, *Statement on the Defence Estimates 1966*, Part 1: *Defence Review*, Cmnd 2901, London, HMSO, 1966, p. 7.
[3] Ibid. p. 14.
[4] Ministry of Defence, *Statement on the Defence Estimates 1967*, Cmnd 3203, London, HMSO, 1967, p. 7.

the Aden base in January 1968'. In the Far East, we had 'decided to reach a reduction of about half the forces deployed in Singapore and Malaysia during 1970–71'.[1]

Table 7.4. *Overseas expenditure on military services, 1960–73*

£ million

	Western Europe	Gibraltar, Malta and Cyprus	Persian Gulf, S. Yemen	Far East	Other	Total
1960	63	39	12	53	36	203
61	73	40	18	57	36	224
62	84	41	19	59	40	243
63	94	40	22	62	32	250
64	101	37	23	71	38	270
65	101	35	25	82	27	270
66	108	34	27	86	28	283
67	107	34	25	78	20	264
68	119	35	14	80	27	275
69	130	40	10	69	33	282
1970	150	41	9	65	36	301
71	169	46	7	55	45	322
72	211	60	—	41	43	355
73	279	70	—	33	47	429

SOURCE: CSO, *United Kingdom Balance of Payments 1971*, table 14, and *1964–74*, table 9.

In February 1968, nine major decisions which the government had taken were listed:

(1) Britain's defence effort would be concentrated mainly in Europe and the North Atlantic area.

(2) The withdrawal of forces from Malaysia, Singapore and the Persian Gulf would be completed by the end of 1971.

(3) Service manpower would be reduced eventually by more than the 75,000 forecast in July 1967, and more quickly.

(4) The carrier force would be phased out and naval construction reduced.

(5) The Brigade of Gurkhas would be run down to 6000 by 1971.

(6) The order for 50 F111 aircraft was cancelled and the Royal Air Force transport force would be cut.

(7) Support facilities, including headquarters and the Ministry of Defence, would be cut.

(8) No special capability for use outside Europe would be maintained.

(9) A general capability, based in Europe including the United

[1] Ministry of Defence, *Supplementary Statement on Defence Policy 1967*, Cmnd 3357, London, HMSO, 1967, p. 5.

Kingdom, would be retained for use overseas as circumstances demanded, and for supporting United Nations operations as necessary.[1]

In a Report dated 1969 it is stated that, in spite of the 1967 devaluation, the sterling cost of our 'local defence expenditure in areas other than Germany will be cut by one-third by 1970/1, and by a further third in 1972/3 compared with the 1967 rate of expenditure'.[2] In addition to such economies achieved in respect of British forces and installations located overseas, reductions in foreign exchange expenditures were achieved by cuts in expenditure on armaments, especially United States military aircraft and missiles.[3]

The defence burden could also be reduced if some means were found of offsetting the foreign exchange costs either by a cash contribution or by 'offset purchases' of British equipment. Cash contributions were obtained to counterbalance expenditure in Germany in the years from 1955/6 to 1960/1;[4] thereafter the Germans helped by means of offset purchases. From 1961 to 1963 roughly half our foreign currency stationing costs were offset by German defence and other contracts. Thereafter the proportion increased, and in 1967/8 there were United States as well as German offset purchases. By 1968/9 about 90 per cent of our costs were offset, the sale of defence equipment playing a substantial part in this achievement.[5]

TAXATION OF OVERSEAS INVESTMENT INCOME

According to the National Plan, the tax system had tended to give too favourable a treatment to overseas compared with domestic investment.[6] This was emphasised by James Callaghan in his budget statement in 1965 in defence of some of the provisions of the new corporation tax which he was introducing. He said that the return we received from our long-term investments overseas was on average considerably less than the return on home investments, because income earned abroad bore tax in the country of origin, so that the benefit to the United Kingdom was measured by what remained after the payment of foreign taxes, whereas in the case of home investment the benefit to the national economy was measured by the return before tax.

[1] Ministry of Defence, *Statement on the Defence Estimates 1968*, Cmnd 3540, London, HMSO, 1968, pp. 2 and 3.

[2] Department of Economic Affairs, *The Task Ahead*, p. 49.

[3] Payments to United States manufacturers for military aircraft and missiles were only £2 million in 1964; they rose to £98 million in 1967 and £109 million in 1968, then declined to £61 million in 1969 and to only £20 million in total in the three years 1970-2 (CSO, *United Kingdom Balance of Payments 1963-73*, London, HMSO, 1974, p. 65).

[4] CSO, *United Kingdom Balance of Payments, 1972*, London, HMSO, 1972, p. 67.

[5] Ministry of Defence, *Statement on the Defence Estimates 1969*, Cmnd 3927, London, HMSO, 1969, p. 49.   [6] Department of Economic Affairs, *The National Plan*, p. 71.

His remedy for this state of affairs comprised three main changes. The first concerned portfolio investment overseas, where he proposed to phase out relief given to a British shareholder for 'underlying' tax – that is, tax levied by overseas governments on the *earnings* (not just the remitted dividends) of his foreign shareholdings.[1] The second change was relevant to direct overseas investment by British companies, and concerned the treatment of dividends paid by British companies out of overseas income; credit for overseas tax paid by the British company would be given only against the corporation tax for which the company was liable, not against the income tax due from a shareholder on his dividends. Thirdly, it was proposed to abolish the special tax treatment of overseas trade corporations, which had been introduced by the Conservative government in 1957.[2]

The Chancellor thought that his new corporation tax would, after the expiration of various transitional arrangements, improve the balance of payments, but by an amount which was 'not easy to quantify'. But he did attempt to quantify the benefit to the revenue, estimating that tax from companies with overseas income would ultimately be increased by about £100 million a year. In the next section we consider estimates of the combined effect on United Kingdom outward investment of the tax changes of 1965 and of various changes made in the 1960s in exchange controls on capital transactions.

EXCHANGE CONTROLS ON CAPITAL TRANSACTIONS

Until about 1969 changes in exchange controls were mostly designed to increase obstacles to capital outflows while avoiding discouragement to capital inflows. Then, with the desired improvement of the balance of payments in 1969, there was some relaxation of controls. In 1971 official policy also became less favourable to capital inflows; indeed, with the flight from the dollar precipitated by President Nixon's speech of 15 August,[3] there was a temporary imposition of completely new regulations to limit certain kinds of short-term capital inflows;[4] these were however repealed by the end of the year. The improvement in

---

[1] Relief on underlying tax continued where the shareholder was a British company owning 25 per cent or more of the shares in an overseas company.

[2] Overseas trade corporations are companies controlled and managed from this country, but having all their actual trading operations abroad. Since 1957 their trading profits earned abroad (though not, of course, dividends paid to British residents) had been free of United Kingdom tax. [3] See page 315 above.

[4] From 27 August banks were not permitted to pay interest on any additional sterling deposits from non-sterling countries; also a prohibition was placed on sales to residents of those countries of sterling certificates of deposit or short-dated public sector securities, and on the accepting by local authorities of further deposits from non-sterling countries (*Midland Bank Review*, May 1972, pp. 22–3).

Britain's balance of payments proved, however, to be short-lived; in 1972 sterling was floated and exchange controls extended to the sterling area; in 1973 a number of new measures were adopted to increase capital inflows.

Oil and miscellaneous investment

United Kingdom official statistics, as shown in tables 7.5 and 7.10, distinguish three categories of overseas investment–'direct', 'portfolio' and 'oil and miscellaneous'. Of these the last is mainly oil.[1] 'Miscellaneous' includes property investment, certain investments by the British insurance industry, London market borrowings by countries outside the sterling area and other minor items.

Sir Alec Cairncross has observed that oil investment continued throughout the 1960s at a remarkably stable rate, with no indication that exchange control was exercising much effect, despite changes in the regulations. There was also no marked divergence between the course of sterling and non-sterling investment.[2]

Portfolio investment outside the sterling area

Throughout the postwar period there have been restrictions on United Kingdom residents acquiring foreign exchange for the purchase of securities denominated in foreign currencies. Prior to 1957 they were permitted to buy such securities from residents of the overseas sterling area, but with the closing of the so-called 'Kuwait gap' in July 1957 sterling might not be used to make net purchases of foreign currency securities from residents outside the United Kingdom. United Kingdom residents have, however, enjoyed considerable freedom to switch from one foreign currency security to another. Moreover, United Kingdom investment trusts and some similar institutional investors have, since the latter part of the 1960s, been fairly readily permitted to buy such securities out of the proceeds of foreign currency borrowing.[3] United Kingdom investors, whether institutional or private, have also been permitted to trade freely among themselves in foreign currency

---

[1] According to CSO, *United Kingdom Balance of Payments 1964–74*, London, HMSO, 1975, table 20, United Kingdom overseas investment in 'oil and miscellaneous' totalled £1145 million in the ten years 1963–72 inclusive. In the same ten years other changes affecting the value of the United Kingdom's overseas 'oil and miscellaneous' assets amounted to an upward revaluation of £90 million (ibid. table 35). Hence the United Kingdom's overseas 'oil and miscellaneous' assets increased in the ten years by £1235 million. But 'oil' assets alone increased from £1100 million at the end of 1962 to £2250 million at the end of 1972 (ibid. table 35). Thus 'miscellaneous' increased by only £85 million.

[2] Sir Alec Cairncross. *Control of Long-term International Capital Movements*, Washington (D.C.) Brookings Institution, 1973, p. 67.

[3] As have also private investors from December 1970, when this permission was extended to 'professional managers of securities' on behalf of resident individual clients.

Table 7.5. *United Kingdom private investment outside the sterling area,^{a} 1960–73*

£ million

	Direct investment^b financed by:			Portfolio investment	Oil and miscellaneous investment	Total
	Unremitted profits^c	Other means	Total			
1960	34	56	90	−24	55	121
61	38	64	102	−39	64	127
62	39	48	87	−34	39	92
63	47	54	101	13	43	157
64	49	53	102	28	82	212
65	66	56	122	−44	91	169
66	94	63	157	−44	49	162
67	95	44	139	18	73	230
68	157	76	233	79	61	373
69	171	65	236	13	44	293
1970	164	152	316	70	115	501
71	181	307	488	80	115	683
72	259	247	506	705	61	1272
73	437	726	1163	215	695	2073

SOURCES: CSO, *United Kingdom Balance of Payments 1971*, tables 26 and 29, and later figures from the CSO (by convention these sources give the figures with reversed signs from those above).

^{a} Up to June 1972 the sterling area comprised the Commonwealth (except Canada), South Africa, the Irish Republic and a number of smaller contries. Membership is taken to be unchanged thereafter.

^{b} Other than oil and miscellaneous. The item 'direct borrowing from financial subsidiaries abroad (net)' in table 7.6 is here treated as disinvestment.

^{c} Profits of subsidiaries and associated companies.

securities, many of which (predominantly ones denominated in United States dollars) have been regularly quoted on the London Stock Exchange. The shortage of such securities relative to the demand for them has usually raised their sterling price in London to a premium over their dollar price in New York divided by the official sterling–dollar exchange rate. This premium, the so-called investment currency premium, rose to 40 per cent or even higher on occasions (chart 7.4).

Originally there were separate switching arrangements for securities denominated in dollars and those denominated in other foreign currencies, but the two categories were amalgamated in 1962 to form 'investment currency' and residents could then switch freely from one foreign currency security to another, provided that it was quoted.[1]

Further changes in the 1960s to the controls on outward portfolio investment were largely in the direction of greater restriction. As from

[1] *Bank of England Quarterly Bulletin*, vol. 7, September 1967, p. 256.

the budget of April 1965, 25 per cent of the proceeds of all sales of foreign currency securities, including sales abroad for the purpose of switching investments, had to be sold on the official exchange market, leaving only 75 per cent available for sale as investment currency (at a premium) or for reinvestment. At the same time United Kingdom residents were no longer allowed to use investment currency to buy property outside the sterling area for private use, as had been permissible since April 1964; instead they had to purchase foreign currency

Chart 7.4. *The investment currency premium, 1961–72*

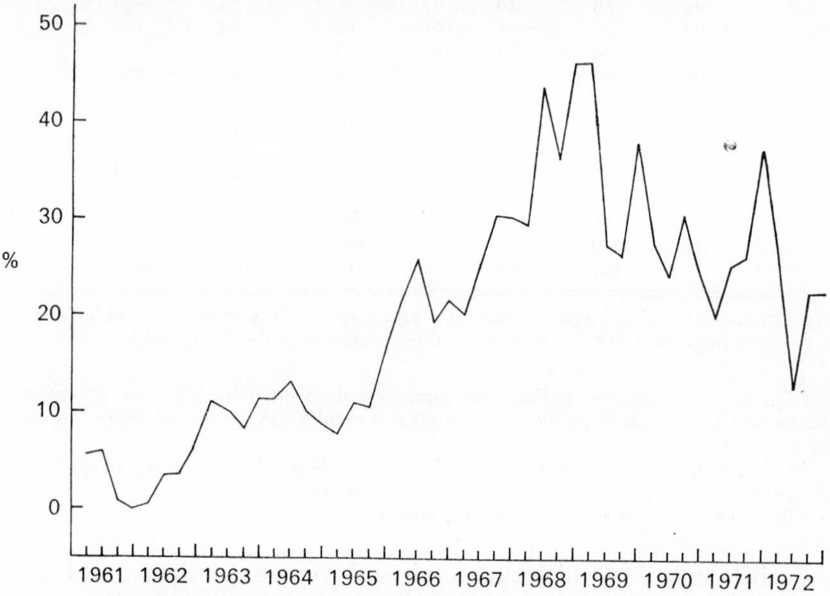

SOURCES: Bank of England, *Statistical Abstract*, no. 1, table 28, and no. 2, table 28.

in a separate 'property currency' market.[1] Then in May 1966 a 'voluntary programme' restricted institutional portfolio investment in the non-sterling area as well as in the four developed countries of the overseas sterling area: institutional investors were asked to ensure that any such investment did no more than balance their disinvestment and foreign currency borrowing. The intention of this restriction was presumably to depress the investment currency premium, and hence to encourage the 'bleeding' of the investment currency pool for financing *direct* investment; as from May 1962 British companies had been permitted to draw on the pool for this purpose.

In 1969 and 1970 there were minor easements in controls: in the

[1] Ibid. pp. 258–9.

1969 budget institutional portfolio investment outside the sterling area was exempted from the voluntary programme, and in August 1970 the property currency pool was once again merged with the investment currency pool.

What effect can be attributed to official actions in the 1960s aimed at discouraging portfolio investment outside the sterling area? The changes in tax arrangements and in exchange controls made by James Callaghan in April 1965 and in May 1966 were not followed by any sustained decrease in such investment, as may be seen from the fourth column of table 7.5. There was admittedly an excess of disinvestment over investment in 1965 and 1966, but this had also occurred in the three years 1960–2, and after 1966 the balance was always in the opposite direction.

Table 7.6. *Methods of financing direct investment[a] outside the sterling area, 1967–72*

£ million

	1967	1968	1969	1970	1971	1972
Eurocurrency borrowing by parent companies from UK banks	35	64	48	138	133	87
Direct borrowing abroad by parent companies	39	46	46	68	97	162
Direct borrowing from financial subsidiaries abroad (net)[b]	..	23	32	17	61	57
Use of investment currency pool (net)	5	−28	−15	−5	−12	−29
Total	..	105	111	218	279	277

SOURCES: CSO, *United Kingdom Balance of Payments 1971*, table 49, *1972*, table 47, and *1963–73*, table 47.

[a] Excluding 'oil and miscellaneous'.
[b] Treated as outward disinvestment in table 7.5.

This net disinvestment in the five years cannot be explained in detail, since the necessary statistics are lacking in the first half of the 1960s, but part of the explanation is that as from May 1962 the investment currency pool could be drawn upon to finance direct investment. However, drawings on the pool for this purpose were not serious as from 1967, when the relevant statistical series starts (table 7.6) – indeed from 1968 direct investment and disinvestment have on balance made a net contribution to the pool. More serious was the bleeding of the investment currency pool by the 25 per cent surrender scheme (table 7.7). Hence the question arises why it was possible for portfolio investment not merely to equal but to exceed portfolio disinvestment, as

Table 7.7. *Yield to United Kingdom official reserves of the 25 per cent surrender scheme, 1965–72*

£ million

	From net sales through investment currency market of:		Other	Total yield
	Portfolio investments	Direct investments		
1965[a]	56	−21	18	53
66	69	3	−2	70
67	58	−2	32	88
68	59	38	7	104
69	126	21	−38	109
1970	52	9	26	87
71	130		−2	128
72	162		−24	138

SOURCE: CSO, *United Kingdom Balance of Payments 1973*, table 25, and *1965–75*, table 20.

[a] Excluding the first quarter.

happened regularly from 1967 onwards. The main answer must be foreign borrowing by institutional investors,[1] and this is broadly confirmed by official statistics of foreign currency borrowing for portfolio investment (see table 7.8).

Table 7.8. *Foreign currency borrowing to finance portfolio investment, 1967–73*

£ million

	Borrowing	Repayments
1967	38·0	—
68	85·0	—
69	96·1	22·2
1970	52·9	3·5
71	111·9	7·5
72	696·7	37·6
73	373·5	221·7[a]

SOURCE: Bank of England.

[a] Excludes £35·6 million repayments with investment currency.

[1] Foreign securities bought with foreign currency borrowing can be switched at will or sold to repay the loan. In either case the transactions do not involve the purchase or sale of sterling; hence the investment currency premium does not apply, nor does the 25 per cent surrender scheme.

Direct (non-oil) investment outside the sterling area

There was a gradual easing of the restrictions on overseas direct investment in the 1950s and by 1956 practically no outward investment which could show a reasonable economic advantage was refused. However, in July 1961 restrictions were tightened on direct investment (other than 'oil and miscellaneous') in countries outside the sterling area and from then on investment qualified for official exchange only if it would yield commensurate benefits to the balance of payments within two or three years.[1] Companies which could not comply with this criterion were, however, permitted to borrow foreign currency to finance their overseas investment. Prior to July 1961 there had been no provision for such borrowing, but thereafter 'long-term' borrowing was permitted for 'non-criterion' projects. By 'long-term' the authorities generally had in mind a period in excess of five years, although in the case of very long-term loans – ten to fifteen years – repayments might start before five years. In any case, however, borrowing could not be repaid except to the extent that benefits from the investment had been received by the United Kingdom in the forms of exports to countries outside the sterling area, of interest, dividends and profits, or of royalties, licence fees, management fees and other payments for technical 'know-how'.

To alleviate the difficulties of companies unable to borrow in foreign currency, it was conceded in May 1962 that direct investment which did not satisfy the July 1961 criterion for finance at the official exchange rate might be financed through the investment currency market at the cost of paying the current premium (then around 3 per cent). This minor easement was, however, followed by changes in the opposite direction in 1965 and 1966. In the first place the 25 per cent surrender scheme introduced in April 1965 was applied to all transactions which could give rise to investment currency, including sales of direct investments outside the sterling area. At the same time the July 1961 criterion for access to foreign exchange at the official rate was tightened up: the extra conditions imposed were that the project must bring a substantial continuing return to the balance of payments and that there should be good prospects that the overall return to the balance of payments would, in the short term, equal or exceed the capital outflow. Where official exchange was denied, investment continued to be financed with investment currency or by long-term borrowing abroad.

Soon after, in July 1965, it was laid down that even projects satisfying the April 1965 criteria could no longer be financed by foreign currency acquired at the official rate, and in May 1966 the same criteria were

[1] *Bank of England Quarterly Bulletin*, vol. 7, September 1967, p. 258.

applied for access to investment currency; henceforth all non-criterion projects had to be financed from foreign currency borrowing.[1] In January 1968 there was a slight easement: the ban imposed in July 1965 was lifted in the case of direct investment outside the sterling area for so-called 'super-criterion' projects; foreign exchange was henceforth obtainable at the official rate for projects directly concerned with promoting British exports up to a limit of £50,000 or half the investment (whichever was the greater) provided that there was a net benefit to the balance of payments within eighteen months and continuing thereafter. This meant that from January 1968 there were three kinds of direct investment project:

(a) 'super-criterion' projects, which could wholly or in part be financed with foreign exchange bought at the official rate;

(b) 'criterion' projects, satisfying the criteria laid down in April 1965, which could be financed only with foreign exchange borrowed 'long-term' abroad, or purchased (more expensively than at the official rate) in the investment currency market;

(c) 'non-criterion' projects, which (if authorised at all) could only be financed by 'long-term' foreign currency borrowing.

In 1971, when the balance of payments had temporarily ceased to be a problem, there were several further easements. From March, categories (b) and (c) were amalgamated, so that *all* projects which did not meet the super-criterion (as well as those that did), could be financed via the investment currency market (as an alternative to borrowing abroad) and from May the upper limit for the finance of 'super-criterion' projects by foreign exchange purchased at the official rate was raised from £50,000 to £250,000. Moreover, in the 1971 budget the previous requirement that foreign currency borrowing had to be 'long-term' was relaxed by permitting 'self-liquidating' borrowing; that is, borrowing might be repaid as soon as it could be shown that equivalent benefits had been received in the United Kingdom from the investment. Then in the 1972 budget statement a further easement was announced in respect of British companies making direct investment in EEC countries, Denmark or Norway.[2]

With the benefit of hindsight and *ex post* statistics, it now seems that neither the tightening of exchange controls on direct outward investment in countries outside the sterling area from July 1961 nor the fiscal discouragement in the 1965 budget had the effect of reversing the rising trend in such investment in the 1960s, or of tilting downwards the more or less level trend in the amount financed otherwise than out of unremitted profits (this is clear from table 7.5); nor to any great

---

[1] Ibid.
[2] This easement was withdrawn in March 1974.

extent did they result in direct investment being financed through the investment currency pool (at least from 1967, see table 7.6). But (not unexpectedly) the tightening of controls was associated with substantial non-sterling borrowing to finance direct investment outside the sterling area (as also shown in table 7.6).

Would the upward trend of direct investment (excluding oil) outside the sterling area have been much steeper in the absence of restrictions and of fiscal deterrents? Sir Alec Cairncross thinks probably not.[1] As we see from table 7.5, the rising trend in the 1960s was roughly matched by a similar increase in unremitted profits, which could in practice be fairly readily applied to financing further investment. The official restriction which applied to such financing was the 'normal' requirement that at least two thirds of after-tax profits should be repatriated, but official statistics show a ratio of much less than two thirds, indeed as little as 46 per cent in the five years 1963–7 and 39 per cent in the following five years.[2]

This is largely because exchange control applies only to companies where voting control lies within the UK, whereas the balance of payments statistics include also figures for earnings of overseas companies where the UK interest is a minority; and because remittances of royalties, management fees and certain other earnings count towards the two thirds requirement, while stock appreciation is generally disregarded in calculating earnings.[3]

Would the amount of direct investment *not* financed out of unremitted profits have shown a rising (instead of a roughly level) trend in the 1960s if tax arrangements and exchange controls had been left unchanged? In Sir Alec's view the figures suggest that the criterion introduced in July 1961 for access to official exchange cannot have been applied very restrictively. This is supported by the fact that the permission given in May 1962 to use the investment currency market led neither to an upsurge of direct investment nor to an increase in the investment currency premium to much more than 10 per cent. As from April 1965 access to both the official and the investment currency markets was progressively tightened and the premium rose much higher, but by then the practice of borrowing overseas to finance direct investment developed very rapidly and restricted access to the currency markets was no insuperable obstacle.[4]

[1] Cairncross, *Control of Long-term International Capital Movements.*
[2] CSO, *United Kingdom Balance of Payments 1963–73*, table 20. The figures relate to British companies' subsidiary and associated companies in the non-sterling area.
[3] Treasury, *Economic Progress Report*, no. 78, September 1976, p. 1.
[4] Cairncross, *Control of Long-term International Capital Movements*, pp. 63–5.

Overseas borrowing to finance overseas investment

The considerable scale of non-sterling borrowing for outward investment, including 'oil and miscellaneous' as well as 'portfolio' and
'direct' (table 7.9), resulted in a state of affairs in which the grand total
of British private investment outside the sterling area was financed in
the second half of the 1960s without leading to any drain on official
reserves. This is clear from the second column of the same table.
Moreover, the weight of evidence appears to support the view that
British investors who had access to facilities for foreign currency
borrowing were not greatly restrained in their overseas investment
outside the sterling area by exchange controls. On this view, the only
important category of overseas investment that was discouraged (to
the extent of becoming substantially negative) was portfolio investment
by private individuals, who were only permitted to borrow abroad for
this purpose as from December 1970.[1]

Table 7.9. *Financing of net private overseas investment outside
the scheduled territories,[a] 1965–73*

£ million

	Borrowing in foreign currency	Effect on total currency inflow
1965	78	21
66	47	21
67	133	55
68	231	4
69	163	44
1970	265	20
71	388	−53
72	980	201
73	869	26

SOURCE: CSO, *United Kingdom Balance of Payments 1965–75*, table 20.

[a] Up to 23 June 1972 the scheduled territories were the sterling area; thereafter they were
the British Isles (see page 337 below).

This outcome seems to have been broadly in line with the objectives
of government policy. It was reliably reported that the aim of
Callaghan's changes in tax and exchange control arrangements in 1965
was an improvement of £150 million a year in the net balance of the
private capital account.[2] At the time it was accepted, and even

---

[1] See footnote 3 on page 326 above.
[2] H. F. R. Catherwood, *Britain with the Brakes Off*, London, Hodder & Stoughton, 1966,
p. 124.

expected, that this could be achieved only by a reduction in the overall level or the rate of growth of such investment. But after the middle of the 1960s, and increasingly from about 1968 onwards, it was apparent to the authorities that British companies were readily able to find international sources of finance; this was, of course, linked with the development of the Euromarkets. The most immediate effect was to make foreign currency borrowing the major basis of financing direct investment and to make it possible to authorise foreign currency borrowing for institutional portfolio investment. Certainly in the last two or three years of the decade the objective of the authorities was no longer to limit overseas investment, but only to ensure that its financing did not impose a strain on the balance of payments; overseas investment which met this requirement was not discouraged.

Investment in the overseas sterling area

Up to May 1966 the British exchange control imposed no impediments to capital movements within the sterling area, except (as from July 1957) in the case of foreign currency securities. However, this did not imply that companies from the overseas sterling area could freely make capital issues on the London market, since there was all the time a control on all overseas capital issues and this has always been highly restrictive. On the other hand, up to May 1966 there was no restriction on United Kingdom portfolio investment in securities issued in the overseas sterling area, nor on bank credit or trade credit to the overseas sterling area, nor on direct investment by British companies in branches, subsidiaries, or associated companies in the overseas sterling area.

Measures taken in May 1966 modified these rules in respect of Australia, New Zealand, South Africa and the Irish Republic. British companies which had plans for direct investment in these sterling area countries which did not satisfy the criteria applied outside the sterling area were asked if the plans could be postponed for the time being; or if that was not practicable, whether finance could be raised from local sources. In addition, institutional investors were asked to refrain from any significant increase in their portfolios of securities in the four countries as well as in all countries outside the sterling area.[1] This 'voluntary programme' was in principle only temporary, but it was renewed from time to time until its termination was announced in the 1972 budget statement.

What was the effect on the United Kingdom balance of payments of the voluntary programme? The Chancellor's statement answered this question in a roundabout way, which the National Institute took to imply that he was hoping for an improvement of perhaps £35 million

[1] *Bank of England Quarterly Bulletin*, vol. 7, September 1967, pp. 259 and 260.

a year.[1] Whether such a saving was in fact achieved cannot be established with any confidence. The relevant official statistics (see table 7.10) do not reveal any sustained discouragement of portfolio investment, either by the budget of April 1965 or by the voluntary programme of May 1966. The statistics do show, in the case of direct investment net of unremitted profits, a run of relatively low annual amounts in 1966–8, but this may have been fortuitous; the 1969 and 1970 figures are higher, despite the fact that tax arrangements continued unchanged and that the voluntary programme remained in operation until April 1972. Thus the *ex post* evidence is inconclusive.

Table 7.10. *United Kingdom private investment in the overseas sterling area,[a] 1960–73*

£ million

	Direct investment[b] financed by:			Portfolio investment	Oil and miscellaneous investment	Total
	Unremitted profits[c]	Other means	Total			
1960	51	109	160	−13	54	201
61	36	88	124	11	51	186
62	56	66	122	−5	33	150
63	71	64	135	−8	36	163
64	98	63	161	−25	51	187
65	101	85	186	−50	63	199
66	89	30	119	−39	61	141
67	95	47	142	41	43	226
68	120	57	177	157	20	354
69	150	163	313	21	52	386
1970	157	73	230	20	35	285
71	148	39	187	−60	25	152
72	208	23	231	−120	—	111
73	410	51	461	−510	−165	−214

SOURCES: CSO, *United Kingdom Balance of Payments 1971*, tables 26 and 29, and later figures from the CSO (by convention these sources give the figures with reversed signs from those above).

[a] Membership of the sterling area taken as unchanged from June 1972.

[b] Other than oil and miscellaneous.

[c] Profits of subsidiaries and associated companies.

In June 1972, when sterling was allowed to float, exchange control was extended to transactions with the sterling area almost as strictly as to countries outside the area.[2] According to Anthony Barber the

[1] *National Institute Economic Review*, no. 36, May 1966, pp. 7–8.

[2] Concessions for investment in the overseas sterling area which remained operative until March 1974 were exemption from the 25 per cent surrender rule for portfolio investment (so that 100 per cent of the overseas currency proceeds of disposals of overseas sterling area securities could be sold at a premium in the investment currency market) and permission

two decisions were related, because a speculative outflow to these countries might follow the float; he announced that pending consultation with the governments concerned he had taken immediate temporary measures to apply exchange control to transactions with the sterling area.[1] However, one is left in some doubt as to whether the two decisions can have been so closely linked; the Chancellor offered no evidence that floating would be likely to provoke a speculative capital outflow to the overseas sterling area, nor have the restrictions he imposed been only temporary.

As a result of the new restrictions, the scheduled territories (the area in which exchange control permitted free capital movements) were reduced from the whole of the sterling area to the British Isles (plus Gibraltar from January 1973). Thus, at last, the step was taken which had been advocated by Day and Shonfield in the 1950s. Since that time the course of events had made the case for it more persuasive, quite apart from the temporary reason adduced by Barber. The whole idea of privileges to the sterling area (other than the Irish Republic) was difficult to reconcile with membership of the EEC; this had been realised as early as 1961. Freedom to invest in the overseas sterling area was also seen as inconsistent with our determination, dating from 1961, to be more discriminating in our official attitude to overseas investment. There had been a heavy capital outflow to Australia and South Africa in 1968 and 1969, which suggested that the 1966 voluntary programme was not very restrictive. This may explain why the programme was abandoned in the budget statement of 1972, only to be replaced by tighter control at the next convenient opportunity.

We have not yet assessed the effect of extending exchange controls to the overseas sterling area and thereby bringing investment in these countries within the scope of the investment currency pool. However, it is probably one of the reasons for the massive portfolio disinvestment in the overseas sterling area in 1973 (table 7.10). The proceeds of such disinvestment could be sold at a premium in the investment currency market (the 25 per cent surrender rule not being applied to the sterling area until March 1974) to finance investment in the non-sterling area, which in 1972 and again in 1973 reached record heights (table 7.5).

Measures to increase the capital inflow

In January 1968 the government adopted a policy of financing our balance of payments deficit by encouraging the nationalised industries and local authorities to borrow in non-sterling currencies. This policy

---

for all direct investment in the overseas sterling area approved by the British authorities to be financed by buying overseas currency at the official rate.

[1] Treasury, *Economic Progress Report*, no. 30, August 1972.

was implemented by introducing forward exchange cover, given by the Treasury, for dollar borrowing by public sector bodies. However, in July 1971, with the improvement in the balance of payments, the cover was restricted to maturities of ten years or more, and at the time of the 1972 budget it was withdrawn altogether.

In March 1973 foreign exchange cover facilities were reintroduced in respect of dollar borrowing by public sector institutions and in October they were extended to other currencies. Much the biggest public sector borrower in 1973 was the Electricity Council, which raised a dollar loan of $1000 million; the total of all public sector non-sterling borrowing in 1973 net of repayments was $2600 million.[1]

Private sector foreign currency borrowing to finance domestic investment was, like public sector borrowing, affected by the improvement in the balance of payments in 1971 and by its subsequent deterioration. In January 1971 a ban was imposed on such borrowing for domestic use by United Kingdom firms with a maturity of less than five years, but in October 1973 the minimum maturity was reduced from five to two years.[2]

EXPORT PROMOTION AND IMPORT-SAVING

Throughout the 1950s a great deal of help, advice and information on selling abroad was available to firms from government sources through the Export Services Branch and the regional offices of the Board of Trade, and through the commercial officers of the Diplomatic Service; credit insurance for exports was available through the Export Credit Guarantee Department (ECGD). In 1964 the Labour government introduced a number of additional measures to promote exports, some of them aimed particularly at smaller firms. The export rebate scheme was introduced,[3] credit insurance facilities were greatly improved and a list of some 400 established exporters willing to help firms making complementary products to export was published – the so-called 'pick-a-back' scheme. Government finance was made available through the British National Export Council to encourage selling missions abroad and buying missions to Britain, and to support collective market research. A study was made of the feasibility of setting up 'a new form of export selling organisation which will give special attention to the needs of those smaller companies which at present export either very little or not at all'.[4] The evolution of the Export Credit Guarantee Department's facilities for medium-term export

[1] *Bank of England Quarterly Bulletin*, vol. 16, March 1976, p. 80.
[2] *Financial Times*, 19 October 1973.
[3] See below page 344.
[4] Department of Economic Affairs, *The National Plan*, p. 73.

credit and of the various other arrangements made between the Bank of England and the commercial banks to improve the credit facilities available to British exporters (and subsequently to British shipbuilders) is set out below in appendix II. The increase in medium-term and long-term credit extended under ECGD guarantees is shown in table 7.11.

Table 7.11. *Increase in medium-term and long-term export credit extended under ECGD guarantees, 1965–73*

£ million

| | Buyer credit schemes | Bank guarantees | |
		Specific	Comprehensive
1965	42	−1	—
66	37	28	—
67	77	34	41
68	116	37	53
69	125	77	40
1970	150	119	62
71	229	124	25
72	259	53	10
73	259	−5	45

SOURCE: CSO, *United Kingdom Balance of Payments 1965–75*, table 22 (by convention this source gives the figures with reversed signs from those above).

Among these new arrangements for export promotion, there was at least one failure: the Overseas Marketing Corporation Limited (which was the 'new form of export selling organisation') did not achieve the expected results and was wound up at the end of 1970 at a loss to the taxpayer of £½ million.[1]

Turning now to import-saving, the National Plan of 1965 refers to 'measures to reduce the growth of manufactured imports';[2] on this issue the Economic Development Committees had already set in hand action to save imports in their fields.[3] Specific mention was made of the work of the Economic Development Committees for machine tools, chemicals and mechanical engineering, and to a Report by the NEDC.[4]

The progress made in import-saving over the subsequent four years or so by the three named industries may be judged from Reports by

[1] Report of the Comptroller and Auditor General in Treasury, *Appropriation Accounts 1972–73* (Classes I–V, Civil), London, HMSO, 1974, pp. xvi and xvii.
[2] Department of Economic Affairs, *The National Plan*, p. 73.
[3] Ibid. p. 46.
[4] NEDC, *Imported Manufactures: an inquiry into competitiveness*, London, HMSO, 1965.

their Economic Development Committees.[1] The impression left is that there were only modest achievements to record and that such as there were owe little to government policy. The share of imports in the home market showed little sign of falling: in machine tools, it was 26 per cent in 1960–5, but seemed 'likely to account for 30 per cent of total home consumption in 1972'; in chemicals, imports were 'expected to continue to grow at $11\frac{1}{2}$ per cent a year', or considerably faster than the rate suggested by the Department of Economic Affairs in 1969 in *The Task Ahead*; in mechanical engineering, imports in 1971 and 1972 were expected to increase at less than the past trend rate, but this had been about 10 per cent a year at constant prices. The only decisive intervention by the government in manufacturing industry in the interests of import-saving was not in any of the three industries specifically mentioned, but in respect of three new smelters in the aluminium industry (see chapter 10).

OFFICIAL TRANSACTIONS IN THE FORWARD MARKET

The traditional instrument for discouraging a capital outflow from London and encouraging an inflow was to increase Bank Rate, which raised the level of short-term interest rates prevailing in London relative to those in other countries. But, as the Radcliffe Committee reported in 1959: 'The general tenor of the evidence submitted to us was that in post-war conditions no large-scale transference of funds was to be expected in response to changes in short-term interest rates unsupported by other measures. Two important influences limiting this response have been fear of official interference with the movement of funds and fear of depreciation of sterling.' In consequence, 'such movement of funds as there has been has almost always, at least until lately, been covered in the forward exchange market; that is to say, the foreign holder of sterling has generally taken the precaution of selling it forward at a discount so as to avoid any larger loss through a possible devaluation of the pound.'[2]

If, however, all short-term investment in London is so covered, in the absence of official support in the forward market there will be a rapid fall in the forward value of sterling to the point where covered investment in London is no more profitable than elsewhere. The monetary authorities can, however, maintain the attractiveness of London by supporting the forward pound, and this is what two witnesses to the

---

[1] NEDO, *Industrial Report by the Chemicals EDC on the Economic Assessment to 1972*, *Industrial Report by the Machine Tools EDC on the Economic Assessment to 1972* and *Industrial Report by the Mechanical Engineering EDC on the Economic Assessment to 1972*, London, 1970.

[2] Treasury, *Radcliffe Report*, para. 697.

Radcliffe Committee recommended should regularly be done.[1] Jasay's evidence recommended official support for the forward rate as a means of making sterling assets adequately attractive *in yield* to investors who have the option of investing in other currencies; his point is that many such investors are (as the Radcliffe Committee believed) interested in comparing covered yields, so that a forward discount on sterling reduces its attraction no less than an unfavourable interest-rate differential. Spraos, on the other hand, had in mind the need to protect the official reserves from a 'speculative attack' on sterling, conducted by transactors seeking to make a capital gain or avoid a capital loss. The Radcliffe Committee's findings gave support (though not very strong support) to the case for forward intervention, but only as a means of retaining a steady clientele of investors in sterling, not as a means of meeting a speculative attack.

The Committee did not spell out its reasons for rejecting the argument put to it by Spraos. It is, however, reasonable to suppose that their view was akin to that of Oppenheimer, who maintained that, in the face of speculation against the pound, the authorities had the choice between holding spot sterling near to its \$2.80 parity either by buying it spot or by buying it forward, and that there was not much to choose as between the two.[2] The case put to the Committee by Jasay was more persuasive since, insofar as investors require forward cover, the yield they get on their sterling investments incorporates the difference between the spot and forward rate; thus, if the latter is not officially supported, a flow of covered investment into sterling will quickly widen the difference to the point at which the covered yield on sterling assets becomes unattractive.

The Treasury's oral evidence to the Radcliffe Committee argued 'that there is bound to be at times some participation by the Exchange Equalisation Account in the forward market. But that is quite a different thing from having a definite policy of supporting the rate, which would cast great doubt, which does not exist at present, over the value of the published figures'.[3] And this seems to represent official policy up to the time of the prolonged sterling crisis which began in November

---

[1] A. E. Jasay, 'Alternative ways of defending the exchange rate' in Radcliffe Committee, *Principal Memoranda of Evidence*, vol. 3, p. 132; J. Spraos, 'Speculation, arbitrage and sterling', *Economic Journal*, vol. 69, March 1959.

[2] Spraos would not accept that there is 'not much to choose', since if the authorities support the spot rate the amount of support needed is revealed in the published figures for official reserves, whereas the amount of forward support is never published. It can therefore be argued that bear speculation against sterling is encouraged more by the knowledge that official support has been needed to hold the spot rate than by the suspicion that official support has been needed to hold the forward rate.

Oppenheimer's views are quoted on page 342, below.

[3] Radcliffe Committee, *Minutes of Evidence*, reply to question 9704.

1964. Thereafter, however, until the devaluation of sterling in November 1967, the Exchange Equalisation Account intervened to prevent the forward rate falling to a serious discount,[1] and the intervention is believed to have been on some occasions on a massive scale.[2]

Thus, there was in November 1964 an important change in official tactics in the forward market. Oppenheimer, writing in February 1966, was clearly rather unhappy about the change of policy, but conceded that 'the authorities did keep some short-term money in London by dint of accumulating vast forward commitments. But they might easily have borrowed more from the central banks instead. In effect, they used part of the central-bank credit arrangements to back their forward commitments. It is these arrangements that were in every way the decisive factor. Forward intervention did not make a great deal of difference'.[3] However, he obviously thought that the authorities had been lucky in 1964/5 and might not be equally so in the future; in the event his misgivings were vindicated in the crisis of 1967, when the support operation failed and the authorities were forced to devalue. On that occasion a policy initially adopted to retain a loyal clientele of foreign investors ended up, in the weeks preceding devaluation, by affording unlimited facilities for bear speculation at the expense of the Exchange Equalisation Account. Moreover, it is difficult to see how this outcome could have been avoided, given that the policy of support had been adopted and become known to market operators. Any subsequent withdrawal of support would have been interpreted as a sure sign that the authorities were no longer committed to avoiding devaluation, and the resulting flight from the pound would have forced the immediate abandonment of the $2.80 peg. After devaluation the Account apparently reverted to its earlier policy of severely limiting its intervention in the forward market.[4]

---

[1] *Bank of England Quarterly Bulletin*, vol. 10, March 1970, p. 39.

[2] The CSO's *United Kingdom Balance of Payments 1972*, p. 7, quotes figures for 'EEA loss on forward commitments' amounting to £105 million in 1967 and £251 million in 1968, or £356 million in total. We are also informed (p. 78) that 'this item records the loss arising from the fact that the forward commitments of the Exchange Equalisation Account with the market entered into before devaluation in 1967 have been recorded as being settled on maturity at the new parity'. Since the parity fell by $\frac{1}{7}$, the implication is that at the time of devaluation the Account had outstanding forward commitments to the tune of $2981 million (the devaluation loss of $\frac{1}{7} = \$854$ million being £356 million at $2.40).

[3] P. M. Oppenheimer, 'Forward exchange intervention: the official view', *Westminster Bank Review*, February 1966, p. 13.

[4] *Bank of England Quarterly Bulletin*, vol. 10, March 1970, p. 39.

PALLIATIVES AFFECTING THE CURRENT BALANCE

Four of the devices used in the 1960s to improve the external balance raised the issue of whether they were compatible with our obligations under the IMF Charter and GATT. They were the travel allowance, the export rebate, the import surcharge and the import deposit scheme.

The travel allowance

Postwar restrictions on expenditure on personal travel abroad had been removed by the end of the 1950s, but they were reimposed in the second half of the 1960s. In July 1966 a basic travel allowance of only £50 a year was introduced for travel in countries outside the sterling area, to operate as from 1 November. A waiver from the IMF was obtained for this restriction, which remained in force until January 1970, when the allowance was raised from £50 a year to the virtually unrestrictive ceiling of £300 a trip. The National Institute, in noting the lifting of the restriction, estimated the effect on the balance of payments in 1970 as something like £40 million, a rather higher figure than that of

Chart 7.5. *The share of overseas travel in consumers' expenditure, 1952–75*

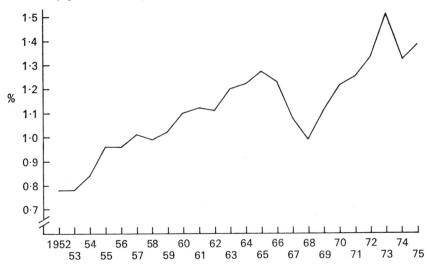

SOURCES: CSO, *United Kingdom Balance of Payments 1965–75*, table 2, and *National Income and Expenditure 1965–75*, table 1.1.

£25 million suggested by official spokesmen.[1] In retrospect, chart 7.5 strongly suggests that the trend of the share of travel in consumers'

[1] *National Institute Economic Review*, no. 51, February 1970, p. 30.

expenditure was deflected by the travel allowance; had the curve followed an horizontal path, corresponding to the actual value of travel debits in 1970 as a percentage of consumption, the total difference in travel debits over the three years 1967–9 would have been some £125 million. This must not, of course, be regarded as an estimate, even an approximate one, of the improvement in the balance of payments achieved by the imposition of the travel allowance, since the measure may well have affected expenditure on things other than overseas travel, and thereby have, directly or indirectly, affected other kinds of external transactions.

The export rebate

The export rebate, introduced in October 1964 and repealed at the end of March 1968, provided for the refund of certain indirect taxes on exports to a value of about 2 per cent of total exports or somewhat more than £80 million a year. It was expected that about £10 million would go to the motor industry, £5½ million to the electrical machinery industry and £1 million to the whisky industry.[1] Its ostensible purpose was to recompense exporters for otherwise unrebated indirect taxes, in particular the hydro-carbon duties, paid on goods 'incorporated' in the products exported. Since we maintained that it was a rebate and not an export subsidy, we were able to claim that it did not contravene our obligations under GATT; all the same it was very unpopular with other parties to GATT and hence was repealed when, thanks to devaluation, it was no longer considered a necessary palliative for our external deficit.

The import surcharge

A temporary surcharge of 15 per cent on the value of imports of most manufactured and semi-manufactured goods was introduced in October 1964. Following strong representations from other countries, especially members of EFTA, it was reduced to 10 per cent in April 1965; in May 1966 the termination of the scheme was announced, and the surcharge duly ended on the last day of November 1966.

The surcharge was undoubtedly in breach of our obligations under GATT, which provides that a country in balance of payments difficulties may temporarily impose quantitative restrictions on imports, but not what was in effect a temporary tariff. Nevertheless the United Kingdom's action was not without precedent, in that Canada had imposed a similar surcharge from June 1962 to April 1963. The action was all the same strongly criticised by other contracting parties.

The imposition of a temporary import surcharge might be expected

---

[1] Department of Economic Affairs, *The National Plan*, pp. 72–3.

to exert at least three distinct effects upon the value of the import bill. First, its temporary nature might have induced some overseas suppliers to shade their prices, thus absorbing part of the surcharge and correspondingly improving the United Kingdom's terms of trade. Secondly, one would expect it to lead to some reduction in the volume of imports. Thirdly, the explicitly temporary nature of the scheme might have exerted some temporary, reversible effects on consumption and purchase of imports for stock, any reduction being made good after the removal of the surcharge. There is, in addition, a tax effect on real disposable incomes to the extent that the surcharge is passed on in higher prices; but this effect has been neglected here, on the grounds that it is shared by other instruments of fiscal policy and is not peculiar to the surcharge *per se*.

Post-mortems have concentrated almost exclusively upon the substitution effects of the scheme; however, the terms of trade effect was not entirely negligible. Cooper notes, for example, that the government of the Irish Republic refunded half the surcharge to its exporters[1] and, from the reaction of the import unit value index for manufactures to the removal of the surcharge, it would seem that suppliers may have absorbed something like 2–3 per cent of the surcharge rate. On this basis, the United Kingdom would have gained something like £40–£50 million per annum from the surcharge by way of an improvement in her terms of trade.

Table 7.12 compares various estimates of the surcharge effect and indicates which method was used to arrive at the result. First there is the 'residuals method', where the technique is to estimate an equation in the demand for imports prior to the surcharge period, and then to forecast with it over the surcharge period using the equation residuals as an estimate of the surcharge effect. In order to deduce an elasticity of demand from the residuals some allowance must be made for the reversible stock effects and for absorption by suppliers of part of the surcharge. The second method is the 'dummy variable' approach, in which the surcharge effect may be identified with the coefficient of a dummy variable in an import demand equation; further modifications are again required to arrive at an estimate of the operative elasticity of demand. The third method employs direct estimates of the elasticity of demand, together with a calculation of the effect of the surcharge on prices, to derive a surcharge effect which, *a priori*, excludes the reversible stock fluctuations. All the methods have disadvantages, but the last is possibly the most satisfactory.

The figures in table 7.12 are on a variety of different price bases, but there is not much difference between them and 'current' prices for

[1] R. N. Cooper, 'The balance of payments' in Caves *et al.*, *Britain's Economic Prospects*.

Table 7.12. *Estimates of the effect of the 1964 import surcharge*

	Price base		Method used	
		Residuals	Dummy variable	Price elasticity
		(£ million)		
Johnston and Henderson ⎫		⎧ 100–150	n.a.	n.a.
Black, Kidgell and Ray ⎬ 1958	⎨ 200	350	n.a.
Burns ⎭		⎩ 300–364	230–300	n.a.
Barker[a]	1960	134	n.a.	462
Treasury[b]	1961	200	330	n.a.
NIESR ⎫ 1963	⎧ n.a.	390	n.a.
Fane and Whitley[c] ⎭	⎩ n.a.	n.a.	200

SOURCES: Johnston and Henderson, 'Assessing the effects of the import surcharge'; I. G. Black, J. E. Kidgell and G. F. Ray, 'Forecasting imports: a re-examination', *National Institute Economic Review*, no. 42, November 1967; T. Burns, 'An econometric analysis of UK imports 1959–68' (London Graduate Business School discussion paper), 1969; T. S. Barker, 'Aggregation error and estimates of the UK import demand function' in Hilton and Heathfield (eds.), *The Econometric Study of the United Kingdom*; NIESR, 'The effects of the devaluation of 1967 on the current balance of payments'; Treasury, *The Determination of UK Imports* by Rees and Layard; Fane and Whitley, 'Imports of goods and services'.

[a] Assumed elasticities −1·1 for manufactures, −1·43 for semi-manufactures.
[b] Assumed elasticities:

	Finished capital goods	Semi-manufactures	Consumer goods
Initial	−0·9	−0·9	−0·8
Under surcharge	−1·3	−1·2	−1·8

[c] Assumed elasticity −0·68 for all goods.

the period of the surcharge; thus, the multipliers to be attached to the figures to bring them to a current price basis (average for 1965/6) appear to vary only within the range of approximately 1·05 to 1·10, so they can reasonably be compared with each other as they stand.

The estimates by Johnston and Henderson are among the lowest.[1] Cooper, who included in his presentation of the Johnston–Henderson results some credit for what appears to be a reversible stock run-down effect at the end of 1966 and thus inflated the result, suggested that the implied elasticities (0·8 for 1965, 0·5 for 1966) were unexpectedly low,[2] and the original authors themselves concluded their investigation by speculating on why the substitution effect was so weak. Most of the remaining estimates give grounds for thinking that the elasticities may

[1] J. Johnston and M. Henderson, 'Assessing the effects of the import surcharge', *Manchester School of Economic and Social Studies*, vol. 35, May 1967.
[2] Cooper, 'The balance of payments'.

have been rather higher than implied by the original Johnston–Henderson investigation, although there is a suspicion in almost all cases that the calculated effects include reversible stock effects. The most recent estimates by Fane and Whitley go further than the others in attempting to confine the calculation to the elasticity effect;[1] the elasticity used in the computation is, however, probably biased downwards, since it relates to total imports of goods and the presumption is that the elasticities of demand for manufactures and semi-manufactures are higher than average; on the other hand, these authors assumed no absorption of the surcharge by overseas suppliers.

The evidence provided by the surcharge episode on the elasticity of demand was thus less than clear-cut for a variety of reasons. The government had in mind an effect of £300 million a year when this scheme was first introduced;[2] this figure should be taken, after adjustment for the subsequent change in the tariff rate and the length of its operation, as something over £440 million.[3] In the light of the estimates in the table, the government figure seems to have been on the optimistic side. The imposition of the surcharge did involve temporary stock run-downs, so that there was quite a powerful immediate effect and some catching up after the end of the scheme. The difficulty of capturing these reactions is one of the reasons why estimates of the effect differ. It does seem that there was a mild terms of trade effect in Britain's favour as a result of the scheme. Taking the Fane–Whitley estimate as a base, but allowing for price absorption of 2–3 percentage points, the combined terms of trade and elasticity effects of the scheme might be said to amount to something like £250 million at current prices over two years; this is an underestimate to the extent of the bias in the overall elasticity calculation.

The temporary import deposit scheme

In November 1968, when a number of additional deflationary measures were taken, details of a new scheme for controlling imports were announced. Importers of certain classes of goods, broadly those which had been covered by the import surcharge, were required to deposit with the government for six months an amount equal to half the value of such goods purchased for import.[4] The scheme was modified in

[1] G. Fane and J. Whitley, 'Imports of goods and services' (unpublished, NIESR), 1973.

[2] House of Commons, *Hansard*, 11 November 1964, cols. 1027–8.

[3] Obtained by scaling the government's initial £300 million estimate by 11·2/15·0 (the ratio of the average rate of surcharge to the initial rate) and doubling to allow for the fact that the scheme ran for just over two years.

[4] Details of the mechanics of the scheme are given in the notice of credit restriction published in the *Bank of England Quarterly Bulletin*, vol. 8, December 1968, pp. 358–9. Technically, the deposits were regarded as Customs duties. The value of imports covered by the scheme at the time of its introduction is put by the Bank at about £2800 million a year.

December 1969 to require a deposit of only 40 per cent of the value of the imported goods; there were further reductions to 30 per cent in May and 20 per cent in September 1970; the scheme ended in December 1970. Perhaps surprisingly, it did not run into difficulties with either the IMF or GATT; somewhat analogous schemes had been used in other countries, though close parallels were denied by the Chancellor.

The scheme may be regarded as having two components. It can be seen as, on the one hand, analogous to a surcharge, on the other, as a monetary measure designed to reduce the rate of importing by creating a shortage of finance unless the overseas sellers could supply it.

The surcharge effects could never have been thought to be particularly severe, for with a deposit rate of 50 per cent the equivalent surcharge rate could not have been more than about 2–3 per cent.[1] To the extent that the equivalent cost of the surcharge was borne by foreign suppliers the United Kingdom would gain a terms of trade advantage; otherwise import demand would be reduced to an extent dependent on the relevant elasticities.

The availability effects of the scheme arose in theory when importers were unable to find the deposit on any tolerable terms. Banks were asked specifically to avoid lending to customers for the purpose of paying the deposit, particularly on imports for stock.[2] However, overseas suppliers might make good the shortage of funds by loaning the deposit to the customer, or by delaying claims for payment. During the first few weeks of the scheme permission to borrow abroad was in fact granted quite freely, but on 18 December the scheme was reinforced, when it was announced that United Kingdom importers would no longer be allowed to borrow foreign currency, or sterling owned by overseas residents outside the sterling area, in order to pay deposits.[3] However, nothing could be done to prevent overseas suppliers from accommodating British importers by delaying settlement.

Official sources were reticent in providing any estimate of the anticipated effects of the scheme. The Bank of England did suggest that they looked for a quick stock run-down in the first six months, as well as for some continuing cost effect.[4] The National Institute suggested an effect on imports in 1969 of some £80 million (at 1958 prices), of which it was anticipated that £20 million would be reversed in the first quarter of 1970. Of the net effect of £60 million, one third was attributed to

[1] The equivalent surcharge rate, s, may be expressed in terms of the duration of the forced loan, l (measured in years), the annual rate of interest for the period of the loan, r, and the deposit rate, d, as $s = d.l.r$; that is, with d and l both 50 per cent, as one quarter of the rate of interest.

[2] *Bank of England Quarterly Bulletin*, vol. 8, December 1968, pp. 358–9.

[3] *Bank of England Quarterly Bulletin*, vol. 9, March 1969, p. 6.

[4] *Bank of England Quarterly Bulletin*, vol. 8, December 1968, p. 343.

the surcharge-like effects of the scheme and two thirds to availability effects.[1]

Very little detailed work providing estimates of the scheme's effects is available. Rees and Layard reported no discernible effect of the scheme on the residuals of their import demand equations, arguing that the effect was so small as to be negligible.[2] The National Institute subsequently reported its inability to detect any post-devaluation effect on imports, so that the question of distinguishing the effects of the scheme from those of devaluation did not arise.[3] Fane and Whitley, however, estimated a total effect over the whole period of the surcharge of £50 million (1963 prices), an estimate arrived at by considering the surcharge-like effects alone; as in the case of their estimate of the import surcharge, the figure was arrived at by applying an elasticity of −0·68 (in this case to the equivalent surcharge rate), and may be biased downwards because the elasticity in question is an aggregate for all goods.

It is probably justified to neglect availability effects, especially in the light of the Treasury's estimates that a significant proportion of import deposits was financed by overseas suppliers. Although the data are admittedly rather inadequate, the Treasury estimate was that about half of the deposits (some £130 million) paid in the first quarter of 1969 were supplied from overseas.[4] Subsequently the balance of payments statistics have recorded a total of £60 million as 'import deposits paid directly from overseas' in 1968 and 1969, which were repaid in 1970 and 1971, and other 'credit received in connection with import deposits' is located in figures for 'import credits received by United Kingdom businesses (other)'; these show a sharp jump upwards in 1968 and 1969 (the figures are: 1967 £9 million, 1968 £50 million, 1969 £70 million, 1970 £12 million, 1971 £12 million, 1972 £17 million).[5] On this basis, then, it might not be too far off the mark to suggest that, of the total outstanding deposits received by the end of 1969 of £544 million (the quarterly peak in outstandings came in mid-1969 at £565 million), more than a quarter was supplied from overseas.

By the same token it would therefore appear that the deposit scheme had much bigger (but reversible) effects on the capital account than it had on the current account. To put it no higher, there is no indication that this was what was initially anticipated or intended.

---

[1] *National Institute Economic Review*, no. 47, February 1969, p. 35.

[2] Treasury, *The Determinants of UK Imports* by R. D. Rees and P. R. D. Layard, London, HMSO, 1972.

[3] NIESR, 'The effects of the devaluation of 1967 on the current balance of payments', *Economic Journal*, vol. 82, March 1972 (supplement).

[4] CSO, *Economic Trends*, no. 188, June 1969, pp. xiv–xv.

[5] CSO, *Economic Trends*, no. 209, March 1971 and no. 242, December 1973.

FINANCING THE DEFICIT

Despite all the efforts made to improve the balance of payments in the 1960s, both by operating on the general level of demand and by the various policies described in this chapter, large deficits had nevertheless to be financed either by drawing on the reserves held by the Exchange Equalisation Account or by other kinds of official financing.

As table 7.2 shows, the deficits in the 1960s were not to any great extent financed by drawing down our reserves, presumably because the authorities thought it harmful to confidence in sterling. Our transactions with the IMF were mainly the result of drawings in 1961, 1964, 1965 and 1968. These drawings were substantial, but involved no new principle; we had made a large drawing in the 1950s to deal with the financial aftermath of the Suez affair, so that by and large it was a matter of following established procedure.

Support from other central banks (table 7.2) did, however, involve recourse to new procedures. The first step was taken in 1961 with the prototype of what came to be known as 'Basle Arrangements'. Following the German and Dutch revaluations by 5 per cent in the first week of March, there was a wave of speculation, which was discussed on 13 March at the normal monthly meeting of central bank governors at the Bank for International Settlements in Basle. The governors reacted to the danger by agreeing on mutual short-term banking accommodation to finance the speculative movement of funds – such accommodation to be repaid either by the reflux of the speculative funds or, if the reflux did not occur reasonably quickly, by recourse to the IMF. Britain duly obtained accommodation under this prototype Basle Arrangement, partly in the form of an exchange of currencies, partly in foreign currency deposits; the largest amount outstanding was £325 million.[1] The repayment of this sum, which had nearly been completed by the end of September 1961, required (as had been foreseen) recourse to the IMF, from which we made a drawing in August. In subsequent balance of payments crises the same scenario was followed, but in addition we were able to get assistance from the United States central banking system under the reciprocal swap network negotiated by the Federal Reserve Bank of New York.

Assistance afforded by one central bank to another conventionally requires repayment within one year[2] and the United Kingdom made every effort to respect this convention, if needs be by following the

---

[1] *Bank of England Quarterly Bulletin*, vol. 1, September 1961, pp. 9 and 10.
[2] R. A. Young, *Instruments of Monetary Policy in the United States*, Washington (DC), International Monetary Fund, 1973, p. 91. This convention did not apply to the 'Basle Group Arrangements' (see page 351 below).

1961 precedent of refinancing any outstanding amount by drawing on the IMF. But continuous balance of payments difficulties from 1964 onwards forced the British authorities on occasions to have recourse to central bank assistance at times when the IMF drawing limit had already been reached. This issue first arose in May 1965, when a drawing of $1400 million following one of $1000 million the preceding December took Britain to the limit of her drawing rights. The May 1965 drawing enabled outstanding debts to be repaid to other central banks and added $343 million to the reserves, but in June borrowing began again from the Federal Reserve Bank of New York. Then in November 1967 a $250 million credit was negotiated (mainly from other central banks) through the good offices of the Bank for International Settlements, so as to permit repayment of the final instalment of the December 1964 drawing. The permitted IMF limit was again reached in June 1968 with another drawing to repay short-term debts, in particular to the Federal Reserve Bank of New York, 'but in the latter part of the year it became necessary to draw again on the Federal Reserve Bank facility, and by the end of December $1150 million (£480 million) was outstanding'.[1]

In addition to the periodic recourse to 'normal' Basle Arrangements, the United Kingdom benefited from the so-called 'Basle Group Arrangements'; the first was negotiated in June 1966 (renewed in March 1967 and March 1968) and the second in September 1968 (likewise renewed at intervals until September 1973). The Basle Group Arrangements were unusual in being specifically intended to counter the threat to United Kingdom reserves arising from the possible conversion of sterling balances held overseas. Under the 1966 Arrangement the central banks of Austria, Belgium, Canada, Italy, Japan, the Netherlands, Sweden, Switzerland and West Germany, and the Bank for International Settlements collaborated in affording the United Kingdom swap facilities to offset most of any reduction in the United Kingdom reserves caused by fluctuations in overseas countries' sterling balances, whether held by monetary authorities or privately. Such fluctuations were to be measured by reference to a base date early in 1966.[2]

Continued nervousness about the pound after devaluation and about the stability of the international monetary system caused sterling area countries to speed up the process of diversifying their reserves and this led to the second Basle Group Arrangement in 1968. This differed from its predecessor in relating only to sterling balances held within the sterling area. The Basle Group of central banks and the Bank for

---

[1] Bank of England, *Report for the year ended 28 February 1969*, p. 12.
[2] *Bank of England Quarterly Bulletin*, vol. 6, September 1966, p. 209.

International Settlements provided a medium-term facility of $2000 million, on which the United Kingdom could draw during a three-year period in order to offset fluctuations below an agreed base level in the sterling balances of sterling area holders, both official and private. Then a series of agreements, mostly for three years with provision for an extension to five, was negotiated between the United Kingdom and individual overseas sterling area countries, whereby each undertook to hold a specified proportion of its reserves in sterling and in return obtained a dollar-value guarantee on its official holdings of sterling in excess of 10 per cent of its total official external reserves. At the same time it was announced that the earlier facility, negotiated in June 1966 and subsequently renewed, which related to fluctuations in all overseas countries' sterling balances, would be progressively liquidated and cease by 1971.[1]

At the conclusion of the negotiations in 1968 the United Kingdom was entitled to draw some $600 million to finance earlier reductions in the sterling balances. In 1969 and 1970, when sterling holdings increased, the United Kingdom's net entitlement was correspondingly reduced.[2] By mid-1969 almost all the amount outstanding under the 1968 facility had been repaid.[3] The facility remained in force until September 1973, when it was replaced by a six-month unilateral guarantee by the United Kingdom on most of the sterling reserves held by the sterling area countries, on terms which afforded compensation to the holders if the pound should, on average over the next six months, fall below $2·4213. The exchange rate guarantee was not in this case underwritten by the Basle Group.

The floating pound was costly for the United Kingdom in respect of both the exchange rate guarantee associated with the Basle Group Arrangement of 1968 and the unilateral guarantee which superseded it in September 1973. The former called for payments totalling £59 million; the latter had cost £80 million before it was in turn superseded in March 1974 by yet another scheme.[4]

The improvement in Britain's balance of payments which eventually followed devaluation permitted the repayment of all borrowing from central banks before the end of the first quarter of 1971 and of all drawings from the IMF by the middle of 1972. Further temporary help from other central banks was needed around the time of the floating of sterling in June 1972, but thenceforth borrowing was not needed again to bolster the official reserves until 1973, when the novel device

[1] Bank of England, *Report for the year ended 28 February 1969*, pp. 13 and 14.
[2] Ibid. p. 14.
[3] *Bank of England Quarterly Bulletin*, vol. 9, September 1969, p. 280.
[4] *The Banker*, vol. 124, April 1974, p. 313.

was adopted of encouraging public sector institutions, such as the Central Electricity Generating Board, to borrow in the Eurocurrency market and to sell the currencies thus acquired to the Exchange Equalisation Account for sterling (table 7.2), forward cover being provided by the Treasury.

CONCLUSION

There had been a succession of balance of payments crises in the 1940s and 1950s – notably in 1947, 1949, 1951, 1955, 1956 and 1957 – and this phenomenon continued, though with less regularity, in the 1960s and 1970s. The main remedies applied had much in common throughout these decades: deflationary demand management to improve the current balance and short-term interest-rate management to help the capital balance. These well-tried devices were supplemented by miscellaneous temporary expedients in the crises of the 1960s – for example, the travel allowance, the export rebate, the import surcharge and import deposits – but these were only minor palliatives.

In addition to measures applied specifically to deal with crises, there were others which were aimed at a permanent improvement, even though in many cases their adoption was immediately triggered by one or other of the crises. Included under this heading are exchange control on capital outflows, which was in operation throughout the postwar period; the dam was made more watertight in the 1960s, but its restrictive effect on outward investment was substantially offset by the growth of facilities for financing it by foreign currency borrowing. Then there was devaluation; this had been resorted to in 1949, but was then eschewed for eighteen years. It was resorted to again, with extreme reluctance, in November 1967 and as from June 1972 the exchange rate was allowed to float. The unwanted side effects of exchange-rate depreciation, though unpalatable, turned out to be less serious than had been feared earlier in the 1960s, but the beneficial effect on the current balance proved to be rather disappointing. Additional, and more novel, measures adopted in the 1960s were the tax changes made in 1965 to discourage overseas investment and the determined efforts made throughout the decade to reduce government expenditure overseas; these measures admittedly did not produce any improvement in the relevant items in the British balance of payments, but may well have served to prevent a deterioration.

APPENDIX I
EFFECTS OF THE 1967 DEVALUATION

Five detailed estimates of the balance of payments effects of the 1967 devaluation of sterling have been published; they are summarised in table 7.13, which also shows the actual changes recorded in various items between 1967 and 1969 or 1970. These latter figures reflect, of course, *all* influences on the United Kingdom current account, not merely the devaluation; they are included for comparison with estimates of the 'devaluation effect', so that the importance of the latter's contribution to the improvement in the United Kingdom balance of payments over this period can be gauged.

The first estimate listed – that made by the NIESR *ex ante* at the time of devaluation[1] – is of historical interest as reflecting a degree of optimism about the balance of payments effects which was soon to be dispelled by events. The NIESR used elasticities for merchandise trade that would have been widely accepted as plausible at the time, and made rough estimates of the effect on invisibles. Various statements by the Chancellor to Parliament and in the Letter of Intent to the IMF, which mentioned a preliminary swing of £500 million in the current account in 1968 and later a surplus of between £300 million and £500 million (implying a swing of between £800 and £1000 million), suggest that official forecasts of the likely effect of devaluation were of the same order of magnitude.

The first *ex post* estimate was made by Worswick in 1970, when the payments figures for 1969 were already available.[2] Estimates of export gains were made by calculating the growth of exports assuming that the pre-devaluation relationship between world and United Kingdom exports continued into 1969, and taking the difference between these calculations and observed exports as the 'devaluation effect'. The results implied a lower export elasticity than that used by the NIESR *ex ante*. Furthermore, it was necessary to assume that devaluation had had no effect on the volume of imports, because an estimate of 1969 imports using an unchanged exchange rate gave a lower figure than the actual level. The NIESR *ex post* estimates for 1970 were a refinement of this approach.[3] A similar assumption was made about imports of goods, but the export figures were estimated from a more detailed examination of United Kingdom shares in world exports of manufactures, while major flows of invisibles were separately

---

[1] *National Institute Economic Review*, no. 42, November 1967, pp. 4 *et seq.*

[2] G. D. N. Worswick, 'Trade and payments' in Cairncross (ed.), *Britain's Economic Prospects Reconsidered.*

[3] NIESR, 'The effects of the devaluation of 1967 on the current balance of payments'.

Table 7.13. *Estimates of the effects of devaluation and actual changes in the balance of payments*

	Estimates of devaluation effects					Actual change in value from 1967 to:	
	For 1969		For 1970				
	NIESR[a]	Worswick	NIESR[b]	LBS[c]	Artus	1969	1970
	(£ million)						
Goods							
Exports	986	1240	1255	1116	1243	1939	2769
Imports	314	880[d]	1125	899	517	1525	2221
Balance	672	360	130	217	726	414	548
Services							
Credits	250	250[e]	390	435 } 240 {		666	1241
Debits	225	180[de]	140	273 }		445	943
Other (net)	128	80[f]	45	89	70	126	162
Invisible balance	153	150	295	251	310	347	460
Current account	825	510	425	468	1036	761	1008
Elasticities[g]							
Exports	−2·0	−1·5	−1·4	−1·2	−1·3	.	.
Imports	−0·7	—	—	—	−0·4	.	.
	(percentages)						
Price changes[g]							
Exports (£)	9·0	7·6	8·5	7·0	6·1	.	.
(\$)	−7·0	−7·8	−7·0	−8·3	−9·1	.	.
Imports (£)	13·5	12·3	16·7	10·0	12·9	.	.

SOURCES: *National Institute Economic Review*, no. 42, November 1967; Worswick, 'Trade and payments'; NIESR, 'The effects of the devaluation of 1967 on the current balance of payments'; Ball, Burns and Miller, 'Preliminary simulations with the London Business School macro-economic model'; Artus, 'The 1967 devaluation of the pound sterling'; CSO, *United Kingdom Balance of Payments 1973*.

[a] *Ex ante* forecasts.   [b] *Ex post* estimates.
[c] Includes additional imports induced by rise in GNP. If GNP was held constant, as in other estimates, estimates for goods imports would be £697 million and for service debits £235 million, giving surpluses of £419 million for visibles, £289 million for invisibles and £708 million on current account.
[d] Goods and services originally calculated together; split estimated here.
[e] Excludes government services.   [f] Investment income only.   [g] Goods only.

estimated in relation to trade, income or some other appropriate indicator.

The estimate for 1970 by the London Business School[1] cannot be compared with others in the table, since, unlike them, it does not assume that policies designed to maintain the level of activity unchanged

[1] R. J. Ball, T. Burns and G. Miller, 'Preliminary simulations with the London Business School macro-economic model' in Renton (ed.), *Modelling the Economy*.

were implemented after devaluation. If imports are adjusted to allow for this, a much larger devaluation effect results than that estimated by the NIESR. This is not due to a fall in the volume of imports – the equations for (disaggregated) imports contain no price terms – but to a much smaller rise in import prices. The NIESR assumed that the changed sterling rate was fully reflected in import prices; the London Business School made import prices a function of the volume of world trade and the level of world prices as well as of the exchange rate.

Artus's more recent estimates for 1970[1] are distinguished by the use of disaggregated import equations with significant price elasticities for manufactures (-3.4 for semi-manufactures and -1.0 for finished goods) implying an average elasticity of -0.4. Here, the fall in the volume of imports implies a smaller rise in their value than in the other estimates and, in turn, yields a 'devaluation effect' more than twice as large as that of the NIESR.

All three 1970 estimates were not only close in the export elasticities and price changes estimated or implied (and hence in the changes in the value of goods exported), but also fairly close in their estimates of the effect on invisibles. They all found evidence to support the existence of the J-curve,[2] though the timing differed from estimate to estimate. The essential difference between the three lies in the calculation of the effect of devaluation on imports, and here Artus's view is now probably most widely accepted. The London Business School can still find no significant price elasticity for imports,[3] but the NIESR, when estimating import equations from data spanning the post-devaluation period as Artus did, has found elasticities of a similar order of magnitude. Thus a significant part, but by no means all, of the change in the United Kingdom current account between 1967 and the early 1970s should, on this evidence, be attributed to devaluation, even though the estimates themselves may be open to criticism for failing to take other influences fully into account or ignoring other consequences of devaluation. But it should also be mentioned that there is still a school of thought that would dismiss all arguments about elasticities and propensities, and would explain the turn-round in the balance of payments by reference to the dramatic change in the government's finances between 1967 and 1970.

---

[1] J. R. Artus, 'The 1967 devaluation of the pound sterling', *IMF Staff Papers*, vol. 22, November 1975.

[2] The J-curve describes the initial deterioration in the balance of payments after a devaluation as import prices rise more quickly than export prices, followed by an improvement as the volume of exports rises and the volume of imports falls in response to price changes.

[3] R. J. Ball, T. Burns and J. S. E. Laury, 'The role of exchange rate changes in balance of payments adjustment', *Economic Journal*, vol. 87, March 1977.

APPENDIX II
MEDIUM-TERM EXPORT CREDIT[1]

October 1960. The ECGD was authorised to 'insure credit on longer terms than the normal maximum where this is necessary to allow a United Kingdom exporter to match terms offered by a foreign competitor with the backing of an export credit guarantee institution or equivalent official support'. 'Part-period cover' (for the first five years only) was introduced for other cases where it was reasonably sure that longer terms were being offered by foreign suppliers and that the order would be lost unless the United Kingdom exporter could compete on terms.

February 1961. The Bank of England announced it would refinance export credits provided by the banks when they reached eighteen months to maturity, provided the loans were originally for between three and five years and were backed by ECGD guarantees. Such credits could be counted as 'liquid assets' in calculating the London clearing banks' liquid asset ratios.

April 1961. Arrangements for direct guarantees to banks were extended to include 'financial guarantees' on loans for more than five years to creditworthy overseas purchasers. This was intended to facilitate the sale by United Kingdom suppliers of large capital projects costing not less than £2 million.

January 1962. The London and Scottish clearing banks agreed to finance export contracts of £100,000 or more of heavy capital equipment for terms of three to five years at a rate of interest fixed at $5\frac{1}{2}$ per cent per annum at least until 1967. Member companies of the British Insurance Association agreed to make £100 million available for loans exceeding five years at an interest rate of $6\frac{1}{2}$ per cent per annum.

January 1965. The banks took over from the insurance companies loans exceeding five years and henceforth would apply their own interest rate of $5\frac{1}{2}$ per cent. The minimum size of contract was reduced from £100,000 to £50,000 and the limitation to capital goods was removed.

Refinancing facilities by the Bank of England were extended to cover whichever was greater of credits maturing within eighteen months or 30 per cent of the total; such credits counted as liquid assets. A supplementary refinancing facility was provided for new loans of over five years to maturity to cover the longer-term

---

[1] SOURCES: *Bank of England Quarterly Bulletin*, vol. 1, March 1961, vol. 2, March 1962, vol. 5, March 1965, vol. 7, June 1967, vol. 9, September and December 1969; *Midland Bank Review*, August 1962 and August 1972.

lending taken over from the insurance companies, but such credits did not count as liquid assets,[1] so that the purpose was not so much to obviate liquidity constraints as to meet the growing concern of the banks that the expansion of longer-term lending was pre-empting too large a proportion of their resources.

April 1965.   The minimum period for medium-term fixed-rate export credit was lowered from three to two years and ECGD cover was increased from 90 to 100 per cent of the finance provided. The minimum size of contract was further reduced to £25,000.

March 1966.   The minimum size of contract was abolished.

May 1967.   The London and Scottish clearing banks extended medium-term fixed-rate financing to shipbuilding contracts in United Kingdom yards backed by Ministry of Technology guarantees. Refinancing facilities by the Bank of England were extended to shipbuilding credits repayable over a period of more than eight years from delivery, 30 per cent of such loans being eligible as liquid assets.

May 1969.   Refinancing facilities were re-negotiated with the banks, so that:

(i) existing arrangements were to be continued for credits which could be counted by the London clearing banks as liquid assets (that is, 30 per cent of all eligible loans or, for export credits, the total repayable within eighteen months if greater);

(ii) other facilities were replaced by a Bank of England commitment to the London and Scottish clearing banks to refinance any eligible lending which might not be treated as liquid in excess of 5 per cent of the bank's total gross deposits.

October 1970.   The fixed rate of interest on medium-term bank financing of exports and shipbuilding was increased from $5\frac{1}{2}$ to 7 per cent.

November 1971.   The fixed rate of interest on financing of exports other than ships was reduced to $6\frac{1}{2}$ per cent; on exports of ships and shipbuilding it remained at 7 per cent.

March 1972.   The fixed rate of interest on financing of exports other than ships was reduced to 6 per cent; henceforth these interest rates were to be determined by the government, which would recompense the banks for the difference between such rates and market rates.

Since medium-term credits were not eligible to be counted towards the new $12\frac{1}{2}$ per cent reserve asset ratio (which superseded the 28 per cent liquid asset ratio in 1971), any excess of

---

[1] Except insofar as the 18 months or 30 per cent arrangement applied to the whole of a bank's export credits under the scheme.

such credits over 18 per cent of a bank's current account deposits were to be refinanced by the ECGD (if for exports) or by the Department of Trade (if for shipbuilding for United Kingdom purchasers).

January 1974. The fixed rate of interest on financing of exports was increased to 7 per cent for loans lasting two to five years and to a range of 6–8½ per cent for longer loans.

CHAPTER 8

INCOMES POLICY

by *F. T. Blackaby*

1960 TO 1964

The period began at the end of an *annus mirabilis* for price stability: on 15 December 1959 the index of retail prices was exactly the same as on 16 December 1958. This remarkable, if short, period of price stability had been helped a little by the fall in import prices during 1958. However, the main reason was a rather extraordinary hiatus in wage claims during 1959, when the index of hourly wage rates rose by a mere 1·2 per cent. 1959 showed a 'Phillips-type' pattern; unemployment, which was at a peak at the beginning of the year, had fallen only gradually and in consequence a number of important trade unions had postponed their wage claims until times got better.

It was partly this brief price stability which made the developments of 1960 and 1961 appear disturbing. Wage rates began to rise again during 1960 and were just over 5 per cent higher by the end of the year. The effect on retail prices was, however, still very small – they went up by a mere 2 per cent through the year. By the first half of 1961 the inflationary process appeared to be speeding up to figures which, although they now look insignificant, seemed disturbing then: in the first half of 1961 hourly wage rates and retail prices were rising at annual rates of 7 per cent and 4 per cent respectively. This was part of the background to the wages pause introduced in July.

It was also part of the background at the time that a number of Reports were published stressing the cost element in inflation. The Council on Prices, Productivity and Incomes, in its Report published in July 1959, emphasised costs rather than demand as a cause of inflation; it also reviewed a number of proposals, such as those for a 'guiding light' and a statutory advisory body, which later became incorporated into the government's incomes policy.[1] In 1961 the OEEC published a Report which concluded that certainly in Britain 'excessive wage

[1] Council on Prices, Productivity and Incomes, *3rd Report*, London, HMSO, 1959; see also *4th Report*, London, HMSO, 1961. Sir Dennis Robertson had been the economist member of the Council when its first two Reports were produced in 1958, laying heavy stress on demand rather than costs. Sir Dennis resigned in 1958 and his place was filled by Professor Phelps Brown; in the third and fourth Reports there was a distinct change of emphasis.

increases constituted both an important and independent inflationary force'.[1] We have evidence about the advice which must have been given to the government in an article by Sir Robert Hall, written shortly after he had retired as Economic Adviser to the government. He comments: 'With the passage of time the number of adherents of extreme positions has diminished and a large body of opinion now thinks that some form of wage policy other than leaving wages to free collective bargaining is necessary, if full employment and stable prices are to be combined. In this connection, the OEEC Report on the problem of rising prices is extremely significant since it is very nearly an agreed document, by highly respected economists from a number of western countries who can certainly not be regarded as all belonging to any particular school of thought.'[2] It is noticeable that in his 1961 budget speech the Chancellor referred specifically to the dangers of accelerating cost-inflation.

It was not surprising, therefore, that when crisis measures had to be taken in July 1961 they included a 'pay pause'. Indeed, it is clear that in the Prime Minister's view it was the pay pause that really mattered; he had little sympathy with the other deflationary measures. In his view the country's difficulties 'were not due to an attempt to run the economy at too great a rate or to the strains upon government expenditure, whether at home or overseas'; they were primarily due to an explosion of wages. It was the wages battle which was all important: 'what is the use of our scraping and scrounging to get £50–£150 million of "economies", if the extra wage and salary bill of £1,000 million or more is presented again?'[3]

The pay pause was announced on 25 July 1961. It required no legislation; the government proposed to use its existing powers and its position as an employer to hold back wage increases in the public sector as best it might, hoping that the private sector would follow. Existing commitments would be honoured; otherwise, the general principle was that Civil Service pay increases would be delayed for seven months. The process of arbitration would continue, but the government would reserve its right to decide when and in what steps to implement the decisions. The government could put considerable pressure on nationalised industries to conform; there was, however, no complete prohibition of wage increases and each case was considered separately. The pay pause was, therefore, very far from being a statutory pay freeze.

The administration of the pay pause can best be described as a

[1] OEEC, *The Problem of Rising Prices* by W. Fellner *et al.*, Paris, 1961.
[2] 'Britain's economic problem', *Economist*, 16 September 1961, p. 1042.
[3] Macmillan, *At the End of the Day*, p. 36.

prolonged and rather ragged battle, with ground being gained in some sectors and lost in others. In some cases arbitration awards were postponed until the end of the pause. The Civil Service unions were particularly disturbed at the interference with arbitration and only mollified with the promise that there would be a return to unfettered arbitration once the pause was over. Some awards by Wages Councils were referred back for reconsideration, but when this was refused the government let the awards through. Part of a Post Office award was allowed through and part held back until the end of the pause. There was a major breach, however, in November, when the Electricity Board, which had informally agreed to offer a maximum increase of 1d. an hour from 1 April, declared after prolonged negotiations that they saw no alternative to offering 2d. an hour from 28 January; they informed the Minister of Power, who protested over the telephone but did nothing. The Prime Minister reprimanded both the Minister and the Board, but privately admitted that 'we have retreated...from the one point in the line which it is in fact impossible to hold, for we have no technically effective method by which electric power could be produced on any reasonable scale in the event of a strike'.[1]

During the pause, the government – and the Prime Minister in particular – were wrestling with the problem of establishing a permanent incomes policy. The Prime Minister was in a constant state of exasperation that the Chancellor and the Treasury were doing nothing about it and it was on this issue that he eventually concluded that Selwyn Lloyd would have to go (page 21). Certainly it was some time before the longer-term incomes policy took shape; not until a year after the beginning of the pay pause was the National Incomes Commission announced.

The incomes policy which emerged had three main constituents: a 'norm', a set of criteria or principles by which wage claims should be judged, and an independent body to pass judgements on particular cases. This framework stayed much the same until 1970. The name and constitution of the independent body was, of course, changed, and its scope was widened to include prices; there were also some changes (though not many) in the principles or criteria. The policy was, however, firmly based on the view that costs were mainly responsible for inflation; if wage increases could be controlled, this would also effectively control prices and profits.

The idea of a 'norm' had been around for a long time. In 1956 a White Paper had advanced the proposition that if incomes rose faster than output prices were bound to rise,[2] and a general 'norm' had been

---

[1] Ibid. p. 47.

[2] Treasury, *Economic Implications of Full Employment*, Cmd 9725, London, HMSO, 1956.

extensively discussed in the Reports of the Council on Prices, Productivity and Incomes.[1] There was therefore no particular difficulty in saying what the norm should be; in January 1962 the Chancellor of the Exchequer sent a letter to the TUC asking for their cooperation in keeping earnings increases within the limit set by the Treasury estimate of the probable rise in productivity. This was calculated at $2\frac{1}{2}$ per cent and it became known as the 'guiding light'.

The criteria which were supposed to govern decisions about income increases were set out in a White Paper in February of that year.[2] This White Paper, like those which followed it, considered that increases in the cost of living ought not to be given 'the same weight as hitherto', thus sharply distinguishing the incomes policy then pursued by the Conservative government from its later forms. Increased productivity was only to be a justification for increases if it had been achieved by more exacting work, more onerous conditions, or the renunciation of restrictive practices; an increase might also be justifiable when 'a build up of manpower in one industry relatively to another is plainly necessary'. These were much the same principles as those of the subsequent Labour period of incomes policy, except that low pay was not mentioned as a criterion. The White Paper quoted the Chancellor's declaration in December 1961 that 'as a part of the incomes policy, appropriate corrective action would have to be taken if aggregate profits showed signs of increasing excessively as compared with wages and salaries', but it is fairly clear that this contingency was thought unlikely.

The final component of this incomes policy – the National Incomes Commission – was eventually announced in July; the Prime Minister had clearly been a little uncertain about the support he would get from his Cabinet and the Conservative Party in the House of Commons; there were a number of Conservatives who had little sympathy with this kind of intervention. He records that he addressed the Cabinet at some length on the need for 'an impartial source of wage assessment operating over the whole field, in place of a series of *ad hoc* arbitrations when one group after another felt itself to be left behind'.[3] The idea of giving the Commission powers of compulsion was considered and rejected, partly because it would only be able to consider a relatively small number of settlements rather arbitrarily selected and partly because a great deal of industrial action was unofficial. The Prime Minister hoped that the Commission's rulings would become effective through the pressure of public opinion after full disclosure of the facts. It was

[1] Council on Prices, Productivity and Incomes, *1st–4th Reports*, London, HMSO 1958–61.
[2] Treasury, *Incomes Policy: the next step*.
[3] Macmillan, *At the End of the Day*, p. 70.

envisaged as a permanent body: 'an incomes policy is, therefore, necessary as a permanent feature of our economic life'.[1]

The National Incomes Commission

The new Conservative incomes policy, having been born with such travail, hardly lived up to expectations. The National Incomes Commission had a short and rather undistinguished life; it certainly did not succeed in focusing the wrath of public opinion on excessive wage awards.

There were a number of reasons for this failure to make much impact. First of all, by October 1962 when the Commission was eventually established, unemployment was rising sharply and retail prices – even by the standards of the time – only very slowly: the retail price rise through 1962 was only $2\frac{1}{2}$ per cent and through 1963 only 2 per cent. Unemployment, on the other hand, passed half a million (seasonally adjusted) in the winter of 1962/3. Not surprisingly, the threat of inflation ceased to be the main preoccupation of the government, or of public opinion in general.

The Commission had very limited terms of reference: to review certain pay matters where the cost was wholly or partly met from the Exchequer if the government asked it to do so, and to examine retrospectively any particular pay settlement which the government referred to it. In its two years it received only one reference under the first head and three under the second, producing five Reports in all on the four references.[2] It condemned as being against the national interest an agreement for Scottish builders, national agreements in the engineering and shipbuilding industries, and an agreement in electrical contracting. It acquitted an agreement for Scottish plumbers and, in its one 'non-retrospective' reference, it recommended salary increases substantially above the norm for university academic staff. However, its 'retrospective' Reports were published well after the wage agreements had been concluded; for example, its interim Report on the engineering and shipbuilding industries came five to six months after the agreement had taken effect and the final Report fifteen months later, after a new national agreement (with some important innovations) had been reached. This was one reason for the lack of impact on public opinion.

---

[1] Ibid. p. 105.
[2] National Incomes Commission, *Report no. 1: Scottish Plumbers' and Scottish Builders' Agreements of 1962*, Cmnd 1994; *Report no. 2: Agreements of Feb.–March 1963 in Electrical Contracting in Heating, Ventilating and Domestic Engineering and in Exhibition Contracting*, Cmnd 2098; *Report no. 3: Remuneration of Academic Staff in Universities and Colleges of Advanced Technology*, Cmnd 2317; *Report no. 4 (interim and final): Agreements of Nov.–Dec. 1963 in the Engineering and Shipbuilding Industries*, Cmnd 2583, London, HMSO, 1963–5.

The Commission's procedure was legal in form – presumably because this was the procedure with which the chairman, Sir Geoffrey Lawrence, QC, was familiar; it invited submissions and evidence, and held hearings. It was thus considerably handicapped when the trade unions refused to cooperate.[1]

The Commission did, however, increase the 'norm'; the government had promulgated 2–2½ per cent, but the Commission raised this to 3–3½ per cent, partly on the grounds that the target growth rate accepted by the NEDC implied a 3·2 per cent growth rate in productivity per head (page 407). However, the more important reason was simply that 2–2½ per cent seemed unattainable and the Commission thought it more sensible to take a figure which had 'some real chance of general acceptance'.

The last months of the Conservative government

In the first half of 1964 unemployment was falling fast; retail prices were beginning to rise significantly, after moving very little during the previous year. The Chancellor tried through the NEDC to get some agreed statement of intent from both sides of industry on price and wage restraint, but he was unsuccessful. The trade unions were in no mood to cooperate with a Conservative government, which had set up the National Incomes Commission without first securing their cooperation and, further, was clearly in its last year of office and preparing for an election. A number of prominent trade unionists went on record as saying that, although they were unalterably opposed to Conservative wage restraint, they saw possibilities of cooperating with a Labour government on the 'planned growth of incomes'.

It also became clear during 1964 that the government was unable to keep wage increases in the public sector below 3–3½ per cent. In June a Court of Inquiry recommended increases for electricity supply manual workers ranging from 5 to 12½ per cent; this was soon followed by awards to London busmen and Post Office workers also well in excess of the norm. Thus, by the end of their period in office the Conservative government's incomes policy was in some disarray. Their manifesto suggests that if they had won the election there would have been further moves of some kind: '...an effective and fair incomes policy is crucial to the achievement of sustained growth without inflation. We shall take a further initiative to secure wider acceptance and effective implementation of such a policy.' It is noticeable that the manifesto does not mention the National Incomes Commission, although it does mention elsewhere the Conservative's other institutional creation, the NEDC.

[1] Some academic staff gave evidence in the hearings on their salaries.

THE LABOUR GOVERNMENT'S INCOMES POLICY

Labour came to power with different ideas about an incomes policy; it abolished the National Incomes Commission and set up its own institution. (This was to become a pattern of behaviour in this field: in turn, the Conservative government abolished the NBPI in 1970 and the Labour government abolished the Pay Board in 1974.) The idea of some kind of incomes policy had been discussed within the Labour Party, and indeed within the TUC, for some two years previously. The 1963 annual Congress had adopted a Report on economic development and planning which the General Secretary, George Woodcock, defended in a speech in which he used the famous phrase: 'We left Trafalgar Square a long time ago.' This TUC Report cautiously endorsed the view expressed by the NEDC that 'there would be a need for policies to ensure that money incomes, wages, salaries, profits as a whole rise substantially less rapidly than in the past'.[1] However, the same Congress also passed a motion declaring 'its complete opposition to any form of wages restraint', despite the General Secretary indicating that it would contradict the General Council s own Report.[2] The 1964 Congress moved a little further in allowing for an incomes policy: a composite motion included a sentence saying that the Congress 'reiterates its opposition to the attempted imposition of an incomes policy which has as its aim the restraint of wage and salary increases', but it also contained a section describing the characteristics of an acceptable incomes policy – for example, 'it must be based on social justice, taking into account all forms of incomes including rent, interest and profit...Congress further believes that an acceptable incomes policy must redress the injustices in the existing wages structure, and that Congress would have to establish its own system of priorities to achieve these aims.'[3]

With this degree of trade union support the Labour Party felt able to include a section on incomes policy in its election manifesto of 1964: 'To curb inflation we must have a planned growth of incomes so that they are broadly related to the annual growth of production. To achieve this a Labour Government will enter into urgent consultations with the Unions and employers' organisations concerned...Labour's incomes policy will not be unfairly directed at lower paid workers and public employees; instead, it will apply in an expanding economy to *all* incomes: to profits, dividends and rents as well as to wages and salaries.'

[1] NEDC, *Conditions Favourable to Faster Growth*.
[2] TUC, *Report of the 95th Annual Trades Union Congress at Brighton, 1963*, p. 409.
[3] TUC, *Report of the 96th Annual Trades Union Congress at Blackpool, 1964*, p. 561.

General characteristics

The Labour government's incomes policy went through a number of phases; between 1965 and 1970 there were no fewer than six distinct policy statements and a number of Prices and Incomes Acts. However, the successive phases had certain characteristics in common.

The policy was conceived as permanent, with permanent institutions, and not as a temporary interruption; it did not begin, therefore, with a wages freeze. So far as incomes were concerned, the general concept was a norm, with the NBPI adjudicating on difficult cases. As the Labour manifesto suggested, the new institution differed from its predecessors in that it was to consider prices as well as incomes. It differed in other ways too: the procedure was no longer an imitation of a Court of law; the Board conducted vigorous research work of its own and considered that it had a duty not simply to comment on prices and incomes, but to make general recommendations about the running of the industries and firms concerned.

It is also important in any assessment to realise that the Labour government's incomes policy was not a comprehensive statutory policy in the same sense as that introduced by the Conservatives in 1972. During Labour's term of office, except for the short period of the freeze, the powers of enforcement were very limited indeed: the government could refer a relatively small number of wage claims to the NBPI and could only delay those awards for varying lengths of time.

The first phase

In the Labour government the general responsibility for prices and incomes policy was given to the new Department of Economic Affairs. Within two months the Secretary of State, George Brown, had persuaded representatives of the TUC and the various employers' associations to sign a joint statement of intent on productivity, prices and incomes. Not much space in this document is in fact given to incomes policy; most of it is about raising productivity and increasing exports – indeed about the general objectives of the National Plan. On incomes policy, the parties agreed to cooperate in establishing new machinery to 'keep under review the general movement of prices and money incomes of all kinds' and to examine particular cases. The document shows how incomes policy was envisaged then – very much as one element in the expansionary policies of the National Plan.

The executive measures followed shortly. The NBPI was set up early in 1965 and in March the TUC General Council agreed to a $3-3\frac{1}{2}$ per cent norm – the same figure as that of the National Incomes Commission. In the beginning there were no supporting statutory powers;

the NBPI – like the National Incomes Commission before it – was intended to educate public opinion. In April, a White Paper laid down the criteria for prices and for incomes:[1] for prices these were new; for wage and salary increases above the norm they were much the same as under the Conservatives, except for the addition of low pay as a new criterion.

The first wholly voluntary phase of incomes policy disappointed the policy-makers, though the trial was a very short one; the rise in the wage-rate index accelerated in the first half of 1965. The first moves to tighten the policy were made towards the end of August. There had been a sterling crisis (page 35) and, according to Harold Wilson, the Secretary to the United States Treasury indicated that it might be difficult to get further central bank aid if Britain had no better safeguard against inflation than a wholly voluntary system.[2] It was also observed that the NBPI had the same weakness as the National Incomes Commission – only income settlements already made and price increases already effective were being referred to it. The first move, therefore, was to produce an 'early warning' system.

The early warning system

The main problem, as with any statutory intervention in this field, was to get some kind of agreement from trade union leaders, who were fundamentally opposed to any kind of legislative interference with free collective bargaining. George Brown, summoned home from holiday, had a marathon session with the TUC General Council and the result was a compromise. The General Council reluctantly agreed to a voluntary system of notification – and indeed of vetting – of wage claims; the government would nonetheless go ahead with a Bill to give it statutory powers. However, the Bill needed an Order in Council to activate those powers, which the government agreed would not be done unless the voluntary system did not work.

The Trades Union annual Congress, which was in progress at the time, was also persuaded to back the new policy, though the majority in favour was much smaller than it had been in the spring, with 5·2 million for and 3·3 million against. The Transport and General Workers' Union was among those which voted against the new policy. A case for it was presented in a powerful speech by the General Secretary, George Woodcock. He accepted that the government had reason to be disappointed with the voluntary policy so far: prices and incomes had gone up rather more than in the period when there was no policy,

---

[1] Department of Economic Affairs, *Prices and Incomes Policy*, Cmnd 2639, London, HMSO, 1965.
[2] Wilson, *The Labour Government 1964–1970*, pp. 131–2.

and the interval between one claim and another was getting shorter. He argued that the only way to avoid legislation was 'to produce something that looks awfully good in the light of the Government's difficulties, an awfully good substitute'; consequently, any voluntary policy must aim to achieve the same objectives and results as legislation.[1]

Under the voluntary system, unions affiliated to the TUC were expected to notify the General Council of all impending claims. These claims were then examined by a special vetting committee set up for the purpose, consisting of one member of the General Council from each of the nineteen trade groups. This committee had a month in which to make no comment, to make written observations, or to invite representatives of the union or unions concerned to meet and discuss the claim. In most cases, therefore, the period of delay was no longer than five weeks: unions were expected to refrain from proceeding until they had heard from the General Council. There was nothing, however, to make them pay attention to any observations which the committee might make. This vetting committee operated from October 1965 to January 1970, with a short break from July to November 1966 during the period of the wages freeze. In many ways, it was this committee, much more than the NBPI, which was the Labour government's instrument of incomes policy. The NBPI dealt with only a selected number of wage claims and, on the whole, the big claims were not referred to it: the TUC vetting committee, on the other hand, considered all the major claims.

The TUC undertook to keep the government informed of developments: presumably it let the Ministry of Labour know the size of claims coming before the vetting committee and whether or not the committee had commented on them. The Ministry of Labour also received information about claims and offers from the employers, and unions and staff associations not affiliated to the TUC were expected to notify the Ministry directly. Thus there was an overlapping procedure of notification.

On the prices side the government did not feel the same need to get the CBI's agreement to an early warning system. Manufacturers of some 75 items were asked to inform the appropriate government department not less than four weeks in advance of any price increases proposed for those items. This notification had to be accompanied by a brief justification for the increase in the light of the criteria set out in the White Paper earlier in the year.[2]

These various arrangements for prices and incomes were described

[1] TUC, *Report of the 97th Annual Trade Union Congress at Brighton, 1965*, p. 470.
[2] Department of Economic Affairs *Prices and Incomes Policy*, Cmnd 2639.

in a White Paper towards the end of November 1965,[1] and were introduced on a non-statutory basis pending legislation. The legislation was in fact introduced: it was, as promised, an enabling Act, creating powers to be held in reserve until needed. However, it lapsed with the dissolution of Parliament in March 1966.

These new institutions – the early warning system and the TUC's vetting committee – do not seem to have made much difference to the rate at which earnings and wage rates were rising in the first half of 1966. The TUC had indicated clearly enough that, in any vetting which they did, their treatment of the norm would be 'flexible'. The NBPI was also discovering some of the difficulties of its role. Most awards which were not referred to the Board were higher than would have been warranted by a strict interpretation of the criteria in the White Paper. If the NBPI held back the few awards which were referred to it, it would find its judgements almost universally disregarded; this was one reason for it stressing the need to finance increases above the norm by productivity arrangements of some kind. (In addition, the chairman, Aubrey Jones, considered that one of the functions of the NBPI was to act as a kind of national management consultancy.) Further, the Board found that it had to compete with other arbiters using more lenient criteria. Early in 1966, when the government approved a substantial award to Scottish teachers on the basis of comparability, the Board reminded the government that, according to the White Paper, comparability was to be given less weight than hitherto. Also, when the Wages Council for the road haulage industry made a 7 per cent pay award, the Board pointed out that it had made 'concessions, not in exchange for improvements in productivity, but for a promise to talk about productivity'; nonetheless, the Minister of Labour endorsed the settlement. At about the same time Lord Kindersley recommended substantial increases for doctors and dentists, accepting the principle of comparability with little question.

The freeze

The government finally decided to stand firm – or more precisely, to encourage employers to stand firm – when the National Union of Seamen called a strike on 26 May 1966 in pursuit of a 17 per cent wage claim. The strike was very damaging; the government set up a Court of Inquiry on 26 May, which offered the seamen the equivalent of $9\frac{1}{2}$ per cent over two years, as opposed to the employers' final offer of $12\frac{1}{4}$ per cent over 3 years. These terms were eventually accepted, but not

---

[1] Department of Economic Affairs, *Prices and Incomes Policy: an 'Early Warning System'*, Cmnd 2808, London, HMSO, 1965.

until 1 July. The strike was one of the factors in the sterling crisis in July; it was by now fairly clear – given the apparent failure of voluntary policies – that the measures taken to deal with the crisis would include more forceful wage and price restraints. Together with the deflationary measures introduced on 20 July (page 38), the government enacted a six-month freeze on wages, salaries, dividends and prices, to be followed by six months of 'severe restraint'. This marked a major change in Labour's incomes policy, which had originally been conceived as a long-term strategy, the national interest being gradually introduced as one criterion of wage bargaining in an economy where output and the standard of living were rising fast. As a short-term crisis measure and part of a package intended to check the rise in output and consumers' expenditure, however, an incomes policy inevitably became identified with restrictions on the rise in the real standard of living.

The government obtained statutory powers for enforcing the freeze by adding an extra section to the Prices and Incomes Bill which was going through Parliament at the time. This Bill was a slightly revised version of the one which had lapsed with the general election in March, providing for compulsory advance notification of price or wage increases. Notification had to be given one month before the increases were implemented and, if during that month the Minister decided to refer the case to the NBPI, the increase could not be implemented until after the Board had published its Report or three months had passed from the date of the reference, whichever was the earlier.[1] The section which was now added gave the government powers to direct that specified prices, charges, or rates of remuneration should not be increased from a certain date; also to enforce recommendations of the NBPI – although this power was never used. As with the rest of the Bill, the powers in this new section could only be brought into operation by an Order in Council and would lapse automatically after twelve months.

The government then encountered – as on other occasions – the problems of interpretation which are associated with a standstill of this kind. They decided to allow 'genuine promotion' and increments due on incremental scales. They dealt with existing commitments, which covered about a quarter of the workforce in one way or another, by saying that they should be honoured after a delay of six months. For the rest, no new agreement could take effect before 1 January 1967.

On 27 July the TUC General Council gave its reluctant support to the freeze. In meetings with Ministers, the Council had outlined all

---

[1] The introduction of this Bill in early June led to the resignation of Frank Cousins from the government.

the various objections: it would involve the dishonouring of agreements already made; it would hit hardest at the lowest paid, many of whom had received no increases for eighteen months; through its application to productivity agreements, it would impose a standstill on 'growth and modernisation'. The Council also seemed doubtful about its effectiveness and disclaimed any responsibility for making sure that it worked; there was much the same reluctant endorsement at the Trades Union annual Congress, where the freeze was accepted by a majority of 4·9 to 3·8 million.

There were in fact very few attempts on the union side to break the freeze. At the end of September the Association of Supervisory Staffs, Executives and Technicians forced the government to activate its statutory powers by bringing a case for the payment of wage increases agreed before the freeze. In fact, however, only seven stand-still orders were made up to the end of January 1967 and they only concerned some 36,000 workers out of a working population of 23 million.

In November the government set out the criteria which were to apply during the period of 'severe restraint' from the end of January 1967 to 12 August of that year.[1] There was to be a nil norm; exceptions might be allowed for productivity agreements strictly interpreted and for some increases to the lowest paid workers. Only in the most exceptional circumstances were the other criteria which had been set out initially – the distribution of manpower and comparability – to be accepted as justification for wage or salary increases. The NBPI was asked to produce a special interim Report suggesting guidelines for judging productivity agreements. This set stringent standards: in particular, payment should not be made before the productivity increases took place and there should be clear benefits to the consumer through a contribution to stable prices.[2] The TUC was strongly hostile to this Report.[3]

The NBPI was also given some 'low pay' references. It had relatively little difficulty in accepting that agricultural workers should receive an increase during the period of severe restraint on this ground. It had more difficulty with the retail drapery, outfitting and footwear trades, where it was anxious that increases should be confined to the lowest paid and tapered as earnings rose. The relevant Wages Council rejected this recommendation, but the Minister drew the employers' attention to the NBPI's view and apparently a number of large employers did in fact pay the increases only to workers on near minimum rates. The

---

[1] Department of Economic Affairs, *Prices and Incomes Standstill: period of severe restraint*, Cmnd 3150, London, HMSO, 1966.

[2] NBPI, *Report no. 36: Productivity Agreements*, Cmnd 3311, London, HMSO, 1967.

[3] TUC, *Report of the 100th Annual Trade Union Congress at Blackpool, 1968*, p. 543.

NBPI also had considerable difficulties with a low pay reference which concerned rather over a million manual workers in local authorities, the National Health Service, and gas and water supply. The conclusion was that the main problem was inefficient use of labour and consequently low productivity; the claim was in fact agreed, but it was argued that there should also be immediate steps to give productivity incentives.

The periods of freeze and severe restraint had the effect, immediately visible in the figures, of checking the rise in wage rates and earnings. From July to December 1966 the weekly wage-rate index did not move at all; from July 1966 to June 1967 there was a rise of only 2 per cent in both the index of weekly wage rates and the monthly index of average earnings. Of course, a good deal of the effect could have been simply postponement; this point is discussed more fully on pages 390–1 below.

The declining phase

Discussions of what should follow the period of severe restraint had already begun towards the end of 1966. In October of that year the TUC General Council published its views on the form a future incomes policy should take. They considered: 'that the TUC should indicate those areas in which the Government could operate effectively and, equally important, those areas which the Government should leave alone. In the General Council's view incomes policy largely fell into the latter category... An incomes policy would need to be in operation for a considerable time before its benefit started to appear, whereas the Government was seeking quick-acting remedies to meet a crisis situation.'[1] They sketched out the kind of voluntary policy they envisaged: their vetting procedures would continue; in addition, each year they would prepare a report on the economic situation, incorporating the General Council's views on the general increase in wages and salaries that would be appropriate, and submit this to a conference of the executives of affiliated unions.

The first such conference was held in March 1967 and endorsed the proposed return to a voluntary policy by a huge majority. The main quantitative guidance which the General Council gave was in interpreting low pay: 'as a first step the General Council decided that they would regard as compatible with incomes policy claims for increases of up to £1.00 a week in national minimum rates which were less than £14.00 a week... The General Council accepted that they would also have to have regard to the need to reward the acquisition of skills and the acceptance of responsibility, and to the relationship between

[1] TUC, *Report of the 99th Annual Trades Union Congress at Brighton, 1967,* p. 322.

supervisors and supervised, but agreed that they should not interpret this as automatically justifying claims based on the maintenance of traditional relativities.'[1] This in effect recognised the great difficulty of raising the income of the low paid without raising the income of the higher paid as well. At the conference the General Secretary stoutly defended the effectiveness of the TUC's voluntary system; he considered that its operation so far had been 'remarkably successful, although apparently no one outside the Trade Union movement thought it was'. Both here and on a later occasion he indicated that the vetting committee could not possibly consider itself tightly bound by the precise criteria of any White Paper: 'above all in this business we need flexibility. We need – I am not ashamed of the phrase at all – room for those shoddy, shabby, dirty compromises which are the essence of practical people trying to do a job. We do not rule out any...considerations...cost of living, comparability, the importance of the need to maintain proper differentials for skill, and so on.'[2]

The government's own statement on prices and incomes policy from mid-1967 was published in March. There was to be no norm: 'there can be no justification at present for returning to the norm of $3-3\frac{1}{2}$ per cent...which in practice tended to be regarded as the minimum increase which everyone expected to receive. Over the twelve months' period beginning 1 July 1967, no-one can be entitled to a minimum increase; any proposed increase...will need to be justified against the criteria set out below'.[3] Basically there was a return to the criteria set out in the initial 1965 White Paper,[4] and these criteria were repeated. A few additional points were made: that twelve months should be regarded as the minimum period between awards; that it might be appropriate for substantial improvements to be achieved by stages; that there should be no attempt to make good increases forgone during the previous year. On enforcement, the government returned in effect to the provisions of the 1966 Act, which enabled them to delay an award while it was referred to the NBPI. However, under a new Bill, it could impose a one-month standstill while examining a claim, order a further delay of up to three months if the proposals were referred to the NBPI and, at the end of three months, if the NBPI so recommended, could impose a further delay of three months, making a total maximum period of delay of seven months. Thus a reference to the NBPI became an essential part of delaying tactics by the government.

[1] Ibid. p. 329.　　　　　　　　　[2] Ibid. p. 539.

[3] Department of Economic Affairs, *Prices and Incomes Policy after June 30, 1967*, Cmnd 3235, London, HMSO, 1967.

[4] Department of Economic Affairs, *Prices and Incomes Policy*, Cmnd 2639.

From mid-1967 to the end of the Labour government's incomes policy there was less and less relationship between the carefully worded criteria set out in the White Paper and actual events. There were many claims of the order 15–17 per cent and many settlements at around 7 per cent – which is roughly the percentage implied by the TUC General Council's recommendation earlier in the year that those earning £14 a week might expect to get an additional £1. There is no evidence of any significant narrowing of relativities. The Trades Union annual Congress passed a batch of motions severely critical of incomes policy and the one motion strongly in favour was lost. A motion urging the government to reassess the functions, purpose and organisation of the NBPI was passed; the trade unions were becoming increasingly dissatisfied with its role.

After devaluation at the end of 1967, the gap between the trade union picture of an incomes policy and government ideas widened even further. By the beginning of 1968 retail prices were rising fast, partly because of devaluation, and, although rises in the cost of living were supposed to be no argument for wage increases, this was certainly not generally accepted by the trade unions. Further, at the beginning of 1968 the TUC's *Economic Review* produced a very optimistic forecast of the possibilities of growth, which it put at 6 per cent for the year ahead; in this light it suggested that a basic 14s. per week increase all round would be in line with incomes policy objectives.[1]

The government reasonably took the view that, if those at the bottom of the income scale got increases of 14s. per week, those higher would get substantially more, and in April they produced a tighter incomes policy, which was to start from 20 March 1968.[2] There was still no norm; all increases in pay would have to be justified by the 1967 criteria, but, in addition, there was a ceiling of $3\frac{1}{2}$ per cent for claims which satisfied the criteria, the only exception being agreements which 'genuinely raise productivity and increase efficiency sufficiently to justify a pay increase above $3\frac{1}{2}$ per cent'. The NBPI's guidelines for judging productivity agreements were repeated. At the same time the government gave notice that, when the relevant sections of the 1967 Act expired on 11 August 1968, they would introduce legislation to enable them to delay price or pay increases for as long as twelve months in the context of a reference to the NBPI; this time these powers would be sought for eighteen months – that is, to the end of 1969.

Since the only justification for an increase above $3\frac{1}{2}$ per cent was

---

[1] TUC, *Economic Review 1968*. See also *National Institute Economic Review*, no. 43, February 1968, pp. 28–9.
[2] Department of Economic Affairs, *Productivity, Prices and Incomes Policy in 1968 and 1969*, Cmnd 3590, London, HMSO, 1968.

now productivity, this became the central point in arguments about the various claims put forward. The stress on productivity was perhaps more marked because in April 1968 responsibility for incomes policy was moved to the Ministry of Labour, which was re-christened the Department of Employment and Productivity. Because Ministers now had to find some productivity justification when they gave way to pressure and allowed increases greater than 3½ per cent, there was a growing laxity over the meaning of productivity agreements, and less and less attention was paid to the stringent guidelines laid down by the NBPI. Thus, in July 1968, although the government at first insisted that there would be no across-the-board increases to railwaymen before a 'copper-bottomed' productivity agreement had been drawn up, after a two weeks go-slow a 3 per cent increase across-the-board was agreed upon vague promises of a productivity agreement; the deal subsequently drawn up in August provided for another 8–9 per cent in return for simplified grade structures and the abolition of job demarcations. In much the same way, in October 1968 the government approved a three-year settlement for the engineering industry which was well above the 3½ per cent ceiling; although it was called a 'productivity deal' it complied with virtually none of the NBPI's guidelines, amounting to little more than the promise of good intentions for the future in such matters as cooperation with job evaluation and shop-floor work-study schemes. It was becoming quite clear that the 3½ per cent ceiling was meaningless. Thus, when the NBPI considered agricultural wages for the second time in 1968, it was faced with the situation that no more than 3½ per cent should be allowed, for there was no possibility of productivity bargains which conformed with the Board's own guidelines. A 3½ per cent increase would, however, have been so unfair compared to the other awards current at the time that the NBPI recommended that the government would be justified in considering 'whether a special exception to the requirements of the White Paper ought to be made in this case',[1] and the government accepted this recommendation.

Not only were the trade unions becoming disenchanted with incomes policy – in September 1968 the motion supporting the TUC voluntary policy scraped home with only the tiny majority of 34,000 – but the government was becoming increasingly disenchanted as well. The view began to take hold that the real problem was the trade unions' inability to control unofficial action by local militants, which was making any incomes policy impracticable. This received some support when the Royal Commission on Trade Unions and Employers'

[1] NBPI, *Report no. 101: Pay of Workers in Agriculture in England and Wales*, Cmnd 3911, London, HMSO, 1969.

Associations eventually published its Report, after three years' work, in June 1968.[1] It stressed how far collective bargaining had become de-centralised: 'Before the war it was generally assumed that industry-wide agreements could provide almost all the joint regulation that was needed, leaving only minor issues to be settled by individual managers. Today the consequences of bargaining within the factory can be more momentous that those of industry-wide agreements'.[2] From mid-1968 the government became more and more concerned with the reform of industrial relations and consequently less concerned with incomes policy. A White Paper was published in mid-January 1969 in which it was envisaged that consultations would proceed up to the end of May, when the drafting of a Bill would begin.[3] Soon afterwards the government decided to accelerate this timetable; one industrial dispute which provoked this was at Ford's, where the management had made an offer well in excess of the $3\frac{1}{2}$ per cent ceiling in exchange for an undertaking not to engage in unofficial strikes. On 11 February the unions voted to accept the terms, but they were almost immediately rejected by shop stewards from 21 out of the 23 Ford plants in Britain. The shop stewards called an unofficial strike, which was subsequently declared official. In mid-March a settlement was reached, which included the full pay increases agreed previously but made no reference to any undertaking on unofficial strikes. The award could not in any sense be called a productivity deal and, in order to save face a little, the Employment Secretary agreed to give it 'provisional approval' only. The government then decided to press ahead with an early Bill on industrial relations; the Prime Minister told the General Council that the public were looking for action against unofficial strikers who 'brought about industrial anarchy'. The events which led to the abandonment of this Bill in exchange for a 'solemn and binding undertaking' from the TUC are set out in chapter 13.

The government, having diverted its attention from incomes policy to legislation on unofficial strikes, found it had insufficient support to get that legislation through and, as a result of this defeat, was no longer in a position to enforce its incomes policy in any way. Indeed, it had already been announced in the budget that the government would not seek to renew its extended powers over prices and incomes when they expired at the end of the year. By the autumn of 1969 Labour's incomes policy was moribund. In October, Aubrey Jones announced his retirement as the chairman of the NBPI. There was no longer any relationship between the size of awards and the criteria they were supposed to

---

[1] This, the *Donovan Report*, and the government reaction to it are discussed in greater detail in chapter 13.   [2] Ibid. p. 14, para. 57.

[3] Department of Employment and Productivity, *In Place of Strife*.

observe; in October both the miners and the dustmen won very large pay increases. Nonetheless there was one last White Paper in December 1969,[1] which indicated the longer-term intention of the government to merge the NBPI with the Monopolies Commission; it also returned to the minor delaying powers (four months only) of the 1966 Act and suggested a norm of $2\frac{1}{2}$–$4\frac{1}{2}$ per cent for 1970. By January 1970 most of the settlements being made were well into double figures and at this point the TUC wound up their vetting committee.

INCOMES POLICY, 1972–4

Introduction

After the fall of the Labour government in June 1970, a period without an incomes policy followed. The Conservative government came to power devoted to the principle of non-intervention in wage negotiations. This period is described in chapter 2 (pages 52–62), which also gives an account of the search for an agreement with the trade unions after the miners' strike in January and February 1972, leading up to the freeze on wages and prices in November of that year. That ground is not covered again here; this section is concerned with the detailed provisions and problems of the three stages of the Conservative government's incomes policy, and with a discussion of their effects.

The general economic background is important (page 63). First, this was a period of reasonably rapid – but certainly not phenomenally rapid – economic expansion. Between the fourth quarters of 1971 and 1973 national output was rising at about 3 per cent a year[2] and from the first quarter of 1972 onwards unemployment fell rapidly. Secondly, throughout this period of incomes policy there was a mounting explosion of import prices helped by the falling exchange rate for sterling. In the second half of 1972 import prices (in sterling terms) rose at an annual rate of 16 per cent; in successive half years after that the rates of increase were 28, 42 and 64 per cent respectively.

The Conservative incomes policy began with a standstill on pay, prices, rents and dividends announced by the Prime Minister on 6 November 1972. This was to take effect immediately and to last 90 days – with provision for an extension of up to 60 days. A number of trade unions, anticipating some kind of restriction on free bargaining, had already negotiated settlements, and some important agreements – in particular that for 100,000 manual workers in the electricity supply

[1] Department of Employment and Productivity, *Productivity, Prices and Incomes Policy after 1969*, Cmnd 4237, London, HMSO, 1969.

[2] The year-on-year estimates are distorted because output fell in the first quarter of 1972 with the miners' strike. Over the same period, total final expenditure rose about 5 per cent a year and the foreign balance worsened sharply.

industry – just managed to get through; so long as the operative date was on or before 6 November, the increase could be implemented. The settlement with the electricity supply workers certainly removed one threat to the early stages of the policy. The main settlements which were caught and had to be deferred to the end of the freeze were for agricultural workers, for those employed by the clearing banks and for employees in the furniture industry; these three groups together involved some 600,000 workers. Wages Council settlements for another 600,000 were also deferred.

The freeze on wages presented the usual problems – increments, merit awards, Christmas bonuses, payment by results, and so on. However, as is usual with short freezes, there was very little leakage; between November 1972 and March 1973 average earnings rose less than 1 per cent.

The freeze on prices excluded fresh foods. There was some provision for firms to apply for increases if material prices rose sharply, and a number of food manufacturers in particular were allowed to raise prices, for between November 1972 and February 1973 the cost of basic material and fuel inputs into food manufacturing rose some 15 per cent. Between November and March the retail price index rose 2·4 per cent. Food prices – particularly for seasonal food – accounted for most of this; excluding food the rise was 0·7 per cent. However, the divergence between the movements of prices and of earnings over this short period prompted the General Secretary of the TUC to say that the proposition that price rises were a consequence of wage increases had been 'blown sky-high'.

For pay the freeze ended partly at the end of February, when deferred settlements whose operating date had been before the end of November 1972 became payable, but mainly at the end of March, when other deferred settlements were payable. This backlog consisted of settlements reached in 1972 when the going figures were high; it is part of the explanation for the relatively large rise in earnings between March and November 1973. For prices the freeze was extended to the end of April to cover the transition to VAT in place of purchase tax.

Throughout November and December 1972 the government had been preparing the next stage of their incomes policy. There were separate consultations with the CBI and the TUC; the latter re-emphasised its opposition to any form of statutory policy. The policy in fact followed the model set up in the United States in August 1971;[1]

---

[1] The American model of incomes policy is analysed in detail in the *National Institute Economic Review*, no. 62, November 1972, pp. 6–11; the designers of that model had in turn attempted to avoid the pitfalls of earlier British experience.

it was very different from the incomes policy of 1964–9, which illustrates the wide range that the term 'incomes policy' covers.

On the wages side the main distinguishing characteristics were as follows. First, the policy was universal and the newly established Pay Board was responsible for ensuring it was observed; there was no question of a few settlements being referred to the Board at the government's discretion. Secondly, the limitation was on the average amount per head actually paid by the firm; in this way the policy dealt with the problem that percentage increases on wage rates agreed in national negotiations often end up as very different percentage increases in actual earnings paid at individual plants. Thirdly, the policy had no productivity provisions, thus avoiding one of the major loopholes of the later stages of Labour's policy. Fourthly, notification requirements were more onerous for big firms than for small ones, the belief being that if the big settlements were held the smaller settlements would be kept in line.

On the prices side too the American model was followed. A separate body – the Price Commission – was set up and again the requirements were more onerous for big firms than for small ones. Price controls were based on two principles: firms could apply for increases on the basis of 'allowable costs per unit'; also, they had a reference level of net profit margins – the average of the best two years of the last five – and were not to exceed that level. Distributors were not controlled by allowable costs, but by a combination of net profit margins and gross percentage margins. Export sales were not controlled. Allowable costs were specified, but not non-allowable costs. Initially, advertising expenditure, depreciation, and research and development were the main non-allowable costs, but later the last two items were allowed. British practice differed from American in its treatment of productivity. The American Price Commission established productivity trends for a large number of industries and used them to calculate the allowable increase in costs per unit, so that a firm whose productivity record was better than average stood to gain. In Britain firms had to demonstrate that their own costs per unit had risen; that is, they gained no advantage in profits per unit from a productivity record better than average (though they might, of course, gain in total profits through an increase in market share). In addition, there was at first a productivity deduction of 50 per cent; that is, only half the rise in wage costs per unit of output was allowable.[1]

---

[1] The Price Commission justified this double deduction with the rather curious argument that, whereas the cost per unit calculation allowed for past increases in productivity, the 50 per cent disallowance allowed for future increases in productivity. This would only be valid if no firm went back to the Price Commission a second time.

Pay policy under Stage II

Under Stage II the pay limit per head – 'the maximum amount by which the average pay per head of the group may be increased in a 12 month period' – was the sum of 4 per cent of the average per head of the group's pay bill for the preceding twelve months and £1 per week. In calculating the total past wage bill non-contractual overtime was excluded and no individual might be paid an increase of more than £250 a year. In administering this policy, a number of employers – for example, the Post Office – found it very difficult to establish a figure for average pay in the past twelve months; in some cases the Pay Board permitted them to use figures from the Department of Employment's *New Earnings Survey*. Once the total sum had been established it could be distributed as the negotiators decided – favouring the low paid if they wished.

How did Stage II of the pay policy in fact work out? The trade union movement reluctantly acquiesced; there was little overt opposition, the number of days lost in strikes being lower not only than in 1972 (when there was the miners' strike), but also substantially lower than in either 1970 or 1971. There was a fairly clear effect on the rise in earnings; in the absence of some kind of incomes policy, there was every reason to think that the rise in money earnings would have accelerated during 1973. Unemployment was coming down quite briskly throughout the year and, pushed by the rise in import prices, retail prices were going up a good deal faster in 1973 than in 1972; nevertheless, the rise in earnings during 1973, excluding the effect of overtime, was significantly lower than during 1972.

However, although it is reasonably certain that the first two stages of incomes policy brought down the rise in money earnings, the increase still seems big when compared with the incomes policy 'norm'. The Pay Board claimed that the average pay increase resulting from approved Stage II settlements was $7\frac{2}{3}$ per cent, but, on national figures and excluding overtime, the increase in average hourly earnings between October 1972 and October 1973 was $13\frac{1}{2}$ per cent. Unlike the Price Commission, which related its figures to the national published series, the Pay Board made no attempt to analyse the reasons for this difference. Part of the explanation clearly lies in settlements postponed by the freeze, which were generally in line with the very large increases in the 1972 wage round. Then, movements towards equal pay could be made outside the pay limit and, according to the Pay Board, nearly three million benefited from this exception. There were also certain reductions in hours and improvements in holidays which were outside the limit, but these were not in fact very important.

How far was the pay code infringed? The Pay Board conducted a number of spot checks to see in particular whether the code was observed in settlements affecting under a hundred employees, which did not need to be reported. In the whole period of Stage II and Stage III spot checks on firms employing 614,000 in all showed that some 40,000, or about $6\frac{1}{2}$ per cent, had been paid too much; the average excess was £1·54, which was 4–5 per cent of average earnings. If we assume that this represents the average degree of non-compliance – and this is a considerable assumption – it still explains only about 0·3 per cent out of the $13\frac{1}{2}$ per cent rise in money earnings. It seems therefore that the settlements postponed by the freeze, the move to equal pay, payments by results systems, increases in overtime and the permitted continuance of incremental awards must explain most of the discrepancy between the national figure and the Pay Board's estimate of the average size of settlements approved.

Stage III

Stage II had an expected life of only seven months – from April to November 1973 – so that from its beginning the government was concerned with the problems of the third stage. The Pay Board was instructed to prepare two Reports, on anomalies and on relativities, and to have the former ready well before November.[1]

Throughout the summer the government discussed the shape of Stage III with the TUC and the CBI – though how much difference the discussions made eventually is uncertain. The TUC agreed to the talks on the grounds that the government ought to be given its views, but one important union, the Amalgamated Union of Engineering Workers, instructed its General Secretary not to join in and at the Trades Union annual Congress the General Council's policy of agreeing to talk was endorsed by only a small majority. In the discussions, the TUC representatives seem mainly to have reiterated their strong opposition to any statutory interference in wage bargaining; during the year various spokesmen for the TUC issued statements suggesting that, while wage increases were held back, price increases were 'let through in droves'.

The government issued a statement in July announcing that it intended to include a threshold clause in the next stage of incomes policy. This idea had been around for a long time, but it represented

---

[1] This was to deal with the unfair situations which had arisen specifically from the standstill introduced in November 1972; the other was to have a wider coverage: 'Within any system for the determination of pay, groups from time to time feel that they deserve special treatment . . . If a policy for controlling inflation is to be effective and fair, it must have procedures for considering such claims objectively' (Pay Board, *Advisory Report no. 2: Problems of Pay Relativities*, p. vi).

a radical change from previous government policies. In the period 1962–9 the official incomes policy had always stressed that price increases were no longer to be considered a justification for wage increases. On occasions the trade unions had put the idea forward and the government had turned it down; this time, it was a government proposal, which had a lukewarm reception from the trade unions.

The government's other main concern was to introduce greater flexibility into the next stage; apart from a general need, there was a specific problem in regard to the miners. The government had early warning of this; at the National Union of Mineworkers' annual conference in July there was unanimous approval for a claim for increases ranging from 22 to 46 per cent.[1] Thus, the provisions for greater flexibility in Stage III had both a general and a specific objective. They included a 1 per cent margin to deal with changes in pay structures or arrangements making possible better use of manpower; also extra payments were allowed for genuine efficiency schemes, but the savings had to be achieved first and the Pay Board presented with evidence from three months' operation. Further progress towards equal pay for women was also permitted, the Pay Board was instructed to produce recommendations on London allowances and (the provision proposed particularly to help the miners) premium payments above the limit were allowed to those working 'unsocial hours'.

Apparently the Prime Minister did attempt to check with the president of the National Union of Mineworkers that the concessions would be sufficient, and was certainly given the impression that they would be. It may be that the latter misjudged his executive committee; it may be that he got the wrong impression that during the negotiations there would be special concessions for the miners alone, rather than general provisions in a code available to all.

The new code for pay came into operation on 7 November 1973; the basic limit on increases was £2.25 per head per week or 7 per cent, with a limit of £350 a year for any individual; groups had to choose either the lump sum or the percentage; the various flexibility provisions described above were also included. Agreements could include the threshold provision, which provided that when the retail price index had risen 7 per cent above the figure for October 1973 a pay increase of 40p a week could be given, and the same increase for every further 1 per cent rise in the index. (This compensated in full on gross earnings of the average worker.) Presumably at the time the threshold was set – probably early in October 1973 – the Treasury price forecast for the

---

[1] The conference set targets for minimum weekly rates of an increase for surface workers from £25.29 to £35, for underground workers from £27.29 to £40 and for face workers from £39.79 to £45.

year from October stood at around 7 per cent; even allowing for the impossibility of forecasting the rise in oil prices, this was rather optimistic, given the increases which had already occurred in other commodity prices and the fall which had already occurred in the sterling exchange rate.

On prices the main change was that all category II firms (in manufacturing, those with sales between £5 million and £50 million a year) were required to notify price increases to the Price Commission. Increases in depreciation were made allowable costs and various safeguards were included to prevent an indefinite erosion of profit margins.

The whole of Stage III was, of course, overshadowed by the struggle with the National Union of Mineworkers. The Coal Board, making full use of the flexibility provisions in the new code, made an offer which was worth about 13 per cent on average, of which the shift premium for 'unsocial hours' accounted for 4·4 per cent. The miners rejected this offer and began an overtime ban on 12 November. The Electrical Power Engineers' Association had also begun a ban on out-of-hours working on 1 November because they considered it impossible under the new code to resolve a dispute over stand-by payments which had begun in December 1972. The sequence of events which led up to the miners' strike and the fall of the Conservative government is set out in chapter 2.

The procedural problem was that Stage III had no adequate mechanism for dealing with special cases on their merits. The Pay Board had to interpret the code as it stood, using only lawyers' ingenuity to see if special payments could not be squared with it. They were empowered to deal with 'anomalies', as recommended in their Report,[1] but these were defined as cases where a clear and identifiable link had been broken by the standstill. The Report on relativities had not yet appeared; when it did appear in January 1974,[2] it recommended a process for selecting and examining cases which could have been used, but by then it was very late. The government did in fact ask the Pay Board to turn itself into a relativities board and consider the miners' case; it reported after the election was over. There was an escape clause in the counter-inflation legislation which provided that, if the Secretary of State for Employment was satisfied that there were exceptional circumstances, he could overrule the Pay Board and give his consent to an increase, but this particular route would have seemed very much a surrender. Apart, then, from all the problems which arose in running an incomes policy to which the trade union movement was hostile,

[1] Pay Board, *Advisory Report no. 1: Anomalies arising out of the Pay Standstill of Nov. 1972*, London, HMSO, 1973.
[2] Pay Board, *Advisory Report no. 2: Problems of Pay Relativities*.

Stage III did not contain adequate mechanisms for dealing with special cases in time.

While the struggle with the miners was going on, the Pay Board proceeded with the administration of the new code – and indeed continued to do so for some months after the change of government. Up to the end of June 1974 it approved settlements covering some $14\frac{1}{2}$ million employees and calculated that the average pay rise was around 9 per cent excluding threshold components. On the whole, negotiating groups preferred the lump sum to the percentage system of calculating the total. Up to the end of June only about a third of the settlements had taken advantage of the threshold provisions; no doubt many of these included threshold provisions later. Perhaps not surprisingly there is evidence of rather more extensive infringement of the code in its dying stages. When infringements were discovered their average size in the quarter to the end of May 1974 was £2.75, against the figure for the whole incomes policy period of £1.54. The Pay Board ceased to exist on 25 July 1974.

AN ASSESSMENT OF INCOMES POLICY

Introduction

Were incomes policies successful? Does the experience of 1960–74 suggest that future governments should continue with experiments of this kind or abandon them?

There are some preliminary points to be made. First, 'incomes policy' covers a wide range of different types of attempt to intervene in the process of fixing incomes; it is not a single instrument like, say, VAT. The incomes policy of 1964–5, with a voluntary statement of intent and the NBPI, whose effect was to be selective and educative, was very different from the statutory £1 plus 4 per cent policy of April–November 1973. Indeed, it is not at all easy to distinguish satisfactorily between periods when incomes policy was 'on' or 'off'. In 1970 and 1971 the Conservative government tried to make each settlement in the public sector 1 per cent lower than the previous settlement – the 'N–1' policy – is this to be counted an 'on' period or not?

Secondly, before discussing the success of any policy, we must establish what policy-makers were trying to do. Clearly their dominant objective was to bring down the rate of inflation, but there were other secondary objectives as well. Most incomes policies were supposed to favour the low paid, so that one measure of success is whether or not the differential between low wages and the average wage narrowed. There are other consequences to be considered: incomes policies may reduce or increase the number of industrial disputes, improve or worsen industrial relations, or (conceivably) affect productivity. However, the main criterion is undoubtedly success or failure in reducing the rate of inflation.

Thirdly, the success of an attempt to change some institution in society must necessarily be judged in a different way from the efficacy of a more conventional instrument, such as a change in tax rates. It may take a long time for new workable institutions to evolve; there can be a slow learning process and the early attempts may be unsuccessful partly because those involved are reluctant to accept the need for change. It is not enough simply to consider the success or failure of early attempts; there is also the question of whether or not these early moves were along a road with a dead end. If incomes policy proves to be an idea with no future, then the early experiments were a waste of time; if, on the other hand, they were steps towards an eventual and necessary acceptance of some form of intervention in free collective bargaining, then the judgement has to be different.

There are therefore basically two questions. First, whether the whole series of attempts at various kinds of incomes policy was a mistake; if so there is little more to be said. If, however, the idea is not wholly rejected, then there is the second question of the lessons to be learned by comparing the various forms of incomes policy which were attempted.

The general argument

The general argument for an incomes policy presented in this country is that without it a very high rate of unemployment would be needed to bring about an acceptable degree of price stability; further, this rate of unemployment was probably higher at the end of the period than at the beginning. Proponents of incomes policy tend to view inflation in terms of wage bargaining; they picture the rate of inflation as being largely determined by trade union bargains in any particular year. Also, a relatively small number of 'leading' wage bargains, which may not be the same ones each year, set the standard which other unions follow, for one of the main concerns of a trade union negotiator is that the group he represents should not be left behind. In any year the leading wage bargains will obviously be strongly influenced by past price rises and increases in real incomes (before or after tax), but not so strictly that they cannot also be influenced by policy, or by willingness or unwillingness to cooperate with the government of the day. Single events can affect the figures; for example, after the successful miners' strikes in 1972 and 1974 the general increase in average earnings was probably much higher than it would have been had the strikes failed. Longer-term trends might also drive the figures up. The advocates of incomes policy see the structure of free collective bargaining in this country, with a very large number of separate bargains following each other throughout the year, as being particularly conducive to high money wage settlements; they therefore believe there may well be some advantage in modifying this institution.

The arguments against incomes policy are that it is, at best, ineffective (except in the very short term) and, at worst, damaging – in preventing desirable changes in relativities. On this view the rate of increase in money earnings is determined by factors which no incomes policy can alter for any appreciable period – predominantly, of course, the demand for labour; governments are therefore wasting their time.

The arguments about incomes policy are part of the wider debate about the desirable degree of intervention in the economy; an incomes policy implies a considerable extension of that intervention, in that, whether the policy is statutory or voluntary, those who negotiate wage or salary increases are subject to constraint. It is natural that those who are anxious to limit government intervention in the working of a market economy should be dubious about incomes policies. There is also a natural disinclination among economists to accept that the rate of increase in earnings cannot be explained in terms of other economic variables – for economists are essentially in the business of explaining the movement of one economic variable in terms of others.

So far as the past is concerned, therefore, the question is whether or not year-to-year movements in average earnings – or some other indicator of income from employment[1] – can be satisfactorily explained using variables which incomes policy could not be expected to influence. If so, there is a strong case for saying that past incomes policies have been ineffective, at least in their main objective of holding back the rise in money incomes. It would not, of course, follow that all forms of incomes policy would necessarily be ineffective; it would simply be evidence on the past performance of the forms tried so far.

The obvious candidate as an economic determinant of the rate of rise in money earnings is the pressure of demand for labour, and in the late 1950s and early 1960s it was widely argued that changes in unemployment adequately explained fluctuations in the increase in money earnings.[2] F. W. Paish was an influential advocate of the view that in this period it was excess pressure of demand for labour which

[1] Attempts at explanation have sometimes used wage rates and sometimes earnings, either hourly or weekly; more recently an attempt has been made to calculate a series for wage settlements. Another possible series is the average wage or salary per unit of employment.

[2] The arguments were generally based on the article by Professor A. W. Phillips, 'The relation between unemployment and the rate of change of money wage rates in the United Kingdom, 1861–1957', Economica, vol. 25 (new series), November 1958. It was from this article that Professor Paish deduced that a rise in unemployment from 1 to 2 per cent would be accompanied by a fall in the rate of increase in wage rates from 9 to 3 per cent a year.

mattered; the demands of trade unions were irrelevant. In a memorandum presented to the Council on Prices Productivity and Incomes in November 1957, he wrote:

The causal factor in the rise in wages and salaries has been, not the demands of Trade Unions, but the ability of employers to grant them without reducing their demand for labour...it is probably true that the very existence of collective bargaining, with its administrative delays, has caused wage rates to rise more slowly than they would have done under similar conditions of excess demand in a free labour market, where there were neither Trade Unions nor employers' associations.[1]

In 1964 Paish put forward the view that if wages increased at an excessive rate when unemployment was below 2 per cent the proper course was to restrain demand, if unemployment was above $2\frac{1}{4}$ per cent a 'wages policy' was unnecessary but harmless, in the narrow area where unemployment lay between 2 and $2\frac{1}{4}$ per cent restriction of demand might be usefully supplemented (though probably not replaced) by a 'wages policy'. At that time he considered the level of unemployment a powerful determinant of the rate of increase in wages and earnings.

However, in the late 1960s and early 1970s unemployment was rising and the increase in money earnings accelerating at the same time. The view that the rise in earnings could be explained by the pressure of demand for labour as measured by unemployment then clearly became untenable. Various amendments were tried. It was argued that with the introduction of earnings-related supplements to unemployment benefit as from October 1966 those who became unemployed were not under the same pressure to find another job immediately and so took longer in their search. Hence, for any given pressure of demand for labour, after October 1966 the figure for unemployment was higher than it had been before. However, subsequent studies showed that not many of the unemployed in fact received earnings-related supplements; a Department of Employment working party concluded that the additional unemployment from this cause in November 1973 'was very probably less than 50,000' males.[2] Another amendment was to add price expectations to the pressure of demand as part of the explanation of the movement of earnings or wage rates,[3] but various difficulties were

[1] Paish, *Studies in an Inflationary Economy*, p. 116. Paish is referring here to the experience of the 1950s; he did not suggest that excess demand for labour was the sole explanation of inflation in the late 1960s, but concluded that trade union activity was an important component in that period.

[2] The Report was summarised in 'The changed relationship between unemployment and vacancies', *Department of Employment Gazette*, October 1976.

[3] This followed the work of M. Friedman in the United States (see, for example, 'The role of monetary policy', *American Economic Review*, vol. 58, March 1968). The inclusion of price expectations is possibly more plausible in the United States, where labour contracts are for a set term, than in the United Kingdom, where they are not.

encountered: first, it was the term for expected prices which then provided virtually all the explanation of the movement in wage rates or earnings, and unemployment tended to drop out of the picture altogether;[1] secondly, since price expectations are usually made to depend on the movement of past prices (or constructed from a series which is heavily dependent on past prices), there is the much more straightforward method of using past prices themselves, which does not bring in the complexity of expectations.

By the early 1970s, therefore, it was becoming less plausible to suggest that the movement of wage rates or earnings basically responded to the pressure of demand for labour. An alternative approach put wage bargaining in the centre of the picture and attempted to model the main forces acting on the wage bargaining process. The suggestion was that negotiators were concerned to make good the loss in real income from the increase in prices since the last settlement and then to add a further sum to ensure some real gain. This view was in some ways a rediscovery of a relationship suggested by Dow as long ago as 1956 – that it seemed reasonable to believe 'that full compensation for price increases is something which trade unions aim at and which both sides to wage negotiations accept as a standard of reference'.[2] One question which arises is whether the negotiators also take account of changes in tax or national insurance deductions, so that they are concerned with the post-tax income of their members.[3] However, neither the demand for labour nor the wage bargaining view provides a good account of the year-to-year movements of money wage rates or earnings, particularly in the 1970s. There were clearly other forces at work.

By the early 1970s none of the main bodies engaged in short-term economic forecasting in Britain were using econometric relationships for forecasting wage rates or earnings. It is reasonable to suppose that a sharp increase in prices will tend to put wage settlements up and that there is some level of unemployment which will tend to push them down, but it is not possible to quantify those influences with any precision. It follows that there is no way of saying what would have happened in the absence of incomes policy; it certainly does not appear that the year-to-year movement of wage rates or earnings is precisely

---

[1] For a general discussion of the problem of various forms of wage equation, see M. J. Artis, 'Is there a wage equation?' in Courakis (ed.), *Inflation, Depression and Economic Policy in the West*. See also the discussion in 'Spare capacity and full employment', *National Institute Economic Review*, no. 79, February 1977, p. 45 *et seq.*

[2] J. C. R. Dow, 'Analysis of the generation of price inflation', *Oxford Economic Papers*, vol. 8 (new series), October 1956.

[3] Equations of this kind are set out in S. G. B. Henry, M. C. Sawyer and P. Smith, 'Models of inflation in the United Kingdom', *National Institute Economic Review*, no. 77, August 1976; also, K. Coutts, R. Tarling and F. Wilkinson, 'Wage bargaining and the inflation process', *Economic Policy Review*, no. 2, March 1976, p. 20.

determined by economic factors which incomes policy could not influence. It also follows that assessments of incomes policy effects have to be rather rough and ready. Chart 8.1 sets out experience in various periods, from which the following conclusions are tentatively suggested.

First, short wage freezes are certainly and undoubtedly effective. The clearest evidence is provided by the period of freeze followed by severe restraint from the middle of 1966 to the middle of 1967. Before and after that period average earnings were rising at roughly 8 per cent a year; during that period they rose only 2 per cent a year. There can

Chart 8.1. *Changes in average weekly earnings, 1959–76*

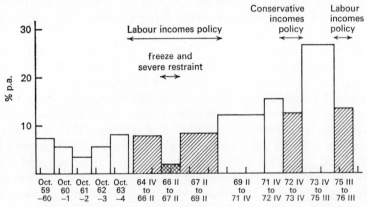

SOURCES: CSO, *Economic Trends, Annual Supplement 1976*; Department of Employment, *British Labour Statistics: historical abstract, 1886–1968*, London, HMSO, 1971, and *British Labour Statistics Yearbook 1972*, London, HMSO, 1974.

Note: For 1959–64 the figures are for male manual workers aged 21 and over in the United Kingdom; from 1964 they are for wages and salaries combined in all industries in Great Britain. The series ran closely together in the period 1964–70 and can be assumed to be comparable.

be no other sensible explanation of that difference. The period of freeze under the Conservative government was even shorter – effectively from November 1972 to March 1973. There was the same sharp deceleration: in the year to November 1972 average earnings rose just on 17 per cent; in the next four months they rose at an annual rate of only 3 per cent.

Assessing longer periods of incomes policy is more difficult. First, they did not achieve the ambitious objectives which their originators set. The basic intention of the Labour government was to bring the rise in money earnings down to a figure close to the trend in national output per head, so that the target was probably an average increase of something like 4–5 per cent a year. In fact, apart from the period of freeze and severe restraint, the rise was roughly 8 per cent a year. During the Conservative government's short incomes policy the objective was probably to bring the rise in earnings down to something like 8 per cent; in fact the figure was about 12½ per cent. However, this is perhaps too severe a criterion of success. The question might rather be whether or not these policies brought the rise in money earnings down to a figure lower than it would otherwise have been.

In any assessment of an incomes policy, it is important to compare the experience of that period not simply with the years that went before, but with the years after as well, because there may well be forces producing a long-term upward trend in the increase in money wages and earnings. Taking the period from the fourth quarter of 1964 to the second quarter of 1969,[1] which included a year of freeze and severe restraint, the annual rise in average earnings was 6½ per cent. This seems very little improvement on the annual rate which prevailed in the two years before the beginning of the period, of around 7½ per cent. However, the period was one in which some of the pressures making for large increases in money earnings were particularly strong; the effect of devaluation on prices and the successive increases in taxation meant that the real post-tax earnings of the average wage earner rose little. The effectiveness of the policy also looks rather different if one takes into account what happened after it ended: the rate of increase in money earnings moved up sharply to 12 per cent a year between mid-1969 and mid-1972, which suggests that up to mid-1969 the policy was having some effect in making trade unions settle for figures lower than they would otherwise have accepted.

To some extent the same kind of assessment applies to the Conservative government's incomes policy. From the fourth quarter of 1972 to the fourth quarter of 1973 average earnings rose about 12½ per cent,[2] which was about the same as the rate of increase during the previous two years. However, again 1973 was a year when one would normally have expected the rise in earnings to accelerate, partly because import prices were rising very fast and partly because output was rising fast and unemployment falling. And again the end of the policy was followed by a very sharp acceleration – to an annual rate of 24 per cent between the end of 1974 and the middle of 1975.

Perhaps the strongest evidence for the effectiveness of incomes policy lies strictly outside the period covered by this book; it is hard to believe that the sharp deceleration in the increase in money earnings which

---

[1] It seems sensible to pick mid-1969 as the terminal date, because during 1969 the government in effect abandoned the incomes policy approach and turned to an attempt to bring the trade unions within the framework of the law (page 377 above).

[2] In the first quarter of 1974 the figure for average earnings fell, mainly because of the effect of the miners' strike.

followed the reintroduction of an incomes policy after mid-1975 would have been so sharp in its absence. Indeed it is highly uncertain whether it would have happened at all.

In sum, if we suppose that over this period there was a variety of forces tending to produce a rising trend in the increase in money earnings, then the experience of the late 1960s and early 1970s is consonant with the view that the two incomes policies during that period were successful, so long as they were in force, in holding back this process. Given that conclusion, it is reasonable to look at the various forms which incomes policy took and the problems which arose to see what lessons can usefully be drawn about different types of attempt at institutional change.

The structure of incomes policies

The problems of incomes policy throughout were not so much conceiving what it should be ideally, but rather the practical and political difficulties of devising machinery which worked. There was the choice between attempting a temporary or a permanent policy and the need to decide on a norm (here the question of compensation for past price rises comes up). Criteria were required for exceptions from the norm; also – and this was easily the most formidable difficulty – some way of administering the policy had to be found; in particular, the choice had to be made between seeking cooperation, imposing a compulsory system, or adopting some mixture of the two. Finally, a decision was needed on any concomitant action on non-wage incomes and prices. In what follows we consider each of these difficulties.

On the choice between temporary and permanent policies, governments alternated between attempts to bring in long-lasting reforms and emergency action to halt inflation. In 1962 the National Incomes Commission was to be a permanent body whose main function was educational. In 1964 the Labour government's initial conception was again a permanent policy, with an annual decision about the norm and the NBPI to adjudicate on cases referred to it. However, in mid-1966 short-term emergency action was superimposed for a year and the more permanent underlying policy had effectively come to an end by the middle of 1969 as government preoccupation moved elsewhere. The Conservative government's policy in 1972 can be labelled 'medium-term temporary'; it was initially envisaged that it would last for perhaps three years.

In neither 1964 nor 1972 was the 're-entry problem' of transition back to free collective bargaining dealt with successfully. Part of the reason is that both policies ended with changes in government. However, clearly a great difficulty with temporary policies is that they are inherently unstable. They tend to be followed by a rash of large claims, with negotiators trying not only to catch up what they think they have lost, but also to obtain a large award before the introduction of the next policy. One of the most obvious things about the rise in money earnings since the mid-1960s is the way in which it accelerated when incomes policies ended. This is part of the case for more permanent institutional changes.

The successive incomes policy White Papers during the 1960s were largely concerned with the theology of the norm and the criteria for exceptions. The norm, both under the Conservatives up to 1964 and under Labour up to 1969, tended to be set theoretically at a figure which would have brought about virtual price stability had it been observed. The initial 'guiding light', set in 1961, was the trend rate of growth in output per head of $2\frac{1}{2}$ per cent. This was later raised by the National Incomes Commission to $3-3\frac{1}{2}$ per cent, partly on the grounds that incomes policy should be geared to the faster rate of growth which it was supposed to help to bring about, but also partly to make the figure a little more realistic. In the period 1964–9 the norm varied between 3 per cent and zero; it was still set at the figure which would bring about virtual price stability. In 1972 the Conservative government's incomes policy was introduced at a time when prices were rising much faster. The objective was the less ambitious one of bringing the rate of inflation down, so that the norm of Stage II was around 7–8 per cent and the Stage III figure if anything rather higher.

Between 1964 and 1972 there was a change of view about indexation. Up to the end of the 1960s it had been emphasised that past price increases should not be considered a justification for future wage increases – this would simply perpetuate the inflationary process. During the early 1970s various means of indexation were being extensively discussed, and Stage III of the Conservative policy permitted negotiators to include in their agreements a guarantee which effectively compensated the average wage earner if the retail price index rose by more than 7 per cent during the year from October 1973 to October 1974. This particular guarantee was most unfortunately timed, since the retail price index passed the 7 per cent threshold in April 1974; indeed the April figure for retail prices was 9·7 per cent above the threshold base and the first three threshold payments were triggered. Under some agreements threshold payments were triggered eleven times during 1974, which shows the danger of any form of indexation in a country with a large foreign trade. If the terms of trade worsen for any reason – because of sharply rising import prices, from devaluation, or from a deliberate 'managed downward float' – real wages and salaries should fall (or rise more slowly) in consequence, but indexation by inhibiting the transfer of real resources into exports prevents the downward movement of the exchange rate from working.

Criteria for exceptions

The main criteria for exceptional pay increases which were put forward at one time or another during this period were as follows:

(1) Low pay: 'where there was general recognition that existing wage or salary levels are too low to maintain a reasonable standard of living'.[1]

(2) The reallocation of labour: 'where it is essential in the national interest to secure (or prevent) a change in the distribution of manpower, and a pay increase would be both necessary and effective for this purpose'.[2] Linked to this criterion was that of comparability – where there was widespread recognition that the pay of some group had fallen out of line with the pay for similar work elsewhere in the United Kingdom – which was behind the Conservative government's proposal to rectify in its Stage III the anomalies brought about by the timing of the freeze in November 1972.

(3) Productivity: initially the principle was that employees had to make a direct contribution by accepting more exacting work or by a major change in working practices, and that some of the benefit should accrue to the community in the form of lower prices. Later, under the Labour government, the NBPI recommended tighter provisions, in particular that the productivity gains should come before the additional payment; this was written into the productivity clauses in the Conservatives' Stage III policy.

Two additional criteria added later were reorganisation of wage and salary structures which could be justified on grounds of economic efficiency and increased productivity (1968), and the implementing of equal pay legislation (1970).

The success of criterion (1) above must be judged on whether or not it in fact improved the position of the low paid in relation to the average. This question can be asked about earnings alone, or about the spread of employment incomes through the economy as a whole; incomes policy was, of course, simply concerned with gross earnings from employment, so that these are the figures which should be used to measure any effect. The figures for the dispersion of gross weekly earnings in fact show a remarkable stability (table 8.1). For both men and women manual workers there is a very slight widening of dispersion between 1960 and 1970, followed by a very slight narrowing between

---

[1] The criterion is described in this way in successive White Papers, for example, Department of Economic Affairs, *Productivity, Prices and Incomes Policy in 1968 and 1969.*
[2] Ibid.

1970 and 1976. However, the movements were very small. For non-manual men (but not for non-manual women) there was some reduction in the relative position of the higher income groups between 1970 and 1976. In general, the figures suggest strongly that it is very difficult to change the distribution of gross earnings, and particularly difficult to improve the relative position of the low paid. This is in spite of the fact that the Conservatives' incomes policy was deliberately designed to help this group; in their Stage II firms were expressly permitted to distribute the total sum available in such a way as to benefit the low paid.

Table 8.1. *Dispersion of gross weekly earnings,[a] Great Britain, 1960–76*

Percentages of median

	Manual workers		Non-manual workers		All workers	
	Highest decile	Lowest decile	Highest decile	Lowest decile	Highest decile	Lowest decile
Men						
1960	145·2	70·6	..	..	..	..
1965	143·9	69·7	..	..	..	..
1970	147·2	67·3	175·1	61·8	160·6	65·4
1974	144·1	68·6	171·6	62·9	157·0	66·8
1976	144·9	70·2	167·5	62·5	159·5	67·6
Women						
1960	138·3	72·0	..	..	..	..
1965	138·7	66·5	..	..	..	..
1970	144·8	69·0	173·7	64·2	170·4	66·4
1974	143·4	69·1	162·0	66·5	159·1	67·7
1976	140·6	67·8	172·9	65·1	165·9	66·1

SOURCES: Department of Employment, *British Labour Statistics Yearbook 1974*, London, HMSO, 1976, and *New Earnings Survey 1976*, London, HMSO, 1977, part A.

[a] For full-time men aged 21 or over and full-time women aged 18 or over, whose pay was not affected by absence.

Criterion (2), although it was available to the NBPI, was in fact hardly ever used. This is perhaps surprising, in that one of the standard arguments against incomes policy is that it abolishes the natural mechanism by which labour is channelled from industries with a low marginal product to industries with a high one. The NBPI tended to take the view that, if there were insufficient workers with the particular skill required for a particular job, a short-term increase in pay was not the best way of increasing the numbers available; the problem was better dealt with by improved long-term prospects, or by an extension of training. The principle of comparability was also used very sparingly; if it were used extensively, an incomes policy might simply reproduce the workings of the existing system, since there is always some comparison which can justify virtually any increase. In the allowance for anomalies made by the Conservatives it was only where the freeze had broken a relationship which was very well established indeed that the case was accepted.

Productivity as a criterion has considerable theoretical attractions, in that its rate of increase in an economy could then be accelerated by an incomes policy. However, productivity agreements fell into some disrepute in the later years of the Labour government; in spite of the fairly stringent conditions which the NBPI attempted to lay down,[1] these were very frequently not observed.[2] From 1968 onwards there was what has been described as 'an uncritical campaign for productivity bargaining',[3] the surveillance of the NBPI was weakened by insufficient and inadequate references, and productivity bargains became one of the main routes by which wage awards evaded control. For this reason stringent criteria were imposed for productivity agreements in the Conservatives' Stage III; in subsequent incomes policies up to mid-1977 no provision for them was made at all.

The incomes policies of this period did not provide an adequate structure for dealing with exceptional cases. The NBPI could only consider the cases which the government chose to refer to it; the intention was that it should establish a kind of case law, but for case law to be effective its rulings have to be copied by other adjudicators and there is no evidence that the TUC vetting committee, for example, took much notice of the principles which the NBPI laid down. The Conservative government's statutory policy did not provide a satisfactory alternative; the Pay Board could do no more than interpret the pay code. A basically judicial system has to have greater coverage than the NBPI had to be effective; on the other hand, a statutory pay code which allows no discretion to the institution administering it is not flexible enough for the later stages of an incomes policy.

The administrative machinery

Part of the attraction of incomes policies is that basically the idea is simple: that there is little point in high nominal wage and salary awards, which lead to higher prices; it is more sensible to have lower money awards all round with smaller price rises. However, the problems which arose from the attempts to find new institutions to bring that result about proved formidable. This section sets out some of the problems encountered and describes the main attempts to find solutions.

---

[1] NBPI, *Report no. 36: Productivity Agreements*.

[2] In a survey of 24 cases of productivity bargaining, Clegg found over half to be either spurious or seriously defective (H. Clegg, *How to Run an Incomes Policy and Why We Made Such a Mess of the Last One*, London, Heinemann, 1971, p. 38).

[3] Ibid. p. 39.

First, there was the choice between a voluntary and a statutory policy. A voluntary policy has the considerable advantage that it can be run in cooperation with the organised trade union movement, which may find it difficult to deliver an incomes policy – particularly a long-term one – but has considerable power effectively to destroy a policy to which it is opposed. The disadvantages of a voluntary policy are that it runs the risk of being weak – little more than a statement of good intentions – and once one union has 'broken through' it is virtually impossible to prevent others (who have the duty to protect the interests of their members) from following. A voluntary policy has to be very simple, so that it can be monitored without difficulty, and such a policy cannot make sufficient allowance for exceptional treatment for one reason or another. The trade union movement is opposed to 'outside bodies' exercising any kind of judicial function in wage negotiations; it was never reconciled to the NBPI.[1] Thus the voluntary incomes policy of the period 1964–9 proved to be weak. It is true that it appears less unsuccessful in retrospect than it did at the time; nonetheless, the norm was exceeded by a very wide margin indeed. However, voluntary policies with a single simple figure and no provision for exceptions have had considerable success.

There are possibilities for mixing statutory and voluntary elements. The period of freeze and severe restraint from mid-1966 to mid-1967 began as a voluntary policy, with the threat of statutory enactment if the policy was broken; in fact one union forced the government to introduce statutory provisions. Another mix is to make the policy basically voluntary for the unions, but in effect statutory on the paying agent. There is indeed no example in any period of statutory policy of a union or union negotiator being penalised for breaking the rules; insofar as there has been any enforcement it has always been on the paying agent, as, for example, under the Conservative government's statutory policy. (The method of enforcement was also very similar in what was labelled a voluntary policy under the Labour government from mid-1975 onwards.) Thus the dividing line between a statutory and a voluntary policy is not distinct.

In fact, the main difficulty of statutory policies proved to be much the same as the main difficulty of voluntary policies – that of making reasonable provision for exceptional treatment where justified. Statutory periods of wage freeze were effective, but the Conservative government did not develop in time any adequate system for dealing with exceptions. Thus, when confronted by the miners' claim to be an

[1] It does not have the same objection to an arbitral body which simply attempts to reconcile the conflicting views of the two sides; the objection is to a body which uses criteria of its own to judge whether a wage award is warranted or not.

exception – a claim which the trade union movement in general supported – they had no adequate machinery; the Pay Board Report on relativities, which suggested such a mechanism, came too late.[1]

Another problem arose from the great complexity of systems of payment in the British economy. In the period 1964–9 the claims and awards considered by the three bodies concerned with the policy – the TUC vetting committee, the Department of Employment and the NBPI – usually arose from national negotiations about changes in basic rates. It was often very difficult to establish what such awards might mean as an annual percentage increase in actual earnings.[2] Incomes policy in this period never grappled with the problem posed by payment by results schemes, for example, although about eight or nine million workers were employed in undertakings where such schemes were used and were directly or indirectly affected by them. The NBPI commented:

The essence of the problem of applying the incomes policy to PBR systems is that a large part of the increase in earnings under them does not arise from 'claims' or 'settlements' in the accepted sense at all. The setting of piece work prices, standard times for new jobs and so forth are not 'settlements' in the accepted sense of the word, and they are often negotiated by individuals or small groups of workers with foremen, rate-fixers or first-line management …Thousands of such bargains are struck every day…we came across only one instance where a firm was attempting to apply the [incomes] policy to PBR earnings in any way.[3]

Later incomes policies attempted to take this problem into consideration. The Conservatives' incomes policies set a limit to the total increase in the wage bill which firms or other paying agents were permitted to make. Labour's policies after mid-1975 fixed sums which were explicitly additions to earnings, not to basic rates.

Finally there is the choice – which has already been touched on in the discussion of statutory or voluntary policies – between simplicity and flexibility. The advantages of a simple policy are clear – there is much less scope for evasion and it is much easier to monitor – therefore, in the short term, it is likely to be more effective. However, simple policies are short-term policies only – they lead to strong pressures either to restore relativities which have been altered by the policy, or to change relativities when new circumstances have arisen – and short-term policies tend to be followed by a rush of very large claims and

---

[1] Pay Board, *Advisory Report no. 2: Problems of Pay Relativities*.

[2] For example, the award to electricity supply workers in February 1971 was claimed by some to represent a rise of some 20 per cent and by others to represent a rise of little over 10 per cent.

[3] NBPI, *Report no. 65: Payment by Results Systems*, Cmnd 3627, London, HMSO, 1968, para. 220 *et seq*.

awards. A long-term policy must have some provision for judging exceptions to the norm. No adequate mechanism for doing this was found during the period: the NBPI (for various reasons) tended to act more as an advocate for industrial reform than as an adjudicator on particular settlements; the Pay Board's Report on relativities suggested a possible mechanism, but too late for it to be tried.

Control of other incomes and prices

The main objective of incomes policies throughout this period was to bring down the size of wage and salary awards, in the belief that these were the driving force in the inflationary process in this country. In the view of those concerned with these policies, there was little risk that moderation in wage increases would lead to excessive increases in profits; price moderation would follow from wage moderation. Evidence about the behaviour of prices in this country strongly suggests that this is true. Nonetheless, all incomes policies concerned themselves with prices as well – indeed a number were presented so as to give the impression that price control was on an equal footing with income control. This was basically a cosmetic exercise, based on the view that income control without price control would not be acceptable to wage and salary earners. In much the same way the policies also laid down rules – admittedly unenforceable – for self-employment incomes and frequently included statutory control of dividends. These additional controls were in the interests of 'fairness', not because the designers of incomes policies believed that these incomes were important in their own right in the inflationary process.

It is true that a view existed that sufficiently tough price control could also serve as an incomes policy – in that if firms were prevented from raising their prices they would be forced to resist excessive wage demands. However, this particular policy was never tried during the period covered in this book, and subsequent experience between April 1974 and June 1975, when there was a weak incomes policy together with price control, was not encouraging.

The guidelines for the various incomes policies normally prescribed that incomes from self-employment should follow the general rules which applied to incomes from employment. However, there was no way of monitoring whether this in fact happened, and certainly no way of enforcing the rules on the self-employed during periods of statutory incomes policy; the one exception was fees charged by professional groups, which could be referred to the NBPI. However, the general assumption was that this was a 'passive' sector.

The policy towards dividends was more active. Up to 1968 companies were requested to exercise moderation; during the standstill and period of severe restraint they were asked not to increase dividends at all and indeed dividends did not rise. In 1968 the government introduced a $3\frac{1}{2}$ per cent limit for dividend increases, which was abolished at the end of 1969. Under the Conservatives' incomes policy there was a statutory 5 per cent limit on dividend increases, administered by the Treasury, which was empowered to consent to companies exceeding the limit under certain circumstances – take-over defence, new companies, newly quoted companies, increases in share capital, recoveries and pre-standstill commitments. It is hard to say what effect the various voluntary and statutory limitations on dividends had, for the usual reason that it is virtually impossible to say what dividends might have been paid in their absence. This was a period when there was fairly general pressure on company profits and their share in national income was falling, so that in any case capital consumption and the financing of stocks (including stock appreciation) and new investment might have been expected to take a larger share of company income. Further, during this period companies were tending to raise new money by issuing fixed-interest stock more than ordinary shares; also, there were successive changes in the system of company taxation, including a period from 1965 to 1972 when distributions were differentially taxed.

The legislation concerning the rents of private housing – the Rent Act 1965 and the Housing Finance Act 1971 – was essentially a separate matter outside the scope of incomes policies. However, the operation of this legislation was modified from time to time in the interests of incomes policy. Thus, under Part III of the Prices and Incomes Act 1968, rent increases during the later half of 1968 and 1969 were spread out. As part of Stage II of the Conservative government's incomes policy, there was a specific modification to the size of the rent rebates and allowances in their Housing Finance Act, so that a low income family living in local authority housing would not have to pay a significant rent increase. Essentially, however, these were marginal modifications to housing legislation which had other objectives. During the first year of the Conservatives' incomes policy, there was also a standstill on business rents, which was extended to May 1974.

The system of price control under the Labour government was, like the system of intervention in incomes, basically a voluntary one. Guidelines were promulgated setting out what were considered to be legitimate justifications for price increases, also indicating the circumstances in which prices should be reduced. Then in November 1965 an early warning system was introduced for prices in parallel with the early warning system for wage increases. For an initial list of about 75 items, firms were required to give four weeks notice of their intention to raise prices; there was a supplementary list of food prices 'under constant watch' by the Ministry of Agriculture, Fisheries and Food. The government could ask a firm to defer a price rise for further enquiry or for reference to the NBPI, but the total period of delay – including any NBPI Report – could not exceed three months. This remained the basic system throughout the period, except during the period of wages and prices freeze, when firms were not expected to raise their prices at all.

The system under the Conservative government was considerably more elaborate: its prices policy, like its pay policy, followed the pattern set by the Americans (see page 379 above). Firms were divided into three categories by size: category I had to give prior notification before raising prices, category II had to submit regular reports, and category III were subject to spot checks. In Stage III of the policy category II firms were also required to notify price rises in advance.

It is doubtful whether the Labour government's early warning system had any substantial general effect; certainly some prices were held back when references were made to the NBPI, but it is quite possible that firms cross-subsidised the prices of the products in the early warning list. The effects of the price code under the Conservative government may have been a little more significant. The Price Commission's own quantification of its effects was probably optimistic, in that it was based on the money consequences of its rejection or amendment of applications for price increases. However, we know from firms whose applications were approved that their actual increases were frequently less than those approved. Further, the Price Commission did not have any apparatus for checking that its rulings were observed.

An inquiry addressed to a small group of firms in May 1976 suggested that the prices of that group were $2\frac{1}{2}$ per cent lower on average than they would have been in the absence of the price code;[1] that was after the code had been in operation for three years. Further, a number of the firms stated that they could have raised their prices within the terms of the code, but that market conditions prevented this. The general conclusion is that the effect of the price code was not substantial.

[1] R. W. Evely, 'The effects of the price code', *National Institute Economic Review*, no. 77, August 1976.

CHAPTER 9

PLANNING

by *P. Meadows*

THE RE-EMERGENCE OF PLANNING IN THE 1960s

In the early 1960s 'planning' re-emerged as one of the themes of government economic policy, having been dormant for more than a decade. During the Labour government's period in office from 1945 to 1951, planning had become identified with physical controls, which, as they were dismantled, were accompanied by the idea of planning. In the 1950s the only surviving institution in any way concerned with the concept was the Economic Planning Board; this consisted of three employers' representatives, three trade unionists and six officials of the departments concerned with finance and industry. It was intended to provide a forum for the exchange of views on economic problems and met seven or eight times a year; it was not an important body.

A number of forces came together to bring about the re-emergence of planning in the 1960s: the growing practice of comparing international growth rates, the observed need for a longer time-horizon in deciding on future public expenditure, the interest shown by the Federation of British Industries, the evangelistic zeal of those concerned with French planning and Harold Macmillan's particular approach to the problems of economic policy.

It was only towards the end of the 1950s that international comparisons of growth rates – particularly comparisons between the United Kingdom and continental countries – began strongly to suggest that these had established, on a permanent basis, a faster rate of economic growth than the United Kingdom (table 9.1). Up to then it had been frequently argued that the differences were simply the result of delayed postwar reconstruction on the continent, which had to recover from a much larger fall in output during the war. By the end of the decade, however, these explanations were clearly no longer valid.[1] One example of these figures being used to suggest policy changes was in a book by Political and Economic Planning published in 1960.[2] This compared

---

[1] The evidence is discussed in D. C. Paige, 'Economic growth: the last hundred years', *National Institute Economic Review*, no. 16, July 1961.

[2] Political and Economic Planning, *Growth in the British Economy*, London, Allen & Unwin, 1960.

Table 9.1. *International comparisons of growth and balance of payments performance, 1956–60*

	Annual change in GNP[a]						Current balance of payments[b]					
	1956	1957	1958	1959	1960	1956–60[c]	1956	1957	1958	1959	1960	1956–60
			(percentages)									
Belgium	2·8	2·4	−0·7	2·2	5·5	2·4	+	+	+	+	+	+
Denmark	2·2	5·1	2·7	6·9	6·2	4·6	−	+	+	+	−	+
Finland	1·9	1·5	−0·1	7·4	10·0	4·1	−	−	+	+	−	+
France	5·0	6·0	2·6	2·9	7·1	4·7	−	−	−	−	+	−
Germany	6·9	5·7	3·2	7·0	8·8	6·3	+	+	+	+	+	+
Italy	4·8	5·4	4·9	6·6	6·3	5·6	−	+	+	+	+	+
Netherlands	3·7	2·9	−0·3	4·9	8·4	3·9	−	−	+	+	+	+
Norway	5·1	0·8	1·2	3·4	3·6	2·8	+	+	−	−	−	−
Sweden	3·1	3·1	2·6	5·6	3·5	3·6	−	−	−	+	−	−
Switzerland	6·0	2·9	−1·8	7·2	5·8	4·0	+	−	+	+	+	+
United Kingdom	2·0	2·1	0·9	3·7	4·8	2·7	+	+	+	+	−	+

SOURCE: OECD, *National Accounts of OECD Countries, 1950–68*, Paris, 1970.

[a] At market prices. [b] + indicates a surplus and − a deficit. [c] Average for the period.

Britain's investment and productivity record with that of other countries, and suggested that one reason for Britain's comparatively poor performance was that there had never been a growth objective at which to aim. 'The mere publication of an estimate of the possible achievement of the economy for a few years ahead, if such an estimate has been carefully drawn up with the cooperation of the people who will be responsible for its realization, may in itself be a potent force making for success.'[1]

Secondly, the idea of medium-term planning arose through criticism of the Treasury system of controlling public expenditure. In 1958 a House of Commons Select Committee caustically concluded that 'it is really an abuse of language to speak of a "system" of Treasury control, if by the word "system" is meant methods and practices that have at one time or another been deliberately planned and instituted'.[2] As a result an internal committee was set up under Lord Plowden, which recommended that public expenditure should be planned for five years ahead and the plan rolled forward each year.[3]

A separate impetus came at the end of November 1960 from a conference of the Federation of British Industries, at which one of the five groups into which the participants divided discussed economic

[1] Ibid. p. 24.
[2] House of Commons, *Select Committee on Estimates, Session 1957–58. Sixth Report: Treasury Control of Expenditure*, London, HMSO, 1958, para. 94.
[3] Treasury, *The Control of Public Expenditure*, para. 12.

growth in Britain. This group's Report concluded, amongst other things, that faster economic growth was not inconsistent with stable prices, low unemployment and an adequate balance of payments, and that indeed these objectives might be helped if the growth rate were faster. The need to make Britain more competitive externally was seen as the dominant short-run problem, and rapid changes in government policy were condemned for the lack of confidence they created. Government and industry together should make a more conscious attempt to formulate, not targets or plans, but assessments of possibilities. However, studies of plans and demands on an industry basis for five to ten years ahead, like those made with some success by the steel industry, might usefully be attempted. The group also suggested that 'government and industry might see if it would be possible to agree on an assessment of expectations and intentions to be placed before the country as a framework for economic effort during the next five years'.[1] Without any specific resolution, this tentative endorsement of some form of forward planning began to emerge during 1961 as the view of the Federation of British Industries.

The French influence came in a series of informal meetings and exchanges with the French planners, which culminated with a conference held in the spring of 1961 in London on economic planning in France; it was organised by the National Institute of Economic and Social Research in association with the Institut de Science Economique Appliquée. A Report of the proceedings was published by Political and Economic Planning.[2] At the conference Pierre Massé outlined the guiding ideas behind French planning. The French procedure was described as stating the growth objective and its consequences for the various sectors of the economy; then all the various interests concerned were confronted with the adjustments, often difficult, which had to be faced to achieve the objective. It was agreed that it was debatable how far planning had been responsible for the faster growth of France, but it was possible that 'the many committees talk themselves into it and have faith in the planners who tell them that such and such a rate of growth is possible'.[3] The participants at the conference included Treasury and other government officials, and leading industrialists. The discussion was summed up by Sir Robert Shone of the Iron and Steel Board, whose planning methods had been commended at the Federation of British Industries conference.

Finally, there was Macmillan's influence in persuading a Conservative Cabinet to allow the word 'planning' back into their vocabulary.

---

[1] Federation of British Industries, *The Next Five Years*, London, 1960, pp. 18–19.
[2] Political and Economic Planning, 'Economic planning in France', *Planning*, vol. 27, 14 August 1961.   [3] Ibid. pp. 234–5.

The idea certainly does not seem to have come from any grass-roots Conservative pressure.[1] Different views have been put forward about the attitude of the Chancellor, Selwyn Lloyd;[2] indeed, given the vagueness of the term 'planning', it is obviously possible for someone to be fully consistent in supporting the idea in some of its senses and opposing it in others. For example, in the November 1960 debate on the *Plowden Report* the Chancellor indicated that he hoped to discuss with industry and the trade unions the value of long-term forecasting of investment intentions. In a debate on 6 February 1961 he stressed that German performance had not been due to centralised planning, and he decried the opposition's suggestion that the government should produce a national plan, on the grounds that it could not be carried out without 'complete direction of labour and consumption, with the lack of liberty that would involve'. He observed that there was already a good deal of planning of investment in the public sector; it was necessary to try to improve this, but he was opposed to having any single plan which would be 'almost certain to go wrong'.

There is much less doubt about the Prime Minister's views. Before the war he had written a book which enthusiastically endorsed some ideas of planning: 'The next step forward...in our social thinking is to move from "piecemeal planning" to national planning – from the consideration of each industry or service separately to a consideration of them all collectively.'[3] He proposed a national economic council, consisting of representatives of the government, unions, employers and economic experts under the chairmanship of a Minister of Economics. It would survey the whole field of economic activity and 'formulate a comprehensive plan for central guidance'.[4] There were obvious similarities between the council which Macmillan suggested then and the NEDC established in 1961. In the Cabinet discussion on the latter in the late summer of 1961, Macmillan notes: 'A rather interesting and quite deep divergence of views between Ministers, really corresponding to whether they had old Whig, Liberal, *laissez-faire* traditions, or Tory opinions, paternalists and not afraid of a little *dirigisme*.'[5]

The idea of establishing the NEDC had been floated, rather tentatively and vaguely, in the Chancellor's speech on the July measures of

---

[1] For example, an editorial in the Bow Group's *Crossbow* in the summer of 1961 summed up the prevailing attitude – support for the principle of the market economy, with no place for planning (*Crossbow*, vol. 3, Summer 1961).

[2] Brittan, in *Steering the Economy* (rev. edn), p. 239, suggests that the Chancellor had come to the conclusion that planning was commonsense; G. Polanyi in *Planning in Britain: the experience of the 1960s*, London, Institute of Economic Affairs, 1967, p. 20, and A. Shonfield in *Modern Capitalism: the changing balance of public and private power*, London, Oxford University Press, 1965, 102–3, suggest that he was out of sympathy with the idea.

[3] H. Macmillan, *The Middle Way*, London, Macmillan, 1939, p. 176.

[4] Ibid. pp. 290–3.   [5] Macmillan, *At the End of the Day*, p. 37.

1961. He said that the time had come for better consolidation of the activities of the various bodies concerned with planning, both in individual industries and in the economy as a whole; he intended to discuss with both sides of industry procedures 'for pulling together these various processes of consultation and forecasting with a view to better coordination of ideas and plans'. Later in the same debate he explained that he wanted 'something more purposeful' than the existing system:

I envisage a joint examination of the economic prospects of the country stretching five or more years into the future. It would cover the growth of national production and distribution of our resources between the main users, consumption, government expenditure, investment and so on. Above all it would try to establish what are the essential conditions for realising potential growth...In other words, I want both sides of industry to share with the government the task of relating plans to the resources that are available.[1]

On 8 August the Chancellor invited both sides of industry to join a body such as he had outlined. The negotiations to form this new body continued through the rest of the year; the TUC deferred its decision about joining because it was nervous that the new body might be used to introduce an incomes policy. The Director General of the new Council (Sir Robert Shone) was appointed in December 1961, the Economic Director (Sir Donald MacDougall) in February 1962 and the first meeting eventually took place on 7 March 1962. The Chancellor was to be chairman, with the Minister of Labour and the President of the Board of Trade also representing the government; the membership consisted of six representatives of the employers, six of the TUC, two of the nationalised industries, two independents and the Director General.

THE NEDC UNDER THE CONSERVATIVES, 1962–4

At the first meeting, the Chancellor defined the NEDC's task as follows:

(a) To examine the economic performance of the nation with particular concern for plans for the future in both private and public sectors of industry.
(b) To consider together what are the obstacles to quicker growth, what can be done to improve efficiency, and whether the best use is being made of our resources.
(c) To seek agreement upon ways of improving economic performance, competitive power and efficiency, in other words, to increase the rate of sound growth.[2]

It was decided that the office organisation (NEDO) should be in two divisions – one to deal with broad economic questions and the other

[1] Selwyn Lloyd in the House of Commons, 26 July 1961.
[2] Lord Bridges, *The Treasury*, London, Allen & Unwin, 1964, p. 219.

with particular industries and sectors of the economy.[1] Its reports, but not its working papers, would be published.

The second meeting on 9 May adopted a proposal that the implications of a 4 per cent annual growth of output between 1961 and 1966 should be examined. Given that the whole rationale of the NEDC was to explore the possibilities of faster growth, the figure to be examined had clearly to be higher than the past trend growth rate (of around 2·7 per cent). Further, since one implicit objective was to raise the rate of growth in Britain to a figure more closely comparable with that in other industrial countries, the discussion of the appropriate figure was influenced by the OECD's recent selection of a target growth rate: in November 1961 it had agreed to a 50 per cent growth target for the ten years 1960 to 1970 (equivalent to 4.2 per cent a year) for the West as a whole. Thus 4 per cent seemed to be a figure which was sufficiently above the existing trend to have some psychological impact, and yet not so high as to be implausible.

The new institution's initial task was to study in particular the implications of a 4 per cent growth rate for seventeen major industries, covering over half of national product; NEDO was also required to prepare a study on the conditions favourable to faster growth. An identical inquiry among the seventeen industries concentrated, since time was short, on finding out about existing plans and expectations, on the implications of a 4 per cent growth rate, and on discussing particular problems foreseen as impeding expansion, with suggestions for meeting them. In their replies, firms and trade associations in general indicated that they considered a 4 per cent growth rate possible, although critics were quick to point out that this sort of questionnaire can lead to over-optimistic answers. In February 1963 the results of the inquiry were presented to the Council in the framework of a general economic assessment.[2] According to the Report, exports would have to increase at 5 per cent a year and productivity at 3·2 per cent. The assessment took the view that the underlying trend in productivity had speeded up in recent years and that this had been hidden by the depression of 1961/2; the high investment of 1960 and 1961 had not shown a return because demand had been held back.

The government took the Report and its implications seriously; for instance, in March 1963 it asked the Central Electricity Generating Board to make its investment plans on the basis of the NEDC growth target. The industry had been planning on the basis of an $8\frac{1}{2}$ per cent annual increase in sales; a 4 per cent growth target, it was estimated, would raise this to 10 per cent.

[1] NEDC, 'History and functions' (unpublished), 1963, p. 6.
[2] NEDC, *Growth of the United Kingdom Economy to 1966*.

In April 1963 the study on conditions favourable to faster growth was published.[1] This outlined possible ways of overcoming eight major obstacles to growth – regional imbalance, shortage of research and development, lack of labour mobility, the balance of payments, the taxation system, wage inflation, and lack of management education and of industrial training for adults.

There were two other developments in the NEDC during the period of the Conservative government. At the beginning of December 1963 it was decided to establish Economic Development Committees for individual industries (later known as 'little Neddies'). Their terms of reference were to:

(a) examine the economic performance, prospects and plans of the industry and assess from time to time the industry's progress in relation to the national growth objectives and provide information and forecasts to the Council on these matters;

(b) consider ways of improving the industry's economic performance, competitive power and efficiency, and formulate reports and records of these matters as appropriate.

Secondly, Reginald Maudling (who had become Chancellor in July 1962) was anxious if possible to use the NEDC to get some kind of declaration of intent about the rise in money incomes – something similar to the declaration subsequently obtained by George Brown (page 367). However, all such attempts failed because of the TUC's unwillingness to allow such questions on the NEDC agenda; when they originally agreed to join the NEDC, they had indicated that they were opposed to any attempt to use it for purposes of wage restraint.

During 1964, with an impending general election, there was no great activity at the NEDC. In March a progress report was published comparing the actual performance of the economy with the planned targets.[2] Although growth had accelerated rapidly in 1963, the average annual increase from 1961 to the end of 1963 was only 3 per cent, so that, to reach the target for 1966, output in the rest of the period would have to grow at 4·8 per cent a year. Given that the Chancellor had indicated in the budget the need 'to achieve a smooth transition from the recent exceptionally rapid rate of growth to the long-term growth rate of 4 per cent', it appeared that the government had in effect decided that the target was not attainable.

---

[1] NEDC, *Conditions Favourable to Faster Growth*.
[2] NEDC, *Report on the Growth of the Economy*, London, HMSO, 1964.

THE ORIGINS OF LABOUR PARTY PLANNING

After successive election defeats, the Labour Party began to realise that, in the voters' minds, it had an unfortunate identification with physical controls; so the rethinking of the meaning of planning began. In 1954 Marris referred to interference with the pattern of production by direct controls as 'a most clumsy, uncertain and painful method for achieving general social objectives or specifically altering the distribution of income'.[1] He suggested that investment should be planned on a national basis over ten or fifteen years, after discussion with industry about the industrial pattern.[2] A Ministry of Economic Policy should be divided into two parts – for short-term tactical control and for long-term strategic policy-making. The idea that British economic policy tended to concentrate on the short term and ignore the medium term became more and more influential during the next decade. Crosland, writing two years later, agreed that detailed physical planning was inefficient: 'the emphasis should now be positive rather than negative; that is, on securing expansion, breaking bottlenecks, and encouraging vital investment, rather than on physical controls designed to restrict day-to-day freedom of industry'.[3]

So, in its 1958 election manifesto the Labour Party stressed that planning did not mean a return to detailed controls; it was, however, very vague about what it did mean. The object would be 'to provide a broad framework within which the creation of new wealth can go smoothly and rapidly ahead, and to ensure that the detailed decisions of industry do not come into conflict with national objectives'.

In 1961, with planning just beginning to come into favour again, the Labour Party elaborated a little further.[4] 'A national plan with targets for individual industries – especially for the key sectors which produce the tools of expansion – would enable every industry and undertaking publicly or privately owned to plan its own development with confidence in the future.'[5] The machinery would consist of a national industrial planning board, which would work out expansion plans for basic sectors of the economy.

After the conversion of the Conservative government to a mild form of planning, it was incumbent on the Labour Party to differentiate their own planning product in some way. This they did by arguing, first, that the procedures for preparing a plan should be brought into the government machine, so that the plan became a government plan;

[1] R. Marris, *The Machinery of Economic Policy*, London, Fabian Society, 1954, p. 23.
[2] Ibid. p. 24.
[3] C. A. R. Crosland, *The Future of Socialism*, London, Cape, 1956, pp. 516–17.
[4] Labour Party, *Signposts for the Sixties*, London, 1961.   [5] Ibid. p. 13.

secondly, that the responsibility for the plan, and indeed for strategic economic decisions, should be given to a new Ministry, not the Treasury. The Treasury began to be pilloried as the body responsible for 'stop–go' policies, with little knowledge of industry and with no commitment to faster economic growth.

Thus Balogh suggested in 1963 that the NEDC's function should be taken over and extended by a Ministry of Planning and Production.[1] He also suggested industrial economic councils, which would collect information for discussion with the national planning authority on the implications for an industry of the national plan and keep the planning agency informed of the industry's investment plans. In September of that year the TUC endorsed the General Council's Report on economic development and planning.[2] This expressed some doubt about the NEDC's ability to meet 'the basic requirements of planning'. It pointed out two possible types of planning machinery:

(1) A government department could draw up a plan and submit it to an advisory council for discussion and subsequent amendment; it would then pass through Parliament and be launched as a government plan.

(2) The plan could be drawn up by an independent staff like NEDO and submitted by a body like the NEDC to Parliament for approval.

Also in 1963 the home policy committee of the Labour Party, under the chairmanship of George Brown, came to the conclusion that the function of overseeing the economy as a whole should be removed from the Treasury; this was a fairly general theme at the time. Thus Paul Johnson wrote: '...a priority of choices based on long-term conceptions of government policy is the direct antithesis of the classic system of Treasury control...[which], while often successful in hampering genuine planning efforts, is too overloaded to prevent real instances of waste';[3] Michael Shanks in much the same way concluded that the qualities needed for the regulation of public expenditure were not the ones required in a department which was to be 'the powerhouse of an economy bent on growth in an age of dynamic technological, social and economic change'.[4]

Thus, in September 1964 Labour's election manifesto announced that they would set up a Ministry of Economic Affairs, with the duty of formulating a national economic plan. It affirmed that 'within the national plan each industry will know what is expected of it, and what help it can expect – in terms of exports, investment, production and

[1] T. Balogh, *Planning for Progress: a strategy for Labour*, London, Fabian Society, 1963, p. 34.

[2] General Council Report 'Economic development and planning' in TUC, *Report of the 95th Annual Trades Union Congress at Brighton, 1963*, para. 19, p. 486.

[3] P. Johnson, 'Tackling the Treasury octopus', *New Statesman*, 14 February 1963, pp. 240–2.

[4] M. Shanks, 'The comforts of stagnation', *Encounter*, July 1963, p. 33.

employment...If production falls short of the plan in key sections of industry...then it is up to the government and the industry to take whatever measures are required.'

PLANNING UNDER THE LABOUR GOVERNMENT, 1964–70

The effective history of planning under the Labour government is brief. The figures in the National Plan were already in doubt by the time it was published,[1] and certainly within nine months of its publication it had clearly ceased to have any relevance to Britain's economic situation. The Department of Economic Affairs was closely identified with the National Plan, so that – although planning was strictly speaking only one of its functions[2] – with economic policy dominated by short-term balance of payments considerations the Department gradually lost its *raison d'être*; its functions were successively given back to other Departments and in October 1969 it disappeared.

The announcement that a five-year National Plan would be prepared in the Department of Economic Affairs was made on 4 November 1964; the Department would consult the Economic Development Committees (the 'little Neddies'), whose number was increased. The output target for the National Plan – a 25 per cent increase in output by 1970 – was announced on 1 February 1965, although the industrial inquiry had hardly begun. By the time the Plan was submitted to the NEDC for comment (in August), and published (in mid-September), the first of the government's mid-year deflationary budgets had already made the numbers look implausible. To achieve the growth target of 4 per cent, the labour force would have to increase by 0·4 per cent a year and productivity by 3·4 per cent. The volume of imports was planned to rise no faster than the national product – by 4 per cent – and the volume of exports by $5\frac{1}{4}$ per cent. For trade movements of this kind to accompany a 4 per cent growth rate, there would have to have been a very substantial improvement in the international competitiveness of British industry; it was the absence (until 1967) of any effective policies to bring this about which undermined the National Plan.

The Plan was passed through the House of Commons on 3 November

---

[1] Department of Economic Affairs, *The National Plan*.

[2] The Department was initially divided into four sections:

(a) the economic planning group, responsible for medium-term and long-term forecasts and for the drawing up of the National Plan;

(b) the economic coordination group, responsible for public expenditure, external relations and prices and incomes policy;

(c) the regional policy group, which coordinated regional physical planning, land use and transport and all the Regional Planning Boards and Councils;

(d) the industrial division, which concerned itself with industrial efficiency and general industrial policies, such as investment and production for export.

1965 without a division – an indication of the sanctity of the word 'planning' at that time. By July 1966 – with the second package of deflationary measures – it was clear that the Plan should either be abandoned or revised; indeed the original intention had been that it should be regularly reviewed.[1] However, partly because the degree of elaboration incorporated in the Plan made any revision a complex and time-consuming task, no such year-by-year revision was undertaken. By the middle of March 1967 the National Institute was advocating a medium-term plan, 'not so much in the sense of target figures for individual industries, but in the sense of a coherent set of economic policies'.[2]

It was not until March 1968 that it was announced that the Department of Economic Affairs and the NEDC would jointly prepare a new medium-term plan. This was finished by the end of the year, discussed by the Prime Minister with employers and trade unionists at a meeting at Chequers in December, and published at the end of February 1969.[3] It described itself as 'a planning document, not a plan' and 'a basis for a further stage in the continuing process of consultation between government and both sides of industry about major issues of economic policy'. It considered alternative growth paths, depending on the degree of success in improving the competitiveness of British industry. However, it had very little impact.

Meanwhile, the Department of Economic Affairs had been losing its functions. Its responsibilities for external policy (in particular, relations with the EEC and negotiations for entry) had been moved to the Board of Trade. In April 1968 its responsibility for incomes policy was transferred to the Ministry of Labour. In October 1969 it was finally abolished, its industrial affairs being transferred to the Ministry of Technology and medium-term planning restored to the Treasury. In 1970 the Treasury issued a revised version of *The Task Ahead*,[4] but this was, of course, overtaken by the change of government.

AN ASSESSMENT

There were two main innovatory ideas in British economic policy in the early 1960s. One was the acceptance that modification of free collective bargaining – an incomes policy of some kind – was needed; that idea has survived and has continued as a recurrent theme of economic policy. The other idea was the need to move towards some

[1] Department of Economic Affairs, *Progress Report*, no. 4, April 1965.
[2] *National Institute Economic Review*, no. 39, February 1967, p. 14.
[3] Department of Economic Affairs, *The Task Ahead*.
[4] Treasury, *Economic Prospects to 1972 – a revised assessment*, London, HMSO, 1970.

form of national planning; that idea has not survived. The word 'planning' has once again been dropped entirely from the Conservative Party's economic vocabulary, and – insofar as it still exists in Labour Party thinking – its meaning is something very different from what it was in the early 1960s.

The main reason for this demise is simply that the experiments in 'indicative planning' of the period 1962–6 are identified with failure. They were supposed to accelerate the rate of growth and did not do so. (It is curious that at a time when the concept of expectations has become so prominent in other areas of economics, there is now universal rejection of the idea that the expectations which largely determine investment plans might be influenced in this way.)

The central idea of indicative planning was that a plan, by helping to raise expectations, could become a self-fulfilling prophecy. The process was succinctly summarised as follows: 'The purpose of the plan was to develop a coordinated, internally consistent set of projections of how the economy might develop to 1970 and thereby create expectations that would induce private economic decisions to conform to the projections.'[1] Indicative planning would help to remove bottlenecks: 'The effect of better communication on problems requiring joint action by independent centres of power, and of more systematic analysis of the problems themselves, is that the typical bottlenecks which are a recurrent feature of a full-employment society are likely to be identified earlier. Again, the habit of looking at them, and taking them seriously enough to do something about them, should make the progress to economic growth smoother.'[2] For example, if a substantial house-building programme was included, the investment plans of suppliers of building materials could be geared to this expectation.

The criticisms of the idea that the growth could be accelerated in this way have been forceful and extensive. One line was summed up by a speaker at a 1974 conference on medium-term planning:

Two conditions are necessary for medium-term planning to be effective [in raising the rate of growth] ... First, one needs to know what factors determine the growth of productive potential. Secondly, one needs to have instruments which affect those factors whose quantitative importance can be predicted. If these conditions exist, then medium-term planning of this kind is possible. It is because they do exist for short-term purposes that short-term forecasting is possible. However, in relation to economic growth the conditions are not satisfied. We don't have instruments whose operation is understood and whose effect is quantifiable. Therefore, quantitative planning on this basis is bogus, and any new round would also be bogus.[3]

[1] Caves *et al.*, *Britain's Economic Prospects*, p. 118. [2] Shonfield, *Modern Capitalism*, p. 172.
[3] G. D. N. Worswick and F. T. Blackaby (eds.), *The Medium Term: models of the British economy*, London, Heinemann, 1974, pp. 180–1.

The same kind of point had been made by Harrod in 1964; if the government has the ability to guarantee that the target will be fulfilled, 'they must have means of their own – apart from indicative planning – of ensuring growth in accordance with potential: then what is the need of such planning? But if they lack such means how can they give the all-important guarantee?'[1] There is nothing particularly implausible about the idea that, if expectations are changed, events may conform to those changed expectations. The problem was rather that indicative planning was a weak instrument for bringing about such a change, and failure was fatal to any repetition of the attempt.

A further argument against the idea is the effect it may have on government expenditure. With a national plan the government is virtually bound to base its own expenditure projections on the assumption that faster growth will be achieved, otherwise it will appear to be doubting its own figures. If, in the event, the acceleration of the growth rate does not occur while government expenditure goes ahead as planned, this will produce an unintended change in the distribution of the rise in output between public and private goods, as in fact happened in the period 1964–70. The one item of expenditure which rose in volume roughly as expected in the National Plan was public authorities' current expenditure on goods and services (table 9.3, page 416).

The arguments against any repetition of the attempt to raise the underlying growth rate by indicative planning are therefore strong: to be effective it would have to be persuasive, and that is unlikely. However, in the reaction against indicative planning there has also been a reaction against any systematic official macroeconomic examination of possible alternative futures. Although some details of short-term Treasury forecasts are now published, and although it is now generally recognised that for the examination of the full consequences of many policies projections have to be made for some years ahead, nonetheless there is very little official material which explores the alternative possibilities for the medium term. The stress at the NEDC tends to be on prospects for individual industries, though obviously these cannot sensibly be examined in isolation from the prospects for the economy as a whole. It is also unfortunate that the nationalised industries now (in 1977) publish, if anything, less about their future plans than they did in the early 1960s, and it is not clear what national growth-rate assumptions they are using as a basis for their investment plans. Indicative planning as a way of accelerating growth rates may have failed; it remains true that investment plans based on assumptions about low rates of growth will help to bring low growth rates about.

[1] Sir Roy Harrod, 'Are monetary and fiscal policies enough?', *Economic Journal*, vol. 74, December 1964, p. 907.

APPENDIX

THE PLANS OF 1962–9: TARGETS AND OUTCOMES COMPARED

The tables which follow summarise some comparisons between the target figures of three successive plans – the NEDC plan for 1961–6, the National Plan for 1964–70, and *The Task Ahead* for 1967–72.[1] A common theme of all three is the failure to predict the rate of increase in the import content of final expenditure.

Table 9.2. *The NEDC plan, 1961–6: target annual growth rates and out-turns*

Percentages

	Target	Revised target	Actual
Macroeconomic variables			
GDP	4·0	4·0	3·0
GDP per person employed	3·2	3·2	2·5
Labour force	0·8	0·8	0·7
Manufacturing investment	3·3	1·4	0·7
Imports of goods	4·0	4·7	4·1
Exports of goods	5·0	5·1	3·9
Consumers' expenditure	3·5	3·6	3·7
Industry figures			
Coal: output	0·9	1·0	− 1·7
Petroleum: inland deliveries	7·6	7·6	9·9
Electricity: sales	10·0	10·0	7·4
Gas: sales	2·8	6·4	7·1
Confectionery: output	0·7	− 0·1	0·2
Chemicals: output	7·6	7·6	5·7
Steel: output	5·5	4·6	2·5
Motor vehicles: output	10·0	9·5	6·4
Paper and board: output	2·5	2·5	2·4
Construction: output	4·1	4·4	3·0

SOURCES: NEDC, *Growth of the United Kingdom Economy to 1966* and *Report on the Growth of the Economy*; CSO, *National Income and Expenditure 1964–74* and *1966–76*, London, HMSO, 1975 and 1977; CSO, *Annual Abstract of Statistics*.

Although the NEDC plan was published in 1963, some of the figures were revised in 1964,[2] and the revised figures are also shown in table 9.2. The actual rise in the labour force was as predicted – unemployment in 1966 was about the same as in 1961. The target for manufacturing investment was revised downwards in 1964 because of the fall in 1962 and 1963; the actual rise was below even the revised figure. The ratio of the growth of imports to the growth of output – put at 1·0 in the first plan – was revised to 1·2; the actual figure was nearer 1·4.

The actual rise in output (tables 9.3 and 9.4) fell even further below the

[1] NEDC, *Growth of the United Kingdom Economy to 1966*; Department of Economic Affairs, *The National Plan* and *The Task Ahead*.　　[2] NEDC, *Report on the Growth of the Economy*.

Table 9.3. *The National Plan, 1964–70: target annual growth rates and out-turns (macroeconomic variables)*

	Target	Actual
	(percentages)	
GNP	3·8	2·2
GNP per person employed	3·4	2·6
Gross fixed capital formation		
Manufacturing and construction	7·5	4·8
Other private industry	3·8	4·6
Nationalised industries	4·5	1·5
Housing	4·8	1·5
Public services	7·7	5·6
Total	5·5	3·5
Defence	1·0	−3·0
Other public authorities' current expenditure	4·0	4·2
Personal consumption	3·2	1·8
Imports of goods	4·0	4·4[a]
Exports of goods	5·3	5·7[b]
	(thousands)	
Labour force	400	−210

SOURCES: Department of Economic Affairs, *The National Plan*; CSO, *National Income and Expenditure 1964–74* and *1966–76*; CSO, *Annual Abstract of Statistics*.
[a] 1964–7, 3·3 per cent; 1967–70, 5·6 per cent.   [b] 1964–7, 2·8 per cent; 1967–70, 8·6 per cent.

Table 9.4. *The National Plan, 1964–70: target annual growth rates and out-turns (industry figures)*

Percentages

	Output		Employment		Output per head	
	Target	Actual	Target	Actual	Target	Actual
Manufacturing	4·4	2·7	0·5	—	3·9	3·0
Mining and quarrying	−0·9	−3·9	−5·1	−7·4	5·4	3·8
Construction	4·6	1·6	0·9	−3·3	3·7	5·1
Gas, electricity and water	8·4	5·0	1·7	−0·9	6·5	6·0
Agriculture, forestry and fishing	3·5	1·8	−2·7	−5·7	6·3	8·0
Transport and communications	4·0	3·2	−1·0	−0·7	5·0	3·9
Distribution	2·8	1·8	0·1	−1·6	2·7	3·5
Insurance, banking and finance	4·2	4·7	2·2	7·0	2·0	−2·1
Professional and scientific services	2·4	3·2	3·0	3·3	−0·6	−0·1
Miscellaneous services	3·3	0·7	0·8	−2·9	2·5	−3·7
Public administration and defence	1·8	0·7	0·9	1·3	0·9	−0·6

SOURCES: Department of Economic Affairs, *The National Plan*; CSO, *Annual Abstract of Statistics*.

target figure in 1964–70 than in 1961–6, as deflationary policies raised the level of unemployment and brought output below capacity.[1] Once again, the volume of imports rose very much faster than planned; the target ratio of their growth to the growth of GNP was 1·05 and the actual figure was 2·0. For the actual movements in import and export volumes, it is useful to consider the figures before and after devaluation separately. In the use of resources, the one category of domestic expenditure which rose roughly in line with the target figures was public current expenditure on goods and services (excluding defence).

The Task Ahead, the final 'planning document' of the Department of Economic Affairs, offered a range of possibilities. The basic rate of output growth was expected to be $3\frac{1}{4}$ per cent, but it could be as high as 4 per cent or as low as 3 per cent; in fact, with rising unemployment, it was 2 per cent. With a 3 per cent rise in output, the volume of imports of goods was projected to rise at $3\frac{3}{4}$ per cent a year, with a volume rise in exports of $5\frac{1}{4}$ per cent. In fact, the volume of imports grew at 6·3 per cent a year and of exports at 7·4 per cent.

[1] A fuller post-mortem of the National Plan is given in M. J. C. Surrey, 'The National Plan in retrospect', *Bulletin of the Oxford University Institute of Economics and Statistics*, vol. 34, August 1972.

CHAPTER 10

INDUSTRIAL POLICY

by *P. Mottershead*

THE ROLE OF INDUSTRIAL POLICIES

Since 1960 governments have become more involved with the structure, conduct and performance of individual industries and individual firms in the private sector. This chapter collects together most of the policies which were intended to affect private industry – that is industries which were not nationalised in 1960. It covers not only continuing and developing policies, such as those concerned with the regulation of competition, but also the range of what might be called specific or *ad hoc* policies, such as the decision to encourage the establishment of aluminium smelters in the United Kingdom. To collect them together is not to suggest that these policies formed a coherent overall strategy towards the private sector. Indeed there was often little coherence and the term 'strategy' implies more forethought and planning than was associated with many of the measures, so that this chapter is about policies rather than a policy. However, despite this, there is a case for looking at the combined effect of the various policies in macroeconomic terms to see whether it was unequivocally in one direction, or whether contradictions and inconsistencies might have cancelled each other out. Even policies with strictly limited aims involve some resources and thus have an opportunity cost in terms of alternatives forgone.

In 1960, when the Conservatives were firmly in power, the boundaries between the private and public sectors seemed relatively firm; the political issue was limited to the steel and road haulage industries, which had been nationalised when Labour was in power and subsequently de-nationalised by the Conservatives; the steel industry was renationalised in 1966. The mixed economy, with some slight disagreements about its exact composition, seemed to be acceptable to both Parties. The Conservatives' view was that intervention in the private sector was in general undesirable, but they accepted a case for a framework of rules to prevent the abuse of monopoly power and restrictive practices, and had passed the Restrictive Trade Practices Act in 1956. They also accepted that in certain instances the private sector on its own did not produce satisfactory results from the national viewpoint. Broadly this was judged true of regional imbalance, particularly as demonstrated by differing regional unemployment rates. Although the improvement of that balance was an objective which had existed since the 1930s, the 1960 Local Employment Act was significant in terms of the priority given to regional problems and the instruments adopted.

On a microeconomic level, specific industrial situations produced selective responses, of which the most important concerned the aircraft and cotton industries. The government was a major purchaser of aircraft and a reduction in state demand, particularly for military aircraft, was foreseen as a result of defence policy changes. They felt it necessary to preserve the industry for defence reasons and thought it desirable that the number of firms should be reduced and their size increased; mergers within the industry were therefore encouraged. Falling demand was also the problem in the cotton industry, in this case exacerbated by fierce import competition from the Asian Commonwealth. The government response, given a reluctance during the late 1950s to introduce formal import restrictions, was to provide financial aid to assist the industry in scrapping outdated machinery and installing modern equipment.

Thus, up to 1964 the Conservatives accepted the existing nationalised industries, but believed in general that the market economy produced desirable outcomes, provided measures were taken to avoid excessive regional imbalance, the abuse of monopoly power and restrictive practices. In this last context, one of their final moves in 1964 was to abolish resale price maintenance, which was seen as hindering the free play of the market. In addition, they were prepared to intervene on a temporary basis in the private sector to help industries with particular problems. Finally, with the setting up of the NEDC in 1962, they recognised that the performance of the economy might benefit from some overall attempt to coordinate the private sector, both on its own and in conjunction with the public sector.[1]

Labour too accepted a government role in competition policy, and one of their first moves was to pass the 1965 Monopolies and Mergers Act, which for the first time introduced some control over mergers. Many of the measures in the Act stemmed from proposals in an earlier Conservative White Paper.[2] Labour's view of the government's relationship with private industry differed, in that planning was more central to their approach and they believed that selective intervention could improve industrial performance. They saw British industry, with

---

[1] See chapter 9.
[2] Board of Trade, *Monopolies, Mergers and Restrictive Practices*, Cmnd 2299, London, HMSO, 1964. See also pages 424–6 below.

exceptions, as scientifically and technologically backward, which was reflected in its poor growth performance and in affording low status and salaries to scientists, which resulted in their emigration to the United States – the 'brain drain'.

New machinery that was established included the Ministry of Technology and the IRC. The former had the overall task of guiding and stimulating a major effort to bring advanced technology and new processes to British industry. The IRC (see page 432) was intended to promote the rationalisation of manufacturing industry in the interests of its international competitiveness. In both cases the emphasis was on selective intervention – also on prodding reluctant companies into improving their methods and performance. Two inquiries were instituted – into the shipbuilding and aircraft industries. Both Reports recommended some temporary assistance, but thought that in the long run the aim should be commercial viability without extra government support.[1]

Another change introduced by Labour which reflected a different approach was to replace investment allowances by investment grants. The government gave four reasons for this change: grants were more readily taken into account when making investment decisions, they helped new enterprises before they started to earn profits, and they provided both quicker reimbursement and a greater certainty of benefit.

But all these measures were to be peripheral to the main instrument of industrial policy – the overall planning of the economy, with the National Plan setting targets for each industry.[2] With the early abandonment of the National Plan, however, the various specific industrial policies were developed in relative isolation.

Labour enthusiastically pursued the regional commitment of previous governments, making certain changes to the boundaries of assisted areas and later introducing the concept of intermediate areas. Incentives for industry were available at various rates in the different categories of assisted area. The regional employment premium was introduced as a labour subsidy and the premium rate of selective employment tax refunded to manufacturing industry was continued to firms in development areas even after it was generally withdrawn in 1967. Investment grants were also differentiated in favour of the regions. By 1970 there was a wider range of regional inducements than any previous government had offered.[3]

The Conservative government which came to office in 1970 had a

---

[1] Ministry of Aviation, *Report of the Committee of Inquiry into the Aircraft Industry*, Cmnd 2853, London, HMSO, 1965; Board of Trade, *Shipbuilding Inquiry Committee 1965–66. Report* [Geddes Report], Cmnd 2937, London, HMSO, 1966.

[2] Department of Economic Affairs, *The National Plan.*

[3] For a full assessment of regional economic policy in the 1960s see A. J. Brown, *The Framework of Regional Economics in the United Kingdom*, Cambridge University Press, 1972.

strongly expressed preference for the market. Apart from ideological considerations, there were considerable doubts about whether government intervention could achieve the things claimed for it; Labour's record was not persuasive in this respect. The new Ministers at the Department of Trade and Industry were committed to repealing the Industrial Expansion Act and drastically modifying the IRC; there was emphasis on the importance of competition and the need to reduce regional imbalance. An early move was the reintroduction of investment allowances instead of grants.

The stopping of open-ended support for companies became known as the 'lame duck' policy, and was seen by the Conservatives as a means of reducing government intervention in specific cases. There was also a commitment to 'hive-off' the peripheral activities of the nationalised industries and bring back to them some element of private capital. The intention of the Conservative government to reduce intervention in industry was not realised in two particular cases described in more detail later in this chapter; both occurred in 1971. The first involved the Rolls-Royce Company and the second Upper Clyde Shipbuilders, at an estimated cost of £190–£195 million and £35 million respectively (at 1971 and 1972 prices).

In 1972 industrial policy changed direction. A new Minister for Industrial Development was appointed and a range of regional investment incentives introduced. A new body, the Industrial Development Executive, was set up to administer the policy, with a system of regional boards to coordinate activity. Under the Industry Act 1972 financial assistance was given to a considerable number of firms and industries, including shipbuilding, computers, machine tools, motor cycles and wool textiles. The three types of cases justified were: high-risk investment which might be in the nation's long-run interest, adjustment assistance and cases where social considerations might warrant support. Following ministerial changes there was a reform of monopolies, mergers and restrictive practices legislation, although the Fair Trading Act 1973 (described in the next section) did not generally show any significant deviation from the style of past legislation.

Broadly, the second Conservative contribution to the government–industry relationship left things much as they were in terms of the various roles which the government filled. Nevertheless this period of office encompassed both attempts to reduce direct detailed intervention in private industry and subsequent measures which, if anything, increased the government's involvement. In some ways the legitimacy, and indeed the inevitability, of government intervention in the private sector was reinforced. Both of these aspects will be discussed in the concluding section of this chapter.

POLICY AND COMPETITION

The position in 1960

Competition policy up to 1960 had resulted in three pieces of legislation: the Monopolies and Restrictive Practices (Inquiry and Control) Act of 1948, the Monopolies and Restrictive Practices Commission Act of 1953 and the Restrictive Trade Practices Act of 1956. The Act of 1948 had set up the Monopolies and Restrictive Practices Commission which, at the request of the Board of Trade, could investigate monopolies and restrictive practices and their effects on the public interest. No formal definition of monopoly or restrictive practice was provided, but where at least one third of goods supplied or processed was in the control of one body or group, or where two or more firms which together supplied at least one third of any market were parties to an agreement or restricted competition, the Commission could investigate and declare undesirable such practices as it thought against the public interest.[1] However, it was the Board of Trade which decided on any action to be taken and the main emphasis of the Commission's work was on investigation.

The Act of 1953 attempted to remedy some practical defects by expanding the membership of the Commission to 25 and making the top posts on its staff permanent and pensionable.

The 1956 Restrictive Trade Practices Act separated the restrictive practices and monopolies functions – a division which has continued. A Registrar of Restrictive Practices was appointed to compile a register of agreements between companies concerning collective discrimination, the fixing of common prices, level tendering and resale price maintenance. Firms were obliged to register such agreements, which had to be abandoned unless they were found to pass through one of the seven justificatory 'gateways' and in addition to provide some positive benefit. Cases were dealt with judicially in the new Restrictive Practices Court. The renamed Monopolies Commission was left only with situations where the criterion of a one third market share applied, and its membership was reduced again to ten.

[1] The public interest provisions related to the need to achieve:
  '(a) the production, treatment and distribution by the most efficient and economical means of goods of such types and qualities, in such volume and at such prices as will best meet the requirements of home and overseas markets;
  (b) the organisation of industry and trade in such a way that their efficiency is progressively increased and new enterprise is encouraged;
  (c) the fullest use and best distribution of men, materials and industrial capacity in the United Kingdom; and
  (d) the development of technical improvements and the expansion of existing markets and the opening up of new markets.'
(Section 14, Monopolies and Restrictive Practices (Inquiry and Control) Act, 1948.)

Conservative policy up to 1964

The early 1960s saw few policy changes. In the early stages of compiling the register there were a large number of restrictive trading agreements to consider; by the deadline for registration in February 1957 details of nearly 1200 agreements had been received by the Registrar, who was given guidance by the Board of Trade on which to consider first. Within that framework he concentrated on what he believed to be test cases in which judgement was likely to affect other agreements. Between 1958 and 1964, 30 cases were dealt with by the Court, twenty of which produced judgements that the agreement should be abandoned. Yet up to June 1963 the register contained details of 2430 agreements, of which nearly a thousand had been brought to an end by the parties concerned and 525 varied to remove all restrictions to which the Act related.[1]

Most agreements which appeared before the Court were found to be against the public interest; the exceptions included agreements in the cement industry, and for the supply of standard metal windows, permanent magnets and glazed tiles.[2] The proportion of successfully defended cases increased over time, but this may have been because manufacturers got to know more about the working of the Court and did not contest cases where the likelihood of success was small.

The Monopolies Commission was given only seven new references between 1956 and 1964, and only five Reports were published between 1958 and 1965. The impression is one of little activity, but the recommendations in those Reports and the Board of Trade's action on them are suggestive of official attitudes towards competition and large companies. Two cases illustrate government responses to the Commission's findings.

The first case concerned cigarettes and tobacco, on which the original reference was made in 1956 and the Report published in 1961.[3] It found that the major company, Imperial Tobacco, supplied nearly two thirds of the domestic market, but concluded that this monopoly position did not operate against the public interest. Imperial also had a shareholding in one of its competitors, Gallahers, and, since the Commission thought that this might operate against the public interest, it recommended that Imperial should divest itself of this shareholding.

[1] Board of Trade, *Registrar of Restrictive Trading Agreements. Report for the period July 1, 1961 to June 30, 1963*, London, HMSO, 1964, p. 10. Agreements remain on the register even after they have been terminated or modified.

[2] For more detailed assessment see D. Swann, D. P. O'Brien, W. P. Maunder and W. S. Howe, *Competition in British Industry*, London, Allen & Unwin, 1974.

[3] Monopolies Commission, *Report on the Supply of Cigarettes and Tobacco, and of Cigarette and Tobacco Machinery*, London, HMSO, 1961.

The Board of Trade entered into negotiations with Imperial, as a result of which it was announced that Imperial had given undertakings which made it no longer necessary for the government to ask the company to dispose of its Gallahers shareholding.

The second case concerned wallpaper, on which the reference was made in 1961 and the Report published in 1964.[1] Wall Paper Manufacturers, which supplied over two thirds of the home market, had followed a policy of taking over smaller companies which manufactured wallpaper. The Commission found that the acquisition of further undertakings by the company might be expected to operate against the public interest, as did the practices of exclusive dealing with distributors and of operating resale price maintenance. The Board of Trade entered into negotiations with the company which, it was announced, gave satisfactory assurances on all three points.

As these two examples illustrate, the Board of Trade was much more likely to seek voluntary assurances from companies than to attempt any stronger action. This attitude provoked some criticism, and the Imperial Tobacco case in particular prompted a private member's Bill, which would have required companies to sell shareholdings where the Commission had ruled them against the public interest. The *Economist* welcomed the Bill 'as an attempt to put even a little stuffing into the Government's flabby attitudes'.[2]

The government was already in the process of revising those attitudes, however, for early in 1962 it was announced that an intensive review of policy towards monopolies was under way. One of the main concerns was the increasing number of mergers, to which the takeover bid for Courtaulds by Imperial Chemical Industries early in 1962 brought considerable publicity. The government's position was stated at that time as: 'It has been the policy of successive governments since 1948 to judge monopolies by their actual effects and not reach a conclusion before a monopoly has come into being. There are no circumstances to make them depart from that policy.'[3]

Some Conservative backbenchers, however, were dissatisfied and in the spring of 1962 their pressure led to the setting up of a subcommittee under Lord Poole. This published its findings in March 1963, and within a short space of time two other pamphlets were published, all three containing proposals for the control of mergers.[4] The Poole proposals suggested a Registrar of Monopolies to be responsible for

[1] Monopolies Commission, *Report on the Supply of Wallpaper*, London, HMSO, 1964.
[2] *Economist*, 17 March 1962.
[3] President of the Board of Trade in *Board of Trade Journal*, 30 January 1962, p. 227.
[4] Conservative Political Centre, *Monopoly and the Public Interest* [Poole Report], London, 1963; Bow Group, *Monopolies and Mergers*, London, Conservative Political Centre, 1963; J. B. Heath, *Still Not Enough Competition*, London, Institute of Economic Affairs, 1963.

referring cases to the Monopolies Commission, which implied a reduction in the Board of Trade's role. Any proposed merger involving assets of £1 million or more would need to be registered and could not proceed unless the Registrar approved.

In January 1964 the government announced a major overhaul of legislation relating to competition policy. There followed the Resale Prices Act 1964, in which the central provision was to make it unlawful for a supplier of goods which were not exempt to fix a price at or below which the goods might not be resold, although he was still free to advertise a recommended maximum price. There was also a White Paper containing detailed proposals for altering the workings of the Monopolies Commission.[1] It proposed a Registrar of Monopolies to be responsible for investigating and setting before the Monopolies Commission the questions and issues of public interest which were involved in a particular situation, making the Commission nearer to a solely judicial body. The Registrar would be able to investigate proposed mergers where a monopoly (in the sense of a one third market share) would be created or added to. Such a merger would be prohibited, or allowed only subject to conditions, if the Commission ruled that it was likely to be against the public interest. The supply of services was also to be included within the Commission's field, and changes were proposed in the restrictive practices legislation which would make so-called 'information agreements' registrable.

The election of October 1964 ended the Conservatives' chance of finishing the overhaul of competition policy which had been outlined and it was left to the new Labour government to complete it.

Labour policy 1964–70

The Monopolies and Mergers Act 1965 introduced major changes, including many proposed in the previous government's White Paper. Perhaps the most significant differences were the omission of the Registrar of Monopolies and the introduction of an asset figure to determine which mergers should be investigated (the White Paper had only proposed investigating mergers which would result in or strengthen a one third market share). The Act stipulated that mergers fell within the scope of the law if the company taken over had assets of £5 million or more, or if the merger involved total assets of £10 million or more.[2] It required the Board of Trade to review mergers above the minimum size and decide whether or not to refer them to the Commission for

[1] Board of Trade, *Monopolies, Mergers and Restrictive Practices*.
[2] An asset figure had been suggested as a criterion in the Poole Report and by the Bow Group (*Monopolies and Mergers*), although they recommended a much lower figure of £1 million.

investigation; if a reference was made the Commission had to report within six months. The Board of Trade could delay a merger pending investigation and stop a merger (or dissolve it) following an adverse recommendation by the Commission. The rule of a one third market share remained applicable to extant monopolies, and now applied to services as well as goods. The Commission was increased to 25 members and allowed to split into subcommittees.

A panel was established of people with experience of the newspaper industry, which the Commission could consult on newspaper mergers. It became unlawful without the written consent of the Board of Trade to transfer a newspaper to a proprietor whose newspapers already had an average daily circulation of 500,000 or more. This consent could only be given following an investigation by the Monopolies Commission, unless the newspaper had a circulation of under 25,000 or the Board felt that a delay might seriously prejudice the proposed merger's chance of success. The inclusion of newspapers as a special case was interesting, but marginal to the Act as a whole, which made possible important changes in competition policy.

The period from 1965 to 1970 showed a marked increase in the Commission's workload. As compared with the seven references between 1956 and 1964, there were nineteen monopoly and general references and fourteen completed merger Reports.

In a study published in 1969 Alister Sutherland concludes that in dealing with monopoly references the Commission's main concern was with anti-competitive behaviour, followed by very high profits and failure to meet demand;[1] they rarely made any recommendations about structure and in general accepted the existing degree of market domination as given. With regard to mergers, he finds that in most cases the potential economies of scale were expected to be small and the overall benefits limited; in fact, it was simply the absence of any detriment to the public interest which explains the acceptance of the five mergers allowed at this time.

However, for changes in competition policy to be effective, changes in attitudes were needed in the Board of Trade. Following a monopoly reference the Board of Trade could (and usually did) negotiate with the company concerned about the Commission's recommendations. And even where the Commission made a very specific request, for example when it wanted Imperial to sell its holding in Gallahers, the Board of Trade could claim that the company had given sufficient undertakings to make the action unnecessary. In the case of a merger

---

[1] Anti-competitive behaviour includes agreements between home producers and foreign suppliers to restrict competition, and agreements which discriminate between customers (A. Sutherland, *The Monopolies Commission in Action*, Cambridge University Press, 1969).

the Commission had to make a definite choice, and if its decision was 'no' it was very difficult for the government not to abide by it. While the Board of Trade had considerable flexibility in deciding which proposed mergers should be referred, merging companies had no guidelines to suggest what aspects of any particular case would influence this decision and once a merger had been referred the flexibility was much reduced.

This situation led to some changes. First, a handbook was published in 1969 outlining the considerations which the Board of Trade took into account when examining mergers.[1] In horizontal mergers these concerned the possible implications for market power, efficiency, the balance of payments, regional policy and redundancy. In vertical and conglomerate mergers, the special concern was with the possible effects on competition and efficiency. In the same year the Board of Trade decided to seek more assurances about the future behaviour of merged companies in such matters as industrial relations, regional policy and possible balance of payments implications; firms were to be deterred from merging with the sole object of acquiring assets without a reasonable expectation that they could use those assets more efficiently.

The 1965 Act made no change in legislation on restrictive practices, but it came into conflict with other aspects of Labour policy and the Restrictive Trade Practices Act of 1968 remedied the position. The conflict was really between planning and competition policy: the first involved firms cooperating to improve efficiency within both their industry and the economy in general; the second was suspicious of collusion. The problem seemed particularly relevant to the 'little Neddies', the Economic Development Committees which covered various industries under the umbrella of the NEDC. The NEDC argued that the rigid interpretation of the law on restrictive agreements was frustrating cooperative action which would be in the national interest; it saw a need for increased scale in British manufacturing industry and supported rationalisation agreements as the first step towards mergers.[2]

Pressure for change of a different sort came from the Registrar himself, who in a Report listed a number of weaknesses in the 1956 Act; the most important were the absence of any effective sanctions on those who failed to register agreements and the exclusion of most information agreements from the need to register.[3]

The 1968 Act provided for both sorts of change – it made information agreements registrable (although it was left to the Board of Trade to

---

[1] Board of Trade, *Mergers: a guide to Board of Trade practice*, London, HMSO, 1969.

[2] National Economic Development Council, 'Rationalisation and the Restrictive Trade Practices Act' (unpublished), 1967.

[3] Board of Trade, *Restrictive Trading Agreements. Report of the Registrar July 1, 1963 to June 30, 1966*, Cmnd 3188, London, HMSO, 1967.

decide what categories should be placed on the register), it imposed a statutory duty to register agreements and it exempted from registration agreements considered to be in the national interest. It also introduced a new 'gateway' through which a registrable agreement could seek approval in Court – that it did not discourage competition to any material degree.

In 1970 the Labour government stated their intention to merge the Monopolies Commission with the NBPI to form a new body, the Commission for Industry and Manpower, thereby developing competition policy in close relation to other government action, particularly incomes policy. A consultative document issued by the Department of Employment and Productivity in January 1970 argued that all oligopoly situations involved potential dangers to the public interest. These need not be related directly to pricing and output decisions, for a firm without much effective competition might grant wage settlements that were in some sense 'excessive', which could frustrate both competition policy and incomes policy. It was hoped that the merged body would provide machinery to deal with all situations of imperfect competition, including the public sector as well as the private.

Conservative policy after 1970

The latest proposals came to nothing with Labour's defeat in 1970, and the NBPI was abolished early in 1971. But, as with the 1965 Act, the incoming government took over many of its predecessor's plans. The Fair Trading Act 1973 strengthened the Monopolies Commission, empowering it to direct its attention to specific issues as well as the traditional wide-ranging monopoly inquiry. On the restrictive practices side the Secretary of State was empowered to 'call-up' various categories of agreements affecting the supply of commercial services by means of an Affirmative Resolution of both Houses of Parliament.

An important institutional change was the establishment of an Office of Fair Trading, under a Director General, which was intended to be the focal point for collecting information and initiating action on competition policy. The Director General took over the role of the Registrar of Restrictive Practices, and this, together with his status as an officer of the Crown, implied that policy would henceforth be more independent of the government. He was given power, in addition to the Secretary of State, to initiate a monopoly reference, although the renamed Monopolies and Mergers Commission reported to the Secretary of State as before. The definition of a monopoly situation was changed from a one third to a one quarter market share, and publicly owned enterprises now fell within the scope of the law, although in such cases the reference had to be made by the Secretary of State, who was bound by the Act to consult first with the relevant Minister for the undertaking. The Director General had no power to refer a proposed merger for investigation, but the Act gave him a watching brief, which in practice meant that he became chairman of the Mergers Panel.[1] With both merger and monopoly reports, he had the duty, when so requested by Ministers, of conducting negotiations with the firms concerned, advising Ministers on the use of their statutory powers and supervising the observance of undertakings or orders. The first Director General was appointed in November 1973.

The Act also changed the public interest clauses, on which the criteria had been unaltered since 1948, and the new provisions had for the first time an explicit commendation of competition. Section 84 of the Fair Trading Act 1973 states that:

The Commission...among other things shall have regard to the desirability:

(a) of maintaining and promoting effective competition between persons supplying goods and services in the United Kingdom;

(b) of promoting the interests of consumers, purchasers and other users of goods and services in the United Kingdom in respect of the prices charged for them and in respect of their quality and the variety of goods and services supplied;

(c) of promoting, through competition, the reduction of costs and the development and use of new techniques and new products, and of facilitating the entry of new competitors into existing markets;

(d) of maintaining and promoting the balanced distribution of industry and employment in the United Kingdom; and

(e) of maintaining and promoting competitive activity in markets outside the United Kingdom on the part of producers of goods, and of suppliers of goods and services in the United Kingdom.

Competition policy in theory and in practice

There has been a difference in emphasis between the two main Parties in regard to competition policy. In general the Conservatives have been keen to stress the positive economic benefits of the competitive process, whereas Labour has been very hard to pin down on the merits of competition, concerning itself much more with the potential dangers of monopoly power.

There is a large volume of economic writing dating at least from Adam Smith which extols the virtues of competition as ensuring a satisfactory distribution of resources through the exercise of consumer choice and the operation of the price mechanism, and stimulating efficiency by forcing companies to keep costs down for fear of losing trade to more efficient competitors. Monopolies and cartels, it is believed, are likely to restrict output and raise prices in order to increase

[1] This is an inter-departmental committee which reviews mergers when first proposed.

profits. The benefits of competition are perhaps summed up in the concept of market efficiency, which monopolistic behaviour is thought to reduce. Politicians have, nevertheless, shown an ambivalent attitude towards large firms, perhaps because size offers possibilities of economies of scale in production, with favourable implications for growth, so that there may be long-run gains in productive efficiency to set against the potential loss of market efficiency. There are also other political and economic issues involved. The size of a large company, relative either to the country as a whole or to a particular region, might mean that its decisions had important consequences for government policy and this could lead to conflicts of interest. It has been suggested that large firms are too powerful and beyond proper democratic control, and that their existence limits the opportunities for small enterprises, which are an important feature of national prosperity. There are also conflicting views about the role of large and small firms in the process of innovation.[1]

On the other hand, a government might have reasons for promoting the growth of large firms. One view is that what matters is the size of a company relative to its international competitors rather than to its national market; another, more political reason is that it is easier for the government to negotiate and exert influence to further its policy by talking to one or two boards of directors than to scores of smaller firms.[2]

Such conflicting influences have resulted in the vacillating attitudes of successive governments towards market power. Before the 1956 Act there was no assumption *a priori* that monopolies or restrictive practices operated against the public interest; each case had to be judged on its own merits. After 1956 restrictive practices which fell within the scope of the Act were presumed to be against the public interest unless they passed through one of the permitted gateways, but even this indicated an uncommitted attitude, in that it was not simply the existence of market power in a structural sense which was considered harmful, but its abuse. This approach contrasts strongly with the American antitrust laws, which adopt a more automatic, more rigid and more hostile attitude to structural market power. There has also been official reluctance to spell out clearly the public interest that is believed to be at stake; while admittedly it is a difficult concept to define, the original

---

[1] A study by the National Institute found no evidence that size had an influence on innovation (L. Nabseth and G. F. Ray (eds.), *The Diffusion of New Industrial Processes*, Cambridge University Press, 1974). See also J. Jewkes, D. Sawers, and R. Stillerman, *The Sources of Invention* (2nd edn), London, Macmillan, 1969; C. Freeman, *The Economics of Industrial Innovation*, London, Penguin, 1974; C. Kennedy and A. P. Thirwall, 'Technical progress: a survey', *Economic Journal*, vol. 82, March 1972; J. E. S. Parker, *The Economics of Innovation*, London, Longman, 1974.

[2] For a fuller discussion of the objectives of competition, see A. Hunter, *Competition and the Law*, London, Allen & Unwin, 1966, pp. 17–21.

drafters of the 1948 Act did not intend to include guidelines at all, and those that were incorporated were very general (page 422 above) and remained unaltered until the 1973 Fair Trading Act.

The controls on mergers introduced in 1965 were therefore important; the government admitted that changes in structure might affect competition and the public interest. But at the same time Labour was aiming to promote mergers in certain industrial sectors and, while it is not necessarily inconsistent to favour some mergers while forbidding others, reasonably explicit criteria are needed to distinguish them.

In statistical terms the effects of controlling mergers look slight; the number of mergers taking place showed little change and the value of assets involved continued to increase. The Board of Trade and its successor the Department of Trade and Industry considered some 875 mergers or proposed mergers between 1965 and 1973. In that time the Monopolies Commission was asked to produce reports on eighteen, of which five concerned newspapers and hence a statutory reference. These five received formal consent, and of the other thirteen only six were forbidden.[1] Six out of 875 might seem trivial, but this is not necessarily a complete measure. There is likely to be a deterrent effect from a reference, with plans being dropped before the investigation, or they may be shelved even before a reference in response to concern by the Department of Trade and Industry. A formal reference to the Commission is, then, the last step.

With regard to firms' behaviour policy has been more definite and more consistent. Since 1956 restrictive trading agreements have had to be justified as being positively in the public interest if they were to be continued. It is possible that this in itself may have led to more mergers, for in some cases a merger may have replaced a cartel, and there is evidence that this did happen.[2] However, such a merger may not reduce competition significantly; if it simply formalises the arrangements of a former cartel there is no change in competitive pressures.

POLICY AND INDUSTRIAL STRUCTURE

Nearly always efforts by the government to stimulate structural change within industry have involved greater concentration through mergers and take-overs. Although earlier governments had seen rationalisation

[1] Ross Group–Associated Fisheries (1966), United Drapery Stores–Montague Burton (1967), Barclays–Lloyds–Martins Banks (1968), Rank–De la Rue (1969), British Sidac–Transparent Paper (1970) and Beechams–Glaxo or Boots–Glaxo (1972). Of these Ross and Associated Fisheries were merged later following action by the IRC and Barclays merged with Martins.

[2] D. Elliott and J. D. Gribbin, 'The abolition of cartels and structural change in the United Kingdom' in A. P. Jacquemin and H. W. de Jong (eds.), *Welfare Aspects of Industrial Markets*, Leiden, Nijhoff, 1977.

as a solution to particular problems, it was the 1964–70 Labour administration which for the first time pursued it as a general policy, principally through the IRC.

The major legislation was, first, the 1966 Industrial Reorganisation Corporation Act, which established the IRC as an independent body to promote rationalisation schemes yielding benefits to the national economy, especially through increased exports and more rapid technological advance. Secondly, there was the 1968 Industrial Expansion Act, providing £100–£150 million to finance industrial investment schemes approved by the House of Commons which would create, expand or sustain capacity, improve efficiency or promote technological advance; it also provided additional finance for Concorde, the QE2, the shipbuilding industry and the National Research Development Corporation.

Labour's rationalisation plans existed in principle before the Party came to power, based on the belief that more advanced technology and scientific knowledge should be disseminated throughout industry. It was hoped that selective intervention to modernise industry would help to solve the balance of payments problem without resorting to devaluation. In practice the policy of stimulating structural change was linked closely with the new Department of Economic Affairs and a group of industrialists assembled there; it was firm enough by September 1965 to be included in the National Plan.

The theme of size and international competition was central to the White Paper proposing the IRC, which maintained that many production units in Britain were too small compared with those abroad, who were able to base their operations on a much larger market.[1] It argued that unit size should be increased in the interests of improving efficiency, exports and the balance of payments, and that there was no evidence that market forces alone could be relied upon to produce the necessary structural changes at the pace required, because existing institutions generally acted only at their client's request and desirable regroupings had failed to occur through lack of initiative and sponsorship. The IRC was intended to fill this gap in the institutional framework. It was to seek the fullest cooperation from industry and financial institutions in pursuing rationalisation and modernisation schemes which offered good prospects of early returns in terms of increased exports or reduced import requirements. It would not support schemes which had no prospect of achieving eventual viability, and would be able to draw up to £150 million from the Exchequer, which could be used for making loans or taking equity holdings. Arrangements would be made to

[1] Department of Economic Affairs, *The Industrial Reorganisation Corporation*, Cmnd 2889, London, HMSO, 1966.

ensure that mergers backed by the IRC would not be referred to the Monopolies Commission.

The IRC came into being in December 1966.[1] In conception it was certainly a novel policy instrument for the United Kingdom, involving the delegation to an independent group of businessmen of the task of promoting mergers and rationalisation schemes, and allowing them to use up to £150 million of public funds with less stringent control than was usual for such quasi-governmental bodies. It faced two immediate tasks: first to establish priorities, so that the effort could be made where it would produce the most impact; secondly to win the confidence of the business community, particularly in those industries with which it wanted to become involved.[2]

In the first year there were no startling results. A survey of the telecommunications industry and its relationship with the Post Office was undertaken at the request of the Postmaster General and the Minister of Technology. Some Chrysler shares were acquired – also at the request of the government – in a move designed to retain at least some British interest in the company, which was coming increasingly under the control of its American parent. And, in June 1967, £15 million was lent to assist the merger between English Electric and Elliott Automation in the field of electronics. But perhaps the most significant intervention in 1967/8 – certainly the largest in terms of IRC money – was the promotion of a merger between the Leyland Motor Corporation and British Motor Holdings; £25 million was lent to the new British Leyland, which now contained the greater part of the indigenously owned motor industry.[3]

A proposal for a merger between the General Electric Company and Associated Electrical Industries was dropped because it became apparent that the latter was likely to oppose it. But subsequently the IRC did back the merger, stating in the offer document to shareholders of Associated Electrical Industries that the proposed combination of the businesses had its full support, but adding that it was for them to decide their own interests. Differences over policy towards this merger led to some changes, and resignations from the IRC board including the managing director.

---

[1] Its functions were set out in section 2 of the Industrial Reorganisation Corporation Act:
'The Corporation may, for the purpose of promoting industrial efficiency and profitability and assisting the economy of the United Kingdom or any part of the United Kingdom –
(a) promote or assist the reorganisation or development of any industry, or
(b) if requested to do so by the Secretary of State, establish or develop, or promote or assist the establishment or development of, any industrial enterprise.'
[2] Department of Economic Affairs, *Industrial Reorganisation Corporation. First Report and Accounts, December 1966–March 1968*, London, HMSO, 1968.
[3] The story of the British Leyland merger is fully documented: see G. Turner, *The Leyland Papers*, London, Eyre & Spottiswoode, 1971.

Dissatisfaction with the IRC's early performance seemed the motive behind the Industrial Expansion Act, which gave the government general powers to intervene and provide finance under less restrictive conditions than those of the IRC. Two industrial investment schemes were sponsored under the Act, in aluminium smelters and in computers. The contrast with the IRC's type of intervention can be seen by looking at the first of these in more detail (the second is described on pages 445–6 below).

In 1968 Britain was importing the bulk of its primary aluminium, whereas most of its industrial competitors had at least some native smelting capacity. Aluminium smelting uses large quantities of power for transforming alumina into aluminium by electrolysis, the amounts involved being of the order of 18,000 kilowatt–hours per ton of metal. Production has therefore tended to be near abundant sources of cheap power, rather than close to the bauxite deposits from which the alumina is extracted.

The prospect of cheap electricity from atomic power stations extended the possibility of smelting in Britain. In 1965 there was talk of electricity at as little as a halfpenny per kilowatt–hour, and Rio Tinto-Zinc, with a small fraction of the United Kingdom market but large bauxite deposits in Australia, started talks with the Atomic Energy Authority and the Board of Trade about the possibility of using this cheap power. The Board of Trade was apparently impressed at the potential import-savings and discussed the idea with two other manufacturers, British Aluminium and Alcan. The IRC was asked to consider various plans proposed by the companies and submitted a confidential Report in January 1968, which apparently favoured the plans of Rio Tinto-Zinc and British Aluminium for smelters of around 100,000 tons annual capacity. Alcan's plan to build a coal-powered smelter was not well received.[1]

The Central Electricity Generating Board's powers did not permit it to sell electricity cheaper to one customer than to another, but the two aluminium companies were allowed to take a nominal slice in the capital costs of the new power stations, which entitled them to receive power at lower rates under long-term contracts. Under the Industrial Expansion Act £33 million was lent to Rio Tinto-Zinc and £30 million to British Aluminium, repayable over 30 and 28 years respectively with a fixed interest rate of 7 per cent. The smelters, sited at Anglesey and Invergordon, also qualified for 40 per cent investment grants and 35 per cent building grants.

---

[1] Alcan decided to press ahead with their coal-powered plan and built a smelter at Lynemouth in the North East. They entered into a long-term contract with the National Coal Board to supply coal for a new power station which they built near the smelter.

The most controversial aspect of the scheme was cheap power. Charges were linked to nominal costs of production with the most advanced type of generating capacity in stations which were not yet in operation and problems had arisen suggesting that the original expectations of cheap electricity were optimistic. The secrecy surrounding the contracts implied to other electricity consumers that the subsidy was high and subsequent evidence suggests that the contracts were at fixed prices. However, the Central Electricity Generating Board claimed in its Annual Report that other proposals by large-scale users of electricity for special long-term contracts would be considered on their merits.[1]

A computers' merger (see pages 445–6) was the only other scheme promoted under the Industrial Expansion Act; after this the Act was not used again, being rendered at least partially redundant by the more positive approach of the IRC after its change of management in 1967. A loan of £1·5 million was made to the Reed Paper Group in February 1968 to help finance two plants which would de-ink and reconstitute printed paper, which was significant because it was the first time that the IRC had provided finance in a non-merger situation (apart from the Chrysler case at the government's request). This change in approach was acknowledged in the following terms:

Whereas in the early months the emphasis was mainly on establishing contacts with companies and hearing their suggestions for possible IRC action, the IRC itself is now more ready to take the initiative in proposing and encouraging action within industry...The IRC s task is to seek out those sectors of industry where structural change should be happening but is not – to identify the obstacles and try to eliminate them.[2]

Although there was only limited scope for large interventions, the IRC involved itself in an increasing number of merger schemes, rationalisations and loans. In the first Report details are given of fourteen projects; in 1968/9 there were 23 and in 1969/70 22; in 1970/1, its last year, mostly under a Conservative government pledged to its drastic modification, there were seventeen. These projects are classified in table 10.1, which also shows the amounts of finance involved. Some of the more controversial interventions are now described in detail.

The IRC had shown itself prepared in the case of General Electric to back one company against an unwilling suitor. In June 1968 it was involved with Cambridge Instruments, a manufacturer of advanced scientific and analytical instruments, for which the Rank Organisation

[1] Ministry of Power, *Central Electricity Generating Board Annual Report and Accounts 1968–69*, London, HMSO, 1969, para. 159.
[2] Department of Economic Affairs, *Industrial Reorganisation Corporation. First Report and Accounts*, p. 6.

Table 10.1. *Projects supported by the IRC, 1966–71*

	Dec. 1966–March 1968	1968/9	1969/70	April 1970–April 1971	Whole period
		(no. of projects)			
Industry surveys (no finance)	2	2	—	—	4
Share purchases/loans where no mergers involved[a]	2	2	2	10	16
Mergers and rationalisation schemes	10	18	18	7	53
(in which no finance)	(4)	(4)	(7)	(2)	(17)
Subsequent assistance	—	1	2	—	3
Total projects[b]	14	23	22	17	76
			(£ million)		
Payments made[c]	*17·2*	*38·3*	*33·6*	*30·9*	*120·0*
Money committed	*31·5*	*10·9*	*6·2*	*12·6*	n.a.

SOURCES: Department of Economic Affairs and Ministry of Technology, *Industrial Reorganisation Corporation, Report and Accounts* (various periods).

[a] All action taken under Section 2(1)(b) of the IRC Act (see footnote 1, page 433).

[b] The number of IRC projects is slightly arbitrary, especially when they were carried over from one year to the next.

[c] Gross payments, which differ from those in the accounts in ignoring repayments of loans.

had made a bid, but the IRC believed that the best match was with George Kent, the largest independent instrument company in the United Kingdom. When attempts to create a company from Cambridge, Kent and the instrument interests of Rank failed, the IRC decided to enter the market and bought enough Cambridge shares to ensure the success of the Kent bid. The decision to intervene actively to ensure the success of a favoured candidate added a new dimension to the IRC's activities.

A second intervention occurred in 1969, as a result of a possible merger between Ransome and Marles, a ball-bearing manufacturer, and the Skefko Ball Bearing Company, which was a subsidiary of a Swedish company, SKF. The IRC feared that this would not leave enough capacity still in British ownership to create a viable British-owned company in the industry, in which there were two other medium-sized firms, Pollard and Hoffmann. It made a successful bid for the shares of Brown Bayley, which owned 60 per cent of Hoffmann's equity capital, and from this base went on to negotiate a three-way merger, which resulted in Ransome Hoffman Pollard.

The IRC also became involved in the trawling industry. The Monopolies Commission had in 1966 ruled against a merger between the Ross Group and Associated Fisheries, but in the IRC's opinion the reasons for such a merger were more pressing by 1969, and the government declared itself satisfied that the public interest would not be threatened. This reversal inevitably aroused comment about the conflict between the IRC's role and the government's merger policy.

In the last months of the Labour government, the IRC intervened in a number of situations which are described below in the sections on the aircraft industry, shipbuilding, science and technology, and the textile industry. After the Conservatives won the 1970 election they announced that the IRC would be wound up and it officially ceased to exist on 21 May 1971, following the transfer of its assets and liabilities to the Secretary of State for Trade and Industry. However, in 1972, when the Conservative government introduced new industrial and regional assistance, the Industrial Development Executive was set up, with practising businessmen among its members, but this differed from the IRC in a number of ways, principally in that it was an advisory body.

The impact of the IRC is difficult to assess. Its aims were to produce structural change in manufacturing industry – generally an increase in unit size. Yet at a time when there was a substantial merger movement anyway, possibly it was simply pushing at an open door. On the other hand, it is probable that certain regroupings would not have occurred without the IRC – the most likely being the controversial interventions already mentioned, Ransome Hoffmann Pollard and Kent – Cambridge. It is also possible that the IRC speeded up mergers in certain situations – British Leyland for example – and it actually suggested the merger between General Electric and Associated Electrical Industries. Thus it can reasonably be concluded that it did make some impact; whether that was the impact desired can perhaps best be assessed by its own declared objectives of improving productivity and the balance of payments in the national interest. There was also a commitment to assist the government's regional policies as far as possible.[1]

It seems clear that the IRC did keep the balance of payments in mind when choosing projects to support. McClelland, who was a director, says, 'The Corporation paid little or no attention to industries, such as building, where there might have been scope for reorganisation but which were not direct importers or exporters on a significant scale.'[2] In particular, the schemes which did not involve mergers usually cited

---

[1] Department of Economic Affairs, *Industrial Reorganisation Corporation. Report and Accounts for the year ended March 31, 1969*, London, HMSO, 1969.

[2] W. G. McClelland, 'The Industrial Reorganisation Corporation 1966/71 – an experimental prod', *Three Banks Review*, no. 94, June 1972.

the balance of payments, import-saving or export promotion as the motive for the intervention. This concern was sometimes expressed in what might be called 'nationalist' solutions: the creation of Ransome Hoffmann Pollard was seen as a counter to the increased presence of SKF in the United Kingdom ball-bearing industry, and the merger between Rowntree and Mackintosh in the confectionery industry was seen as preferable to letting General Foods, an American company, proceed with their bid for Rowntree.

Improving productivity was seen largely in terms of increasing unit size, although the IRC claimed it did not believe in size for the sake of it. It did believe, however, that mergers provided the basis on which more successful companies could be built through better plant utilisation, concentrated effort in export markets, financial strength and economies of scale in research and development and in new investment programmes.[1] Certainly McClelland admits that size was the IRC's principal aim: 'in the main, "reorganisation" was a euphemism for creating larger units'.[2] In pursuit of this goal the IRC concentrated on some sectors more than others. Electrical engineering and electronics received considerable attention, especially in the earlier years, based, said the IRC, on the great importance of the sector to the country's export effort, the rapid pace of its technological change, and the intense competition from powerful companies in the United States, Europe and Japan. In the electrical industry, the merger between General Electric and Associated Electrical Industries was encouraged because it strengthened General Electric's competitive position in the international market, and because, in pursuit of greater productivity, the new company could prune its workforce considerably. This did not provoke such extreme reactions as subsequent redundancies, but more concern for the effect of rationalisation on employment was shown by the IRC in its later years.

Support of the government's regional policies was, in practice, very much in third place. Most of the schemes do not mention any regional effects as the motive, although the loan to the Reed Paper Group for a waste paper de-inking plant in Scotland was justified as a contribution to regional policy.

Overall, it is still probably too early to produce more than an interim judgement. Mergers and rationalisations can take many years before the potential benefits are realised; there is also a considerable problem in deciding how to measure the effects. Measurement by linking the companies' previous results and comparing them with post-merger

---

[1] Ministry of Technology, *Industrial Reorganisation Corporation. Report and Accounts for the year ended March 31, 1970*, London, HMSO, 1970.
[2] McClelland, 'The Industrial Reorganisation Corporation'.

results may be distorted in the short run because the costs of rationalisation tend to occur in the early years. Any assessment should really contain some comparison with manufacturing industry in general, or at least some sample of it.

The total injection of £120 million by the IRC in its active years between 1967 and 1970 is fairly small in comparison with total manufacturing investment over the period, which was some £7000 million. Certainly it was not enough to make more than a marginal difference to manufacturing as a whole, and could not outweigh the broader cyclical patterns of investment influenced by the general state of the economy. But by selective intervention the IRC believed it could make an impact. Its own preliminary assessment was that of the 90 or so projects with which it was substantially involved at least 75 were turning out as expected.[1]

The IRC was aware that its policy of promoting mergers at a time when the government had also introduced powers to control them meant that there was a possible conflict, but not all members of the board regarded this as serious. Its managing director believed that at certain times an industry might need stimulating and at others sedating, and the Board of Trade was the coordinator to see that only one drug was applied at a time.[2] However, firms in a merger situation might try to get IRC approval to guard against investigation by the Monopolies Commission; certainly Weinstock believed that the IRC had helped to ease the passage of the General Electric merger.[3] But if criticism is warranted it should surely be of the government, rather than the IRC, which was, after all, carrying out stated government policy.

The IRC has been much discussed. A House of Commons Committee found that the majority of its witnesses were in favour of an agency of this kind. The arguments were, first, that businessmen were better able than Civil Servants to handle the problems, secondly, that independence from government had advantages and, thirdly, that the government's backing gave the agency more authority than a private institution.[4]

SCIENCE AND TECHNOLOGY POLICY

Government involvement in science, both in this country and others, has been strongly influenced by the increasing size and science-based content of defence expenditure and by the desire to obtain some civil

[1] Ministry of Technology, *Industrial Reorganisation Corporation. Report and Accounts covering the period April 1, 1970 to April 30, 1971*, London, HMSO, 1971.

[2] Sir Charles Villiers quoted in *Management Today*, October 1969, p. 194.

[3] House of Commons *Sixth Report from the Expenditure Committee, Session 1971–72. Public Money in the Private Sector*, vols. 2 and 3: *Minutes of Evidence*, London, HMSO, 1972.

[4] Ibid. vol. 1: *Report*.

spin-off. This tendency has been apparent since the 1939–45 war, when scientists were involved in weapon development and policy planning on a scale unknown before and technical advances seemed to promise that science could make a significant contribution to peacetime progress if sufficient resources were devoted to it.

By 1959 a basic agreement between Conservatives and Labour that civil science should be encouraged had given way to policy disputes which focused on three main problems. The first was the shortage of qualified manpower, particularly industrial engineers, which was not helped by the 'brain drain'; the second was the generally low level and uneven spread of industrial research, which was concentrated mainly in those industries involved in substantial defence contracting; the third was the haphazard system of government support for civil science, which left individual agencies – some very large such as the Atomic Energy Authority – outside any central control.

A Minister for Science had been appointed in 1959, but defence expenditure on research and development, still much the largest source of such funds, remained outside his control. A special committee was set up in 1958 to look at how government departments controlled research and development. The resulting Report made recommendations on managerial techniques in research stations, but could not, under its terms of reference, comment on the division of responsibilities between the agencies and departments involved.[1] The increasing amount of scientific research, the growing scale of individual projects and the proliferation of research agencies, together with Treasury concern over the control of expenditure, led to the appointment of another committee in March 1962 to examine the organisation of civil science.

The Trend Committee reported in October 1963,[2] at a time when the Labour opposition was vigorously propounding a scientific revolution as the cure for Britain's problems. It recommended that the Department of Scientific and Industrial Research, which was the main vehicle for government promotion of industrial research and development, should be replaced by three new Research Councils, one for science, one for natural resources and one for industrial research and development (to include the National Research Development Corporation). It also recommended that the Minister for Science should have more powers and staff and, in addition, be made responsible for higher education.

The government, however, decided not to split higher and lower

---

[1] Office of the Minister for Science, *Report of the Committee on the Management and Control of Research and Development* [Zuckerman Report], London, HMSO, 1961.
[2] Office of the Minister for Science, *Committee of Enquiry into the Organisation of Civil Science* [Trend Report], London, HMSO, 1963.

education, and in February 1964 formed a new Department of Education and Science. They indicated that the Department of Scientific and Industrial Research would be replaced by the three new research councils and the National Research Development Corporation transferred to the Board of Trade, but these changes had not been made by the October election.

The Conservatives' contribution to relieving the shortage of scientific and technical manpower also took place amid controversy. By 1960 the postwar population 'bulge' had begun to reach university age and there was a growing demand for higher education. Plans for a new university in Sussex had been announced in 1958, but the predictions continued to suggest that demand for places would exceed supply. The whole question of higher education was the subject of the *Robbins Report*,[1] which recommended an expansion of existing universities, the creation of six new ones and the upgrading of Colleges of Advanced Technology, Scottish central institutions and colleges of education to university status. The government accepted these recommendations and voted extra grants in 1964.

Labour had decided early in the 1960s that science was a subject on which to take issue with the government. An extensive campaign had been mounted, concentrating on the 'brain drain', the poor status of scientists and technologists, and the meanness of the government in sponsoring scientific and technical research. The status problem seemed significant for, despite the high overall demand for student places and the need for more qualified manpower, there were still vacancies in some Colleges of Advanced Technology and university engineering departments. The Labour Party's science policy was launched at the 1963 annual conference; the plan was aimed at producing more scientists, keeping them in this country and using them more intelligently, also encouraging the wider application of scientific research in industry. This was to be done by devoting more resources to research for industrial purposes, which would stimulate production and concurrently provide more status and prospects for scientists. The 'white-hot technical revolution' became a slogan associated with Harold Wilson and with Labour's election campaign throughout 1964. In their election manifesto Labour promised 'a Ministry of Technology to guide and stimulate a major national effort to bring advanced technology and new processes to industry'.

Under the new Labour government the establishment of the new Ministry involved a number of administrative and organisational changes, which largely embodied the proposals of the *Trend Report*.

[1] Ministry of Education, *Higher Education. Report* [Robbins Report], Cmnd 2154, London, HMSO, 1963.

The Minister was made responsible for the Atomic Energy Authority, the National Research Development Corporation and those parts of the Department of Scientific and Industrial Research which were concerned with research and technical development in industry. The Ministry was also to sponsor machine tools, electronics, telecommunications and computers. Under the Science and Technology Act 1965, a Science Research Council and a Natural Environment Research Council were established under the Department of Education and Science. Some of the functions of the Department of Scientific and Industrial Research were transferred to the Science Research Council, but the majority came to the Ministry of Technology. The Act also extended the powers of the Atomic Energy Authority to engage in non-nuclear research and provided the means for the Ministry to sponsor scientific research in industry, partly by means of shared development contracts, in which the government contributed some of the costs and received benefits in the form of sales levies if the development work was successful. In June 1965, under the Development of Inventions Act, the financial provision for the National Research Development Corporation was increased from £10 million to £25 million.

The Ministry of Technology grew in importance throughout Labour's period in office, at least when measured by its domain. The functions of the Ministry of Aviation were transferred to it early in 1967, and those of the Ministry of Power, together with sponsorship for several other industries, in 1969. The work of such a wide-ranging Ministry is difficult to describe briefly, so three of the functions it discharged from the beginning will be looked at in more detail: in machine tools and computers, and the provision of general technical services to industry.

The machine tool industry

In 1960 an official committee had investigated the machine tool industry and found that it was unable to respond quickly to rises in demand, had a poor export performance and was generally slow to adopt modern techniques and designs. The main problem seemed to be lack of qualified manpower.[1] Labour Party statements since the early 1960s had pointed to machine tools as just the sort of industry which needed a large dose of science and technology to bring it up to date. A Labour policy document even suggested new publicly owned companies to specialise in types of machine tool which existing firms were not producing satisfactorily.[2]

The main problem facing the industry in 1964 was a cyclical pattern of demand, common among capital goods. Capacity was insufficient to

[1] Board of Trade, *The Machine Tool Industry. Report*, London, HMSO, 1960, para. 117.
[2] Labour Party, *Signposts for the Sixties*.

cope with the peaks of demand, so that imports increased during the upswing, but manufacturers were discouraged from developing new, more sophisticated models because they knew demand would fall away as the cycle turned down. The government aimed to help the industry to develop and produce more of the most advanced and effective types of machine tool by increasing research and development contracts, and by orders for pre-production models. They encouraged arrangements which associated machine tool manufacturers with electronics and control engineering firms; they also believed that by concentrating the industry into stronger units it would better meet the demands of manufacturing in general.

Under the pre-production order scheme the Ministry bought advanced models and placed them out on free loan for industrial trial and evaluation by potential purchasers. Another scheme was designed to stimulate the use of numerically controlled machine tools: users could purchase such machines knowing that they could be returned for a guaranteed repurchase price, when the National Research Development Corporation would pay the manufacturer for the cost of reconditioning and re-selling the machine.

The pre-production scheme was provided with an extra £5 million in April 1967, the timing being intended to produce counter-cyclical effects. Then, in August 1967, the clearing banks announced that they were prepared to make special medium-term loans available to purchasers of machine tools manufactured in the United Kingdom. The loans were to be for up to five years at normal overdraft rates, but repayments could be small to start with, rising as the return on the machine increased.

In 1969 the IRC arranged loans to Marwins and to Herbert-Ingersoll, and announced its willingness to do likewise for other technically advanced companies. It also encouraged concentration in the numerically controlled sector, giving financial support to a group comprising Plessey, Airmec and Ferranti, and later to Kearney and Trecker. But perhaps the most interesting IRC aid was the provision in June 1970 of £10 million to British Leyland, which was to use the money together with its own finances 'for the purchase of machine tools to modernise and expand its production facilities'.[1] It is difficult to see how the IRC could ensure that this loan resulted in additional orders for the home industry and generally it seemed a rather roundabout way of assisting it.

To assess the effect of these various measures on the machine tool industry is difficult. A committee recommended in 1971 that the pre-production scheme should be a continuing feature of government

---

[1] Ministry of Technology, *Industrial Reorganisation Corporation. Report and Accounts covering the period April 1, 1970 to April 30, 1971*, p. 20.

support.[1] Likewise the Machine Tool Trades Association, in evidence to Parliament, said that the scheme was the only form of aid specifically for machine tools which had had any real success.[2] The accolades of the industry are not, however, necessarily a good guide to the success of the scheme from the government's point of view. The Department of Trade and Industry estimated that its cost up to May 1972 had been £5·5 million net of associated receipts,[3] which is relatively small over a period of seven years compared to the output of the industry. The money seems to have been spread over a considerable number of projects, but at the same time was centred mainly on the firms which had been involved in mergers, in line with government policy.

Table 10.2. *Expenditure on research and development in the machine tool industry, 1964/5–1972/3*

£ million

1964/5	1966/7	1967/8	1968/9	1969/70	1972/3
2·6	5·4	5·4	5·2	4·2	1·6

SOURCE: CSO, *Research and Development Expenditure*, London, HMSO, 1973.

The amount of research and development in the industry also ought to be a guide to the impact of the policy, and the figures in table 10.2 show that total expenditure did rise after 1964/5 but declined somewhat by 1969/70. An even more dramatic fall is apparent by 1972/3 and, although the run of figures is not long enough to make firm judgements, it does suggest that the cycle is an important influence.

Another part of the government's plan was to encourage the use of numerically controlled machine tools and estimates suggest that the stock of such tools in Britain rose from about 1000 in 1966 to 3200 in 1970.[4] The only scheme specifically for this purpose did not, however, seem to have much effect; of a sample of user firms, only two fifths reported that government assistance had influenced their decision in favour of numerically controlled machines.[5] The National Research Development Corporation, which administered the scheme, reported in 1968/9 that sales were disappointing and in April 1970 the scheme was withdrawn.

[1] Department of Trade and Industry, *The Machine Tool Industry. Report of the Machine Tool Expert Committee*, London, HMSO, 1971, p. 76.
[2] Memorandum to the Trade and Industry Sub-Committee in House of Commons, *Sixth Report from the Expenditure Committee, Session 1971–72*, vol. 3, p. 698.
[3] Ibid. p. 736.
[4] Nabseth and Ray, *The Diffusion of New Industrial Processes*, p. 31; Machinery and Production Engineering, *Survey of Machine Tool Statistics 1951–1970 Inclusive*, Brighton, Machinery Publishing Co, 1971.   [5] Nabseth and Ray, *The Diffusion of New Industrial Processes*, p. 42.

Overall the impact of the Labour government's science policy on the industry seems small. The only scheme which was well received was pre-production ordering, and this was on such a small scale that it could make no difference to the problems arising from the cyclical demand for the industry's products.

The computer industry

In the early 1960s the computer industry was facing competition from United States manufacturers such as IBM, Honeywell and Burroughs, which received large government research contracts in connection with the American defence and space programmes, and with this backing were able to compete strongly in European markets. Aid for the industry was announced to Parliament on 1 March 1965, and almost immediately put into effect.

The Computer Advisory Service within the Ministry of Technology was started in April 1965; all proposed central government purchases of computers for civil purposes had to be appraised by the Service before procurement could be authorised. An increased procurement programme for universities and colleges was expected to cost £30 million over six years. Government support for research and development was increased and the Ministry of Technology instituted a number of cost-sharing development contracts. The National Computing Centre was established in July 1966. It was an independent company, with the objectives of standardising and simplifying the programming of computers, and advising on the training of systems analysts and programmers. The Ministry gave grants to this venture which increased from £290,000 in 1966/7 to £610,000 in 1971/2.[1]

The main manufacturers in the industry had been International Computers and Tabulators, English Electric and Elliott Automation, of which the last two merged in June 1967. A merger between the remaining two companies in 1968 resulted in International Computers Ltd.

The government planned to finance International Computers' operations to the extent of £17 million over a period of five years; £13½ million of this was to be grants for research and development and £3½ million deferred ordinary shares. At the same time the government adopted a single tender policy for large computers, so that International Computers would supply all central government requirements; in practice some smaller systems would also have to be bought from that company because of compatibility. Between 1968 and 1971 government purchasing from International Computers amounted to

[1] Treasury, *Civil Appropriation Accounts (Classes I–V) 1966–67*, London, HMSO, 1968, and *Appropriation Accounts (Classes I–V, Civil) 1971–72*, London, HMSO, 1973.

£36 million, 76 per cent of its total orders for computers; the company's turnover for a similar period was £367·75 million,[1] so that the government's orders represented some 10 per cent of total turnover.

General technical services to industry

In 1964 the Ministry of Technology had taken over from the Department of Scientific and Industrial Research several research stations, as well as the sponsorship of many industrial research associations. Using these as a base, the Ministry expanded the number of services it offered.

One scheme was the Industrial Liaison Service, under which an officer was appointed to a university or college with responsibility for maintaining contact with local firms and encouraging the wider use of existing scientific and technical knowledge. The cost was borne jointly by the institution and the government. The scheme had only just started when Labour took office and, concentrating mainly on the Colleges of Advanced Technology, the number of Industrial Liaison Centres grew to over 60 by 1968, and eventually to 75.

Another scheme which the Ministry of Technology adopted in its infancy was the dissemination of the idea that innovation is not necessarily expensive. A number of Low-Cost Automation Centres were established, again using colleges, polytechnics and universities, to provide appreciation courses on the benefits of low-cost automation, practical courses on applications, demonstrations of equipment, and advisory and consultancy services on a fee-paying basis.

The Industrial Liaison Officers and the Ministry's regional network could advise industry on several other services, including the Production Engineering Advisory Services, the British Calibration Service, the National Computing Centre, the Numerical Control Advisory and Demonstration Service, and the Central Unit for Scientific Photography. Some of these services were run by other departments or various industrial bodies rather than directly by the Ministry. A pilot scheme run by the Board of Trade in Bristol and Glasgow subsidised consultancy services for small firms, paying half of the cost up to a maximum of £5000 per business, but this scheme was not continued.

The Ministry of Technology also sponsored a number of industrial units, which were sometimes based in colleges or universities. These units specialised in research on topics of basic interest to the engineering industry in particular. Some of the topics were new. 'Mintech even dreamed up some sciences of its own...tribology and terotechnology were coined with the aid of the compilers of the Oxford Dictionary, the first referring to the problems of friction between rubbing surfaces –

---

[1] International Computers' financial year runs to end-September. The figure given includes the total turnover for 1968/9 and 1969/70, plus half each for 1967/8 and 1970/1.

everything from bearings to brakes – the second, the maintenance of plant.'[1]

Any success in spreading the gospel of science and technology to industry depended on publicity as well, and a monthly news sheet, *New Technology*, was started, which contained information about improvements in technology and the services available to industry. It was distributed free.

The worth of these services is almost impossible to gauge. Sir Richard Clarke, assessing them, said that they added up to 'a large effort and this must have been a profitable use of resources for the national economy. Indeed, most of these services have survived the very critical appraisal to which they were subjected in the first year or so of the DTI'.[2] An alternative view was expressed by the Bolton Committee, which believed that 'all Management Advisory Services, whether in the public or private sector, should be self-supporting, since the readiness of clients to pay and the ability of the service to survive on this basis are the only reliable indicators of their value'.[3] The only exception they made was an information and referral service to advise businessmen on sources of advice, which they thought could legitimately be provided by the government.

Science policy after 1970

Labour's policy derived from an overall philosophy which favoured government intervention in industry. The Conservative government in 1970, however, had a very different view, with a theme of 'disengagement'. This showed in their early dealings with some of the industries which had received help from Labour. The Report on the machine tool industry, for example, stated that 'the present government have since made clear their intention to create a suitable climate for industry to operate in, rather than intervene directly in the affairs of industry'.[4] Again with computers, the Conservatives honoured their predecessors' commitments, completing the purchase of the government shareholding in International Computers and the final instalment of the research grant. That done, however, 'the government sees no need for further support of these kinds'.[5]

In the field of research and development generally, the new govern-

---

[1] T. Lester, 'The unmaking of Mintech', *Management Today*, November 1973, p. 198.

[2] Sir Richard Clarke, 'Mintech in retrospect – II', *Omega*, vol. 1, April 1973, p. 146.

[3] Department of Trade and Industry, *Report of the Committee of Inquiry on Small Firms* [Bolton Report], Cmnd 4811, London, HMSO, 1971.

[4] Department of Trade and Industry, *The Machine Tool Industry*, p. ii.

[5] Memorandum by the Department of Trade and Industry in House of Commons, *Select Committee on Science and Technology, Session 1970–71, Fourth Report. The Prospects for the United Kingdom Computer Industry in the 1970s*, vol. 2: *Minutes of Evidence*, London, HMSO, 1971, p. 140.

ment was concerned at the large amounts of public money being spent without yielding identifiable returns. The reorganisation of central government late in 1970, which created the Department of Trade and Industry and the Department of the Environment, also established a Central Policy Review Staff, and this body was asked to examine the whole area of government support for research and development. The resulting *Rothschild Report* maintained that 'applied R and D, that is R and D with a practical application as its objective, must be done on a customer–contractor basis. The customer says what he wants; the contractor does it (if he can); and the customer pays'.[1] The government, in their introduction to the Report, firmly endorsed this principle.

There were, however, certain difficulties in identifying a 'customer' for research with a general objective of improving the spread of scientific and technical knowledge and practices. An attempt to overcome these was the creation of requirement boards,[2] which have overall responsibility for research in their particular area and examine proposals from research associations and firms. About half the board members are senior industrialists, 15 per cent academics and the rest government officials.

These changes in the system of financing government research and development, particularly in the industrial sector, were aimed at producing a better control over the funding of projects, and were in line with policy in regard to the more mundane technical services to industry, where a review was instituted of 'the size and methods of the various services now provided to help industry in order to determine whether they are a proper charge on the state'.[3] However, the overall Conservative industrial policy of disengagement was largely reversed following the events concerning Upper Clyde Shipbuilders and Rolls-Royce, and the change was embodied in the 1972 Industry Act.

In the computer industry a decline in new orders during 1971 and 1972 put considerable strain on the development programme of International Computers and the company decided not to pay an interim dividend in July 1972. The government stepped in with a short-term grant of £14·2 million; they also said they were examining the prospects of a link-up with European firms, but that any such

[1] Civil Service Department, *A Framework for Government Research and Development*, Cmnd 4814, London, HMSO, 1971, para. 6.

[2] Boards were established for ship and marine technology, engineering materials, mechanical engineering and machine tools, metrology and standards, chemicals and minerals, computer systems and electronics, and fundamental standards. There is a Chief Scientist's Board and a separate Requirements Committee to cover the work of the government chemist. Subsequently the board for fundamental standards was wound up. Also, in 1975, a board was established for the garment and allied industries.

[3] Cabinet Office, *The Reorganisation of Central Government*, Cmnd 4506, London, HMSO, 1970, p. 8.

association would have to leave control of the company in this country.

For machine tools too declining orders presented problems, and in March 1972 the government announced a scheme of accelerated and additional public purchases amounting to some £9–£10 million. The figures for home orders did show a marked rise through 1972, but it is quite likely that demand was already picking up independently of the government action.

Conservative support for the machine tool industry does not seem to have had any technological motive, although the support for International Computers might be said to reflect concern for the promotion of science and technology. Probably, however, the greatest impact was made by the Rothschild reforms, which were aimed at obtaining better results for money rather than cutting back on the government's research and development programme. Figures on research and development are available only periodically, with considerable delay, so no effect is measurable yet, but there are no indications that the Conservatives reduced the commitment to industrial research.

To sum up, in the early 1960s science became more of a political topic than it had been before. Government continues to be significantly involved in science and technology and both Parties seem to accept this, particularly the provision of research funds (table 10.3 shows the sources of funds for a number of years). But there have been considerable differences of emphasis between the two Parties, especially regarding the role of science and technology in industry.

The Labour government's 'scientific revolution' argued the need for the wider industrial application of scientific and technical knowledge, and the determination of the priorities for scientific research other than by defence spending. The vehicle for Labour's policy, the Ministry of Technology, became by the end of Labour's office a very large Ministry indeed; whether or not its effects were particularly beneficial is difficult to assess. The Ministry's semi-official biographer has said that 'it could not be claimed that the Ministry had succeeded in its original assignment of "stimulating a major national effort to bring advanced technology and new processes into British industry": it never had anything approaching the resources which would have been required for this purpose'.[1] Lester suggests that: 'Mintech's contribution to the country's economic development has to be assessed strand by strand; and if only a few of the strands turn out to have been strong enough for the job, they should not be despised.'[2] But even to judge strands criteria are needed and it is not clear which are appropriate. With regard to

[1] Clarke, 'Mintech in retrospect', p. 162.   [2] Lester, 'The unmaking of Mintech'.

Table 10.3. *Sources of finance for scientific research and development,*
1958/9–1969/70

	1958/9	1961/2	1964/5	1966/7	1967/8	1968/9	1969/70
	(percentages)						
Government							
Defence	49·0	36·7	32·6	26·7	23·9	21·5	20·9
Civil							
Research councils	3·7	4·4	5·6	5·8	6·0	6·2	6·9
Other	14·2	16·4	16·4	19·3	21·4	22·9	23·9
Total government	66·9	57·5	54·6	51·8	51·3	50·6	51·7
Universities	0·3	0·2	0·2	0·5	0·6	0·6	0·6
Public corporations	1·6	3·5	3·5	3·8	4·6	4·5	4·8
Private industry	28·5	37·0	36·9	38·2	37·5	39·0	37·9
Overseas }	2·7	1·8	2·7	2·8	3·1	3·6	3·6
Others }			2·1	2·9	2·9	1·7	1·4
	(£ million)						
Total	*477·8*	*657·7*	*771·4*	*926·3*	*962·1*	*1016·6*	*1018·9*
Total at 1970 prices	*811·0*	*909·7*	*982·7*	*1093·6*	*1102·1*	*1128·3*	*1151·0*

SOURCES: 1958/9 from Office of the Minister for Science, *Annual Report of the Advisory Council on Scientific Policy 1959–60*, Cmnd 1167, London, HMSO, 1960; other years from CSO, *Research and Development Expenditure*, table 2.

interventions in specific industries, the examples of machine tools and computers were not exactly wild successes, and with regard to general services, the Bolton Committee at least was sceptical.

The Conservatives in 1970 wanted to change their predecessors' policy of specific intervention and, in keeping with their general industrial approach, favoured attempts to produce the right market framework with a set of rules of general application. This they tried both for industry and for government-funded research and development, but in industry they reversed the change in 1972, returning to more detailed intervention in certain cases. The implications of this are important, for if public money is to be spent on supporting firms in difficulties – firms which are not necessarily in the vanguard of scientific development – then it is likely that less will be available for alternative scientific and technical projects.

INTERVENTION IN SPECIFIC INDUSTRIES

The aircraft industry

The present structure of the United Kingdom aircraft industry was determined largely by government policy in the late 1950s. Mergers in 1959 and 1960 inspired by the government (table 10.4) left five main producers, of whom the two in aero-engines, Rolls-Royce and Bristol Siddeley Engines, subsequently merged in 1966. The government was motivated partly by defence policy, which since 1957 had envisaged more guided weapons with a corresponding decline in manned military aircraft, and partly by the realisation that civil aircraft were becoming larger and more costly, resulting in the poor record of government-sponsored civil projects since the war.[1]

Table 10.4. *Changes in the structure of the aircraft industry, 1958–60*

1958	1960
Airframe manufacturers	
Hawker Siddeley Blackburn Folland de Havilland	Hawker Siddeley*
Bristol Aircraft English Electric Aviation Vickers Armstrong Hunting Aircraft	British Aircraft Corporation*
Westland Bristol Helicopter Fairey Saunders Roe	Westland Aircraft*
Auster Miles	Beagle
Handley Page	Handley Page
Scottish Aviation	Scottish Aviation
Short Bros. & Harland	Short Bros. & Harland
Aero-engine manufacturers	
Bristol Aero-Engines Armstrong-Siddeley de Havilland Engines Blackburn Engine	Bristol Siddeley Engines*
Rolls-Royce	Rolls-Royce*

SOURCE: K. Hartley, 'The mergers in the UK aircraft industry 1957–60', *Journal of the Royal Aeronautical Society*, vol. 69, December 1965.

* 5 major producers.

The increasing length and expense of projects had important implications for both civil and military aircraft. The average cost per unit fell significantly if the development costs (which were largely fixed) could

[1] Aircraft and aero-engine projects started between 1945 and 1951 involved an outlay by the government of £71 million, of which, by 1965, some £20 million had been recovered in levies on sales (Ministry of Aviation, *Report of the Committee of Inquiry into the Aircraft Industry*, appendix G).

be spread over increased sales. This effect was reinforced by the reduction, through the learning process, in labour input per unit as production increased; it had been known as early as 1936 that this applied to aircraft production.[1]

The government felt that there would not be enough orders to keep all the existing firms in work and decided to encourage mergers in the industry, using government procurement policy to exert pressure. The Minister of Aviation announced in February 1960 that government orders would, in normal circumstances, be concentrated on the five major groups (table 10.4); also that civil and military requirements would be harmonised with a view to increasing the domestic market for transport aircraft. Aid for civil aircraft projects was to be limited to 50 per cent of the original estimated cost and a standard procedure was established for government recoveries from sales, which had previously been negotiated individually for each project. Military projects continued to be financed mainly on a cost-plus basis.

The government placed contracts for the development of a small number of civil transport aircraft during 1961 and 1962; launching aid was given on the 50 per cent basis to the Trident, the VC10 and the BAC 1-11. Contracts were placed with the two airframe companies, British Aircraft Corporation and Hawker Siddeley, which was consistent with the announced policy, as was the government's refusal to allow the Royal Air Force to buy Herald aircraft from Handley Page early in 1962 on the grounds that the company had refused to involve itself in the merger movement.

The only other new project on the civil side was the development of a supersonic airliner, which from the start the government would consider only in collaboration with the French government and aircraft industry. In March 1962 the two governments announced a joint design study, involving the British Aircraft Corporation in this country and Aerospatiale in France. The reasons for such a project are not clear; a common view is that, the British industry having lost its technological superiority to the United States, it was hoped that this would restore the balance. A Ministry of Aviation witness soon after said it was thought that 'without a project of this kind we should not retain a first class aircraft industry at all'.[2] Costs do not seem to have been much of a consideration. The decision to develop Concorde, as the supersonic airliner was to be called, was made by the two governments in November 1962, committing the United Kingdom to an estimated expenditure

[1] See S. G. Sturmey, 'Cost curves and pricing in aircraft production', *Economic Journal*, vol. 74, December 1964.

[2] House of Commons, *Second Report from the Estimates Committee, Session 1963–64. Transport Aircraft*, London, HMSO, 1964, para. 83.

on development of £75–£85 million. Yet in the same year the government had already cancelled on cost grounds the Rotodyne, a vertical take-off and landing project, and the Blue Water missile.

Indeed, the government seemed to want at least a limited contraction of the industry, for a meeting was held in March 1963 between the Ministry of Aviation, the state airlines and the main aircraft producers, at which it was announced that there would be no new orders in the near future, so that effort should be scaled down.[1] At the time it was thought that this might mean the cancellation of another military project – the TSR-2, designed as both a high altitude bomber and a low-level strike plane – estimates of the cost of which had risen from £80–£90 million in December 1959 to £175–£200 million in January 1963. In September 1963, however, the British Aircraft Corporation were authorised to begin buying parts, which signified the government go-ahead for production. In October the Australian government cancelled an order for the TSR-2 in favour of an American alternative.

The government's financial dealings with the industry featured in two separate Reports early in 1964. The first highlighted the cost of producing the Bloodhound guided missile and found discrepancies relating to the costings used by the firm involved, Ferranti, for the purpose of determining the mark-up allowed on the cost-plus contracts.[2] The Ministry of Aviation set up a committee to examine the position and Ferranti agreed to repay to the government £4½ million of excess profits.

The second Report concerned the whole range of government support for the aircraft industry.[3] The Concorde project was the biggest single item in the Report, which expressed surprise that the contract with the French government contained no 'break clause' to allow for termination by either party, and even more surprise that the Treasury had not authorised the project before the agreement had been made. Concern was also expressed at the possibility that the government might, in the interests of the aircraft industry, exert pressure on the state airlines to buy aircraft they did not want.

During the run-up to the 1964 election the government decided to import United States Phantom jets for the Navy – the first major import of combat aircraft since the immediate postwar years. The balance of payments cost was partially offset by the fact that the engines were made by Rolls-Royce, but the decision was questioned in the Labour election manifesto, which argued that, despite the large sums of money spent on the aircraft industry, lurches in strategic policy,

---

[1] *Economist*, 23 March 1963, p. 1139.

[2] Treasury, *Civil Appropriation Accounts (Classes I–V) 1962–63. Report of the Comptroller and Auditor General*, London, HMSO, 1964, paras. 49–53.

[3] House of Commons, *Second Report from the Estimates Committee, Session 1963–64*.

wrong priorities and mistakes in the choice of aircraft had left a situation in which obsolete types had not been replaced and the country was dependent on the United States.

In December 1964 the new Minister of Aviation established a Committee of Inquiry to look into the aircraft industry. In January 1965 the government announced that Concorde would go ahead. Among the military projects under consideration, the P1154, a strike aircraft intended as a replacement for the Hunter, was cancelled on the grounds that it would not be in service quickly enough and American Phantom jets were ordered instead. The HS681, a transport aircraft, was also judged to be too late to meet requirements and cancelled in favour of an American alternative. On a more positive note, Royal Air Force orders were placed for the vertical take-off and landing Harrier and for an aircraft later called Nimrod for use by Coastal Command. In April 1965 the government announced that TSR-2 was to be cancelled. In the light of these decisions, the Plowden Committee, reporting in December 1965, concluded that if the government did not act to keep the aircraft industry in existence, 'Britain would suffer a serious loss';[1] they hoped and believed, however, that the industry would ultimately be able to thrive with no more support than comparable industries.

Early in 1966 the government announced that it fully accepted the case for a substantial aircraft industry, both civil and military. Negotiations between Rolls-Royce and Bristol Siddeley Engines were under way, leading to a single aero-engine company, but no merger took place between the British Aircraft Corporation and Hawker Siddeley despite press reports of progress, neither was any state shareholding taken in either company as had been recommended by the Plowden Committee.

The rest of the period under Labour was concerned primarily with collaborative projects. Apart from Concorde, for which estimates of development costs rose steadily, there were plans to produce a variable geometry or 'swing-wing' fighter aircraft jointly with France,[2] but despite initial approval in January 1967 the French withdrew in July. The Anglo-French Jaguar, a dual-purpose advanced trainer strike-fighter, was started in 1965 and given a firm endorsement by both governments in 1968; a variable geometry multi-role combat aircraft involving Britain, West Germany and Italy was also started in 1968; a European airbus was started between Britain, France and West Germany, but Britain subsequently withdrew.

At this time Rolls-Royce were developing an engine for the new

[1] Ministry of Aviation, *Report of the Committee of Inquiry into the Aircraft Industry.*
[2] The term refers to the aircraft's ability to alter the angle of its wings during flight.

generation of wide-bodied airbuses which were being designed both in Europe and America. Work had started in 1961 and several innovations, including carbon fibre material instead of metal for the engine fan, seemed to promise a favourable power-to-weight performance. The government provided launching aid at the exceptional rate of 70 per cent of the estimated cost and in March 1968 the Lockheed Company in America ordered this RB 211 engine for its Tri-Star airbus. However, the contractual obligations undertaken by Rolls-Royce in the deal with Lockheed were formidable, given that the engine was to be much more powerful than anything previously produced by the company and the project depended on the success of a number of technological and design improvements. In fact, development problems put a severe financial strain on Rolls-Royce, which led to a high level of temporary borrowing by the company and, in October 1969, to a reduced interim dividend, which, when announced, caused the share price to fall sharply.[1] In August 1969 the government had asked the IRC to enquire into the company's finances. Following prolonged discussions it was announced in May 1970 that the IRC would make a convertible loan of £10 million to Rolls-Royce subject to the company providing regular financial information and the IRC being allowed to nominate a director to the Rolls-Royce board. The IRC also agreed to provide another loan of up to £10 million during 1971.

The government was also involved in other firms in the industry, although in none on the scale of Rolls-Royce. In particular, the Belfast firm of Short Bros. and Harland had been in financial difficulties since the early 1960s. The government already owned a majority shareholding in the company and in 1961 the Northern Ireland government had made a loan of £5 million to help develop the Belfast transport aircraft, of which the Royal Air Force ordered ten. It was later confirmed that the unemployment situation had been a factor influencing this contract.[2] In 1962 Shorts were promised work for at least another year, and in 1963 Westminster and Stormont agreed a £10 million grant to the company – £7½ million from the former and £2½ million from the latter. Although the government did not place any direct orders with Shorts, it arranged for work on orders placed with Hawker Siddeley to be subcontracted to them. In 1966 Shorts again had financial problems: first, an interest-free loan of £2½ million was provided by Westminster and a grant of £325,000 by the Northern Ireland government; Westminster provided further assistance, making a total of £4·45 million in loans and grants during 1966/7 and £3·15 million the following

---

[1] A 38p fall to £1.51 on the day.

[2] Treasury, *Civil Appropriation Accounts (Classes I–V), 1965–66. Report of the Comptroller and Auditor General*, London, HMSO, 1967, para. 87.

year. It was also arranged for some of the work on the RB 211 programme to be subcontracted to Shorts.

In 1966 the Beagle light aircraft company, which had run into difficulties with its Bassett aircraft for the Royal Air Force, the performance being below the stipulated requirements, was taken into public ownership. The government's short-term aim was to maintain employment, but in 1969 the company was allowed to fold, at a total cost to public funds of about £8 million. Another liquidation at about the same time was that of Handley Page.

Following the Conservative election victory in June 1970, the aircraft industry was specifically exempted from their policy of disengagement. Rolls-Royce joined in consultations with the new government over technical problems regarding the RB 211 and the additional cash needed to complete the programme. In November 1970 an agreement was reached providing an extra £60 million: £42 million from the government, £5 million each from the Midland Bank and Lloyds Bank, and £8 million from the Bank of England. Further technical problems and delays, however, led to a steadily worsening situation and in February 1971 Rolls-Royce petitioned for a receiver; the government announced their intention of taking some of the company's assets into public ownership. The principal reason for this move was to escape from the stringent contractual obligations of the deal with Lockheed. The government had clearly decided that the company's involvement in home and collaborative defence projects made it too important to sacrifice, but the device of nationalisation gave them a chance to renegotiate the RB 211 deal. The new agreement, which came into force in September 1971, involved among other things the United States government giving loan guarantees to Lockheed, and Lockheed and their airline customers agreeing to price increases and the forfeit of compensation for late delivery. Estimates made in late 1971 of the cost to the United Kingdom government of this package suggested an outlay of £190–£195 million.

The Concorde project had progressed steadily. The whole picture of estimated costs from the beginning is shown in table 10.5. The French prototype made its maiden flight in March 1969 and the British one in August of the same year; pre-production models were also under construction. The aircraft's development was, however, not without problems, particularly because of its noise level; there were fears that some countries might refuse it permission to land. The effect of this and other uncertainties was that the only firm orders were for nine aircraft from the captive French and British markets, although publicists played up as much as possible interest expressed by China and Iran. The price of the aircraft was not made public, although the figure of

Table 10.5. *Estimates of Concorde's total development cost*

£ million

Date made	At current prices	At constant (1970) prices
November 1962	150–70	200–25
July 1964	280	360
June 1966	500	590
May 1969	730	790
October 1970	825	820
April 1971	885	820
March 1972	970	820
June 1973	1065	820
January 1974	1070	760

SOURCE: House of Commons, *Sixth Report from the Expenditure Committee, Session 1971–72*, vol. I, p. 29.

£13 million was mentioned in the House of Commons and the government stated early in 1972 that this price would include some return on research and development costs. Successive answers to Parliamentary questions in 1972 and 1973 continued to state that there would be some return over production costs, although it was admitted that this would be only a proportion of development costs. Throughout 1972 there were still only nine confirmed orders; nevertheless production continued and in September 1972 the French and British governments authorised an increase in production from ten to sixteen aircraft. By March 1974 the number of firm orders had still not increased. Joint development costs were estimated at £1070 million of which the United Kingdom had still to spend £130 million;[1] none of these costs would be recovered. Losses on production were estimated at between £200 million and £225 million on the sixteen existing aircraft. British Airways considered that operating Concorde could substantially worsen their financial results. In July 1974 the British government agreed with the French not to authorise any further production for the time being.

Assessments of government support for the aircraft industry have often claimed that it is in a different category from other industries, because its role in supplying defence requirements could not for strategic reasons be filled from overseas.[2] Support for the military side need not

---

[1] Both figures at 1974 prices.

[2] This argument for supporting an indigenous military aircraft industry is not questioned here, because defence matters are beyond the scope of this chapter. But it has been elsewhere; see, for example, K. Hartley, *A Market for Aircraft*, London, Institute of Economic Affairs, 1974.

imply support for the civil side, but it is frequently suggested that the marginal cost of supporting civil production, given the defence commitment, is more than outweighed by the advantages. Before discussing any possible advantages, it is worth attempting some rough estimate of that marginal cost.

The Department of Industry's figures for the industry's sales are broken down by markets. Apart from direct government purchases, home civil sales are basically to the state-run airlines, so it seems reasonable to view exports as the only non-government market. On this basis government purchases have ranged from a maximum 80 per cent of total sales in 1964 to 50 per cent in 1974, with a general downward trend. A breakdown of government aid to civil projects is given in table 10.6, where it can be seen that a total of £772·8 million at current prices (£757·7 million at 1970 prices) has been spent in the fourteen years covered, most of that expenditure having gone on two projects, Concorde and the RB 211.

In 1971 the Department of Trade and Industry were asked by a

Table 10.6. *Government assistance to civil aerospace projects, 1960/1–1973/4*

£ million

	Gross expenditure							Receipts
	Airframes		Aero-engines			Total		
	Concorde^a	Other	Concorde^a	RB 211^b	Other	Current prices	1970 prices	
1960/1 to 1964/5	..	..	..	..	..	54·8	73·4	6·6
1965/6	9·2	2·1	10·0	—	1·5	22·8	27·8	1·5
1966/7	18·2	1·2	15·9	—	1·5	36·8	43·4	2·3
1967/8	24·0	9·0	20·5	0·5	2·3	56·3	64·5	1·6
1968/9	31·1	8·3	24·6	10·2	0·9	75·1	83·4	2·3
1969/70	31·0	6·8	19·9	28·2	0·1	86·0	91·5	5·0
1970/1	44·0	4·9	20·5	15·2	0·4	85·0	83·1	6·5
1971/2	40·1	0·9	27·0	69·0	—	137·0	120·7	2·2
1972/3	45·4	0·1	26·9	50·1	3·6	126·1	101·5	3·4
1973/4	47·6	1·4	20·8	20·1	3·0	92·9	68·4	4·9
Total^c	290·6	34·7	186·1	193·3	13·3	772·8	n.a.	36·3
Total^d	277·6	37·4	183·8	172·7	12·8	n.a.	757·7	37·5

SOURCE: Department of Industry, *Business Monitor M9: Survey of the United Kingdom Aerospace Industry, 1975,* London, HMSO, 1975.

^a In addition to the amounts shown there were payments of £12·9 million for capital expenditure and £48 million for other intra-mural expenditure at government establishments.
^b Repayments for short-term production financing are not deducted from amounts shown.
^c At current prices.
^d At 1970 prices.

House of Commons Committee to give reasons for continuing to support the industry.[1] The defence side, they said, was a matter of government policy. For the civil industry there were two principal reasons: the benefit to the balance of payments of export sales and import-savings, and the need to maintain technological skills across the whole field of engineering. The maintenance of employment, although mentioned, was generally regarded as a minor consideration.

It is probably true that employment has not been a prime motive. Two factors suggest that it would be less important for aerospace than for some other industries which the government supports: first, the industry is spread widely throughout the country;[2] secondly, there is a high proportion of skilled and semi-skilled workers compared with the average for manufacturing. Thus, redundancy is less likely to be a long-term problem. Employment has, nevertheless, fallen from 286,000 in 1959 to 210,000 in 1974 – that is by 27 per cent compared with an average fall for manufacturing of 2·5 per cent.

The industry itself relies mainly on the balance of payments argument for continued government support. The Society of British Aerospace Companies maintains that launching aid to civil projects should be regarded as the price paid by the government to allow the industry to earn and save foreign currency, given that all home aircraft sales are indispensable and would otherwise be imported. There is evidence that the government accepts this argument, for in the Department of Trade and Industry's memorandum to the House of Commons Committee the column for home civil sales is, in fact, called 'import-savings'. Table 10.7 shows the crude trade balance for the industry's products, which over the period has invariably been positive.

On the technology side, the industry commands a large proportion of the resources spent on research and development. In 1969/70, the total cost of research and development in private industry was £636 million, of which £169 million (27 per cent) was in the aerospace sector, whereas the weight of the industry in the index of industrial production is 19·81 per 1000. Most of the research and development in the industry relates to military objectives, and its assessment is thus not strictly the task of this chapter. Nevertheless, there are frequent claims by the industry that the national economy benefits from such expenditure through the wider application of new techniques and innovations. However, it seems reasonable to disregard such 'spin-off', on the grounds that, as a side effect, it should not be considered a prime justification for any expenditure; further, it is probably true that

[1] House of Commons, *Sixth Report from the Expenditure Committee, Session 1971–72*.

[2] For example, of the Concorde labour force only 1 per cent was located in special development areas and 4 per cent in intermediate areas.

Table 10.7. *Trade in aerospace products,*[a] *1960–74*

£ million

	Exports[b] f.o.b.	Imports[b] c.i.f.	Crude trade balance
1960	141·7	66·3	75·4
61	150·3	45·5	104·8
62	119·4	47·0	72·4
63	122·1	41·7	80·4
64	102·2	43·4	58·8
65	151·3	47·3	104·0
66	217·1	57·1	160·0
67	204·5	109·1	95·4
68	298·8	240·1	58·7
69	315·7	273·2	42·5
1970	247·4	151·3	96·1
71	303·2	214·1	89·1
72	384·2	225·5	158·7
73	487·9	319·3	168·6
74	595·4	355·4	240·0

SOURCE: Department of Trade.

[a] Excluding guided weapons.
[b] Including returned goods and goods for process.

technological improvements in any sector are more likely to follow from direct work than from spin-off from another sector.

What is clear from the experience of the United Kingdom industry and its competitors is that the development of new aircraft, both military and civil, has become increasingly costly and increasingly lengthy; also there are significant reductions in unit costs over long production runs of individual aircraft. The home market alone is not large enough to provide these cost reductions, which has led the United Kingdom to seek collaboration with other European countries possessing similar markets. Collaborative projects, both military and civil, have not, however, been without problems. The military projects are not easily evaluated, but there are reasonable grounds for thinking that, first, the process of international collaboration itself involves extra costs of development through the organisational constraints which are imposed and, secondly, that the expected gains from spreading costs over a larger number of sales may not materialise if several variants of a basic design are produced to conform with different countries' national requirements. On the civil side collaborative experience has been dominated by Concorde, which must surely be considered a financial disaster. The United Kingdom government has since shown itself unwilling to finance further major civil projects.

Overall, despite the military complications and the consequent problems of determining the actual benefit to the balance of payments, the basic argument for supporting this industry is not much different from that for other industries; the issue is still whether the resources could be of more benefit to the national economy if used elsewhere. It is likely that resources released would be used elsewhere, but whether this would be more beneficial, particularly in terms of the balance of payments, is not clear. Perhaps, given the strength of the military and industrial lobby, it is unrealistic to envisage much reduction in support, but the government might consider spreading its largesse, instead of concentrating on one or two expensive projects. (After the 1974 elections, the Labour government decided to take the industry into public ownership, and British Aerospace formally took control in April 1977.)

The shipbuilding industry

Since the war the significance of shipbuilding in British manufacturing industry has declined, but it is still very important in the regions where it is concentrated, particularly on the Clyde and in the North East of England. Against a background of rapidly rising world output – world launchings increased from 3·6 million gross tons in 1951 to 8·3 million in 1960 – the British industry failed to increase its output and by 1960 its share of world tonnage launched had fallen to 16 per cent compared with 37 per cent in 1951; employment had declined from 216,000 in 1957 to 190,000 in 1960. This concerned the government, both because it affected the areas where regional unemployment was already above the national average and because of the adverse effect on our balance of payments. Other aspects of the industry causing concern were the organisation of its research effort and its poor labour relations. Between 1949 and 1959, shipbuilding and ship-repairing lost more days per employee through strikes than any other industry, a high proportion of them involving demarcation issues between craftsmen of different unions.

A subcommittee of the Shipbuilding Advisory Committee, a body with representatives of shipowners, shipbuilders and unions, was therefore set up in February 1960 to examine the industry's prospects and it reported in April 1961.[1] Its most important proposals concerned credit for new ships. The United Kingdom, like other shipbuilding countries, offered credit to foreign buyers; Japan in particular had led the way in cheap credit for ships, with favourable fixed interest rates and longer-term loans than were generally available. In the United Kingdom loans from the commercial banks were backed by guarantees

---

[1] Ministry of Transport, *Shipbuilding Advisory Committee. Report of the Subcommittee on Prospects*, London, HMSO, 1961.

from the Export Credit Guarantee Department of the Board of Trade. The Report argued that, when even the most efficient yards in the United Kingdom were failing to get orders because their competitors could offer better credit terms, there was a strong case for enabling home producers to meet those terms. It also suggested that any forthcoming naval orders should be placed quickly to help the industry over what was seen as a temporary lean spell. For the industry itself, it urged action to achieve better labour relations and suggested amalgamations between yards where feasible.

A number of other Reports followed, and early in 1962 the credit situation for exports (including ships) was eased when the banks agreed to provide medium-term finance for up to five years at a fixed $5\frac{1}{2}$ per cent interest rate. The Bank of England also extended its scheme (introduced in 1961) for refinancing certain loans for exports, thus encouraging the banks to continue to make export credit available. For shipbuilding this meant that Britain could compete more favourably for foreign orders, although there were anomalies, in that home owners could not get such good credit terms as foreign buyers and might well be encouraged to place orders abroad. In the light of this situation, and in the face of a continuing fall in employment and orders, a scheme was introduced in June 1963 whereby United Kingdom owners ordering from British yards could obtain credit of up to 80 per cent of the value of the ship, repayable over five to ten years at rates of interest related to the government borrowing rate, which in fact varied between $4\frac{1}{2}$ and $5\frac{3}{8}$ per cent. The scheme had a limit of £30 million, but this was quickly reached and in July it was raised to £60 million; in October it was raised to £75 million specifically to finance the Q4 liner for Cunard. Unlike the loans for foreign buyers of ships, which were made through the banks, the money for this scheme came from the government under the Shipbuilding Credit Act 1964. The loans were swiftly taken up and no new loans were considered after 31 May 1964.

In 1964 the Labour government transferred the industry to the Board of Trade, appointed a Minister with special responsibility for shipping and shipbuilding and set up an independent inquiry (the Geddes Committee). Before the Committee reported there was little scope for action, although in October 1965 the government lent £1 million to Fairfields to keep the yard in operation until the Geddes proposals were known. The loan did not last long enough and in December 1965 the company again approached the government. A rescue was organised in which the government, private industry and the trade unions all provided capital for the venture; one of the hopes was that this tripartite involvement might lead to better labour relations.

The *Geddes Report*, published in March 1966, took the view that reasons such as defence, the balance of payments and employment were not in themselves sufficient to justify state intervention, so that if the industry could not expect to become competitive and profitable it might be better to let it decline.[1] However, the Committee thought that a growing world demand for merchant tonnage provided the chance of a successful future for British shipbuilding – a chance which depended on the reorganisation of existing yards into larger units to benefit from economies of scale. They recommended temporary financial help to effect such a reorganisation, administered by a Shipbuilding Industry Board with a life of five years. Money should be available to pay for consultants' advice on regroupings, to provide loans to help with working capital and extra investment during amalgamation, and to compensate for any transitional losses. A temporary credit scheme with a limit of £30 million should give British shipowners the same terms as those available to foreign buyers. There should also be relief from indirect taxation for home shipbuilding similar to that existing for exports in the export rebate, on the grounds that shipbuilding competed in a truly international market, with no distinctions between production for export or home buyers; further, other shipbuilding countries provided similar indirect tax relief. Finally, the Report recommended that the government's naval work should be concentrated on specialist yards, rather than spread around, as it had been previously.

In May 1966 the government announced their acceptance of these proposals, and the Shipbuilding Industry Board began work in August, although the Shipbuilding Industry Act setting it up was not passed until the following year. In September 1966 the government introduced the indirect tax refund known as 'shipbuilders' relief', amounting to 2 per cent of the gross value of ships completed. During the first months of its life the Shipbuilding Industry Board helped two amalgamations: the first concerned four Tyneside yards and created Swan Hunter and Tyne Shipbuilders, the only money involved being a small grant towards consultancy expenses; the second involved five yards on the Upper Clyde and formed Upper Clyde Shipbuilders in August 1967, with the Shipbuilding Industry Board providing small consultancy grants and a loan of £3½ million.

Further regroupings took place during 1968, and in its Report for the year ending March 1969 the Shipbuilding Industry Board announced that, of the 27 shipbuilding undertakings covered by the *Geddes Report*, 21 had merged into seven groups and two were no longer building ships.[2] These and subsequent amalgamations are shown in

---

[1] Board of Trade, *Shipbuilding Inquiry Committee 1965–66. Report.*

[2] Ministry of Technology, *Shipbuilding Industry Board. Report and Accounts for the year ended March 31, 1969*, London, HMSO, 1969.

table 10.8. The remaining yard, which did not lend itself to regrouping because of its geographical isolation, was Harland and Wolff in Belfast. The Board nevertheless encouraged the company to modernise and expand its facilities, and provided loans and grants to aid the construction of a new dock in which very large ships could be built.

Also under the Shipbuilding Industry Act there was a credit scheme with a limit of £200 million – considerably greater than the £30 million recommended by the Geddes Committee. The credit was

Table 10.8. *Changes in the structure of the shipbuilding industry, 1966–71*

1966	1971
East Scotland	
Robb ⎫ Caledon ⎬ Burntisland ⎭	Robb Caledon
Lower Clyde	
Scotts ⎫ Lithgows ⎬ Greenock Dockyard ⎭	Scott Lithgow
Upper Clyde	
John Brown ⎫ Chas. Connell ⎪ Alex. Stephen ⎬ Fairfield ⎪ Yarrow (Shipbuilders)* ⎭	Upper Clyde Shipbuilders
Tyne/Tees	
Vickers (Walker Naval Yard) ⎫ Swan Hunter ⎪ Hawthorn Leslie ⎪ John Redhead ⎬ Furness ⎪ Smith's Dock ⎭	Swan Hunter
Wear	
Austin & Pickersgill ⎫ Bartram ⎬	Austin & Pickersgill
Doxford ⎫ James Laing ⎬ J. L. Thompson ⎭	Doxford & Sunderland
Southampton	
John I. Thorneycroft ⎫ Vosper ⎬	Vosper Thorneycroft

SOURCE: Shipbuilding Industry Board, *Shipbuilding Industry Board 1967–1971*, London, 1971.
  * Subsequently disengaged.

provided in the same way as export credit – through the banks at a fixed $5\frac{1}{2}$ per cent interest rate – and was available to British ship-owners buying from British yards and with guarantees given by the Ministry of Technology on the recommendation of the Shipbuilding Industry Board.[1]

Export and shipbuilding credit was specifically exempted from the restrictions following devaluation in November 1967, and the combined effect of the credit scheme and the change in exchange rates was a rise in orders during 1967 and 1968, especially new orders for export. Home orders soon reached the limit of £200 million for loan guarantees and, in December 1968, the government raised the limit to £400 million. The Shipbuilding Industry Board concluded that there was no doubt that the scheme provided a powerful stimulus for United Kingdom owners to place orders in British yards.[2]

Despite this rise in orders for the industry as a whole, Upper Clyde Shipbuilders were in serious difficulties; there were losses on both current and new contracts caused by cost increases and late completions. In February 1969 the Shipbuilding Industry Board provided further grants, while requesting the company to produce a plan for achieving eventual viability. The first plan was not acceptable, but after negotiations a revised plan was produced and accepted. The Shipbuilding Industry Board provided a further £2 million in grants and £3 million to purchase shares in the company; the board of directors was reconstituted and a managing director appointed who was considered to have a background of success in shipbuilding. By this stage the Shipbuilding Industry Board had injected approximately £6 million in grants, nearly £5 million in loans and £3 million in shares into Upper Clyde Shipbuilders and its subsidiary Yarrow (Shipbuilders).

In the autumn of 1969 Upper Clyde Shipbuilders again approached the Shipbuilding Industry Board for help, but this was refused on the commercial grounds required by the Act. However, the government decided to provide a further loan of £7 million 'in view of the wider economic, regional and Scottish considerations'.[3] Yarrow (Shipbuilders), which specialised in naval work, also had poor financial results and early in 1970 it was agreed that Yarrow, which had sold a 51 per cent shareholding to Upper Clyde Shipbuilders on the group's formation, should repurchase this and withdraw from the group. This withdrawal was under way but not completed by the general election of June 1970.

---

[1] See appendix II to chapter 7 above.

[2] Ministry of Technology, *Shipbuilding Industry Board. Report and Accounts for the year ended March 31, 1969*.

[3] House of Commons, *Hansard*, 11 December 1969, col. 666.

Another company in trouble in early 1970 was the Merseyside firm of Cammell Laird, where shipbuilding losses threatened the rest of the company's activities in engineering. The government asked the IRC to investigate; the IRC insisted as a precondition that the shipbuilding section should become independent of the rest of the group. This having been done, the IRC made loans of £3·8 million to the Laird Group and purchased shares at a cost of £1·2 million. The money was used to make good losses on shipbuilding and the government itself purchased for £1·5 million 50 per cent of the shares in the shipbuilding company, which retained the name of Cammell Laird.

There were also plans in January 1970 to increase the credit scheme to £600 million and it was decided to give the Shipbuilding Industry Board, which was due to close at the end of 1970, a further year of life. In July 1970, following the election, the Conservative government announced that they would introduce legislation similar to that planned by Labour to increase the credit limit for home shipowners; in February 1971 the limit was raised to £700 million. Even this appeared insufficient and in August 1971 the limit was raised to £1000 million; however there was no attempt to prolong the Shipbuilding Industry Board's legal life beyond the end of 1971. The policy of 'disengagement' was put to the test in a minor way in September 1970, when the Conservative government decided not to continue a subsidy to the small Palmers ship-repair yard at Hebburn-on-Tyne.

In late 1970 Harland and Wolff was also in financial difficulties and approached the Shipbuilding Industry Board, which agreed to provide grants of £3·5 million on the understanding that the government would also provide funds. The chairman of the company resigned in December 1970; then the government took control of the yard and invited tenders for it. Of the four offers considered the one chosen was that which left the existing owners in control. The Northern Ireland government announced their support in principle and, in July 1971, subscribed £4 million for shares, with the intention of disposing of the shareholding at an appropriate time, and promised a grant to cover the losses on existing fixed price contracts and a further £2–3 million aid in the future. In May 1972 they provided a grant of £13·9 million to cover previous losses and announced that the modernisation programme costing £35 million was to receive government support.

In October 1970 the Department of Trade and Industry withheld any new credit guarantees for shipowners wishing to order vessels from Upper Clyde Shipbuilders on the advice of the government's director on the board. The board, however, continued to explore other solutions to their problems, including negotiating with customers for increases in contract prices. In February 1971 the government announced that Yarrow (Shipbuilders) had been hived-off, and that, because of the importance of its naval work, the Ministry of Defence had arranged a loan of £4·5 million to cover this company's financial difficulties; the broad lines of a capital reconstruction for Upper Clyde Shipbuilders had also been agreed and credit guarantees for the company would soon be resumed.

That company, however, continued to have difficulties with working capital and in June 1971 approached the government with a request for £5–£6 million of immediate aid, without which it could not continue to trade. The government rejected the appeal and Upper Clyde Shipbuilders petitioned for a liquidator. The government appointed a committee to examine the prospects for regrouping the Upper Clyde yards and their Report recommended that, of the four yards left after the withdrawal of Yarrow, shipbuilding should continue at Govan (formerly Fairfields) and Linthouse; the other two yards, at Clydebank and Scotstoun, should be disposed of by the liquidator. The government accepted these recommendations, but the workforce occupied the yards, demanding that all four should be kept in operation. The government went ahead with the proposals for Govan Shipbuilders, as the new company was to be called, but agreed that proposals for the inclusion of the Scotstoun yard could be reconsidered. The Clydebank yard featured during the latter part of 1971 and early 1972 in several well-publicised attempts to arrange a buyer. Eventually, in February 1972, the Department of Trade and Industry agreed to provide an undisclosed sum to the Marathon Company of Texas under the Local Employment Act, and in April that company took over the yard for the purpose of building off-shore oil drilling equipment. £35 million was injected into Govan Shipbuilders, which was to include the Scotstoun yard – £17 million for losses on Upper Clyde Shipbuilders' contracts and £18 million for reconstruction.

Further assistance was also given to Cammell Laird: in August 1971 a loan of £3 million while the company's future was reviewed, a further loan of £3 million in April 1972 and, in September 1972, a loan of up to £14 million under the Industry Act for a modernisation programme.

The 1972 budget had included a scheme which gave grants to shipbuilders of 10 per cent of the contract value of work undertaken during 1972; the grants were tapered and the rate was to be 3 per cent in 1974, when the scheme was to end. In addition, there were possibilities of further loans under the Industry Act, which provided for the credit limit for home shipbuilding to be increased by Order from £1000 million to £1400 million in future if considered necessary. A White Paper announced an appraisal of the long-term prospects for shipbuilding, and the consultants Booz-Allen were commissioned to undertake this.[1] There were also important changes in the system of providing credit: the banks would continue to provide the initial finance, but if the combined total of shipbuilding and export loans exceeded 18 per cent of the banks' current account deposits, the excess would be refinanced.[2]

The Booz-Allen Report, published in May 1973, examined the state of world shipbuilding and the record of the United Kingdom industry.[3] It looked at five possible future situations for British shipyards in the light of different combinations of government support and industry performance. At one extreme it predicted that, if the United Kingdom industry failed to achieve any significant increase in efficiency and received little government support, it would decline until by 1982 its annual output was 600,000 gross registered tons and employment only 25,000 (at the time employment in shipbuilding was about three times this figure and 1972 output was 1·2 million gross registered tons). The most optimistic assumptions – improved performance and a high level of government support – produced estimates for 1982 of an output of 2·5 million gross registered tons and employment of 39,000; the government's contribution to capital costs would then have to be £250 million up to 1977 and £27 million a year thereafter to 1982. All the predictions involved a decline in employment, and even the lowest level of support still meant £60–£65 million in previous commitments.

Neither side of the industry accepted the Booz-Allen estimates on employment. Following an upturn in orders after the Report was prepared the government too was more optimistic. Aid was made available under the Industry Act, which allowed support for individual projects in the assisted areas. Under the Act the most favourable terms were for projects which increased employment, but in view of the Booz-Allen call for big improvements in output per man, these favourable terms were made available to shipbuilding projects even if they did not increase employment. In October 1973 a loan of £9 million was made to Sunderland Shipbuilders to modernise its Pallion Yard.

In May 1973 it was announced in Belfast that the United Kingdom government's contribution to the Harland and Wolff modernisation programme announced earlier was to be £23·5 million in loans and grants. The company's progress was, however, considerably delayed by a serious strike during the latter part of 1973, and towards the end of the year it was announced that £10 million of the company's debt to the government would be converted into shares and a loan guarantee

[1] Department of Trade and Industry, *Industrial and Regional Development*, Cmnd 4942, London, HMSO, 1972.
[2] See pages 358–9 in chapter 7 above.
[3] Department of Trade and Industry, *British Shipbuilding 1972*, London, HMSO, 1973.

of up to £10 million would be provided. No significant change was planned in the modernisation programme, which implied that the total input of public funds was likely to be greater than the previous estimate.

Looking at the overall picture, many different forms of assistance have been used, which makes a coherent summary of financial aid to the industry difficult. Table 10·9 gives most of the expenditure, totalling £167·9 million at current prices, £153·2 million at 1970 prices, over the period 1965/6 to 1973/4, although it does not include all the payments made through the Northern Ireland government to Harland and Wolff. In addition there were two further forms of assistance: relief from duty on imported goods used in the manufacture of ships and (more important) subsidised credit for home shipowners. Although the latter involves no direct financial assistance to the shipbuilder, it almost certainly increases demand and diverts it to the home producer. Introduced briefly in 1963/4, the scheme started in earnest in 1967. By the end of 1971 the Shipbuilding Industry Board had recommended guarantees in respect of ships with a contract value of about £1095 million. Since only a proportion of the total cost is lent (up to a maximum of 80 per cent) and not all of the orders would materialise, the actual guarantee figure is somewhat less; guarantees totalling £642

Table 10.9. *Government assistance to the shipbuilding industry,* *1965/6–1973/4*

£ million

	Expenditure in Appropriation Accounts	SIB loans	Other payments	Ship-builders' relief	Total	
					Current prices	1970 prices
1965/6	1·5	—	—	—	1·5	1·8
1966/7	—	—	—	0·4	0·4	0·5
1967/8	0·4	3·5	—	3·5	7·4	8·5
1968/9	5·8	5·9	—	3·6	15·3	17·0
1969/70	16·7	3·6	—	3·7	24·0	25·5
1970/1	8·5	2·6	3·8[a]	4·7	19·6	19·1
1971/2	10·2	3·0	18·4[b]	5·2	36·8	32·4
1972/3	23·3	—	—	4·8	28·1	22·7
1973/4	28·5	—	—	6·3	34·8	25·7
Total	94·9	18·6	22·2	32·2	167·9	153·2

SOURCES: Treasury, *Civil Appropriation Accounts*; Northern Ireland Government, Department of Finance, *Appropriation Accounts*; Ministry of Technology, *Shipbuilding Industry Board Report and Accounts*; Exchequer and Audit Department, *Defence Accounts*, London, HMSO (annual to 1973–74); Customs and Excise, *Report of the Commissioners*.

[a] Loan by the IRC to the Laird Group in respect of Cammell Laird shipyard.

[b] £4·5 million loan by the Ministry of Defence to Yarrow plus £13·9 million grant by the Northern Ireland government to Harland and Wolff.

million (net of repayments) were current on 31 March 1974.[1] The element of government subsidy is extremely difficult to assess. Indeed, before 1972 the banks themselves provided the credit at a fixed rate and the Bank of England undertook the refinancing, so that no costs were borne directly by the state. In the two financial years 1972/3 and 1973/4, the Department of Trade and Industry refinanced loans total- ling £145 million, of which £80 million represented an increase in the banks' entitlement and £45 million a transfer from the Bank of England of loans already refinanced by them. Also, from 1972 the government agreed to 'top up' the difference between the fixed interest rate and the market rate; the scale of this subsidy was revealed in October 1974, when the government paid the banks £25·5 million to clear the arrears that they were owed. Calculations suggest that this is consistent with the banks receiving approximately the Bank of England minimum lending rate, although probably slightly more in 1972/3 when the minimum lending rate was lower. If the various credit schemes had not existed, finance for shipowners would have had to be provided at market rates and, while these vary between different classes of borrowers, they would probably have been 1½–2 per cent above the minimum lending rate.

Looking at the distribution of government aid, it is clear that Upper Clyde Shipbuilders, Harland and Wolff, and Cammel Laird have benefited to a far greater extent than their competitors. The motive for supporting these particular companies seems to have been a desire to avoid the effects of their collapse on local employment. Certainly the support for the industry announced in July 1973 was framed more in terms of shipbuilding's importance to areas of high unemployment than its intrinsic importance to the national economy; so regional considera- tions have been paramount.

Employment has, nevertheless, continued to fall and by 1974 was less than 70 per cent of the 1960 level (compared with a fall of 2·5 per cent over the same period in manufacturing employment as a whole). Increased productivity has been a call common to the various Reports on the industry and, although this kept broadly in step with the average for manufacturing industry up to 1970, since that date it has shown a significant divergence. In some degree this reflects the extent to which the large fall in employment in the industry took place in the early 1960s; by 1970, in contrast, the labour force had been largely stabilised and it has declined only slightly since then. There is clearly a conflict between the objectives of increasing productivity and maintaining employment when the market is declining.

Apart from protecting employment, other reasons have been put

[1] Department of Industry, *Industry Act 1972. Annual report for the year ended March 31, 1974,* London, HMSO, 1974.

forward to justify government support of shipbuilding: for example, that for defence purposes it is important to have a home shipbuilding capability. The government's naval work, however, (apart from that carried out in its own dockyards) is almost exclusively contracted to three specialist companies, Vosper Thorneycroft, Vickers and Yarrow, so even the strategic motive does not help to explain the size and breadth of government aid that has been given. It has also been suggested that because the British shipping industry is large there should be the capacity to supply it, and this is often linked to the benefit to the balance of payments – a ship built at home is one less imported. A longer view suggests that if protection was abandoned and the home industry declined it would be costly to revive and, with foreign suppliers in a strong position, they could then charge higher prices with less risk of competition. However, the main justification for the government's support has been the high level of aid in other major shipbuilding countries, most of which have some or all of a range of subsidies similar to those given here. The OECD set up a working party with the aim of progressively reducing indirect and direct subsidies to shipbuilding, passing a resolution to this effect in 1972, but the British government, while declaring agreement, has increased support for the industry in recent years. Probably the government was genuinely in favour of reducing the commitment, but once an industry in an area of high unemployment has received support it becomes increasingly difficult to withdraw.

Certainly it is clear that government involvement in shipbuilding has increased significantly since the early 1960s. Whatever the stated intentions of the two political Parties, at the end of 1973 the government owned Govan Shipbuilders entirely, also 50 per cent of Cammell Laird and 47·6 per cent of Harland and Wolff. The Labour government elected in February 1974 had plans to nationalise the industry. These were realised, after considerable delays, with the creation of British Shipbuilders in July 1977.

The textile industry

In the 1960s the cotton industry was affected by falling demand at home and abroad, and by increasing penetration of the home market by cheap imports from the Asian Commonwealth. In these circumstances there was an understandable reluctance to replace outmoded machinery for, even if demand increased, there was plenty of spare capacity which could be reintroduced at low cost, particularly in the prevailing conditions of high unemployment and low wages. The industry, through its representative body the Cotton Board, continually urged the government to stem the flow of cheap imports, and although compulsory restrictions were refused on the grounds that they would conflict with Commonwealth Preference, so-called 'voluntary' quotas were negotiated with Hong Kong, India and Pakistan. The government considered the industry a special case for assistance because of its geographical concentration in Lancashire,[1] where employment in textiles had fallen from about 330,000 at the end of 1954 to 250,000 four years later.[2]

In 1959 the Cotton Industry Act was passed, introducing schemes to reduce excess capacity and encourage re-equipment. Firms were compensated for scrapping existing machinery, the cost being met two thirds by the government and one third from compulsory levies on the industry; then 25 per cent grants were available towards approved re-equipment. Unlike an earlier scheme in 1948, there was no attempt to impose any particular pattern of change on the industry; any manufacturer who complied with the schemes' requirements could obtain the compensation and grants. The schemes were administered through the Cotton Board and the government seems to have followed the industry's advice fairly closely in framing this assistance. The estimated cost of the schemes was £30 million over five years, but the outlay on re-equipment was smaller than expected and actual expenditure was some £25 million in current prices, £33·7 million in 1970 prices (table 10.10).

At the end of 1962 the voluntary agreements with Hong Kong, India

Table 10.10. *Costs of the cotton industry reorganisation schemes,*
1959/60–1966/7

£ thousand

	Compensation	Re-equipment	Total Current prices	Total 1970 prices
1959/60	941	—	941	1,374
1960/1	8,248	180	8,428	12,074
1961/2	1,375	1,765	3,140	4,343
1962/3	408	2,772	3,180	4,274
1963/4	371	2,901	3,272	4,305
1964/5	75	3,094	3,169	4,037
1965/6	2	2,622	2,624	3,204
1966/7	—	73	73	86
Total	11,420	13,407	24,827	33,697

SOURCE: Treasury, *Civil Appropriation Accounts* (various years).

[1] Board of Trade, *Reorganisation of the Cotton Industry*, Cmnd 744, London, HMSO, 1959, para. 5.
[2] Cotton Board estimates quoted in C. Miles, *Lancashire Textiles*, Cambridge University Press, 1968.

and Pakistan were re-negotiated for a further three years, but this only partly alleviated the industry's continuing concern over cheap imports. Imports increased throughout 1963 and 1964 and this, although partly due to a cyclical upswing, together with the approaching end of the voluntary agreements, led the Cotton Board to present the government in July 1964 with a memorandum, which argued that more effective control of imports was needed to help the industry continue the process of modernisation and restructuring.[1]

The need for further stability in the home market was accepted; the general election in October 1964 forestalled Conservative plans, but the Labour government adopted a similar policy. Although a tariff on imports was not acceptable, quantitative restrictions were imposed for five years from January 1966 to prevent imports from low-cost countries rising further as a percentage of home consumption.

At this time reorganisation and restructuring in the industry were linked primarily to the activities of the major firms, which had nearly all acquired smaller companies engaged in different processes, thus increasing vertical concentration. Between 1960 and 1966 six major companies in the industry bought from 100 to 150 smaller companies.[2]

Courtaulds and Imperial Chemical Industries were important producers of synthetic fibres and the latter, although not engaged in acquiring smaller companies, in 1962 attempted unsuccessfully to take over the former. Considerable pressure for some control of mergers followed this, but in July 1964, in reply to a question in Parliament concerning the behaviour of Courtaulds and Viyella, the contribution to the modernisation of the industry made by vertical integration was emphasised.[3]

The Labour government, however, referred the supply of man-made cellulosic fibres to the Monopolies Commission in June 1965; meanwhile Courtaulds continued to acquire smaller companies. The Monopolies Commission found that a monopoly situation did exist,[4] and their main recommendations were that import duties on cellulosic fibres should be reduced; also that Courtaulds should sell to all customers only at published prices, end their agreements with EFTA competitors and not, without Board of Trade permission, make further acquisitions in any sector of the textile and clothing industries if their share of capacity would then be too large (the figure mentioned was 25 per cent).

[1] *Board of Trade Journal*, 31 July 1964.
[2] Miles, *Lancashire Textiles*, p. 93. The six companies were Courtaulds, English Sewing Cotton, Viyella, Calico Printers Association, Carrington and Dewhurst, and Ashton Brothers.
[3] *Board of Trade Journal*, 7 August 1964.
[4] Monopolies Commission, *Man-made Cellulosic Fibres. Report on the Supply*, London, HMSO, 1968.

Monopolies Commission recommendations carry no force in themselves and the government failed to act upon these proposals. The President of the Board of Trade said that he was reviewing the tariff on cellulosic fibres, but that other decisions would have to await a forthcoming study by the Textile Council (which had in 1967 replaced the Cotton Board). Courtaulds were also permitted to take over Ashton Brothers, itself one of the larger firms in the industry, in June 1968; in at least one sector – cotton spinning – this involved adding to a market share which was already more than 25 per cent.

The Report of the Textile Council published in March 1969 recommended a dismantling of quotas and their replacement by a tariff;[1] in July 1969 it was announced that this would be done with effect from January 1972. The trend towards increasing vertical integration in the industry was seen by the Report as likely to create a strong yet competitive situation provided that some medium and small firms remained. The Council thought that there was still scope for rationalisation in the industry, particularly among smaller companies.

By early 1969, following further concentration in the industry, the major companies were Courtaulds, Coats Paton, English Calico, Viyella, Carrington and Dewhurst, and Imperial Chemical Industries. A bid for English Calico by Courtaulds was withdrawn pending an inquiry into the industry's structure, which concluded that there should be no further mergers between any of the large firms for the time being, although there was still scope for rationalisation involving smaller firms, or the transfer of capacity between the larger companies.[2] Late in 1969, however, Imperial Chemical Industries decided to acquire Viyella – an important customer for its fibres – and to merge it with Carrington and Dewhurst, another important customer. Following a special Report, the government approved the merger subject to three conditions: Imperial Chemical Industries should not have more than a 35 per cent holding in the combined Carrington Viyella company, this holding should not influence the new company in its choice of fibres and the new company should have an independent chairman.[3]

One of the last moves of the Labour government in June 1970 was to ask the IRC to consider applications for finance for re-equipment by medium-sized and smaller companies in the cotton and allied textiles industry. It was envisaged that under the scheme loans might total £10 million, with the smallest loan £100,000.

The Conservatives were pledged to reduce the government's involve-

[1] Textile Council, *Cotton and Allied Textiles: a report on present performance and future prospects*, Manchester, 1969.
[2] House of Commons, *Hansard*, 30 June 1969, cols. 41–3.
[3] Ibid. 25 March 1970, cols. 1432–4.

ment in private industry, but in textiles direct involvement was not great. A time-limit was placed on the IRC scheme to finance re-equipment, but in any case its take-up had been poor. It was also decided in February 1971 to dissolve the Textile Council from March 1972.

A tariff on Commonwealth imports was introduced in January 1972; quota restrictions were also retained in order to avoid disruption of the home market by a surge of imports from many sources. Part of the problem was that the United States had agreed voluntary restraints on imports with certain Asian countries and the British government feared that goods might be diverted to the United Kingdom if quotas were lifted. It was also anticipated that retaining quotas would make for smoother adjustment to a common EEC policy, because the other Community members were generally more protectionist than the United Kingdom.

The other important intervention by the Conservative government was in wool textiles. Following the 1972 Industry Act and consultations with the Wool Textile Economic Development Committee, the government announced in July 1973 a scheme to encourage firms to modernise their machinery and rationalise their facilities.[1] Grants and loans of varying amounts were made available under the Industry Act for projects which involved re-equipment, rebuilding, more comprehensive development and the elimination of marginal capacity. The scheme was open until the end of 1975 provided work would be completed by the end of 1977. Projects below a minimum size did not qualify.

Looking at the industry's performance overall, output per head has increased faster than in manufacturing as a whole, especially since 1966, and employment has fallen by about half between 1960 and 1974. Government support has concentrated on those sectors which have been in the most rapid decline – cotton spinning and weaving and, latterly, woollen and worsted. The scale of direct assistance has not been particularly great: expenditure under the 1959 Act of £33·7 million at 1970 prices, a small amount of assistance under the IRC scheme and commitments at 31 March 1974 of some £3 million under the Industry Act's wool textile scheme. But since 1958 the country has become increasingly protectionist with regard to textiles: moving from a situation where imports from the Commonwealth came in duty-free, through various stages of voluntary restrictions and formal quotas, to both tariffs and quotas from 1972. New developments will be worked out in conjunction with our EEC partners, but as other EEC countries have generally protected their textile industries more than we have

[1] Ibid. 19 July 1973, cols. 715–17.

there seems little likelihood that the trend will be reversed. The textile trade is covered by GATT and the EEC hopes to put forward a common policy when the agreement comes up for renewal at the end of 1977.

Table 10.11. *Crude trade balance^a in textiles and clothing, 1963–73*

£ million[b]

	Textile fibres	Textile yarns, fabrics, etc.	Clothing
1963	−159·2	+115·0	−24·7
64	−170·7	+106·2	−29·0
65	−140·4	+131·3	−7·2
66	−129·4	+111·9	−15·3
67	−116·2	+76·5	−19·1
68	−126·2	+78·1	−25·6
69	−108·6	+121·9	−16·0
1970	−87·5	+140·4	−6·3
71	−62·7	+100·9	−48·7
72	−105·6	+75·7	−74·5
73	−150·3	+74·6	−154·0

SOURCE: *Board of Trade Journal | Trade and Industry.*

[a] Exports f.o.b. and imports c.i.f.
[b] At current prices.

The effect of the import restrictions is difficult to assess. Table 10.11 shows the crude trade balance in textiles and clothing. The overall situation was relatively stable through most of the 1960s, with some tendency for the deficit on fibres to fall as man-made fibres replaced the traditional ones. The surplus on yarns and fabrics fell in the mid-1960s, but recovered towards the end of the decade. The deficit on clothing was fluctuating with no clear trend up to 1970, but since then there has been a rapid rise in imports, because clothing is not covered by the restrictions. Since 1971 the balance on fibres, yarns and fabrics also seems to have deteriorated. There has been a gradual fall in imports of woven cotton piece goods and the percentage share of the main individual Asian suppliers taken as a whole has remained broadly the same; the restrictions seem to have achieved their object here. But for the industry as a whole the restrictions have not been a significant barrier in recent years because of the growth in imports of made-up articles.

Government influence on the structure of the industry reflects at first a neutral attitude, and then positive approval of the trend to increasing vertical integration, which proceeded rapidly in the middle 1960s. But by the late 1960s official opinion was that the trend had gone far enough, and since then the structure has remained reasonably stable among the larger firms.

Vertical integration has been seen, particularly by the fibre producers, as a means of ensuring a continued demand for their products in fluctuating market conditions. The possible disadvantages to the consumer pointed out by the Monopolies Commission include the restriction of choice by the fibre-using subsidiaries, who would be expected to use only the products of the parent company, and the deterrent to any new firm thinking of entering fibre production.[1] The government seems to have shown less concern than the Monopolies Commission for the possible disadvantages, however, for neither Party has made any attempt to reverse the trend. And even after the Labour government decided to call a halt in 1969, at what was a quite advanced stage of vertical integration within the industry, the Conservatives in 1971 still permitted Imperial Chemical Industries to take over four of its yarn-texturising customers.

THE LESSONS OF INDUSTRIAL POLICY

This chapter has outlined the most important developments in a period of considerable growth in government involvement in private industry. There is a distinction between making rules to govern the behaviour of industrial companies and policies which involve the government more directly in industry – between holding the ring and putting on the boxing gloves – and if it is the latter role which has received more attention, that is partly because increasing intervention has been characteristic of the period. (Table 10.12 draws together from earlier tables government expenditure on certain industries, illustrating the rising cost of such selective assistance.) However, the development of this approach can have repercussions for the government's other role as industrial referee, because its ability to maintain a credible, impartial system for policing conduct in industry generally could be prejudiced by its own direct involvement in certain cases. Although conflict between the two roles is not inevitable, the possibility clearly exists.

The government's role as industrial referee is expressed principally through competition policy, whereby the state establishes rules to govern the operation of the market – rules which, since 1965, have included powers to stop mergers. The interventionist role is exemplified at least in part by policies to promote structural change in manufacturing industry – through the IRC and through specific schemes in shipbuilding, aircraft and computers. It is clear that, for conflict to be avoided between promoting some mergers and constraining others,

[1] Monopolies Commission, *Man-made Cellulosic Fibres.*

Table 10.12. *Summary of government expenditure on intervention in industry, 1960/1–1973/4*

£ million[a]

	Aerospace	Shipbuilding	Textiles	IRC[b]
1960/1–1963/4	57·1	—	25·0	—
1964/5–1969/70	326·9	53·3	7·3	97·9
1970/1–1973/4	373·7	99·9	—	30·2
Total	757·7	153·2	32·3	128·1

SOURCES: tables 10.1, 10.6, 10.9 and 10.10.

[a] At 1970 prices.

[b] These figures differ from those in table 10.1 because the latter are at current prices.

consistent criteria are needed. The evidence suggests that the controls on mergers were exercised in a somewhat haphazard way and with such little impact that only six mergers were stopped out of 875 reviewed up to 1974.[1] The stimulus to merge was similarly based on rather vague criteria – in this case the possibility of significant economies of scale, evidence on the existence of which is not particularly conclusive; there is also the possibility of diseconomies.[2] As between encouraging mergers to promote structural change and constraining them to pre-serve competition, the encouragement has clearly outweighed the constraint. Yet a lingering attachment to competition is illustrated by the preservation of two firms in several reorganisations prompted by the government. Examples are the aircraft mergers in 1959/60, the IRC s decision in 1969 to support two nuclear power groups in prefer-ence to a single consortium and the decision to back two aluminium smelters in 1968. Nevertheless, the balance between refereeing industrial conduct and intervening more directly has shifted, and this shift has been reinforced by interventions in various 'crisis' situations involving the rescue of firms in difficulties. In these cases governments have found it progressively harder to refuse appeals for help, because of the growing tendency for the shortcomings of industry to be seen as failures of government policy.

It is clear that new objectives have not been an important cause of the increase in direct intervention. Attempts at rationalisation and modernisation have aimed principally at the usual objectives of economic policy – full employment, growth, stable prices and a satisfactory external balance. It is from persistent lack of success in achieving these objectives that the stimulus for more intervention has come. Various additional objectives – broadly regional and tech-

[1] See page 431 above.

[2] See S. J. Prais, *The Evolution of Giant Firms in Britain*, Cambridge University Press, 1976.

nological – have been present, but these have frequently been reflections of failure on the wider front. They have usually been associated with 'crisis' interventions, and the most commonly cited have been the preservation of regional employment (shipbuilding and textiles), aiding the balance of payments (shipbuilding, aircraft and aluminium), supporting technology (aircraft and computers) and protecting home industry from unfair foreign competition (shipbuilding and textiles). In many instances a combination of these motives was apparent and frequently the government claimed that support would be temporary.

To subsidise employment in particular industries instead of allowing its transfer to a more profitable use is prima facie undesirable. In practice, however, ailing industries such as shipbuilding and textiles may be geographically concentrated in areas of high unemployment, and in the short run it may then be better to subsidise continued production if the subsidy is less than the costs of redundancy pay and unemployment benefit. With the general rise in unemployment nationally, it is likely that resources released in areas of above-average unemployment will remain unused for a significant time.

One argument in favour of supporting domestic production is that the alternative would be to import the goods, with harmful effects on the trade balance; the argument against is that welfare would be increased by importing the goods more cheaply and diverting resources at home to an alternative use. Provided that domestic resources can be quickly diverted there would seem little to be said for subsidies, although if the overseas supplier then has a monopoly there would be no guarantee that import prices would remain low.

The argument for assistance for technological reasons is broadly that a developed economy needs a wide range of skills associated with certain industries, for example aerospace, and a decline in such industries would cut off a source of expertise which could otherwise flow to the rest of industry. This argument seems dubious; if what is required is technological development across a large part of industry, then a more direct way to achieve it is to invest in research and development across the whole range, as indeed the government already does to a limited extent.

Finally, there is the argument that unfair competition from abroad justifies assistance to the home industry. In some cases it is possible to take action under anti-dumping legislation; this, however, may not be practicable in all cases where an industry in another country is being subsidised. Again the arguments turn on whether or not overall welfare would be increased by importing the subsidised product and transferring the resources released at home to other uses. An alternative approach, which has been tried with shipbuilding, is an international agreement to reduce subsidies in all countries, but this has met with little success so far. In textiles international negotiation has led to the GATT multi-fibre agreement to regulate trade.

Looking now for the lessons to be learned from the government's industrial policy, it seems that the major problems have arisen in connection with the 'crisis' interventions. This is not to say that competition policy was entirely successful, but firm action was possible if the government had wished to take it. Nor was the IRC an unqualified success, but it was an interesting development and arguably not a failure. The other interventions, however, have little on the positive side. To mention just two: the Shipbuilding Industry Board did not succeed in establishing a strong independent shipbuilding industry – individual firms and the industry as a whole came back to the government for help time and time again; likewise, the creation of a single computer company, International Computers, has resulted in persistent claims on government funds rather than a company capable of holding its own in world markets. In more general terms, one of the problems of rescue operations is that support is usually offered on a temporary basis, yet the subsidy becomes permanent. As suggested above, support may be justified in the short run, but its continuation will surely discourage a desirable redistribution of resources.

These experiences suggest two alternatives – intervene better or don't intervene. The choice need not be so stark, for one could argue in favour of less intervention *and* better intervention, but for convenience the alternatives will be considered separately. To refrain from intervention must appeal to governments sometimes, but it seems not to be a course which they believe politically possible. To quote Christopher Chataway as Minister of Industrial Development in the Conservative government: 'To say that government had better leave it all alone because it is sure to get the answers wrong is a counsel of despair in the modern world, for all governments are bound to be involved.'[1] There are, of course, those who argue that less – and different – intervention is needed. Prais, for example, believes that there is a case for discouraging large and encouraging small firms, on the grounds that overall concentration in the United Kingdom is higher than in our industrialised and more successful competitors, and the number of small firms much lower.[2] The methods he suggests include social audits on large firms to establish whether any of their activities could be hived-off and a progressive corporation tax. Such policies would swing the balance away from selective intervention and towards reliance on the market mechanism.

[1] C. Chataway, *New Deal for Industry*, London, Conservative Political Centre, 1972, p. 15.
[2] Prais, *The Evolution of Giant Firms in Britain*.

But if the aim is to intervene better, there are various improvements which can be suggested. First, crisis interventions require swift decisions with little time to consider alternatives; a better industrial monitoring system to provide early warning of impending problems therefore seems worthwhile. Secondly, criteria for selecting the interventions most likely to benefit the economy, established in advance of any specific rescue, would reduce *ad hoc* decision-making. Thirdly, the creation of a single mechanism of intervention might improve on a situation where each case requires separate legislation and individual organisation. Fourthly, a systematic check on the results of intervention would seem to be required.

It is worth looking at how developments in recent industrial policy relate to these suggestions. None of them has really helped much to provide a monitoring system. The National Enterprise Board for example, established by the 1975 Industry Act, is required to promote industrial efficiency, employment and the balance of payments (objectives very similar to those of the IRC before it). It is specifically enjoined to invest only in projects which it believes will be profitable. It can bring problems to the government's attention, but it is not required to look out for such problems. The 1975 Act also established the concept of planning agreements – voluntary agreements under which firms and the government exchange information about plans. This system if it became widespread could help the flow of information to the government, but as the first agreement was reached only in March 1977, the early evidence suggests a very limited effect. One possible way of providing a monitoring system would be to adapt and increase the role of government departments in their position as sponsor to each industry. The exact meaning of this role has never been fully clear and there is a case for some monitoring to be included. This would require some development in the industrial expertise of the relevant departments.

The second suggestion concerns criteria for intervention. That there should be some guidelines is perhaps as important as their exact nature, for without them the government is moved along by events rather than having any semblance of a strategy. Recent developments in policy are set out in two government publications.[1] The main strategy seems unimpeachable: 'the broad thrust of the Government's selective assistance policy is to invest in success'. It is recognised, however, that 'it will no doubt remain necessary for the Government itself to consider a number of problem cases involving actual or potential insolvency'.[2]

---

[1] Treasury, *An Approach to Industrial Strategy*, Cmnd 6315, London, HMSO, 1975; 'Criteria for assistance to industry', appendix A to Department of Industry, *Industry Act 1972. Annual Report for the year ending March 31, 1976*, London, HMSO, 1976.

[2] Ibid. para. 26.

Three types of rescue operation are acknowledged as acceptable: first, a limited number of important undertakings where it is immediately clear that the government should intervene to ensure that the capability is maintained; secondly, cases where it is thought that with a reasonable amount of assistance the company can be made viable; thirdly, exceptional cases where modest assistance to a company in receivership may make all the difference between continuing operation and liquidation. These criteria go some way towards what is needed, but they are only valuable insofar as the government acts in accordance with them. An early test was the case of Chrysler UK, to which assistance would have had to be justified under the second criterion above, as the first and third did not apply. Yet, although the government was advised by its own Industrial Development Advisory Board that the proposals did not offer a prospect of viability, support was granted on grounds of employment and the balance of payments.[1]

The third suggestion – that a single mechanism for interventions should be created – was in fact one task of the 1968 Industrial Expansion Act, but a task which it never fulfilled. Subsequent developments within the IRC led the government to ask that body to carry out most of its interventions. The National Enterprise Board, although in many ways successor to the IRC, is hedged about with more guidelines and controls (in particular the restriction to undertake only profitable investment unless directed by the Secretary of State), which limits its ability to intervene on a wide front.

The last suggestion is for a system of reviewing the results of intervention, and presumably this would best be done by a body independent of the intervention agency. The Comptroller and Auditor General provides such a service for all government expenditure and an expansion of his coverage, perhaps augmented with more specific industrial expertise, would be one way of achieving this aim. It is perhaps interesting that he does not at the moment have direct access to the books and records of the National Enterprise Board.

Continued failure to achieve the broad objectives of economic policy has been one of the significant reasons for the increase in government intervention, but it is clear that increased intervention has in turn made little contribution to improving our economic performance. The experience of industrial policy suggests that direct intervention is not generally successful; in rescue cases it is very likely to be unsuccessful. And the increase in direct intervention, whether successful or not, effectively precludes greater emphasis on the more general control of market forces through competition policy. It could be said that in this

---

[1] House of Commons, *Eighth Report from the Expenditure Committee, Session 1975–76. Public Expenditure on Chrysler UK Ltd*, vol. 1: *Report*, London, HMSO, 1976, para. 151.

country governments have intervened against market forces, rather than trying to improve the functioning of the market.

Despite the lack of success of industrial policies in general, intervention is apparently unavoidable, so that changes in the method of intervention along the lines suggested in the previous paragraphs might have some effect in improving the record. It is, however, difficult to see how such changes would make more than a small impression on the overall performance of the economy, if only because the scale of resources which the government can utilise within the framework of the present mixed economy is unlikely ever to be large enough to influence decisively the broad movements of variables such as manufacturing investment, employment and growth.

In conclusion, then, industrial policies seem limited to a peripheral role of tidying up at the edges of the economy, rather than providing any central thrust to alter and improve industry's performance and that of the economy as a whole.

CHAPTER 11

POLICY TOWARDS
THE NATIONALISED INDUSTRIES

by *K. Jones*

INTRODUCTION

By the beginning of the 1960s the general pattern of nationalisation in British industry had stabilised. Briefly, in 1960 fuel and power were largely nationalised, the exceptions being petroleum and the merchanting of coal, and so was a large part of transport and communications.[1] These industries had been nationalised by the Labour government between 1946 and 1949; iron and steel had also been nationalised, but was de-nationalised in 1954.

The performance of these industries was an important factor in the management and rate of growth of the economy. Their output was approximately 10 per cent of gross national product, they employed 8 per cent of the labour force and their capital expenditure programmes were 18 per cent of gross fixed investment. Moreover, they were mainly basic industries whose output was an input into manufacturing industry, or a vital service.

In fuel and power the National Coal Board controlled the whole of its industry. Electricity was controlled in England and Wales by the Electricity Council with supervisory duties, the Central Electricity Generating Board being concerned with power production and the area boards with distribution; there were also two boards in Scotland. The gas industry had a federal structure, with the Gas Council coordinating area boards covering the whole country.

The British Transport Commission controlled the nationalised part of transport – railways, docks, waterways and parts of the road haulage industry. There were also the two airlines, British European Airways and the British Overseas Airways Corporation.

Between 1960 and 1974 there were a number of changes in the structure of these industries and one major addition, iron and steel, as

[1] The following were nationalised: coalmining, electricity and gas, the railways, docks and inland waterways, some parts of road passenger transport and the road haulage industry, London transport, international telecommunications and air transport. The Bank of England had also been nationalised in 1946, but it is not covered in this chapter.

[484]

a result of renationalisation. The transport industries were twice restructured. The Transport Act of 1962 broke up the British Transport Commission into the British Railways Board, the British Waterways Board and the British Transport Docks Board, together with a Transport Holding Company. The 1968 Transport Act created new corporations in the shape of the Passenger Transport Executives in the conurbations, the National Bus Company, the Scottish Transport Group and the National Freight Corporation. In air transport a new body, the British Airports Authority, took over the international airports in 1966. The transformation of the Post Office from a government department to a public corporation began in 1962 and was completed in 1969. The two airlines were merged into British Airways in 1972.

In fuel and power the main change was in the gas industry, where a highly decentralised structure was modified over the years. The Gas Act of 1965 gave the Gas Council powers of coordination, and to manufacture, acquire and supply gas, which it had not had before; in 1972 the area boards were abolished. There were also plans for restructuring the electricity industry, but these were deferred with the change of government in 1970.[1]

The industries were beset by critical problems – created in some industries by strongly increasing demand, in others by falling demand. In many cases the technology was changing and the decade was one of controversy about national fuel and transport policy.

In fuel, the argument was focused on the Labour government's attempt to formulate agreed principles. The 1960s were years of almost continuous decline in coalmining and some decisions were made specifically to protect coal from strong competition from oil, or to assure parts of its market. Nevertheless, it was generally accepted that the contraction of the coal industry was inevitable; a decision to develop nuclear reactors played some part in this. In 1965 the government accepted the need for special financial measures to deal with the situation and decided that, because the National Coal Board had pursued a policy of expansion with active government support, it should be relieved of debt for investments which had turned out unnecessary. In the second half of the decade, following the discovery of North Sea gas, the government decided to run down the coalmines at a much faster rate.[2]

The 1960s were also years of change in the public transport system and, in particular, years of crisis for the railways. In 1963 Dr Beeching began to reshape the railways in the hope that much of their deficit

---

[1] There were also some changes in the structure of suppliers, for example a regrouping of nuclear plant constructors and a rationalisation of heavy electrical equipment.

[2] Ministry of Power, *Fuel Policy*, Cmnd 3438, London, HMSO, 1967.

would be eliminated by 1970, but it gradually became clear that this was unachievable. In 1966 the government laid down basic themes of better planning of investments, priority for the improvement of traffic conditions in towns, the key role of public transport and the need to take account of social as well as economic needs.[1] There followed a major capital reconstruction and a distinction between the commercial and non-commercial sectors of the railways in the 1968 Transport Act.

The following sections examine the application of the government's economic and financial objectives for the nationalised industries. First there is a description of the situation as it had developed in the 1950s and the unsatisfactory financial position which led to a re-examination of the government's objectives as they had been laid down in the nationalisation statutes. The next section describes the new criteria which were set out in White Papers in 1961 and 1967.[2] There follows an examination of the new criteria in practice and of the attitudes of the industries' boards to their adoption. A final section attempts to assess how far the government achieved its aims.

ECONOMIC AND FINANCIAL OBJECTIVES

During the 1960s each industry had its own special problems, but in addition there were general problems affecting all the nationalised industries. These were connected with the role of the industries in the economy and their relation to Ministers and to Parliament. The government's objectives had been set out in the nationalisation statutes: first, the boards had a duty to raise revenues that, taking one year with another, would be not less than sufficient to meet all items properly chargeable to revenue, including interest, depreciation, the redemption of capital and a contribution to the provision of reserves; secondly, the industries were to be operated in the public interest.

The phrase 'not less than' had been generally taken to imply the minimum performance not the maximum; it was accepted that the industries were simply expected to pay their way and not to make large and regular surpluses. Apart from this the industries had been left without economic guidance; in particular, no statutory guidance was given about what was proper provision for depreciation and the renewal of assets, or what constituted proper allocations to general reserves. There was no indication of pricing and investment criteria, nor of the extent to which the industries should finance capital improve-

---

[1] Ministry of Transport, *Transport Policy*, Cmnd 3027, London HMSO, 1966.
[2] Treasury, *Financial and Economic Obligations of the Nationalised Industries*, Cmnd 1337, London, HMSO, 1961, and *Nationalised Industries: a review of economic and financial objectives*, Cmnd 3437, London, HMSO, 1967.

ments and expansion from accumulated trading surpluses rather than by raising new capital from the market.

The boards had been made responsible to Parliament for the overall financial position, while Ministers had power to control investment and borrowing. Different boards pursued different policies – some aiming to simply pay their way and others to secure surpluses.

Dissatisfaction with the conduct of the industries had begun in the 1950s and had found expression in Parliamentary debates and questions in the House of Commons about the industries' objectives, their accountability and the practice of ministerial control. Outside Parliament these matters were also discussed in a critical way by academic economists and others. Within the government too, Ministers and officials were concerned: there was confusion about purposes and methods of control, an absence of coherent principles among departments and little or no guidance to the boards on questions of policy, but an increasing tendency to encroach on the details of management. Government control was exercised primarily through the departments, with the statutes giving the Treasury only a secondary role in relation to the approval of investment and borrowing; general programmes of capital development were the responsibility of the Minister, who was also empowered in the statutes to authorise borrowing, *with Treasury approval*. This had led in practice to great independence for the boards, with Ministers and governments unable to instruct, only to persuade.

Parliament's dissatisfaction with the position led to the setting up of the Select Committee on Nationalised Industries in 1956. Its terms of reference were 'to examine the Report and Accounts of the Nationalised Industries established by statute whose controlling Boards are appointed by Ministers of the Crown and whose annual receipts are not wholly or mainly derived from moneys provided by Parliament or advanced from the Exchequer'. There were thus no restrictions on its work and the Committee could choose its subjects of inquiry; it immediately embarked upon a series of investigations into each undertaking.

As far as the government was concerned the main problem was the financial position of some of the industries. Both the National Coal Board and the British Transport Commission had made large losses in early years. For the nationalised industries as a whole the deficits on current account were not particularly large, bearing in mind they were arrived at after the payment of interest on stock, but all the industries needed investment on a very large scale as a result of years of inadequate provision for renewal of capital equipment and for expansion. Added to the deficits this made the borrowing requirement very large in some years. Table 11.1 shows the total borrowing requirement of the nationalised industries and how it was financed.

Table 11.1. *Central government finance for the nationalised industries,*[a]
1948–73

£ million

	Subsidies	Borrowing requirement			Debt to government written off[b]
		Government loans	Other (net)	Total	
1948	—	− 1	111	110	—
49	—	− 22	113	91	—
1950	—	− 15	165	150	—
51	—	16	138	154	—
52	—	42	231	273	—
53	—	34	225	259	—
54	—	85	210	295	—
55	—	112	377	489	3
56	—	231	36	267	—
57	—	550	10	560	—
58	—	532	7	539	—
59	—	584	6	590	—
1960	115	456	8	464	—
61	137	485	45	530	—
62	141	452	21	473	10
63	136	378	24	402	432
64	123	541	18	559	—
65	142	613	11	624	525
66	143	768	38	806	—
67	174	1040	− 37	1003	—
68	180	957	− 166	791	19
69	125	715	− 228	487	1258
1970	113	674	128	802	255
71	104	971	156	1127	—
72	298	905	− 53	852	350
73	323	514	385	899	543

SOURCES: CSO, *National Income and Expenditure*; NIESR estimates.

[a] Fuel and power, transport and communications, iron and steel.

[b] The implications for the annual interest charge of the writing-off of debt are not available.

In early years it was thought that the needs of the nationalised industries could be met from borrowing through the market by issuing stock. From the first this was done under government supervision; under the statutes investment plans had to be approved and borrowing had to have government consent. So the Corporations borrowed with the support of a Treasury guarantee; the exception was the National Coal Board which received funds through the Ministry of Fuel and Power. The Treasury guarantee meant that if subscriptions for stock fell short the Exechequer would and did support the issue.

Between 1948 and 1954 the annual amount of stock issued (net) fluctuated between £50 million and about £200 million, but in 1955 the borrowing requirement reached nearly £500 million, of which over

£300 million was borrowed on the market. The issue of this amount of stock interfered with the Exchequer's national debt operations; there was increased difficulty in selling the stock to the public and a succession of issues had to be taken up by the Bank of England. The effect was directly contrary to the policy at that time of restricting credit and, for that purpose, keeping the liquidity of the banking system as near to the conventional minimum as possible. It was therefore decided to introduce a new system and from then on the nationalised industries were required to borrow from the Treasury. However the Treasury still had to borrow, so that the main gain seems to have been in the timing of the operations. The Radcliffe Committee subsequently approved of this arrangement.[1]

The gap between undistributed income and gross fixed investment continued to rise and was over £500 million in each of the years 1957–9. Consequently, Treasury officials began working on the ideas subsequently published in the White Paper of 1961.[2] One source on which they no doubt drew was the Report of the Radcliffe Committee and the ideas presented by some of the witnesses. The Report itself drew attention to the fact that the industries were free in law to include in the prices of their products some margin to allow for additions to their capital equipment as well as its replacement. The Committee was not optimistic that price rises for transport and coal would increase receipts enough to allow a margin for all the capital development of those industries, but thought there might be room for some further margin in the electricity industry. R. F. Harrod was more emphatic on this point, stressing the importance of the problem of funding finance and arguing that the only solution was to get the nationalised industries to rely mainly on self-finance. This would presumably involve a once-for-all rise in prices and greater freedom in pricing policy in the future, but it would be a sacrifice worth making.[3]

Harrod was not the first economist to criticise the pricing policy of the nationalised industries; most of them had begun by basing their prices on average costs, but a number of economists objected to the practice. A long controversy about the merits of rival pricing rules had begun as early as the 1930s.[4] At first the debate was for the most part on a highly theoretical plane concerned with basic welfare principles, but gradually it shifted to more concrete consideration of pricing systems.[5] The

[1] Treasury, *Radcliffe Report*.

[2] Treasury, *Financial and Economic Obligations of the Nationalised Industries*.

[3] Radcliffe Committee, *Principal Memoranda of Evidence*, vol. 3, p. 112.

[4] O. Lange and F. Taylor, *On the Economic Theory of Socialism*, Minneapolis, University of Minnesota Press, 1938.

[5] See N. Ruggles, 'Recent developments in the theory of marginal cost pricing' in R. Turvey (ed.). *Public Enterprise: selected readings*, Harmondsworth, Penguin, 1968, for references.

budgetary implications of marginal cost pricing were examined by Meade and Fleming,[1] and the theory was developed in a more general form by Lerner.[2] Other economists entered the debate and considerable controversy ensued.[3] Broadly, those who advocated marginal cost pricing and differential pricing among consumers did so on economic grounds. They conceived of the nationalised industries as very large firms and expected them to be primarily concerned with the maximisation of economic advantage for the community through the proper allocation of resources.

At the practical level, the problems of the coal industry were the first to claim attention. In 1952 the Ridley Committee was equally divided between those who favoured marginal and those who favoured average costs.[4] About the same time a powerful argument for marginal cost pricing as soon as shortages had been overcome was put forward by I. M. D. Little.[5] Pricing soon became a key issue in the other nationalised industries.

During the 1950s there was a stream of White Papers and reports by independent committees on the various nationalised undertakings. A number of the latter made recommendations relevant to the nationalised undertakings as a whole. One of the most important, because of its thorough-going recommendation of commercial principles, was the Report of the Herbert Committee on electricity supply.[6] This carried the debate well beyond the issue of pricing policy and concluded that efficiency should be measured in strictly economic terms. It recommended that the price of electricity should be related to the cost of supply and where costs to some (for example, rural) consumers were greater, they should be charged more. Moreover the Committee considered that plant should be purchased in the cheapest market and no preference should be given to British manufacturers, while retail selling should be as commercial as that of other concerns.

Even before the White Paper of 1961 the Treasury was encouraging a change in attitude towards pricing policy in the nationalised industries. Price control had traditionally been imposed because most of

[1] J. E. Meade and J. M. Fleming, 'Price and output policy of state enterprise: a symposium', *Economic Journal*, vol. 54, December 1944.

[2] A. P. Lerner, *The Economics of Control*, New York, Macmillan, 1944.

[3] For example, T. Wilson, ' Price and output policy of state enterprise: a comment', *Economic Journal*, vol. 55, December 1945; R. H. Coase, 'The marginal cost controversy' and 'The marginal cost controversy: some further comments', *Economica*, vol. 13 (new series), August 1946, and vol. 14 (new series), May 1947.

[4] Ministry of Fuel and Power, *Report of the Committee on National Policy for the Use of Fuel and Power Resources*, Cmd 8647, London, HMSO, 1952.

[5] I. M. D. Little, *The Price of Fuel*, Oxford, Clarendon Press, 1953.

[6] Ministry of Fuel and Power, *Electricity Supply Industry. Committee of Inquiry Report*, Cmd 9672, London, HMSO, 1956.

them were quasi-monopolies, but by the late 1950s the view had developed that this control had been a factor in the deficits of some industries and in others a lack of sufficient surpluses to provide for any self-financing of capital expenditure.[1] For example, the price of electricity to personal consumers rose only by 26 per cent between 1948 and 1955, compared with a rise of 43 per cent for consumer goods and services as a whole and a rise of 50 per cent in fuel used in manufacturing. The Treasury therefore hoped that a change of attitude would improve the ratio of prices to costs and reduce deficits or, as for example in the electricity industry, enable the boards to achieve a substantially greater degree of self-financing. There followed a greater emphasis by the government on commercial viability, which led in some cases to the cutting out of unprofitable activities, particularly in the railways. At the same time this tended to bring into the open the cross-subsidisation which had existed for many years prior to nationalisation. A number of attempts had been made to stop cross-subsidisation where it led to so-called unfair competition with private industry, but not much progress had been made by 1961.

THE NEW CRITERIA

The 1961 White Paper

In the 1961 White Paper the government attempted to formulate official doctrine on the operation of the nationalised industries and to present a new framework in which they were to work. It was emphasised that, although the industries had obligations of a national and non-commercial kind, they were not and ought not to be regarded as social services absolved from economic and social justification. It was noted that some boards were not making large enough provision to cover the replacement cost of assets having regard to inflation and obsolescence. Further, it was pointed out that in consequence of the low returns obtained by some industries they were depending heavily on the savings of others to finance their investment.

The White Paper explained how the statutes should be interpreted:

(1) The boards' duty to pay their way should be applied over a five-year period, thus giving a more precise interpretation to the phrase 'taking one year with another'.

(2) Industries should make provision from revenue sufficient to cover depreciation calculated on a replacement cost basis (as distinct from historic cost) and an adequate allocation to general reserves, to be available *inter alia* as a contribution to capital development and as a safeguard against premature obsolescence and similar contingencies.

[1] Treasury, *Financial and Economic Obligations of the Nationalised Industries.*

For this purpose financial objectives would be agreed for each industry in the light of its own circumstances, needs and capabilities.

(3) The government's arrangements for investment reviews were to be codified and the Minister was to be informed of general plans for preventing poor performance.

(4) The existing arrangement, whereby chairmen of the boards ascertained in advance the views of their Ministers on changes in prices, was confirmed. If a board decided to modify its proposals in the light of a Minister's views, then it could require a written statement of those views and ask for a revision of the financial objective where the modification in prices would impair the board's ability to achieve that objective.

(5) The original financial objectives would take account of unprofitable activities carried out by the boards at the government's request and, if further activities were imposed from outside, a board would be entitled to ask for an adjustment of its financial objective.

Following the publication of the White Paper, specific financial objectives were drawn up for most of the industries for periods of up to five years; these were in terms of a percentage rate of return on average net assets before interest and either before or after depreciation. But for the National Coal Board the target was to break even and for British Rail it was to reduce the deficit and break even as soon as possible. The main emphasis was thus on financial targets. The role of the Treasury was to remain a limited one, its powers still being confined to the approval of capital expenditure programmes and of borrowing to meet them, also the authorising of payments to meet continuous deficits. The prime role in the relationship of the industries with the government remained with the sponsoring departments.

The White Paper was the first attempt to formulate some official doctrines for the nationalised industries. It seems likely that its drafting helped to clarify the views of officials and Ministers. It was regarded as a step in the direction of applying commercial standards, but this was heavily qualified in the last paragraph, which referred to the wider obligations of these industries than of commercial concerns in the private sector. However, it was not long before the disadvantages of the emphasis on financial targets became clear. For one thing their calculation was not as simple as was made out. Moreover, because of the concentration on end results, little guidance was given about how those results were to be achieved, in terms of either proper pricing policies or investment policies.

The financial performance of the industries showed little improvement after 1961. There was some increase in their gross trading surplus, which led to a slight fall in the borrowing requirement for 1962 and

1963, but by 1964 gross fixed investment was again running well ahead of undistributed income and the borrowing requirement was again rising rapidly. During these years, therefore, work was begun on improving the framework, in particular the methods of investment appraisal. In 1964 the Labour Chancellor announced the government's acceptance of the system of financial objectives, but also its intention of developing further the methods used to guide the industries on investment and pricing policies. Another influence towards greater precision and clarity was increasing concern about public expenditure; from 1964 the government spent more and more time trying to decide on priorities as the planned level of public expenditure had to be revised downwards. This made it more natural to ask the purpose of subsidies, so that they could be compared with other ways of spending money. Outside advice was taken on methods of appraisal, from both industrial and academic circles, and the methods selected were then discussed with departments and tested out in practice on two specific projects – the freight area at Heathrow airport and electrification of the London to Bournemouth railway. A meeting was held early in 1965 with all the nationalised industries and sponsoring departments to discuss discounted cash flows as a method of appraising investments; this was followed by a series of smaller meetings to discuss points in more detail. Discussions were also proceeding with the departments on new financial objectives and ways of achieving them, and the industries were consulted about pricing policy and its relationship to the new targets. The outcome of all this was another White Paper in 1967.[1]

The 1967 White Paper

The new White Paper started from the position that nationalised industries should be operated basically as commercial concerns and aim at promoting an efficient allocation and use of resources. It laid down principles to guide pricing policies and the criteria to be used in investment decisions.

The main proposals were:

(1) Investment programmes should be based on consistent criteria and projects should normally show a satisfactory return in commercial terms. The best possible methods of appraisal should be used and this meant discounted cash flows for all important projects; 8 per cent was prescribed as the test rate of discount.

(2) Common pricing policies should be applied. In addition to covering total costs, prices should relate to the costs of particular products or services to eliminate undesirable cross-subsidisation, although it was recognised that in some cases there would be good commercial reasons

[1] Treasury, *Nationalised Industries: a review of economic and financial objectives.*

for charging prices which differed from costs. For example, if persistent spare capacity existed, either for relatively long periods or at certain times, places or seasons, it might be desirable to reduce prices to stimulate demand. Similarly, if peak loads were a problem, the pricing system should provide incentives to users to shift from peak to off-peak, provided off-peak charges did not fail to cover variable costs.

(3) In addition to covering accounting costs, prices should be reasonably related to costs at the margin, the main consideration being long-run marginal costs, including provision for the replacement of fixed assets together with a satisfactory return on capital employed.

(4) Provided that the industries could meet their targets over a period of years, they should comply with the government's general policy on prices and incomes. As price stability in the nationalised industries was of special importance to the economy, in future all their major price increases would be referred to the NBPI.

(5) Critical attention should be paid to reducing costs and there should be a continuous drive to increase efficiency and productivity. The NBPI had already been given powers to inquire into the efficiency of industries whose proposals for price increases were referred to it.

(6) The system of financial targets should continue, but be interpreted more flexibly, taking into account the investment, pricing and efficiency policies outlined.

The most striking feature of the White Paper was the transition from control by means of an objective expressed as an end result to control by criteria. In their evidence to the Select Committee in 1967 the Treasury suggested that financial objectives would continue to be necessary 'so that success or failure of management over a period may be assessed.'[1] But they believed that it was essential that the new objectives should provide more definite guidance on investment and pricing. It was stated that there was nothing magic about a target figure and no 'right' target to which all industries should aim. For example, where an industry had a very heavy investment programme, the chances were that being an expanding industry prices stood relatively high in relation to marginal costs; therefore there would be a good return, so that a high financial objective could be set. On the other hand, in an industry with little prospect of expansion or even facing a decline, prices would be low in relation to marginal costs and the financial objective correspondingly lower. The fact that it might not always be possible in practice to reconcile the criteria was fully understood and recognised, but it was thought that they did automatically imply a higher level of self-financing in expanding industries.

[1] House of Commons, *Select Committee on Nationalised Industries, Session 1967–68. Ministerial Control of the Nationalised Industries*, vol. 2, London, HMSO, 1968.

THE CRITERIA IN PRACTICE

The 1967 White Paper showed how investment, pricing and efficiency policies would be taken into account in setting the financial objectives. In the following years financial targets survived as an instrument, and the investment criteria came increasingly to be adopted as a useful discipline. Marginal cost pricing has generally played a smaller role; in overall pricing policies it has never got off the ground. However, in problems of relative prices, peak prices and differential tariffs it has played a greater part in working out more consistent policies.

Investment criteria

After 1967 considerable progress was made in developing the various techniques of investment appraisal; in particular the use of discounted cash flows became widely accepted. The test discount rate was increased to 10 per cent in August 1969, the change being occasioned by evidence that the private sector of industry was looking for a return on marginal low-risk investment equivalent to a pre-tax rate of 10 per cent.

The government has continued to operate a standard procedure for considering the nationalised industries' investment programmes, which is done regularly in annual investment reviews. Since 1969 these have been arranged so that the capital expenditure of the nationalised industries can be included in the annual review of public expenditure. Every year each industry submits to its sponsoring department proposed capital expenditure for a five-year period. Discussions then take place between the department and the board and the department and the Treasury, which include the general prospects for the industry and the relationship of the investment programme to issues of current concern to the government. The discussions also have regard to the general responsibility of the Minister concerned for the wise use of advances to the boards from the National Loans Fund and for the efficiency of the industries. In considering a capital development programme, a department must be satisfied that it is related to a sound strategy for the industry; also any issues that are of concern to the government must be brought to the attention of Ministers.

Individual projects are identified to a varying degree. For the electricity industry proposals for the construction of major generating stations and area boards' projects over £50,000 are shown. The Gas Council shows projects costing £100,000 or more. The National Coal Board shows mining projects costing over £1 million and other projects over £250,000. The airlines specify projects over £1 million. The British Steel Corporation has much the highest figure, identifying projects over £2 million. To some extent this pattern reflects the nature of each industry. It also helps the departments to understand the programmes and provides opportunities for testing methods of appraisal.

If for any reason a board does not use the best available methods of investment appraisal for a project, or proposes an investment which does not comply with the test discount rate, it is expected to report the fact and justify it. The department only goes through the detailed appraisals in selected cases for the purpose of examining the techniques as such. The department will enquire about the assumptions on which the proposal is based, the relation of the scheme to the industry's operations and strategy, and the degree of risk involved. It will also be concerned with the effects on employment and on other industries.

Nevertheless, the primary responsibility for assessing what investment is required rests with the board. In some industries discounted cash flows are not straightforward to apply and there was some resistance to this technique. Most boards now appear to have developed their own methods of appraisal, including discounted cash flows, but in many cases adapted to suit their particular industry.

For example, in the electricity industry the decisions involve a plant programme to minimise the cost of meeting a demand forecast for some years ahead and the test discount rate is used in these calculations. But it is necessary to simulate the working of the whole system to evaluate capital and running costs with and without the addition of the plant under consideration. Standard appraisal procedures are supplemented by a range of computer studies designed to assist decisions, taking account of risk and security of supplies and the economic merits of long-term developments in transmission.

In the gas industry a variety of approaches is adopted using discounting techniques in different forms. Assessment of a direct return on new capital investment is applied only to a small part of expenditure, because most projects are essential links in an investment chain joining North Sea wells with the final consumer. For these projects the lowest-cost solution is sought from the feasible alternatives and discounted cash flows are the method of assessment most usually employed. The test discount rate is applied to all low-risk investment, but is adjusted in the light of experience.

The National Coal Board faces a similar situation, in that much investment is in maintenance to keep a pit open, so that the whole colliery needs to be involved in the appraisal. The procedure used to be to compare the expected profit of the whole pit as a percentage of the total investment proposed with the actual result for the year before the investment was to take place. The National Coal Board was reluctant to abandon its arrangements and sought the advice both of the Ministry of Power and the Treasury on how best to apply discounted cash flows in the mining industry, but progress appears to have been slow. It was found very difficult to project the results of a particular colliery over ten to fifteen years because of unknowns in geology and the state of the market. Since 1968/9, however, considerable experience has been gained in the use of discounted cash flows and proposed investments are always appraised in these terms. At the same time the improved results with the investment continue to be compared with what was being achieved without it.

The criteria for capital investment in British Railways were discussed with the Ministry of Transport in 1962 and 1963 and agreement was reached on essentials. But the claim made by the British Railways Board in their evidence to the Select Committee in 1967 that discounted cash flow techniques were applied to all major projects where it was considered appropriate did not accord with the experience of the Ministry and indeed was not consistent with the policy described in the Board's own paper.[1] Of the 57 projects submitted to the Minister for approval in 1966 only ten were accompanied by a discounted cash flow assessment when originally submitted and in three more it was added at the Ministry's request. The Board did not use these methods for appraising replacement investment. Since then things have improved and in 1972 the Department of the Environment stated that in submitting investment projects the Railways Board normally included a discounted cash flow assessment, showing the net present value, the internal rate of return and a break-even year.[2] Recently considerable progress has been made in the refinement of appraisal techniques and a comprehensive system of project control based on individual accountability has been instituted. In cases where the justification for a project is wholly or partly social, the proposal is accompanied by a cost–benefit appraisal unless it has previously been agreed that the department should take primary responsibility for assessing the social benefits.

Among other transport industries, the airlines use discounted cash flows for about 90 per cent of their capital expenditure; for the rest the pay-off period is used. Investment by the National Freight Corporation is mainly in vehicles and discounted cash flows are used. The British Transport Docks Board also applies discounted cash flows.

The Post Office aims to use discounted cash flows and the test discount rate where practicable, but it too faces the complication that the system is an integrated one and revenue is derived from the operation

[1] House of Commons, *Select Committee on Nationalised Industries, Session 1967–68. Ministerial Control*, vol. 1.
[2] House of Commons, *Select Committee on Nationalised Industries, Session 1973–74. First Report. Capital Investment Procedures*, London, HMSO, 1974.

as a whole. Consequently it is not feasible or sensible to carry out a full present value analysis on every individual project.

Finally, the British Steel Corporation applies discounted cash flows and, until investment grants were abolished, a test discount rate of 15 per cent – a self-imposed rate higher than the government's because, unlike the other nationalised industries, the Corporation received investment grants.

Pricing policies

The difficulties of applying the pricing policy were accepted in the White Paper and circumstances were recognised in which there would have to be a departure from long-run marginal cost pricing. For example, if there was spare capacity, prices should be lowered to short-run marginal costs; if, on the other hand, there was excess demand, prices should be increased as a rationing device. Problems of dynamic adjustment were also recognised. Thus, if technological progress reduced long-run marginal costs, it was recommended that prices should be brought into line gradually and large changes avoided.

Developments since the White Paper have demonstrated clearly the difficulties experienced by a number of boards in applying the principles to their industries in practice. Even where there was spare capacity there has been reluctance to lower prices if it was thought to be a short-term problem, partly on the grounds that alterations in prices would be disliked by customers. Most of the boards have failed to make much progress in applying long-run marginal costs in pricing; they have had more success in using short-run marginal costs for periods (or types of service) where there is spare capacity, with the result that there has been a considerable increase in price discrimination among different consumers. In electricity and gas, with their expanding markets, the boards began to work towards gearing tariffs to long-run marginal costs, but this was by no means straightforward. Academic writers appeared to have underestimated the practical difficulties of measuring marginal costs and choosing a detailed price structure. In the first place it is not always easy to decide which is the marginal unit; in the second, the ideal tariff would be impossibly complicated. The following description of electricity charging illustrates some of the problems.

Tariffs in electricity are set at two levels: for electricity sold by the Central Electricity Generating Board to the area boards (and direct to several very large consumers) under the terms of the bulk supply tariff, and for electricity sold by the area boards to final consumers.[1]

---

[1] For a fuller discussion of the problems of electricity pricing see R. L. Meek, 'The new bulk supply tariff for electricity' and 'Electricity costs: a reply', *Economic Journal*, vol. 78, March and December 1968; P. E. Watts, 'CEGB's bulk-supply tariff and long-run marginal

The bulk supply tariff is meant to indicate to the area boards the varying costs of supplying electricity at different times of the day and the year; to be successful in guiding consumer choice on the basis of relative costs this tariff must be reflected in the tariffs of the area boards. It was announced that from 1967/8 it was intended to base the bulk supply tariff firmly on marginal principles, with the aim of achieving a smooth transition from average to marginal costing by 1970/1. Three separate running rates and two capacity charges were distinguished, but these were not sophisticated enough to provide the necessary incentives; in addition, there were administrative problems in putting more sophisticated pricing into operation, so that the area boards appear to have had difficulties in putting these charges into practice.

The application of marginal cost pricing is complicated by the fact that the demand for electricity fluctuates considerably, both daily and seasonally. Because output cannot be stored, peak demand can only be met if capacity is not less than that demand. For large industrial consumers most area boards have a maximum demand tariff in two parts – a charge per kilowatt of demand, the demand being the maximum registered in a particular period, and a charge per unit of electricity consumed. The first part of the charge is varied seasonally, in some cases monthly and in some cases according to time of day or month or year. The application of this sort of tariff to small commercial and domestic consumers would be costly in terms of metering, so that usually they have had two-part and block tariffs, which reflect costs less closely than the industrial tariffs. However, area boards have been able to develop off-peak tariffs, either with a special meter and circuit for storage space heaters, or with a white meter distinguishing a night and a day rate.

The application of more complex tariffs to reflect marginal costs is costly and one which fully reflected marginal costs would be impossibly so; the benefits have had to be considered against the higher costs of operation. For a number of industries, therefore, it seems likely that tariffs can only rarely be expected to be much more than poor indicators of marginal costs. However, certain reforms should lead to better pricing, as appears to have happened in some industries; for example time-differentiated tariffs are now used for electricity, telephones, railways and airlines, although differential charging is not carried to an optimal marginal cost solution.

In coalmining the application of long-run marginal costing was found

---

cost' and 'Electricity costs – a reply', *Economic Journal*, vol. 78, March and December 1968; R. Turvey, 'Electricity costs: a comment', *Economic Journal*, vol. 78, December 1968, and *Optimal Pricing and Investment in Electricity Supply*, London, Allen & Unwin, 1968; M. V. Posner, *Fuel Policy: a study in applied economics*, London, Macmillan, 1973.

to be very difficult because the situation was complicated by many factors – the range of products, declining output, unknown cost performance in the future, a highly monopolistic market with one large buyer (the electricity industry) and the opportunity of making long-term contracts. The National Coal Board wished to retain a formal price structure with flexibility and the Ministry of Power did not worry too much about whether or not prices were below long-run marginal costs, because the electricity industry was already being made to pay much more for coal than for competing fuels. Pricing policy was thought to be of secondary importance compared with the problem of ensuring the progression to a smaller, more efficient industry and the elimination of pits showing heavy losses.

Among the transport industries the problems were also found to be acute. The best the Railways Board found they could do was to try to ensure that prices moved with inflation, or when justified by new investment which improved services as opposed to replacement. But even this was difficult. Early in 1970 a steering group, on which the Treasury, the department and the Board were represented, concluded that demand and supply conditions were such that there was no set of prices which would yield enough revenue to cover total costs. The need for financial support becomes greater as the railway system shrinks.

The National Freight Corporation has generally rejected marginal cost pricing and continues to aim to cover average costs. But, in a very competitive market, the Corporation is aware that some traffic does no more than cover direct costs and tries to price out these goods. The British airlines are part of an international cartel and are not therefore free to pursue their own price policies, although they can influence the policy of the cartel. There has been no apparent pressure for a move to marginal cost pricing, even in domestic fares.

The Post Office has also found itself unable to adopt long-run marginal costs as a basis for setting tariffs. In 1968 the NBPI reported that relatively little analysis of long-run marginal costs had been undertaken and recommended that a team should be set up to analyse the whole postal and telecommunications systems.[1] By 1969 the Post Office started on studies of the long-run marginal cost of each service, but these have not yet been completed.[2]

When the British Steel Corporation took over ownership of the bulk of the steel industry, prices of steel products had been set by the Iron and Steel Board. The system took into account current costs and also something described as new plant costs, which was the Board's inter-

[1] NBPI, *Report no. 58: Post Office Charges*, Cmnd 3574, London, HMSO, 1968.
[2] By 1974.

pretation of the concept of long-run marginal costs.[1] The Corporation carried out a comprehensive review of prices and devoted a lot of attention to costs of production in their plants and to long-run marginal costs as they saw them. A set of proposals was agreed with the government. The intention was to adopt long-run marginal costs, but it is now recognised that this has failed because of the government's restraint on increases in steel prices in the years since the proposals were agreed.

Costs and efficiency

The measurement of improvements in efficiency is not simple, because efficiency embraces complex relationships resulting from multiple activities. However, some estimates can be made of changes in output per man. In coalmining there had been little increase in output per man–shift during the 1950s, but in the 1960s progress was rapid. By 1971 about 2·4 tons per man–shift were being produced, compared with about 1·3 tons in the late 1950s. Similarly, in terms of output per employee, there was a considerable increase in productivity in electricity generation. In the gas industry comparisons are difficult because of sharp technological discontinuities; also, productivity changes in surface transport are difficult to measure because of alterations in measures of output and in organisation. But in both industries there is evidence of substantial increases in output per man.

All these industries experienced great technical changes during the 1960s: the spread of coal-cutting by machinery and of power loading of coal; larger electricity generators and the introduction of nuclear generation; the change to natural gas; and the electrification of the railways. There has also been a transformation in telecommunications. These developments have all aided labour productivity, but the question which remains is whether the degree of improvement reflects adequately the resources that have been invested. An attempt has been made to measure how far the rise in labour productivity in public enterprises is due to the substitution of capital for labour, using an index of growth of output per unit of labour and capital combined.[2] Tentative results showed that in the period 1958 to 1968 output per unit of labour and capital together increased more slowly than output per man, but there were still substantial gains in productivity per worker even when capital was taken into account.

It has also been argued that these increases compare favourably with trends in manufacturing industry, but not very well with com-

[1] House of Commons, *Select Committee on Nationalised Industries, Session 1972–73. First Report: British Steel Corporation*, London, HMSO, 1973.
[2] R. Pryke, *Public Enterprise in Practice*, London, MacGibbon & Kee, 1971, pp. 109–14. Mr Pryke used the method described in W. B. Reddaway and A. D. Smith, 'Progress in British manufacturing industries in the period 1948–54', *Economic Journal*, vol. 70, March 1960.

parable industries in continental Western Europe. International comparisons are complicated by different conditions, but Pryke concluded that in Germany (the only other country in Western Europe with a sizable production of coal) coal productivity was higher than in Britain; also, British electricity productivity was somewhat less than in Germany and France and well below that in the United States. An earlier study also found that British coal-fired stations were less productive than either French or American ones.[1] British railways compare poorly in terms of productivity partly because of a different pattern of demand.[2]

Financial targets

Tables 11.2 and 11.3 show two sets of financial targets and the actual results. The industries were all below their targets in the first period – most of them only slightly below, but coal and the railways well below. The target of both the National Coal Board and British Railways was to break even as soon as possible. In the case of the former the capital

Table 11.2. *Financial objectives of the nationalised industries, period I*

		Rate of return	
	Period	Objective	Actual annual average
		(%)	(%)
Post Office	1963/4–1967/8	8·0[a]	7·7[a]
Gas Council	1962/3–1966/7[b]	10·2[c]	9·8[c]
Electricity Council			
England and Wales	1962/3–1966/7	12·4[c]	12·0[c]
South Scotland[d]	1962/3–1966/7	12·4[c]	10·4[c]
British European Airways	1963/4–1967/8	6·0[a]	5·7[a] (deficit, £m.)
National Coal Board	1963/4–1967/8	to break even[e]	12·0
British Railways Board	1963/4–1966/7	to reduce deficit	137·0

SOURCES: Annual Reports of the nationalised industries.

[a] On average net assets, before interest but after historic cost depreciation.

[b] The objective of 10·2 per cent was retained in 1967/8 and 1968/9, and rates of return of 7·7 and 10·9 per cent were achieved in those years.

[c] On average net assets, before interest or depreciation.

[d] North Scotland, as an interim measure, had to apply such tariff increases as would give the same percentage increase in revenue as the tariff increases applied by South Scotland.

[e] After interest and depreciation, including £10 million for the difference between historic and replacement cost depreciation. The inclusion of the £10 million was suspended in 1964/5 and 1965/6.

[1] F. P. R. Brechling and A. J. Surrey, 'An international comparison of production techniques: the coal-fired electricity generating industry', *National Institute Economic Review*, no. 36, May 1966.   [2] Pryke, *Public Enterprise in Practice*.

Table 11.3. *Financial objectives of the nationalised industries, period II*

		Rate of return	
	Period	Objective	Actual annual average
		(%)	(%)
Post Office			
Postal services	1968/9–1972/3	2·0[a]	−6·6[a]
Telecommunications	1968/9–1972/3	8·25[b]	8·3[b]
Gas Council	1969/70–1973/4	7·0[c]	6·8[c d]
Electricity Council			
England and Wales	1969/70–1973/4	7·0[c]	5·2[c e]
British Overseas Airways	1966/7–1971/2	12·5[a]	··
British European Airways	1968/9–1972/3	8·0[a]	··
British Airports Authority	1969/70–1971/2	14·0[b]	··
			(deficit, £ m.)
National Coal Board	1969/70–1970/1	to break even	13·3
British Railways Board	1968 onwards	full self-sufficiency	17·4[f]
British Steel Corporation	1967–73	to break even	11·3[g]

SOURCES: as table 11.2.
[a] On total expenditure, after interest and depreciation.
[b] On average net assets, before interest but after historic cost depreciation.
[c] On average net assets, before interest but after depreciation.
[d] Period 1969/70–1972/3.   [e] Period 1969/70–1971/2.
[f] Period 1969–72.   [g] Loss before extraordinary items.

reconstruction of 1965 had reduced the burden of interest charges, but these soon rose again as the Board had to increase its borrowing from the government to finance investment. Similarly the capital reconstruction of British Railways following the 1962 Transport Act was meant to enable the Board to achieve its financial objective and break even eventually. In this case, however, it was recognised that it would take time and the Minister of Transport was empowered to make grants of up to £450 million until the objective was achieved.

There were some delays in fixing the next set of objectives and these ranged over the years to 1973/4, so that it is not possible in all cases to compare the results with the targets. For the most part they are similar to the earlier targets, although sometimes expressed in a different way, but British European Airways' target was increased. Until 1970 electricity and gas, the Post Office and the airlines were reasonably on target and the National Coal Board's finances improved a little. There was some check to the rate of loss by the British Railways Board, mainly as a result of direct support for certain passenger services following the 1968 Transport Act.

The significance of the targets has been discussed at some length both by the Select Committee and elsewhere. They have been justified on a number of grounds: because, first, pricing rules are difficult to define precisely and in any case the merit of marginal cost pricing depends on the assumption that it is applied throughout the economy, a condition we know is not fulfilled in practice; secondly, it might be better to allow the price of electricity or gas to be a little above its long-run marginal cost than to raise some other form of tax; thirdly, it is not clear that a given test discount rate on new assets uniquely defines the capital charge – new investment should be capable of earning it, but there is no reason why it should be earned on the value of existing assets.

However, the targets have also come under attack; they are determined by the sponsoring department after consultation with the boards and are in some sense predictions of what it is possible to achieve rather than targets. But in any event they may prove difficult or impossible to achieve because of the economic situation at the time or a change in government policy. It has been suggested that it is more appropriate to regard them as management tools than as instruments of control. In evidence to the Select Committee in 1967 some departments suggested that the fixing of the objectives had made the industries more efficient, but the Select Committee concluded that they should not set out to achieve their targets at the price of departing from agreed policies; if market circumstances changed it might be the objective that should be adjusted, not necessarily the policies.[1] Nevertheless the Committee thought that the financial targets could still be valuable in three ways: first, they would provide a rough test against which the performance of the industries could be judged; secondly, they would be indicators of the financial consequences of the policies adopted; thirdly, they would be useful as management tools within the industries.

The controversy about the significance of financial targets has continued, with the Select Committee trying hard to throw some light on the matter and asking questions about them at almost every investigation. The view of the Treasury expressed in evidence to the Committee is that the objectives are something better than the old requirement to break even, and should facilitate a contribution to self-financing and reserves while still taking account of the circumstances of the industry.[2] It was suggested that if the financial criteria were not pursued in one form or another then there would be difficulties in effectively assessing performance.

---

[1] House of Commons, *Select Committee on Nationalised Industries, Session 1967–68. Ministerial Control*, vol. 1.

[2] House of Commons, *Select Committee on Nationalised Industries, Session 1973–74. First Report.*

THE EFFECTIVENESS OF POLICY

The main objectives of government policy towards the nationalised industries during the 1960s have been identified as an improvement in their financial performance and a greater degree of self-financing in order to reduce the burden of their borrowing on the Exchequer. It was hoped that the methods by which these aims were to be achieved, namely the application of marginal cost pricing and discounted cash flows, and a continuous drive to increase efficiency, improve productivity and reduce costs, would lead to a more effective allocation of resources.

Financial performance

The gross trading surplus of the nationalised industries as a whole improved steadily throughout the 1960s (table 11.4) but, as the proportion taken in interest and taxes was rising, the increase in undistributed income was rather less. Gross fixed capital formation was rising rapidly up to 1967, but then levelled out.

Table 11.4. *Financial performance of the nationalised industries, 1960–73*

	Annual averages		
	1960–4	1965–9	1970–3
		(£ million)	
Gross trading surplus[a]	774	1235	1732
Interest and taxes[b]	340	520	821
Undistributed income[c]	434	715	911
Capital formation[d]	920	1458	1834
Borrowing requirement	486	743	923
		(percentages)	
Borrowing requirement as a percentage of capital formation	*52.8*	*50.9*	*50.2*

SOURCES: CSO, *National Income and Expenditure 1974*, London, HMSO, 1974; NIESR estimates.

[a] Including rent and non-trading income, but before provision for depreciation and stock appreciation.　　[b] Mainly interest.

[c] Before provision for depreciation and stock appreciation.

[d] Includes gross fixed capital, stocks and net lending.

The degree of self-financing did not start to rise until the late 1960s. Exchequer loans to the electricity industry fell from 1966/7 onwards; to coal, gas and transport they fell from 1967/8 (table 11.5). But loans to the Post Office and the British Steel Corporation continued to rise and for the industries as a whole the borrowing requirement remained at about 50 per cent of gross fixed investment. Table 11.6 shows that one of the reasons for the higher ratio of self-financing in the late 1960s was in fact a fall in gross fixed investment between 1967/8 and 1969/70, much of which was accounted for by a fall in the fuel and power industries in 1968/9 and 1969/70. In the transport industries the situation was more variable, with investment fluctuating from year to year. In the Post Office and steel there was a continued upward trend.

Table 11.5. *Exchequer loans to the nationalised industries (net),[a] 1960–74*

£ million[b]

	60/1	61/2	62/3	63/4	64/5	65/6	66/7
NCB	3	24	−26	−17	30	39	43
Electricity	181	228	231	302	361	333	440
Gas	20	13	21	69	50	61	164
Aviation	32	32	15	5	7	2	3
Surface transport	182	157	79	13	40	62	36
Post Office	40	40	35	65	85	95	130
BSC	—	—	—	—	—	—	—
Total	458	494	355	437	573	592	816

	67/8	68/9	69/70	70/1	71/2	72/3	73/4
NCB	76	20	−11	−28	44	117	19
Electricity	380	204	321	242	194	115	−116
Gas	262	206	158	133	188	173	−38
Aviation	17	30	−20	24	43	−36	−36
Surface transport	88	44	16	40	45	2	35
Post Office	200	240	240	253	297	423	313
BSC	175	−19	31	43	145	143	−3
Total	1198	725	735	707	956	937	174

SOURCES: CSO, *Annual Abstract of Statistics* and *Financial Statistics*.

[a] Some of the industries also borrowed abroad, but the amounts were relatively small until 1973, when other identified borrowing by the public corporations was £839 million.
[b] At current prices.

The Treasury's interpretation of these results was that during the 1960s there was a discernible improvement in the financial performance of the industries as a whole. It was felt that the relationship of the financial results to managerial and labour efficiency was more complicated, and that those were matters for the sponsoring department rather than the Treasury.[1]

Financial performance is not necessarily a good indicator of efficiency. It is also difficult to see how it can measure whether or not the application of the economic criteria succeeded in reducing excessive investment. But certainly in the years between 1967 and 1970 the industries' demands for Exchequer financing fell. What is less certain

[1] Ibid.

is whether this has led to any more efficient allocation of resources. In any case it seems unlikely that the efficient use of resources would require the industries to achieve particular levels of self-financing.

The success of government policy towards the nationalised industries in the 1960s was thus very limited, the increase in self-financing being

Table 11.6. *Capital expenditure by the nationalised industries, 1960–74*

£ million[a]

	60/1	61/2	62/3	63/4	64/5	65/6	66/7
NCB[b]	92	91	82	83	87	88	85
Electricity[b]	333	379	432	511	602	660	719
Gas[b]	42	44	57	92	89	119	234
Total fuel	*467*	*514*	*571*	*701*	*826*	*850*	*1079*
Aviation	46	36	24	34	38	31	40
Surface transport	198	169	129	112	132	155	127
Post Office	105	122	127	162	182	216	275
BSC	—	71	28	15	6	2	7
Total	816	912	879	1024	1184	1254	1528

	67/8	68/9	69/70	70/1	71/2	72/3	73/4
NCB[b]	80	58	59	73	79	79	74
Electricity[b]	670	562	475	481	489	497	544
Gas[b]	280	224	203	197	149	120	140
Total fuel	*1061*	*790*	*682*	*769*	*712*	*768*	*672*
Aviation	49	102	71	124	123	68	88
Surface transport	176	127	110	138	105	81	173
Post Office	320	349	401	470	575	671	727
BSC	62	80	102	195	210	256	252
Total	1668	1448	1366	1696	1725	1844	1912

SOURCES: CSO, *National Income and Expenditure 1975*, London, HMSO, 1975; HM Treasury.

[a] At current prices.

[b] Expenditure on fixed assets only; excludes other capital expenditure included under 'total fuel' (increase in value of stocks, sales of fixed assets, net lending to private sector).

confined to a short period and even then not applying to all the industries. The reasons for this are complicated, but a number of factors can be identified. In the first place the application of the commercial solution was controversial and in some cases difficult to apply. A further complication was the reluctance of some boards to apply the criteria, and this could only be overcome gradually because they resented interference in what they described as detailed management decisions. Finally, and perhaps most important, the commercial criteria conflicted from time to time with national policy, when inevitably they were modified or temporarily shelved.

The commercial solution

The nationalised industries are required by statute to pay attention to the public interest, which obliges them to work for something more than the good of themselves. This has been taken to imply that the industries' policies should conform with the broad economic policy of the country, so that their success must be harmonised with other developments. The main administrative appeal of the commercial approach lay in its clarity; it provided as a test of the success of a policy an unmistakable criterion, which could also be used to compare dissimilar activities. Its economic appeal lay in the fact that, if only projects that pay are taken up and services are economically priced, then resources will eventually be allocated more efficiently. The protagonists of the commercial approach argued that, even if commercial standards could not be applied without exception, the principle would provide a recognisable and practicable distinction between the responsibilities of the boards, which should be entirely commercial, and those of the government, which may take other considerations into account. This was the view of the Herbert Committee and has repeatedly been emphasised by the Select Committee on Nationalised Industries.

However the identification of social costs was not always straightforward. For example, the extension of overhead electricity cables on pylons raised the question of when it becomes worthwhile to put them underground, although the cost is on average ten times as great. Should the consumer bear this cost or should it come out of taxation, since it is a benefit to the public as a whole that the appearance of the countryside should not be marred by overhead systems. Another illustration affected the National Coal Board. Many pits in Scotland were operating at relatively high cost, but their closure would involve unemployment and distress in mining towns and villages, with social capital becoming redundant in those places and new social capital necessary in the places to which ex-miners moved. But the problem of social costs was probably most acute in the transport industries, where the closing down of branch railway lines became a political as well as a local issue. During the 1960s, however, there was a considerable advance in techniques of measuring social costs as a result of the research done in connection with the new Victoria tube line in London.[1]

Associated with the problem of identifying social costs and the decision on how far these should be financed by government subsidy was the whole question of cross-subsidisation. From the start nationalised industries had engaged in cross-subsidisation (indeed they had inherited

[1] C. D. Foster and M. E. Beesley, 'Estimating the social benefit of constructing an underground railway in London', *Journal of the Royal Statistical Society* (series A), vol. 126, pt 1, 1963.

systems where it had been applied). Some part of it was unavoidable – as in any business operation not all sales can be costed and sometimes prices have to be announced in advance before all costs are known. But there were many cases where it was practicable to avoid it, although in some the administrative costs of doing so were high and in others there were special reasons for retaining it. Cross-subsidisation has varied objectives: revenue from one very profitable service may enable a board to offer keen prices on another service where it faces sharp competition; it may enable an industry to keep up services which are expected to be viable in the future, but which could not easily be restarted if once discontinued, or embark on pioneering activities which are expected to pay eventually. The possibility of the government being willing openly to subsidise certain activities may lead a board to retain these in the hope of agreeing a subsidy. Generally it has become accepted that there are advantages in making it clear to everyone that a particular service is being subsidised.

The problem of combining social and commercial ends is an awkward one. In practice it is difficult to measure the financial cost of non-commercial actions imposed on the boards when they have a combination of activities producing very different returns. Also, it may not be easy to decide whether a particular service which the government wishes to be maintained is one that the industry might reasonably seek to eliminate on commercial grounds.

For all these reasons the commercial solution has not been universally regarded as the right one. In any case the view is held by some that all industry, whether nationalised or not, has social responsibilities. Industrial decisions should involve social as well as commercial values and it has been argued that public industries should take the lead in this. There is a movement in the United States and Britain against defining business objectives in simple terms and it would be paradoxical if at this juncture a 'commercial' rule, based solely on the money profits of each concern separately, were to be prescribed for the nationalised industries.

The attitude of the boards and the system of control

The criteria were set out as guiding principles only and no legal enforcement followed. The 1967 White Paper came nearest to an order in its request that investment plans should be put forward in the form of discounted cash flows. At first there was resistance to this; evidence to the Select Committee in 1967/8 and subsequently revealed considerable reluctance by some of the boards to using this technique. The main reason was inability to produce all the figures necessary and the application is often highly specific to the technology of the industry.

Gradually these difficulties seem to have been overcome and by 1973 all the boards claimed that they used this technique for investment appraisal.

Similarly, the actual working out of long-run marginal costs can be very complicated, requiring a sophisticated simulation of the system. Accepting the principle is only a start, and the interpretation is more often than not a very detailed matter, complicated in some industries by the problem of peak demand. The adoption of marginal cost pricing was consequently even slower than the adjustment of investment appraisal, but by 1973 most of the expanding industries had achieved a closer relation between prices and short-term marginal costs, often as a result of urging by the NBPI. However, for coal and the railways, which faced a major long-term decline in demand, there was no solution to their problems through marginal cost pricing.

The adoption of the criteria was consequently a gradual process and not universal. Because of the constitutional position of the industries the departments could only persuade. Moreover, the role of the Treasury remained a secondary one; the main financial powers rested with the sponsoring departments, although it was the Treasury which was most anxious to improve the industries' performance.

The main way in which the Treasury carries out its function in relation to the industries (apart from housekeeping questions connected with the terms of borrowing and the form of the accounts) is through the machinery to combine their investment programmes, which is all done through the departments and not directly with the boards. No system has ever developed for the Treasury itself to collect the investment programmes and appraisals, and to recommend how investment might be reallocated; this was felt to be inconsistent with departmental Ministers' Parliamentary accountability for particular industries. However, the idea grew that the government should secure a better oversight of efficiency, and in 1967 it was announced that the NBPI would carry out a study of each industry whenever a proposed price increase was referred to it, and would review the industry's machinery for keeping down costs. Between 1967 and 1971 some studies were undertaken in areas which were considered to show the greatest scope for improvement, but by and large responsibility remained with the industries themselves.

Conflicts with national economic policies

The nationalised industries were expected to cooperate to the full with the current economic policy of the government of the day. During the 1960s wages, prices and investment programmes all had to be adapted to comply with emergency measures to meet critical economic problems. The political and administrative power of the government ensured that the industries did not neglect or evade these duties; indeed they were often expected to be a good example to private industry.

There had been interventions in the 1950s and there were more during the 1960s – mainly of two types. In the first place, in the interests of short-term demand management the industries were asked to reduce or defer their investment programmes for the financial years 1961/2, 1966/7, 1967/8 and 1968/9; in 1971 they were asked to accelerate their programmes for the years 1972/3 and 1973/4. It seems unlikely that the cuts had any material effect on profitability; for one thing the amounts were small in relation to the total of the programmes, for another they were generally delays rather than cuts and for a third the boards themselves considered the effects marginal. The effects of these short-term adjustments to capital expenditure are traced in chapter 3: the 1961/2 cuts had no demonstrable effect and nor had those for 1966/7 and 1967/8; there may have been some small reductions in 1968/9; the acceleration from 1972 to 1974 was also ineffective.

The second group of interventions, which related to the government's prices and incomes policy, had much more serious effects on the industries. Raising prices has never been simple for industries in public ownership because of the need to obtain the government's approval, which has often been difficult to secure and has sometimes involved costly delays. But in the late 1960s the situation became more difficult as prices and incomes policies were intensified. In 1966/7 the industries were forced to delay price increases in line with the pay freeze. From 1970 to 1973 price restraint exercised at the government's request brought the industries' finances into greater difficulties than ever before and a number of them accumulated large deficits.[1] In these ways the industries' economic and financial objectives were sacrificed to the government's wider economic objectives.

Other broad government objectives related to transport and fuel policy have sometimes conflicted with the Treasury's general objectives for the boards. For example, it was argued that prudence dictated special care of the coal industry, in view of the uncertainty about supplies and costs of imported fuels which must always prevail in circumstances of rising world demand. Arguments of this kind were used in the discussions on national fuel policy in the 1960s and secured limited acceptance; they were one factor in the government support which slowed the running down of the industry. Similarly, consideration of future transport needs implied that an efficient railway system would be needed, despite the fact that in the 1960s it could not have

---

[1] The effect of restraint has been estimated at £146 million for 1971–3 and £300 million in 1973/4 (House of Commons, *Hansard*, 20 March 1974, col. *126*; *Economist*, 30 March 1974).

been sustained as a going concern by commercial operation, even when loss-making services retained for social reasons were financed by the government. An uncontrolled run-down of the coal industry and the closure of some railway lines would also have conflicted with the government's regional policy.

Finally, it is pertinent to consider whether the government's emphasis on growth led to any excessive investment in the nationalised industries in the 1960s. As part of the procedure for the annual investment review the Treasury provides each industry, through its sponsoring department, with basic assumptions about the growth of the economy over the five years ahead; if any industry needs assumptions for a longer period the Treasury does its best to provide them. The industries like to have a lead in this way for their own forecasts, but it is known that in some cases they modify the assumed growth rates. For example, when the Electricity Council decided that the growth rates in the National Plan were not going to be achieved, the electricity industry began to make its own forecasts of future growth.[1] The British Railways Board has also admitted to making variations in the Treasury's forecasts.[2] However, the unreality of the growth targets was recognised fairly quickly, so that although there may have been some excessive investment as a result of over-optimistic government forecasts of the rate of growth, this is unlikely to have been substantial. Where excess capacity has occurred it is more likely to have been the result of over-optimism about the demand for the industry's products than about the overall growth rate.

CONCLUSION

The role of the government in relation to the nationalised industries is a very special one.[3] It is involved in their affairs in four different ways. First, it is concerned as a producer in the output and efficiency of the industries and their 'profitability' however defined. Secondly, it is concerned with the effects on consumers of the industries' policies and performance. Thirdly, since these industries are monopolies, it is concerned, as with private monopolies, to ensure that their monopolistic position is not exploited. Finally, it is concerned with the influence of the industries on its economic and social policies as a whole,

---

[1] In 1966/7 a downward revision to the forecast rate of economic growth led to the postponement of a number of projects; there may even so have been some over-investment during the year 1965/6.

[2] House of Commons, *Select Committee on Nationalised Industries, Session 1973-74. First Report.*

[3] A recent Report examines the role in detail and concludes that most nationalised industries feel strongly that government intervention is excessive (NEDO, *A Study of UK Nationalised Industries*, London, HMSO, 1976).

for example through labour relations in the industries. These different aspects of government involvement are at the root of the issues discussed in this chapter, which has attempted to assess the effectiveness of government policy towards the nationalised industries in the 1960s. The broad conclusion is that the government has achieved only a limited success in its objectives; the main reasons are lack of clarity in the aims, limitation of the instruments of control and conflicts with other objectives of government policy.

The first two reasons are closely related. The controversy about commercial principles, which was a symptom of confusion about the aims of nationalisation, has proceeded since the 1950s and is still not settled satisfactorily. The doctrine that non-commercial activities should be allowed so long as they are at the behest of the government now seems to have been accepted, but it does not answer all the problems. Managers are still faced with the need to take decisions which involve social criteria and which require a broader approach than simply a distinction between commercial and non-commercial activities. A former Treasury official sees the issues as among the most important in the public sector today and concludes that more satisfactory ways must be found of combining the commercial and social objectives of the industries.[1]

Even if the objectives had been capable of more satisfactory definition, it seems doubtful if the economic criteria set out in the White Papers could have been the means to their achievement. The investment criteria provided a useful discipline but little more, and marginal costs turned out to be too simple a formula for the complicated pricing problems of most of the industries. The annual accounts with their financial out-turns have remained the main criteria of success – also one of the main disciplines, as there is a universal dislike of going into deficit, which means more questioning and more interference by the sponsoring department and the Treasury. Such a financial constraint provides a strong incentive for reducing costs and the various forms of investigation are a stimulus to efficiency. But more useful criteria of success are needed.

It is difficult to imagine a set of rules which would be appropriate in all circumstances; what is needed is a supervisory body with discretion to adapt rules to different industries and changing circumstances. In some cases the constraints imposed on the industrial management would be ones a competitive market would impose; in other cases they would be political. The nationalised industries should not be profit maximisers; because competition is weak, prices need to be limited or

[1] Civil Service Department, *The Developing System of Public Expenditure, Management and Control* by Sir Samuel Goldman, K.C.B., London, HMSO, 1973.

controlled. Pricing policy should therefore be an important part of the role of the supervisory body because changes in tariffs need to be justified. There is also a need for some form of efficiency audit which would include indicators of quality, standards of service and managerial efficiency. A major objective should be to ensure that the abuses of monopoly power are checked.

However, detailed interference in the running of the industries by government departments, as is now the practice, should be eliminated. Conflicts with other objectives of policy may recur and there should be some recognised means by which the corporations can act as agents of the government's social policies without it reflecting in the measures of the industries' economic performance.

CHAPTER 12

COMMERCIAL POLICY[1]

by *A. D. Morgan*

The late 1950s and the 1960s saw the biggest change in British commercial policy since free trade was finally abandoned in favour of protection and Imperial Preference in 1932. What started as a largely defensive reaction to the creation of the EEC evolved into a Europe-oriented policy pursued for its own sake. In purely commercial terms, the aim of policy-makers was to establish preferential trading arrangements with the EEC. Partly in pursuit of this aim, and following the lead given by the United States, the tariff protection given to British industry was drastically reduced. At the same time, and again partly in preparation for EEC membership, the system of agricultural protection was reorganised.

BACKGROUND TO POLICY IN THE LATE 1950S

As a founder-member of the GATT and OEEC, Britain in the mid-1950s was committed to reducing barriers to international trade on a multilateral, non-discriminatory basis within the limits imposed by balance of payments constraints, but this commitment was something less than whole-hearted. The potential gain from greater freedom to import, an important consideration in postwar commercial policy, no longer appeared to have much (if any) influence on official thinking. Tariff cuts and the abolition of quotas were seen as a means of securing easier access to foreign markets, and GATT as a referee, whose role was to police 'unfair practices' that could lead to undercutting of British prices.[2] The government equally felt it had a duty to give away as little protection for British industries as it could, whether the pro-

---

[1] This chapter covers those measures primarily intended to regulate the long-run conduct of trade with other countries. The use of non-discriminatory commercial instruments, for example the import surcharge, to influence the balance of payments in the short run is outside its scope, as are measures such as production subsidies that protect industries against import competition but were introduced for reasons of domestic policy. In the case of agriculture, however, deficiency payments and subsidies were, for most of the period covered, the main instrument of protection in the United Kingdom and they are therefore treated as elements of commercial policy.

[2] See, for example, a speech by the Minister of State at the Board of Trade reported in the *Board of Trade Journal*, 10 December 1955.

tection took the form of restrictions on imports into the United Kingdom or preferential treatment for British exports to the Commonwealth. Speaking at the opening of the Geneva Round in 1956, Frank Lee, the Permanent Secretary of the Board of Trade, declared that the British government did not accept the argument that tariffs in some countries were excessively high. 'We take, quite frankly, a pragmatic line'.[1]

The United Kingdom was, in fact, one of the most highly protected markets in Western Europe in respect of manufactured goods. Although quota restrictions remained important only in respect of a few sensitive products and in trade with the dollar area, Japan and the Sino-Soviet bloc, tariffs were another matter. The United Kingdom's most-favoured-nation tariff was one of the highest in Europe,[2] higher probably than any others save the French and Italian tariffs; it was notable also for the number of very high duties on manufactures, ranging upwards from 30 per cent *ad valorem*. The protective effect of the tariff was, however, mitigated by the Commonwealth Preference system, under which zero or very low duties were charged on almost all goods imported from Commonwealth countries and the Irish Republic. In consequence the bulk of food and raw material imports entered the country duty-free. Commonwealth manufactures were equally eligible for preference, but in practice this was of much less importance, since few countries in the preference area had an export trade in manufactures. The share of cheap Asian textiles and other simple manufactures in the British market was nevertheless beginning to rise sharply – a development that was arousing much anxiety in the Lancashire cotton textile industry and some others. In turn, United Kingdom products received tariff preferences in certain Commonwealth countries, notably Canada, Australia and New Zealand, and in the Irish Republic; but most African and several Asian Commonwealth countries gave no preferences to British goods, while elsewhere the preferences by no means applied to all British products.

Commonwealth Preference was not unique (France gave and received more substantial preferences in its Associated Overseas Territories), but it affected a larger volume of trade than any comparable system, and attracted a corresponding degree of criticism from non-participants. The most unusual feature of British commercial policy was the method of protecting agriculture, but since it was less restrictive of trade than the range of state trading, quotas, tariffs and so on deployed in many

[1] Reported in the *Board of Trade Journal*, 28 January 1956. As an example of the pragmatic approach – the United Kingdom voted in favour of Japan's accession to the GATT and promptly invoked article xxxv allowing it to refrain from honouring GATT obligations in respect of Japanese goods. The United Kingdom was, of course, not alone in its reluctance to allow unrestricted entry to Japanese products.

[2] This was in practice the general tariff applied to all non-Commonwealth goods.

other countries it did not arouse the same hostility abroad as the tariff preferences.

Because of Commonwealth Preference the tariff gave British farmers little or no protection against competing imports; the only duties that really protected British, as opposed to Commonwealth, producers were those on fruit and vegetables. But production of major crops and livestock products was subsidised through the system of deficiency payments, whereby the difference between market prices realised and an agreed guaranteed price was made up by payments from the Exchequer. The object was twofold – to maintain farm incomes and to ensure to United Kingdom producers as large a share of the market as they were physically capable of satisfying. The commitment to make up the guaranteed price was open-ended for most products, since the whole of domestic production was eligible for deficiency payments, but payments on liquid milk were limited to a 'standard quantity'. Here additional protection was provided by giving the Milk Marketing Board a monopoly of off-farm purchases of milk (apart from sales by producer-retailers), so that imports were effectively nil. Sugar imports were also controlled; but Commonwealth producers received a high guaranteed price for fixed quantities of sugar exported to the United Kingdom under the Commonwealth Sugar Agreement. Butter imports were intermittently subject to quotas, which were imposed in the interests of major overseas suppliers rather than of United Kingdom producers, since Britain was a favourite dumping ground for surpluses. By the early 1960s these quotas had been put on a permanent basis and 'voluntary' quotas had been negotiated on cheese.

The composition and direction of British trade reflected the pattern of commercial policy, more especially Commonwealth Preference. In 1955 food, drink and tobacco accounted for over one third and manufactures for less than one fifth of total imports – significantly higher and lower proportions respectively than in any other major European country[1] – while nearly one half of total imports and more than half of exports originated in or were destined for the preference area. However, there were reasons to expect that the Commonwealth bias in United Kingdom trade would become less pronounced over the next few years. Britain's share in Commonwealth markets, and its dependence on Commonwealth supplies, had been inflated by quotas and currency controls, postwar shortages elsewhere and the lack of purchasing power in European markets. It was clear that, as trade with other areas revived under the stimulus of postwar recovery, Commonwealth trade must become relatively less important for Britain; while the dismantling of sterling area controls on non-sterling area imports would leave trade

[1] Part of the difference is attributable to differences in the structure of production.

both ways, but especially British exports to the Commonwealth, more exposed to competition. Moreover, changes in tariff schedules, the erosion of margins on specific tariffs and changes in the commodity composition of trade had greatly reduced the extent and effectiveness of Commonwealth Preference as compared with the position before the war.[1]

In the postwar period the United Kingdom's share in the imports and exports of the rest of the Commonwealth had held up well, but in 1956 its share in trade both ways dropped sharply and continued to do so thereafter. This was the more worrying in that the British share of world exports of manufactures to all destinations had already begun to fall, not merely from the inflated level of 1950/1, but below the prewar level.

By 1955, then, it was becoming apparent that Britain's trading situation was changing, although there was as yet no sign that these trends would prompt any major rethinking in commercial policy. In June of that year, however, the situation altered dramatically when the six member-countries of the European Coal and Steel Community (ECSC) agreed at Messina to establish a Common Market, entailing the creation of a customs union with internal free trade and with a common external tariff and a commercial policy discriminating against all non-union suppliers. As an associate of the ECSC Britain was invited to send observers to the preparatory conference of the Six in Brussels, but after two months the observers were withdrawn, for what was proposed ran counter to the whole pattern of British policy and not on matters of trade alone. The evolution of Britain's commercial policy from then on stems directly from attempts to join the 'Europe' from which it had voluntarily retired.

CHRONOLOGY

The development of commercial policy since 1955 falls into six phases of unequal length. From 1955 to 1958 it was concerned with unsuccessful negotiations for a free trade area embracing all OEEC members; 1959 and early 1960 saw the formation of EFTA in the vain hope of bridgebuilding; this was followed by the first attempt, under a Conservative government, to secure British membership of the EEC, which ended in the French veto of late 1963. During 1964 and 1965 commercial policy was in the doldrums and there were no fresh initiatives; 1966 and 1967 saw the second abortive attempt, under Labour, to enter the Community, once again vetoed by the French. In the final

---

[1] See Sir Donald MacDougall and R. Hutt, 'Imperial preference: a quantitative analysis', *Economic Journal*, vol. 64, June 1954.

phase Britain at last negotiated entry into Europe: a Treaty of Accession was signed on 22 January 1972, and on 1 January 1973 the United Kingdom formally joined the EEC.

Negotiations for a free trade area

The original proposals for a free trade area emerged in response to the changing situation in continental Europe. Early in 1956 the British government appointed an inter-departmental committee to examine alternative policies that might be adopted to meet the situation created by the plans, now well in hand, to form a European Economic Community or Common Market. The committee was instructed to consider the possibilities of promoting some organisation based on either NATO or the OEEC; from the alternatives put forward, the government picked Plan G – the creation of a Europe-wide industrial free trade area comprising all OEEC members. On the evidence available it seems unlikely that Plan G differed radically from any of the alternatives proposed; according to Harold Macmillan's memoirs application for EEC membership was not at issue.[1]

In January 1957 an OEEC working party that had been established the previous summer reported in favour of establishing a free trade area and at the meeting of the OEEC Council of Ministers in the following month it was agreed that the member-countries should embark on formal negotiations. A bare two weeks later the Treaty establishing the EEC was signed in Rome.

The British view of what the free trade area should be, neatly tailored to British interests, was clearly set out in a memorandum circulated to other OEEC members and subsequently published as a White Paper.[2] Free trade should be limited to industrial goods, foodstuffs being wholly excluded not merely from tariff reductions but from any trade arrangements. Tariffs and quotas should be eliminated on intra-European trade according to a fixed timetable, but members should continue to levy duties fixed without reference to other members on imports from third countries. Moreover, they should have the right (under escape clauses) to take unilateral action on trade policy in the event of serious balance of payments difficulties. While common rules of origin would be necessary,[3] and some strengthening of rules of 'fair competition' might be needed to avoid deflection of trade[4] and the substitution of cartels or similar arrangements for tariff and quota

[1] H. Macmillan, *Riding the Storm 1956–1959*, London, Macmillan, 1971.

[2] Treasury, *A European Free Trade Area*, Cmnd 72, London, HMSO, 1957.

[3] Rules of origin determine what goods are deemed to have originated in a customs union or free trade area and therefore qualify for preferential treatment.

[4] The importing of goods from third countries into member-states with high tariffs via low-tariff members.

restrictions, common policies such as characterised the EEC on, for example, social regulations were not required. Institutional arrangements should be kept to a minimum, following in general the OEEC pattern, rather than the EEC system with its provisions for a strong central administration and for increasing resort to a form of majority voting, though limited departures from the unanimity rule within the free trade area were envisaged. The White Paper referred to the likelihood of closer cooperation in future on balance of payments policies, invisible trade, intra-area movements of capital and labour, social policies and the avoidance of marked divergences in economic and financial policies – cooperation that might arise either spontaneously or as a result of deliberate policy – but this was the only concession to the 'European' view that free trade was impossible without simultaneous coordination of policy in a number of areas. In the words of an official memorandum on Plan G: 'The proposals would be entirely consistent with the collective approach to freer trade and payments, and to convertibility; they would represent one step forward towards the world-wide reduction of trade barriers.'[1]

There was much in this that was unacceptable not merely to the Six but to other OEEC countries as well. In the course of the long drawn-out negotiations, the British government was forced to abandon, or at least modify substantially, its original position. Perhaps the most significant concession was that it agreed that agriculture should be covered, not to the extent of freeing trade (which would have suited no one), but at least to the extent of accepting measures that would promote intra-European trade in foodstuffs and perhaps lead to reduced protection. Britain also accepted rules comparable to those in the Treaty of Rome on non-tariff matters wherever it felt able to do so, agreed in principle to more restrictive procedures on origin than originally envisaged and, of its own volition, swung round in favour of a majority voting system to prevent abuse of escape clauses. But on the question of tariff autonomy it remained adamant – Britain was not prepared to enter into a customs union.

On their side, the Six, with the possible exception of the Germans, were not prepared to accept anything that would seriously weaken or dilute the EEC. During the course of 1958 it became apparent that the French at least would accept nothing less than some form of customs union. The moribund negotiations were given the *coup de grâce* in November, when the French government bluntly told the press (without having first told its partners in the EEC, or any of the other participants in the negotiations) that it was not possible to establish a free trade area of the kind desired by Britain.

[1] Macmillan, *Riding the Storm*.

During this period there were few other developments of any significance in British commercial policy. The United Kingdom participated in the 1956 Geneva Round of GATT tariff negotiations, but the results were disappointing. Together with the Canadians, the British government promoted what was intended to be a major Commonwealth conference on trade and finance in Montreal; the outcome of this oddly timed meeting – the free trade area negotiations were still under way – was little more than a collection of pious platitudes. The simultaneous British suggestion of an Anglo-Canadian free trade area came to nothing. Commonwealth countries were, indeed, beginning to move away from close association with Britain: both Australia and New Zealand negotiated agreements that allowed them to reduce preferential tariff margins on British goods.

The only legislative change was the passage of an Anti-Dumping Act early in 1957. This gave the Board of Trade power to impose additional duties on dumped and subsidised imports when satisfied that it was in the national interest to do so. However, the most important anti-dumping measures were taken in the interest of New Zealand butter producers; as a general rule, little use was made of these powers. Over the next twelve years 73 cases were investigated; anti-dumping duties were imposed in fourteen and other remedies, for example an agreement with the offending exporter that he should raise his prices, were found for a further twenty cases; the remaining applications were rejected, as were a considerable number of others where there was no prima facie evidence of dumping.[1]

The formation of EFTA

The idea that if the negotiations for a wider free trade area collapsed the outsiders should go it alone was first mooted not by governments but by industrialists in Britain and Scandinavia during the spring of 1958; it was put forward again when the negotiations indeed collapsed and quickly taken up by governments of the 'Other Six' – Scandinavians, British, Austrians and Swiss – as well as by the Portuguese. Inter-governmental discussions began early in the new year, in July 1959 a full-dress ministerial meeting was held in Stockholm to evolve a draft plan and by November the Stockholm Convention establishing a European Free Trade Association had been signed.

It was natural that the 'Other Six' should attempt some common action: they had a common interest in finding some way of living with the EEC, they had cooperated to a considerable degree during the free trade area negotiations and they were more likely to be able to put pressure on the Six together than singly. It is less clear why they

[1] *Board of Trade Journal*, 23 July 1969.

should have decided to form their own free trade area. EFTA in itself had little to recommend it, or so it appeared. All the members did more trade with the EEC than with each other and they entirely lacked the geographical cohesion of the Six. In the press release issued after the draft plan had been agreed in July it was stated that: 'The object of this association would be to strengthen the economies of its members by promoting expansion of economic activity, full employment, a rising standard of living and financial stability.' But, more to the point: 'Ministers affirmed that in establishing a European Free Trade Association it would be their purpose to facilitate early negotiations with the European Economic Community...These negotiations would have as their object to remove trade barriers and establish a multilateral association embracing all members of OEEC.'[1] The creation of an organisation such as EFTA was seen at that time as preventing any one country from doing a deal with the Six at the expense of the rest, which it was feared might lead to the development of a network of bilateral agreements.

In the light of hindsight it is easy to see that the formation of EFTA hindered rather than helped agreement with the EEC so far as Britain was concerned, but at the time this was less apparent. The 'Other Six' needed some cement and there was a readymade formula to hand. It has been suggested, no doubt correctly, that the British government believed that EFTA would not only hold the Other Six together in negotiations with the EEC, but also would demonstrate to the Six that a free trade area was a practical proposition.

The Stockholm Convention came very close to reproducing the original British plan for a wider European free trade area. It laid down a precise programme for the abolition of tariffs and quotas on intra-EFTA trade in industrial products (including industrial raw materials originating in the area), which was intended to be carried through between 1 July 1960 and 1 January 1970, but in fact was completed ahead of schedule by 1 January 1967.[2] It specified rules of origin, requiring for the most part no more than a certain 'EFTA content' to qualify goods for free trade treatment. It covered escape clauses, rules of competition, coordination of policy, invisibles and capital movements only in broad terms. Generally speaking rules and procedures were kept to a minimum and so far as possible followed OEEC practice. In one respect alone did it depart from the pattern originally laid down:

[1] Treasury, *Stockholm Draft Plan for a European Free Trade Association*, Cmnd 823, London, HMSO, 1959.

[2] As a consequence of the EFTA rules on quotas, the import licensing system for synthetic organic dyestuffs was abolished and replaced by a duty of 33⅓ per cent *ad valorem*. This is almost the only occasion during the decade when a high duty was introduced into the British tariff.

under pressure from the Danes and the Norwegians trade in agricultural and fisheries products was covered. Concrete measures on this front were, however, limited for the most part to the abolition of selected tariffs; they did not entail any change in Britain's agricultural policy.

During 1959 and early 1960, Britain and other major European countries where imports were still subject to significant quota restrictions virtually completed the liberalisation of intra-European and dollar imports. Thus by 1961 the only important physical restrictions on non-food imports that remained, apart from a few dollar quotas, were on imports from Japan and the Sino-Soviet bloc. Independently of the liberalisation programme, moves were being made to increase trade with the Soviet bloc. Following Harold Macmillan's visit to Moscow in February 1959, a five-year Anglo-Soviet trade agreement was signed, which was expected to lead to an increase in exports of Russian raw materials to the United Kingdom, substantial Russian orders for British industrial equipment and new opportunities for trade, still under quota, in consumer goods.

However, at the same time as official controls were being lifted on trade with other industrial countries, Britain was introducing unofficial restrictions on imports of low-cost cotton textiles from the developing countries. The government had been under pressure from Lancashire for several years to restrict imports from Asian Commonwealth countries. It steadfastly refused to introduce a tariff or to impose quotas unilaterally, but it gave its blessing to the cotton industry's efforts to secure 'voluntary' limitation of exports by manufacturers in Hong Kong, India and Pakistan. After two years of haggling, agreement was finally reached in September 1959, and the United Kingdom industry simultaneously received additional indirect protection with the introduction of the cotton industry reorganisation scheme. The quotas marked the beginning of a new protective policy, for negotiations with the three major suppliers were soon to be extended to other Asian Commonwealth countries and later to 'new' non-Commonwealth suppliers.

The first approach to the EEC

During the eighteen months following the collapse of the original free trade area negotiations, the British government remained officially committed to the idea of building a bridge between the EEC and EFTA that would lead to the creation of a wider association, if not quite the one they had formerly hoped for. But the ink was scarcely dry on the Treaty that was to make bridgebuilding possible before it became clear that it would not produce a solution to the problem of relations between the United Kingdom and the Six. Reconciliation on the terms envisaged by Britain foundered on the rocks of EEC opposition and mistrust of British motives. The government was faced with the alternatives of seeking reconciliation on terms acceptable to the Six (more accurately, to the French) or of developing some new positive approach. It chose to do the former.

The crucial change in Britain's policy appears to have originated during the first half of 1960, when Harold Macmillan and a number of leading Civil Servants were converted to the idea that, sooner or later, Britain must join the EEC. Until then, although the political implications of the EEC had not been ignored, the government had chosen to treat relations with the Community largely as a commercial problem. (It is significant that the department chiefly concerned with the negotiations of 1957/8 and 1959 was the Board of Trade.) This approach appears to have arisen partly from the preoccupation of the Foreign Office and the Treasury with problems elsewhere and from their innate dislike of 'Europe', partly from misunderstanding of what the Six were doing and partly from disbelief that they could go as fast and as far as they intended – even on the economic side. Much of the Treaty of Rome consists of statements of intent – indeed almost all of it save the plans for a customs union and the institutional framework of the Community – while proposals for a political union were cloudier still. This being so, it was perhaps not wholly unreasonable to treat United Kingdom–EEC relations as a matter of commercial policy, leaving time to show how, if at all, relations in other fields would be affected. But the failure of an almost purely commercial approach and the successful launching of the Common Market forced the British government to think again.

Once again an inter-departmental committee was charged with the task of examining the problem of relations with the EEC and the alternative policies open to the British government. This time, however, the committee took a wider view than in 1956. The conclusion reached – that Britain should when the time was ripe seek to join the Community – was based far more on political than on economic arguments. From now on the departments mainly concerned with negotiations were the Foreign Office and the Treasury.

Though the Prime Minister and some other members of the Cabinet agreed with the committee's conclusion, there was still a long way to go before this change of heart could be translated into action. The doubters in the government had to be convinced, political support drummed up, the Commonwealth and EFTA consulted and if possible squared, and soundings taken about the American reaction; some assurance had to be obtained from the Six that an application for membership had a reasonable chance of success and proposals for dealing with some of the problems bound to arise in any negotiations had to be evolved. All this was in fact to be achieved within the next twelve months. Meanwhile the immediate aims of policy as described by Selwyn Lloyd to the House of Commons in July 1960 were to develop trade with EFTA and the EEC, and to work for reduced discrimination between the two trade blocs, more particularly by playing an active part in the forthcoming Dillon Round of GATT tariff negotiations. For the longer term, the government was publicly committed to some form of close association between the United Kingdom and the Six, probably involving a customs union and certainly having some political content.

During the latter part of 1960 and the first part of 1961 the idea that Britain should apply for EEC membership began to command increasingly wide support within the government. Partly this arose from the recognition that any 'close association' short of entry was likely to have all the disadvantages of full membership without the power to influence the Community's evolution, partly it arose in consequence of moves towards political union among the Six themselves and partly because the idea was there. Once the government stopped saying 'in no circumstances can Britain join the EEC', once entry became a genuine alternative, it naturally attracted support. Moreover, industry as represented by the Federation of British Industries was strongly in favour of closer relations with the Six. There was still considerable opposition inside and outside the government, but opponents of the idea signally failed to put up a convincing case for any alternative policy.

By mid-1961 the time was judged to be ripe, and at the end of July Harold Macmillan announced to the House of Commons that Britain was to apply for membership of the EEC. A little over two months later Edward Heath was in Paris setting out for the Six the reasons for the application and the British view on the problems that membership would create for which special solutions must be found during the course of negotiations.[1] These were trade relations with the Commonwealth, United Kingdom agriculture, and arrangements with those EFTA countries that did not wish to join the Community. In respect of the first problem a combination of association (after the pattern adopted for former French colonial territories), special protocols to maintain duty-free entry to the United Kingdom and tariff-free quotas (both of which already existed in respect of a small part of the trade of existing member-countries) and straightforward tariff reductions were proposed. In the case of temperate foodstuffs, that is those competing directly with European agricultural products, Commonwealth countries should

---

[1] See Foreign Office, *The United Kingdom and the European Economic Community*, Cmnd 1565, London, HMSO, 1961.

in principle receive 'comparable outlets' to those they enjoyed in Britain for their exports. Given the value of the trade involved, Britain was in fact asking for a fairly substantial adulteration of Community preference in favour of the Commonwealth; for the rest it was prepared to accept the customs union as it stood, while tacitly endorsing the proposal for a 20 per cent cut in the common external tariff in the forthcoming Dillon round of GATT negotiations.

The EFTA problem was, in fact, never seriously discussed during the negotiations and that of British agriculture, though extensively discussed, was not finally resolved. It is clear, however, that the British government was prepared to go a long way to reach a compromise acceptable to the Six on this point. Arrangements for dealing with Commonwealth trade were virtually completed and here Britain gave a great deal away. In place of 'comparable outlets' for temperate foodstuffs it accepted the vague promise of 'reasonable access', backed up by assurances that the enlarged Community would declare in favour of discussions on international commodity agreements and a price policy that would contribute to a 'satisfactory' level of world trade. It failed to achieve any significant tariff or quota concessions on manufactures from the older Dominions and Asian Commonwealth countries. Only for those African and West Indian countries prepared to accept association (and many were not) did Britain secure anything like the terms asked for.

While the negotiations for EEC entry dragged on in Brussels, the Dillon Round of GATT negotiations had been completed in the spring of 1962. They had originated in American efforts to secure a substantial reduction in the EEC's common external tariff, and had been warmly welcomed by Britain. The government 'hoped that negotiations at the conference would lead to substantial reductions in trade barriers'; the United Kingdom was 'ready to exchange important tariff reductions over a wide range of our imports for comparable reductions in tariffs against our exports'.[1] The chief participants in the Dillon Round, including Britain, did in fact reduce duties on many industrial goods by one fifth, but for all industrial products the average was much less – estimated at between 7 and 11 per cent of the basic tariff. The cuts were put into effect at the beginning of November 1962, except for duty reductions on imported passenger cars, which were to be implemented in three stages in line with similar reductions by the EEC.

Another tariff change made during the period, though not significant in itself, was a portent for the future. Since the publication of the Haberler Report[2] the developing countries had been pressing for more generous

[1] *Board of Trade Journal*, 10 June 1960.
[2] GATT, *Trends in International Trade: a report by a panel of experts*, Geneva, 1958.

treatment of their exports by the industrial countries, including the elimination of both revenue and protective duties on tropical products. In the 1962 budget duties on sugar, cocoa and coffee were reduced to zero for Commonwealth produce and to a level that maintained the margin of Commonwealth Preference on imports from all other countries.

A move in the direction of non-discrimination was the signing of an Anglo-Japanese Commercial Treaty on 14 November 1962, under which the United Kingdom agreed to give Japan most-favoured-nation treatment, subject to safeguards against 'disruptive' import competition, and the retention of import controls or 'voluntary' export quotas on certain sensitive items; controls on sensitive items other than textiles and clothing were to be regularly eased and finally abolished by the end of 1967. This programme was largely carried out, so that by 1968 only major textile products, clothing and pottery remained subject to export quotas.

On the other hand, the United Kingdom maintained and strengthened the system whereby imports of cotton textiles from the less developed countries were restricted or controlled; it was a party to the GATT Long-Term Cotton Agreement on condition that it was exempt from the obligation to increase quotas annually.[1] Moreover, while professing its desire to remove obstacles to the exports of the developing countries, the government was not prepared to make concessions unmatched by similar concessions elsewhere. The United Kingdom was, of course, a good deal more generous already in its treatment of developing countries' products, including cotton textiles, than were other industrial countries.

The government's generally liberal approach to commercial policy was partly dictated by the desire to minimise discrimination against British exports should negotiations with the EEC fail. But it was not solely a response to external pressures; there was now a real commitment to greater freedom for international trade. Replying to a Parliamentary question in March 1962 which tacitly asked for the encouragement of import replacement, the President of the Board of Trade said: 'It would not make economic sense to increase domestic production in order to save imports unless the goods could be produced here more cheaply and more efficiently than they can be bought from abroad. Our prosperity depends on the expansion of international trade, and trade is a two-way process.'[2]

[1] The Agreement, which came into effect in 1962, was designed to regulate the growth of cotton textile exports from developing to developed countries; it incorporated provisions for regular increases in import quotas.

[2] *Board of Trade Journal*, 6 April 1962.

Marking time

In January 1963 General de Gaulle slapped his veto on the Brussels negotiations, thus not only defeating Britain's first attempt to enter the EEC but coming close to wrecking the Community itself for a time. With the Six embroiled in a long drawn-out crisis, which effectively lasted until the following December, there was little that the British government could do in the way of sorting out relations with the EEC, and in 1964 the general election and the balance of payments crisis crowded Europe off the stage. For the time being there was neither opportunity nor energy for developing new initiatives in commercial policy. Nevertheless, these two years saw the beginning of the most important changes (apart from the creation of EFTA) that actually occurred during the 1960s in the level and method of protection.

The first major change was initiated with the opening of the Kennedy Round of GATT negotiations in May 1963. Though multilateral in form, the Kennedy Round was essentially a bilateral bargain between the United States and the EEC. Britain was, however, an enthusiastic and active participant, both under the Conservative government and under the Labour administration that replaced it. As in the Dillon Round, its interest was to secure the maximum international reduction in tariffs so as to minimise discrimination in the EEC market. Initially it lined up behind the United States in support of equal percentage tariff cuts rather than larger cuts on higher tariffs and kept its list of exceptions short, though the other major EFTA countries went one better by submitting no lists of exceptions at all; in the end it made considerable concessions on steel and agreed to cut some high chemical tariffs by more than half.[1]

The Kennedy Round was not completed until June 1967, after Britain had made its second application to join the Community, but the results of the negotiations may conveniently be summarised here. They far surpassed those of all previous GATT rounds, even if the 50 per cent across-the-board cut envisaged in the United States Trade Expansion Act was not achieved. The main participants agreed that duties on a high proportion of industrial goods should be reduced by half, with smaller cuts for most other items, bringing the average reduction for all manufactures to between 35 and 40 per cent of the base level. The biggest reductions applied to machinery and vehicles and to chemicals, though in the latter case the full cuts by Britain and the EEC were conditional on the abolition of the American selling price

[1] For an account of the Kennedy Round negotiations see E. H. Preeg, *Traders and Diplomats*, Washington (DC), Brookings Institution, 1970.

system and have not in fact been implemented; the smallest cuts were in respect of simple textiles and other manufactures exported by the developing countries. The United Kingdom made its first cuts, two fifths of the total reduction agreed, on 1 July 1968; these were followed by successive reductions of one fifth of the total at the beginning of 1970, 1971 and 1972. Apart from the conditional reductions, the Kennedy Round programme of tariff cuts has been completed.

The second change, which arose largely from domestic budgetary considerations, involved the level of support and hence of protection given to domestic agricultural production. With growing farm output and fluctuating world prices, the cost of open-ended support through the guaranteed price system was becoming too large and too erratic for comfort. Hence, in March 1963 it was announced that the amount of domestic output qualifying for guaranteed prices would be restricted to 'standard quantities' in future, while negotiations would be held with major overseas suppliers with the object of limiting their exports to this country.

The Agriculture and Horticulture Act of 1964 gave formal expression to the new system, making provision for the introduction of minimum import prices, enforced where necessary by levies on imports below the minimum. Following negotiations with major suppliers, a minimum import price system was introduced for the major cereals in 1964, but attempts to negotiate limitations on beef and lamb imports failed. Support arrangements for cattle and sheep were therefore left unaltered; standard quantities were introduced only for wheat and barley. Pig-meat was dealt with rather differently, the volume of imports being regulated by negotiated quotas under the 'bacon market understanding' of November 1963; domestic producers were thus given an assured share of the market.

The third strand in post-Brussels policy was an attempt to secure easier access to industrial markets for developing countries, especially in the Commonwealth – a move which would at once help the countries concerned and encourage them to devote less attention to the United Kingdom market. (This policy could be pursued with more vigour now that there was no risk of prejudicing negotiations with the Six.) A minor step in this direction was the conclusion of an agreement with the EEC in September 1963 first to suspend and then to abolish duties on tea and tropical hardwoods. The most important policy development in this area, however, was the stand taken by the British government at the first UNCTAD. In his opening speech to the conference in April 1964, Edward Heath proposed a number of commercial and financial measures to assist the developing countries; several did no more than reiterate points already under discussion in GATT, but the

United Kingdom government also proposed the granting of generalised tariff preferences by the industrial countries to the exports of the developing countries. For the United Kingdom itself this meant the substitution of general preferences for Commonwealth Preference so far as the developing countries in the Commonwealth were concerned.

In its last months in office, the Conservative government took fresh steps to 'normalise' trading relations with Communist countries. East European countries were offered further trade liberalisation and the removal of a wide range of quantitative restrictions on their exports in return for definite safeguards for British industry against disruptive dumping and increased opportunities for British exporters. The government also drew up plans to establish a new export trade promotion organisation following the dissolution of the Western Hemisphere Export Council. Its final measure in commercial policy was the introduction of a new system controlling imports of jute manufactures, which involved the return of part of the trade to private hands, an increase in the range of goods to be imported by the Jute Control, and a reduction in the mark-up (in effect an import levy) charged on imported cloths.

The second approach to the EEC

In its first months in office the Labour government had its hands too full with other problems to be concerned with the grand strategy of commercial policy. In broad outline it continued the policy of its Conservative predecessor; though there were some shifts in emphasis, on the whole they were of more sentimental than practical importance. In particular, British support for the Kennedy Round was maintained. In the budget debate of November 1964, Douglas Jay, the new President of the Board of Trade said: 'We mean to press on strenuously with the Kennedy Round and the international long-term effort to reduce protective tariffs and restrictions throughout the world...We must learn to distinguish sharply between...short-term emergency measures ...and permanent restrictive barriers.'[1] This, in fact, was something the Labour government did; despite pressure from some of its supporters it did not renege on its long-term commitments to GATT and EFTA, even if some of its temporary measures bent the rules almost to breaking point.

Meanwhile, it was assumed that, even should the government opt for entry into the EEC, any direct approach was blocked while General de Gaulle remained in power. For the time being, therefore, the emphasis was laid on cooperation, including technological cooperation and participation in joint production programmes; but how the government

[1] *Board of Trade Journal*, 20 November 1964.

would choose between long-term policy alternatives was far from clear.

During the 1964 election campaign a good deal had been said about the importance of revivifying the Commonwealth. After a ritualistic mention of closer links with Europe, the election manifesto stated categorically that 'the Labour party is convinced that the first responsibility of a British government is still to the Commonwealth'. Furthermore, it promised that a Labour government would 'build a firmer basis for expanding trade by entering into long-term contracts and commodity agreements providing guaranteed markets for Commonwealth primary produce at stable prices'. Once Labour was in office little more was heard of this idea. The wranglings at the 1965 Commonwealth Prime Ministers' Conference put paid to any serious efforts to reconstruct commercial policy on the basis of the Commonwealth connection.

EFTA was a less visionary alternative and gestures were made in the direction of encouraging further development, combined with bridge-building between the Six and the Seven (see page 521). Wilson attended the EFTA ministerial meeting in Vienna in May 1965, when various possibilities were discussed, but nothing constructive emerged, partly because the Seven were at odds among themselves about EFTA's future, partly because the Six remained hostile to anything that would dilute Community preference.

During the course of 1965 the tone of official and unofficial references to the Community became steadily warmer and policy statements more ambiguous. The Conservative Party once again came out strongly in favour of EEC membership, even before Edward Heath succeeded Sir Alec Douglas Home as leader; opinion within the Labour Party was moving in favour of entry, as was opinion in the country at large. Whereas in July 1960 only 49 per cent of replies to a Gallup Poll inquiry were in favour of approaching the EEC, 60 per cent on average were in favour in the autumn of 1965;[1] and this despite the fact that the Community was again embroiled in a crisis – the most serious in its history. By early 1966 the government was coming very close to adopting a policy of actively seeking entry into Europe.

The sole new policy that was implemented in 1965, however, had nothing directly to do with the EEC, though the possibility of future membership obviously influenced not merely the British government but that of the other country concerned – the Irish Republic. The Republic had never lost its preferences in the United Kingdom market and continued to give (less generous) preferences to British goods. This

[1] Gallup Poll, 'British attitudes to the EEC, 1960–63' and 'Public opinion and the EEC' *Journal of Common Market Studies*, vol. 5, September 1966, and vol. 6, March 1968.

partial and lop-sided system was now replaced by a Treaty, signed in December, which established an Anglo-Irish free trade area giving all Irish goods not already admitted freely under the Commonwealth Preference system duty-free entry into the United Kingdom with effect from 1 July 1966 and guaranteeing access for agricultural exports to the United Kingdom market. In return, the Republic was to abolish almost all protective duties on imports from the United Kingdom over a ten-year period starting in mid-1966.

With the EEC crisis resolved and the British elections out of the way in March 1966, things began to move. This time Labour's election manifesto had stated that: 'Labour believes that Britain, in consultation with her EFTA partners, should be ready to enter the European Economic Community, provided essential British and Commonwealth interests are safeguarded.' In the new Labour administration, George Brown (long a committed European) was charged with special responsibility for economic relations with Europe. He became chairman of a committee that was once more to examine the economic and social consequences of EEC membership, while, together with George Thomson at the Foreign Office, he was to 'probe' European minds on possible terms of entry. By the autumn Harold Wilson had made up his mind, and persuaded the doubters in his Cabinet that Britain should make a new high-level approach to see whether and on what terms negotiations might be conducted. Early in the new year Wilson and Brown set off on a tour of European capitals; finally, on 2 May 1967 the Prime Minister announced that Britain was formally to apply for EEC membership.

In his account of his administration Harold Wilson records that the Cabinet considered three alternatives: a North Atlantic free trade area, EEC entry, or go it alone. The first proposal initially included the United States, Canada, the United Kingdom and the rest of EFTA, but was envisaged as extending later to all developed countries. It had originated some years earlier with the private Canadian–American committee and was effectively publicised on both sides of the Atlantic. It attracted considerable attention and some support in this country, particularly among those who disliked the protectionist element in the EEC. The Cabinet, however, agreed that the North Atlantic free trade area was not a real alternative because it was not negotiable; it was, in fact, never official policy in the United States. Going it alone was regarded as a fallback if entry could not be negotiated; though the reasons for this view are not set out, they are not hard to guess. That, of course, left EEC entry as the only acceptable choice.

The difficulty was to get the British case heard. The French refused to allow it to be submitted to the Commission and the British government was reduced to delivering it via the back door in the form of a speech by George Brown to the West European Union Council of Ministers, in which he set out the United Kingdom's negotiating stance.[1] In form this speech was similar to that made by Edward Heath at the beginning of the previous negotiations; having given the reasons for Britain's application, it turned to the problems involved. They were the same as before, but had shrunk in the intervening years, some almost to vanishing point. Only a one-year standstill at the beginning of the transition period was asked for to facilitate negotiations with the EFTA countries and the Irish Republic; the chief concern on agriculture was with the financing of the Common Agricultural Policy; in relation to the Commonwealth it was with imports of Commonwealth sugar and New Zealand butter. For the developing Commonwealth in Africa and the Caribbean the proposals, in effect, were to revive the agreements reached in the 1961–3 negotiations. In short, the British government was now asking for no more than very limited exceptions to the Community preference system.

During the summer, the EEC Commission was asked by the Council to give a formal opinion on Britain's application and reported in favour in early October. The French, pursuing their customary delaying tactics, stalled discussion in the Council of Ministers and early in November Wilson, in a speech at the Guildhall, attempted to give fresh impetus to the pre-negotiations by proposing a European technological community. He advocated the development of a specifically European technology as 'a catalyst to a deeper and closer economic integration'.[2] Among his suggestions were bilateral projects, both government and private, in computers, electronics and the civil application of nuclear energy, multilateral discussions on technology with 'our European partners', and a multilateral European institute of technology. Throughout the pre-negotiations Wilson had emphasised the great accretion of technological know-how that British membership would bring to the Community, and equally, of course, the opportunities for Britain to deploy its skill. This approach was not original – British Ministers had often tried to tempt European appetites with the bait of British know-how – but the importance given to it was new. But it was all to no avail. Shortly after devaluation the French government once more vetoed Britain's application. It had been clear almost since the British decision was announced that General de Gaulle was simply waiting for a suitable opportunity to say 'No' once more.

The second British application for EEC membership was never

---

[1] Cabinet Office, *The United Kingdom and the European Communities*, Cmnd 3345, London, HMSO, 1967.

[2] Quoted in U. Kitzinger, *The Second Try: Labour and the EEC*, Oxford, Pergamon, 1968.

formally withdrawn and both major Parties remained committed to seeking entry, but until the General disappeared from the European scene there was nothing to be done. This time there was no question of falling back on EFTA; indeed, Britain's relations with its partners were strained by its lack of consideration for their interests. The Kennedy Round had, for the time being, exhausted any possibility of fruitful negotiations between the industrial countries, while negotiations for generalised preferences for the developing countries were bogged down in Paris and Geneva. All that the government could do was wait for something to turn up on the international scene and devote itself to tidying up some minor aspects of commercial policy.

In *The National Plan*,[1] and again in *The Task Ahead*,[2] the importance of substituting domestic goods for imports was emphasised and some faint efforts in this direction were made by the Labour government. Most of them, for example the proposal to build three aluminium smelters,[3] fall outside the field of commercial policy proper. However, in order to assist plans to replace £250 million worth of agricultural imports annually, the government abandoned the standard of quantity of wheat eligible for deficiency payments in 1967 and of barley in 1968, thus, of course, increasing the protective effect of the deficiency payments system. In other respects they left protection of agriculture unchanged. The Conservative Party was, by 1966, advocating the extension of the levy system to other products, but at that time Labour would have none of it, though like the Conservatives the government professed itself in favour of international commodity agreements.

In 1967 the Queen's speech promised the introduction of stronger anti-dumping legislation, but it was not till 1969 that the Customs Duties (Dumping and Subsidies) Act was passed, consolidating the 1957 Act with the provisions of the Amendment Act of 1968. The main purpose of the new legislation was to allow the Board of Trade to take (provisional) action against dumped goods before, rather than after, investigating the case, and to give it additional powers to determine 'comparable domestic prices' for goods from state-trading countries. The Board, however, continued to put a strictly limited interpretation on dumping and material injury.

Also in 1969, the Textile Council proposed and the government agreed that, with effect from the beginning of 1972, the use of quotas to protect the cotton industry should be abandoned except in special cases, and a duty at the level of 85 per cent of the most-favoured-nation rate should be imposed on imports from the Commonwealth. This was a major change in principle; previous measures had diluted Common-

---

[1] Department of Economic Affairs, *The National Plan*.
[2] Department of Economic Affairs, *The Task Ahead*.   [3] See chapter 10, page 434.

wealth Preference, but not since 1932 had an import duty actually been introduced on a major Commonwealth export. On the other hand, the remaining controlled trade in jute manufactures was returned to private hands, though the industry remained heavily protected by tariffs and quotas.

The final negotiations

Even after the resignation of General de Gaulle in April 1969, the French insisted that the EEC should deal with the problems of 'completion' (that is the financing of the Common Agricultural Policy), 'deepening' and 'enlarging' the Community in that order. It was not until the end of 1969 that the Six agreed that preparations should be made for negotiations with Britain to begin in the following summer – an arrangement that was confirmed with the Labour government in May. But when the negotiations opened on 30 June the Conservatives were back in power and it was Anthony Barber who presented the British case. There was, however, no difference of substance between what he said and what George Brown had said three years previously. Barber's speech was, perhaps, more confident and forward-looking in tone,[1] but he listed almost exactly the same problems: agriculture and the financing of the Common Agricultural Policy, Commonwealth sugar, New Zealand and certain other Commonwealth questions. Fisheries policy, which had not reached the EEC's agenda in 1967, was added. These, together with the length of the transition period, were the main points at issue during the negotiations. EFTA had ceased to be a problem.

By July 1971 all the crucial issues apart from access to coastal fisheries had been dealt with, and the British government issued a White Paper setting out the terms agreed.[2] The most important points relating to trading arrangements were:

(1) Tariffs on trade between the United Kingdom and the EEC were to be abolished in five equal stages, beginning on 1 April 1973 and ending on 1 July 1977, assuming that Britain formally joined the Community at the beginning of 1973. United Kingdom tariffs on imports from the rest of the world were to be adjusted to bring them into line with the common external tariff over the same period, but with a year's delay before the first two fifths of the difference between the two tariff-rates was eliminated.

(2) Britain would adopt the EEC system of agricultural support

[1] Cabinet Office, *The United Kingdom and the European Communities*, Cmnd 4401, London, HMSO, 1970.

[2] Cabinet Office, *The United Kingdom and the European Communities*, Cmnd 4715, London, HMSO, 1971.

(entailing the introduction of fixed domestic intervention prices, as well as minimum import prices and levies for major products) in the first year of membership; deficiency payments would be phased out and United Kingdom prices, initially lower, would be adjusted to EEC prices in six stages during the transition period.

(3) The scale of British contributions to the Community budget would rise from 8·64 per cent of the Community total in 1973 to 18·92 per cent in 1977; full integration with the EEC budgetary system was postponed until 1980 under an agreement limiting the rise in United Kingdom contributions during 1978 and 1979.

(4) A guaranteed but diminishing market, at guaranteed prices, was ensured for New Zealand butter and cheese during the transition period, with a promise of 'suitable measures' to maintain special treatment of butter after 1977; but the Community's 20 per cent duty was to apply to lamb.

(5) The Commonwealth Sugar Agreement was to remain in operation until 1974. Thereafter special arrangements for Commonwealth sugar would be made within the framework of association or trading agreements with the enlarged Community.

(6) Independent Commonwealth countries in Africa and the Caribbean might choose between association under a renewed Yaoundé convention (the agreement governing trade and aid between the Six and their former colonies in Africa), a more limited form of association such as was already enjoyed by Kenya, Uganda and Tanzania under the Arusha convention, or a straightforward trading agreement. All dependent territories in the Commonwealth, with the exception of Hong Kong and (at its own request) Gibraltar, were to be associated with the enlarged Community.

(7) Commonwealth countries in Asia, apart from Hong Kong, were promised that their trade problems would be 'examined' by the enlarged EEC. All of them, including Hong Kong, would participate in the Community's generalised preference scheme for imports of industrial goods from developing countries.

(8) Suspended or reduced tariffs or duty-free quotas were to be introduced for woodpulp, lead bullion, phosphorus, aluminium, plywood and wattle extract. The United Kingdom would share in enlarged Community quotas for newsprint, refined lead and zinc.

(9) The United Kingdom would accede to the association and preferential trading agreements between the Community and Greece, Turkey, Tunisia, Morocco, Israel, Spain and Malta.

The White Paper is generally less precise on other aspects of EEC membership, such as financial and monetary issues – necessarily so since a firm Community policy had yet to be agreed. Some of the commitments undertaken were, however, expected to affect Britain's trade position, notably the switch to VAT and other amendments that might be required in indirect taxation. The change to VAT was not dependent on EEC membership, of course, since the tax was in any case to be introduced in 1973.

Similarly, the switch in the system of agricultural protection was less drastic than it appeared, since the government was already moving to a comparable system. Even before the election, at the time of the 1970 farm price review, discussions were under way in preparation for the introduction of minimum import prices for beef, backed up as necessary by import levies, and minimum import prices for eggs had been introduced. The new Conservative government's declared aim was 'to adapt the present system of agricultural support to one relying increasingly on import levy arrangements'.[1] To this end it extended the levy system to beef and veal, and to dairy products other than butter and cheese, revised minimum import prices and levies for cereals, and introduced duties on imports of mutton and lamb from all sources other than the Irish Republic. It was thus developing to their logical conclusion the measures introduced in 1963 and 1964.

Finally, the change from Commonwealth Preference for manufactures to generalised preferences had already occurred. Generalised preferences were introduced in the EEC on 1 July 1971 and in the United Kingdom on 1 January 1972. The EEC system was slightly less generous than the United Kingdom's, since quota ceilings were imposed on sensitive products and it did not extend zero duties to a number of non-manufactures as the United Kingdom did. On the other hand, the EEC was more generous on textiles and clothing, which were mostly excluded from the British scheme.

Following the United Kingdom's formal accession to the Community on 1 January 1973 the government made the necessary changes to tariffs and to the system of agricultural protection according to plan. On 1 February 1973 the elaborate price mechanism of the Community was introduced for British agricultural products and British import levies were replaced by Community import levies related to the threshold prices fixed for the United Kingdom market. Imports from the Six original members were free of levy and under the transitional arrangements were, in fact, being subsidised by the Six through what were known as 'accession compensatory amounts'; in addition 'monetary compensation amounts' were paid on sales by the Six to offset the effect of the decline in value of the pound during the course of the year. At the beginning of April the first 20 per cent cut in duties on imports

---

[1] Ministry of Agriculture, Fisheries and Food, *Agriculture Acts 1947 and 1957. Annual Review and Determination of Guarantees 1971*, Cmnd 4623, London, HMSO, 1971.

from the Six was made. Duties on imports from other areas remained unchanged till the beginning of 1974, when in most cases 40 per cent of the difference between the 'basic duty' (the United Kingdom's most-favoured-nation and Commonwealth Preference tariffs) and the common customs tariff[1] of the EEC was eliminated; where rates of duty differed by less than 15 per cent of the common customs tariff, the British tariff was adjusted to the common customs tariff. The United Kingdom also switched from its own to the Community's generalised preference system. However, for 'associable' Commonwealth territories (the EEC's original associates and Mediterranean countries enjoying preference within the EEC), duties were only changed if the new rate was lower than that charged under the basic tariff, while most manufactured goods imported from EFTA and the Republic of Ireland continued to enjoy duty-free entry. In sum, therefore, the United Kingdom's tariff was significantly reduced once more at the cost of introducing new tariff schedules of bewildering complexity.

POLICY MOTIVES

The motives for Britain's approach to Europe cannot be discussed in the context of commercial policy alone, for the mainspring of the whole endeavour was political. Even in the early days of the free trade area negotiations, political considerations – the desire to build an organisation that would embrace all European countries – gave added force and urgency to the government's plans; for some policy-makers, notably Harold Macmillan himself, the likely political consequences of success or failure in the negotiations were more important than the economic outcome. From the time of Macmillan's conversion to the idea of joining the Community, political motives were paramount. Opening the debate on Britain's application for membership in 1961, he declared: 'I believe that our right place is in the vanguard of the movement towards the greater unity of the free world and that we can lead better from within than outside.'[2] To hold aside risked splitting Western Europe into two opposing groups and would in no way lessen the political dangers involved.

The political emphasis is most pronounced in Edward Heath's application speech of 1961; indeed, the economic motives for joining the Community were barely mentioned.[3] George Brown devoted more time to economic affairs in his 1967 speech, but in stating the reasons for Britain's application he emphasised that 'some of the most decisive

---

[1] As the common external tariff had been renamed.
[2] House of Commons, *Hansard*, 2 August 1961, col. 1483.
[3] See Foreign Office, *The United Kingdom and the European Economic Community*.

considerations for us have been political'.[1] The Labour government envisaged a less rapid evolution into a political community than had the Conservatives in 1961. Speaking at the Guildhall on 29 July 1969, Harold Wilson said: 'The immediate task of this generation is to work, as we are pledged to work, for that degree of political unity which is within our immediate grasp.'[2] He pointed out, however, that British membership of the Community would of itself have major political consequences and he reiterated his belief that 'the political arguments are even stronger' than the economic case.

Since the end of the war, Britain had been inextricably involved in the security and defence of Western Europe. Policy-makers had been haunted by the fear of a political breakdown on the continent, or alternatively the emergence of a new super-state based on the Community. At the same time it had been borne in upon them that Britain's influence in world affairs was dwindling, and that the country could no longer support an independent politico-strategic role based on leadership of the Commonwealth. Circumstances conspired to ram home Britain's political and economic weaknesses (and the consequences of the latter for the former) first to Macmillan and then to Wilson. In 1959–61 it was the collapse of East–West *détente*, the foreign exchange crisis, South Africa's enforced withdrawal from the Commonwealth and the cancellation of the Blue Streak missile; under the Labour government it was Rhodesia, the perennial sterling crisis, the problems of Britain's new high-technology industries and the withdrawal of British troops from east of Suez.

This is not to say that government policy was purely defensive. On the contrary, consciously or unconsciously, there was a strong positive motive for entry – the enticing prospect of providing Europe with 'leadership' (whatever else had gone with the Empire, the fundamental British belief in their own superior qualifications for this role remained intact) – though, naturally enough, this was a view of the case that was seldom officially acknowledged. There was also, of course, a vocal minority who were genuinely converted to the idea that the nation-state was outdated and must be superseded in Europe by a close-knit political organisation that would transcend national frontiers. But for the most part British policy evolved under the pressure of events and a growing recognition of the country's weakness: 'If you can't beat 'em, join 'em.'

To quote an unsympathetic but acute critic:

The British people can doubtless see more and more clearly that, in the great movement which is carrying the world, faced with the enormous power

[1] Cabinet Office, *The United Kingdom and the European Communities*, Cmnd 3345.
[2] *The Times*, 30 July 1969.

of the United States, the growing power of the Soviet Union, the resurgent power of the continentals, the new power of China, and keeping in mind the increasingly centrifugal trends that are appearing in the Commonwealth, the structure and norms of Britain's activities and even her national personality are now at stake. And furthermore, the serious economic, financial and monetary difficulties with which she is at grips make her aware of this day by day. Hence, within herself, a tendency to seek a framework, even a European one, that would help her to save, to safeguard her own substance, that would enable her still to play a leading role and lighten part of her burden.[1]

That this is not merely the interpretation of a prejudiced and interested onlooker may be demonstrated by reference to George Brown's memoirs, in which there are two strands to his political thinking about Britain's relations with the EEC. First, there is a carefully argued case: Europe must be an equal partner in a defensive Atlantic alliance; Europe must be politically united, for this is the only way to contain both the Germans and domestic revolutionary pressures; British membership of the EEC will help towards the wider end of creating such a Europe. Yet running through this sober statement there is another line of thought – that Britain is the only possible, the predestined leader of a Europe 'which would have the same power and influence in the world as the old Commonwealth'.[2]

The political reasons for joining Europe had much to do with the rejection of all alternative policies. Neither a reinvigorated Commonwealth trading system nor a North Atlantic free trade area, even had they been negotiable, had the political potential associated with EEC membership, and still less did a policy of 'go it alone'. Yet even had policy been framed solely in the light of commercial and economic objectives, these alternatives would probably in the end have been discarded in favour of an application to the Community in view of the pattern of trade developments and the economic motives underlying the British approach to Europe.

Throughout the period under review, Britain's share in world exports of manufactures, and especially of exports to the Commonwealth and sterling area, was falling. From almost 21 per cent in 1955, its share of all exports from major industrial countries fell to something over 17 per cent in 1960 and to less than 12 per cent by the end of the decade. The corresponding figures for exports to the Commonwealth were 43, 34 and 19 per cent. Given this situation, the prime economic objective of Britain's European policy was to ensure that there would be no tariff discrimination against British exports in an important and rapidly

[1] General de Gaulle at his press conference of 27 November 1967, quoted in Kitzinger, *The Second Try*.
[2] Brown, *In My Way*.

growing market. This was the first advantage of creating a free trade area that Harold Macmillan put forward in his opening speech in the 1956 debate on the decision to launch negotiations. Speaking to the Institute of Public Administration two years later, Edgar Cohen, then Second Secretary, Board of Trade, said that initially, in his view, the defensive reaction 'was uppermost in most people's minds',[1] but that as time went on the desire to maintain intra-European cooperation assumed increasing importance. Changing circumstances and a better understanding of the potential benefits of European economic integration reduced the fear of discrimination in the 1960s; it has, however, remained an element in policy formation.

At the time of its inception the EEC was proposing to surround itself with a high tariff. The Dillon and Kennedy Rounds significantly reduced rates in the common external tariff, thereby reducing the margin of discrimination on British sales to the Community, while the virtual abolition of quota restrictions around 1960/1 reduced the risk of massive diversion of industrial goods still further. During this same period, however, the proportion of British exports going to the Six increased very rapidly. From 14·5 per cent in 1956, it rose to 17·3 per cent in 1961; on a revised definition, including trade in diamonds which was formerly excluded, it rose from 18·1 per cent in 1961 to a high of 21·5 per cent in 1963, and subsequently remained at around 20 per cent. By the end of the decade it was moving up again, to 21·8 per cent in 1970, when for the first time the Community overtook the Commonwealth as Britain's largest market. It is hardly surprising that the fear of 'exclusion' from EEC markets was a major element in British commercial policy.

At the same time, the proportion of exports going to the Commonwealth was falling steadily, from 38·9 per cent in 1956 to 34·0 per cent in 1961; and on the revised definition, from 32·9 per cent in 1961 to 21·0 per cent in 1970. As was feared in 1955, the Commonwealth proved a less expansionary market than Europe, the erosion of Commonwealth Preference continued and Commonwealth countries showed themselves much more concerned to secure a larger flow of aid and investment from Britain than to promote two-way trade.

The other economic motives for seeking to join the EEC were more positive. At one time or another successive governments have expressed the view that British participation in European free trade, whether in a wider free trade area or in the EEC, would provide new export opportunities for British industry; promote international specialisation, and hence greater efficiency; give lethargic British industries a salutary competitive shock; encourage the exploitation of economies of scale;

[1] Quoted in *Board of Trade Journal*, 7 November 1958.

create circumstances in which Britain could develop soundly based high-technology industries; stimulate the sluggish British economy by close association with the fast-growing, high-investment economies of the Six; and in any or all of these ways promote a higher rate of economic growth in Britain.

Clearly these ideas and possibilities are interrelated, so that, just as the fear of 'exclusion' from the Community lived on into the 1970s, most of the potential gains from European free trade listed above can be found expressed embryonically in statements made in 1956. But the emphasis has shifted to and fro, as shifts in political and intellectual fashions have put more weight on this potential benefit or that.

The economic case for joining Europe was originally set out modestly enough, with the emphasis on specialisation and economies of scale in a larger 'home' market. The White Paper published at the initiation of free trade area negotiations states: 'With a population of 250 million, there is clearly a great opportunity that Europe can seize provided that the free circulation of goods is not impeded by tariffs and quantitative restrictions';[1] and 'the establishment of a Free Trade Area... will raise industrial efficiency by the encouragement it will afford to increased specialisation, large-scale production and new technical and industrial developments'; but 'the Free Trade Area should be formed in such a way as to be wholly consistent with the existing objective of a collective approach to the widest possible system of multilateral trade and payments'.[2]

Speaking to the press some months earlier, Harold Macmillan had said very much the same thing:

If Western Europe, including the United Kingdom, could develop into a free trading area, this would undoubtedly be a great source of strength – a common market of nearly 250 million people. It would, over a period, be able to provide for this country the full advantages of large-scale production which tend in the modern world to be associated with big economic units, such as the United States and now the USSR.

And he went on to point out that the proposed free trade area was fully compatible with existing policies – 'the policy of trying to reduce trade barriers and to build more opportunities for trade over as wide an area as possible'.[3]

The economic case put forward in 1961 differed radically from that of 1956 in one important respect: of necessity it dropped the proviso that policy should be 'wholly consistent with... a collective approach to the widest possible system of multilateral trade and payments'. Instead,

---

[1] Treasury, *A European Free Trade Area*, para. 1.   [2] Ibid. para. 8.
[3] *Board of Trade Journal*, 13 October 1956.

ministerial statements tended to dwell on the importance of getting into the Community to keep it liberal and outward-looking. Apart from this, what was said in 1961 might equally well have been said in 1956: 'an island placed as ours is... cannot maintain the high standards of life that we want for our people in an isolated protective system'.[1] And, 'It will be possible for us to support new industries which demand heavy investment and a much larger market than Britain alone can provide.'[2] Less was said about specialisation, but rather more about the benefits expected from a sharp increase in competition and the gains to come from a freer exchange of technical and commercial ideas. However, the political arguments were so dominant that no one apparently bothered to refurbish the economic arguments.

In the middle and late 1960s the Labour government gave pride of place to the importance of membership for Britain's high-technology industries. Presenting the British case at Strasbourg, George Brown said: 'We are none of us big enough as individual countries to provide all the resources for development and research for which the sophisticated products of our times call with mounting insistence.'[3] This argument was partly intended, of course, to enhance Britain's standing as a candidate, for he went on to point out that Britain had a great deal to contribute in this line, but there is no doubt that the idea of providing a European base for Britain's technologically advanced industries had assumed a new and outstanding importance – witness Wilson's proposals for a technological community and his 1969 Guildhall speech: 'Year by year, the technological threshold gets higher, so that no one in Europe can undertake the research, the development, and the financial risks of research and development on a continental scale unless they have a potential market going far beyond the limited 50 millions or so represented by the purchasing power of a single nation state in Europe.'[4]

The government's 'technological case' for EEC membership was most fully elaborated in the 1970 White Paper (described as an economic assessment), where it was flatly stated that 'the future of the so-called high technology industries...depends decisively on whether or not it proves possible to create an enlarged Community'.[5] As compared with the high-technology industries in the United States, European industries suffer, it said, from the small scale of government

---

[1] Macmillan in the debate on EEC negotiations (House of Commons, *Hansard*, 2 August 1961, col. 1489).

[2] Alan Green, Minister of State, Board of Trade (*Board of Trade Journal*, 19 October 1962).

[3] Cabinet Office, *The United Kingdom and the European Communities*, Cmnd 3345, para. 6.

[4] *Board of Trade Journal*, 6 August 1969.

[5] Treasury, *Britain and the European Communities: an economic assessment*, Cmnd 4289, London, HMSO, 1970.

spending on research and development, small markets that cannot generate the necessary financial and other resources, and the lack of companies of sufficient size. None of the other advantages accruing from British membership are dealt with in such detail; the way the economic arguments for entry are put forward can only be described as impressionistic. There is rather more enthusiasm than in *A European Free Trade Area*, but the nature of the arguments has barely changed.

The final White Paper in the series, in July 1971, may be taken as representing the view of the Conservative administration.[1] It is a remarkable document; though more sophisticated in tone (and with less strident emphasis on technology) than its immediate predecessor, it rehearses all the old arguments for membership and, under the guise of a description of the Community's experience, presents them in a new form – the growth of EEC intra-trade has promoted faster growth of investment and productivity in manufacturing, and membership will do the same for Britain.

The abolition of tariffs provided a strong and growing stimulus to the mutual trade of Community countries...The consequent increase in intra-trade was accompanied by important changes in the performance of manufacturing industries in the Six countries. Those industries which competed with imports faced an intensification of competitive pressure as tariffs fell, obliging them to seek ways of raising efficiency and reducing costs. By the same token, prospects for exporting dramatically improved. Import competition and export expansion were closely associated with a growth in investment. The outcome of these processes was a significant improvement in the rate of growth of manufacturing productivity, and, therefore, higher national incomes in the Community than the member countries believe they would have enjoyed otherwise.[2]

It would hardly be unfair to say that membership of the EEC has been hawked around as the panacea for every failure in Britain's long-term economic policy. If the objective is political strength and stability – join the Community; if it is a larger share of world trade – join the Community; if the industrial climate is sluggish and you believe in competition, if the National Plan collapses and you want high-technology industries, if the economy stagnates and you want export-led growth – join the Community. If quantitative assessments of the impact effects of membership are unfavourable, sweep them aside (as the 1971 White Paper did those of the 1970 'economic assessment') and rely on the dynamic effects.

To this barrage the opponents of EEC membership could find no adequate reply, for either they spoke a different language or they were

[1] Cabinet Office, *The United Kingdom and the European Communities*, Cmnd 4715.
[2] Ibid. para. 50.

policy-makers themselves, subject to the same preoccupations and constraints as the government of the day. Apart from the lunatic fringe of Empire loyalists, no one could treat Commonwealth free trade as an alternative; and apart from latter-day Little Englanders no one wished to revert to a tightly protected economy. Wider regional trade groupings, multilateral or unilateral free trade were damned because they lacked political content. No one, apart from a few professional economists, seriously envisaged more than two alternatives – join, or leave things to slide while Britain more and more lost the power to shape its own foreign and commercial policies.

BRITAIN AND EUROPE – THEORY AND POLICY

At the time when the United Kingdom government launched the plan for a free trade area, two approaches to the theory of economic integration had been elaborated. The first, based on rather restrictive assumptions and essentially static in character, was derived from Viner's and Meade's analyses of the allocative effects of customs unions.[1] In brief, they argued that when tariffs between members of a union are abolished costly domestic products are displaced by cheaper imports from partner-countries. Trade is created and welfare is increased to the extent that costs are reduced. Moreover, there may be an additional gain to the consumer, whose range of choice among goods widens as the tariff disappears. On the other hand, a common tariff against the rest of the world may entail the replacement of imports from third countries by more costly products of partner-countries; thus trade is diverted and welfare reduced. The desirability of forming a custom union depends on whether or not trade creation is likely to exceed trade diversion. There may be additional gains to member-countries deriving from the possible increase in the scale of production in a wider protected market and from an improvement in the union's terms of of trade *vis-à-vis* the rest of the world, but neither Viner nor Meade thought that such effects were likely to be important in practice.

Both authors elaborated a list of conditions in which the formation of a customs union was likely to increase rather than diminish welfare. Cost savings would be greater:

(*a*) the larger the economic area concerned and hence the greater the potential for increased division of labour;

(*b*) the greater the degree of rivalry in protected industries between members of the union, or the less the pre-union degree of complementarity;

---

[1] J. Viner, *The Customs Union Issue*, New York, Carnegie Endowment for International Peace, 1950; J. E. Meade, *The Theory of Customs Unions*, Amsterdam, North-Holland, 1955.

(*c*) the greater the difference in unit costs in protected industries of the same kind within member-countries;

(*d*) the greater the range of protected industries with potential scale-economies that might be realised within the union.

Meade added a further condition particularly relevant to Europe – welfare was more likely to increase where countries forming a customs union were the principal suppliers to each other of goods actually traded. But, though he declared a prejudice in favour of customs unions, Meade argued that non-discriminatory tariff reductions were a more desirable policy goal and was for hastening slowly.

It is reasonable to suppose that Meade's analysis had considerable weight with policy-makers in the middle and later 1950s, when his retirement from the Cabinet Office was fairly recent. (Besides, his conditions and qualifications fitted well with the trend of official thinking.) The origin of the argument in the 1957 White Paper that international specialisation as a result of freer trade would promote greater efficiency can be traced to the pure theory of customs unions.[1] Yet, although this argument remained embedded in official statements, it is doubtful if the pure theory had the slightest influence on policy in subsequent years.

There are three reasons for this view. As a guide to policy-makers the theory of customs unions has the grave defect that its results are equivocal. In its original form it offered no *a priori* arguments for preferring union membership to independence, and the later development of the theory has done nothing to alter this. Secondly, the initial attempts to measure increases in welfare that might follow from the elimination of tariffs in intra-European trade suggested that they would be disappointingly small – at most equivalent to about 1 per cent of GNP.[2] While the precise figures were suspect, it was shown that, given the share of trade in output and existing tariff levels, it was unlikely that the gain from increased allocative efficiency would be of sufficient magnitude to provide on its own a convincing argument in favour of British entry into Europe; nor, equally, could it offer powerful arguments for staying out. But the most serious weakness of the pure theory of customs unions as a guide to policy-makers is its static and limited character. Economists and policy-makers were united in the belief that the dynamic consequences of integration would outweigh the static effects; they were concerned in practice with something much more than a simple customs union or free trade area.

The alternative approach to the problem of economic integration

[1] See Treasury, *A European Free Trade Area*, para. 8.

[2] See, for example, H. G. Johnson, 'The gains from freer trade with Europe: an estimate', *Manchester School of Economic and Social Studies*, vol. 26, September 1958.

initiated by Scitovsky was less rigorous, more congenial (for it was building on ideas already familiar to policy-makers of the superiority of large economic units over smaller, as exemplified by the prosperity and high productivity of the United States) and hence, it may be supposed, more influential. Scitovsky argued that changes in methods of production due to the exploitation of scale-economies and increased competition would raise productivity, and that such changes, together with those consequent upon the reallocation of resources between industries, would increase the efficiency of investment. Furthermore, integration would ease the constraints imposed on investors by small markets and by the additional risk and uncertainty attached to investing in export capacity, though the benefits would be long in coming and their full realisation would require a degree of integration closer than that obtaining in a pure customs union.[1]

Though Scitovsky did not explicitly deal with the effect of integration on the growth rate, it is this line of reasoning that supports the argument that integration promotes faster economic growth. No economist has claimed that integration as such will step up the growth rate; faster growth is a consequence of the greater efficiency that can be achieved in an integrated market. However, the fact that Scitovsky's case for integration could be, and by some later writers was, linked to a discussion of growth made it all the more attractive to governments.

The pure theory assumed that domestic economies were perfectly competitive and hence did not consider the effects of union on competition, but for Scitovsky the increase in competition that he expected to follow on the freeing of trade was the essential benefit of integration. In fact he came close to offering a rationale for the 'competitive shock' argument – the view that greater competition acts as a stimulus to harder, more effective work on the part of management. This view did not obtain wide currency when it was first propounded, largely because there was little evidence to support it. Latterly, however – in the wake of the development of the concept of 'X-efficiency' by Liebenstein[2] – it has reappeared in some of the literature. Liebenstein argued that in the absence of competitive pressure resources are under-utilised because people prefer an easy life and the cost of enjoying it is not high. When competition increases the cost of idleness also increases, and so people work harder and more effectively. From a scattering of empirical evidence Liebenstein and others have concluded that the gains from greater 'X-efficiency' may be sizable. However, Liebenstein himself

[1] See T. Scitovsky, *Economic Theory and Western European Integration*, London, Allen & Unwin, 1958.

[2] H. Liebenstein, 'Allocative efficiency vs. "X-efficiency"', *American Economic Review*, vol. 56, June 1966.

did not relate 'X-efficiency' to economic integration and, as Corden has pointed out, it still has to be demonstrated that all producers will experience greater competition as a result of integration; there may be more competition from producers within the customs union but less outside it or from outsiders.[1]

For the most part those who developed Scitovsky's analysis of customs unions gave a different emphasis to competition, linking it with economies of scale, partly because in empirical work it has proved impossible to disentangle their effects. Scale-economies are treated in the pure theory of customs unions as deriving solely from economies of plant size. Scitovsky and those who followed him adopted a wider definition, exemplified by Balassa, who argued that both individual industries and the economy as a whole benefited from internal and external economies made possible by the larger size of the market – from keener competition and from greater certainty, which led to more and better-quality investment;[2] he also discussed the importance of scale in research and development expenditure. Like Scitovsky, Balassa and later writers have appealed to a variety of empirical evidence that supports the connection between market size, economies of scale (in their widest sense) and efficiency. Few would now dispute that there are scale-economies to be reaped from integration, but the vital question – how large they would be – was and still is unanswerable.[3]

As a guide to policy-makers the analysis of the effects of integration stemming from the work of Scitovsky shares one of the major defects of the pure theory of customs unions – it is inconclusive. In this case, however, it is not that the results might go either way; their direction is known, but their magnitude, even in some cases their existence, is uncertain. As things have turned out the uncertainty about the scale–competition effects of integration is crucial, for the reallocative and revenue effects of joining the customs union plus the commitment to the Common Agricultural Policy are probably unfavourable. Thus, professional economists opposed to British entry into the EEC have been able to demand proof that the 'dynamic' gains would outweigh the

[1] W. M. Corden, 'The efficiency effects of trade and protection' in I. A. McDougall and R. H. Snape (eds.), *Studies in International Economics*, Amsterdam, North-Holland, 1970.

[2] B. Balassa, *The Theory of Economic Integration*, London, Allen & Unwin, 1962.

[3] The variant of the scale argument that was given so much emphasis in the 1970 White Paper – that a Europe-wide market is required as a base for high-technology industries – has not been seriously discussed, for the very good reasons that it has yet to be shown that the existence of heavily subsidised, high-technology industries will increase European welfare or that the EEC will promote the growth of supra-national enterprises in this field. The technology argument for integration is the preserve of a few enthusiasts and the politicians. Similarly the export-led growth argument of the 1971 White Paper has not been seriously advanced by professional economists as a justification for integration, since it is not necessary to invoke it to explain dynamic gains, nor does integration necessarily induce larger total exports.

static losses (while at the same time, of course, freely expressing their belief that they would do no such thing), and have concentrated their attack on specific aspects of the EEC – the terms of entry, the Common Agricultural Policy (which has nothing to do with free or freer trade) and the risks inherent in plans for monetary integration in the Community.[1]

What then can be said about the influence of economic theory and the work of professional economists on the making of government policy towards Europe? It has already been suggested that both the pure theory of customs unions and Scitovsky's approach via competition and scale did influence policy in the 1950s, helping in its formation and providing sanction for the course of action proposed. But during the 1960s the former certainly and the latter probably had very little influence. Partly, of course, this was because the overriding motive for seeking closer relations with Europe was political. However, it was also due in part to the character of the theories concerned and to the failure to supply empirical estimates of the effects of entry before policy had been finally decided – that is before 1967. Economists did little more than provide the government with arguments that they could use or not as they chose. Of the three roles they might have performed in relation to policy-making – providing analysis yielding reasonably firm conclusions as a basis for action, consistent and constructive criticism, and useful assessments of the likely effects of proposed policies – the first and second were neglected from the late 1950s on, and it is only in the last few years that the third has been seriously attempted.

Estimates of the static balance of payments and welfare costs to Britain of joining the EEC that have been made in recent years were conveniently summarised in an article by M. M. Miller.[2] The estimated balance of payments cost ranges from £266 million to £1095 million at 1969 prices – the latter figure being derived from very unfavourable and somewhat unrealistic assumptions – while the welfare cost ranges from £389 million to £1144 million. The median estimate of the balance of payments cost is of the order of £350 million; for the welfare cost it lies within the range £550 million to £700 million, that is something over 1 per cent of GNP. These figures may be wide of the mark, but the calculations demonstrate conclusively that there is a cost involved in membership.

The main elements in the balance of payments cost calculations are:

(1) The change in the balance of trade on manufactures following

[1] See, for example, N. Kaldor, 'The truth about the dynamic effects', *New Statestman*, 12 March 1971.

[2] This appeared first in the *National Institute Economic Review*, no. 57, August 1971, and then, revised and updated, as 'Estimates of the static balance-of-payments and welfare costs compared' in J. Pinder (ed.), *The Economics of Europe*, London, Charles Knight, 1971.

from tariff changes, which was uniformly expected to be unfavourable, though not in most cases seriously so.

(2) The effect of applying the Common Agricultural Policy, which is further subdivided into three:

(a) A saving on food import expenditure at 1969 prices, since the Common Agricultural Policy gives higher producer prices to British farmers, inducing them to produce more, while consumers reduce their purchases. The extent of the saving depends on the supply and demand elasticities – the higher they are the greater the saving. It was generally expected that these savings *at 1969 prices* would exceed the loss on manufactures.

(b) Because the Common Agricultural Policy diverts British purchasing to European sources of supply and can normally be expected to keep European prices above world prices – that is, after all, its object – the price of imported food is higher than it would have been had Britain continued to import food at world prices. This cost is equivalent to a tax on food, the proceeds of which are transferred to farmers in the Community. The smaller the gap between European and world prices the smaller the tax.

(c) Levies charged on food imported from the rest of the world have to be transferred to the Community budget to finance the Common Agricultural Policy, though there is some offset in the form of support payments to British farmers.

(3) The payment of revenue from customs duties to the Community budget, again largely to finance the Common Agricultural Policy, which, like the payment of levy revenue, is a straight transfer to the Community.

(4) Possible payments of VAT into the Community budget to offset any shortfall in revenue from food levies and customs duties.

(5) Possible receipts from the Community under regional and other 'structural' policies, which were usually assumed to offset VAT payments.

These same elements, plus an estimated gain from trade creation, enter into the computation of welfare costs, that is the resource cost of correcting for the changes in the balance of payments. For the balance of trade in manufactures and import-saving on food, the welfare change is equivalent to the change in the terms of trade required to restore balance. The welfare multiplier is smaller the higher are the elasticities; unless they are very small it is well below unity and the welfare cost is less than the balance of payments cost. For transfer payments, the welfare multiplier takes into account the direct cost of the transfer, that is the actual payment, plus the effect on trade of the consequent change in British and other Community incomes and the required change in the terms of trade; thus the multiplier always exceeds unity and welfare costs are greater than balance of payments costs. The larger the transfer costs of entry in relation to the trade-balance costs in terms of any given total of balance of payments costs the greater the net welfare costs of entry.

Despite the wide range of the estimates of costs, there are two features common to all of them. First, the direct effects on the trade balance of joining the Community are relatively small. Secondly, the transfer costs (which are inescapable) are several times as large as any gain accruing from changes in the (constant-price) trade balance.[1] So, if the British economy is to benefit from membership of the Community, it can only be through 'dynamic' gains large enough to outweigh the static costs.

Only one attempt has been made, by Williamson, to calculate the order of magnitude of the dynamic gains, assuming of course that there will be such gains.[2] His 'central guess' is that economies of scale, competition and additional investment generated by larger exports would each contribute something of the order of $\frac{1}{2}$ per cent of GNP by the end of the transition period – a total of $1\frac{1}{2}$ per cent of GNP, or 0·3 per cent annually on the rate of growth – with possibly some further gains after the end of the period. On this reasonably optimistic assessment the dynamic gains would surpass the static costs, though not by any wide margin.

Apart from an optimistic early assessment of British prospects in a Europe-wide free trade area made by the Economist Intelligence Unit,[3] there is only one detailed study of the impact of integration on individual British manufacturing industries by Han and Liesner.[4] They ranked 230 products according to performance in United Kingdom–EEC trade during the period 1965–7, and made a supplementary comparison of performances in non-European markets, grouping their results in five classes from the most to the least competitive. The striking feature of their findings is the extent to which products of major industries are distributed across performance classes. This, and the fact that the ranking changes as different criteria are used, makes it virtually impossible to summarise their results. Only two industries are consistently placed – the transport industries among the most competitive and the chemical industries among the least – a result which later experience hardly confirms.

[1] Even when the adverse trade-balance effect is enlarged by allowing for the influence of an induced wage–price spiral, transfers are larger than pure trade effects.

[2] J. Williamson, 'Trade and economic growth' in Pinder (ed.), *The Economics of Europe*.

[3] Economist Intelligence Unit, *Britain and Europe*, London, 1957.

[4] S. S. Han and H. H. Liesner, *Britain and the Common Market: the effect of entry on the pattern of manufacturing production*, Cambridge University Press, 1971.

In sum, the likely effects of Community membership on the British economy are still very uncertain. A greater proportion of trade will, of course, be conducted with Europe. Trade in agricultural products will be most affected, but here the consequences are particularly uncertain because of trends in world and Community prices and possible reforms in the Common Agricultural Policy. But much depends on developments outside the field of commercial policy and above all, as successive governments have rightly argued, on the unquantifiable political consequences of membership from which further economic consequences may well derive.

EFFECTS OF COMMERCIAL POLICY CHANGES

Changes in commercial policy can affect trade in three ways: they may make the economy more or less open, increasing or decreasing the ratio of imports to output; they may alter the composition of trade by varying the degree of protection given to different sectors of the economy and hence the degree to which imports are substituted for domestic production; they may affect the direction of trade either directly, through changes in preferential treatment given to goods originating in different areas, or indirectly, as a consequence of changes in the composition of trade. But to measure these effects with any degree of precision is extremely difficult, the more so during the period under review since other influences have been working in the same direction as the changes in commercial policy previously described.

Between 1955 and 1973 there were profound changes in the pattern of United Kingdom imports. First, the ratio of imports to GNP in real terms increased at an accelerating rate throughout the period. Measured in 1970 prices, imports were equivalent to 16 per cent of GNP in 1955 and 25 per cent in 1973. (The exceptional increase in the last two years of the period is mainly attributable to additional imports of manufactures.) Measured in current prices, changes in the import ratio were offset by the decline up to 1972 in import prices relative to domestic prices, particularly in the late 1950s, so that the current-price import ratio fell until 1967 and rose only gradually in the next five years. It was not till 1973, when relative import prices rose sharply, that it exceeded the 1955 level. These developments are illustrated in chart 12.1.

Movements in the total import ratio mask divergent movements in the ratio of imports of different classes of goods. Whether measured at current or at constant prices, the ratios of food, drink and tobacco and of raw materials have fallen almost without interruption, while those for manufactures and more especially finished goods have risen. The remaining class, fuels, shows a negligible fall measured at current prices, but a rise when measured in constant prices (table 12.1). The behaviour of raw materials and fuels may be used to illustrate the importance of factors other than commercial policy in influencing trade. In the former case protection has always been negligible and, though such tariffs as exist have been reduced or abolished, the effect on trade was probably minimal. The importance of raw material imports has diminished because of technological changes, leading to lower con-

Chart 12.1. *Ratio of imports to GNP and relative import prices, 1955–73*

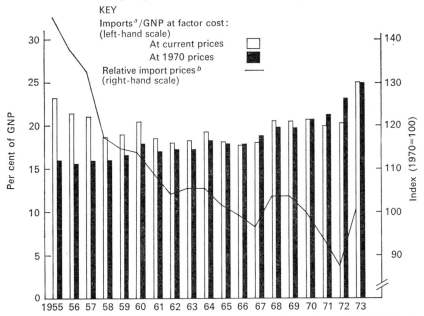

SOURCES: CSO, *Annual Abstract of Statistics, National Income and Expenditure* and *United Kingdom Balance of Payments: Board of Trade Journal / Trade and Industry.*

[a] C.i.f. excluding tariffs.
[b] Current-weighted unit value of imports divided by the implicit GNP deflator.

sumption per unit of final output, the replacement of natural products by synthetics which are classed as semi-manufactures, and changes in the structure of industry. In fuels there has been no change in protection; the import ratio rose because of the growth of road transport and because of a deliberate switch to imported oil from domestically produced coal in electricity generation.

Partly as a consequence of the changes in the commodity composition of trade, but even more as a result of differences in the rate of export growth among supplying countries, there have been equally important changes in the origin of United Kingdom imports, which are illustrated

Table 12.1. *Changes in the ratio of imports by category to GNP at factor cost, 1955–72*

Percentages

	Food, drink and tobacco	Raw materials	Fuels	Semi-manu-factures	Finished goods	Total[a]
At current prices						
Actual: 1955	8·4	8·5	2·4	2·6	1·2	23·2
1971	4·4	4·3	2·5	3·6	4·9	20·0
1972	4·3	4·0	2·3	3·8	5·7	20·3
Change: 1955–9	−1·3	−2·8	−0·2	−0·5	+0·6	−4·2
1959–63	−1·0	−0·9	−0·2	+0·4	+0·6	−0·7
1963–7	−1·1	−0·4	+0·1	+0·4	+1·0	−0·2
1967–71	−0·6	−0·2	+0·4	+0·7	+1·5	+1·9
1971–2	−0·1	−0·3	−0·2	+0·2	+0·8	+0·3
At constant prices[b]						
Actual: 1955	6·5	5·8	1·6	1·9	1·1	16·9
1971	4·6	4·6	2·3	4·1	5·4	21·3
1972	4·6	4·7	2·3	4·7	6·7	23·2
Change: 1955–9	+0·3	−0·4	+0·1	—	+0·6	+0·7
1959–63	−0·6	−0·5	+0·4	+0·6	+0·7	+0·7
1963–7[c]	−0·6	−0·2	+0·4	+0·6	+1·2	+1·6
	(−0·5)	(+0·3)	(−0·6)	(−0·1)	(—)	(−1·1)
1967–71	−0·5	−0·4	+0·4	+1·1	+1·8	+2·5
1971–2	—	+0·1	—	+0·6	+1·3	+1·9

SOURCES: Customs and Excise, *Annual Statement of Trade of the United Kingdom*; Department of Trade, *Overseas Trade Statistics of the United Kingdom*; as chart 12.1.

[a] Includes also unclassified goods, but not United States military aircraft.
[b] At 1963 prices to 1967; thereafter at 1970 prices.
[c] Figures in brackets show the effect in 1967 of the change from 1963 to 1967 prices.

in table 12.2. The share of imports originating in the Commonwealth more than halved between 1955 and 1973, while the EEC's share more than doubled. EFTA too gained ground, while the United States share over the period as a whole has remained fairly constant, as has (since 1959) that of other countries. Changes in the direction of trade began well before any significant changes were made in British commercial policy. Though the growth of trade with EFTA countries undoubtedly owed something to the formation of the Association, the rise in the EEC's import share continued more or less regardless of the state of negotiations with the Six or of generalised reductions in most-favoured-nation duties on manufactures; the biggest rise in any four-year period covered by the table came in 1963–7 when negotiations were moribund. However, it has been suggested that some of the increase may have been due to anticipation of entry into the EEC, particularly perhaps the rise since 1971.

Table 12.2. *Changes in the origin and destination of United Kingdom imports and exports, 1955–73*

Percentages[a]

		Common-wealth[b]	EEC (Six)	EFTA	United States	Other places
Imports						
Actual:	1955	39·8	12·6	11·5	10·9	25·2
	1971	22·3	21·4	15·9	11·1	29·3
	1972	19·3	24·5	17·5	10·5	28·2
	1973	17·2	26·4	17·9	10·2	28·3
Change:	1955–9	−4·2	+1·4	+0·3	−1·6	+4·1
	1959–63[c]	−3·9	+2·1	+0·7	+1·1	—
		(−0·2)	(−0·2)	(−0·3)	(−0·2)	(+0·9)
	1963–7	−6·7	+3·7	+2·4	+2·3	−1·7
	1967–71	−2·5	+1·8	+1·3	−1·4	+0·8
	1971–2	−3·0	+3·1	+1·6	−0·6	−1·1
	1972–3	−2·1	+1·9	+0·4	−0·3	+0·1
Exports[d]						
Actual:	1955	40·6	14·1	11·8	6·6	26·9
	1971	21·9	21·0	15·0	11·8	30·3
	1972	18·9	22·9	16·1	12·4	29·7
	1973	16·6	24·7	16·6	12·1	30·0
Change:	1955–9	−4·2	+0·7	−0·3	+4·4	−0·6
	1959–63[c]	−7·2	+5·9	+2·0	−2·5	+1·8
		(−1·1)	(+0·8)	(−0·3)	(+0·7)	(−0·1)
	1963–7	−4·3	−1·5	+1·8	+3·0	+1·0
	1967–71	−1·9	+1·0	—	−0·4	+1·3
	1971–2	−3·0	+1·9	+1·1	+0·6	−0·6
	1972–3	−2·3	+1·8	+0·5	−0·3	+0·3

SOURCES: Board of Trade, *Commonwealth and Sterling Area Statistical Abstract 1962*, London, HMSO, 1963; as table 12.1.

[a] Proportion of total imports or exports.
[b] South Africa excluded throughout and Rhodesia since 1966. If South Africa was included in 1955 it would raise the Commonwealth share of imports by 2·1 per cent and of exports by 5·6 per cent (rather more if trade in diamonds were included).
[c] There is a break in the series in 1961 owing to the inclusion of diamonds, previously excluded. Figures in brackets show the effect of the change in coverage.
[d] Including re-exports.

Changes in the direction of exports, shown in the lower half of the table, were broadly similar to import changes, notably the fall in sales to the Commonwealth and the rise in the EEC's share over the period as a whole, despite a temporary drop in the mid-1960s – possibly due to diversion of trade in the Community. Only trade with the United States shows any marked difference in the development of import and export shares and that only in the late 1950s. In respect of exports little influence can be attributed to changes in the commodity composition of trade, but differences in rates of market growth as between the Commonwealth (much of it in the developing world and principally exporters of primary products) and the industrial economies of Europe and the United States were clearly of major importance. Throughout the period exchanges between industrial countries have been the most rapidly growing sector of world trade.

It is against this background that changes in commercial policy, or more precisely changes in the protection given to agriculture and manufacturing, are to be measured and their effect assessed. It is difficult to measure the extent of protection of agriculture, because of the use until recently of deficiency payments as the main intrument of protection and because of the non-quantifiable effect of such arrangements as the 'bacon market understanding' (see page 529) on the volume and price of domestic output. The incidence of import duties on total imports of food was small at the beginning of the 1960s – 3 per cent at its maximum – and had fallen to less than 2 per cent in the early 1970s; because of the rise in world market prices, the incidence of import levies, of which scant use was made prior to 1972/3, was smaller still, as is shown in table 12.3.

In measuring the trend of deficiency payments and other Exchequer support to agriculture, we have followed a method devised by Sharp and Capstick,[1] which related the cost of Exchequer support to the value of domestic output at market prices. Until 1963/4 deficiency payments fluctuated in the region of 13 to 14 per cent of the value of output, though rising sharply in some exceptional years; since then they have fallen with only occasional interruption. This fall and the simultaneous rise in the absolute value of other Exchequer support, which in terms of its percentage incidence was more or less steady, was in part the consequence of the changes in policy inaugurated in 1963 and 1964 (see pages 528–30 above). But in practice it seems probable that it was possible to reduce deficiency payments so drastically only because average market prices for cereals and livestock (accounting for most of the output covered by the guaranteed price system) have risen every year since 1962/3. They jumped by 18 per cent from 1962/3 to 1964/5, then rose gradually to 1967/8 and more steeply though erratically thereafter. It is clear that such large increases were not anticipated by the authorities, for in most years since the mid-1960s forecast expenditure on deficiency payments has considerably exceeded actual expenditure. Thus market developments reinforced policy; prices received by farmers were kept on a rising trend, with an increasing proportion of the total return coming from the market and a decreasing proportion from deficiency payments, as the government intended.

Although the percentages relating to deficiency payments and other

[1] G. Sharp and C. W. Capstick, 'The place of agriculture in the national economy', *Journal of Agricultural Economics*, vol. 17, May 1966.

Table 12.3. *Agricultural protection, 1955/6–1973/4*

	Exchequer support		Proportion of adjusted gross output^a		Duties	Levies	Proportion of import values in the class^b	
	Deficiency payments	Other support^c	Deficiency payments	Other support^c			Duties	Levies
	(£ million)		(%)	(%)	(£ million)		(%)	(%)
1955/6	138·6	62·2	12·9	5·8	27·9	—	2·2	—
1956/7	156·4	78·1	14·2	7·1	33·5	—	2·4	—
1957/8	200·7	77·8	17·9	6·9	38·1	—	2·9	—
1958/9	154·7	80·9	13·2	6·9	41·7	—	3·0	—
1959/60	154·7	95·6	12·9	8·0	42·2	—	3·0	—
1960/1	151·2	105·0	12·5	8·7	40·7	—	2·9	—
1961/2	225·5	108·1	18·6	8·9	36·1	—	2·7	—
1962/3	190·1	110·0	14·5	8·4	35·5	—	2·5	—
1963/4	178·9	104·7	13·6	8·0	35·3	—	2·2	—
1964/5	146·1	108·5	9·6^d	7·2^d	34·2	0·1	2·2	—
1965/6	121·7	104·8	7·6	6·5	33·8	—	2·1	—
1966/7	108·8	108·4	6·6	6·6	33·9	—	2·1	—
1967/8	135·0	113·8	7·8	6·6	36·1	—	2·2	—
1968/9	127·2	124·5	7·3	7·2	33·5	0·3	2·0	—
1969/70	127·9	135·4	6·8	7·1	34·6	0·5	2·0	—
1970/1	93·5	157·7	4·4	7·4	35·5	0·7	1·9	—
1971/2	140·9	175·7	6·2	7·7	38·8	6·1	1·9	0·3
1972/3	86·2^e	173·7	3·1	6·4	40·9	20·2^f	1·8	0·9
1973/4	113·5^e	182·8	..	..	40·3	25·4	1·4	0·9

SOURCES: Ministry of Agriculture, Fisheries and Food, *Agriculture Acts. Annual Review*; Customs and Excise, *Report of the Commissioners* and *Annual Statement of Trade of the United Kingdom*; CSO, *Annual Abstract of Statistics*; Department of Trade, *Overseas Trade Statistics of the United Kingdom*.

^a Gross output of agriculture as officially defined, less Exchequer support and miscellaneous receipts.

^b Refers to all imports of food, drink and tobacco, including horticultural and tropical products, and processed food.

^c Excludes administrative expenses and grants exclusively for horticulture, for which a complete run of figures is not available. By 1973/4 horticultural grants had risen to £10·1 million.

^d Owing to a change in the definition of gross output there is a break in the series in 1964/5. Calculated on the old basis, deficiency payments were 10 per cent and other support 7·2 per cent of adjusted gross output in that year.

^e Includes exceptional payments to milk producers of £30·8 million in 1972/3 and £103·8 million in 1973/4; since then these have been treated as consumer subsidies.

^f Levies under the Agriculture and Horticulture Act 1964 to end-January 1973; EEC levies under the Common Agricultural Policy thereafter.

Exchequer support in table 12.3 indicate, like an *ad valorem* tariff, the extent to which prices to domestic producers can exceed the landed price of competing imports, they are not comparable as a measure of protection. The deficiency payment system ensured that all domestic output could be sold; imports were a residual closing the gap between domestic supply and demand. If importers attempted to increase their share of the market by reducing prices, the unit deficiency payment was raised to cover the increased difference between market and guaranteed prices, in contrast to the situation with an *ad valorem* tariff, where the duty paid falls as the import price falls. The extent to which imports were in fact reduced by protection could only be measured if the supply elasticity of British agricultural output were known. Taking a figure of 0·5 by way of illustration,[1] and allowing for the effect of all Exchequer support though not of import duties, the value of output was at most some £150 million greater in 1971/2 than it would have been without protection. Net import-saving was less because of imported inputs into domestic production.

The fact that deficiency payments reserved to British farmers as much of the market as they could physically supply, together with the growing importance of other non-tariff protection of agriculture, explain the otherwise paradoxical circumstance that as the cost of protection to the Exchequer fell the degree of self-sufficiency increased. Official figures for the ratio of domestic output to supplies, which have been calculated since 1962/3, are shown in table 12.4. It appears from these data that market forces have had more effect on trade in food-stuffs than any changes in the level of protection. Until 1970/1 consumption (more or less equivalent to total supplies) and self-sufficiency were both rising gradually. In 1971/2 and subsequently retail food prices started to rise faster than consumer prices in general, consumption and imports dropped and the self-sufficiency ratio rose.

Measurement of the effects of commercial policy on trade in manufactures is, in principle, simpler, since the tariff has been the main instrument used, but in practice there are serious conceptual and practical problems in constructing an indicator of the height of the 'average' tariff. However, to calculate the direction and the proportionate size of the change in the tariff level turns out to be simpler in the present instance, since different methods of calculation give similar results.

In an article by the author two methods were used to calculate a time-series showing the change in protection given to semi-manufactures and finished goods from 1955 to 1972;[2] the first series was an average of duties potentially chargeable on imports and the second was based on the incidence of tariff revenue on the value of imports.[3] Though the

---

[1] Half way between the two extremes applied in Cabinet Office, *The United Kingdom and the European Communities*, Cmnd 4401.

[2] A. D. Morgan, 'Tariff reductions and UK imports of manufactures: 1955–1971', *National Institute Economic Review*, no. 72, May 1975.

[3] Both series referred to nominal tariffs. Such evidence as is available suggests a similar fall in 'effective tariffs' on average; cf. Treasury, *Tariffs, Taxes and Trade in the UK: the effective protection approach* by N. Oulton, London, HMSO, 1973.

Table 12.4. *Production, imports and self-sufficiency in food, 1962/3–1973/4*

	Indigenous-type supplies			Share of home output in total supplies[a]	
	Home output	Imports	Total	Constant prices	Current prices
	(indices of volume)[b]			(percentages)	
1962/3	100·0	100·0	100·0	64·0	64·9
1963/4	100·9	101·8	101·2	63·8	63·6
1964/5	102·1	99·7	101·2	64·6	64·1
1965/6	103·0	101·4	102·4	64·4	64·9
1966/7	102·7	103·5	103·0	63·9	65·0
1967/8	105·2	101·0	103·7	65·0	66·2
1968/9	106·2	104·2	105·5	64·5	65·4
1969/70	107·9	101·3	105·5	65·5	66·6
1970/1	109·4	100·4	106·1	66·0	66·9
1971/2	110·4	95·5	105·0	67·3	66·8
1972/3	111·7	92·1	104·7	68·4	66·8
1973/4	..	..	..	..	68·2

SOURCES: CSO, *Annual Abstract of Statistics*; Ministry of Agriculture, Fisheries and Food, *Food Facts*, 30 April 1975.

[a] Indigenous-type.   [b] Value at constant 1962/3–1964/5 average prices.

two series differed significantly in absolute value, because of differences in weighting and because of the exemption of certain dutiable goods from payment of duty, they proved to be closely correlated. Both showed a fall of the order of 50 per cent in the average tariffs on semi-manufactures and finished goods between 1959, the last year before major duty cuts were introduced, and 1972, when the final Kennedy Round cuts had been implemented.

Table 12.5 summarises the figures given by the two series for the beginning and end of the tariff-cutting period. It also shows in terms of the tariff series how much of the fall was due to EFTA and to the GATT reductions. (No similar estimate can be made for the revenue series.) For both classes of manufactures the Dillon Round accounted for 10 per cent or less of the cuts, but EFTA was responsible for just over half the fall in the average for semi-manufactures, while the Kennedy Round accounted for almost 60 per cent of the fall in duties on finished goods. At the beginning of the period almost 70 per cent of all duties levied on semi-manufactures and 90 per cent of those on finished goods were 15 per cent *ad valorem* or more. By 1972 these proportions had dropped to less than 30 per cent and less than 20 per cent respectively.

In the article referred to above the tariff revenue series was used in regressions of imports on the level of demand and relative import prices to estimate the increase in United Kingdom imports attributable

Table 12.5. *Reduction in average United Kingdom tariffs on manufactures, 1959–72*

Percentages ad valorem

	Semi-manufactures	Finished goods
Average tariff 1 Jan. 1960	12·1	18·0
Fall in		
Dillon Round	0·5	1·0
Kennedy Round	2·6	5·6
EFTA	3·2	2·9
Total	6·3	9·5
Average tariff 1 Jan. 1972	5·8	8·5
Average duty incidence		
1959/60	8·1	13·3
1972/3	4·5	6·5

SOURCE: Morgan, 'Tariff reductions and UK imports of manufactures'.

to tariff reductions over the period 1959–71. The equations have since been further modified and re-estimated for the period 1959–72.[1] The results suggest that for semi-manufactures rather more than one third of the increase in the volume of total imports (£444 million out of a total increase of £1225 million measured at constant 1961 prices) was due to tariff reductions. For finished goods the corresponding proportion was over a quarter (£442 million out of £1605 million). These estimates allow both for the direct effect of the tariff in reducing prices and for a once-and-for-all shift in the import function as tariff cutting was initiated under the three different programmes. Such a shift could be caused by the expectation of a permanent fall in the tariff-paid price of foreign goods relative to domestic prices and by the disappearance of near-prohibitive duties (duties which are high enough to inhibit all but a very small flow of imports); once duties are reduced below a critical threshold level imports react very sharply – more sharply indeed than they would to the complete abolition of a low tariff. In the light of the reduction in the number of high tariffs during the 1960s, our calculations provide strong support for the existence of such an effect in the import market for finished goods; the evidence for semi-manufactures is perhaps not quite so good, but is still persuasive.

Although tariff reductions appear to have been a major influence on imports of manufactures, it is apparent that they were only one among many and that other influences were, in all, more important. The regressions gave elasticities with respect to industrial production for imports of semi-manufactures and with respect to expenditure on

[1] For a description of the revised equations, see the appendix to this chapter.

finished goods for imports of finished goods that were well in excess of two. These elasticities reflect not only the effect of rising incomes on imports, but also the pronounced growth of intra-industry trade experienced by all industrial countries in consequence of such influences as shifts in consumer preference, product diversification and the growth of multi-national corporations.

Table 12.6. *The proportion of imports in the total supply of manufactures,[a] 1955–71*

Percentages

	1955	1963	1968	1971
Chemicals	8·8	9·8	14·4	15·6
Metals	5·5	3·9	6·1	6·7
Machinery and vehicles	3·4	6·6	13·1	13·4
Textiles and clothing	4·5	8·8	12·4	15·1
Other	6·3	6·9	9·0	9·1
Total	5·1	7·0	10·7	11·9

SOURCES: CSO, *Input–Output Tables for the United Kingdom, 1954, 1963* and *1968*, and *Economic Trends*, no. 258, April 1975; Board of Trade, *Report on the Census of Production for 1954* and *Report on the Censuses of Production for 1955, 1956 and 1957*; Customs and Excise, *Annual Statement of Trade of the United Kingdom*; NIESR estimates.

[a] Total output free of duplication, plus imports.

The rise in the ratio of imports of manufactures to GNP discussed above has, in fact, been matched by relatively very large increases in the share of imports in total supplies of manufactures. In table 12.6 we show estimates of the increase for all manufacturing and for broad sectors of industry. Between 1955 and 1971 the import share for all manufactures rather more than doubled. It rose nearly fourfold for machinery and vehicles and more than trebled in the case of textiles and clothing. (In terms of consumption the rise would have been still greater owing to an increase in the proportion of output exported.) It is interesting that between 1968 and 1971 there was a sharp drop in the annual rate of increase – the effect of devaluation. If more up-to-date figures were available, however, they would certainly show a higher rate of rise in the last few years of the period under review.

Thus, while commercial policy and market forces have worked together to make the United Kingdom slightly more self-sufficient in agriculture, they have worked strongly in the opposite direction where manufactures are concerned. Likewise, by its influence on imports of manufactures, commercial policy has reinforced the swing in the origin of imports away from the Commonwealth and towards Western

Europe. The reciprocal tariff cuts made by other industrial countries under the EFTA and GATT tariff-cutting programmes similarly reinforced the change in the direction of exports induced by the more rapid growth of industrial, and particularly West European, markets for manufactures. Membership of the EEC will promote further changes in both direction of trade and in import ratios, but no attempt is made to estimate these here, since they fall outside the period covered by this study.

APPENDIX

ESTIMATES OF EFFECTS OF TARIFF CUTS ON UNITED KINGDOM IMPORTS OF MANUFACTURES

In the article referred to in the text[1] the regression equations used to estimate the effect of tariff changes were of the form:

$$\log M = a + b \log Y + c \log PT_i$$

where M referred to an index of the volume of imports of semi-manufactures or finished goods; Y referred to industrial production or expenditure on finished goods; PT_i referred to the unit value of imports, adjusted for the incidence of tariff revenue and the 1964–6 import surcharge, relative to an index of domestic wholesale prices for the relevant classes of manufactures.

This equation performed well for semi-manufactures over various time-periods and also when the variables were transformed into logarithms of first differences, but the results for finished goods were much less satisfactory. It was found that the latter (though not the former) could be greatly improved by the inclusion of a dummy variable from 1968 onwards to allow for a shift in the import function, which might have been produced by the initiation of the Kennedy Round tariff cuts.

If, however, the shift was due to the Kennedy Round and not to other causes, then similar shifts, proportionate to the size of the planned tariff reductions, might have occurred in connection with the EFTA and Dillon Round cuts. The equations for both semi-manufactures and finished goods were therefore modified to allow the value of the dummy to rise in proportion to the influence on the tariff, as illustrated in table 12.5 above, of successive tariff-cutting programmes. The effect of this modification was to improve the fit and stabilise the coefficients in both cases, although the dummy for semi-manufactures was only significant at the 95 per cent confidence level when the variables were in level form (it was significant at the 99 per cent level in first difference

[1] Morgan, 'Tariff reductions and UK imports of manufactures'.

form). On the other hand, the fact that the dummy for 1968 alone performed badly in the equations for semi-manufactures, while the split dummy performed reasonably well, was consistent with the greater influence of EFTA than of the Kennedy Round on imports of semi-manufactures. It appeared, therefore, that the equation with the split dummy should be used in estimating the effects of tariff cuts for both classes of manufactures.

The equations estimated for 1959–72 were (t-statistics in brackets):

Semi-manufactures

$$\log M = 2 \cdot 28 + 2 \cdot 22 \log Y - 1 \cdot 74 \log PT_i + 0 \cdot 19D \qquad \bar{R}^2 \ 0 \cdot 992, \ \text{SE } 0 \cdot 03,$$
$$\qquad\quad (14 \cdot 36) \qquad (9 \cdot 60) \qquad\quad (2 \cdot 67) \qquad\qquad \text{DW } 1 \cdot 505$$

$$\Delta \log M = 2 \cdot 77 \Delta \log Y - 1 \cdot 78 \Delta \log PT_i + 0 \cdot 23D \qquad \bar{R}^2 \ 0 \cdot 903, \ \text{SE } 0 \cdot 03,$$
$$\qquad\quad (13 \cdot 14) \qquad (8 \cdot 35) \qquad\quad (4 \cdot 21) \qquad\qquad \text{DW } 1 \cdot 610$$

Finished goods

$$\log M = - 1 \cdot 68 + 2 \cdot 79 \log Y - 1 \cdot 44 \log PT_i + 0 \cdot 29D \quad \bar{R}^2 \ 0 \cdot 998, \ \text{SE } 0 \cdot 02,$$
$$\qquad\quad (35 \cdot 05) \qquad (8 \cdot 13) \qquad\quad (8 \cdot 52) \qquad\qquad \text{DW } 2 \cdot 299$$

$$\Delta \log M = 2 \cdot 44 \Delta \log Y - 1 \cdot 44 \Delta \log PT_i + 0 \cdot 25D \qquad \bar{R}^2 \ 0 \cdot 828, \ \text{SE } 0 \cdot 03,$$
$$\qquad\quad (10 \cdot 23) \qquad (5 \cdot 96) \qquad\quad (3 \cdot 97) \qquad\qquad \text{DW } 2 \cdot 523$$

The equations in level form were used in calculating the estimates in the text.

CHAPTER 13

INDUSTRIAL RELATIONS AND
MANPOWER POLICY

by *R. Elliott*

INDUSTRIAL RELATIONS

Pressures for reform in the 1950s

The dominant tradition in British industrial relations, supported by employers, unions and governments, has been 'voluntarism'. This tradition is based on three closely related preferences: first, for collective bargaining over other methods of regulating conditions of employment; secondly, for voluntary non-legalistic regulation; thirdly, for autonomy in the relationship between the bargaining parties and the minimum of third party intervention.[1] This approach to industrial relations is reflected in the Ministry of Labour's *Handbook* which states: 'It has been conscious policy for many years to encourage the two sides of industry to make agreements and to settle their differences for themselves.'[2]

The legal framework to industrial relations in this country derived essentially from the Conspiracy and Protection of Property Act 1875 and the Trade Disputes Act 1906, which gave trade unions and persons acting in contemplation or furtherance of a trade dispute a number of important immunities. 'Anomalous privileges and statutory immunities from judge-made liabilities thus became the distinguishing characteristic of the law of industrial conflict in Britain.'[3]

While the philosophy of 'voluntarism' was very much an *ex post* rationalisation of many events which occurred over a long period, it was eventually elevated to an ideological belief common to both sides of industry and to the government. However, after a long period in which this voluntary system was regarded as a sign of the healthy and mature state of British industrial relations, a number of criticisms emerged in the 1950s. The main areas of concern were the effect of unconstitutional and unofficial strikes on Britain's industrial output

[1] A. Flanders, *Management and Unions*, London, Faber & Faber, 1970, p. 174.
[2] Ministry of Labour, *Industrial Relations Handbook*, London, HMSO, 1961.
[3] R. Lewis, 'The historical development of labour law', *British Journal of Industrial Relations*, vol. 14, March 1976, where the term 'collectivist *laissez-faire*' was first used to describe this framework.

and competitiveness in export markets,[1] the inhibiting effect of 'restrictive practices' on productivity and industrial change, and the contribution of union-backed wage demands to the problem of inflation. Views varied as to which constituted the major problem: some saw the inflationary threat as more important than the loss of working days and stressed the need for a voluntary or statutory wages policy;[2] others saw little evidence as yet that trade union bargaining power was 'independent of the normal forces of supply and demand in the economy'[3] and were more concerned with the disruptive effect of unofficial strikes led by shop stewards, which were the subject of several Committees of Inquiry.[4]

There was similar disagreement on the remedies to these problems. One school of thought argued that it was the very power of trade unions that was the cause of the trouble, and urged that this power, or at least that of certain sections of the unions such as shop stewards, should be curbed. This viewpoint was expressed in the pamphlet *A Giant's Strength*,[5] which advocated a new legal framework of trade union registration to force unions to exert greater control over their officers and members.[6] (Registration was to be central to later Conservative policies on industrial relations.) Another school of thought saw current industrial relations problems as merely a symptom of the unsatisfactory nature of institutions and procedures in industry and urged the need for the reform of collective bargaining; they did not see any need to curb union power, but stressed rather that effective collective bargaining required strong trade unions.[7]

Another source of concern in the 1950s, less immediately related to economic policy, was the impact of trade unions on the rights of

[1] Unconstitutional strikes are strikes that breach the agreed procedure on grievances in a particular industry or establishment; unofficial strikes are strikes that do not have the official approval of the union headquarters. It is by no means inevitable that an unconstitutional strike is unofficial, or that an unofficial strike is unconstitutional. Many strikes are never formally condemned or approved by union headquarters; rather they are short strikes and over before headquarters have heard of them.

[2] B. C. Roberts, 'Trade unions in the welfare state' and D. J. Robertson, 'Trade unions and wages policy', *Political Quarterly*, vol. 27, January–March 1956.

[3] *Economist*, 8 February 1958.

[4] For example, Ministry of Labour, *Unofficial Stoppages in the London Docks, Report of a Committee of Inquiry* [Legget Report], Cmd 8236, London, HMSO, 1951, and *Report of a Court of Inquiry into the Causes and Circumstances of a Dispute at Briggs Motor Bodies Limited, Dagenham*, Cmnd 131, London, HMSO, 1957.

[5] Inns of Court Conservative and Unionist Society, *A Giant's Strength*, London, 1958 (one of the authors of this pamphlet was Sir John Donaldson, later to be president of the National Industrial Relations Court).

[6] This approach was also advocated by the *Economist*, 22 February 1958, and by B. C. Roberts, *Trade Unions in a Free Society*, London, Institute of Economic Affairs, 1959.

[7] A. Flanders and H. Clegg (eds.), *The System of Industrial Relations in Great Britain*, Oxford, Blackwell, 1954.

individuals, particularly through the 'closed shop'. This was reflected in several Court cases, notably Huntley v. Thornton [1957] and Bonsor v. Musicians' Union [1956], which upheld the rights of individuals against the union, contrary to former legal practice. Some groups pressed for the abolition of the closed shop,[1] but others sought ways of providing individuals with a right of appeal while still maintaining the practice.[2] This concern with the rights of individuals was not wholly unrelated to fears about the growing economic powers of trade unions; there was a tendency to imply that their disruptive potential would be less if the mass of individual 'moderate' members had more influence over the militant and 'unrepresentative' leaders.[3] Such inferences often coexisted somewhat ambivalently with the assumption that many industrial relations problems would be solved if top union officials exerted more rather than less control over the membership.

These competing and frequently contradictory diagnoses of the nature of Britain's industrial relations problems were at the root of most policy disagreements during the 1960s and the 1970s, and indeed accounted for some of the ambiguities within specific policies and programmes.

The strike pattern in Britain since the 1950s

Since strikes, particularly unofficial strikes, have been a central pre-occupation in government policy towards industrial relations, it is useful to analyse briefly the pattern of strikes during the relevant period.

The Ministry of Labour did not keep separate figures on unofficial strikes until 1960, and even then did not officially publish them, so that precise calculation of trends in such strikes is not possible. However, the Royal Commission on Trade Unions and Employers' Associations was given access to the figures, and from their Report it appears that far from soaring in numbers in the 1960s, as the media and indeed governments tended to imply, unofficial strikes displayed no consistent upward or downward trend (table 13.1). What is significant in the pattern is that, from the late 1950s onwards, industrial conflict, once heavily concentrated in the coalmines, tended to become more dispersed. As one commentator remarked: 'It is especially significant that the metal working complex is tending to replace mining as the most strike-prone sector of the economy.'[4] Strike activity had essentially shifted from a declining to an expanding sector (table 13.2).

[1] For example, the Inns of Court Conservative and Unionist Society in *A Giant's Strength*.

[2] C. Grunfeld, *Trade Unions and the Individual*, London, Fabian Society, 1957.

[3] Inns of Court Conservative and Unionist Society, *A Giant's Strength*.

[4] H. A. Turner, *Is Britain Really Strike Prone?*, Department of Applied Economics, University of Cambridge, 1969.

Table 13.1. *Official and unofficial strikes, 1960–7*

	Official strikes[a]	Unofficial stoppages[b]
1960	68	2764
61	60	2626
62	78	2371
63	49	2019
64	70	2454
65	97	2257
66	60	1877
67	108	2008

SOURCE: Derived from Department of Employment and Productivity, *In Place of Strife*, appendix 2, paras. 2 and 5.

[a] Declared official beforehand or while in progress.
[b] Includes a small number of lock-outs and strikes by non-union members.

Table 13.2. *Workers involved and days lost in stoppages, 1957–73*

	Stoppages beginning in year			No. of workers involved	Aggregate no. of working days lost
	Coalmining	Other	Total		
				(000s)	(000s)
1957	2224	635	2859	136	841
58	1963	666	2629	52	346
59	1307	786	2093	65	527
1960	1666	1166	2832	81	303
61	1458	1228	2686	77	305
62	1203	1246	2449	442	580
63	987	1081	2068	59	176
64	1058	1466	2524	88	228
65	740	1614	2354	88	293
66	553	1384	1937	54	240
67	394	1722	2116	73	279
68	221	2157	2378	226	469
69	186	2930	3116	167	685
1970	160	3746	3906	180	1098
71	135	2093	2228	118	1355
72	218	2252	2470	171	2390
73	301	2553	2854	152	717

SOURCE: *Department of Employment Gazette* (various issues).

Analysis of strike data from the 1950s to the late 1960s confirms that the predominant type of dispute was a short, small, unofficial strike; there were relatively few protracted national disputes involving large numbers of workers in a particular industry.[1] This trend in size, duration and frequency of strikes, which can be traced back to 1926, was

[1] For a fuller analysis see R. Hyman, *Strikes*, Glasgow, Fontana-Collins, 1972, p. 26.

accompanied by a change of emphasis in the causes of strikes as classified by the Department of Employment.[1] In the twenty years since
1940 the proportion of strikes about 'wage-questions other than demands
for increases' and about 'working arrangements, rules and discipline'
rose markedly, from one third to three quarters of all stoppages. Since
these kinds of dispute imply some attempt 'to submit managerial
discretion and authority to agreed – or failing that, customary – rules',[2]
they have been pointed to as evidence of the need for procedural reform
in industrial relations at plant and company levels.

However, as Hyman has pointed out, 'the trend of British strikes has
been anything but simple'[3] (a fact not always recognised by some
concerned to find simple solutions to industrial relations problems),
and developments in the later 1960s were markedly different from those
of the previous decades. The proportion of disputes over wage issues
again increased sharply, so that by 1970 disputes concerned primarily
with wage increases accounted for 62 per cent of all recorded stoppages.[4] There was also a change in the size and duration of strikes:
official national disputes involving large numbers of workers became
increasingly frequent. From the late 1960s onwards, except in 1969 and
1970, the number of strikes 'increased only gradually and then not
steadily, [but] the number of employees involved doubled...The
total number of working days lost increased even more dramatically
and the number of working days lost per employee involved trebled...
Strikes then have become longer and larger in recent years and this
has occurred at a time of government incomes policies of various kinds
for most of the period. In most recent years large national disputes,
particularly of public sector workers, in response to such policies have
dominated the strike picture.'[5] This change in the pattern of strikes
was to have important implications for government policies towards
industrial relations.

Policies before the 'Donovan Report'

While certain sections of the Conservative Party were among the most
vocal in criticising the growing power of trade unions, in the 1950s
and early 1960s the Conservative government 'resisted pressures from
the right and centre of their own party to revise the Trade Union

---

[1] See W. E. J. McCarthy, 'The reasons given for striking', *Bulletin of the Oxford University Institute of Statistics*, vol. 21, February 1959.

[2] H. A. Turner, *The Trend of Strikes*, Leeds University Press, 1963, p. 18.

[3] Hyman, *Strikes*, p. 26.

[4] Ibid. p. 117.

[5] B. Weekes, M. Mellish, L. Dickens and J. Lloyd, *Industrial Relations and the Limits of the Law*, Oxford, Blackwell, 1975, p. 214. The proportions are for 1970–3 compared with 1963–6.

Acts...afraid both of losing their own growing trade union support and of reviving the fortunes of the Labour Party at the same time'.[1] The Conservatives were 'leaning over backwards to get the top trade union leaders to cooperate with them in the task of running the country'.[2] However, towards the end of its period of office, the Conservative government appeared to calculate that it might increase its public support, including that from trade unionists, if it appeared willing to take action on the 'abuse' of trade union power. In March 1964 the Minister of Labour indicated his support for the idea of an inquiry into trade unions and employers' associations: 'Recent decisions in the Courts have focused attention on the present state of the law affecting trade unions and employers associations, which was last reviewed nearly 60 years ago. The government are of the opinion that the law should again be reviewed.'[3] It was in line with future Conservative policy that the emphasis was on the role of the law in industrial relations.

However, disagreements between the TUC and the government delayed the setting up of this proposed inquiry. In the case of Rookes v. Barnard [1964], a Court decided that section 3 of the 1906 Trade Disputes Act did not give immunity in the case of *threats* to induce a breach of contract; the case also raised questions of wider legal liabilities which might have restricted industrial action. The TUC maintained that this violated the spirit of the 1906 Act and wanted immediate legislation to remove the new restrictions. The Conservative government refused, however, and were only prepared to concede a general inquiry on the state of trade union law. This deadlock persisted until the Labour government came to power and introduced legislation (the Trade Disputes Act 1965) to meet the TUC's demands. At the same time the TUC agreed to a 'broad enquiry into trade unions and society'.[4]

The first terms of reference for the Royal Commission specifically mentioned what the government presumably saw as the most urgent problems in industrial relations, such as productivity and restrictive practices. However, the TUC objected to this specificity and the final terms of reference were much more general: 'to consider relations between managements and employers and the role of trade unions and employers' associations in promoting the interests of their members and in accelerating the economic and social advance of the nation, with particular reference to the law affecting the activities of these bodies'.

[1] W. Pickles, 'Trade unions in the political climate' in B. C. Roberts (ed.), *Industrial Relations: contemporary problems and perspectives*, London, Methuen, 1962.

[2] *Economist*, 8 February 1964.

[3] *Hansard*, 19 March 1964, col. 1598.

[4] TUC, *Report of the 97th Annual Trades Union Congress at Brighton, 1965*.

From the beginning of their period of office the Labour government's approach to industrial relations diverged considerably from the 'voluntary' tradition, particularly in regard to the assumption that the bargaining parties in industry should enjoy autonomy in their relationships. The Ministry of Labour became more active in disputes than ever before; it began to intervene in a number of unofficial strikes, where previously the convention had been that third party intervention would undermine the established authority of unions and employers. Undoubtedly the most significant challenge to the voluntary tradition was the government's prices and incomes policy, which introduced new legal constraints into collective bargaining and reflected a growing feeling that no government could afford to take an attitude of 'formal indifference' to wage settlements. In terms of legal policy, the Prices and Incomes Act 1966, which stipulated criminal sanctions against those using direct industrial action to contravene government orders to delay pay awards, was a revolutionary development. Even in wartime the government had previously stopped short of such direct interference with the substantive outcome of collective bargaining and had instead favoured compulsory arbitration and the compulsory direction of labour.[1]

The Reports of the Prices and Incomes Board, which frequently stressed the role of chaotic pay structures in encouraging inflationary 'leap-frogging', provided further backing for the arguments of those who saw the development of orderly and well-defined collective bargaining procedures as a prerequisite for the reform of industrial relations.

The Royal Commission was therefore set up 'at a time when the basic principles of our system of industrial relations [were] in question: should they be restored, revised, or replaced?'.[2] The oral and written evidence submitted to the Commission suggested that unions, employers and the relevant government departments favoured retaining the main features of the voluntary tradition, perhaps with slight revision, rather than its replacement by a fundamentally different system of legal regulation. The CBI expressed doubts about the wisdom of making collective agreements legally enforceable and did not advocate legislation that would involve the prosecution of individuals; they favoured the conferring of extended powers on the Registrar of Trade Unions to ensure that union rules were specific on such matters as the authority to call strikes and the penalties to be imposed by the union for breaches of the rules. The attraction of such a scheme was that any penalties on unofficial strikers would be 'imposed by the union itself on its

---

[1] Lewis, 'The historical development of labour law'.
[2] *Donovan Report*, para. 45.

members according to its rules';[1] there would be a minimum of legal or government intervention.

The Ministry of Labour expressed a similar attitude in their evidence.[2] They too did not favour legislation that would involve the prosecution of individuals, but felt that it was desirable 'in the national interest that pressure should be exerted on trade unions to give more attention to the activities of shop stewards and other subordinate bodies'. They proposed that, in the case of unofficial strikes, 'the trade union concerned should be subject to defined penalties, according to the length of time the unofficial strike lasted, unless they could show to some independent tribunal that they had taken all steps open to them to prevent the unofficial strike taking place, or to bring it to an end as soon as possible'. However, they also recognised the need to tackle causes as well as symptoms, and questioned whether current procedures had kept pace with developments in collective bargaining.

The TUC strongly defended the voluntary system and argued that the introduction of a more legalistic framework could 'have a serious and damaging effect on the generally enlightened approach to industrial relations which has been evolved in this country over the years'.[3]

The Conservative Party showed consistently more enthusiasm than either employers or unions for a comprehensive new legal framework that would fundamentally reconstruct the traditional system of industrial relations. In their 1966 election manifesto they pledged themselves to introduce a wide-ranging industrial relations act, and chastised the 'frightened Socialist Government' for its inaction.[4] They published a fuller account of their proposals in April 1968, laying their cards on the table shortly before the Royal Commission. They had been able to draw on the published evidence of the Commission and had also conducted their own studies and research. The pamphlet *Fair Deal at Work* stressed that reform in industrial relations was 'absolutely crucial to economic progress', and laid primary emphasis on the role of a new and comprehensive legal framework in bringing about this reform by creating 'an environment in which responsible voluntary action within industry would have more opportunity and more incentive to succeed'.[5] This new framework was to regulate both internal union affairs and the relations between unions and employers.

[1] Royal Commission on Trade Unions and Employers' Associations, *Minutes of Evidence: Witness Confederation of British Industry, 7 December 1965*, London, HMSO, 1966.

[2] Royal Commission on Trade Unions and Employers' Associations, *Written Evidence of the Ministry of Labour*, London, HMSO, 1965.

[3] TUC, 'Trade unionism' in *Selected Written Evidence Submitted to the Royal Commission*, London, HMSO, 1968.

[4] S. Abbott, *Industrial Relations: Conservative policy*, London, Conservative Political Centre, 1966.   [5] Conservative Political Centre, *Fair Deal at Work*, London, 1968.

The Conservative proposals were largely derived from *A Giant's Strength*, the pamphlet mentioned above;[1] the emphasis on registration as the major tool for regulating the behaviour of unions and their members was now developed to become a cornerstone of policy. The objective was to ensure that certain democratic principles were applied in the internal conduct of trade unions. Their rule books would be expected to make explicit reference to the rights of individual members in matters such as elections or disciplinary procedures; they would also be expected to delineate precisely the status, responsibilities and authority of officials at all levels in the union. In addition to protecting the rights of individuals, this was intended to ensure that union officials did not act without regard to constitutional checks and balances. It was assumed that once trade unions had precise and unambiguous constitutions and rules there could be no legitimate excuse for anyone transgressing those rules, and any who did (say by engaging in unofficial industrial action) might justly expect to be disciplined by the union.

The legal framework proposed in *Fair Deal at Work* also aimed to provide new forms of regulation for union–employer relations and to restrict industrial conflict. The central proposal was that collective agreements should be legally binding, one implication of which was that a union failing to do all in its power to prevent breaches of agreements by members would be liable in the Courts. It was also proposed to restrict the legal immunities enjoyed by strikers by narrowing the definition of a trade dispute to exclude inter-union disputes, secondary boycotts and strikes to enforce the closed shop. The proposals also included new forms of government intervention in industrial disputes where they were of such magnitude as to endanger the national interest. The Minister of Labour was to be empowered either to apply for an injunction to stop industrial action for a specified period (a 'cooling-off' period), or to call for a secret ballot to ascertain whether the industrial action had the support of the majority of union members.

These proposals were strongly influenced by American labour law and industrial relations practice, as was the whole approach of *Fair Deal at Work*, which laid great stress on the fact that, while Britain's strike record compared quite favourably with that of the United States, the United States had one major advantage – with legally binding fixed-term contracts containing no-strike clauses, strikes were eminently predictable. 'The threat of action comes after one contract has expired without agreement on the terms of the next. Thus, employers may anticipate trouble well in advance and, if necessary, prepare for it. In these circumstances, there is less likelihood of an early impact on their customers, on other industries, or on the public at large.'[2]

---

[1] See page 565.   [2] Conservative Political Centre, *Fair Deal at Work*.

While the predominant emphasis of *Fair Deal at Work* was on constitutional reform, it also made brief reference to institutional reform – commenting on the need to review and overhaul collective bargaining procedures, particularly at plant level. An independent body was to be established to encourage and stimulate reform; a code of industrial relations practice was also advocated.

The 'Donovan Report'

While the matter of institutional and procedural reform was very much an addendum to *Fair Deal at Work*, it was central to the whole analysis behind the Report of the Royal Commission, which was published in June 1968. The Commission felt that much of the industrial unrest which some sought to solve through legal remedies was a symptom of disorder in industrial relations institutions; consequently permanent solutions could only be found by reforming those institutions, and short-term legal remedies and restrictions might inhibit this reform.

The Commission maintained that there existed two systems of industrial relations – the formal one 'embodied in the official institutions and industry-wide collective agreements', and the informal one 'created by the actual behaviour of trade unions and employers' associations, of managers, shop stewards and workers' – and that these two systems undermined and conflicted with each other (para. 149). The assumption that formal industry-wide agreements control industrial relations had led companies to neglect their own industrial relations policies; consequently regulation at company and plant level had developed in a disorderly and *ad hoc* manner, so that procedures at these levels were inadequate. The Commission argued that only through the development of clear-cut company and plant procedures could order be restored; industry-wide agreements should be limited to matters they could regulate effectively, which might include the setting of guidelines for acceptable company or plant agreements (para. 101).

The Commission felt that management must take the initiative in this reform (para. 168), but their Report reflected the growing disenchantment with pure 'collectivist *laissez-faire*' by advocating a much wider role for third party intervention. It proposed that companies of a certain size should register their collective agreements with the Department of Employment to enable progress and the nature of the problems to be assessed. A commission was also proposed to stimulate the process of reform; this body would carry out general investigations within a factory or an industry, as well as dealing with specific references on union recognition (paras. 198–201). The Royal Commission felt that formalising plant and company bargaining would do much to ease the problems both of restrictive practices (which were encouraged by a reliance on 'custom and practice' – para. 305) and of inflationary wage pressures derived from competitive bargaining within fragmented pay and bargaining structures (paras. 207–11).

The Commission rejected wide-ranging legal sanctions against strikers, since the evidence suggested that unofficial strikes were only a symptom of the general inadequacies of the conduct of industrial relations at plant and company level. 'They will persist so long as companies pay inadequate attention to their pay structures and personnel policies and the methods of negotiations adopted at the workplace remain in their present chaotic state. They will also persist so long as neither employers nor trade unions are willing adequately to recognise, define and control the part played by shop stewards in our collective bargaining system.' (para. 454.) The Report stressed that breaches of procedure could not be contained merely by disciplining shop stewards or even members; the problem could only really be solved through the development of procedures commanding the respect and confidence of all involved, from the rank and file upwards.

Many of the changes in law that had been suggested to the Royal Commission, including provisions for cooling-off periods or secret ballots at the discretion of the government, were rejected in the final Report as simplistic, irrelevant or unworkable (paras. 418–26). The Report also argued that to make collective agreements legally enforceable would be undesirable and indeed self-defeating until such agreements had been reformed and formalised (para. 475).

As regards the regulation of internal union affairs, the Commission agreed with the Conservatives that there was a need for the Registrar of Trade Unions to be given extended powers to scrutinise union rule books, and to require the rules covering such issues as entry, discipline, disputes, elections, voting and the responsibilities of shop stewards to be more specific. To encourage unions to register, a majority of the Commission proposed to limit the protection of the first part of the Trade Disputes Act (giving statutory immunity from inducing breach of contract) to registered unions. In contrast to the subsequent policy of the Conservatives, however, they did not advocate any further legal disabilities for unregistered unions. Moreover, they did not think it would be wise to deal with complaints concerning breaches of trade union rules through the Courts (as was to happen in later Conservative legislation); rather it was proposed that a new review body should be set up to deal with individual workers' complaints against unions and with any differences that might arise between unions and the Registrar (paras. 648–58).

To give further protection to individuals, the Commission proposed a legal remedy against unfair dismissal (para. 546). At the same time it was stressed that safeguards for individuals should not be allowed to undermine orderly and effective collective organisation; if collective bargaining was to be the preferred way of regulating industrial relations supported by the government, then this must involve some restrictions on individual freedom. This approach was well illustrated in the Commission's attitude to the closed shop, where both the role that it can play in supporting stable and orderly collective bargaining and the practical problems of abolishing it were acknowledged. It was proposed, therefore, that the closed shop should continue, but that if the security of an individual's job was threatened by its operation he should have the right to complain to a labour tribunal (para. 614).

The Commission's concern to strike a balance between individual rights and the promotion of stable collective bargaining was also reflected in the recommendation that individuals should not be given a statutory right *not* to belong to a union. It was argued that the right to belong and the right not to belong were not equivalent, since one was designed to promote collective bargaining in accordance with public policy, while the other would tend to frustrate it – a distinction ignored later by the Conservative government, with potentially serious consequences for the stability of collective bargaining arrangements.

In many respects, the Commission's recommendations followed the 'voluntary' tradition; they reflected preferences for collective bargaining over other methods of regulating management–employee relations and for a non-legalistic process of reform, whereby managers and trade unions together should agree on the nature of the problems facing them and devise adequate institutional solutions. However, some of the Report's proposals, such as the majority recommendation in favour of confining the statutory immunity from inducing breach of contract to registered unions only, did constitute significant deviations from the tradition of the 1906 Trade Disputes Act. Moreover, although it was proposed that collective agreements should retain their non-contractual status in the immediately forseeable future, the Donovan Commission nevertheless recommended that legal enforcement of procedural agreements should be considered if unconstitutional strikes continued as a problem after the reform of collective bargaining (paras. 508–18). A fundamental critique of the tradition of British industrial relations came in Andrew Shonfield's note of reservation, which called for a much greater degree of legal intervention in industrial relations.

Those politicians and those sections of the press that shared Shonfield's view were highly critical of the Royal Commission's Report. Iain Macleod called it a 'blueprint for inaction',[1] and press comments included 'appallingly complacent' (*Daily Telegraph*) and 'a report to

[1] *Hansard*, 16 July 1968, col. 1260.

forget' (*Economist*). *The Times*, on the other hand, applauded it for 'diagnosing with deadly accuracy what has gone wrong with Britain's system of industrial relations' and the *Guardian* regarded it as 'notable rebuff for the magic wand school of thought. The Commission is not to be condemned for its failure to provide a neat package of answers.'

However, not all the Commissioners had complete faith in a largely voluntary process of reform as a solution to the immediate problems of the government and of industry. Lord Donovan in an addendum suggested there might be a need for 'some interim remedy which would be both workable and just'. Similar feelings were expressed in supplementary notes by four other Commissioners, who advocated that voluntary compliance alone should not be relied upon in certain areas. These minority views attracted considerable support in subsequent policy debates and the search for this elusive 'interim remedy' that would 'give Donovan teeth' became one of the most contentious issues following the publication of the Report.

'In Place of Strife'

The Labour government's proposals on the reform of industrial relations, set out in a White Paper in January 1969,[1] broadly accepted the diagnosis and prescriptions of the Royal Commission, including the registration of collective agreements, the setting up of the CIR[2] and the registration procedures for trade unions (although the idea of restricting legal immunities to registered unions was rejected). However, while it was stressed that without procedural reform there could be 'no fundamental solution to the problem of unofficial strikes', the government clearly felt the need for interim remedies which could help in the immediate future to protect the economy from the disruptive effects of certain strikes. Hence the ill-fated 'penal clauses'.

These clauses included a modified version of the conciliation pause or cooling-off period. Where the effects of an unconstitutional strike were likely to be serious, the Secretary of State was to have discretionary power to secure a conciliation pause of 28 days. This was clearly an attempt to provide a short-term remedy for what has been called Britain's 'real strike problem' – the occasional unconstitutional strike which 'causes a disproportionate amount of damage to the national economy and results in large numbers of workers who are not involved being laid off'.[3] The White Paper also proposed that the government should have power to call for a secret ballot in an official dispute where 'the support of those involved may be in doubt' and where there might

---

[1] Department of Employment and Productivity, *In Place of Strife*.   [2] See page 58.
[3] W. E. J. McCarthy, 'The nature of Britain's strike problem', *British Journal of Industrial Relations*, vol. 8, July 1970.

be a 'serious threat to the economy or the public interest'. The CIR was also to be given legal powers to enforce a settlement in an inter-union dispute where the TUC had failed to bring about a voluntary agreement. This hard-line approach was undoubtedly influenced by the stress the Conservatives were placing on their intention to withdraw legal immunities from such disputes, and by the extensive press coverage of current inter-union disputes (for example, that at the Girling brake factory, which had caused thousands of men in the motor industry to be laid off). The final 'penal clause' was directed more against employers: if an employer refused to accept the recommendations of the CIR on a recognition case, he could be ordered to recognise and negotiate with the appropriate union.

These 'interim remedies' in fact satisfied no one. The President of the CBI complained that the package 'failed miserably to deal with the problems of unofficial strikes'; the TUC deplored the penal clauses, and there was also strong opposition from some Labour members of Parliament. In the House of Commons debate of 3 March, 57 Labour members voted against the government and an estimated 30 more abstained. As the *Guardian* prophetically commented of the penal clauses: 'They will probably occupy more parliamentary and public time than they are worth.'[1] Yet the Prime Minister appeared to stake the credibility of the government's whole industrial relations policy on the acceptance of those clauses. In a speech on 14 March in his constituency he denounced:

...strike after strike frustrating the efforts of government, signalling the question mark to those industrialists who are attracted by the inducements the government provide and who are considering establishing themselves here...I want it to be understood that we mean business about these proposals. All that has happened in the last three weeks provides powerful support for the measures we shall be introducing in Parliament.[2]

In spite of growing opposition within the Labour Party, reflected in a national executive vote of sixteen to five against legislation based on *all* the proposals in the White Paper, the government decided to legislate immediately for selected parts of the proposals, including the penal clauses (except the proposed ballot which was dropped). The announcement came in the budget speech of 15 April 1969, which suggested an important shift in Labour Party policy. Roy Jenkins expressed the view that no counter-inflation policy could succeed in the face of the 'irresponsible industrial action' that characterised British industrial relations. The curbing of such action was now seen as a major

[1] *Guardian*, 18 January 1969.
[2] P. Jenkins, *The Battle of Downing Street*, London, Charles Knight, 1970, p. 61.

objective of government economic policy: 'No observer of the British economy can doubt that the present climate of industrial relations is a serious obstacle to the attainment of our economic objectives, and that the improvement of that climate should be a major aim of policy.'[1] Some people, however, viewed this announcement as indicative not so much of a well thought out shift in policy, but as a pragmatic attempt at 'using anti-strike measures to boost confidence in the economy and appease the International Monetary Fund'.[2]

Indeed the proposed Bill, unveiled on 16 April, revealed none of the overall strategy for the long-term reform of industrial relations set out in the Royal Commission's Report and in *In Place of Strife*. Its major focus was the penal clauses, suggesting that the government's objective had shifted from the long-term reform of collective bargaining to short-term action on unofficial strikes. When announcing the Bill, however, Barbara Castle made it clear that the government did not see legislation as the only way forward. She stressed that 'the Government will still be prepared to consider any alternative proposals from the TUC for achieving its purpose equally effectively and urgently'.[3]

The TUC did indeed respond by producing its own proposals for amending its own rules to give the General Council more scope for intervention in unconstitutional and inter-union disputes. While the Prime Minister expressed satisfaction with the proposals on inter-union disputes, he questioned whether the proposals for dealing with unconstitutional strikes provided a viable alternative to the government's proposals.[4] The point at issue in the tense meetings between the government and the TUC over the next month was what the TUC was prepared to do in unconstitutional strikes to ensure that 'their members returned to work and remained at work during negotiations'.[5]

The government was anxious to drop their legislation, since there was clearly little chance of carrying a Bill containing any penal clauses in the Commons.[6] Yet a compromise was not easy, since the government had exalted the Industrial Relations Bill to a symbol of its capacity to rule and to take firm measures to deal with the worsening economic crisis. Harold Wilson seemed determined to demonstrate his ability to take a tough stand, regardless of popularity, on important issues of policy. As he remarked in an interview on television: 'We have got to go on and do what is right, regardless of popularity.' As a compromise became increasingly inevitable, the government's main concern was to seek one that would not utterly destroy this 'tough' image. If the

[1] *Hansard*, 15 April 1969, col. 1006.
[2] Jenkins, *The Battle of Downing Street*, p. 93.
[3] *Hansard*, 16 April 1969, col. 1187.
[4] TUC, *Report of the 101st Annual Trades Union Congress at Portsmouth, 1969*.
[5] Ibid.　　　　　　　　　[6] *Financial Times*, 17 June 1969.

legislation was to be dropped in favour of the TUC proposals, the government had to be convinced, as the Prime Minister put it, of the 'saleability to the country' of these proposals. Clearly the issue had ceased to be one of economic policy and was now a question of political expediency.

The necessary 'saleable' compromise was found on 18 June, when the TUC offered a 'solemn and binding undertaking' as to the action they would take during an unconstitutional dispute to ensure a return to work.[1] In return the government dropped their Bill and its penal clauses, promising a new and comprehensive Bill in the next session. But this Bill, published in April 1970, was a disappointingly piecemeal collection of measures, lacking any coherent overall policy, and it lapsed with the dissolution of Parliament.

The only surviving element of Labour policy on industrial relations was the CIR, which had been set up in March 1969. However, this body also was a casualty to some extent of the tension caused by the Labour government's first Industrial Relations Bill. In the early months of its existence few cases were referred to it: 'there was not a suitable industrial climate prevailing in which to carry out investigation'.[2] After the demise of the Bill there was a steady flow of references (25 by the end of June 1970),[3] but the change of government at this point meant that the CIR did not function in its voluntary role for long enough to make possible any meaningful assessment of its success in stimulating the kind of reform advocated by the Royal Commission. Soon after the beginning of the Conservative period of office several members resigned in protest against the new government's proposals for an Industrial Relations Act, and the TUC initiated a policy of non-cooperation. The CIR therefore ceased to function in the manner intended by the Royal Commission.

Conservative policy 1970–4

The Conservative Party manifesto had made it clear that if elected they would regard legislation along the lines set out in *Fair Deal at Work* as a matter of high priority. Within four months, on 5 October, the Department of Employment and Productivity published a 'consultative document' on a proposed Industrial Relations Bill. The Bill itself was published in December. While it was in many respects based on *Fair Deal at Work*, it also took account of the recommendations and diagnosis of the Royal Commission by laying much greater emphasis on the need for the reform and formalisation of fragmented and informal collective bargaining arrangements.

[1] For a detailed analysis of these events see Jenkins, *The Battle of Downing Street*.
[2] CIR, *First General Report*, Cmnd 4417, London, HMSO, 1970.   [3] Ibid.

The main objectives of the Bill were the restriction of industrial conflict, the reform of collective bargaining and the promotion of individual liberties. The first two objectives were closely linked to economic policy, while the third had its origins more in traditional Conservative ideology and concern with individual freedom. The three were not always to prove mutually compatible, as later sections illustrate. The next section describes the instruments chosen to achieve the various objectives of the Bill.

The Industrial Relations Bill

Registration was the key to achieving all the objectives of the Bill. Unions would have to register to bring themselves within the legal definition of a 'trade union'. It would be a condition of registration that union rule books met certain minimum standards. The aim was to prevent the abuse of power by ensuring that there were precise and unambiguous rules governing all union procedures, with adequate safeguards for individual rights and a clear delineation of the responsibilities and functions of all officials and members of the union.[1] Various incentives were offered to encourage unions to register, thereby subjecting their rule books to the scrutiny of the Registrar and to the stipulations in section 65 and schedule 4 of the Bill. Unregistered unions could not benefit from the provisions of the Bill regarding union recognition, disclosure of information and agency or approved closed shops; they also lost certain tax concessions and became subject to unlimited fines in the Courts. Moreover, individuals had no right to belong to an unregistered union.

Many of the stipulations concerning union rules aimed to protect the rights of individual members, who could complain to the Courts if a union acted contrary to the principles set out in the Bill's guidelines. The other main concern was that rules should be specific on the right to call for industrial action. Registered unions must clarify the powers and duties of all officials and bodies, and must specify any body and any official by whom industrial action might be ordered on behalf of the union and the circumstances in which such orders might be given. Rules must also specify the exact penalities that would follow from an infringement of the rules. It was expected that unions would be unwilling to give shop stewards full authority to call strikes in all circumstances and would prefer to modify their rules to limit that authority; they would then have no option but to discipline stewards who infringed the rules, which would have the effect of restricting unofficial industrial action. However, this was not to be the effect of the Bill in practice.

[1] Part IV of the Bill covered this area.

It was in the sections on the legal regulation of industrial action that the Bill drew most strongly on the analysis of *A Giant's Strength* and *Fair Deal at Work*, and diverged most markedly from the Royal Commission.[1] The clear objective was to curb industrial action by limiting the legal immunities enjoyed by trade unions. Since such immunities have been the way in which British law grants a right to strike,[2] their limitation indicated an attempt to solve the 'strike problem' by severely restricting the right to strike, rather than by seeking, as did the Royal Commission, to identify and resolve some of the underlying causes of strikes. The abolition of the Trade Union Act and the Trade Disputes Act, and the establishment of the NIRC[3] meant a totally new approach to the legal regulation of industrial conflict.

Industrial action, including irregular industrial action short of a strike, was declared an 'unfair industrial practice' in a number of circumstances related to other provisions of the Bill (for example, recognition procedures and the closed shop), and would be actionable in the NIRC.[4] Section 96 made it illegal for anybody but a registered union or its officials acting within their authority to induce a breach of contract in contemplation or furtherance of a trade dispute; since many contracts may be broken during a dispute, this had wide-ranging implications. Moreover, section 98 declared illegal any sanctions to prevent an 'extraneous' party in a dispute performing his contract with the employer involved in the primary dispute, with sweeping implications for blacking and picketing. These sections comprised the strongest attack since the last century on rights of collective organisation and collective action. The right to strike was nominally guaranteed by section 147, which laid down that if notice of a strike was given the same period in advance as that required to terminate the contract of employment, then the strike did not count as a breach of contract under section 96. However, even if due notice had been given, a strike still constituted a breach of contract if there was a restriction on the right to strike incorporated into the individual's contract of employment. The right to strike therefore became highly vulnerable and precarious. The emergency procedures that could be invoked by the Secretary of State (sections 138–45) placed further potential restrictions, albeit of a temporary nature, on industrial action. These provided for versions of the cooling-off period and the secret ballot so unsuccessfully proposed by the Labour government.

Part III of the Bill set out various procedures which aimed to reform

[1] Parts V and VIII of the Bill.

[2] K. W. Wedderburn, 'Labour law and labour relations in Britain', *British Journal of Industrial Relations*, vol. 10, July 1972.   [3] See page 57.

[4] See R. Lewis, 'Unfair industrial practices', *Industrial Relations Review and Report*, no. 15, September 1971.

collective bargaining. The *Industrial Relations Code of Practice*, first issued in June 1971, was intended to act as a guide and stimulus to the process of reform.[1] The criteria and guidelines it contained reflect the *Donovan Report's* emphasis on written agreements and procedures to provide clear rules and a sound basis for resolving conflicts. The main architects of the Bill consistently stressed their concern with the Royal Commission's objective of voluntary reform. Robert Carr maintained: 'We are not attempting to replace the voluntary system, but seeking to reform and strengthen it';[2] Geoffrey Howe commented: 'People are fond of suggesting that this approach is in direct contrast with that recommended by the Donovan Commission...Nothing could be further from the truth...I should judge that the major part of the Government's proposals are directly in line with Donovan's recommendations.'[3] Where the Conservatives' approach diverged from Donovan was in the emphasis on law as the 'main instrument' in achieving reform,[4] and in the influence of American industrial relations practices on the 'goals' of the process of reform.

The most important instruments for the reform of collective bargaining contained in the Bill were the procedures for determining bargaining agents and units, and the provision that collective agreements made in writing would be presumed to be intended to create legal relations unless there was an express clause to the contrary.

The statutory recognition procedure (sections 44–5) required the CIR not only to recommend a sole bargaining agent but also an appropriate bargaining unit. There were initial fears that the criteria which the CIR were required to consider when determining an appropriate bargaining unit – the nature of the work performed by groups, and their professional or other qualifications (section 48) – would increase the fragmentation of bargaining procedures by encouraging registered professional bodies to seek representational rights for small groups.[5] In practice, however, the CIR laid greater emphasis on the more comprehensive criteria set out in the *Industrial Relations Code of Practice*, which included 'the need to fit the bargaining unit into the pattern of union and management organisation' and 'the need to avoid disruption of any existing bargaining arrangements that are working well'.[6]

The provision that all collective agreements should be presumed to

[1] Department of Employment, *Industrial Relations Code of Practice*, London, HMSO, 1972.

[2] Robert Carr, speech to the third annual forum of the Institute of Collective Bargaining and Group Relations, New York, 25 May 1971.

[3] Sir Geoffrey Howe, speech to the Industrial Law Society, 21 November 1970.

[4] Department of Employment and Productivity, *Industrial Relations Bill: consultative document*, London, 1970, para. 2.

[5] R. Lewis and G. Latta, 'Bargaining units and bargaining agents', *British Journal of Industrial Relations*, vol. 10, March 1972.

[6] Department of Employment, *Industrial Relations Code of Practice*, para. 78.

be intended to be legally enforceable unless otherwise stipulated (section 34) reflected a clear lack of confidence in voluntary procedural reform; it had obvious relevance to the restriction of industrial conflict as well as to the reform of collective bargaining. The aim was to establish a legal sanction that could be used against 'disruptive' elements. As Weekes points out, 'if agreements were legally binding, an employer would have a legal remedy against any signatory union which failed to take all reasonable steps to ensure that members understood and upheld the terms of the agreement'.[1] The same impatience with voluntary reform was revealed by the sections concerned with non-existent or defective procedures which inhibited the maintenance of 'orderly industrial relations' (section 39). In such situations the CIR was empowered to 'promote and assist discussions between the parties with a view to obtaining their agreement on new or revised provisions...so formulated as to be capable of having effect as a legally enforceable contract'. If, however, agreement was not reached, a Court could make the procedure drawn up by the CIR legally binding on both parties. The usefulness of this provision, with its assumption that if management could not secure the workforce's compliance through collective bargaining they might feel they could secure it through legal sanctions, was questioned from the start, and in fact it soon became virtually a dead letter.[2]

The Bill's concern with the promotion of individual liberty challenged the dominance of collective over individual values in industrial relations. Potential tensions between individual liberties and the reform of collective bargaining were evident in a number of provisions. For example, an individual could challenge the continuance of existing collective bargaining arrangements by requesting that recognition be withdrawn from a particular bargaining agent (section 51). Similar tensions were evident in section 5, which established both the right of an individual to belong to a registered union of his choice, and his right not to belong to either a registered or an unregistered union. The Donovan Commission's argument that the right to belong and the right not to belong were not equivalent, since one was designed to promote collective bargaining in accordance with public policy, while the other would tend to frustrate it, was rejected. One consequence of this approach was that closed shops became inconsistent with these new rights: pre-entry closed shop agreements were explicitly made void by section 7, and section 33 made it an unfair industrial practice to attempt to enforce a closed shop of any kind.

The Bill did not, however, totally ignore the potential of the closed

---

[1] Weekes *et al.*, *Industrial Relations and the Limits of the Law*, p. 157.
[2] Ibid. p. 171.

shop in promoting orderly collective bargaining and reducing multi-unionism. The concept of the 'agency shop' was introduced as an alternative means of achieving these ends.[1] With an agency shop, the individual's right to join the union of his choice, which clearly might encourage multi-unionism, could be legally curtailed. In contrast to a closed shop, however, individuals opposed to membership of any union were allowed to pay dues to the union without becoming members, or to pay an equivalent sum to a charity; thus loss of union membership need not mean loss of a job. The disciplinary function of the closed shop, whereby members transgressing rules could lose their membership and eventually their jobs, was not provided for in the agency shop. In the light of the Conservative's concern with the rigid enforcement of union rules, this weakening of unions' disciplinary power was in some respects paradoxical.

Provisions that were the subject of less contention were the new safeguards against unfair dismissal (sections 22–6). Here the Conservatives broadly accepted the recommendations of the Royal Commission. The legal procedure was available to full-time employees with over two years' service, and tribunals could award compensation for unfair dismissal of up to £4160, or recommend re-engagement. The first stage of procedure involved conciliatory attempts to settle the case out of Court, but if it went to a tribunal the onus was on the employer to provide a good reason for dismissal. These provisions were clearly relevant to the objective of restricting industrial conflict over discipline and dismissal.

Trade union reaction to the Bill

The TUC's opposition to the proposals was intense; the supervision of union rules by the state was denounced and the Bill was seen as an attack on 'the very root of a union's bargaining strength – its power to bring pressure to bear on the employer – and the very root of the union's democratic strength – its responsiveness to the wishes of the rank and file members'.[2] Vic Feather also attacked the *Code of Practice* as 'shabby and paternalistic'; he said that, although it purported to support the principle of collective bargaining, it ignored the fact that strong trade union organisation was an essential prerequisite. The TUC published its own guide in December 1971, laying primary stress on the role of strong trade unions in resolving inevitable conflicts of interest at the workplace.[3] Largely in response to these and other criticisms, the

---

[1] For a fuller description of these provisions, see Weekes *et al.*, *Industrial Relations and the Limits of the Law*, pp. 36–7.

[2] TUC, *Reason: the case against the government's proposals on industrial relations*, London, 1970.

[3] TUC, *Good Industrial Relations: a guide for negotiators*, London, 1971.

final draft of the *Code of Practice*, laid before Parliament on 19 January 1972, placed much greater emphasis on the role of trade unions and virtually dropped the notion of consultative committees independent of trade union organisation that had featured in earlier drafts.

The TUC organised a special conference in March 1971 to develop its policy in opposition to the Bill. It was decided that all affiliated unions should be 'strongly recommended' not to register; that unions should not sign legally binding contracts; that trade unionists should not serve on the NIRC or the CIR and should withdraw from industrial tribunals; that unions should continue to observe the Bridlington principles[1] and the TUC disputes procedure, and should not apply to the NIRC for recognition or agency shop rights; that assurances should be sought from the Parliamentary Labour Party on the repeal by a Labour government of any law based on the Bill. The TUC stance on registration was later strengthened at the Blackpool conference in September 1971, where the majority voted in favour of a motion that unions should be 'instructed' not to register, rather than 'strongly recommended' not to. This meant that affiliated unions were liable to expulsion if they did register.

In January 1972 the TUC published its *Handbook* giving advice to unions on how to maintain normal trade union activities under the new legal circumstances.[2] By this date 82 unions had complied with the instruction to de-register and ten more were in the process of doing so. Several unions that failed to de-register were to change their minds during the docks crisis in the summer of 1972; other unions eventually decided to de-register because they missed the protection of the Bridlington principles, which applied only to unions affiliated to the TUC. Thus while 32 unions were suspended for non-compliance at the 1972 Congress, only twenty were finally expelled at the 1973 Congress.[3]

Since registration was, in the eyes of Conservative policy-makers, 'of central importance in the reform of industrial relations',[4] the success of the TUC's campaign was bound to frustrate many objectives of the legislation. It also raised questions about the liability of unregistered unions to which the drafters of the Bill had given insufficient attention. During the debate on section 96 the Solicitor General was asked whether unregistered unions would be faced with legal responsibility under that

[1] These principles are a set of procedures adopted at the 1939 Trades Union Congress designed to minimise disputes between unions over membership questions. They lay down procedures by which the TUC can deal with complaints by one organisation against another and consider disputes between unions. They were devised by the trade union movement to ensure the development of stable and rational collective bargaining machinery.

[2] TUC, *Handbook on the Industrial Relations Act*, London, 1972.

[3] For more details on the TUC non-registration policy see Weekes *et al.*, *Industrial Relations and the Limits of the Law*, appendix v, p. 252.

[4] *Hansard*, 14 December 1970, col. 976.

section of the Act and he answered: 'I cannot believe that this problem will arise in that way.'[1] The government had clearly not envisaged a concerted policy of trade union non-cooperation with the Act.

Implementing the legislation

The only major amendment made to the Bill before it became law was the insertion of provisions for an approved closed shop. These provisions, added in March 1971, were the direct result of representations made by Equity and the National Union of Seamen, who persuaded the government that only through the operation of closed shops and some form of entry control could they operate effective collective bargaining machinery.

The Bill received the royal assent on 5 August 1971 and on 11 August a timetable for implementing it was announced as follows:

1 October 1971.   The office of the Chief Registrar of Trade Unions and Employers' Associations to open.

1 November 1971.   The CIR to be reconstituted as a statutory body.

1 December 1971.   The NIRC to be established, consisting of three judges and nine lay members (seven of these were company or personnel directors because of trade union non-cooperation). With the setting up of the NIRC the provisions on agency and closed shop agreements, most of the provisions on the reform of collective bargaining, and the emergency procedures were to come into force.

28 February 1972.   The *Code of Practice* to come into force; it was not to be legally binding but would be taken into consideration by the Courts. The final stages of the Act were also to be implemented on this date, including the provisions on individual rights and the restrictions on industrial action. The only parts of the Act still not to be implemented were those applying to disclosure of information, on which the government was awaiting a CIR report.

The government and the Industrial Relations Act

It was not long before the government tested out their new emergency powers in the context of the rail dispute in the spring of 1972. In April the government sought to postpone a threatened work-to-rule and ban on overtime and rest day working, and to encourage further negotiations by applying to the NIRC for a cooling-off period. A fourteen-day cooling-off period was ordered, with which the unions complied, but only four hours' negotiation took place during this period, which suggests that the major objective was not achieved. On 10 May the unions

[1] B. Hepple, 'Union responsibility for shop stewards', *Industrial Law Journal*, vol. 1, December 1972.

instructed their members to resume the work-to-rule, and the Secretary of State decided to invoke the other emergency procedure created by the new Act and to call for a ballot to ascertain whether or not the membership supported the industrial action. There seemed to be a strong feeling in the government, reflected in sections of the media, that the dispute provided a prime example of moderate and reasonable trade unionists being forced into industrial action by militant, irresponsible and unrepresentative leaders.[1] However, the results of the ballot released on 30 May revealed a six-to-one majority in favour of further industrial action. This was only avoided finally by renewed negotiations, which had been inhibited by the invocation of the emergency procedures. Neither emergency procedure therefore achieved its stated objective.

These events, taken in association with those in the docks in the summer of 1972, clearly weakened the government's confidence in their own legislation. The dispute in the docks, which centred on the blacking and picketing of certain container and transport firms, was to call into question the efficacy of the law in curbing unofficial action, and to demonstrate that the disciplining of 'leaders' did not necessarily cause industrial action to cease. In particular, the various judgements given in the case of Heatons Transport showed that the question of 'union responsibility' was not so simple as the legislation had implied.[2] It is significant that the government made no attempt to use their emergency powers in July 1972. They were clearly becoming increasingly aware that strikes were not always led by unrepresentative and militant minorities; they were doubtless motivated also by a desire to obtain cooperation in implementing an incomes policy.

Talks about an incomes policy, which continued throughout the summer and autumn of 1972, represented a fundamental change in government policy and had profound implications for industrial relations. When the Conservative government first took office, industrial relations policy was viewed as a means of combating inflation through curbing the power of trade unions; a certain hostility from unions might have to be tolerated in order to achieve this objective. However, with the gradual move towards a formal incomes policy, operating if possible with the cooperation of management and labour, the Industrial Relations Act became an increasing embarrassment. The government's changed attitude was revealed in press releases in the summer of 1972; symptomatic of the change was a speech by Robert Carr, in which, while maintaining the need for a strong and well-enforced framework of law which would apply to trade unions as well as to everyone else,

[1] See, for example, *Economist*, 20 May 1972.
[2] Weekes *et al.*, *Industrial Relations and the Limits of the Law*, p. 227.

his tone was highly conciliatory. The government, he said, must develop a long-term strategy and stick to it, but 'not stick to it in every detail with the pig-headed obstinacy of the weak'; they must be prepared to 'modify the details in the light of new experience'.[1]

Possible amendments to the Act were among the issues discussed at talks in Downing Street and at Chequers, and at subsequent talks on Stages II and III of the counter-inflation policy.[2] Amendments discussed were:

(a) the abolition of the system of registration;

(b) the legalisation of the closed shop;

(c) the creation of a buffer organisation (probably the government) that could restrain employers or individuals from appealing direct to the NIRC;

(d) an assurance from the government that the emergency powers would never be used again.

No official concessions were made, although there was considerable evidence that if the Conservatives had remained in office the distinctions between registered and unregistered unions would have been amended. Moreover, there is evidence that tacit concessions were made on some of the other points.

It was widely believed by the managers and trade unionists whom we interviewed that, from the end of 1972 onwards, the government wanted to avoid as far as possible the use of the controversial parts of the Act by management or individuals. Some managers told us that the Department of Employment had actively discouraged any use of the Act's collective bargaining provisions.[3]

All the evidence suggests that the government had little stomach for using the emergency powers again, and no use was made of them in any official strikes during the period of an incomes policy. Since these powers were most relevant to the major disputes of the early 1970s – chiefly large official disputes associated with the operation of an unofficial or official incomes policy – the government's unwillingness to use them meant that the Act had little impact during that period.

An assessment of Conservative industrial relations policy

There can be little doubt that Conservative policy fell far short of success. Nevertheless, it is important to identify the reasons for failure; also to examine whether those provisions of the Industrial Relations Act which received less publicity than those on industrial action did achieve some measure of success.

[1] *Economist*, 5 August 1972.
[2] See TUC, *The Chequers and Downing Street Talks – July to November 1972: report*, London, 1972, and *Economist*, 13 January 1973 and 12 May 1973.
[3] Weekes *et al.*, *Industrial Relations and the Limits of the Law*, p. 228.

Conservative policy has been criticised with considerable justification for its 'confusion of thought and contradiction of aims'.[1] One root of this confusion was the eclectic manner in which the policy developed. As already indicated, some parts of Conservative policy were derived from the analysis put forward in the 1950s in the pamphlet *A Giant's Strength*, which suggested that the only effective way to solve our industrial problems (and in particular the problems of industrial unrest) was to curb the ever-increasing power of the unions. However, Conservative thinking also assimilated the analysis of the Royal Commission, with its diagnosis that industrial unrest had its sources in the fragmented, disorderly and informal bargaining procedures characteristic of major sections of industry, and thus could only be curbed through institutional reform. These two analyses are, of course, not necessarily incompatible in terms of policy-making. While institutional reform might be the only way to tackle the underlying causes of industrial unrest, such reform is clearly a long-term policy; in the short term it might well be maintained that crude curbs on union power are the only way to make an immediate impact. The danger is, however, that this short-term approach may inhibit gradual voluntary reform by decreasing the willingness of the parties in industry to cooperate. The events of the 1960s and early 1970s suggested that neither the Conservatives nor the Labour Party were clear as to whether short-term or long-term objectives should have priority, and this weakened considerably the effectiveness of their policies on both time-scales.

In any Act that has multiple objectives, like the Industrial Relations Act, there needs to be some assigning of priorities, particularly if there is a potential trade-off between certain objectives. Such a trade-off clearly exists between the objective of promoting strong and orderly collective bargaining arrangements in industry and the objective of safeguarding individual rights, since collective bargaining must inevitably impose certain constraints on individual freedom. Yet the Act failed to be explicit about its priorities in this area and, as a result, there were considerable tensions; many of the 'rights' given to individuals to protect them from the oppressive power of unions were liable to inhibit the development of orderly and non-fragmented collective bargaining, which other parts of the Act aimed to promote.

There is abundant evidence that the task of the judges charged with applying the new law was made immeasurably harder by the existence of such potentially conflicting provisions within the Act. This was particularly evident in cases where members of unrecognised unions sought to obtain organising rights using section 5. Clearly there was a potential conflict between individual rights and the promotion of

[1] Ibid. p. 220.

orderly collective bargaining, and the Court had to make some compromise. In the case of the Post Office *v.* Crouch [1973], the Appeal Court ruled that the unrecognised Telecommunications Staff Association was entitled under section 5 to 'organising rights' within the Post Office, including the representation of individuals in the grievance procedure, but not to 'negotiating rights' if the Post Office preferred to negotiate with the Union of Post Office Workers. However, the Courts clearly recognised that the dividing line between 'organising rights' and 'negotiating rights' was a narrow one, and that organising rights might be a 'small step towards ultimately securing negotiating rights'.[1] A union might indeed take all their members' salary complaints individually through the procedure, so effectively establishing negotiating rights. 'As eventually interpreted, s. 5 of the Act gave individuals who were members of unrecognised but registered unions the right to challenge and upset the collective bargaining arrangements of employers and unions even where, in accordance with the guiding principles of the act, such arrangements were aimed at promoting orderly industrial relations.'[2]

Sir John Donaldson found himself in a similar dilemma of being unable to satisfy simultaneously two objectives of the Act when he made his judgement in the Langston case. Joseph Langston, who broke a tacit closed shop agreement at the Chrysler plant at Ryton by resigning from the Amalgamated Union of Engineering Workers, was eventually dismissed by Chrysler, who were unprepared to face the industrial disruption that his continued employment would cause. Chrysler conceded that it was technically an 'unfair' dismissal and paid the required compensation. When explaining why Langston could not be reinstated, Sir John indicated that it was the responsibility of the NIRC not only to safeguard individual rights but also to promote 'good industrial relations', and he implied that in his opinion the latter must be the prime objective: 'The plain fact is that no industrial tribunal could possibly in the general climate which exists recommend that Chrysler, as a good employer, ought to take you back...If you were to go back to Chrysler it would not improve industrial relations.'[3] An Act that claims to provide certain safeguards, which then prove inoperable because they conflict with other objectives of the Act, is not likely to earn respect, let alone be effective.

Some critics of Conservative policy have argued that the drafters of the Act were well aware of the incompatibility of certain professed objectives within the Act; they imply that the predominant objective of Conservative policy, despite lip-service to the Royal Commission's recommendations and to the safeguarding of individual freedom, re-

[1] Ibid. p. 302.   [2] Ibid. p. 303.   [3] Ibid. p. 61.

mained that of curbing the strength of the unions. 'The strike for the closed shop may have been forbidden in order to protect the non-unionist, but the effect, perhaps the purpose of the prohibition, seems to be to curb the power of the union.'[1] Suspicions that the Conservatives were 'disguising' attacks on trade union strength by presenting them in the form of new rights for individuals were further roused by the amendments to the Contracts of Employment Act 1963 (sections 9–21). As well as extending periods of notice, these sections placed new obligations on employers to refer employees in their written statements under the Contracts of Employment Act to full details of grievance procedures available to them. This could mean that any 'peace obligations' laid down in collective agreements were incorporated through this process into an individual's contract of employment, when the main legal effect could be to place new obligations on employees and unions rather than on employers. Weekes *et al.* suggest 'there is little doubt that this was the purpose of amendments to the 1963 Act introduced by the Industrial Relations Act'.[2]

Other aspects of Conservative policy on industrial relations would appear to confirm this view that their major objective was to curb the power of unions and their capacity to engage in industrial action, and that the championing of individual freedom or union democracy was not infrequently only instrumental. For example, the Conservatives tended to extol grass-roots union democracy when they felt that the result would be to moderate the policies of 'militant' leaders (as they mistakenly thought in the rail dispute); when the grass-roots were clearly strongly in support of industrial action of which their leaders disapproved (as in the docks) the government became less ardent. This lack of clarity or openness as to the priorities assigned to the various objectives in the Industrial Relations Act, whether intentional or unintentional, did nothing to help the judiciary in implementing the Act and aroused considerable distrust and suspicion, which was not conducive to harmonious industrial relations.

Another source of weakness in the Act was that some of its assumptions were not so much confused as plainly mistaken, and unsubstantiated by the bulk of research on industrial relations. An example is the implicit assumption that strikes are 'led' by militant officers, who coerce the union membership into action to which they are not fully committed, and that consequently 'disciplining' the leaders will curb the industrial action. While this may be true in some situations, there was ample evidence in the published research papers of the Royal Commission that breaches of procedure and industrial action originate as often with

---

[1] O. Kahn-Freund, *Labour and the Law*, London, Stevens, 1972.
[2] Weekes *et al.*, *Industrial Relations and the Limits of the Law*, p. 243.

BBE

the membership as with union officials or lay officials.[1] In such situations the disciplining of leaders is as likely to intensify as to curb industrial action, as events in the docks illustrated.

Another oversimplified assumption of the Act was that unions are hierarchical organisations where power and authority flow entirely from the top. The failure of those drafting the Act to recognise that a shop steward can have dual responsibilities and act on the authority of the members as well as of the union led to considerable complications in the containerisation dispute in the docks. The situation there was exacerbated rather than resolved by attempts to impose an oversimplified 'model' of relations within unions on the complexities of real life. By insisting that the Transport and General Workers Union discipline the stewards involved in the blacking, the NIRC was trying to force the union to readopt the authoritarian style of a Deakin or a Bevin – a style which had indeed been a *cause* of many of the problems that were now facing the docks.[2] Because the Act was based on a simple one-dimensional model of power and responsibility in unions, legal judgements could not easily be adapted to reflect a more complex situation without giving rise to unacceptable legal and political developments, as the Appeal Court judgement on the Heatons case indicated. The Appeal Court, reversing the decision of the NIRC, held that shop stewards had dual responsibilities and that in the particular instance under consideration they were acting on the authority of the membership.[3] However, within the framework of the new law this meant that unions were no longer liable for the actions of their stewards, so that legal proceedings could be initiated against individual stewards, possibly leading to their imprisonment. This possibility was postponed once by the timely intervention of a previously little known character, the Official Solicitor, but such eleventh-hour interventions could not take place indefinitely and eventually five dockers were imprisoned for contempt.[4] The industrial chaos caused by this (at one time 170,000 workers were on strike) was only averted by a hurried reversal of the Appeal Court decision in the House of Lords; the union was deemed once more to be liable for the actions of its stewards and the unrepentant dockers were released. This volte-face aroused suspicions of political manoeuvring, as did the interventions of the Official Solicitor, tending to bring the law into disrepute.

---

[1] See Royal Commission on Trade Union and Employers' Associations, Research Paper no. 1: *The Role of Shop Stewards in British Industrial Relations. Survey of existing information and research* by W. E. J. McCarthy, London, HMSO, 1966, p. 73.

[2] Hepple, 'Union responsibility for shop stewards'.

[3] Ibid. for a fuller discussion of these judgements.

[4] For a full chronology of the docks crisis see Weekes *et al.*, *Industrial Relations and the Limits of the Law*, p. 278.

Episodes like the docks dispute tended to support the argument that complex industrial relations problems are not easily solved by the application of an inflexible legal formula. The unofficial action was finally ended not by legal injunctions but by negotiations with the container firms on the employment of dock labour – negotiations that were preceded by an assurance from the firms that they would make no further use of the law. For example, on 13 January, Midland Cold Storage withdrew its complaints to the NIRC to smooth the way for talks about the employment of registered dockers. Similar assurances were given by Heatons.[1]

There is evidence that the NIRC itself became increasingly less confident about the efficacy of legal injunctions and sought to shift the emphasis to conciliation. Between January and September 1972 there were twelve applications for injunctions, eight of which were granted. However, out of ten applications between October 1972 and June 1973, only one injunction was granted, and even this had a delayed effect.[2] On the whole, recourse by both employers and employees to the law on industrial relations problems was slight, suggesting little confidence in its ability to solve such problems.

Employers and employees were equally reluctant to use the collective bargaining provisions of the Act. A study of employers' attitudes found that those who suffered from problems of multi-unionism or a fragmented bargaining structure did not regard the law as an effective tool for reforming their collective bargaining arrangements. 'Collective bargaining in their view could be reformed only by negotiation or by changing the balance of power. And neither passing an Act of Parliament, nor the making of legal judgements that could not be enforced, affected the balance of industrial power.'[3]

Of the many provisions in the Act relating to collective bargaining the recognition procedures were most used, but since these procedures were restricted to registered unions the number of unions involved was small; 31 of the applications came from either the National Union of Bank Employees or the Union of Bookmakers' Employees. However, about half the individual objections to bargaining arrangements under section 51 were in effect attempts by unregistered unions acting through individual members to get recognition through legal procedures.[4] This suggests that many unions would welcome procedures for recognition within a legal framework other than that provided by the Conservatives' Act.

As regards recourse by individuals to the legal remedies provided for them in the new law, little use was made of the rights in section 5,

---

[1] Ibid. p. 293.   [2] Ibid. p. 198.
[3] Ibid. p. 183.   [4] Ibid. p. 148.

suggesting either 'that compulsory trade union membership is not generally viewed by workers as an oppressive restriction on individual freedom' or that 'if it is so viewed, then individuals are generally unwilling to face the combined opposition of fellow workers, the union and the employer in taking legal action'.[1] This would seem to suggest that a right of appeal to a review body of the kind advocated by the Royal Commission might be more successful in practice than litigation in giving individuals access to meaningful remedies.

Considerable use was made by individuals, however, of the provisions of the Act on unfair dismissal, and in fact these sections led to more litigation and case law than any other part of the Act. It is significant that this was the only part that the TUC and the Labour Party proposed to maintain in their statement of February 1973 pledging the repeal of the Conservatives' Act. The Department of Employment reported over 17,000 claims of unfair dismissal notified between February 1972 and the end of 1973.[2] This figure was, however, still well below estimates of likely caseloads before the Act became law. Virtually half of all applicants received some remedy, either at the conciliation stage or at a Court hearing, although in the vast majority of the cases the remedy was compensation rather than re-engagement. The provisions in fact did little to guarantee employment security, but rather provided 'compensation for loss of employment'.[3] One study of the use of these provisions suggests that, where workers are well organised, they may well prefer to deal with this situation through collective bargaining and collective sanctions rather than through legal remedies. Certainly 'those working in areas where unions are strongly organised made less use of the law'.[4]

Of course it might be argued that the law was always meant to play a residual role in reforming industrial relations and that the provisions on unfair dismissal focused the attention of employers and trade unions on the need to improve disciplinary procedures. As Robert Carr commented, 'law forms opinion and influences behaviour'.[5] Certainly the object of the *Code of Practice* was to set out guidelines and standards for voluntary reform. Reform is inevitably a slow process, so that it is not surprising that the evidence gathered during the operation of the Act is not encouraging. As regards the *Code of Practice*, most large companies clearly felt that they conformed to the standards already; among small companies many had never seen the *Code* and

[1] Ibid. p. 61.

[2] *Department of Employment Gazette*, June and July 1974, gives detailed figures.

[3] S. D. Anderman, *Unfair Dismissals and the Law*, London Institute of Personnel Management, 1973, p. 105.

[4] Weeks *et al.*, *Industrial Relations and the Limits of the Law*, p. 32.

[5] Speech to the Conservative Party annual conference, Brighton, October 1969.

some had never heard of it.[1] Weekes *et al.* found no evidence in the vast majority of top companies where they conducted interviews that management was encouraging the negotiation of formal procedures at any level, although some had reviewed their dismissal procedures to protect themselves against proceedings for unfair dismissal; they concluded that the impact of the Act on voluntary reform was negligible.[2]

This reluctance by management to take the initiative in reforming industrial relations at plant and company level would seem to confirm the need for some independent third party to do so. The CIR was originally established to fill this role, but was unable to function adequately because it was too closely implicated in administering legislation that did not have the whole-hearted support of either side of industry.

Conclusions

The 1960s and early 1970s saw a major rethinking of the traditional British voluntary approach to industrial relations. 'Collective *laissez-faire*' was increasingly seen to be incompatible with government policies in other related areas. Both Labour and Conservative Parties took the view that, given the major repercussions of industrial relations practices on key economic issues like inflation, industrial productivity and competitiveness, no government could stand aside and leave industrial relations solely to the two sides of industry; government had a role and responsibility to promote orderly collective bargaining through public agencies like the CIR. Moreover, prices and incomes legislation, taken together with the penal clauses of *In Place of Strife* and the Industrial Relations Act, were evidence of a much greater willingness on the part of both political Parties to introduce legal sanctions into collective bargaining. The Labour government approached the role of law in a more selective way, seeing it as a short-term instrument for dealing with specific forms of industrial action that threatened to be particularly disruptive; their main emphasis in the longer term was on voluntary reform of collective bargaining. The Conservatives, on the other hand, favoured a much more extensive use of law to regulate collective bargaining and the activities of trade unions, and indeed saw the law as the main instrument for achieving reform.

An assessment of the policies pursued by both governments suggests that, insofar as new forms of legal regulation contained provisions designed to curb industrial action by imposing new constraints on

---

[1] CIR, *Report no. 69: Small Firms and the Code of Industrial Relations Practice*, London, HMSO, 1974.

[2] Weekes *et al.*, *Industrial Relations and the Limits of the Law*, p. 174.

unions, this certainly did not help, and indeed possibly hindered, the longer-term objective of reforming collective bargaining practices and institutions. Such measures tended to exacerbate industrial conflict in a way that was politically counter-productive, and proved particularly harmful when the government concerned was trying simultaneously to develop an effective counter-inflation policy.

It is significant that during the period under consideration industrial relations policies were closely linked to counter-inflation policies, which themselves had a gradual but profound effect on the nature of the 'problems' that industrial relations policies were designed to tackle. For, as incomes policies, official or unofficial, became a virtually permanent feature of the economic scene, unofficial strikes were superseded as the major industrial problem by large-scale, frequently official strikes related to the administration of incomes policies.[1] Many of the industrial relations prescriptions developed during the 1950s and early 1960s were particularly unsuited to dealing with this new problem; introducing restraints on trade union power could only hamper an incomes policy, particularly if this was to be voluntary rather than statutory.

A weakness of the policies pursued by both governments was that industrial relations legislation and reform, and incomes policies tended to be seen as *alternative* ways of dealing with the impact of trade unions on economic policy. The Labour government dropped incomes policy legislation for *In Place of Strife* and the Conservatives initially eschewed an incomes policy in favour of industrial relations legislation, only to find this a considerable embarrassment when they later became persuaded of the need for a formal incomes policy. That some lessons may have been learnt from this experience was reflected in the 'social contract' between the unions and the Labour Party, which attempted to devise an integrated approach to a range of industrial relations and economic issues.

A significant feature of policy in the 1970s has been the emphasis on reforming industrial relations by giving unions more rather than less power at all levels of the economy – by involving them in tripartite discussions on economic policy at national level and by establishing procedures at plant and company level that enable them to influence a much wider range of management decisions. The assumption behind these new policies is that, if unions are involved more in decision-making, they will feel a more positive commitment to the decisions that emerge, and will be less inclined to take a negative and disruptive stance. It is significant that the industrial relations legislation of the Labour government since 1974 has been directed to strengthening the

---

[1] See chapter 8.

power of trade unions in the context of collective bargaining, and extending industrial democracy at all levels of the economy. While the Conservatives are critical of many of the extensions of trade union power, they too are strongly committed now to an increase in industrial democracy as a way of tackling industrial relations problems, although the emphasis is on participation by employees rather than unions.

MANPOWER POLICY

Although the 1950s were characterised by a tight labour market and a high level of demand for labour, with consequent shortages of workers in many skilled occupations, manpower questions were still viewed as the responsibility of industry more than of government. In the early 1960s, however, there was a significant change in approach, and a growing emphasis on the need for a more active government role in manpower policy. This change was reflected in two influential Reports, by the National Joint Advisory Council and the NEDC.[1]

The Report of the National Joint Advisory Council stressed the dire consequences that shortages of skilled labour could have for economic performance. It pointed out that, except for brief periods of recession, there had been a shortage of workers in most skilled occupations since the end of the war. In September 1961 there was an excess of unfilled vacancies over unemployed in nearly all the main skilled trades, making an apparent shortage of over 30,000 workers, including about 20,000 engineering craftsmen and 10,000 building craftsmen. Since the main shortages were in building and engineering, industries of basic importance to the economy, the Report considered that the effects of these shortages would extend far beyond these industries. It concluded that in order to maintain 'an expanding and competitive economy...The government may in future have to play a larger role in the whole field of industrial training.'

The NEDC publication of 1963 also pointed to the inadequacy of current training arrangements and stressed the importance of manpower policy in achieving faster growth. It urged the need for policies to facilitate the mobility of labour and suggested that the government should evolve a national scheme for reducing the financial hardship of redundancy, as well as improving the grants available under the Ministry of Labour's resettlement transfer schemes to help redundant workers seeking new jobs.

The following sections trace the development through the 1960s and

---

[1] National Joint Advisory Council, 'Report of the working party on the manpower situation', *Ministry of Labour Gazette*, vol. 70, February 1962; NEDC, *Conditions Favourable to Faster Growth*.

early 1970s of government policies designed to tackle some of the manpower problems raised in these Reports.

Government policies to facilitate labour mobility

In 1961 the Conservative government published a booklet, *Security and Change*.[1] This did not, however, advocate any government intervention in this sphere; rather it urged firms to formulate their own redundancy payments schemes. It was not until the Labour government came to power in 1964 that proposals for a government scheme of redundancy payments, which led to the Redundancy Payments Act 1965, were put forward. The basic provisions of this Act were as follows.

(1) Employees over 18 dismissed through redundancy after two years of service were entitled to lump sum compensation from their employers at the rate of $1\frac{1}{2}$ weeks' pay for each year of service between the ages of 41 and 65, one week's pay for each year of service between the ages of 22 and 40, and half a week's pay for each year of service between the ages of 18 and 21.

(2) In calculating redundancy pay, earnings of more than £40 a week and continuous employment of more than 20 years were disregarded.

(3) A central fund for redundancy payments was levied from employers by an addition of 4d. a week for men and 2d. a week for women to the national insurance contributions. Employers could claim back from the fund two thirds of the amount paid for each year of service over the age of 41 and half the amount paid for each year of service below this age.

(4) Employers were required to inform local employment exchanges two or three weeks in advance of redundancies, to allow time for the workers to be redeployed.

In 1966/7 there was a sharp increase in the number of people claiming under the Act – largely attributable to the effects of the measures of July 1966 – and this put a severe strain on the finances of the redundancy fund. Consequently, in February 1967 the employers' contribution was raised to 1s. 3d. for men and 7d. for women. Continued financial difficulties led to further amendments in 1967, when the Redundancy Rebates Act was passed. This eliminated the distinction between the amount employers could claim back from the central fund for years of service over and under the age of 41; they could now claim back only half the compensation paid in respect of all age groups.

As a survey in 1969 pointed out, the Act

...was designed to fulfil two main purposes, one economic and the other social. On the economic side, it was intended to facilitate a more effective

[1] Ministry of Labour, *Security and Change: progress in provision for redundancy*, London, HMSO, 1961.

utilisation of manpower by reducing the economic consequences of redundancy to those affected. On the social side, it was recognised that the individual has some rights in his job, in the same way as the employer holds rights in his property, and that these accumulate in value over time. The purpose of the Act in this sphere was to provide some notional compensation for the losses individuals may suffer as a consequence of redundancy.[1]

Another measure taken by the Labour government to reduce the financial hardship of redundancy was the introduction of earnings-related unemployment benefits. The scheme, whereby during the first six months of unemployment employees receive a supplement of about one third of their average weekly earnings between £9 and £30 a week, was introduced in October 1966, and is financed by graduated contributions from employers and employees. One objective of the scheme was to increase the willingness of those with higher earnings – often the more skilled – to accept the increased risks of unemployment associated with changing jobs, and thereby to stimulate the mobility of skilled labour. As a further inducement to labour mobility, the grants available to workers moving to new jobs under the Ministry of Labour's transfer resettlement schemes were raised in 1965.

An assessment of policy on mobility

The outstanding feature of the British government policy for encouraging labour mobility, during the 1960s at least, was the overwhelming emphasis on statutory compensation for the loss of an existing job. In other European countries compensation is typically a matter for negotiation between employers and trade unions, and the major emphasis of government policy is on measures to ensure the easiest possible movement of the redundant individual to a new job.[2] British policy during the 1960s reflected a faith in the efficacy of market forces in redeploying shaken-out labour, which clearly had its roots in the tight labour market of the 1950s and early 1960s. It was assumed that once statutory compensation for the loss of a job had reduced working people's resistance to change, 'there would be freer flows of manpower in response to signals from the market indicating where such resources could be most profitably employed'.[3] Any assessment of government policy on labour mobility must therefore begin by considering the effectiveness of the Redundancy Payments Act in achieving its social and economic objectives.

The social objective of the Act was, as Ray Gunther its main architect

---

[1] Department of Employment, *Effects of the Redundancy Payments Act* by S. R. Parker *et al.*, London, HMSO, 1971, p. 4.

[2] S. Mukherjee, *Through No Fault of Their Own: systems of handling redundancies in Britain, France and Germany*, London, Macdonald, 1973, p. 17.   [3] Ibid. p. 94.

indicated, to provide financial compensation for loss of security, loss of possible earnings and loss of fringe benefits, as well as for the uncertainty associated with, and the anxiety caused by, a change in jobs.[1] There can be no question that the Act guaranteed financial compensation to many for the first time, and meant vastly increased compensation for others. At the same time, a number of redundant workers still did not receive compensation, either because they were under 18, or because they had not been in their jobs for the two-year qualifying period. In 1968 a Department of Employment estimate put the annual number of unpaid redundancies at between 500,000 and 750,000.[2] This was roughly double the number of paid redundancies in that year (see table 13.3). The two-year qualifying period also meant that those once made redundant became immensely vulnerable to unpaid redundancy in the first two years in their new jobs. Daniel found, in a study of redundant workers in Woolwich, that '10 per cent of those who managed to find jobs had been made redundant again between the time of their dismissal and their interview, on average a two-year period'.[3] As Fryer notes: 'as the period of operation of the Act lengthens and workers find themselves declared redundant for a second or third time, so the proportion excluded by the two-year qualifying period might be expected to increase'.[4]

The other major weakness of the Act in relation to its social objective was its implicit assumption about the correlation between age and

Table 13.3. *Payments made under the Redundancy Payments Act, 1966–73*

	No. of payments	Amounts paid		
		By fund	By employers	Total
	(000s)	(£ thousand)		
1966	137	19,876	6,612	26,488
67	242	37,721	12,492	50,213
68	265	46,377	15,460	61,837
69	251	38,579	23,307	61,886
1970	276	38,956	33,585	72,541
71	370	57,094	51,155	108,249
72	297	50,772	46,739	97,511
73	178	34,521	32,052	66,573

SOURCE: *Department of Employment Gazette* (quarterly statistics).

[1] *Hansard*, 26 April 1965, col. 33.
[2] See R. H. Fryer, 'The myths of the Redundancy Payments Act', *Industrial Law Journal*, vol. 2, March 1973.
[3] W. W. Daniel, *Whatever Happened to the Workers in Woolwich?*, London, Political and Economic Planning, 1972, p. 50.
[4] Fryer, 'The myths of the Redundancy Payments Act', p. 13.

length of service and the hardships and losses suffered by individuals made redundant. Since the compensation was meant partly to cover loss of property rights in a job, such as seniority, fringe benefits and so on that typically accrue with length of service, the linking of compensation with length of service had a certain logic. The linking of compensation with age is, however, harder to justify; it assumes that the hardships of redundancy increase with age, but as an OECD study has pointed out 'a redundancy may be worse hardship at age levels when family expenditure for children and amortisation of housing are highest'.[1] Mukherjee has suggested that the higher compensation for older workers and the provisions in the 1965 Act for a larger refund to employers in respect of redundant workers over the age of 41 may have done such workers more harm than good. It may have lessened their ability to resist redundancy and singled them out as the principal target for employers slimming down their labour force.[2]

However, in spite of these shortcomings, by providing compensation the Act undoubtedly did something to reduce working people's fear of redundancy – a fear which, as the NEDC pointed out, could act 'as a brake on industrial expansion, whether it causes strikes, restrictions or resistance to change'.[3] By reducing such resistance, the Act paved the way for the achievement of its economic objective – a more rational and efficient use of manpower. The evidence gathered by the 1969 survey suggests that within firms the Act did facilitate the adoption of more rational manpower policies. For example, it provided some incentive for employees to let go of the principle of 'last in, first out', which can lead to a gradually ageing workforce, and enabled managements to take a more flexible approach in selecting individuals for redundancy.[4] Interviews conducted with both managers and trade union officers suggested that 'statutory payments have made redundancy more acceptable to those employees affected and thereby allowed management greater flexibility in their manpower policies';[5] there was also a decline in strike activity over redundancy issues following the introduction of the Act.[6]

There has certainly been a marked increase in the number of redundancies since 1965, although how much this can be attributed to a reduction in resistance to redundancy is questionable. There are no firm data on the number of redundancies before the Act, but a Ministry of Labour estimate suggested between 470,000 and 590,000 in 1962.[7] By 1970 the

[1] OECD, *Manpower Policy in the United Kingdom*, Paris, 1970.
[2] Mukherjee, *Through No Fault of Their Own*, p. 108.
[3] NEDC, *Growth of the United Kingdom Economy to 1966*, para. 144.
[4] Department of Employment, *Effects of the Redundancy Payments Act*, p. 10.
[5] Ibid. p. 21.   [6] Ibid. p. 13.
[7] Mukherjee, *Through No Fault of Their Own*, p. 28.

figures for paid redundancies in table 13.3, taken with the Department of Employment estimates of yearly unpaid redundancies, suggest that the total number of redundancies had risen to between 775,000 and 1,025,000.

Assuming that the Act made it easier for employers to adopt more rational manpower policies and to shake out non-productive labour, the question remains whether this promoted a more effective use of manpower in external as opposed to internal labour markets. Was the right sort of labour shaken out, and was it redirected to those areas where it could be used most effectively? The evidence here is less favourable. Most studies of redundancy suggest that the workers shaken out were not, in general, those who could be most easily redeployed elsewhere. Certainly few of them were the skilled workers who were in such short supply. Their very scarcity meant that firms were loath to release them even when demand dropped; instead they were kept on short time, on the assumption that skilled labour would be even more scarce when an upturn in demand occurred.[1] There is little evidence that the Act did anything to break this habit of labour hoarding. Mackay's study of the shake-out of labour in the Midlands following the measures of July 1966 found a high proportion of semi-skilled among the redundant, but little evidence 'of a shake-out which bit especially hard on more specialised employees'; he concluded that 'the shake-out does not appear to have released redundant employees whose skills promised easy redeployment'.[2] The Act had a built-in tendency to increase redundancy among older workers – who are usually less suited for redeployment or retraining – because compensation increased with age and because a greater proportion of the sum paid was reclaimable. In one sample nearly 70 per cent of those receiving redundancy payments were over 40,[3] and this finding is repeated in other studies.[4] This bias against older workers remained despite the modifications of the Redundancy Rebates Act.

The linking of compensation to length of service with one employer could also have inhibited improved use of manpower in external labour markets. Such a link is hardly likely to be conducive to increased labour mobility. As the OECD study points out, an employee 'may see an opportunity for a better job, but prefer to stay where he is so as not to forfeit his right to a large redundancy payment by leaving voluntarily'.[5] This serves to highlight certain conflicts between the

---

[1] 'The act and fact of redundancy', *Business*, vol. 96, December 1966.

[2] D. I. Mackay, 'After the "Shake-out"', *Oxford Economic Papers*, vol. 24 (new series), March 1972, p. 106.

[3] Department of Employment, *Effects of the Redundancy Payments Act*, p. 75.

[4] Mackay, 'After the "Shake-out"', p. 92, and Mukherjee, *Through No Fault of Their Own*, p. 99.   [5] OECD, *Manpower Policy in the United Kingdom*, p. 180.

social and the economic objectives of the Act. The social objective to compensate the individual for loss of property rights in a job, which it was assumed increase in value with length of service and age, tended to impede the achievement of the economic objective of promoting the optimum deployment of manpower.

All the studies of redundancy suggest that the major weakness of government policy, during the 1960s at least, was its emphasis on statutory compensation for redundancy and its comparative neglect of measures to assist redundant workers to find suitable new employment, if necessary by retraining. Market forces alone were clearly insufficient to redirect redundant workers to jobs most suited to their skills and capabilities. In the study by Parker et al., a third of the sample 'regarded their first post-redundancy job as a stop-gap' and 'finding another suitable job was reported as the greatest problem of redundancy'.[1] Similarly, Mackay's sample contained a high proportion who regarded their first jobs as providing 'interim employment while they looked around for more satisfactory and rewarding work'.[2] These studies point to the need for a vastly improved employment service to counter-act the individual's imperfect knowledge of the labour market. In 1965 employment exchanges still accounted for no more than a quarter of all placements. Although the Contracts of Employment Act 1963 made it compulsory for employers to notify employment exchanges at least two weeks in advance of dismissal, and a similar obligation was included in the Redundancy Payments Act, this period was far too short to allow for effective job-placement or retraining programmes, and employers were not required to give the kind of detailed occupational description of redundant employees needed for effective job-placement. Moreover, many employers failed to fulfil their obligations.[3]

While establishing a statutory right to financial compensation for the loss of a job through redundancy was in itself an admirable develop-ment, a comparison of government spending on compensation and on other aspects of policy that might contribute to the more effective deployment of manpower highlights the disproportionate emphasis on the compensation aspect. Mukherjee has estimated that while the government spent £381 million over the six years ending 1971 on individual cash compensation, expenditure on adult retraining and on public employment services that could contribute to redeployment totalled only £100 million.[4] During the 1970s steps were taken to redress this imbalance. The need for more effective industrial training

---

[1] Department of Employment, *Effects of the Redundancy Payments Act*, p. 31.
[2] Mackay, 'After the "Shake-out"', p. 107.
[3] Mukherjee, *Through No Fault of Their Own*, p. 158.
[4] Ibid. p. 17.

policies was demonstrated especially by the failure of both the Redundancy Payments Act and earnings-related unemployment benefits to release the skilled labour that was in such short supply. This implied that damaging bottlenecks in key skills could only be avoided by training more skilled workers.

Government policy on training

Up to the 1960s industrial training was approached on an entirely voluntary basis; it was seen as the responsibility of individual firms and, in spite of the continuous shortages since the war of labour in many key skilled occupations, no government had evolved any positive policy. This lack of government concern was reflected in the decline in the number of Government Training Centres: in 1946 there were 65 centres with training places for nearly 24,000 trainees, by 1950 the number of centres was down to 24 and the level of training places had fallen to about 4000, with nearly two thirds of the trainees disabled. This low level of provision persisted throughout the 1950s.

The late 1950s saw some glimmer of interest in training as a national policy, with the publication of the *Carr Report*.[1] The focus of this Report was, however, highly specific – the problem of providing training for the 'bulge' generation arising from the increased birth rate of the 1940s. Reaction to the Report was firmly set in the tradition of non-intervention – an independent Industrial Training Council was established jointly by the British Employers' Confederation, the TUC and the nationalised industries. This body had all the weaknesses of the voluntary approach – insufficient funds to make any real impact, 'no right to press its advice on firms, and no one was under any obligation to pay attention to what it said'.[2]

The move towards increased government intervention was heralded by the 1962 Report on the manpower situation, which concluded that in future the government might have to play a much larger role.[3] That the government was beginning to endorse this view was demonstrated by the publication in December 1962 of a White Paper on industrial training.[4] This echoed the arguments of the Report and stressed that: 'It will be impossible to secure the objective of a steadier and more rapid rate of economic growth unless skilled manpower is

[1] Ministry of Labour, *Training for Skill: recruitment and training of young workers in industry*, London, HMSO, 1958.

[2] S. Mukherjee, *Changing Manpower Needs: a study of Industrial Training Boards*, London Political and Economic Planning, 1970.

[3] National Joint Advisory Council, 'Report of the working party on the manpower situation'.

[4] Ministry of Labour, *Industrial Training: government proposals*, Cmnd 1892, London, HMSO, 1962.

available on a growing scale. This means that the rate of industrial training must be increased.' The quality and quantity of industrial training could no longer be left 'to the uncoordinated decisions of a large number of individual firms'. The government's objectives were three-fold:

(a) to enable decisions on the scale of training to be better related to economic needs and technological developments;

(b) to improve the overall quality of industrial training and to establish minimum standards;

(c) to enable the cost to be spread more fairly.

In order to achieve these objectives, it was proposed to set up Industrial Training Boards to be responsible for all aspects of training in individual industries; they would be empowered to draw up policy for training within the industry, to set minimum standards, to provide advice and assistance to firms, and to establish their own training centres if necessary. They would collect money from all establishments in the industry by means of a levy, and grants could be then paid back to firms in relation to the quality and quantity of training carried out. Firms with adequate training might get back all the levy in grants; firms with little or no training might receive no grant. The administration of the system was left to the discretion of the Boards.

The Industrial Training Act, embodying the proposals of the White Paper, became law in March 1964. An advisory body, the Central Training Council, was also appointed, to advise the Minister 'on the exercise of his functions under this Act, and on any other matter relating to industrial or commercial training which he may refer to it'. The Council consisted of members from employers' associations, trade unions, the boards of nationalised industries, and the Industrial Training Boards. The old Industrial Training Council, set up in 1958, was abolished.

While the Act placed the major responsibility for industrial training on industry itself, the government at the same time indicated a commitment to expanding its own training facilities:

Improvements in the quality of training and increases in the numbers trained should result from the Act. This will, however, take time, and meanwhile the economic well-being of the country demands an early increase in the numbers of skilled men, particularly in the engineering and construction industries, to meet persistent shortages. The training facilities in Government Training Centres are therefore being more than doubled as a contribution towards this.[1]

In 1963 the government also established a Manpower Research Unit within the Ministry of Labour, with the task of studying 'the future

[1] *Ministry of Labour Gazette*, May 1964.

manpower requirements of the various sectors of the economy and of particular industries – in the light of past trends and likely developments, including the effects of technological change'. An important part of the Unit's work was to be to 'provide information to assist in the planning of industrial training by the Industrial Training Boards... and of courses to be provided in Government Training Centres, but it will also have a wider role in relation to manpower planning in general.'[1]

While the Labour Party made some criticisms of the Act, notably its failure to establish a central authority with wide executive powers,[2] they were committed to its broad principles and developed the policies initiated by the Conservatives throughout their period of office. The facilities in Government Training Centres were also steadily expanded (see table 13.4).

Table 13.4. *Numbers trained under the government's vocational training scheme, 1962–71*

	Government Training Centres		Colleges of Further Education, etc.	Employers' establishments	Total
	Standard courses	Sponsored by employers			
1962	3,336	—	758	55	4,149
63	3,375	—	827	31	4,233
64	4,410	—	1,047	83	5,540
65	6,724	—	1,042	56	7,822
66	8,781	—	872	53	9,706
67	10,620	—	830	55	11,505
68	12,040	23	923	45	13,031
69	12,591	587	834	64	14,076
1970	12,623	3,043	939	43	16,648
71	12,759	3,816	1,624	203	18,402

SOURCE: Department of Employment, *Training for the Future*.

Between 1964 and 1969, 27 Industrial Training Boards were set up. The major concern of all the Boards was with the quality and quantity of apprenticeship training; the objective was to train craftsmen whose skills were broad-based rather than company specific, so that several Boards stressed the value of 'off-the-job' training in special centres or technical colleges. The Engineering Industry Board developed a 'module' system as a way of providing flexible training that could be built on in later life:

[1] *Ministry of Labour Gazette*, October 1963.
[2] Labour Party, *Industrial Training*, London, 1967. This criticism was shared by the TUC.

The modules chosen for a given trainee will depend on his capacities and the requirements of the employer, and they will not necessarily be within the same 'trade' as previously demarcated. Nor will each module require the same amount and length of training. The total period of training of the craftsman or technician of the future will not be the same in all trades regardless of the skills required. There should be no reason why a recognised craftsman should not undergo further modules to develop or modify this initial training later on in his career.[1]

In early years the main stress had definitely been on the quality of training, but by 1967 the Central Training Council was expressing concern that the quantitative aspects were being neglected.[2] A major preoccupation also was with the levy and grant system which posed many problems; the administrative burdens for both companies and the Boards were immense, and many Boards were soon in financial difficulties.[3] The levy could constitute a severe drain on the resources of small firms with small training requirements and little hope of grants; to meet this problem, many Boards experimented with differential levies according to size of firm. Another problem was whether grants should be related to a firm's particular training needs, or to the training needs of the industry as a whole; the Engineering Industry Board adopted a two-part grant system as an attempt to meet both these requirements.[4] Yet these refinements all led to more administrative work; consequently some Boards began to question the further usefulness of the system. In its 1970 Report, the Engineering Industry Board expressed the view that the system had served its purpose as a 'carrot and stick' mechanism for prodding employers into action, but was now ready for overhaul. It proposed that standards should be set for each firm; if they were met the firm should be exempt from both levy and grant and only become liable again if training fell below standard; eventually the whole levy and grant system would wither away.[5]

When the Conservative government came to review the functioning of the 1964 Act in 1972, they expressed a similar attitude to the levy and grant system.[6] They suggested that the system had provided 'an essential "shock treatment" which has led to a major change in the attitude of large sections of British industry to systematic training', but

[1] Ministry of Labour, *Central Training Council. Second Report to the Minister*, London, HMSO, 1967.

[2] Ibid.

[3] *Sunday Times*, 20 September 1970.

[4] See Ministry of Labour, *Engineering Industry Training Board Report and Statement of Accounts for the Period ended March 31, 1967*, London, HMSO, 1967.

[5] See Ministry of Labour, *Engineering Industry Training Board Report and Statement of Accounts for the Period ended March 31, 1970*, London, HMSO, 1970.

[6] Department of Employment, *Training for the Future*, London, 1972.

that it should now be phased out if it was not to obstruct the effective development of the other work of the Boards.[1] It was also suggested that the second and third objectives of the 1964 Act had been achieved with more success than the first. There could be little doubt about the influence of the Boards 'on the quality and efficiency of training, which have improved substantially since 1964';[2] also as great a redistribution of costs as was administratively feasible had already occurred. The Boards had, however, been less successful in directing training to national economic needs; their very structure meant that they were ill-suited to coping with training needs that transcended industry boundaries or cut across them.

In order to fill these 'gaps' in the system, it was proposed to establish a National Training Agency – a hived-off body outside the Civil Service – which could fulfil the functions to which the Boards were ill-suited. The Boards would continue to set standards and develop model schemes for training in their industries and, with the phasing out of the levy and grant system, would still make selective grants to encourage training of key importance to either industries or the national economy.

The role of training in satisfying individual as well as national economic needs was also stressed, and it was proposed that 'the Vocational Training Scheme under which 16,650 men and women were trained in 1970 will be developed into a Training Opportunities Scheme which will aim at a target of 100,000 men and women a year, and as a first step to train not less than 60–70,000 people a year by 1975'.[3] Whereas existing government training courses had concentrated mainly on skilled manual trades, the new range of courses was to be much broader and to cater for professional and further educational needs. The new National Training Agency was to assume responsibility for the Training Opportunities Scheme in close cooperation with the employment services of the Department of Employment. The idea of a national 'council on manpower services' was also raised, which could coordinate the activities of all manpower services. However, it was envisaged that this body would have advisory powers only, and no direct relationship with the National Training Agency.

Towards an integrated manpower policy

While the CBI broadly supported the government's proposals contained in *Training for the Future*, the TUC was critical and proposed amendments that were to have a substantial influence on the direction of manpower policy. The TUC attacked especially the proposed abolition of the levy and grant system, quoting the results of a recent

[1] Ibid. p. 16. [2] Ibid. p. 52. [3] Ibid. p. 46.

survey which reported that many Boards found the administration of the system provided invaluable opportunities for contact with firms, when advice on training could be offered.[1] It was feared that if the Boards were to adopt a purely advisory function they would lose contact with firms; at the very least the levy system should not be phased out until the Boards had had time to establish better advisory procedures.

The most fundamental criticism by the TUC was directed at the preoccupation of the government proposals with training alone. The case was argued for a much more integrated manpower policy, geared to 'promoting and maintaining employment and the creation of suitable machinery to achieve that purpose'.[2] The proposed central manpower council was seen as a step in the right direction, but was nevertheless felt to be inadequate. The TUC advocated a national manpower board consisting of representatives from both sides of industry, with wide executive powers that would enable it to 'bring together the present separate machinery for training, vocational guidance, job-placement and publicly financed job creation'. These arguments reflected a new emphasis that was to become increasingly important in the following years, on manpower policy as a technique for combating unemployment in the changed economic climate of the late 1960s and early 1970s. As one speaker at a TUC conference on the subject commented:

The Industrial Training Act was passed and the Boards were set up at a time when we had all come to think of full employment as a permanent characteristic of our economy. We do not now have full employment. We have an endemic condition of unemployment with a figure of one million unemployed. This is a very important factor in the whole approach to the future of industrial training.[3]

The Conservative government, anxious to maintain the cooperation essential to the success of their counter-inflation policy, were fairly receptive to the TUC recommendations and gradually came round to the idea of a national board or commission representing the interests of employers, unions, local authorities and educational establishments, which would administer the work both of the public employment services and of the proposed National Training Agency, although they did not endorse the emphasis put by the TUC on the job-creating functions of such a body. On 22 November 1972 the government announced its intention to establish the Manpower Services Commission; the Central Training Council would be wound up.

A White Paper explaining the structure of the proposed new

[1] TUC, *Trade Unions and Training for the Future*, London, 1972, p. 9.
[2] Ibid. p. 16.　　　　　　　　[3] Ibid. p. 42.

machinery was published early the following year.[1] This made some concessions on the abolition of the levy and grant system, proposing to preserve the Industrial Training Boards' statutory right to impose a levy on firms should they so wish, provided that this did not exceed 1 per cent of the payroll after 1973–4. The Boards would also have the right to exempt from payment of the levy firms whose training standards were deemed adequate. Limited powers of job creation were also conceded to the Manpower Services Commission; the Minister could direct it to exercise on his behalf his powers to provide 'temporary employment for unemployed people'.[2] In the field of manpower forecasting, however, the Commission's responsibilities remained limited; the Manpower Research Unit was to remain within the Department of Employment, despite recommendations from the TUC to the contrary.

The National Training Agency was to become an executive arm of the Manpower Services Commission and was renamed the Training Services Agency. Responsibility for public employment services was to be transferred from the Department of Employment to the new Commission, and the Employment Services Agency was to be the Commission's second executive arm. The task of the Commission was to coordinate various aspects of manpower policy and to 'make arrangements as it considers appropriate for assisting people to select, train for, obtain and retain employment, and for assisting employers to obtain suitable employees'.[3]

The importance to manpower policy of effective employment services had already been recognised in the government's proposals for their reform published in December 1971.[4] The reforms were intended to 'provide the positive and dynamic public service required as an effective instrument of manpower policies in modern employment conditions'.[5] No steps were to be taken to compel employers or employees to use public employment services, but the proposed reforms were expected to attract far greater numbers to them. The 'dole queue' image was to be banished through separating the administration of unemployment benefit from employment work, and a new network of well-designed and well-located employment offices was planned. Furthermore, the Professional and Executive Register was to be restyled, and employers were to be asked to pay for its services. While in 1971 employers notified only about 2 million vacancies a year

---

[1] Department of Employment, *Employment and Training: government proposals*, Cmnd 5250, London, HMSO, 1973.   [2] Ibid. para. 29.   [3] Ibid. para. 5.
[4] Department of Employment, *People and Jobs: a modern employment service*, London, HMSO, 1971.
[5] Paul Bryan, Minister of State for Employment, quoted in *Financial Times*, 15 December 1971.

to the public employment services, it was hoped that the reforms would induce notification of at least 4 million vacancies a year.[1] The need for greater cooperation between the employment services and other manpower services such as industrial training was also stressed. The inclusion of the Employment Services Agency within the Manpower Services Commission would clearly facilitate such cooperation.

The Manpower Services Commission was established on 1 January 1974 and the Training Services Agency on 1 April 1974. The transfer of the Employment Services Agency was delayed until October 1974, after the administration of unemployment benefits had been separated from employment services.

Some indication of how the new bodies proposed to work together to develop an integrated and coherent manpower policy was given in the Training Services Agency's *Five Year Plan* published in 1974. In the case of redundancies, the Training Services Agency would

... cooperate with the ESA to ensure that advance information on redundancies collected through the ESA's early warning system is made known to the Agency's staff in the area concerned, and that there is TSA representation in the project teams set up by the ESA to operate in the premises of firms carrying out redundancies. Secondly, it will work closely with employers involved in redundancies to make special arrangements for retraining... or to persuade them of the desirability of releasing those declared redundant before the actual date of redundancy if training places are available.[2]

The Manpower Services Commission was certainly the kind of machinery through which the government could remedy the key defect of redundancy policy discussed earlier – namely the lack of assistance given to redundant workers seeking new employment. This change in approach was also reflected in the Labour government's Employment Protection Bill published later in 1974. This Bill required all employers to carry out effective consultation with trade unions in the event of redundancies; it also required them to notify the Department of Employment between two and three months in advance of any individual notices of redundancy, depending on the numbers involved. Employees were also to be given the right to reasonable time off to seek new employment.

An assessment of training policy

Although reliable evidence is scarce, what there is suggests that the Industrial Training Act was more successful in achieving some of its three objectives than others.[3]

---

[1] *Financial Times*, 15 December 1971.
[2] Department of Employment, *Training Services Agency. Five Year Plan*, London, HMSO, 1974, p. 29.   [3] See page 605 above.

The major objective in redistributing the costs of training was to remedy the 'poaching' which it was assumed existed prior to the Act, whereby some (larger) firms bore all the training costs, while other firms merely poached trained labour from them. As Lees has commented, however, 'no one knows the actual extent of the so-called "poaching" of trained labour'.[1] Similarly, the *Bolton Report* commented that there was 'no evidence which suggests that small firms were, on the whole, net "poachers" of labour, but there is very little available information on this subject'.[2] In the face of such uncertainties it is hard to assess to what extent the Act achieved this objective, or indeed whether it was a valid one.

That the work of the Industrial Training Boards has resulted in some redistribution of training costs in industry cannot be doubted, since the Act created no additional funds for training and both training grants and administrative expenses were met out of the levy. The key question is whether the redistribution was sufficiently fair to justify the massive bureaucratic administration that the system entailed. The *Bolton Report* argued that small firms were unfairly discriminated against in various ways. They could not afford the extra staff to deal with the administrative burden and often had to write off the levy as 'tax'. The system of a levy every year on *all* employees was particularly hard on small firms with a low labour turnover and consequently less need for continuous training. Cash flow problems caused by delay between payment of the levy and receipt of grants also tended to be more acute for small firms. Many Boards recognised these problems and gradually modified their policies to alleviate them as far as possible. Just as small firms with a low labour turnover could suffer under the system, so large firms with high labour turnover and consequently high training needs could gain disproportionately from it. It could provide a mechanism for 'effective subsidies...to firms with poor labour relations and high labour turnover.'[3]

While it would seem that the redistributive process generated by the levy and grant system was one of rough justice rather than equity, there is evidence that the Act did lead to a greater willingness on the part of *all* firms to accept training responsibilities and to bear training costs. The *Bolton Report* concluded that 'the Industrial Training Act has increased training in small firms as elsewhere'. It stressed, however, that this benefit was of a 'once-and-for-all nature' and was 'unlikely to be significantly improved by continuing the present cumbersome

---

[1] D. Lees and B. Chiplin, 'The economics of industrial training', *Lloyds Bank Review*, no. 96, April 1970, p. 39.

[2] Department of Trade and Industry, *Bolton Report*.

[3] Lees and Chiplin, 'The economics of industrial training', p. 34.

system'. Similar judgements have been made by other studies,[1] by the government in *Training for the Future*, and by those Boards which were themselves planning to phase out the levy system before the publication of this discussion document. It was indeed inherent in the carrot and stick principle of the levy and grant system that it would become self-defeating in time. The phasing out of the levy can be seen, therefore, as an indication not so much of its failure, as some critics would suggest, but of its success. It is hard to imagine that without the levy system some firms could ever have been prompted to accept their responsibilities for training.[2] Fears were expressed by bodies like the TUC that the phasing out of the system might lead to some firms neglecting their training responsibilities once more. Whether or not these fears have been proved right is virtually impossible to assess, given that the new measures were introduced during a recession, when training undertaken by employers inevitably declines. A major task facing the new Training Services Agency will be to devise mechanisms for countering the impact of such cyclical factors on training programmes.

As regards the improvements in the quality of industrial training brought about by the Act, there are no clear-cut indicators on which to base an assessment. But in general it seems inevitable that some raising of standards must have followed the new systematic approach to training illustrated by the redesigning of apprenticeship training on the module system used by the Engineering Industry Board. There are other indicators that would also seem to point to a general raising of standards, such as the increase in the number of training officers and qualified instructors. In engineering the number of full-time training staff employed increased from 6430 in 1965 to 10,582 in 1968, whilst the number of part-time training staff rose even more dramatically from 4838 to 20,268. Intensive courses for instructors organised by the Department of Employment increased their output from 500 in 1964 to over 2000 in 1968. Also likely to be beneficial in quality terms was the increase in off-the-job training. In shipbuilding, for example, 45 per cent of all first-year apprentices were trained off-the-job in 1968 compared with 24 per cent in 1965.

Of course, the emphasis placed by the Boards on precise approved specifications for training methods and training content was not always necessarily conducive to increases in quality from the point of view of a particular employer. This approach could encourage 'training for the sake of training'.[3] An employer might adhere to the standards

---

[1] See Lees and Chiplin, 'The economics of industrial training'.
[2] This is not to argue that there is no longer any problem as regards the fair distribution of training costs. The Training Services Agency is clearly still preoccupied with this issue.
[3] Ibid. p. 39.

because he ensured himself of a grant that way, not because the specifications were most appropriate to the needs of his labour force. One benefit of the phasing out of the levy and grant system may be the relaxing of slavish adherence to standards whether appropriate or not and the introduction of a degree of flexibility,[1] although the danger will remain of too much flexibility, resulting in training that is geared purely to the immediate needs of an individual employer, rather than to national needs.

Studies and assessments of the working of the Act give a general impression that there has been some increase in the *quantity* of industrial training, although it is hard to point to its precise nature: 'There is no one statistical series which unambiguously demonstrates this; indeed, the lack of comparable and meaningful statistics is a major problem in an attempt to evaluate the progress achieved under the Act.'[2] This lack of meaningful statistics was also pointed out by the Training Services Agency: 'No one knows how many employees undergo some form of training each year, although the *New Earnings Survey* suggests that about 1·2 million people may be undergoing training at any one time.'[3]

One useful indicator of the level of training is the Department of Employment's statistical series on boys and girls entering employment by class of employment entered. While these figures suggest some increase in the number of boys undergoing apprenticeship training, the figures on other forms of training for young people show no significant change (see table 13.5). Statistics collected by the Department of Employment on the number of workers under training in manufacturing industry are somewhat more encouraging, and reveal a 15 per cent increase between 1964 and 1969.[4] However, as the *Bolton Report* pertinently points out, 'some of this increase may have been more apparent than real; firms now have an incentive to keep a full record of the training element in their everyday business, whereas before the Act there was no financial incentive to record every act which contributed towards training. This meant that a great deal of "on the job" training went unrecorded.' That there was a slight but not outstanding increase in the quantity of industrial training is also suggested by the reports of the individual Industry Training Boards. The Engineering Industry Board reveals that in the two years to March 1968 the proportion of employees undergoing some form of training rose from 23 to 28 per cent, and the Man-Made Fibres Industry Board reported an increase from 15 to 20 per cent in the same period. However, the general

---

[1] Mukherjee, *Changing Manpower Needs*, p. 104.
[2] Lees and Chiplin, 'The economics of industrial training', p. 33.
[3] Department of Employment, *Training Services Agency. Five Year Plan*, p. 4.
[4] Lees and Chiplin, 'The economics of industrial training', p. 33.

Table 13.5. *Classes of employment entered by boys and girls, 1964–74*

	1964		1970		1972		1974[a]	
	(ooos)	(%)	(ooos)	(%)	(ooos)	(%)	(ooos)	(%)
Boys								
Apprenticeships	114·4	36	104·8	42	100·2	39	118·1	43
Professional	5·2	2	3·3	1	3·4	1	3·5	1
Clerical	34·0	11	19·8	8	18·4	7	19·2	7
With planned training:[b]								
Over 12 months	30·5	10	20·7	8	23·8	9	26·4	10
8 weeks–12 months	16·5	5	14·6	6	18·8	7	20·5	8
Other	114·2	36	85·0	34	94·3	37	86·9	32
Total	314·8	100	248·2	100	258·9	100	274·8	100
Girls								
Apprenticeships	16·9	6	15·8	7	18·0	8	15·5	6
Professional	5·0	2	4·1	2	3·9	2	4·2	2
Clerical	114·9	39	89·5	40	78·3	34	96·3	40
With planned training:[b]								
Over 12 months	13·3	5	11·0	5	12·6	6	13·5	6
8 weeks–12 months	24·4	8	23·0	10	28·0	12	27·5	12
Other	119·0	40	80·4	36	87·4	38	80·8	34
Total	293·5	100	223·8	100	228·2	100	237·8	100

SOURCE: Department of Employment, Training Services Agency, *Vocational Preparation for Young People: a discussion paper*, London, 1975.

[a] Figures for this year probably affected by the raising of the school-leaving age in 1973.

[b] Includes training of all types – on-the-job, off-the-job and simple training – and provision for further education in some cases.

failure of the Boards to produce comparable statistics in any standardised form has added to the difficulties of making quantitative assessments of the success of training policy.

Of course, the objective of the 1964 Act was not purely to increase the quantity of training *per se*; the increase was to be related to economic needs and technological developments. And it is in this respect that the Industrial Training Boards failed most noticeably. One key economic need was to alleviate shortages of skilled manpower, and there is little evidence that the Boards made any real impact on this problem. There was some gain in the number of young persons entering apprenticeships, but little or no attention was paid to the training of adult workers in craft skills. The major contribution here came from the efforts of the Government Training Centres, which turned out in the region of 55,000 skilled workers between 1964 and 1969. As Mukherjee concluded: 'The object of the Act in terms of training craft-level manpower for "economic needs" is being met in part, but not by the machinery created by the 1964 Act.'[1]

As Mukherjee also points out 'the imbalance between vacant jobs and available manpower is only partly a matter of shortages of craftsmen. As often as not it arises from an absence of skills at sub-craft level among those people who are in search of employment.'[2] Yet here too the Boards failed to address themselves to this problem, remaining on the whole preoccupied with setting standards for training in highly traditional craft skills. Once more it was left to the government to modify their own training facilities, to provide not only for training in traditional craft skills but also for training in the new skills that would be required by on-going technological developments. The new Training Opportunities Scheme introduced a vastly expanded range of courses, with heavy emphasis on technical and management skills. By 1973 the scheme was training 40,000 a year – roughly double the numbers trained in 1971 (see table 13.4).

Studies of the working of Industrial Training Boards tend to confirm the view that too often they assessed training against employers' existing needs, rather than themselves promoting training against a demand they foresaw in the future. This suggests that there is a vital role to be played by the new Training Services Agency in setting out, as it does in its *Five Year Plan*, areas of training priority in the light of technological and economic developments.

That the Boards should fail adequately to relate patterns of training to economic and technological needs was to some extent inherent in their structure. Many problems of economic and technological development, such as the need to retrain redundant workers from declining industries for redeployment in expanding industries, cross industrial boundaries. In the absence of any effective coordinating machinery it was virtually impossible to tackle such problems. As Mukherjee points out, 'The boards have no avenue of approach to those people in their industries who are either unemployed or about to become unemployed ...Entry into an ITB established training pipeline requires that the individual be already employed by a firm within the scope of that training board.' To obtain retraining to equip them for new employment individuals have 'to drop out of the industrial system and resort to Government Training Centres'.[3] The Engineering Industry Board was in fact approached by the Ministry of Labour in 1966 to initiate a programme of retraining to cope with the shake-out in the motor industry caused by the July measures, but the Board declined to take up this proposition; it felt that the task was not part of its proper function.[4]

[1] Mukherjee, *Changing Manpower Needs*, p. 109.   [2] Ibid. p. 96.
[3] Ibid. p. 95.   [4] Ibid. p. 87.

In principle, the new Manpower Services Commission should be able to develop integrated manpower policies that could overcome many of these shortcomings, although the success of the new machinery will depend to a large extent on the willingness of the Industrial Training Boards and the employers to cooperate, and on the size of funds made available by the government. While the levy and grant system of the 1964 Act was a cumbersome way of influencing the training policies of firms, it has yet to be seen whether the new institutions can devise effective alternative mechanisms for ensuring that training policies reflect not only immediate industrial needs but also long-term national needs.

Conclusion

In contrast to the bitter policy disagreements on industrial relations, the attitudes of Conservative and Labour governments towards manpower issues reflected a broadly similar progression towards the development of more active, interventionist and integrated policies that could help promote steady growth and full employment.

The early 1970s saw a move away from a policy of detailed intervention at the micro level through the Industrial Training Boards towards a policy of stronger intervention at macro level through the Manpower Services Commission. Although policy in the 1960s relied on intervention across the board through the bureaucratic administrative procedures of the levy and grant system, this approach was gradually abandoned in favour of more selective intervention at both micro and macro levels where particular firms failed to reach adequate training standards, or where particular training programmes needed development to meet specific economic, social or technological needs.

This shift in emphasis as to means was accompanied by a shift in the objectives of manpower policy. In the early 1960s the stress was on easing shortages of skill that could inhibit growth in a situation of full employment and a tight labour market. While the elimination of mismatches between unfilled vacancies and unemployed individuals remained significant, the rising unemployment of the late 1960s and early 1970s meant that manpower policies were increasingly viewed as an instrument for *achieving* full employment and counteracting the effects of unemployment through retraining and job creation. This change in emphasis can also be illustrated in attitudes to redundancy. In the early 1960s it was implicitly assumed that all redundancies were good in themselves insofar as they contributed to mobility in tight labour markets. In the 1970s, however, redundancy was less clearly desirable in social or economic terms, and this was reflected in measures like the temporary employment subsidy, introduced in 1975 and designed to forestall or postpone redundancies.

Given the underlying upward movement in unemployment levels since 1967 (in no year since has the unemployment rate been under 2·2 per cent, as opposed to the average of 1·5 per cent for the period 1959–63), this emphasis on manpower policy as an instrument for alleviating unemployment is likely to become increasingly important.

CHAPTER 14

GENERAL APPRAISAL

by *F. T. Blackaby*

INTRODUCTION

It is generally accepted that the performance of the British economy during this period was relatively poor as measured by the standard criteria normally used for assessing economic success or failure. This proposition has been widely documented and it is not the purpose of this book to review the evidence at length. The attempts to accelerate the British growth rate failed. The objective in the early 1960s was the modest one of getting the figure up from about 3 to about 4 per cent a year; in the event, the rise in real national product from 1960 to 1973 stayed at 2·9 per cent a year.[1] Britain's share in world trade in manufactured goods[2] fell in every year from 1960 to 1973, with only one exception (1971); at the beginning of the period this share was 16 per cent, by 1973 it was down to 9½ per cent. There does not appear to have been much compensation elsewhere for these failures in economic growth and in foreign trade. Consumer prices rose rather faster, if anything, than the average for other industrial countries and Britain's record on unemployment was no better than average.

This relative failure is an important part of the background to the appraisal of economic policy. By their own criteria, economic policy-makers in Britain have been unsuccessful. The natural conclusion has been that the economy was mismanaged and that the policies which successive governments followed were wrong. Perhaps more than in any country, we have had, as a consequence, a very wide range of alternative diagnoses and prescriptions. It does not, of course, strictly follow that because the policies adopted failed in their objectives they were wrong. It is possible that the defects of the British economy are relatively unamenable to management and that no conceivable policy in this period could have made a substantial difference to performance. While it is not an inevitable conclusion that there were other policies which would have been more successful, it is, however, incontrovertible

---

[1] This is the average of the three estimates of the rate of change of GDP at constant factor cost (CSO, *Economic Trends*, no. 276, October 1976, p. 127).

[2] This is the United Kingdom share in the dollar value of exports of manufactures from the eleven main manufacturing countries.

that the policy-makers were wrong in thinking that the particular methods they chose would be powerful enough to transform the economic situation.

The purpose of this chapter is twofold: to survey and comment on some of the various views which have been put forward about British economic policy in this period, and at the same time to summarise some of the conclusions reached in preceding chapters.

Prefatory questions

There are certain prefatory questions to be answered. One concerns how far the different views about the way the British economy should have been managed arise from the fact that their proponents have different valuations of the main objectives of policy. To the extent that they do, the assessment of those views becomes much more complicated. If it is agreed, for example, that one set of policies leads to high unemployment and a low price rise, while another leads to low unemployment and a high price rise, then the choice between those two policies depends on the valuation put on the objectives, so that there is little more to be said. However, the disagreements about economic policy in Britain have not on the whole taken this form. Most proponents of particular economic strategies have tended to claim that if their prescription were followed British economic performance would be better under most of the various heads, certainly in the medium term. There have been differences of emphasis in the valuation put on objectives, but these have not been central to the different views about policy. To give two examples: Paish, in arguing that the economy should be run with a slightly wider margin of spare capacity, suggested that this would not only reduce the rate of increase in prices and help the balance of payments, but would also accelerate the underlying rate of growth.[1] The argument here was that a relatively small sacrifice in the full-employment objective would give a substantial improvement in the other main objectives. Again, the proponents of export-propelled growth argued that, once the economy had entered the 'virtuous circle', its performance would be better on all fronts.

There is, however, a rather different 'complication of valuations' which makes the comparison of alternative policy recommendations more difficult. There is a certain basic difference which permeates a great deal of policy discussion and applies not so much to the objectives of policy as to the type of instruments used. Among policy-makers and economists there are those who strongly prefer that, if possible, the state should not intervene; also, that any intervention should be as far as possible general rather than selective. At the other end of the

[1] Paish, *Studies in an Inflationary Economy*.

spectrum there are those who are by nature enthusiastic for a greater degree of state intervention. This difference was particularly important in the field of industrial policy, where there were, on the one hand, those who argued that the main requirement for greater industrial success was to reduce state interference in industry and to allow managers and owners to obtain higher post-tax rewards for success, and, on the other hand, those who argued that without state intervention British industry would not invest enough, or in the right pattern. This tension shows up in discussions of short-term policy as well. Those who object to constant government attempts to adjust the level of demand do so at least partly because they want to reduce the overall level of state intervention in the economy; this is one of the advantages claimed for the 'simple rules' (page 636 below).

Apart from this general question – of intervention or non-intervention – the differences in views about economic policy have arisen mainly from disagreements about the likely effects of various actions. This raises the question why it is not possible to take the different policy recommendations, put them into one of the existing models of the British economy and compare the results obtained. There are, after all, a number of models of the British economy which are used both for forecasting and for simulating the effects of alternative policies.

For a number of reasons this would not settle the arguments. First, the different models themselves, although they may during some of the period have had a certain family resemblance, are in no way identical and, since they are in a fairly constant state of flux, the differences change from year to year. To take one example, the forecast for the rise in average money earnings has, at various times and in various models, been made to depend essentially on the demand for labour – either the level of unemployment, or the level of unemployment together with price expectations – alternatively, it has been made to depend on variables which represent the pressures on the wage bargainers – the past movements of prices and post-tax real earnings – again, the figures have been put in exogenously on the grounds that there is no good wage equation at all. These different views of inflation lead to different conclusions about policy. The first may suggest measures which raise unemployment, the second measures which accelerate the rise in post-tax real earnings, and those who take the third view probably allow to a greater extent than the others for the possibility of an effective incomes policy.

Linked in some ways to the different views about inflation, the effects of devaluation have also been modelled in different ways. In one model it is the relative movement of wage costs per unit of manufacturing output which is the important variable; in another it is export prices.

Different conclusions are reached about the reaction of imports to changes in relative prices and about the extent to which a competitive advantage obtained by devaluation is automatically eroded by higher wage increases. These differences naturally lead to a different view on the effectiveness of devaluation as an instrument of policy.

The Cambridge Economic Policy Group held for a time a view about the behaviour of the private sector which had strong implications for fiscal policy: this was that, for the private sector as a whole (the company sector and the personal sector taken together) the net acquisition of financial assets was stable and predictable. Consequently, it was argued that fiscal policy – the public sector's net acquisition of financial assets – should be 'set', not in relation to a short-term forecast, but in such a way that it equalled 1–2 per cent of GNP at full employment (depending on the rate of inflation and the balance of payments objective), so that it would balance the full-employment net acquisition of financial assets by the private sector. This prescription was, of course, peculiar to a model embodying this particular constancy.

The problem of reaching an agreement on policy did not arise simply because existing models of the British economy differed. There were critics of the policies adopted since 1960 who did not accept that any of the existing models properly described the workings of the British economy. This is perhaps particularly true of those who criticised the Treasury model or the National Institute model for 'ignoring monetary factors'.[1] These critics did not generally advance an alternative fully fledged model themselves; they put forward certain individual relationships, such as a lagged one from the movement of the money supply first to output and then to prices. Insofar as they were not prepared to specify a full alternative model fitted to past data, and to use it for regular forecasts of the real future, their position was perhaps not a strong one. Nonetheless they were not prepared to accept the results of policy simulations on any of the models extant during this period.

The second reason that it is impracticable to draw incontrovertible conclusions from feeding policies into current models is that those models can only deal with the consequences of policy instruments which can be assumed to have quantifiable and identifiable short-term effects. They cannot, for example, settle arguments about what policies (if any) might have been successful in accelerating the growth rate. They have no satisfactory way of dealing with the underlying productivity trend in the economy – the most usual assumption is simply to extrapolate the past trend into the future[2] – and obviously they cannot then be

---

[1] The reply was that monetary factors were treated like any other variable in the construction of the models; they were incorporated when they were found to be significant.

[2] Worswick and Blackaby (eds.), *The Medium Term*.

used to evaluate policies which, as their advocates argue, would accelerate economic growth.

The third point, linked to the previous one, is that econometric models cannot in general deal with the consequences of institutional changes designed to have medium-term or long-term effects. Increasingly over this period economic policy has consisted in attempts at institutional change, policy-makers becoming less concerned with the traditional instruments of demand management. There is no model of the economy which can estimate the effects of the IRC or the Industrial Relations Act, or which can forecast the consequences of a new set of incomes policy institutions. Further, there are some policies which, though not institutional changes, have effects which depend heavily on how certain institutions react to them. For example, in the debate about the relative merits of import restrictions and devaluation, one argument is that other countries, rationally or irrationally, are more likely to retaliate against the first of these than against the second. This is a crucial assumption; however, there is no way by which a model can indicate whether or not it is correct.

Fourthly, a model is basically a statement of past relationships; it cannot predict with any certainty when the economy moves into previously uncharted territory. The most obvious example is the rate of inflation. Towards the end of the period prices were rising at a rate which had no recent peacetime precedent and there was no reason to suppose that relationships between the rate of inflation and other variables which held when the rate was 5 per cent a year would necessarily hold when it was 25 per cent.

The main decisions during this period were strategic choices between different types of economic policy. Thus, there was a succession of choices between incomes policy and some alternative; there was the decision in 1972 to attempt to combine a faster rate of growth with a floating exchange rate as a way of avoiding the balance of payments constraints which had halted earlier attempts to raise the growth rate; there were decisions about the forms and the extent of industrial intervention, and about the desirability of attempting to join the EEC; there were attempts at trade union reform. These policies could not be evaluated by running them through some agreed model of the economy, even if such a model existed.

A final prefatory point concerns the difference between diagnosis and prescription. Obviously the analysis of the causes of some phenomenon – such as Britain's slow growth – is a necessary preliminary to any decision about what should be done, but the analysis of causation does not by itself settle the question of policy. Some causes – or predisposing factors – may be virtually unalterable; policy has to concentrate on those which can be altered by government action. For example, it is often argued that British exports are uncompetitive, not because of their relative price, but because of uncertain delivery dates, or poor design, or inadequate salesmanship. Nonetheless, the appropriate government policy to deal with a lack of competitiveness may be a devaluation, since relative price is something which the government can alter, and alter quickly; it may have no instruments to deal with uncertain delivery dates or poor design, and relatively low prices may compensate for other deficiencies. This distinction between the analysis of causes and policy prescription is important in assessing the attempts made to accelerate Britain's growth rate.

One large group of suggested causes for Britain's slow growth is concerned, in one way or another, with the social structure of British manufacturing industry – with, for example, the relatively low level of education of British management, or the failure of the workforce to identify with management's objectives. It is argued later that economic policy should have been more concerned with such matters. Nonetheless it is understandable that policy-makers, even if they agreed that these were the major causes of Britain's slow growth, might still search for policies to affect other minor causes, on the grounds that the major predisposing factors were ones which government policy would find it very difficult to alter.

A brief conspectus

Before turning to a critique of the various economic strategies pursued by successive governments during this period, it is perhaps useful to summarise very briefly what they were.

The beginning of the period (1960) coincided with the end of a short expansion – short and unsatisfactory, in that the rise in output per man tapered off rather quickly and the balance of payments ran into a deficit which led to a run on the pound in the following year. It was a time of growing dissatisfaction with Britain's slow rate of economic growth and with the orthodox techniques of demand management. The government, at the same time as it was taking restrictive measures to stop the run on sterling in 1961, was also beginning the first experiments with planning and incomes policies. Rising unemployment, which passed the then crucial figure of half a million in the winter of 1962/3, set off expansionary policies again; the government indicated it was prepared to accept a temporary loss of gold and foreign exchange reserves in order to keep the expansion going. However, the size of the current deficit which developed in 1964 was unexpectedly large.

The period of the Labour government was one of sharp contrast between the initial intended economic strategy and the actual policy the government was forced to follow. The intention was to follow a long-term strategy based on a national plan, with a permanent voluntary incomes policy and an active industrial policy. Actual policy was dominated by, first, the attempt to hold the exchange rate and, secondly, after November 1967, the attempt to defend the new exchange rate; it consisted largely in a succession of crisis measures whose main aim was to reassure foreign opinion. Only in its last year – from mid-1969 onwards – was the government free of its preoccupation with the balance of payments and, in this last year, dissatisfied with the apparent failure of its incomes policies, it made a tentative move towards some legal restraint on unofficial strikes, but was forced to withdraw by lack of Party support.

The Conservative government, coming to power in June 1970, inherited a strong balance of payments. Initially it was not particularly concerned with demand management; its main object was to reduce the role of government and, with its Industrial Relations Act, to bring the operations of the unions more fully within the framework of the law. The government was not anxious to reduce unemployment until the rapid increase in wage rates and earnings had been moderated; it adopted a partial, covert incomes policy in the public sector. The continuing rise in unemployment and the defeat of the public sector incomes policy by the miners' strike led to a change of strategy in 1972. An expansionary fiscal and monetary policy with a floating exchange rate was adopted, together with an attempt at a voluntary incomes policy, which led to a statutory prices and incomes policy when the government failed to reach agreement with the TUC; this strategy evolved into one more attempt to accelerate the growth rate. In the remainder of its period of office the government was largely pre-occupied with the successive stages of its incomes policy; it also moved towards more intervention in industry.

The pattern of criticisms

There is a large number of alternative views about the way in which economic policy should have been conducted – some covering one part of economic policy only and others more general. One group of criticisms is concerned with the short-term demand adjustments made mainly with employment or the balance of payments as objectives. Some of these criticisms are radical, in that they argue that the whole procedure was, in one way or another, misconceived; others simply take issue with the size or timing of the reflationary or deflationary stimuli applied in certain years. Another group of alternative views is more concerned with the policies adopted to accelerate the underlying rate of growth.

DEMAND MANAGEMENT

At the beginning of the 1960s, when *The Management of the British Economy* was written,[1] the idea that the government should 'manage' the economy by intervention based on forecasts was widely accepted. 'Demand management' is, however, something of a portmanteau term and different parts of the procedure have been criticised. Indeed, some criticisms seem to be directed to procedures which were not in fact followed, or to beliefs which were not in fact held. This section first describes and discusses 'demand management' as it was practised during this period; it then considers criticisms and alternative views.

Forecasts and policy actions

The basic idea is that from time to time a forecast is made of the likely trends in the economy for some period ahead; the policy-makers are then able to judge whether or not the performance of the economy, according to the objectives which they have in mind, is likely to be satisfactory or not. If the prospect is considered unsatisfactory, then some of the various instruments available are used to try to improve it. Thus the principles of demand management are the same as the principles of economic policy in general.

The 'normal' process of demand management, which is behind the preparation of a normal rather than an emergency budget, begins with a forecast probably for some eighteen months to two years ahead. This would indicate in particular the expected course of output, employment and unemployment, prices, and the balance of payments on unchanged policies. It would certainly include the tabular material which is normally presented in the regular forecasts published in the *National Institute Economic Review*. The 'budget judgement', of course, involves other considerations too, but, so far as demand management is concerned, it is essentially whether policy intervention can bring about some improvement on balance in the prospect for certain short-term objectives. Obviously there may be a conflict of objectives; a tax change may improve the prospect for output and employment, but worsen the prospect for the balance of payments. Chapter 4 gives examples of the judgements that were made from time to time: for instance, that on unchanged policies output was rising in line with productive potential, so that the budget should make no net change in demand; or, that the pressure of demand showed signs of becoming excessive, so that taxes should be increased; and so on.

It is difficult for any critic to argue with the basic framework of this process – that the government should consider the course which the

[1] Dow, *The Management of the British Economy, 1945–60*.

economy is taking, compare this with certain objectives and intervene to get a better mix of objectives if it can. The critics are, for the most part, not denying that this should be done; they are saying that, in one way or another, the government's picture of the working of the economy has been wrong or incomplete. Essentially they are criticising the models of the British economy which have prevailed in economic policy-making in this country since the war, their criticisms centring mainly on the working of the public sector and the treatment of money. It is therefore useful to describe in general terms how these were treated in the official forecasting process. Obviously the precise methods used evolved substantially during the fourteen years from 1960 to 1974, but the basic structure does not seem to have altered radically.

The forecast of the main categories of expenditure at constant prices has been central to the structure. In this basic forecast the whole public sector does not appear as a single item. The various components are incorporated in ways which seem most appropriate: public authorities' current spending on goods and services appears as a separate item; transfer payments to individuals and taxes on persons are incorporated in the calculations which lead up to a forecast of consumers' expenditure; investment grants are considered in relation to fixed investment in the private sector, so too are tax allowances on investment. On this disaggregated approach the pattern of any changes in government expenditure or in taxation will be important. It will make a difference, for example, whether a given change in the public sector's financial deficit is caused by an increase in an investment programme, a reduction in capital gains tax, or an increase in old age pensions, because these changes, when incorporated into the forecasting process, have different effects on effective demand and on output; consequently any policy adjustment required is also different. Thus the case for this treatment of the components of public sector expenditure is that:

the output-generating (or, in the case of taxes, output-destroying) content differs from item to item. In some 'extreme' cases, for example imports of missiles wholly constructed in the United States, the domestic output content may be zero, and in others, for example the services of school teachers, the output content may be 100 per cent. Similarly, the output generated by public expenditure as a whole may be judged greater than the reduction in competing demands on output implicit in a matching amount of tax revenues raised by the public sector.[1]

There are two main comments on this procedure. First, while it is perfectly possible to produce a measure of the 'push' given by the public sector as a whole, the appropriate measure is not simply the

[1] Artis, 'Fiscal policy for stabilization', p. 294.

public sector financial deficit as it stands, but the 'weighted' budget deficit (page 184), the figures for which are essentially the same as those embodied in the forecast tables. Thus, the production of a weighted budget deficit is not an alternative method of preparing a forecast, but an alternative way of presenting some of the figures. It can also be calculated on a full-employment basis, which helps to establish how far the deficit may simply be due to a recession (pages 183–4).

Secondly, it is possible to deduce from the forecast a set of figures for 'net acquisition of financial assets' by the government sector, the personal sector, the company sector and the overseas sector; towards the end of the period Treasury forecasts produced these figures explicitly. The sum of the balances must, of course, be zero, which is simply a way of saying that each transaction is both a debit and a credit item.[1] In the ordinary process of forecasting consumers' expenditure and private investment, a judgement will already have been made about the plausibility of the savings figures for those sectors; so it is generally unlikely that, when the figures for the balances of each of the four sectors are deduced, they will lead to a revision of the forecasts – certainly a revision has not often been necessary in the National Institute process of forecasting.

'Monetary factors' were incorporated into the forecasting procedure when they were found, on the basis of historical relationships, to have significant effects. These effects were limited (page 291), the main areas of expenditure which were found to have some sensitivity to interest rates being private housing and capital inflows from abroad; changes in hire purchase terms also had effects. Private industrial investment appears to depend heavily on the degree of capacity working and not to respond much to interest-rate changes. Prices were not forecast from the money supply, but from movements in labour costs, import prices and indirect taxes. Wage costs, in turn, which in earlier years were assumed to respond to unemployment, were later forecast on the basis of an *ad hoc* assessment of the situation. Altogether monetary factors were peripheral rather than central to the forecast mainly because examination of past relationships suggested that their influence was not strong.

The model of the economy employed in the forecasts had certain properties with important implications for policy. It had no powerful self-righting properties to bring the economy back without intervention to some natural growth path; it was also one in which changes in government expenditure and taxation had effects on real demand, and did not set in train processes which cancelled out automatically any

[1] Except for the residual error – the difference between the income and expenditure estimates of GDP.

effect on output. Certainly an increase in government expenditure might raise the pressure of demand and, under certain circumstances – particularly in the early part of the period, when the level of unemployment was low – this would lead to higher forecasts of wage rates and prices; but it would not lead to a reduction in private expenditure – for example, because the increased government borrowing led to an increase in the rate of interest and so to a reduction in private investment. The effect would depend on the degree of spare capacity in the economy; if the economy was at less than full employment, an increase in public expenditure would normally lead to a rise, not a fall, in private expenditure. Finally, an increase in government expenditure (or a reduction in taxation) would normally, other things being equal, worsen the balance of payments by increasing imports and possibly also affecting exports; but again there was no process by which an increase in government expenditure automatically led to a worsening of the balance of payments of the same order of magnitude.

However, the model was not such as to lead the policy-makers to suppose that, simply by demand management, they could simultaneously achieve all the traditional objectives. They would generally be unable to engineer simultaneously an adequate balance of payments surplus and full employment, so there could very well be circumstances in which the balance of payments was an effective constraint on the use of demand management to achieve full employment. Further, in the later part of the period the rise in earnings was treated as exogenous in the forecasting process – that is, within a fairly wide range of unemployment figures, it was not substantially influenced simply by demand management, so that clearly on this model some other instrument had to be used when prices began to accelerate.

A monetary rule

One main alternative proposed as a short-term management technique is a monetary rule: the government should set a target for the rate of growth of the money supply and allow the rate of interest to clear the market.

The monetarist approach to economic management is centrally concerned with inflation. The argument, it is true, is that once the economy is on a stable path with firm monetary targets, unemployment will settle at the 'natural rate' and output will grow in line with productive capacity. However, the main stress has been on a monetary regime as a corrective for high rates of inflation; hence its greater prominence in recent years.

The basic proposal is that the government should announce targets for the rate of growth of either M_1 or M_3 or both, equal to the trend growth of productive capacity plus an 'acceptable' rate of inflation. Adjustments should not be made on each month's figures, but on a moving average of three or four months. The government should attempt to set the public sector borrowing requirement so that it does not conflict with the monetary growth target; otherwise control should essentially be through the rate of interest.

In some presentations of monetary policy it is stressed that the government should announce its monetary target and emphasise its determination to keep to it. This, it is argued, would discourage trade unions from making claims which are clearly out of line, for if they collectively succeeded in forcing money wages up excessively, this would force up interest rates, which would reduce the growth of output and create unemployment. This unemployment would then be seen to be the responsibility of the trade unions rather than of the government.

This particular prescription for short-term management has not been tried in this country; there is, therefore, no postwar experience which can be used to assess its effectiveness. Experience in other countries is not an adequate substitute, since financial institutions and trade union structures differ a great deal. Such a policy is dependent on the assumption that there is a stable demand function for 'money', on one or other of its definitions, but it is difficult to establish such a function which holds both before and after 1970 (page 300). There is the further possibility that once particular aggregates of liquid assets, such as M_1 or M_3, are subject to tight control, they cease to act as good indicators because other forms of liquid asset are devised or developed which fall outside the controlled definition.

The money supply is, strictly speaking, an indicator and not an instrument of policy, since the term 'instrument' should be kept for changes which the government can itself make directly, such as changes in its purchases or sales of bonds or in the minimum lending rate. The money supply is therefore an intermediate variable, or an indicator of the setting of policy, and as such the information it provides is limited; so long as the demand function for money is stable, it should give an indication of the rate of increase of national expenditure in money terms, but it says nothing about the separate contributions of real output and of prices to any such increase. Thus a figure for the money supply which is observed in practice, although it may be based on a certain rate of real growth and a certain rate of inflation, will not necessarily bring about that particular combination. Even assuming there is a stable demand function for money on some definition or combination of definitions, all that is controlled is a figure of national expenditure in money terms, which can be brought about by a wide range of combinations of output and price changes.

The 'announcement effect' of a monetary target on trade union wage claims and wage awards is, of course, something which has not been tried. Although it might have some plausibility if the trade union movement negotiated as a whole, it is less plausible as a moderating influence on each individual union, which may well consider that its own position is exceptional, and that its above-average wage claim will be offset by below-average wage claims elsewhere. There is also the political question of how far the government could claim that it was the trade unions which were responsible for high unemployment; it might be argued that, if trade union structures or negotiating procedures were such as to lead to high unemployment, then it was the government's responsibility to change them. 'To "leave it to the Trade Unions" to determine the level of unemployment has no more to be said for it than to leave it to Trade Unions to determine the rate of inflation.'[1]

It is not at all certain what kind of variations in the rate of interest would have to be permitted to make a monetary rule effective. One of the objections to the use of monetary policy in this way, as against the use of fiscal policy, is, first, that there is not much evidence on the quantitative effects of interest-rate changes; secondly, those effects are in any case likely to fall heavily in the first instance on particular sectors of expenditure – such as private investment in general and private investment in housing in particular – which the government may not wish to discriminate against. Many of the self-righting characteristics claimed for a regime in which a monetary target is strictly observed arise from the assumption that expenditure is highly sensitive to interest-rate changes. Thus, if a reduction in the public sector borrowing requirement is needed, it is argued that this will not necessarily be deflationary, since at the same time interest rates can be reduced, which will stimulate private investment sufficiently to offset the effects of the reduced public expenditure or higher taxes. However, the sensitivity of expenditure to changes in the rate of interest is difficult to validate; when rates of interest are included in the equations which attempt to explain the movement of investment, stockbuilding, or consumers' expenditure, they are not in general found to have a strong effect.

In the period 1960–74 monetary policy was not in fact called on to do a great deal. The main quantifiable effects were those of changes in direct controls (on hire purchase terms and bank advances), though failure to discern any more general effects is not, of course, proof that they do not exist. It was the personal sector which felt the main brunt of monetary policy – in both directions – and, given the government's decision to shield and subsidise corporate investment, there was some

[1] G. D. N. Worswick, 'The end of demand management?', *Lloyds Bank Review*, no. 123, January 1977.

justification for this. However, it is also true that by 1971 the system of bank lending controls had become very difficult to manage and there was a case for more flexible arrangements. There were large swings in monetary policy (as in fiscal policy), leading – particularly in 1972/3 – to large changes in asset prices, with possible long-lagged effects of which we know little. As with fiscal policy, there is a case for small, more frequent adjustments, as against large infrequent ones.

The public sector financial deficit

Another line of criticism of the process of demand management suggests that policy-makers, rather than coming to an *ad hoc* judgement on the basis of each successive forecast, should follow some fiscal rule. One set of alternative 'rules' concerns the public sector's financial deficit – that is, it brings together out of the forecast both the revenue and the expenditure elements of the public sector, including the current surpluses and capital expenditure of the nationalised industries.

This formulation, which came to be known as the 'New Cambridge' view, is 'that tax rates should be set, not by reference to a short-term forecast, but in such a way that the full-employment yield of taxes falls short of public expenditure by an amount equal to 1 or 2 per cent of GNP'.[1] The rationale for this proposition is that the private sector as a whole increases its expenditure (on both current and capital items) over a period of two years in line with any increase in its disposable income and that its net acquisition of financial assets tends to be predictably 1–2 per cent of GNP. Consequently, given that the net acquisition of financial assets by the private, public and overseas sectors must add to zero, if the net deficit of the public sector exceeds the private sector's net acquisition, there must be a deficit in the balance of payments. Setting tax rates in the way suggested, it is argued, is a necessary (but not sufficient) condition for ensuring that the return to full employment does not lead to a balance of payments deficit. It is not a sufficient condition, because the competitive position of the country may be such that at full employment there is no prospect that exports will be sufficient to finance full-employment imports; that competitive deficiency would have to be dealt with by other instruments.

A further claim made for this approach to demand management is that it avoids constant intervention – 'fine-tuning'. It is argued that it is possible to calculate from the medium-term public expenditure forecasts what full-employment expenditure will be and thus to specify a set of tax rates which will deliver a certain figure of government revenue at full employment. Once these tax rates have been set, it will

---

[1] *Economic Policy Review*, no. 2, March 1976, p. 47. The proposition has a footnote added to it which reads 'depending on the balance of payments target and the rate of inflation'.

not be necessary to change them; given appropriate policies to deal with the balance of payments, this setting of tax rates will bring the economy back to full employment and keep it there.

There are various difficulties with this formulation. First, the relationship between disposable income and expenditure which appears to hold for the private sector as a whole does not appear to hold for the personal sector and the company sector taken separately. It is not easy to see why this should be, or what transactions between the personal and company sectors provide the offsetting effect. Secondly, the relationship between income and expenditure is not wholly straightforward; expenditure depends, not simply on the disposable income of the current and the preceding year, but also on changes in hire purchase debt, bank advances and the book value of stocks.[1]

Secondly, the rule clearly does not hold at times when prices are rising fast; indeed the proponents of the rule recognise that there is a problem here, particularly with stock appreciation. The private sector's net acquisition of financial assets, which was 2·6 per cent of GNP in 1974, rose to 6·2 per cent in 1975 and 5·5 per cent in 1976; clearly any forecast depends very heavily on the assumption which is made about rates of inflation. Further, it is not at all certain that if the rate of inflation returns to a more normal level the private sector's net acquisitions will necessarily return to 1–2 per cent of GNP.

Thirdly, the 'full-employment yield of taxes' is not an unambiguous concept. The return to full employment can take a number of different routes, with different patterns of expenditure and different rates of inflation leading to different revenue outcomes (also different expenditure outcomes). They will vary with different mixes of consumption and investment, and of personal and company income.

If one starts from a position of fairly substantial unemployment, so that it may take some years to return to full employment, it is not easy to see why it should necessarily be right to set tax rates now so that they would be appropriate in two or three years' time when full employment is regained – unless it is considered that there is a very substantial cost in changing tax rates. It is not easy to demonstrate that such a course is better than, for example, reducing taxes now to quicken the early stages of a return to full employment and then increasing them later. The choice between the two policies may depend on the weight given to the unfortunate consequences of unemployment now, as against the possible consequences of too rapid a return to full employment. This is a matter of valuation and there may well be no uniquely 'right' economic answer.

It is not clear that the use of this rule – that tax rates should be set

[1] House of Commons, *Ninth Report from the Expenditure Committee, Session 1974*, p. 3.

so that at full employment the surplus of the public sector is equal to the expected deficit of the private sector – is superior to the following rather less impressive-sounding suggestion: that when the economy is under-employed, policy-makers should look for a succession of fiscal stimuli which, together with measures to safeguard the balance of payments, will produce a reasonably rapid return to full employment, without leaving the economy with a balance of payments deficit when full employment is regained. Sets of measures can be tested using the normal forecasting model to see what the results would in fact be.

Stabilisation

It is probably true that the policy-makers' ideal or Utopian economy, at which they might say they were aiming in the long run, was one of stability in a certain sense; that is, it would be an economy with a steady (rapid) growth rate, a steady level of unemployment, a steady low (or nil) rise in prices,[1] and a balance of payments current surplus which (given stability in the world outside) was roughly constant, or which (in the absence of external stability) fluctuated not too widely around some target figure.[2] However, although this combination of long-term objectives might be summed up as 'stabilisation', this was not in fact a term which was often used by policy-makers themselves – in budget speeches, for example – to describe what they aimed to do.

There are a number of reasons for this. First, the concept of an eventual stable equilibrium of this kind is rather a visionary one and policy-makers' immediate objectives were usually much less ambitious; they were probably doubtful (and probably rightly) whether a stable equilibrium of this kind could be attained with the instruments at their disposal. Secondly, the concept of stabilisation does not include the acceleration of the growth rate, which was one of the objectives of economic policy, including demand management policy. As part of their attempts to accelerate the growth rate, governments on more than one occasion deliberately took action which risked 'destabilising' the balance of payments. Thirdly, on a large number of occasions when governments intervened, the problems of short-term policy did not present themselves as the need for some kind of general stability; rather the situation was that something had to be done, imperatively, about either the balance of payments or unemployment, and action was taken in the full knowledge that an attempt to stabilise one objective was likely to destabilise others.

---

[1] Perhaps the last serious advocacy of the desirability of a gently falling price level was in Council on Prices, Productivity and Incomes, *1st Report*, para. 109.

[2] When targets for the United Kingdom balance of payments were stated, they were usually for a current surplus in order to improve the ratio of short-term assets to liabilities.

The question whether government intervention did or did not reduce the degree of fluctuation of output around its trend is therefore one to ask about policy – but certainly not the only one, since stabilisation of the trend of output is one of many objectives of demand management. (It would be quite possible, for example, for it to be accompanied by steadily rising unemployment, and there seems no particular reason to assume it has any connection with stable prices.)

The various attempts to answer the question whether or not policy has on balance stabilised or destabilised the trend of output are not conclusive.[1] There are two difficulties: first, it is not at all easy to define precisely what non-intervention would be, either for fiscal or for monetary policy; secondly, given some definition of non-intervention, it is not easy to say with any assurance what would have happened on various occasions if the government had not intervened. The short-term models of the economy in use through most of this period show a certain tendency for the rise in output to flatten out if the models are run on into the medium term; it is not clear how far this is due to the way the models were constructed, or whether it represents what in fact the British economy would do.

For example, from July 1971 the government intervened to stimulate demand – first in a small way and then with a substantial reflationary package in the 1972 budget. If none of these stimuli had been applied, would the economy have recovered on its own, or would it simply have continued with a slow rise in output accompanied by steadily increasing unemployment?

Another approach to the question of stabilisation is to compare the United Kingdom's fluctuation in output around its trend with the experience of other industrial countries; the rather surprising conclusion is that output fluctuations in Britain were usually less marked than elsewhere.[2] Of course, this may not be the consequence of British economic policy; it may be that the British economy is itself in some way less volatile. However, it does suggest that the problem with the British economy was not so much any 'stop-go' pattern imposed by government policy, but rather the slowness of the rise in the underlying trend in output. Possibly the 'stop-go' pattern appeared more marked in the United Kingdom because in other industrial countries output was still rising significantly when it was below trend, whereas in Britain there tended to be virtually no rise at all in the 'stop' phases.

[1] See references on page 210, footnote 2.
[2] NEDO, *Cyclical Fluctuations in the United Kingdom Economy*, London, 1975; Whiting, 'An international comparison of the instability of economic growth'.

Fine-tuning

The objections to what has been called 'fine-tuning' are somewhat mixed. Sometimes the term appears to be used as a synonym for demand management, so that the objection is really to any kind of discretionary intervention. Certainly, if it is believed that the economy is self-regulating with some simple rule, then on this view it is a mistake to intervene at all. However, the observance of a simple rule will not necessarily reduce the *number* of government interventions; it will only make them less discretionary. Thus, if the government were to adopt some target figure for the growth of one of the monetary magnitudes, the observance of this rule would probably require frequent interventions in open-market operations, in calls for Special Deposits, or in changes in the minimum lending rate.

Alternatively, the objection may be to the view that it is possible, simply by the adroit manipulation of demand, to steer the economy with a considerable degree of precision on a desired course and, by demand management alone, to bring about a state in which all the major objectives of policy are achieved. Given the experience of the past fifteen years the case against any such view is indeed a strong one, but it is rather difficult to say who held it. Not many of the practitioners of demand management believed that it was an all-purpose technique. From the early 1960s onwards it was doubted whether it could by itself be effective in dealing with inflation, except at a very high cost in unemployment. From the later 1960s onwards there were also not many people who believed that demand management by itself had much to contribute to accelerating the rate of economic growth.

Thirdly, the objection may simply be to the frequency of intervention. This is different from objections to constant reversals of general economic strategy (page 652), such as the alternations between belief and disbelief in an incomes policy, or the changes in industrial policy. The issue here is not whether demand management interventions are needed; it is rather whether it is better for them to be frequent or infrequent. The argument against frequency is that, given the unreliability of economic forecasts, it is better to wait until it is quite clear that action is needed rather than to intervene every time that there are tentative signs of a divergence from the target figures for the objectives. In addition, it is argued that not enough weight is given to the costs imposed on the economy by policy changes – for instance, the constant disturbance to forward plans for production of cars or consumer durables which resulted from the frequent changes in hire purchase controls (pages 226–7).

There is here a difficult problem of balance. It is true that policy interventions have costs (though some create much less disturbance than others) and that forecasts are uncertain. However, although there are some examples during the period of rapid changes in the direction of demand management interventions after short intervals (for example, with public expenditure between 1970 and 1973, pages 117–23), such rapid changes are not all that usual. The National Institute, in its policy appraisals, has tended to take the view it is better to make small frequent adjustments than large infrequent ones. This was on the grounds that there were often fairly long time-lags before policy actions had their effects, and if intervention was left too long there was a danger that it would eventually be excessive. Thus, during the period from July 1970 to the budget of 1972, the National Institute argued consistently for the early application of small stimuli to demand to bring the rise in output in line with productive capacity; it is arguable that this would have produced rather better results than the course actually followed, of giving a very substantial demand stimulus in the budget of 1972.

Other aspects of fiscal policy

On the revenue side of the public sector accounts there was substantial structural reform in the period 1960–74. There was a reduction in the number of rates of both indirect and company taxes, although there was a difference of emphasis here between the two Parties: Labour governments tended to prefer a larger number of rates (and consequently more discrimination) and Conservative governments preferred to reduce the number. The tax base was extended through VAT and capital gains tax. There was also a move towards administrative simplification of income tax, so that the tax threshold is now one of the lowest among industrial countries and the threshold rate of tax by far the highest. On the other hand, the indirect tax system became administratively more complex, first with selective employment tax and then with VAT. Finally, there was a move in the 1970s towards more public consultation about tax reform (through Green Papers).

Particularly in later years, the tax-mix shifted substantially towards direct taxation, as a combined consequence of more rapid inflation, a progressive direct tax system and an indirect tax system relying heavily on specific taxes. This development was hardly a deliberate policy decision; it strengthened demands for *ad valorem* instead of specific indirect taxes and for indexation of tax allowances and thresholds.

On the expenditure side there are the separate questions of the control of public expenditure in the medium term and its use as an instrument of short-term demand management. In the period 1960–74, the public sector, by any measure, expanded a good deal faster than the economy as a whole. In the early and mid-1960s the basic strategy was that public expenditure should rise in volume rather faster than GDP – and the assumption about the future growth of that product was optimistic. In 1969/70 the medium-term strategy shifted to one in which public expenditure, in cost rather than in volume terms, should rise simply in proportion to a less optimistic forecast of the rise in GDP. Finally, there has been a shift to the view that public expenditure, again in cost terms, should rise more slowly than total output. However, these medium-term strategies have tended to be disrupted by short-term interventions. Further, public expenditure planning throughout most of this period was in constant price terms, with an implicit undertaking to finance inflation; it was only after the very sharp rise in relative wages and prices in the public sector between 1972/3 and 1974/5 that cash limits were introduced.

Although most governments agreed in principle with the conclusions of the *Plowden Report*, that short-term changes in public expenditure should be 'a tool of the last resort',[1] nonetheless such interventions were, if anything, probably more frequent at the end of the period than at the beginning. The general picture is one of an unreliable conjunctural instrument, whose timing often proved not to be counter-cyclical in the event. There was, however, no general rule that expenditure cuts were ineffective; sometimes they were under-implemented and sometimes over-implemented. Control over investment by nationalised industries and in housing proved unreliable; it was also difficult to implement cuts in local authority current spending, where control was indirect and incomplete. On the other hand, control over local authority capital programmes (other than housing) proved fairly reliable. In the reflationary counter-cyclical use of public expenditure there was some tendency for a ratchet effect – for counter-cyclical increases to shift the schedule of medium-term expenditure plans upwards as well.

This is one reason for a more extensive use of the concept of the 'full-employment' budget. If each time after a counter-cyclical intervention the long-run full-employment budget was recalculated, this would help to show how far the effects of that intervention were likely to be temporary and how far permanent, which has never been entirely clear in the past, and thus to give some advance warning of any conflict between stored-up resistance to expenditure cuts and equal resistance to tax increases (page 134 and footnote 1, page 190).

---

[1] Treasury, *The Control of Public Expenditure.*

Price inflation

The amount of academic analysis of inflation during this period was, of course, enormous. So far as policy was concerned, the important issue was between, on the one hand, those who considered that inflation could be controlled by some form of macroeconomic strategy and, on the other, those who thought that free collective bargaining would have to be modified in some way.

The arguments about the nature of inflation – whether it was cost-push or demand-pull, or a mixture of the two, or indeed whether the two were distinguishable – continued in a massive literature. Here only one or two of the more influential examples are noted. Some early work by Dow and Dicks-Mireaux suggested that the movement of past prices was more important in explaining the movement of wage rates than the pressure of demand[1] – a doctrine that was later rediscovered – and that trade union pushfulness was an important independent influence.[2] Those who argued for the importance of the pressure of demand turned their attention away from the goods market towards the labour market; the most influential articles during this period were by Phillips, who presented a study of the relationship over a hundred years between the movement of wage rates and the level of unemployment,[3] and Paish, who concluded that a very modest increase in unemployment, to a figure of around $2\frac{1}{4}$ per cent, would be sufficient to produce price stability.[4] However, others disputed the meaning of this apparent relationship between the level of unemployment and the rate of change in wage rates or earnings; they argued that in the short periods when unemployment was rising trade unions postponed or moderated their demands with every intention of pressing them harder when unemployment began to fall again. It was wrong, therefore, to infer from short periods of relatively high unemployment what would happen to wage rates if the relatively high unemployment persisted for some time.

The state of the debate at the beginning of the period of this book – so far as policy-making was concerned – can be seen in the Reports of the Council on Prices, Productivity and Incomes, a body set up in

---

[1] 'It seemed reasonable to believe that full compensation for price increases is something which trade unions aim at and which both sides accept as a standard of reference' (Dow, 'Analysis of the generation of price inflation').

[2] L. A. Dicks-Mireaux and J. C. R. Dow, 'The determinants of wage inflation: United Kingdom, 1946–56', *Journal of the Royal Statistical Society* (series A), vol. 122, pt 2, 1959.

[3] Phillips, 'The relation between unemployment and the rate of change of money wages in the United Kingdom, 1861–1957'.

[4] Paish, *Studies in an Inflationary Economy*.

1957 with the hope that it would clarify matters. The first two Reports came out categorically upon the side of those who stressed excess demand: 'Viewing the period as a whole, we incline to think that the main cause of the rising trend of prices and incomes has been an abnormally high level of demand for goods and services in general, maintained for an abnormally long stretch of time.'[1] The third and fourth Reports expressed a rather different conclusion: 'How can inflation be stopped? It has sometimes been due to the pull of excess demand, but experience has shown that removing excess demand is not of itself enough. We have been brought to the conclusion that inflation has another cause, an upward push as rates of pay are raised and profit margins are maintained by raising prices. This "cost push" comes into play through a myriad of decisions on wages, salaries and prices.'[2]

Certainly from about 1961 up to the late 1960s anti-inflationary policy was mainly directed at trying to find ways of moderating trade union demands – that is, it concentrated on the cost-push side. However, in 1966 the Labour government tacitly accepted an upward shift in the level of unemployment to around $2\frac{1}{2}$ per cent in the hope that easing the pressure of demand would be of some help. And from the end of the 1960s theorists had to explain why the rate of inflation and the level of unemployment rose together, which was obviously rather more difficult for those who stressed the pressure of demand. Price expectations were added to the explanation, also a term to represent the increased benefit resulting from the earnings-related supplement introduced at the end of 1966. The hypothesis was that, with a higher ratio of unemployment benefit to average earnings, those who became unemployed would take longer to search for a new job, so that the level of unemployment corresponding to any given 'pressure of demand' would be raised. However, the figures for the actual number of unemployed persons receiving earnings-related benefit do not provide much support for this view.[3]

An alternative view – not dissimilar to the one put forward by Dow and Dicks-Mireaux 25 years earlier – was that inflation could be better explained by assuming that trade unions bargained on each occasion to recover what they had lost in real income by the rise in prices since their last settlement and then added something to give themselves a real

---

[1] Council on Prices, Productivity and Incomes, *1st Report*, para. 78.

[2] Council on Prices, Productivity and Incomes, *4th Report*, para. 8.

[3] 'Throughout virtually the whole period from November 1966 to November 1970 the number of men receiving ERS was less than 100,000. Even if it was supposed that receipt of ERS doubled the length of an individual's spell out of work...then the increase in the level of unemployment would be 50,000' (*Department of Employment Gazette*, October 1976). See also *National Institute Economic Review*, no. 79, February 1977, p. 15.

increase; it was further suggested that they looked at the movement of their post-tax rather than their gross earnings.[1] This hypothesis helped to explain the very big increase in money earnings which followed a number of years under the Labour government when real earnings net of taxes and national insurance contributions had hardly risen at all; if it was correct, the level of unemployment was relatively unimportant and the main way to keep down inflation would be to ensure a reasonable rate of increase in post-tax real earnings.

However, neither of these suggestions provide a close explanation of the movement of money earnings – particularly for the period after 1972. It appears that money earnings are not so strictly determined that they cannot be influenced by policy – or by the willingness or unwillingness of the trade union movement to cooperate with the government of the day. In any case, any relationships are presumably partly the product of the particular system of pay bargaining in force, so that there is no reason to think that they would necessarily hold if the system were modified or changed.

Because of the absence of any good wage equation, it is not possible to say what would have happened to money earnings in the absence of any incomes policy; it follows that it is not possible to prove any statement about whether such policies were effective or not. A crude examination of the figures suggests that periods of freeze were effective: for example, between the second quarters of 1966 and of 1967 average weekly earnings rose only 2 per cent. For the longer periods of incomes policy, if one assumes that there were long-term forces tending to push up the rise in money earnings during the whole period, it certainly appears that the rise was held back when an incomes policy was in force, with a rebound when the incomes policy was abandoned.

However, during this period – in spite of a number of attempts to create new incomes policy institutions – no progress was in fact made towards any permanent modification of free collective bargaining. This was partly the consequence of the damaging alternation of policies (page 366), in which new governments reversed the decisions of their predecessors, instead of trying to build on to them. Some things were learnt: it is probably true that, particularly after 1974/5, more trade unionists accepted that there was a connection between wage and price increases, and the experience of 1973/4 showed how dangerous indexation could be when the terms of trade turned against the United Kingdom. Conclusions could also be drawn about how to reconcile an incomes policy with plant bargaining and about the problems posed by productivity agreements. The general assessment, however, must be

---

[1] See Coutts, Tarling and Wilkinson, 'Wage bargaining and the inflation process'; Henry, Sawyer and Smith, 'Models of inflation in the United Kingdom'.

one of failure to develop any satisfactory institutional modifications. There were also, of course, the attempts to use legislation to reduce the incidence of strikes and to set industrial relations more generally within a legal framework. Once again no lasting reforms were achieved.

The exchange rate

In the early 1970s probably most British economists concerned with macroeconomic policy would have agreed that the use of the exchange rate was a desirable addition to the instruments of economic policy; it seemed that a lesson had been drawn from experience. It is true that the apparent effects of devaluation had taken a long time to arrive, but the eventual swing into surplus in 1969 and 1970 was a strong one. Those who had argued that devaluation would have catastrophic effects on Britain's invisible earnings had been proved wrong; in fact it appeared to have had a stronger effect on invisible than on visible credits. Consequently, the main criticisms of exchange-rate policy current in the early 1970s were that the pound should have been devalued earlier and the rate moved down more.

The next decision about the exchange rate was rather different. When in 1972 the Chancellor of the Exchequer indicated that he would not let a fixed exchange rate stand in the way of economic expansion, it was assumed that he had in mind a further devaluation to a fixed rate if necessary. When in fact the pound was floated, it was presented as (and probably intended as) essentially a temporary measure, as a prelude to a new fixed rate. It subsequently proved to be a more radical change in exchange-rate policy.

Further, whereas the arguments at the time of the 1967 devaluation were essentially about whether Britain should or should not devalue, the arguments about the move to floating rates were not specifically in the British context; they were rather concerned with the worldwide breakdown of the system of fixed exchange rates and the desirability or otherwise of floating rates in the world system of trade and payments.

Experience since 1972 has served to shake the consensus of the early 1970s. Certainly there are still strong advocates of exchange-rate changes as the best method available for balance of payments adjustment. However, there are now strong critics as well; a number of economists who strongly favoured devaluation in the 1960s now favour import controls instead, and some take the line that in the long term (though the time-period is not always specified) devaluation does not improve the balance of payments at all.

There are a number of points at issue. First, there is the problem of assessing the size of the price elasticities which indicate the likely balance of payments response to an exchange-rate change; for example, there is a good deal of disagreement about the extent to which British imports of manufactures are sensitive to price changes. Secondly, there are questions about the pricing policies of firms, particularly with a floating rate; it has been suggested that more firms now increase their export prices (expressed in sterling) quickly as the sterling exchange rate falls, and if this is so the effect of a downward floating rate on exports depends on firms' reactions to a possible higher profit margin on exports than on home sales. Thirdly, there is the problem for a devaluing country of holding its competitive advantage; by putting up import prices, devaluation increases the pressure on wages (insofar as they respond to past price movements), which raises the possibility of a cumulative process, in which devaluation helps to bring about a continuation of the relatively rapid price rise which occasioned it in the first place. Thus, in countries where the exchange rate floats down, higher rates of inflation may tend to persist, and so the downward float continues. The critics have suggested that there is a good deal in world experience since 1972 to suggest some cumulative process of this kind.

The experience of floating rates since 1972 – particularly the experience of sterling – does not suggest that the market moves exchange rates smoothly to some point of long-term equilibrium. Those responsible for movements in and out of sterling (including those who can delay or accelerate payments on imports or exports) appear to take short views, often reacting to rather ephemeral items of news; since the amount of funds which can be moved in this way far exceeds the funds which the authorities can use to moderate exchange-rate movements (at least in a downward direction), the course of sterling's exchange rate since June 1972 has been anything but smooth.

ECONOMIC GROWTH

Throughout the period widely conflicting lessons were drawn about the reasons for Britain's slow rate of economic growth – and, again, behind these conflicting views lay different pictures of the medium-term or long-term behaviour of the economic system. A number of commentators have pointed out how difficult it is to validate any conclusions here. At least with short-term policies there is some hope of disentangling and quantifying the consequences of, say, a tax change. It is very hard to see how one could successfully disentangle the consequences of the various policies whose objective was to raise the rate of economic growth. First of all, there are usually quite a number of such policies in existence at any time, with long but varying time-lags assumed before they might become effective, and throughout the period these policies were frequently changed. The basic observation of the last fifteen years is that a large number of policies were attempted – some for a short time, some for longer – and there is no evidence that the growth rate of productive capacity was faster at the end of the period than at the beginning. It is still, of course, open to the proponents of various policies to argue that they were not persisted with for long enough, or that there were other policies being pursued simultaneously which prevented them from being effective, or indeed that without them economic growth would have been even slower still.

International comparisons between fast-growing and slow-growing countries are not particularly helpful. There are relatively few observations and a very large number of possible relevant ways in which an economy (and for that matter a society) like that of Japan differs from an economy (or society) like that of Britain. Further, as Beckerman has pointed out, it is extremely difficult to separate causes and effects, 'since almost anything that might be expected to contribute to growth might equally well be caused by growth'.[1]

The lessons drawn at various times about the causes of Britain's slow economic growth can be put into two groups. First, there are views which lead to the conclusion that there is some central, or general, policy change which could accelerate the growth rate; that is, there are, as it were, some levers which the government can pull which would bring about a change in the underlying rate of growth. Here three such approaches are considered – of Kaldor, of Beckerman and of Bacon and Eltis.[2] Secondly, there is a rather more heterogeneous collection of views – views perhaps of economic historians rather than econometricians – which stress a multitude of assorted institutional factors leading to a multitude of assorted inefficiencies.

Growth and the supply of labour

Kaldor's thesis maintained that the driving force behind rapid economic growth was in the manufacturing sector; further – following Verdoorn – the faster the rise in manufacturing output, the faster the increase in productivity, with the direction of causation from output to productivity. He laid great stress on the need for an elastic supply of labour, pointing out that in France, Germany and Italy the industrial sector could draw on reservoirs of labour either from agriculture or from the poorer countries of Western Europe, whereas in Britain the

---

[1] W. Beckerman, 'The determinants of economic growth' in P. D. Henderson (ed.), *Economic Growth in Britain*, London, Weidenfeld & Nicolson, 1966, p. 57.

[2] Kaldor, *Causes of the Slow Rate of Economic Growth of the United Kingdom*; W. Beckerman, 'Demand, exports and growth' in W. Beckerman and Associates, *The British Economy in 1975*, Cambridge University Press, 1965; R. W. Bacon and W. A. Eltis, *Britain's Economic Problem: too few producers*, London, Macmillan, 1976.

reduction in the agricultural labour force had already occurred and there were powerful social arguments for checking the immigration from Commonwealth countries. Thus, Kaldor argued, a rise in manufacturing output in Britain was constantly checked by severe labour shortages which emerged during economic expansions, and this caused the United Kingdom's recurring balance of payments crises, with imports rising faster than exports during periods of growth. This view had some influence on policy; one of the arguments behind the selective employment tax was that it would raise the relative price of labour in service occupations and so free workers for manufacturing industry.

A number of difficulties have emerged with this approach to the causes of Britain's slow growth. The relationship which Kaldor observed in 1966 between manufacturing output and productivity appears not to have held since that date; also, it has been suggested that his comparisons were heavily influenced by the figures for a single country (Japan).[1] Secondly, the conclusion that British manufacturing industry was starved of labour during the postwar period conflicts with a number of industry studies, which show that British plants were overmanned in relation to their continental counterparts. Thirdly, it has been argued that both the productivity potential and the export potential are as high in many service industries as in manufacturing; this does not appear from national accounts statistics simply because there is no adequate way of measuring productivity in many service industries. Kaldor himself now takes the view that the United Kingdom's poor performance may be explained more by lack of international competitiveness than by inability to recruit sufficient labour into manufacturing industry.

'Export-propelled growth'

The phrase 'export-propelled growth' is shorthand for a group of views which became prominent in the early 1960s and had some influence on economic policy in the period of planning. The basic proposition was that more rapid economic growth could be brought about if businessmen expected demand for their products to rise quickly; in countries such as the United Kingdom they would only expect this to happen if there was a sufficiently large export content in the expected rise in demand for there to be little risk of a balance of payments 'stop'. A good deal of the discussion was concerned with possible reasons for relatively fast economic growth in some countries and slow growth in others.

[1] R. E. Rowthorn, 'What remains of Kaldor's Law?', *Economic Journal*, vol. 85, March 1975.

Thus, in February 1962, in a chapter on policies for faster growth, the *National Institute Economic Review* commented:

A number of explanations have been put forward for low growth rates – for instance, too much demand, too little demand, an unfavourable structure of output, slothful entrepreneurs, or legacies of the past – such as having come relatively unscathed out of the war. ...none of these factors by itself seems to provide an adequate explanation.

The only important point that can be established is that a necessary, and almost sufficient, condition for rapid growth is for businessmen in general to expect that the demand for their products will continue to grow rapidly... For businessmen to hold confident expectations about the long-run demand for their products, they must also be confident that total demand in the economy as a whole will expand unhampered by balance of payments difficulties or excessive price rises.[1]

The chapter went on to argue that this 'export-propelled' acceleration of the growth rate could come about if Britain achieved and maintained competitiveness for its goods; it also described the concept of the 'virtuous circle', 'by which initial competitiveness brings growth through rapidly rising exports, growth brings a faster rise in productivity, and this faster rise in productivity helps to keep prices stable and so to maintain or indeed increase competitiveness'.[2]

It is, of course, not easy to establish directly that investment responds to businessmen's demand expectations, because there is no quantitative measure of those expectations. Beckerman treats this essentially as a proposition of obvious commonsense.[3] He cites evidence that changes in sales have been shown to have an overridingly important influence on the rate of investment and comments that the past rate of change of sales must be regarded as the variable most likely to be highly correlated with expectations. However, although fluctuations in demand expectations may well explain fluctuations in investment in individual countries, it does not necessarily follow that different levels of investment in different countries are explained in the same way. Further, in one country a businessman's demand expectations may cover only the next year or two, while in another he may be looking ten years ahead. For example, a Report on the comparative experience of the British and Japanese motor cycle industries suggested that one of the reasons for the decline of the British industry was that it only looked at short-term sales prospects.[4]

---

[1] *National Institute Economic Review*, no. 19, February 1962, pp. 55–6.
[2] Ibid. p. 56.
[3] Beckerman, 'Demand, exports and growth'.
[4] Department of Industry, *Strategy Alternatives for the British Motorcycle Industry*, London, HMSO, 1975.

Although the proponents of export-propelled growth laid stress on the connection between demand expectations and investment, they did not argue that investment alone could explain the differences in growth rates between countries. Beckerman showed that differences in investment ratios between countries explain only a relatively small part of differences in growth rates: in fast-growing countries a given increase in the stock of capital appears to yield a much higher increase in output, the incremental capital–output ratio being much lower than in slow-growing countries.

The second main element in the strategy of export-propelled growth was an improvement in competitiveness. Many of those who put forward this general view envisaged that it should come about through a devaluation. This was not because they necessarily believed that price competitiveness was all-important in exports, although in the period 1951–61 differences in export performance between countries appear to have been closely related to movements in export prices.[1] (After 1961 the relationship is much less close.) Rather it was because they considered that the government had an instrument in devaluation to alter prices relative to those of other countries, whereas it had no short-term instruments to improve design, delivery dates, or the provision of servicing facilities. However, the proponents of this view tended to refer in general terms to the need to improve competitiveness and then maintain that improvement; they did not put numbers to the requirement.

From 1960 to 1967 there was no improvement in price competitiveness; indeed Britain's relative position worsened.[2] The various attempts at incomes policy during this period did not prove (as some people hoped) an adequate substitute for devaluation. The devaluation at the end of 1967 produced a competitive margin, but by 1970 this had been significantly eroded. It is possible that the advocates of devaluation did not pay enough attention to the problem of preventing such erosion; it was unfortunate that the year of 'freeze and severe restraint' had preceded devaluation, so that it was very difficult to prevent a wage reaction to the rise in import prices. Between 1970 and 1974, partly because of revaluations elsewhere and partly because of the downward float of sterling after mid-1972, there were further improvements in United Kingdom competitiveness measured in this way.

The improvement seems to have accelerated the rate of increase in exports: from 1953/4 to 1966/7 – that is, up to devaluation – the annual

---

[1] Beckerman and Associates, *The British Economy in 1975*, p. 59.

[2] The series used for these propositions is the movement of wage costs per unit of output in manufacturing in Britain compared with the weighted average for other industrial countries, both measured in dollars. This series is used, rather than export prices, since part of the mechanism of export-propelled growth was considered to be the improvement of profit margins on export sales.

average rate of increase in the volume of exports of goods and services was
$3\frac{1}{2}$ per cent; from 1966/7 to 1973/4 it was double that – 7 per cent.
However, this appears to have been largely due to faster growth in
world trade – the rate of fall in the United Kingdom's share in world
exports of manufactures stayed much the same – and it failed to bring
about 'export propulsion'. Part of the reason may have been that this
export rise did not produce adequate balance of payments surpluses;
the rise in exports was insufficient to finance both the turning of the
terms of trade against the United Kingdom (partly the consequence of
the falling value of sterling) and also the acceleration in the rise in
import volume. The comparable figures for the rise in the volume of
imports of goods and services were 4 per cent (1953/4 to 1966/7) and
7 per cent (1966/7 to 1973/4). The balance of payments was only
briefly in significant surplus and the second stage of export-propelled
growth – the effect on investment – did not occur; from 1966/7 to
1973/4 the volume of fixed investment in manufacturing industry rose
less than 2 per cent a year.

The idea that indicative planning might help to accelerate economic
growth was in some ways linked to the idea of export-propelled growth;
it was also put forward forcefully in the early 1960s and intended to
work on businessmen's expectations. The statement of an output target,
with a government commitment to try to reach that target, would, it
was hoped, lead firms to expand their capacity and so bring the higher
growth rate about. The experiment with indicative planning, coinciding
as it did with a period when the government took a long succession of
deflationary measures in defence of the exchange rate, was an obvious
failure. Unfortunately all forms of national medium-term planning were
discredited in consequence, so that there is – for instance – now very
little official material published about the possible evolution of the
economy in the medium term.

Market and non-market sectors

The thesis presented by Bacon and Eltis[1] has a certain similarity to that
put forward by Kaldor in 1966. However, whereas Kaldor was arguing
that the manufacturing sector had been starved of labour, Bacon and
Eltis suggest that the market sector has been squeezed by the non-
market sector – that is, essentially, the public sector.

There are a number of points on this thesis. First, insofar as the rise in
the public sector share is considered to be a trend factor which has been
damaging to economic growth, it is perhaps rather unfair to include the
year 1974, which was the first year of a recession when the share of the
public sector can naturally be expected to be off-trend.

---

[1] Bacon and Eltis, *Britain's Economic Problem.*

Secondly, the distinction is perhaps not drawn sufficiently emphatically between the different economic effects of the resources which the government uses itself and the resources it transfers within the private sector. If the government itself employs more people in the health or education services, then obviously it is reducing the productive resources available for the market sector. If the government transfers purchasing power from producers to non-producers in the private sector, the effect is simply to transfer the ability to purchase the output of the market sector from one group to another, which has no *direct* effect on the output of that sector (except insofar as different groups may purchase different types of product, pensioners having a different pattern of consumption from people in the labour force, for example). The effect of this transfer, such as it is, is indirect, presumably arising from the unwillingness of the producers happily to accept the transfer to non-producers.

In the postwar period there has been no substantial increase in the share of resources which the public authorities take for their own direct expenditure. Public authorities' current and capital expenditure on goods and services (excluding public corporations) was, at current prices, 24 per cent of GDP at factor cost in the early 1950s and 27 per cent in 1973. A rise of this order over twenty years is hardly powerful enough to be much of an explanation for slow growth, nor is the share particularly high in comparison with most industrial countries.

The marked change in the postwar period has been the increase in transfers within the private sector. These are not exclusively transfers from producers to non-producers; a significant part comes back to the producers themselves, as housing subsidies, food subsidies and subsidies to the prices of nationalised industries, for example. The argument is that producers have been unwilling to accept the burden of these transfers, which have resulted in a rising incidence of taxation on their earnings, and this unwillingness has been one of the driving forces behind wage demands and consequently behind accelerating inflation. This view is another presentation of the 'real wage' theory of inflation, discussed on page 641 above – that wage explosions tend to occur after a period when the real post-tax wage has failed to rise. The essential strength of the argument is, therefore, the strength of the 'real wage' hypothesis and that hypothesis is far from conclusive.

Further, although the slow rise in the real post-tax wage since 1970 may help to explain the acceleration in inflation in the last few years of this period, it can hardly be considered an explanation of the relatively slow rate of growth over the whole postwar period. For this, it is reasonable to look for some factor which distinguishes the British economy from fast-growing economies and it does not appear that the burden of taxation is such a characteristic. Taxes, including social security contributions, are a lower proportion of GNP in the United Kingdom than in many other industrial countries; further, the aggregate tax burden in the United Kingdom fell quite sharply between 1969 and 1973, whereas in most other countries it rose.[1]

'Generalised inefficiency'

Finally, there is a line of thought about Britain's economic growth which starts not so much with models of the economy but with economic history; it moves on to look not primarily at aggregate statistical series but rather at comparative industry case studies, concerning itself with a certain 'generalised inefficiency' in British industry compared with the situation in competing countries.

This particular approach has a long history: comparisons between British industries and their competitors, to the detriment of the British, date back to the turn of the century and beyond, with comments on Britain's excessive reliance on coal and textiles, on her failure to achieve economies of scale in the iron and steel industry and on her relative weakness in electrical, chemical and metallurgical industries.

There are obvious difficulties in drawing general conclusions from analyses of this type. First, it is always the problem industries which tend to get most attention and they are clearly atypical; secondly, it is always possible that one of the less efficient British firms is being compared with one of the more efficient foreign ones. Further, there is a very large number of facets in the detailed comparisons of firms' behaviour in different countries. Comparisons can be made of innovative ability and of design; of research and development expenditure; of capital stock per worker and of the age of installed equipment; of the organisation and manning of the productive processes; of the proportions of management to other staff; of delivery dates; of the effort put into the study of markets, and into salesmanship and after-sales service. The one thing that all these items have in common is that they are basically the responsibility of the management. However, management obviously works under a set of constraints – such as those imposed by government policy towards industry and government tax policy, by the availability of sources of finance for expansion, or by the 'countervailing power' of trade union organisations.

This line of thought leads to inquiries into such matters as management education and training, the rewards and status of industrial managers in comparison with those afforded by universities or the Civil Service, and the factors which contribute to, or detract from, management–worker cooperation in matters of efficiency. Economists have not given a great deal of attention to questions of this kind, tending to con-

[1] CSO, *Economic Trends*, no. 277, November 1976, p. 109.

sider that they fall outside their field. To quote G. C. Allen: '...economists tend, very naturally, when dealing with practical problems, to direct their attention to facets that can be illuminated by the methods of inquiry they find congenial. Their instruments are efficient within a range; but they often choose to ignore what lies outside it...so it happens that, on occasions, their inquiries do not penetrate beyond the periphery of fundamental problems.'[1] Nor have these matters been in any sense in the forefront of economic policy. There are no obvious instruments at hand to deal with them and any action which the government might take could only begin to have effects over the very long term.

Governments, in their industrial policies, have not given great prominence during the last fifteen years to promoting competition as a way of improving efficiency. Indeed, particularly in the early 1960s, there was a good deal of positive encouragement to mergers; as between encouraging mergers to promote structural change and constraining them to preserve competition, the encouragement clearly outweighed the constraint. Otherwise, direct intervention by governments in industry has largely consisted in rescue operations to preserve employment or to support technology, many of which, initially intended to be temporary (as with shipbuilding), have become permanent. They cannot be said to have made any major contribution to the improvement of economic performance.

Successive governments also found difficulty in adopting coherent policies for industries for which they were more directly responsible – that is, the nationalised industries. The commercial criteria which were elaborated during this period frequently came into conflict with social objectives; they also came into conflict with national economic strategy – notably when the nationalised industries were required to hold their prices down and so run substantial deficits. Since many nationalised industries are monopolies, their pricing policies (and for that matter their general wage and salary decisions) can hardly be left entirely without some supervision. However, the form of supervision during this period was less than ideal; the degree to which the government intervened in detail varied a great deal from time to time and from industry to industry. There is a possible case for some general supervisory body to set a coherent pattern of constraints within which the management of nationalised industries should operate – whether they are commercial criteria, social objectives, or the requirements of national economic policy. It could also conduct efficiency audits.

[1] G. C. Allen, *The British Disease*, London, Institute of Economic Affairs, 1976.

CONCLUSIONS

One main strand of criticism is that there was no continuity of economic policy during this period, mainly because of changes in government, and that this was damaging, particularly to economic growth. This lack of continuity, it is argued, added to the uncertainties of the time; if firms are sufficiently uncertain about the future they will tend not to initiate new ventures and uncertainty about government policy is clearly one element in the total. So the argument has been presented that frequent policy changes – and particularly policy reversals – have a damaging effect on confidence.

There is in addition the cost of policy changes. The public expenditure costs – of creating or altering some institution, for example – are not usually very big. The costs to the economy as a whole are often much greater, since, for example, with a change in company taxation, firms have to devote resources to learning the new rules, and there may well be significant costs of compliance. To take another example, the main costs of running a price control system fall not so much on the central government (in the costs of the Price Commission), but rather on the firms who have to do additional work to meet the requirements of the new laws.

Certainly, in most of the areas of economic policy covered in this book, there were a great many changes, and indeed frequent reversals, in policy. Perhaps anti-inflationary policy is the best example. There was no continuity in the attempt to establish institutions to modify the system of free collective bargaining. The 1964 Labour government abolished the National Incomes Commission and created the NBPI; the 1970 Conservative government abolished the NBPI and two years later created the Price Commission and the Pay Board; the 1974 Labour government abolished the Pay Board. Anti-inflationary policy is not the only example: in fiscal policy, the system of corporate taxation was changed in 1958, changed back again in 1965, and changed once more in 1973; there was also the change from investment allowances to investment grants and back again and, in the field of indirect taxation, there was the introduction and abolition of selective employment tax. In industrial relations there were the attempts to 'bring the trade unions within the framework of the law'; this legislation too was subsequently repealed. In policy towards the nationalised industries there was alternation between encouraging them to act as independent commercial concerns and forcing them to charge low prices in the interests of the government's anti-inflationary policy. In industrial policy the institution of one government – the IRC – was abolished by the next one. One of the few areas where there was a certain consistency was in commercial policy, where it was common ground between successive governments that Britain should if possible join the Common Market; but the reasons were primarily political – the economic gains or losses from EEC membership are uncertain.

There is no way of putting numbers on the effects of these policy changes; nor is it easy to demonstrate in a quantitative way that policy changes were more frequent in Britain than in other major industrial countries. However, the fact that effects cannot be quantified does not mean that they are non-existent; for example, multi-national companies considering in what country to expand must surely give some weight to continuity in economic policy.

Policy-makers in Britain have been faced with the problem of trying to compensate for the fact that Britain has a long history of relative lack of success as an industrial society. In a world where trade barriers have been falling, British industry has not competed successfully in world trade in manufactures: imports have risen very fast and Britain's share in world exports has fallen year by year. In consequence, it has proved increasingly difficult to combine full employment with an adequate balance of payments. Moves aiming at full employment, particularly towards the end of the period, tended to raise the volume of imports to such an extent that exports – with their share in the world market continuing to decline – were unable to finance them.

The second main problem, again emerging particularly towards the end of the period, was the tendency of the particular form of free collective bargaining which exists in Britain to deliver very high figures for the annual increase in money earnings. No doubt there would have been some level of unemployment which would have moderated this tendency, but it is difficult to say what it would have been, except that it would have been very high. Variations in unemployment within a lower range appeared to have little effect on the rate of increase in earnings. Under these circumstances it was not possible simply by demand management to obtain a reasonable combination of the standard objectives of economic policy. This is not to deny that demand management was, in a limited way, effective; that is, that changes in taxation or in government expenditure had effects on the level of employment which were not automatically cancelled by any consequent effects on the price trend (because the rate of inflation was relatively insensitive to unemployment over a wide range). The constraint on the use of demand management was essentially the balance of payments, which hampered moves towards full employment. At the same time, given the insensitivity of the rise in earnings to variations in the pressure of demand for labour, it was not practicable to use demand management to slow down the rise in earnings.

In an attempt to deal with the balance of payments constraint, the government, after initial reluctance, turned to the exchange rate – an instrument whose effectiveness depends, of course, on the reactions of import and export volumes to changes in relative prices.[1] It was not easy, either before or after devaluation, to calculate the size of these price effects; there tended to be a certain alternation of elasticity optimism and elasticity pessimism. The conclusion towards the end of the period was that a shift in relative prices, if maintained, was efficacious in a limited way. The problem with the use of the exchange rate was to retain the competitive advantage – that is, to prevent the rise in import prices triggering off such an acceleration in the rise in earnings that the advantage was rapidly lost. Particularly in the period of floating exchange rates, there appeared to be some danger of a vicious circle, by which a downward float led to an accelerating rate of inflation, so that the exchange rate fell again, and so on.

The problem of dealing with the excessively high increases in money earnings by means other than demand management led to episodic attempts at incomes policy. However, the alternation of policies was such that by the end of the period no permanent modification to the institutional structure had evolved. It is probably true that there had been a certain evolution towards recognising the need for something, but no significant advance to any consensus about what that 'something' should be.

The policy approach to the problems of low productivity, or generalised inefficiency, or low competitiveness – however it might be labelled – was relatively uncertain. This is perhaps not surprising, since it is not at all clear what measures might be effective. Both in the mid-1960s and the early 1970s it was hoped that, given a good prospect of rising demand coupled with an adequate balance of payments, these supply problems would dwindle in importance. How far this might have been true it is hard to say, since the condition of an adequate balance of payments over a reasonably long period of time was never met. In the first period this approach of 'going for growth' was coupled with an experiment in indicative planning, in the hope that this would induce confidence and, by persuading businessmen that faster growth was possible, would encourage them to increase investment and so help to bring it about.

There were not many policy measures *directly* addressed to the problems of low productivity. It is true that throughout the period fiscal encouragement to investment – either in the form of grants or tax allowances – was substantial. The main device tried for improving the general level of management was to encourage mergers (during the

---

[1] Or to changes in the profit margin on exports relative to the profit margin on home sales.

period of the Labour government) and to give a good deal of weight to selecting the best management team for the merged concern. Otherwise, there were a number of studies of the general level of efficiency or competitiveness in various industries. On the industrial relations side an attempt was made (by the Labour government) to impose some legal restraint on unofficial strikes. It failed, and the more extensive attempt to put certain legal limits on unions' industrial action by the Conservative government (the Industrial Relations Act) was also eventually abandoned. There were no government moves during this period to put forward legislation on workers' participation.

In sum, the problem of devising policies appropriate for a country with a relatively inefficient manufacturing sector and an unreformed pay bargaining system remained unsolved.

LIST OF WORKS CITED

I. BOOKS, ARTICLES AND PERIODICALS

ABBOTT, S. *Industrial Relations: Conservative policy*, London, Conservative Political Centre, 1966.

ALLEN, G. C. *The British Disease*, London, Institute of Economic Affairs, 1976.

ALLEN, R. I. G. and SAVAGE, D. 'Inflation and personal income tax', *National Institute Economic Review*, no. 70, November 1974.

ANDERMAN, S. D. *Unfair Dismissals and the Law*, London, Institute of Personnel Management, 1973.

ANDERSON, L. C. and JORDAN, J. L. 'Monetary and fiscal actions: a test of their relative importance in economic stabilization', *Federal Reserve Bank of St. Louis Review*, vol. 50, November 1968.

ARENA, J. J. 'Postwar stock market changes and consumer spending', *Review of Economics and Statistics*, vol. 47, November 1965.

ARTIS, M. J. 'Short-term economic forecasting at NIESR' in Hilton and Heathfield (eds.), 1970, q.v.

— 'Fiscal policy for stabilization' in Beckerman (ed.), 1972, q.v.

— 'Monetary policy in the 1970s in the light of recent developments' in Johnson and Nobay (eds.), 1974, q.v.

— 'Is there a wage equation?' in Courakis (ed.) (forthcoming), q.v.

ARTIS, M. J., KIERNAN, E. and WHITLEY, J. D. 'The effects of building society behaviour on housing investment' in Nobay and Parkin (eds.), 1975, q.v.

ARTIS, M. J. and LEWIS, M. K. 'The demand for money, stable or unstable?', *The Banker*, vol. 124, March 1974.

— 'The demand for money in the United Kingdom 1963–1973', *Manchester School of Economic and Social Studies*, vol. 44, June 1976.

ARTIS, M. J. and MEADOWS, P. 'Lending requests' and 'Lending requests: addendum' (unpublished NIESR working papers), 1974.

ARTIS, M. J. and NOBAY, A. R. 'Two aspects of the monetary debate', *National Institute Economic Review*, no. 49, August 1969.

ARTIS, M. J. and WALLACE, R. H. 'Assessing the fiscal impact' in N. Runcie (ed.), *Australian Monetary and Fiscal Policy: selected readings*, London University Press, 1971.

ARTUS, J. R. 'The 1967 devaluation of the pound sterling', *IMF Staff Papers*, vol. 22, November 1975.

ATKINSON, A. B. and SKEGG, T. C. 'Anti-smoking publicity and the demand for tobacco in the UK', *Manchester School of Economic and Social Studies*, vol. 41, September 1973.

BACON, R. W. and ELTIS, W. A. *Britain's Economic Problem: too few producers*, London, Macmillan, 1976.

BAIN, A. D. *The Control of the Money Supply*, London, Penguin, 1970.

BALASSA, B. *The Theory of Economic Integration*, London, Allen & Unwin, 1962.

BALL, R. J. 'The case against devaluation of the pound', *The Bankers' Magazine*, vol. 203, April 1967.

BALL, R. J., BURNS, T. and LAURY, J. S. E. 'The role of exchange rate changes in balance of payments adjustment', *Economic Journal*, vol. 87, March 1977.

BALL, R. J., BURNS, T. and MILLER, G. 'Preliminary simulations with the London Business School macro-economic model' in Renton (ed.), 1975, q.v.

BALL, R. J. and DRAKE, P. D. 'The impact of credit control on consumer durable spending in the United Kingdom, 1957–1961', *Review of Economic Studies*, vol. 30, October 1963.

BALOGH, T. 'Differential profits tax', *Economic Journal*, vol. 68, September 1958.

— *Planning for Progress: a strategy for Labour*, London, Fabian Society, 1963.

BALOPOULOS, E. T. *Fiscal Policy Models of the British Economy*, Amsterdam, North-Holland, 1967.

The Banker (monthly).

BARKER, T. S. 'Aggregation error and estimates of the UK import demand function in Hilton and Heathfield (eds.), 1970, q.v.

BECKERMAN, W. 'Demand, exports and growth' in Beckerman and Associates, 1965, q.v.

— 'The determinants of economic growth' in P. D. Henderson (ed.), *Economic Growth in Britain*, London, Weidenfeld & Nicholson, 1966.

— (ed.) *The Labour Government's Economic Record 1964–1970*, London, Duckworth, 1972.

BECKERMAN, W. and Associates. *The British Economy in 1975*, Cambridge University Press, 1965.

BEVERIDGE, W. H. *Full Employment in a Free Society*, London, Allen & Unwin, 1944.

BIRKENHEAD, Earl of. *The Prof in Two Worlds: the official life of Professor F. A. Lindemann, Viscount Cherwell*, London, Collins, 1961.

BLACK, I. G., KIDGELL, J. E. and RAY, G. F. 'Forecasting imports: a re-examination', *National Institute Economic Review*, no. 42, November 1967.

BLINDER, A. S. and SOLOW, R. M. 'Analytical foundations of fiscal policy' in *The Economics of Public Finance*, Washington (DC), Brookings Institution, 1974.

BOATWRIGHT, B. D. and RENTON, G. A. 'An analysis of United Kingdom inflows and out-flows of direct foreign investment', *Review of Economics and Statistics*, vol. 57, November 1975.

Bow Group. *Monopolies and Mergers*, London, Conservative Political Centre, 1963.

— *Crossbow* (quarterly).

BRANDON, H. *In the Red: the struggle for sterling, 64/66*, London, Deutsch, 1966.

BRECHLING, F. P. R. and CLAYTON, G. 'Commercial banks' portfolio behaviour', *Economic Journal*, vol. 75, June 1965.

BRECHLING, F. P. R. and LIPSEY, R. E. 'Trade credit and monetary policy', *Economic Journal*, vol. 73, December 1963.

BRECHLING, F. P. R. and SURREY, A. J. 'An international comparison of production tech-niques: the coal-fired electricity generating industry', *National Institute Economic Review*, no. 36, May 1966.

BRECHLING, F. P. R. and WOLFE, J. N. 'The end of stop–go', *Lloyds Bank Review*, no. 75, January 1965.

BRIDGES, Lord. *The Treasury*, London, Allen & Unwin, 1964.

BRISTOW, J. A. 'Taxation and income stabilisation', *Economic Journal*, vol. 78, June 1968.

BRITTAN, S. 'The selective employment tax', *The Banker*, vol. 116, June 1966.

— 'Money supply: the great debate', *Financial Times*, 25 October 1968.

— 'Four propositions about the money supply', *Financial Times*, 23 January 1969.

— *Steering the Economy: the role of the Treasury* (rev. edn), London, Penguin, 1971.

BROWN, A. J. *The Framework of Regional Economics in the United Kingdom*, Cambridge University Press, 1972.

BROWN, C. V. and LEVIN, E. 'The effects of income taxation on overtime: the results of a national survey', *Economic Journal*, vol. 84, December 1974.

BROWN, G. *In My Way*, London, Gollancz, 1971.

BUCHANAN, J. M. 'Easy budgets and tight money', *Lloyds Bank Review*, no. 64, April 1962.

BURNS, T. 'An econometric analysis of UK imports 1958–68' (London Graduate Business School discussion paper), 1969.

Business (monthly).

CAIRNCROSS, Sir Alec (ed.) *Britain's Economic Prospects Reconsidered*, London, Allen & Unwin, 1970.

— (ed.) *The Managed Economy*, Oxford, Blackwell, 1970.

— *Control of Long-Term International Capital Movements*, Washington (DC), Brookings Institu-tion, 1973.

CATHERWOOD, H. F. R. *Britain with the Brakes Off*, London, Hodder & Stoughton, 1966.

CAVES, R. E. and Associates. *Britain's Economic Prospects*, London, Allen & Unwin, 1968.

CHATAWAY, C. *New Deal for Industry*, London, Conservative Political Centre, 1972.

CHESTER, T. E. 'The public sector – its dimensions and dynamics', *National Westminster Bank Review*, February 1976.

CHOWN, J. F. *The Reform of the Corporation Tax*, London, Institute for Fiscal Studies, 1971.

CHOWN, J. F. 'The reform of the corporation tax: some international factors', *British Tax Review*, no. 4, 1971.

CLARKE, Sir Richard. *The Management of the Public Sector of the National Economy*, London, Athlone Press, 1964.

— 'Mintech in retrospect – II', *Omega*, vol. 1, April 1973.

CLEGG, H. *How to Run an Incomes Policy and Why We Made Such a Mess of the Last One*, London, Heinemann, 1971.

COASE, R. H. 'The marginal cost controversy', *Economica*, vol. 13 (new series), August 1946.

— 'The marginal cost controversy: some further comments', *Economica*, vol. 14 (new series), May 1947.

COGHLAN, R. L. 'Special Deposits and bank advances', *The Bankers' Magazine*, vol. 216, August 1973.

— 'Bank competition and bank size', *Manchester School of Economic and Social Studies*, vol. 43, June 1975.

COHEN, L. 'An empirical measurement of the built-in flexibility of the individual income tax', *American Economic Association Papers and Proceedings*, vol. 49, May 1959.

Confederation of British Industry. *Industrial Trends Survey* (3-monthly).

Conservative Political Centre. *Monopoly and the Public Interest* [Poole Report], London, 1963.

— *Fair Deal at Work*, London, 1968.

COOPER, R. N. 'The balance of payments' in Caves *et al.*, 1968, q.v.

COPPOCK, D. J. and GIBSON, N. J. 'The volume of deposits and the cash and liquid assets ratios', *Manchester School of Economic and Social Studies*, vol. 31, September 1963.

CORDEN, W. M. 'The efficiency effects of trade and protection' in I. A. McDougall and R. H. Snape (eds.), *Studies in International Economics*, Amsterdam, North-Holland, 1970.

COURAKIS, A. S. (ed.) *Inflation, Depression and Economic Policy in the West: lessons from the 1970s*, Oxford, Blackwell (forthcoming).

COUTTS, K., TARLING, R. and WILKINSON, F. 'Wage bargaining and the inflation process' *Economic Policy Review*, no. 2, March 1976.

CROCKETT, A. D. 'Timing relationships between movements of monetary and national income variables', *Bank of England Quarterly Bulletin*, vol. 10, December 1970.

CROSLAND, C. A. R. *The Future of Socialism*, London, Cape, 1956.

CROUCH, R. L. 'A re-examination of open-market equations', *Oxford Economic Papers*, vol. 15 (new series), July 1963.

— 'The inadequacy of "new orthodox" methods of monetary control', *Economic Journal*, vol. 74, December 1964.

— 'Special Deposits and the British monetary mechanism', *Economic Studies*, vol. 5, February 1970.

DANIEL, W. W. *Whatever Happened to the Workers in Woolwich? A survey of redundancy in SE London*, London, Political and Economic Planning, 1972.

DEAN, A. J. H. 'Earnings in the public and private sectors 1950–1975', *National Institute Economic Review*, no. 74, November 1975.

DEATON, A. S. 'Wealth effects on consumption in a modified life-cycle model', *Review of Economic Studies*, vol. 39, October 1972.

DENNISON, S. R. 'Investment in the nationalised industries' (paper given to the Manchester Statistical Society, 11 February 1959).

DICKS-MIREAUX, L. A. and DOW, J. C. R. 'The determinants of wage inflation: United Kingdom, 1946–56', *Journal of the Royal Statistical Society* (series A), vol. 122, pt 2, 1959.

DORRINGTON, J. C. and RENTON, G. A. 'A study of the effects of direct taxation on consumers' expenditure' in Renton (ed.), 1975, q.v.

DOW, J. C. R. 'Analysis of the generation of price inflation', *Oxford Economic Papers*, vol. 8 (new series), October 1956.

— *The Management of the British Economy, 1945–60*, Cambridge University Press, 1964.

Economist (weekly).

Economist Intelligence Unit. *Britain and Europe*, London, 1957.

ELLIOTT, D. and GRIBBIN, J. D. 'The abolition of cartels and structural change in the United Kingdom' in A. P. Jacquemin and H. W. de Jong (eds.), *Welfare Aspects of Industrial Markets*, Leiden, Nijhoff, 1977.

EL-MOKADEM, A. M. *Econometric Models of Personal Saving. The United Kingdom, 1948–1966*, London, Butterworths, 1973.

EVELY, R. W. 'The effects of the price code', *National Institute Economic Review*, no. 77, August, 1976.

FANE, G. and WHITLEY, J. D. 'Imports of goods and services' (unpublished NIESR working paper), 1973.

Federation of British Industries. *The Next Five Years*, London, 1960.

FELDSTEIN, M. S. and FANE, G. 'Taxes, corporate dividend policy and personal savings: the British postwar experience', *Review of Economics and Statistics*, vol. 55, November 1973.

FISHER, D. 'The instruments of monetary policy and the generalised trade-off function for Britain, 1955–1968', *Manchester School of Economic and Social Studies*, vol. 38, September 1970.

— 'Targets and indicators of British monetary policy', *The Bankers' Magazine*, vol. 216, August 1973.

FLANDERS, A. *Management and Unions*, London, Faber & Faber, 1970.

FLANDERS, A. and CLEGG, H. (eds.) *The System of Industrial Relations in Great Britain: its history, law and institutions*, Oxford, Blackwell, 1954.

FLEMMING, J. S. *Inflation*, London, Oxford University Press, 1976.

FOSTER, C. D. and BEESLEY, M. E. 'Estimating the social benefit of constructing an underground railway in London', *Journal of the Royal Statistical Society* (series A), vol. 126, pt 1, 1963.

FREEMAN, C. *The Economics of Industrial Innovation*, London, Penguin, 1974.

FRIEDMAN, M. 'A monetary and fiscal framework for economic stability', *American Economic Review*, vol. 38, June 1948.

— 'The role of monetary policy', *American Economic Review*, vol. 58, March 1968.

— 'A theoretical framework for monetary analysis', *Journal of Political Economy*, vol. 78, March–April 1970.

FRIEDMAN, M. and MEISELMAN, D. 'The relative stability of monetary velocity and the investment multiplier in the United States 1897–1958' in Commission on Money and Credit, *Stabilization Policies*, Englewood Cliffs (NJ), Prentice-Hall, 1963.

FRIEDMAN, M. and SCHWARTZ, A. J. 'Money and business cycles', *Review of Economics and Statistics*, vol. 45, February 1963.

FRIEDMAN, M., WINCOTT, H. and TOOBY, F. 'The money supply debate', *The Banker*, vol. 118, December 1968.

FRY, R. 'Government spending overseas: how it has risen', *The Banker*, vol. 118, June 1968.

FRYER, R. H. 'The myths of the Redundancy Payments Act', *Industrial Law Journal*, vol. 2, March 1973.

GALBRAITH, J. K. *The Affluent Society*, London, Hamish Hamilton, 1958.

Gallup Poll. 'British attitudes to the EEC, 1960–63', *Journal of Common Market Studies*, vol. 5, September 1966.

— 'Public opinion and the EEC', *Journal of Common Market Studies*, vol. 6, March 1968.

GARGANAS, N. 'An analysis of consumer credit and its effects on purchases of consumer durables' in Renton (ed.), 1975, q.v.

GIBSON, N. J. 'Special Deposits as an instrument of monetary policy', *Manchester School of Economic and Social Studies*, vol. 32, September 1964.

— 'Monetary credit and fiscal policies' in A. R. Prest (ed.), *The UK Economy: a manual of applied economics* (2nd edn), London, Weidenfeld & Nicolson, 1968.

GODLEY, W. A. H. 'The measurement and control of public expenditure', *Economic Policy Review*, no. 2, March 1976.

GODLEY, W. A. H. and SHEPHERD, J. R. 'Long-term growth and short-term policy', *National Institute Economic Review*, no. 29, August 1964.

GOODHART, C. A. E. 'Monetary policy in the United Kingdom' in K. Holbik (ed.), *Monetary Policy in Twelve Industrial Countries*, Boston (Mass.), Federal Reserve Bank of Boston, 1973.

— 'Problems of monetary management: the UK experience' in Courakis (ed.) (forthcoming), q.v.

GOODHART, C. A. E. and CROCKETT, A. D. 'The importance of money', *Bank of England Quarterly Bulletin*, vol. 10, June 1970.

GRIFFITHS, B. 'Resource efficiency, monetary policy and the reform of the UK banking system', *Journal of Money, Credit and Banking*, vol. 5, February 1973 (pt I).

GROOME, D. R. and JOHNSON, H. G. (eds.) *Money in Britain 1959–1969*, London, Oxford University Press, 1970.

GRUNFELD, C. *Trade Unions and the Individual*, London, Fabian Society, 1957.

HACCHE, G. 'The demand for money in the United Kingdom: experience since 1971', *Bank of England Quarterly Bulletin*, vol. 14, September 1974.

HALL, Sir Robert. 'Britain's economic problem', *Economist*, 16 and 23 September 1961.

HAN, S. S. and LIESNER, H. H. *Britain and the Common Market: the effect of entry on the pattern of manufacturing production*, Cambridge University Press, 1971.

HARRIS, L. 'The Chicago school of thought', *The Bankers' Magazine*, vol. 208, July 1969.

HARROD, Sir Roy. 'Are monetary and fiscal policies enough?', *Economic Journal*, vol. 74, December 1964.

HARTLEY, K. 'The mergers in the UK aircraft industry 1957–60', *Journal of the Royal Aeronautical Society*, vol. 69, December 1965.

— *A Market for Aircraft. A critique and a proposal for radical reconstruction of British Government procurement policy*, London, Institute of Economic Affairs, 1974.

HEATH, J. B. *Still Not Enough Competition*, London, Institute of Economic Affairs, 1963.

HECLO, H. and WILDAVSKY, A. *The Private Government of Public Money*, London, Macmillan, 1974.

HENRY, S. G. B., SAWYER, M. C. and SMITH, P. 'Models of inflation in the United Kingdom', *National Institute Economic Review*, no. 77, August 1976.

HEPPLE, B. 'Union responsibility for shop stewards', *Industrial Law Journal*, vol. 1, December 1972.

HERRINGTON, P. R. 'Walters on money – a review article', *The Bankers' Magazine*, vol. 208, July 1969.

HICKS, J. R. 'Mr. Keynes and the "Classics": a suggested interpretation', *Econometrica*, vol. 5, April 1937.

— *After the Boom: thoughts on the 1966 economic crisis*, London, Institute of Economic Affairs, 1966.

HICKS, U. K. 'Plowden, planning and management in the public services', *Public Administration*, vol. 39, Winter 1961.

HILTON, K. and CROSSFIELD, D. 'Short-run consumption functions for the UK, 1955–66' in Hilton and Heathfield (eds.), 1970, q.v.

HILTON, K. and HEATHFIELD, D. F. (eds.) *The Econometric Study of the United Kingdom*, London, Macmillan, 1970.

HINES, A. G. and CATEPHORES, G. 'Investment in UK manufacturing industry, 1956–67', in Hilton and Heathfield (eds.), 1970, q.v.

HODJERA, Z. 'Short-term capital movements of the United Kingdom, 1963–1967', *Journal of Political Economy*, vol. 79, July–Aug. 1971.

HOPKIN, W. A. B. and GODLEY, W. A. H. 'An analysis of tax changes', *National Institute Economic Review*, no. 32, May 1965.

HUNTER, A. *Competition and the Law*, London, Allen & Unwin, 1966.

HUTCHISON, T. W. *Economics and Economic Policy in Britain, 1946–1966: some aspects of their interrelations*, London, Allen & Unwin, 1968.

HUTTON, J. P. 'A model of short-term capital movements, the foreign exchange market and official intervention in the UK, 1963–1971' (mimeo.), 1974.

— 'A model of short-term capital movements, the foreign exchange market and official intervention in the UK, 1963–70', *Review of Economic Studies*, vol. 44, February 1977.

HYMAN, R. *Strikes*, Glasgow, Fontana-Collins, 1972.

Inns of Court Conservative and Unionist Society. *A Giant's Strength: some thoughts on the constitutional and legal position of Trade Unions in England*, London, 1958.

JAKOBSSON, U. 'On the measurement of the degree of progression', *Journal of Public Economics*, vol. 5, Jan.–Feb. 1976.

JENKINS, P. *The Battle of Downing Street*, London, Charles Knight, 1970.

JEWKES, J., SAWERS, D. and STILLERMAN, R. *The Sources of Invention* (2nd edn), London, Macmillan, 1969.

JOHNSON, H. G. 'The gains from freer trade in Europe: an estimate', *Manchester School of Economic and Social Studies*, vol. 26, September 1958.

JOHNSON, H. G. and NOBAY, A. R. (eds.) *Issues in Monetary Economics*, London, Oxford University Press, 1974.

JOHNSON, P. 'Tackling the Treasury octopus', *New Statesman*, 14 February 1963.

JOHNSTON, J. and HENDERSON, M. 'Assessing the effects of the import surcharge', *Manchester School of Economic and Social Studies*, vol. 35, May 1967.

KAHN-FREUND, O. *Labour and the Law*, London, Stevens, 1972.

KALDOR, N. *Essays on Economic Policy*, London, Duckworth, 1964.

— *Causes of the Slow Rate of Economic Growth of the United Kingdom*, Cambridge University Press, 1966.

— 'Productivity and growth in manufacturing industry: a reply', *Economica*, vol. 35 (new series), November 1968.

— 'The new monetarism', *Lloyds Bank Review*, no. 97, July 1970.

— (ed.) *Conflicts in Policy Objectives*, Oxford, Blackwell, 1971.

— 'The truth about the dynamic effects', *New Statesman*, 12 March 1971.

KENNEDY, C. and THIRLWALL, A. P. 'Technical progress: a survey', *Economic Journal*, vol. 82, March 1972.

KENNEDY, M. C. 'How well does the National Institute forecast?', *National Institute Economic Review*, no. 50, November 1969.

— 'Employment policy: what went wrong?' in Joan Robinson (ed.), *After Keynes*, Oxford, Blackwell, 1973.

KEYNES, J. M. *The General Theory of Employment, Interest and Money*, London, Macmillan, 1936.

KINDLEBERGER, C. P. *International Economics* (3rd edn), Homewood (Ill.), Irwin, 1963.

KING, M. A. 'The United Kingdom profits crisis: myth or reality?', *Economic Journal*, vol. 85, March 1975.

KIRSCHEN, E. S. (ed.) *Economic Policies Compared: West and East*. Vol. I: *General Theory*. Amsterdam, North-Holland, 1974.

KIRSCHEN, E. S. *et al. Economic Policy in Our Time*. Vol. I: *General Theory*, Amsterdam, North-Holland, 1964.

KITZINGER, U. *The Second Try: Labour and the EEC*, Oxford, Pergamon, 1968.

Labour Party. *Signposts for the Sixties*, London, 1961.

— *Industrial Training*, London, 1967.

LAIDLER, D. E. W. 'The influence of money on economic activity – a survey of some current problems' in G. Clayton, J. C. Gilbert and R. Sedgwick (eds.), *Monetary Theory and Monetary Policy in the 1970s*, London, Oxford University Press, 1971.

LAIDLER, D. E. W. and PARKIN, J. M. 'The demand for money in the United Kingdom 1956–1967: preliminary estimates', *Manchester School of Economic and Social Studies*, vol. 38, September 1970.

LANGE, O. and TAYLOR, F. *On the Economic Theory of Socialism*, Minneapolis, University of Minnesota Press, 1938.

LEES, D. and CHIPLIN, B. 'The economics of industrial training', *Lloyds Bank Review*, no. 96, April 1970.

LERNER, A. P. *The Economics of Control: principles of welfare economics*, New York, Macmillan, 1944.

LESTER, T. 'The unmaking of Mintech', *Management Today*, November 1973.

LEWIS, R. 'Unfair industrial practices', *Industrial Relations Review and Report*, no. 15, September 1971.

— 'The historical development of labour law', *British Journal of Industrial Relations*, vol. 14, March 1976.

LEWIS, R. and LATTA, G. 'Bargaining units and bargaining agents', *British Journal of Industrial Relations*, vol. 10, March 1972.

LIEBENSTEIN, H. 'Allocative efficiency vs. "X-efficiency"', *American Economic Review*, vol. 56, June 1966.

LITTLE, I. M. D. *The Price of Fuel*, Oxford, Clarendon Press, 1953.

— 'Higgledy piggledy growth', *Bulletin of the Oxford University Institute of Statistics*, vol. 24, November 1962.

Local Government Finance (monthly).

London and Cambridge Economic Bulletin (quarterly).

McCARTHY, W. E. J. 'The reasons given for striking: an analysis of official statistics, 1945–1957', *Bulletin of the Oxford University Institute of Statistics*, vol. 21, February 1959.

— 'The nature of Britain's strike problem', *British Journal of Industrial Relations*, vol. 8, July 1970.

McCLELLAND, W. G. 'The Industrial Reorganisation Corporation 1966/71: an experimental prod', *Three Banks Review*, no. 94, June 1972.

MacDOUGALL, Sir Donald and HUTT, R. 'Imperial Preference: a quantitative analysis', *Economic Journal*, vol. 64, June 1954.

Machinery and Production Engineering. *Survey of Machine Tool Statistics 1951–1970 Inclusive*, Brighton, Machinery Publishing Co., 1971.

MACKAY, D. I. 'After the "Shake-out"', *Oxford Economic Papers*, vol. 24 (new series), March 1972.

MACMILLAN, H. *The Middle Way*, London, Macmillan, 1939.

— *Riding the Storm, 1956–1959*, London, Macmillan, 1971.

— *Pointing the Way, 1959–1961*, London, Macmillan, 1972.

— *At the End of the Day, 1961–1963*, London, Macmillan, 1973.

Management Today (monthly).

MARRIS, R. *The Machinery of Economic Policy*, London, Fabian Society, 1954.

MEADE, J. E. 'The case for variable exchange rates', *Three Banks Review*, no. 27, September 1955.

— *The Theory of Customs Unions*, Amsterdam, North-Holland, 1955.

MEADE, J. E. and FLEMING, J. M. 'Price and output policy of state enterprise: a symposium', *Economic Journal*, vol. 54, December 1944.

MEEK, R. L. 'The new bulk supply tariff for electricity', *Economic Journal*, vol. 78, March 1968.

— 'Electricity costs: a reply (1)', *Economic Journal*, vol. 78, December 1968.

Midland Bank Review (quarterly).

MILES, C. *Lancashire Textiles: a case study of industrial change*, Cambridge University Press, 1968.

MILLER, M. H. 'An empirical analysis of monetary policy in the UK, 1954–1965' (unpublished PhD thesis, Yale), 1971.

— 'Money, output and inflation: a critique of some recent monetarist developments in the UK', *Manchester School of Economic and Social Studies* (forthcoming).

MILLER, M. M. 'Estimates of the static balance-of-payments and welfare costs compared' in Pinder (ed.), 1971, q.v.

MODIGLIANI, F. 'The life cycle hypothesis of saving twenty years later' in Nobay and Parkin (eds.), 1975, q.v.

— 'The channels of monetary policy in the Federal Reserve–MIT–University of Pennsylvania econometric model of the US' in Renton (ed.), 1975, q.v.

MORGAN, A. D. and MARTIN, D. 'Tariff reductions and UK imports of manufactures: 1955–1971', *National Institute Economic Review*, no. 72, May 1975.

MORGAN, D. R. *Over-taxation by Inflation*, London, Institute of Economic Affairs, 1977.

MOSLEY, P. 'Towards a "satisficing" theory of economic policy', *Economic Journal*, vol. 86, March 1976.

MUKHERJEE, S. *Changing Manpower Needs: a study of Industrial Training Boards*, London, Political and Economic Planning, 1970.

— *Through No Fault of Their Own: systems of handling redundancies in Britain, France and Germany*, London, Macdonald, 1973.

MUSGRAVE, R. A. 'On measuring fiscal performance', *Review of Economics and Statistics*, vol. 46, May 1964.

MUSGRAVE, R. A. and MILLER, M. H. 'Built-in flexibility', *American Economic Review*, vol. 38, March 1948.

MUSGRAVE, R. A. and MUSGRAVE, P. B. 'Fiscal policy' in Caves *et al.*, 1968, q.v.

— *Public Finance: in theory and practice*, London, McGraw Hill, 1975.

MUSGRAVE, R. A. and THIN, T. 'Income tax progression, 1929–48', *Journal of Political Economy*, vol. 56, December 1948.

NABSETH, L. and RAY, G. F. (eds.) *The Diffusion of New Industrial Processes: an international study*, Cambridge University Press, 1974.

National Institute Economic Review (quarterly).

National Union of Conservative and Unionist Associations. *Verbatim Report: 88th Conservative Conference, Blackpool 1970*, London, 1970.

NEILD, R. R. and SHIRLEY, E. A. '*Economic Review:* an assessment of forecasts, 1959–1960', *National Institute Economic Review*, no. 15, May 1961.

NEILD, R. R. and WARD, T. *The Budgetary Situation: an appraisal*, Department of Applied Economics, University of Cambridge, 1976.

NEWLYN, W. T. 'The supply of money and its control', *Economic Journal*, vol. 74, June 1964.

NICKELL, S. 'Tax structure and financial policy' in M. J. Artis and A. R. Nobay (eds.), *Studies in Modern Economic Analysis*, Oxford, Blackwell, 1977.

NIESR. 'The effects of the devaluation of 1967 on the current balance of payments', *Economic Journal*, vol. 82, March 1972 (supplement).

NOBAY, A. R. 'A model of the United Kingdom monetary authorities' behaviour 1959–1969' in Johnson and Nobay (eds.), 1974, q.v.

NOBAY, A. R. and PARKIN, J. M. (eds.) *Contemporary Issues in Economics*, Manchester University Press, 1975.

NORTON, W. E. 'Debt management and monetary policy in the United Kingdom', *Economic Journal*, vol. 79, September 1969.

OAKLAND, W. H. 'Budgetary measures of fiscal performance', *Southern Economic Journal*, vol. 35, April 1969.

OHERLIHY, C. St J. and SPENCER, J. E. 'Building societies' behaviour, 1955–70', *National Institute Economic Review*, no. 61, August 1972.

OPPENHEIMER, P. M. 'Is Britain's worsening trade gap due to bad management of the business cycle?', *Bulletin of the Oxford University Institute of Economic & Statistics*, vol. 27, August 1965.

— 'Forward exchange intervention: the official view', *Westminster Bank Review*, February 1966.

ORHNIAL, A. J. H. and FOLDES, L. P. 'Estimates of marginal tax rates for dividends and bond interest in the United Kingdom, 1919–1970', *Economica*, vol. 42, February 1975.

OUTRAM, Q. 'The significance of public expenditure plans' (unpublished working paper, Centre for Studies in Social Policy), 1975.

PAIGE, D. C. 'Economic growth: the last hundred years', *National Institute Economic Review*, no. 16, July 1961.

PAISH, F. W. *Studies in an Inflationary Economy: the United Kingdom 1948–1961*, London, Macmillan, 1962.

PARKER, J. E. S. *The Economics of Innovation: the national and multinational enterprise in technological change*, London, Longman, 1974.

PARKIN, J. M. 'Where is Britain's inflation going?', *Lloyds Bank Review*, no. 117, July 1975.

PARKIN, J. M., GRAY, M. R. and BARRETT, R. J. 'The portfolio behaviour of commercial banks' in Hilton and Heathfield (eds.), 1970, q.v.

PEACOCK, A. T. and SHAW, G. K. *The Economic Theory of Fiscal Policy*, London, Allen & Unwin, 1971.

PEACOCK, A. T. and WISEMAN, J. *The Growth of Public Expenditure in the United Kingdom*, Princeton University Press, 1961.

PECHMAN, J. A. 'Yield of the individual income tax during a recession' in National Bureau of Economic Research, *Policies to Combat Depression*, Princeton University Press, 1956.

PHILLIPS, A. W. 'The relation between unemployment and the rate of change of money wage rates in the United Kingdom, 1861–1957', *Economica*, vol. 25 (new series), November 1958.

PICKLES, W. 'Trade unions in the political climate' in B. C. Roberts (ed.), *Industrial Relations: contemporary problems and perspectives*, London, Methuen, 1962.

PINDER, J. (ed.) *The Economics of Europe: what the Common Market means for Britain*, London, Charles Knight, 1971.

PISSARIDES, C. A. 'A model of British macroeconomic policy, 1955–1969', *Manchester School of Economic and Social Studies*, vol. 40, September 1972.

POLAK, J. J. 'Monetary analysis of income formation and payments problems', *IMF Staff Papers*, vol. 6, November 1957.

POLANYI, G. *Planning in Britain: the experience of the 1960s*, London, Institute of Economic Affairs, 1967.

Political and Economic Planning. *Growth in the British Economy: a study of economic problems and policies in contemporary Britain*, London, Allen & Unwin, 1960.

— 'Economic planning in France', *Planning*, vol. 27, 14 August 1961.

POOLE, W. 'Optimal choice of monetary policy instruments in a simple stochastic macro model', *Quarterly Journal of Economics*, vol. 84, May 1970.

PORTNEY, P. R. 'Congressional delays in U.S. fiscal policymaking: simulating the effects', *Journal of Public Economics*, vol. 5, April–May 1976.

POSNER, M. V. *Fuel Policy: a study in applied economics*, London, Macmillan, 1973.

PRAIS, S. J. *The Evolution of Giant Firms in Britain*, Cambridge University Press, 1976.

PREEG, E. H. *Traders and Diplomats: an analysis of the Kennedy Round of negotiations under the General Agreement on Tariffs and Trade*, Washington (DC), Brookings Institution, 1970.

PREST, A. R. *The Capital Gains Tax and the Corporation Tax*, London, Woolwich Polytechnic, 1967.

— 'Sense and nonsense in budgetary policy', *Economic Journal*, vol. 78, March 1968.

— 'The Select Committee on corporation tax', *British Tax Review*, no. 1, 1972.

— *Public Finance: in theory and practice*, London, Weidenfeld & Nicolson, 1st edn. 1965 and 5th edn. 1975.

PRICE, L. D. D. 'The demand for money in the United Kingdom: a further investigation', *Bank of England Quarterly Bulletin*, vol. 12, March 1972.

PRICE, R. W. R. 'Some aspects of the progressive income tax structure in the UK', *National Institute Economic Review*, no. 65, August 1973.

— 'A model of the indirect tax system in the UK, 1956–72' (unpublished NIESR working paper), 1977.

PRYKE, R. *Public Enterprise in Practice*, London, MacGibbon & Kee, 1971.

REDDAWAY, W. B. 'The productivity effects of selective employment tax – a reply', *National Institute Economic Review*, no. 57, August 1971.

— *Effects of the Selective Employment Tax: final report*, Cambridge University Press, 1973.

REDDAWAY, W. B. and SMITH, A. D. 'Progress in British manufacturing industries in the period 1948–54', *Economic Journal*, vol. 70, March 1960.

RENTON, G. A. (ed.) *Modelling the Economy*, London, Heinemann, 1975.

ROBERTS, B. C. 'Trade unions in the welfare state', *Political Quarterly*, vol. 27, Jan.–March 1956.

— *Trade Unions in a Free Society*, London, Institute of Economic Affairs, 1959.

ROBERTSON, D. J. 'Trade unions and wages policy', *Political Quarterly*, vol. 27, Jan.–March 1956.

— Introduction to a symposium on the British balance of payments, *Scottish Journal of Political Economy*, vol. 13, February 1966.

ROWTHORN, R. E. 'What remains of Kaldor's law?', *Economic Journal*, vol. 85, March 1975.

ROY, A. D. 'Short-term forecasting for central economic management of the UK economy' in Hilton and Heathfield (eds.), 1970, q.v.

RUBNER, A. 'The irrelevancy of the British differential profits tax', *Economic Journal*, vol. 74, June 1964.

RUGGLES, N. 'Recent developments in the theory of marginal cost pricing' in R. Turvey (ed.), *Public Enterprise: selected readings*, Harmondsworth, Penguin, 1968.

SANDFORD, C. T. *Economics of Public Finance: an economic analysis of public expenditure and revenue in the United Kingdom*, Oxford, Pergamon, 1969.

SANDFORD, C. T. and DEAN, P. N. 'Public expenditure: the paradox of control', *The Banker*, vol. 120, April 1970.

SCHWARTZ, A. J. 'Why money matters', *Lloyds Bank Review*, no. 94, October 1969.

SCITOVSKY, T. *Economic Theory and Western European Integration*, London, Allen & Unwin, 1958.

SCOTT, M. FG. 'What should be done about the Sterling Area?', *Bulletin of the Oxford University Institute of Statistics*, vol. 21, November 1959.

— 'Should the pound be devalued?', *The Bankers' Magazine*, vol. 203, April 1967.

SEERS, D. and STREETEN, P. 'Overseas development policies' in Beckerman (ed.), 1972, q.v.

SHANKS, M. 'The comforts of stagnation', *Encounter*, July 1963.

SHARP, G. and CAPSTICK, C. W. 'The place of agriculture in the national economy', *Journal of Agricultural Economics*, vol. 17, May 1966.

SHEPHERD, J. R. and SURREY, M. J. C. 'The short-term effects of tax changes', *National Institute Economic Review*, no. 46, November 1968.

SHONFIELD, A. *British Economic Policy since the War*, Harmondsworth, Penguin, 1958.

— *Modern Capitalism: the changing balance of public and private power*, London, Oxford University Press, 1965.

SIMS, C. A. 'Money, income and causality', *American Economic Review*, vol. 62, September 1972.

SPRAOS, J. 'Speculation, arbitrage and sterling', *Economic Journal*, vol. 69, March 1959.

STONE, R. 'Private saving in Britain, past, present and future', *Manchester School of Economic and Social Studies*, vol. 32, May 1964.

STURMEY, S. G. 'Cost curves and pricing in aircraft production', *Economic Journal*, vol. 74, December 1964.

SUMNER, M. T. *The Effect of Taxation on Corporate Saving and Investment*, London, Institute for Fiscal Studies, 1976.

SURREY, M. J. C. 'Personal incomes and consumers' expenditure' in Hilton and Heathfield (eds.), 1970, q.v.

— 'The National Plan in retrospect', *Bulletin of the Oxford University Institute of Economics & Statistics*, vol. 34, August 1972.

SUTHERLAND, A. *The Monopolies Commission in Action*, Cambridge University Press, 1969.

SWANN, D., O'BRIEN, D. P., MAUNDER, W. P. and HOWE, W. S. *Competition in British Industry: restrictive practices legislation in theory and practice*, London, Allen & Unwin, 1974.

Textile Council. *Cotton and Allied Textiles: a report on present performance and future prospects*, Manchester, 1969.

THORNEYCROFT, P. 'Policy in practice' in *Not Unanimous*, London, Institute of Economic Affairs, 1960.

TINBERGEN, J. *Economic Policy: principles and design*, Amsterdam, North-Holland, 1956.

TOBIN, J. 'Money and income: post hoc ergo propter hoc?', *Quarterly Journal of Economics*, vol. 84, May 1970.

— 'Friedman's theoretical framework', *Journal of Political Economy*, vol. 80, Sept.–Oct. 1972.

Trades Union Congress. *Reason: the case against the government's proposals on industrial relations*, London, 1970.

— *Good Industrial Relations: a guide for negotiators*, London, 1971.

— *The Chequers and Downing Street Talks – July to November 1972: report*, London, 1972.

— *Handbook on the Industrial Relations Act*, London, 1972.

— *Trade Unions and Training for the Future*, London, 1972.

— *Economic Review* (annual).

— *Report of the Annual Trades Union Congress*.

TURNER, G. *The Leyland Papers*, London, Eyre & Spottiswood, 1971.

TURNER, H. A. *The Trend of Strikes*, Leeds University Press, 1963.

— *Is Britain Really Strike Prone? A review of the incidence, character and costs of industrial conflict*, Department of Applied Economics, University of Cambridge, 1969.

TURVEY, R. 'Electricity costs: a comment', *Economic Journal*, vol. 78, December 1968.

— *Optimal Pricing and Investment in Electricity Supply: an essay in applied welfare economics*, London, Allen & Unwin, 1968.

VEVERKA, J. 'The growth of government expenditure in the United Kingdom since 1790' in A. T. Peacock and D. J. Robertson (eds.), *Public Expenditure: appraisal and control*, Edinburgh, Oliver & Boyd, 1963.

VINER, J. *The Customs Union Issue*, New York, Carnegie Endowment for International Peace, 1950.

WALTERS, A. A. *Money in Boom and Slump*, London, Institute of Economic Affairs, 1969.

WATERS, J. A. 'Money supply and credit – theory and practice', *National Westminster Bank Review*, November 1969.

WATTS, P. E. 'CEGB's bulk-supply tariff and long-run marginal cost', *Economic Journal*, vol. 78, March 1968.

— 'Electricity costs – a reply (2)', *Economic Journal*, vol. 78, December 1968.

WEDDERBURN, K. W. 'Labour law and labour relations in Britain', *British Journal of Industrial Relations*, vol. 10, July 1972.

WEEKES, B., MELLISH, M., DICKENS, L. and LLOYD, J. *Industrial Relations and the Limits of the Law*, Oxford, Blackwell, 1975.

WHITE, W. R. 'Some econometric models of deposit bank portfolio behaviour in the United Kingdom' in Renton (ed.), 1975, q.v.

WHITING, A. 'An international comparison of the instability of economic growth', *Three Banks Review*, no. 109, March 1976.

WHITLEY, J. D. and WORSWICK, G. D. N. 'The productivity effects of selective employment tax', *National Institute Economic Review*, no. 56, May 1971.

— 'The productivity effects of selective employment tax – a rejoinder', *National Institute Economic Review*, no. 58, November 1971.

WILLIAMS, D., GOODHART, C. A. E. and GOWLAND, D. H. 'Money, income and causality: the UK experience', *American Economic Review*, vol. 66, June 1976.

WILLIAMSON, J. 'Trade and economic growth' in Pinder (ed.), 1971, q.v.

WILSON, H. *The New Britain: Labour's plan*, Harmondsworth, Penguin, 1964.

— *The Labour Government 1964–1970: a personal record*, London, Weidenfeld & Michael Joseph, 1971.

WILSON, T. 'Price and output policy of state enterprise: a comment', *Economic Journal*, vol. 55, December 1945.

WOLFE, J. N. 'Productivity and growth in manufacturing industry', *Economica*, vol. 35 (new series), May 1968.

WORSWICK, G. D. N. 'Fiscal policy and stabilization in Britain', in Cairncross (ed.), *Britain's Economic Prospects Reconsidered*, 1970, q.v.

— 'Trade and payments' in Cairncross (ed.), *Britain's Economic Prospects Reconsidered*, 1970, q.v.

— 'The end of demand management?', *Lloyds Bank Review*, no. 123, January 1977.

WORSWICK, G. D. N. and BLACKABY, F. T. (eds.) *The Medium Term: models of the British economy*, London, Heinemann, 1974.

YOUNG, R. A. *Instruments of Monetary Policy in the United States: the role of the Federal Reserve system*, Washington (DC), International Monetary Fund, 1973.

II. OFFICIAL PUBLICATIONS

(a) United Kingdom[1]

Ministry of Agriculture, Fisheries and Food. *Agriculture Acts 1947 and 1957. Annual Review and Determination of Guarantees.*

— *Food Facts*, 30 April 1975.

Ministry of Aviation. *Report of the Committee of Inquiry into the Aircraft Industry*, Cmnd 2853, HMSO, 1965.

Bank of England. *Bank of England Quarterly Bulletin.*

— *Report [and Accounts]* (annual).

— *Statistical Abstract*, no. 1, 1970, and no. 2, 1975.

Cabinet Office. *The United Kingdom and the European Communities*, Cmnd 3345, HMSO, 1967.

— *The United Kingdom and the European Communities*, Cmnd 4401, HMSO, 1970.

— *The Reorganisation of Central Government*, Cmnd 4506, HMSO, 1970.

— *The United Kingdom and the European Communities*, Cmnd 4715, HMSO, 1971.

Central Statistical Office. *Research and Development Expenditure*, HMSO, 1973.

— *Annual Abstract of Statistics.*

— *Economic Trends* (monthly).

— *Economic Trends, Annual Supplement.*

— *Financial Statistics* (monthly).

— *Input–Output Tables for the United Kingdom 1954, 1963* and *1968*, HMSO, 1961, 1970 and 1973.

— *National Income and Expenditure* (annual).

[1] All published in London unless otherwise stated.

— *National Income and Expenditure 1963–73, 1964–74, 1965–75* and *1966–76*, HMSO, 1974–7.
— *United Kingdom Balance of Payments* (annual).
— *United Kingdom Balance of Payments 1963–73, 1964–74* and *1965–75*, HMSO, 1974–6.
Civil Service Department. *A Framework for Government Research and Development*, Cmnd 4814, HMSO, 1971.
— *The Developing System of Public Expenditure Management and Control* by Sir Samuel Goldman KCB, HMSO, 1973.
Commission on Industrial Relations. *First General Report*, Cmnd 4417, HMSO, 1970.
— *Report no. 69: Small Firms and the Code of Industrial Relations Practice*, HMSO, 1974.
Council on Prices, Productivity and Incomes. *1st Report*, HMSO, 1958.
— *2nd Report*, HMSO, 1958.
— *3rd Report*, HMSO, 1959.
— *4th Report*, HMSO, 1961.
Customs and Excise. *Annual Statement of Trade of the United Kingdom*.
— *Report of the Commissioners* (annual).
Ministry of Defence. *Statement on the Defence Estimates:*
   1965, Cmnd 2592, HMSO, 1965.
   1966, Part I: *Defence Review*, Cmnd 2901, HMSO, 1966.
   1967, Cmnd 3203, HMSO, 1967.
   1968, Cmnd 3540, HMSO, 1968.
   1969, Cmnd 3927, HMSO, 1969.
— *Supplementary Statement on Defence Policy 1967*, Cmnd 3357, HMSO, 1967.
Department of Economic Affairs. *Prices and Incomes Policy*, Cmnd 2639, HMSO, 1965.
— *The National Plan*, Cmnd 2764, HMSO, 1965.
— *Prices and Incomes Policy: an 'Early Warning System'*, Cmnd 2808, HMSO, 1965.
— *Investment Incentives*, Cmnd 2874, HMSO, 1966.
— *The Industrial Reorganisation Corporation*, Cmnd 2889, HMSO, 1966.
— *Prices and Incomes Standstill: period of severe restraint*, Cmnd 3150, HMSO, 1966.
— *Prices and Incomes Policy after June 30, 1967*, Cmnd 3235, HMSO, 1967.
— *Productivity, Prices and Incomes Policy in 1968 and 1969*, Cmnd 3590, HMSO, 1968.
— *Industrial Reorganisation Corporation:*
   First Report and Accounts, December 1966–March 1968, HMSO, 1968.
   Report and Accounts for the year ended March 31, 1969, HMSO, 1969.
— *The Task Ahead (Economic Assessment to 1972)*, HMSO, 1969.
— *Progress Report* (monthly).
Department [Ministry] of Education [and Science]. *Education in 1960*, HMSO, 1961.
— *Higher Education. Report* [Robbins Report], Cmnd 2154, HMSO, 1963.
— *Education and Science in 1974*, HMSO, 1975.
Department of Employment [and Productivity]. *In Place of Strife: a policy for industrial relations*, Cmnd 3888, HMSO, 1969.
— *Productivity, Prices and Incomes Policy after 1969*, Cmnd 4237, HMSO, 1969.
— *Industrial Relations Bill: consultative document*, 1970.
— *Report of a Court of Inquiry into a Dispute between the Parties Represented on the National Joint Industrial Council for the Electricity Supply Industry. Industrial Courts Act 1919*, Cmnd 4594, HMSO, 1971.
— *British Labour Statistics: historical abstract, 1886–1968*, HMSO, 1971.
— *Effects of the Redundancy Payments Act: a survey carried out in 1969 for the Department of Employment* by S. R. Parker *et al.*, HMSO, 1971.
— *People and Jobs: a modern employment service*, HMSO, 1971.
— *Report of a Court of Inquiry into a Dispute between the National Coal Board and the National Union of Mineworkers. Industrial Courts Act 1919*, Cmnd 4903, HMSO, 1972.
— *Industrial Relations Code of Practice*, HMSO, 1972.
— *Training for the Future*, 1972.
— *Employment and Training: government proposals*, Cmnd 5250, HMSO, 1973.
— *Training Services Agency. Five Year Plan*, HMSO, 1974.
— Training Services Agency, *Vocational Preparation for Young People: a discussion paper*, 1975.
— *British Labour Statistics Yearbook, 1972* and *1974*, HMSO, 1974 and 1976.

— *Department of Employment Gazette* [formerly *Ministry of Labour Gazette*] (monthly).
— *New Earnings Survey* (annual).
Department of the Environment. *Local Government Finance. Report of the Committee of Enquiry* [Layfield Report], Cmnd 6453, HMSO, 1976.
Exchequer and Audit Department. *Defence Accounts* (annual to 1973/4).
Foreign Office. *The United Kingdom and the European Economic Community*, Cmnd 1565, HMSO, 1961.
House of Commons. *Select Committee on Estimates, Session 1957–58. Sixth Report. Treasury Control of Expenditure*, HMSO, 1958.
— *Second Report from the Estimates Committee, Session 1963–64. Transport Aircraft*, HMSO, 1964.
— *Seventh Report from the Estimates Committee, Session 1967–68. Overseas Aid*, HMSO, 1968.
— *Select Committee on Nationalised Industries, Session 1967–68. Ministerial Control of the Nationalised Industries*, vols. 1 and 2, HMSO, 1968.
— *First Report from the Select Committee on Procedure, Session 1968–69. Scrutiny of Public Expenditure and Administration*, HMSO, 1969.
— *Third Report from the Expenditure Committee, Session 1970–71. Command Papers on Public Expenditure*, HMSO, 1971.
— *Report from the Select Committee on Corporation Tax*, HMSO, 1971.
— *Select Committee on Science and Technology, Session 1970–71. Fourth Report. The Prospects for the United Kingdom Computer Industry in the 1970s*, vol. 2: *Minutes of Evidence*, HMSO, 1971.
— *Third Report from the Expenditure Committee (Public Expenditure (General) Sub-Committee), Session 1971–72. Changes in Public Expenditure*, HMSO, 1972.
— *Sixth Report from the Expenditure Committee, Session 1971–72. Public Money in the Private Sector*, vol. 1: *Report*, and vols. 2 and 3: *Minutes of Evidence*, HMSO, 1972.
— *Seventh Report from the Expenditure Committee, Session 1971–72. Public Expenditure and Economic Management*, HMSO, 1972.
— *Fifth Report from the Expenditure Committee, Session 1972–73. The White Paper 'Public Expenditure to 1976–77' (Cmnd 5178)*, HMSO, 1973.
— *Tenth Report from the Expenditure Committee, Session 1972–73. House Improvement Grants*, vol. 1: *Report*, HMSO, 1973.
— *Eleventh Report from the Expenditure Committee, Session 1972–73. The May 21st Expenditure Cuts*, HMSO, 1973.
— *Select Committee on Nationalised Industries, Session 1972–73. First Report. British Steel Corporation*, HMSO, 1973.
— *Expenditure Committee (General Sub-Committee), Session 1973–74:*
   Minutes of Evidence, Nov. 12, 1973. Control of Road Programme Expenditure, HMSO, 1973.
   Minutes of Evidence, Dec. 3, 1973. Public Expenditure in 1972–73 and 1973–74: forecasts, revisions and out-turn, HMSO, 1973.
   Minutes of Evidence, Monday, Jan. 28. Public Expenditure to 1977–78 (Cmnd 5519). Public Expenditure and the Balance of Resources, HMSO, 1974.
— *Select Committee on Nationalised Industries, Session 1973–74. First Report. Capital Investment Procedures*, HMSO, 1974.
— *Fourth Report from the Expenditure Committee, Session 1974. Expenditure Cuts in Health and Personal Social Services*, HMSO, 1975.
— *Ninth Report from the Expenditure Committee, Session 1974. Public Expenditure, Inflation and the Balance of Payments*, HMSO, 1975.
— *Fifth Special Report from the Expenditure Committee, Session 1974–75. Public Expenditure, Inflation and the Balance of Payments*, HMSO, 1975.
— *Twelfth Report from the Expenditure Committee, Session 1974–75. Cash Limit Control of Public Expenditure*, HMSO, 1975.
— *Eighth Report from the Expenditure Committee, Session 1975–76. Public Expenditure on Chrysler UK Ltd*, vol. 1: *Report*, HMSO, 1976.
— *Debates [Hansard]* (weekly).
Ministry of Housing and Local Government. *Housing in England and Wales*, Cmnd 1290, HMSO, 1961.
— *The Housing Programme 1965–1970*, Cmnd 2838, HMSO, 1965.
— *Report* (annual).

Department of Industry. *Industry Act 1972:*
    Annual Report for the year ended March 31, 1974, HMSO, 1974.
    Annual Report for the year ended March 31, 1976, HMSO, 1976.
— *Strategy Alternatives for the British Motorcycle Industry,* HMSO, 1975.
— *Business Monitor M9: Survey of the United Kingdom Aerospace Industry* (annual).
Inland Revenue. *Report of the Committee on Turnover Taxation* [Richardson Report], Cmnd 2300, HMSO, 1964.
— *Inland Revenue Statistics* (annual).
— *Report of the Commissioners* (annual).
— *Survey of Personal Incomes* (annual).
Ministry of Labour. *Unofficial Stoppages in the London Docks, Report of a Committee of Inquiry* [Legget Report], Cmd 8236, HMSO, 1951.
— *Report of a Court of Inquiry into the Causes and Circumstances of a Dispute at Briggs Motor Bodies Limited, Dagenham,* Cmnd 131, HMSO, 1957.
— *Training for Skill: recruitment and training of young workers in industry,* HMSO, 1958.
— *Industrial Relations Handbook,* HMSO, 1961.
— *Security and Change: progress in provision for redundancy,* HMSO, 1961.
— *Industrial Training: government proposals,* Cmnd 1892, HMSO, 1962.
— *Central Training Council. Second Report to the Minister,* HMSO, 1967.
— *Engineering Industry Training Board:*
    Report and Statement of Accounts for the Period ended March 31, 1967, HMSO, 1967.
    Report and Statement of Accounts for the Period ended March 31, 1970, HMSO, 1970.
Monopolies Commission. *Report on the Supply of Cigarettes and Tobacco and of Cigarette and Tobacco Machinery,* HMSO, 1961.
— *Report on the Supply of Wallpaper,* HMSO, 1964.
— *Barclays Bank Ltd, Lloyds Bank Ltd and Martins Bank Ltd. Report on the Proposed Merger,* HMSO, 1968.
— *Man-made Cellulosic Fibres. Report on the Supply,* HMSO, 1968.
National Board for Prices and Incomes. *Report no. 34: Bank Charges,* Cmnd 3292, HMSO, 1967.
— *Report no. 36: Productivity Agreements,* Cmnd 3311, HMSO, 1967.
— *Report no. 58: Post Office Charges,* Cmnd 3574, HMSO, 1968.
— *Report no. 65: Payment by Results Systems,* Cmnd 3627, HMSO, 1968.
— *Report no. 101: Pay of Workers in Agriculture in England and Wales,* Cmnd 3911, HMSO, 1969.
National Economic Development Council. 'History and functions' (unpublished), 1963.
— *Conditions Favourable to Faster Growth,* HMSO, 1963.
— *Growth of the United Kingdom Economy to 1966,* HMSO, 1963.
— *Report on the Growth of the Economy,* HMSO, 1963.
— *Imported Manufactures: an inquiry into competitiveness,* HMSO, 1965.
— 'Rationalisation and the Restrictive Trade Practices Act' (unpublished), 1967.
National Economic Development Office. *Value Added Tax,* HMSO, 1969.
— *Cyclical Fluctuations in the United Kingdom Economy,* 1975.
— *A Study of the UK Nationalised Industries: their role in the economy and control in the future,* HMSO, 1976.
— Economic Development Committees:
    Industrial Report by the Chemicals EDC on the Economic Assessment to 1972, 1970.
    Industrial Report by the Machine Tools EDC on the Economic Assessment to 1972, 1970.
    Industrial Report by the Mechanical Engineering EDC on the Economic Assessment to 1972, 1970.
— Building and Civil Engineering Economic Development Committees. *The Public Client and the Construction Industry,* HMSO, 1975.
National Incomes Commission. *Report no. 1: Scottish Plumbers' and Scottish Builders' Agreements of 1962,* Cmnd 1994, HMSO, 1963.
— *Report no. 2: Agreements of Feb.–March 1963 in Electrical Contracting in Heating, Ventilating and Domestic Engineering and in Exhibition Contracting,* Cmnd 2098, HMSO, 1963.
— *Report no. 3: Remuneration of Academic Staff in Universities and Colleges of Advanced Technology,* Cmnd 2317, HMSO, 1964.

National Incomes Commission. *Report no. 4: Agreements of Nov.–Dec. 1963 in the Engineering and Shipbuilding Industries, interim*, HMSO, 1964 and *final*, Cmnd 2583, HMSO, 1965.

National Joint Advisory Council. 'Report of the working party on the manpower situation', *Ministry of Labour Gazette*, vol. 70, February 1962.

Northern Ireland Government, Department of Finance. *Appropriation Accounts*, Belfast, HMSO (annual).

Pay Board. *Advisory Report no. 1: Anomalies arising out of the Pay Standstill of Nov. 1972*, HMSO, 1973.

— *Advisory Report no. 2: Problems of Pay Relativities*, Cmnd 5535, HMSO, 1974.

— *Special Report: Relativity Pay of Mineworkers*, Cmnd 5567, HMSO, 1974.

Post Office. *Post Office Report and Accounts* (annual).

Ministry of [Fuel and] Power. *Report of the Committee on National Policy for the Use of Fuel and Power Resources* [Ridley Report], Cmd 8647, HMSO, 1952.

— *Electricity Supply Industry. Committee of Inquiry Report* [Herbert Report], Cmd 9672, HMSO, 1956.

— *Fuel Policy*, Cmnd 3438, HMSO, 1967.

— *British Steel Corporation Annual Report and Accounts*.

— *Central Electricity Generating Board Annual Report and Accounts*.

Prime Minister's Office. *The Economic Situation. A Statement by Her Majesty's Government*, HMSO, 1964.

— *Machinery of Prices and Incomes Policy*, Cmnd 2577, HMSO, 1965.

Ministry of Reconstruction. *Employment Policy*, Cmd 6527, HMSO, 1944.

Royal Commission on Taxation of Profits and Income. *Second Report*, Cmd 9105, HMSO, 1954.

— *Final Report*, Cmd 9474, HMSO, 1955.

Royal Commission on Trade Unions and Employers' Associations 1965–1968. *Written Evidence of the Ministry of Labour*, HMSO, 1965.

— *Minutes of Evidence: Witness Confederation of British Industry, 7 December 1965*, HMSO, 1966.

— *Research Paper no. 1: The Role of Shop Stewards in British Industrial Relations. Survey of existing information and research* by W. E. J. McCarthy, HMSO, 1966.

— *Report* [Donovan Report], Cmnd 3623, HMSO, 1968.

— *Selected Written Evidence Submitted to the Royal Commission*, HMSO, 1968.

Office of the Minister for Science. *Annual Report of the Advisory Council on Scientific Policy 1959–60*, Cmnd 1167, HMSO, 1960.

— *Report of the Committee on the Management and Control of Research and Development* [Zuckerman Report], HMSO, 1961.

— *Committee of Enquiry into the Organisation of Civil Science* [Trend Report], HMSO, 1963.

Shipbuilding Industry Board. *Shipbuilding Industry Board 1967–1971*, 1971.

Ministry of Technology. *Industrial Reorganisation Corporation Report and Accounts for the year ended March 31, 1970*, and *covering the period April 1, 1970 to April 30, 1971*, London, HMSO, 1970–1.

— *Electricity Council. Annual Report and Accounts*.

— *Gas Council. Annual Report and Accounts*.

— *National Coal Board. Report and Accounts* (annual).

— *Shipbuilding Industry Board. Report and Accounts* (annual).

Department [Board] of Trade [and Industry]. *Report on the Census of Production for 1954*, HMSO, 1958–9.

— *Report on the Censuses of Production for 1955, 1956 and 1957*, HMSO, 1959.

— *Reorganisation of the Cotton Industry*, Cmnd 744, HMSO, 1959.

— *The Machine Tool Industry. Report*, HMSO, 1960.

— *Commonwealth and Sterling Area Statistical Abstract 1962*, HMSO, 1963.

— *Monopolies, Mergers and Restrictive Practices*, Cmnd 2299, HMSO, 1964.

— *Registrar of Restrictive Trading Agreements. Report for the period July 1, 1961 to June 30, 1963*, HMSO, 1964.

— *Shipbuilding Inquiry Committee 1965–66. Report* [Geddes Report], Cmnd 2937, HMSO, 1966.

— *Restrictive Trading Agreements. Report of the Registrar July 1, 1963 to June 30, 1966*, Cmnd 3188, HMSO, 1967.

— *Mergers: a guide to Board of Trade practice*, HMSO, 1969.
— *Consumer Credit. Report of the Committee* [Crowther Report], Cmnd 4596, HMSO, 1971.
— *Report of the Committee of Inquiry on Small Firms* [Bolton Report], Cmnd 4811, HMSO, 1971.
— *The Machine Tool Industry. Report of the Machine Tool Expert Committee*, HMSO, 1971.
— *Industrial and Regional Development*, Cmnd 4942, HMSO, 1972.
— *British Shipbuilding 1972. Report to the Department of Trade and Industry by Booz-Allen and Hamilton International BV*, HMSO, 1973.
— *British Airports Authority Annual Report and Accounts*.
— *British European Airways Corporation Annual Report and Accounts*.
— *British Overseas Airways Corporation Annual Report and Accounts*.
— *Overseas Trade Statistics of the United Kingdom* [formerly *Trade and Navigation Accounts*] (monthly).
— *Trade and Industry* [formerly *Board of Trade Journal*] (weekly).
Ministry of Transport. *Shipbuilding Advisory Committee. Report of the Subcommittee on Prospects*, HMSO, 1961.
— *Transport Policy*, Cmnd 3027, HMSO, 1966.
— *British Railways Board. Annual Report and Statement of Accounts*.
— *British Transport Commission. Annual Report and Accounts*.
Treasury. *Economic Implications of Full Employment*, Cmd 9725, HMSO, 1956.
— *A European Free Trade Area*, Cmnd 72, HMSO, 1957.
— *Stockholm Draft Plan for a European Free Trade Association*, Cmnd 823, HMSO, 1959.
— *Committee on the Working of the Monetary System:*
    Report [Radcliffe Report], Cmnd 827, HMSO, 1959.
    Minutes of Evidence July 11, 1957 to April 30, 1959, HMSO, 1960.
    Principal Memoranda of Evidence, vols. 1–3, HMSO, 1960.
— *Public Investment in Great Britain*, Cmnd 1203, HMSO, 1960.
— *Financial and Economic Obligations of the Nationalised Industries*, Cmnd 1337, HMSO, 1961.
— *The Control of Public Expenditure* [Plowden Report], Cmnd 1432, HMSO, 1961.
— *Public Investment in Great Britain:*
    October 1961, Cmnd 1522, HMSO, 1961.
    October 1962, Cmnd 1849, HMSO, 1962.
    October 1963, Cmnd 2177, HMSO, 1963.
— *Incomes Policy: the next step*, Cmnd 1626, HMSO, 1962.
— *Public Expenditure in 1963–64 and 1967–68*, Cmnd 2235, HMSO, 1963.
— *Taxation of Capital Gains*, Cmnd 2645, HMSO, 1965.
— *Corporation Tax*, Cmnd 2646, HMSO, 1965.
— *Public expenditure: planning and control*, Cmnd 2915, HMSO, 1966.
— *Nationalised Industries: a review of economic and financial objectives*, Cmnd 3437, HMSO, 1967.
— *Public Expenditure in 1968–69 and 1969–70*, Cmnd 3515, HMSO, 1968.
— *Economic Report on 1967*, HMSO, 1968.
— *Public Expenditure: a new presentation*, Cmnd 4017, HMSO, 1969.
— *Public Expenditure 1968–69 to 1973–74*, Cmnd 4234, HMSO, 1969.
— *Britain and the European Communities: an economic assessment*, Cmnd 4289, HMSO, 1970.
— *New Policies for Public Spending*, Cmnd 4515, HMSO, 1970.
— *Investment Incentives*, Cmnd 4516, HMSO, 1970.
— *Economic Prospects to 1972 – a revised assessment*, HMSO, 1970.
— *Effects of the Selective Employment Tax. First Report: the distributive trades* [Reddaway Report], HMSO, 1970.
— *Public Expenditure 1969–70 to 1974–75*, Cmnd 4578, HMSO, 1971.
— *Value Added Tax* [Green Paper], Cmnd 4621, HMSO, 1971.
— *Reform of Corporation Tax* [Green Paper], Cmnd 4630, HMSO, 1971.
— *Reform of Personal Direct Taxation*, Cmnd 4653, HMSO, 1971.
— *Public Expenditure 1969–70 to 1975–76*, Cmnd 4829, HMSO, 1971.
— *Taxation of Capital on Death. Possible Inheritance Tax in Place of Estate Duty*, Cmnd 4930, HMSO, 1972.
— *Reform of Corporation Tax* [White Paper], Cmnd 4955, HMSO, 1972.

Treasury. *Proposals for a Tax-Credit System*, Cmnd 5116, HMSO, 1972.
— *Public Expenditure to 1976–77*, Cmnd 5178, HMSO, 1972.
— *The Determinants of UK Imports* by R. D. Rees and P. R. G. Layard, HMSO, 1972.
— *Public Expenditure White Papers: handbook on methodology*, HMSO, 1972.
— *Price and Pay Code. Consultative Document*, Cmnd 5247, HMSO, 1973.
— *Price and Pay Code for Stage 3. A Consultative Document*, Cmnd 5444, HMSO, 1973.
— *The Counter Inflation Policy: Stage 3*, Cmnd 5446, HMSO, 1973.
— *Public Expenditure to 1977–78*, Cmnd 5519, HMSO, 1973.
— *Tariffs, Taxes and Trade in the UK: the effective protection approach* by N. Oulton, HMSO, 1973.
— *Public Expenditure to 1978–79*, Cmnd 5879, HMSO, 1975.
— *An Approach to Industrial Strategy*, Cmnd 6315, HMSO, 1975.
— *The Government's Expenditure Plans*, Cmnd 6721, HMSO, 1977.
— *Appropriation Accounts* [formerly *Civil Appropriation Accounts*] (annual).
— *Economic Progress Report* (monthly).
— *Financial Statement* [*and Budget Report*] (annual).

(b) *International*

European Communities. Monetary Committee. *Monetary Policy in the Countries of the European Economic Community. Supplement 1974 (The United Kingdom)*, Brussels, 1974.
General Agreement on Tariffs and Trade. *Trends in International Trade: a report by a panel of experts*, Geneva, 1958.
Organisation for Economic Co-operation and Development [formerly European Co-operation]. *The Problem of Rising Prices* by W. Fellner *et al.*, Paris, 1961.
— *Fiscal Policy for a Balanced Economy: experience, problems and prospects* by W. Heller *et al.*, Paris, 1968.
— *Fiscal Policy in Seven Countries, 1955–1965* by B. Hansen, Paris, 1969.
— *Manpower Policy in the United Kingdom*, Paris, 1970.
— *National Accounts of OECD Countries 1950–68*, Paris, 1970.
— *Public Expenditure Trends in OECD Countries* by M. Garin-Painter, Paris, 1970.
— *Capital Movements in the OECD Area: an econometric analysis* by W. H. Branson and R. D. Hill, Paris, 1971.
United Nations. *Monthly Bulletin of Statistics*.

INDEX

(after page numbers, ch = chart, n = text footnote, t = table)

PUBLICATIONS OF THE
NATIONAL INSTITUTE OF ECONOMIC
AND SOCIAL RESEARCH

published by
THE CAMBRIDGE UNIVERSITY PRESS

Books published for the Institute by the Cambridge University Press are available through the ordinary booksellers. They appear in the five series below:

ECONOMIC & SOCIAL STUDIES

* At present out of print.

OCCASIONAL PAPERS

* At present out of print.

STUDIES IN THE NATIONAL INCOME AND EXPENDITURE OF THE UNITED KINGDOM

Published under the joint auspices of the National Institute and the Department of Applied Economics, Cambridge.

* At present out of print.